COMMON THREADS

CORE READINGS BY METHOD AND THEME

COMMON THREADS

CORE READINGS BY METHOD AND THEME

Ellen Kuhl Repetto

Jane E. Aaron

BEDFORD / ST.MARTIN'S
Boston ■ New York

For Bedford/St. Martin's

Executive Editor: Daniel McDonough
Senior Developmental Editor: Nathan Odell
Senior Production Editor: Bridget Leahy
Production Supervisor: Victoria Sharoyan
Marketing Manager: Lisa Erdely
Editorial Assistant: Nicholas McCarthy
Copy Editor: Lisa Wehrle
Photo Researcher: Sheri Blaney
Permissions Manager: Linda Winters
Senior Art Director: Anna Palchik
Text Design: Janis Owens
Cover Design: Donna Lee Dennison
Cover Photo: Scott Darling, *Blue Ribbons.* © Scott Darling. Courtesy of Apostrophe.
Composition: Jouve North America
Printing and Binding: RR Donnelley and Sons

President, Bedford/St. Martin's: Denise B. Wydra
Presidents, Macmillan Higher Education: Joan E. Feinberg and Tom Scotty
Editor in Chief: Karen S. Henry
Director of Development: Erica Appel
Director of Marketing: Karen R. Soeltz
Director of High School: Paul Altier
Production Director: Susan W. Brown
Associate Production Director: Elise S. Kaiser

Manufactured in the United States of America.
1 2 3 4 5 6   17 16 15 14 13

For information, write: Bedford/St. Martin's, 75 Arlington Street, Boston, MA 02116
(617-399-4000)

ISBN 978-1-4576-2531-2 (Student Edition)
ISBN 978-1-4576-4759-8 (Teacher's Edition)

Acknowledgments

Acknowledgments and copyrights are continued at the back of the book on pages 469–73, which constitute an extension of the copyright page. It is a violation of the law to reproduce these selections by any means whatsoever without the written permission of the copyright holder.

PREFACE

Common Threads is an affordable, class-tested collection of informational texts for teaching close reading and academic writing. Carefully aligned to the Common Core State Standards and intended as a supplement to literature, this book is specifically designed to help high-school teachers restructure their English language arts curricula to facilitate college and career readiness for students.

The structure is simple and easy to use. Five introductory chapters in Part One guide students through the processes of critical reading, writing, and working with sources. Ten chapters of readings in Part Two focus on the rhetorical methods of development, with each chapter's brief selections both illustrating a method and centering on a common theme. An Appendix offers tips on speaking and listening effectively and also presents a sampling of foundational American speeches.

Flexible, rigorous, and comprehensive, the readings and instructional support in *Common Threads* work together to address the nonfiction requirements in each anchor strand of the new Common Core State Standards: reading, writing, speaking and listening, and language.

Reading

Common Threads combines three readers in one brief volume: a short-essay reader, a rhetorical reader, and a thematic reader. Remarkably thorough given its size, the book complements extensive reading opportunities with helpful guidance.

Range of Readings

The core of *Common Threads* is its selections. Thirty-five short essays, twenty annotated paragraphs, ten stand-alone visuals, and five historic speeches provide interesting reading that will enliven class discussion and spark good writing.

- **A rich variety of material** demonstrates argumentative, informative, and narrative texts from multiple genres, such as memoir, opinion, speech, journalism, and analysis. A wide range of topics and disciplines includes culture, language, media literacy, science, technology, and social studies—from historical contexts to current issues. The selections showcase works by favorite writers such as Amy Tan, David Sedaris, Walter Mosley, and Pat Mora. They also reflect the diversity of American experiences: Half of the readings are by women, and more than a third are by multicultural writers.

- **A range of complexity** ensures that students will find readings that are both challenging and suited to their abilities. Many of the essays and speeches hail directly from the Common Core list of exemplar texts; others feature works from writers endorsed by the Standards; the rest exemplify the kinds of writing and levels of complexity recommended for grades 9 and 10. Arranged in each chapter from least to most complex, the essays average just two to four pages apiece so that students can read them quickly, analyze them thoroughly, and emulate them successfully. A few longer pieces, such as Barbara Kingsolver's "Stalking the Vegetannual," help students make the transition to more demanding material.

- **A unique dual organization** shows how rhetorical considerations shape writing while encouraging the integration of knowledge and ideas. Each of the ten chapters in Part Two shows a rhetorical method—narration, example, comparison, argument, and so on—at work in varied styles for varied purposes. At the same time, each chapter has an overlapping thematic focus that shows the method developing the same general subject and provides diverse perspectives to stimulate students' critical thinking, discussion, and writing.

Instruction and Scaffolding

The selections in *Common Threads* are supported by thorough yet unobtrusive instructional guidance that helps students develop and master the rigors of close reading.

- **An introductory chapter on critical reading** explains and demonstrates the reading process, showing a student's annotations on a sample passage and providing a detailed model analysis of a

classic essay, Barbara Lazear Ascher's "The Box Man." A concise discussion of reading visuals, accompanied by sample images with
interpretive comments, highlights the parallels between critical reading and visual analysis.

- **A practical introduction to each of the ten rhetorical
  methods** discusses the concepts to look for when reading and analyzes two sample paragraphs that illustrate the method. The introductions draw connections among purpose, subject, evidence, and
  method, helping students analyze and respond to any text. A final
  "Note on Thematic Connections" explains how the chapter's visual
  image, paragraphs, and essays relate to one another.

- **Headnotes introducing the authors and the essays** place
  every selection in a context that helps focus students' reading.

- **Gloss notes** explain allusions, historical references, and specialized
  vocabulary that students may not understand without help.

- **Extensive text-dependent critical reading questions** following every essay and speech are keyed to the college and career readiness anchor standards for reading to guide students' independent
  analysis of key ideas and details, craft and structure (including language), and integration of knowledge and ideas.

Writing

Common Threads features an emphasis on the connection between reading and writing that carries through the entire book.

Text Types and Purposes

Brief but thorough instructional materials in every chapter carefully guide
and support students as they learn to develop the kinds of writing emphasized by Common Core.

- **A focus on argumentation throughout.** The introductory
  chapters on writing and revising in Part One, as well as the introduction to every chapter in Part Two, stress the importance of forming
  a thesis, discuss the many ways evidence can be used to develop a
  point, and offer suggestions for organizing claims, reasons, and supporting details. An extended chapter on argument and persuasion

explains how arguments work; introduces the uses of ethical, emotional, and rational appeals; outlines the processes of inductive and deductive reasoning; and shows students how to recognize and avoid faulty logic.

- **Detailed explanations of the methods of development** walk students through the rhetorical strategies that writers commonly use to inform and explain. Each chapter in Part Two suggests specific strategies for developing an essay, from choosing a subject through editing the final draft. The essays in these chapters then offer clear models for writing with each method.

- **Visual texts** are addressed in a discussion of interpreting images in Chapter 1, in advice on incorporating visual evidence into a draft in Chapter 3, and in tips for using multimedia in presentations in the Appendix. Several of the readings, such as Jarrod Ballo's "Women and Children First," David Brooks's "People Like Us," and Charlie Le Duff's "End of the Line," model using visuals as evidence as well.

- **A glossary** at the end of the book defines and illustrates more than a hundred terms, with specific cross-references to longer discussions in the text.

Production and Distribution of Writing

Although the chapters in Part Two address each rhetorical method separately, *Common Threads* is careful to acknowledge that writers rarely use one method at a time and stresses that the methods are tools to be used and combined for particular purposes. The book is built around an understanding that writing is a process that is often messy and unpredictable.

- **Three chapters on the writing process** stress the roles of audience, purpose, and context in developing informative and argumentative essays while following a student as she responds to an essay, writes a first draft, and revises and edits her work. "Developing an Essay" covers the initial stages of composing, from assessing the writing situation through drafting. The next chapter, "Revising," explains the goals of revision, from rethinking the thesis through reshaping paragraphs, adding supportive evidence, and adjusting tone. And a chapter on editing shows how to correct and polish a finished piece of writing.

- **Multiple writing suggestions accompanying every reading** ask students to make inferences and extend, respond to, and synthesize ideas in the text. At least one question explicitly connects the reading to another, encouraging students to compare writers' approaches, techniques, ideas, or arguments.

- **Additional writing topics** appear at the end of each chapter of readings. "Writing with the Method" lists ideas for applying the chapter's method of development, and "Writing about the Theme" suggests ways to draw on the chapter's resources to explore its topic.

- **Method-specific revision and editing checklists** in each rhetorical chapter emphasize the importance of rewriting and focus students on the problems most likely to need attention when working with a particular method.

Research to Build and Present Knowledge

The questions and assignments in *Common Threads* assume not only that students will analyze and write in response to what they read, but also that good writing often draws on and synthesizes sources. The book therefore includes ample support for student researchers.

- **A full chapter on working with sources** outlines the basics of using textual evidence and conducting research—in libraries and online—to support writing. Emphasizing the essential skills of summarizing, paraphrasing, quoting, avoiding plagiarism, and using MLA documentation, Chapter 5 shows students how to evaluate sources and synthesize information and ideas from their reading to develop and support their own conclusions. The chapter ends with an annotated student essay that illustrates the elements of researched argumentative writing.

- **Focused, short-term research projects** suggested in many of the writing prompts that accompany the readings encourage students to expand their understanding of a subject or issue by asking questions, locating and evaluating appropriate sources, and writing or speaking about what they learn.

Speaking and Listening

The readings in *Common Threads* were selected not only for their value as models of good writing, but also for their capacity to spark lively, productive discussions. Accordingly, the book offers advice and guidance to help students develop their oral communication skills.

- **Pointed guidelines for speaking and listening**, in Chapter 2, emphasize the role of discussion in developing ideas for writing and explain how to interact with others effectively. At least one question following each reading highlights a core issue or theme and prompts students to prepare for focused group or class discussion.

- **An overview of speeches and tips for speaking** in the Appendix stress the importance of active listening and offer help with preparing, rehearsing, and delivering speeches and multimedia presentations.

- **Print versions of five iconic speeches**, also in the Appendix, provide exemplary models of persuasive speaking. Questions following these speeches encourage students to analyze both the content and the speakers' rhetorical choices.

Language

Recognizing that grammar, punctuation, and usage is best addressed in the context of students' own reading and writing, *Common Threads* provides ample guidance and opportunities for practice with editing and with analyzing writers' individual choices.

- **A detailed chapter on editing** explains the conventions of standard English and nuances of craft targeted in the Common Core State Standards—among them grammar, clarity, emphasis, word choice, and punctuation. Simple explanations, multiple examples of weak and revised sentences, and a boxed editing checklist teach students to recognize and repair the most common sentence-level problems.

- **"Focus" boxes** in the introductions to each rhetorical method highlight elements of language and usage especially relevant to that method, such as verbs in narration, parallelism in comparison and contrast, and tone in argument and persuasion. Each box discusses the editing skill in the context of the chapter's readings and gives students an opportunity to practice it themselves, followed by a Weblink to related interactive exercises in *Exercise Central* (*bedfordstmartins.com/exercisecentral*).

- **Vocabulary lists** accompanying every essay and speech encourage students to determine meaning from context and confirm their understanding by looking the words up in a dictionary and then using them in sentences of their own.

- **At least one question after each reading** directs students to analyze a particular aspect of the writer's use of language, extending their appreciation of the nuances of meaning and style.

Resources for Teachers

Common Threads comes with a manual that aims to help high school teachers integrate the book into their curricula and use it in class. It includes a correlation guide to the Common Core State Standards, an overview of the book's organization and chapters, ideas for combining the reader with other textbooks and with additional print and multimedia materials, suggested lesson units, answers to the practice exercises in the book's "Focus" boxes, and varied resources for each selection: teaching tips, a list of thematically related literary works, a comprehension quiz, a vocabulary quiz, and detailed answers to all the critical-reading questions.

In addition, Bedford/St. Martin's provides several online teaching tools at no charge. At the companion Web site for *Common Threads* (*bedfordstmartins.com/commonthreads*), teachers will find *Teaching Central*, a rich library of reference works, teaching advice, and classroom materials; *High School Bits*, an archive of creative ideas for teaching in an easily searchable blog; *The Bedford Bibliography for Teachers of Writing*; and an electronic version of the teacher's manual.

Multimedia Supplements

Students have access to a range of helpful resources. At *Re:Writing* (*bedfordstmartins.com/rewriting*), they can visit *Exercise Central* and practice editing with over nine thousand interactive writing and grammar exercises. Students can also find additional advice on citing sources in *Research and Documentation Online* by Diana Hacker; view sample papers and designed documents; take the *St. Martin's Tutorial on Avoiding Plagiarism*; watch videos of writers talking about writing; and learn more about reading and using visuals.

Common Threads can also be packaged with a variety of innovative tools at a significant discount. VideoCentral is a growing collection of videos that capture real-world, academic, and student writers talking about how and why they write. *Re:Writing Plus* upgrades the basic version of *Re:Writing* with hundreds of model documents, the first ever peer-review game, and full access to VideoCentral. And the *i-series* on CD-ROM and online offers interactive exercises on key rhetorical and visual concepts (*ix*), multimedia argument tutorials (*i·claim*), and hands-on practice with research and source citation (*i·cite*). To learn more, contact your Bedford/St. Martin's sales representative, e-mail sales support at sales_support@bfwpub.com, or visit *bedfordstmartins.com/highschool/commonthreads/catalog*.

Acknowledgments

Many teachers helped to shape *Common Threads*, thoughtfully answering detailed questions, generously sharing insights from their experience, and offering creative suggestions for making the book as useful as possible. Grateful thanks to Stacy Aronow, Souderton Area High School (Pennsylvania); Jim Burke, Burlingame High School (California); Jennifer Dooley, Edmonson County High School (Kentucky); John Golden, Cleveland High School (Oregon); Sheryl Miller Hosey, Council Rock High School South (Pennsylvania); Victor Jaccarino, Herricks High School (New York); Diane Jenkins, Charles County Public Schools (Maryland); Dawn Kowalksi, Grant High School (California); Kyle Krol, Mattawan High School (Michigan), Lynn Leschke, Wachusett Regional High School (Massachusetts); Brian Sztabnik, Miller Place High School (New York); Daria Waetjen, Orange County Department of Education (California); and Sarah Wessling, Johnston High School (Iowa). Special thanks in particular to Emily Richardson, Naperville North High School (Illinois), who not only participated in the focus group and review program, but also contributed greatly to the teacher's manual, with advice on integrating *Common Threads* into English language arts and with suggested literature connections. Her enthusiasm for this project from the start has been a constant source of inspiration.

The always wonderful people at Bedford/St. Martin's contributed greatly to this project as well. Denise Wydra, Nancy Perry, and Karen Henry provided encouraging leadership. Daniel McDonough and Lisa Erdely suggested the need for a reader aligned to Common Core and helped to conceive its structure and features. Nathan Odell, assisted by Nicholas McCarthy, fine-tuned the initial ideas, pushed for improvements, averted crises, and cheerfully managed details too numerous to count. Bridget Leahy deftly shepherded the manuscript through production on an impossible schedule. Deep and happy thanks to all.

CONTENTS

5 ▶ WORKING WITH SOURCES   63

PART TWO
SHORT ESSAYS BY METHOD AND THEME   91

6 ▶ NARRATION
GROWING UP   92

8 ▶ EXAMPLE
USING LANGUAGE   150

COMMON THREADS

CORE READINGS BY METHOD AND THEME

PART ONE

GUIDE TO READING AND WRITING

GUIDE TO READING
AND WRITING

1

READING

▶

This collection of essays has one purpose: to help you become a better reader and writer. It combines examples of good nonfiction writing with explanations of the writers' methods, questions to guide your reading, and ideas for your own writing. In doing so, it shows how you can adapt the processes and techniques of other writers as you learn to communicate clearly and effectively.

Writing well is not an inborn skill but an acquired one: you will become competent only by writing and rewriting, experimenting with different strategies, listening to the responses of readers. How, then, can it help to read the work of other writers?

- *Reading introduces you to new information.* People routinely share facts, ideas, discoveries, and ways of thinking in writing. Reading what others have to say lets you learn about subjects and perspectives that would otherwise remain unknown to you, gives you knowledge worth exploring further, and can spark ideas for your own writing.

- *Reading gives you insight on your own experience.* As many of the essays collected here demonstrate, personal experience is a rich and powerful source of material for writing. But the knowledge gained from reading can help pinpoint just what is remarkable in your own world and help you understand where you fit in the scheme of things. Such insight not only reveals subjects for writing but also improves your ability to communicate with others whose experiences naturally differ from your own.

- *Reading exposes you to a broad range of strategies and styles.* Just seeing that these vary as much as the writers themselves should assure you that there is no fixed standard of writing, while it should also encourage you to find your own strategies and style. At the same time, reading will help you see how writers make choices to suit their subjects, their purposes, and especially their readers. Writing is rarely easy, even for the pros; but the more models you have to choose from, the more likely you are to succeed at it.

- *Reading makes you sensitive to the role of audience in writing.* As you become skilled at reading the work of other writers critically, discovering intentions and analyzing choices, you will see how a writer's decisions affect you as audience. Training yourself to read critically is a first step to becoming a better writer.

Reading Attentively

This chapter offers strategies for making the most of your reading in this book and elsewhere. These strategies are reinforced in Chapters 6–15, each of which offers opportunities for careful reading with a visual image, two paragraphs, and three short essays. Each chapter also introduces a method of developing a piece of writing:

narration	process analysis
description	comparison and contrast
example	definition
division or analysis	cause-and-effect analysis
classification	argument and persuasion

These methods correspond to basic and familiar patterns of thought, common in our daily conversations as well as in writing for all sorts of purposes and audiences: homework assignments, lab reports, and research papers; blogs, social-networking pages, and online discussion boards; business surveys and reports; letters to the editors of newspapers; articles in magazines.

As writers we use the methods, sometimes without realizing it, to give order to our ideas. For instance, a writer narrates, or tells, a true story of her experiences to understand and share the feeling of living her life. As readers, in turn, we have expectations for these familiar methods. When we read a narrative of someone's experiences, for example, we expect enough details to understand what happened, we assume that events will be told primarily in the order they occurred, and we want the story to have a point—a reason for its being told and for our bothering to read it. Building an awareness of readers' expectations can sharpen your skills as a critical reader and as a writer.

A full chapter on each method explains how it works, shows it in action in paragraphs, and gives advice for using it to develop your own essays. The essays in each chapter provide clear examples that you can analyze and learn from (with the help of specific questions) and can refer to while writing (with the help of specific writing suggestions).

To make your reading more interesting and also to stimulate your writing, the images, sample paragraphs, and essays in Chapters 6–15 all focus on a common subject, such as nature, popular culture, or stereotypes. You'll see how flexible the methods are when they help five writers produce five unique pieces on the same theme. You'll also have a springboard for producing your own unique pieces, whether you take up some of the book's writing suggestions or take off with your own topics.

Reading Critically

When we look for something to watch on television, we often flip from one channel to another before settling on a choice. Much of the reading we do is similar: we skim a newspaper, magazine, or Web site, noting headlines and scanning paragraphs to get the gist of the content. But such skimming is not really reading, for it allows neither a deep understanding of the subject nor an appreciation of the writer's unique ideas and craftwork.

To get the most out of reading, we must invest something of ourselves in the process, applying our own ideas and emotions and paying attention not just to the subject but also to the writer's interpretation of it. This kind of reading is **critical** because it looks beneath the surface of a piece of writing. (The common meaning of *critical* as "negative" doesn't apply here: critical reading may result in positive, negative, or even neutral reactions.)

Critical reading can be enormously rewarding, but of course it takes care and time. A good method for developing your own skill in critical reading is to prepare yourself beforehand and then read the work at least twice to uncover what it has to offer.

▶ Preparing

Preparing to read may involve just a few minutes as you form some ideas about the author, the work, and your likely response:

- *What is the author's background? What qualifications does he or she bring to the subject? What angle is he or she likely to take?* The biographical information provided before each essay in this book should help answer these questions; many periodicals, Web sites, and books include similar information on their authors.

- *What does the title suggest about the subject and the author's attitude toward it?* Note, for instance, the quite different attitudes hinted at by these three titles on the same subject: "Safe Hunting," "In Touch with Ancient Spirits," and "Killing Animals for Fun and Profit."

- *What can you predict about your own response to the work?* What might you already know about the author's subject? Based on the title and other clues (such as headings or visuals), what do you expect to learn, and do you think you will agree or disagree with the author's views? Why?

▶ Reading Actively

After developing some expectations about the piece of writing, read it through carefully to acquaint yourself with the subject, the author's reason for writing about it, and the way the author presents it. (Each selection in this book is short enough to be read in one sitting.) Try not to read passively, letting the words wash over you, but instead interact directly with the work to discover its meaning, the author's intentions, and your own responses.

One of the best aids to **active reading** is making notes to yourself, a practice often called **annotation**. If allowed, you could make notes right in your book, but generally you will have to use sticky notes, a separate piece of paper, or an electronic file. As you practice annotating, you will probably develop a personal code meaningful only to you. As a start, however, try this system:

- Underline or bracket passages that you find particularly effective or that seem especially important to the author's purpose.

- Circle words you don't understand so that you can look them up when you finish.

- Put question marks in the margins next to unclear passages.

- Jot down associations that occur to you, such as examples from your own experience, disagreements with the author's assumptions, or connections to other works you've read.

When you have finished such an active reading, your annotations might look like those below (the paragraph is from the end of the essay reprinted on pp. 9–12):

The first half of our lives is spent stubbornly deny- *true?*
ing it. As children we acquire language to make ourselves
understood and soon learn from the blank stares in
response to our babblings that even these, our saviors, our
parents, are strangers. In adolescence when we replay earlier dramas with peers in the place of parents, we begin
the quest for the best friend, that person who will receive
all thoughts as if they were her own. Later we assert that   *What about his own? Audience = women?*
true love will find the way. True love finds many ways, but
no escape from exile. The shores are littered with us,
Annas and Ophelias, Emmas and Juliets, all outcasts from   *Ophelia + Juliet from Shakespeare. Others also?*
the dream of perfect understanding. We might as well
draw the night around us and find solace there and a
friend in our own voice.   *In other words, just give up?*

To answer questions like those in the annotations above, count on reading an essay at least twice. Multiple readings increase your mastery of the material; more important, once you have a basic understanding of a writer's subject, second and third readings will reveal details and raise questions that you might not have noticed on the first pass. Reading an essay several times also helps you understand how the different parts of the work—for instance, the organization, the tone, the evidence— contribute to the author's purpose.

▶ Using a Reading Checklist

When rereading an essay, start by writing a one- or two-sentence summary of each paragraph—in your own words—to increase your mastery of the material (see p. 68). Then let the essay rest in your mind for at least an hour or two before approaching it again. On later readings, dig beneath the essay's surface by asking questions such as those in the checklist on the next page. Note that the questions provided after each essay in this book offer more targeted versions of the ones included here.

CHECKLIST FOR **Critical Reading**

- Why do you think the author chose this subject?

- Who is the intended audience? What impression does the author wish to make on readers?

- What is the author's point? Can you find a direct statement of the thesis (main idea), or is the thesis implied?

- What details does the author provide to support the thesis? Is the supporting evidence reliable? complete? convincing?

- How does the author organize ideas? What effect does that arrangement have on the overall impact of the work?

- What do language and tone reveal about the author's meaning, purpose, and attitude?

- How successful is the work as a whole, and why?

Analyzing a Sample Essay

Critical reading—and the insights to be gained from it—can best be illustrated by examining an actual essay. The paragraph on page 7 comes from "The Box Man" by Barbara Lazear Ascher. The entire essay is reprinted here in the same format as other selections in this book, with a biographical note on the author and an introductory note on the essay.

Barbara Lazear Ascher

Born in 1946, American writer Barbara Lazear Ascher is known for her insightful, inspiring essays. She graduated from Bennington College in 1968 and Cardozo School of Law in 1979. After practicing law for two years, Ascher turned to writing full-time. Her essays have appeared in the *New York Times*, *Vogue*, the *Yale Review*, *Redbook*, and *National Geographic Traveler*. Ascher has also published a memoir about her brother, who died of AIDS, *Landscape without Gravity: A Memoir of Grief* (1993), and several collections of essays: *Playing after Dark* (1986), *The Habit of Loving* (1989), and *Dancing in the Dark: Romance, Yearning, and the Search for the Sublime* (1999). She lives in New York City.

The Box Man

In this essay from *Playing after Dark*, the evening ritual of a homeless man inspires Ascher's thoughts on being alone. By describing the Box Man alongside two other solitary people, Ascher distinguishes between chosen and unchosen loneliness.

The Box Man was at it again. It was his lucky night. 1

The first stroke of good fortune occurred as darkness fell and the 2 night watchman at 220 East Forty-fifth Street neglected to close the door as he slipped out for a cup of coffee. I saw them before the Box Man did. Just inside the entrance, cardboard cartons, clean and with their top flaps intact. With the silent fervor of a mute at a horse race, I willed him toward them.

It was slow going. His collar was pulled so high that he appeared 3 headless as he shuffled across the street like a man who must feel Earth with his toes to know that he walks there.

Standing unselfconsciously in the white glare of an overhead light, 4 he began to sort through the boxes, picking them up, one by one, inspecting tops, insides, flaps. Three were tossed aside. They looked perfectly good to me, but then, who knows what the Box Man knows? When he found the one that suited his purpose, he dragged it up the block and dropped it in a doorway.

Then, as if dogged by luck, he set out again and discovered, behind 5 the sign at the parking garage, a plastic Dellwood box, strong and clean, once used to deliver milk. Back in the doorway the grand design was revealed as he pushed the Dellwood box against the door and set its cardboard cousin two feet in front—the usual distance between coffee table and couch. Six full shopping bags were distributed evenly on either side.

He eased himself with slow care onto the stronger box, reached 6
into one of the bags, pulled out a *Daily News*, and snapped it open
against his cardboard table. All done with the ease of IRT Express passengers whose white-tipped, fair-haired fingers reach into attaché cases
as if radar-directed to the *Wall Street Journal*. They know how to fold it.
They know how to stare at the print, not at the girl who stares at them.

That's just what the Box Man did, except that he touched his tongue 7
to his fingers before turning each page, something grandmothers do.

One could live like this. Gathering boxes to organize a life. Wander- 8
ing through the night collecting comforts to fill a doorway.

When I was a child, my favorite book was *The Boxcar Children*. If I 9
remember correctly, the young protagonists were orphaned, and rather
than live with cruel relatives, they ran away to the woods to live life on
their own terms. An abandoned boxcar was turned into a home, a bub-
bling brook became an icebox. Wild berries provided abundant desserts
and days were spent in the happy, adultless pursuit of joy. The children
never worried where the next meal would come from or what February's
chill might bring. They had unquestioning faith that berries would
ripen and streams run cold and clear. And unlike Thoreau,[1] whose deliberate living was self-conscious and purposeful, theirs had the ease of
children at play.

Even now, when life seems complicated and reason slips, I long to 10
live like a Boxcar Child, to have enough open space and freedom of
movement to arrange my surroundings according to what I find. To turn
streams into iceboxes. To be ingenious with simple things. To let the
imagination hold sway.

Who is to say that the Box Man does not feel as Thoreau did in his 11
doorway, not "crowded or confined in the least," with "pasture enough
for . . . imagination." Who is to say that his dawns don't bring back
heroic ages? That he doesn't imagine a goddess trailing her garments
across his blistered legs?

His is a life of the mind, such as it is, and voices only he can hear. 12
Although it would appear to be a life of misery, judging from the bandages and chill of night, it is of his choosing. He will ignore you if you
offer an alternative. Last winter, Mayor Koch[2] tried, coaxing him with

---

[1] Henry David Thoreau (1817–62) was an American essayist and poet who for two
years lived a solitary and simple life in the woods. He wrote of his experiences in
Walden (1854). [Editors' note.]

[2] Edward Koch was the mayor of New York City from 1978 through 1989. [Editors'
note.]

promises and the persuasive tones reserved for rabid dogs. The Box Man backed away, keeping a car and paranoia between them.

He is not to be confused with the lonely ones. You'll find them 13 everywhere. The lady who comes into our local coffee shop each evening at five-thirty, orders a bowl of soup and extra Saltines. She drags it out as long as possible, breaking the crackers into smaller and smaller pieces, first in halves and then halves of halves and so on until the last pieces burst into salty splinters and fall from dry fingers onto the soup's shimmering surface. By 6 p.m., it's all over. What will she do with the rest of the night?

You can tell by the vacancy of expression that no memories linger 14 there. She does not wear a gold charm bracelet with silhouettes of boys and girls bearing grandchildren's birthdates and a chip of the appropriate birthstone. When she opens her black purse to pay, there is only a crumpled Kleenex and a wallet inside, no photographs spill onto her lap. Her children, if there are any, live far away and prefer not to visit. If she worked as a secretary for forty years in a downtown office, she was given a retirement party, a cake, a reproduction of an antique perfume atomizer and sent on her way. Old colleagues—those who traded knitting patterns and brownie recipes over the water cooler, who discussed the weather, health, and office scandal while applying lipstick and blush before the ladies' room mirror—they are lost to time and the new young employees who take their places in the typing pool.[3]

Each year she gets a Christmas card from her ex-boss. The envelope 15 is canceled in the office mailroom and addressed by memory typewriter.[4] Within is a family in black and white against a wooded Connecticut landscape. The boss, his wife, who wears her hair in a gray page boy, the three blond daughters, two with tall husbands and an occasional additional grandchild. All assembled before a worn stone wall.

Does she watch game shows? Talk to a parakeet, feed him cuttle- 16 bone, and call him Pete? When she rides the buses on her Senior Citizen pass, does she go anywhere or wait for something to happen? Does she have a niece like the one in Cynthia Ozick's story "Rosa," who sends enough money to keep her aunt at a distance?

---

[3] Before personal computers became commonplace, many businesses hired people—usually women—to type the handwritten letters, memos, and other documents prepared by higher-level employees. The group of secretaries was known as the typing pool. [Editors' note.]

[4] An early word processor. [Editors' note.]

There's a lady across the way whose lights and television stay on all   17
night. A crystal chandelier in the dining room and matching Chinese
lamps on Regency end tables in the living room. She has six cats, some
Siamese, others Angora and Abyssinian. She pets them and waters her
plethora of plants—African violets, a ficus tree, a palm, and geraniums
in season. Not necessarily a lonely life except that 3 a.m. lights and television seem to proclaim it so.

The Box Man welcomes the night, opens to it like a lover. He moves   18
in darkness and prefers it that way. He's not waiting for the phone to ring
or an engraved invitation to arrive in the mail. Not for him a PO number. Not for him the overcrowded jollity of office parties, the hot anticipation of a singles' bar. Not even for him a holiday handout. People have
tried and he shuffled away.

The Box Man knows that loneliness chosen loses its sting and claims   19
no victims. He declares what we all know in the secret passages of our
own nights, that although we long for perfect harmony, communion,
and blending with another soul, this is a solo voyage.

The first half of our lives is spent stubbornly denying it. As children   20
we acquire language to make ourselves understood and soon learn from
the blank stares in response to our babblings that even these, our saviors, our parents, are strangers. In adolescence when we replay earlier
dramas with peers in the place of parents, we begin the quest for the
best friend, that person who will receive all thoughts as if they were her
own. Later we assert that true love will find the way. True love finds
many ways, but no escape from exile. The shores are littered with us,
Annas and Ophelias, Emmas and Juliets,[5] all outcasts from the dream of
perfect understanding. We might as well draw the night around us and
find solace there and a friend in our own voice.

One could do worse than be a collector of boxes.   21

Even read quickly, Ascher's essay would not be difficult to comprehend: the author draws on examples of three people to make a point
at the end about being alone. In fact, a quick reading might give the
impression that Ascher produced the essay effortlessly, artlessly. But
close, critical reading reveals a carefully planned work whose parts
function independently and together to achieve Ascher's purpose.

---

[5]These are all doomed heroines of literature. Anna is the title character of Leo
Tolstoy's novel *Anna Karenina* (1876). Emma is the title character of Gustave Flaubert's
novel *Madame Bovary* (1856). Ophelia and Juliet are in Shakespeare's plays—the
lovers, respectively, of Hamlet and Romeo. [Editors' note.]

One way to uncover underlying intentions and relations like those in Ascher's essay is to answer a series of questions about the work. The following questions proceed from the specific to the general—from word choice through method and structure to overall meaning—and they parallel the more specific questions following the essays in this book. Here the questions come with possible answers for Ascher's essay. (The paragraph numbers can help you locate the appropriate passages in Ascher's essay as you follow the analysis.)

▶ Vocabulary

How does the author use words to express and clarify meaning? If you don't know the definitions of any words, can you figure them out or do you need to look them up?

One reason Ascher's essay works is that she uses concrete and specific words to portray her characters—she shows them to us—and to let us know what she thinks about them. The Box Man comes to life in warm terms: Ascher watches him with "silent fervor" (paragraph 2); he seems "dogged by luck" (5); he sits with "slow care" and opens the newspaper with "ease" (6); his page turning reminds Ascher of "grandmothers" (7). In contrast, the isolation of the two other solitary people comes across as a desperate state in paragraph 20, where Ascher uses words such as "blank stares," "strangers," "exile," "littered," and "outcasts." The contrast in language helps to emphasize Ascher's point about the individual's ability to find comfort in solitude.

Occasionally, you may need to puzzle over some of an author's words before you can fully understand his or her meaning. Some of the vocabulary in Ascher's essay is difficult, and you may not know the meaning of words such as "fervor" (2), "dogged" (5), "exile" (20), or "solace" (20). When you come across an unfamiliar word while reading, try to determine the word's meaning from its context first, then check your guess in a dictionary. (To help master the word so that you know it next time and can draw on it yourself, use it in a sentence or more of your own.)

▶ Key Ideas and Details

What is the main idea of the essay—the chief point the writer makes about the subject, to which all other ideas and details relate? What are the supporting details that contribute to the main idea?

Ascher states her main idea (or **thesis**) near the end of her essay: in choosing solitude, the Box Man confirms the essential aloneness of human beings (paragraph 19) but also demonstrates that we can "find solace" within ourselves (20). (Writers sometimes postpone stating their main idea, as Ascher does here. Perhaps more often, they state it near the beginning of the essay. See pp. 28–31.) Ascher leads up to and supports her idea with three examples—the Box Man (1–7, 11–12) and, in contrast, two women whose loneliness seems unchosen (13–16, 17). These examples are developed with specific details from Ascher's observations (such as the nearly empty purse, 14) and from the imagined lives these observations suggest (such as the remote, perhaps nonexistent children, 14).

▶ Craft and Structure

What strategies or methods does the author use to express the main idea, and how do those strategies help the author develop the main idea and organize supporting points? How does the author use language to convey his or her attitudes toward the subject and to make meaning clear and vivid?

As writers often do, Ascher relies on more than a single method to develop her ideas. The primary support for her thesis consists of three examples (see Chapter 8)—specific instances of solitary people. Relying on examples especially suits Ascher's subject and purpose because it allows her to show different responses to being alone: one person who seems to choose it and two people who don't. She develops her examples with description (see Chapter 7), vividly portraying the Box Man and the two women, as in paragraphs 6–7, so that we see them clearly. Paragraphs 1–7 in the portrayal of the Box Man involve retelling, or narrating (see Chapter 6), his activities. Ascher uses division or analysis (see Chapter 9) to examine the elements of her three characters' lives. And she relies on comparison and contrast (see Chapter 12) to show the differences between the Box Man and the two women in paragraphs 13 and 17–18.

While using many methods to develop her idea, Ascher keeps her organization fairly simple. She does not begin with a formal introduction or a statement of her thesis but instead starts right off with her main example, the inspiration for her idea. In the first seven paragraphs she narrates the Box Man's activities and describes him. Then, in paragraphs 8–12, she explains what appeals to her about the Box Man's lifestyle. Still delaying a statement of her main idea, Ascher contrasts the

Box Man and two other solitary people, whose lives she sees as different from his (13–17). Finally, she returns to the Box Man (18–19) and zeroes in on her main idea (19–20). Though she has withheld this idea until the end, we see that everything in the essay has been leading toward it.

Notice that Ascher occasionally uses incomplete sentences (or **sentence fragments**, see p. 49) to stress the accumulation of details. For example, in paragraph 10 the incomplete sentences beginning "To" sketch Ascher's dream. And in paragraph 18 the incomplete sentences beginning "Not" emphasize the Box Man's withdrawal. Both of these sets of incomplete sentences gain emphasis from **parallelism**, the use of similar grammatical form for ideas of equal importance (see p. 55). The parallelism begins in the complete sentence just before each set of incomplete sentences—for example, ". . . I long to live like a Boxcar Child, to have enough open space and freedom of movement. . . . To turn streams into iceboxes. To be ingenious with simple things. To let the imagination hold sway." Although incomplete sentences can be unclear, these and the others in Ascher's essay are clear: she uses them deliberately and carefully, for a purpose. (Inexperienced writers often find it safer to avoid any incomplete sentences until they have mastered the complete sentence.)

▶ Integration of Knowledge and Ideas

Why did the author write the essay? Who seems to be the intended audience? What did the author assume about the knowledge and interests of readers, and how are these assumptions reflected in the essay? What inferences can readers make about the work as a whole?

Ascher seems to have written her essay for two interlocking reasons: to show and thus explain that solitude need not always be lonely and to argue gently for defeating loneliness by becoming one's own friend. In choosing the Box Man as her main example, she reveals perhaps a third purpose as well—to convince readers that a homeless person can have dignity and may achieve a measure of self-satisfaction.

"The Box Man" appears to be written for a general audience of people who have experienced, or expect to experience, loneliness at some point in their lives. Ascher assumes that her readers, like her, are people who have homes, people to whom the Box Man and his life might seem completely foreign: she comments on the Box Man's slow shuffle (paragraph 3), his mysterious discrimination among boxes (4), his "blistered legs" (11), how miserable his life looks (12), his bandages (12), the cold night he inhabits (12), the fearful or condescending approaches of strangers (12, 18). Building from this assumption that her readers will find the Box Man strange, Ascher takes pains to show his dignity—his "grand design" for furniture (5), his resemblance to commuters (6), his grandmotherly finger licking (7), his refusal of handouts (18).

Several other apparent assumptions about her readers and their knowledge also influence Ascher's selection of details, if less significantly. First, she assumes some familiarity with literature—at least with the writings of Henry David Thoreau (9, 11) and Cynthia Ozick (16), with the *Boxcar Children* books (9–10), and with the characters named in paragraph 20. Second, Ascher seems to address women: in paragraph 20 she speaks of each person confiding in "her" friend, and she chooses only female figures from literature to illustrate "us, . . . all outcasts from the dream of perfect understanding." Finally, Ascher seems to address people who are familiar with, if not actually residents of, New York City: she refers to a New York street address (2); alludes to a New York newspaper, the *Daily News*, and a New York subway line, the IRT Express (6); and mentions the city's mayor (12). However, readers who do not know the literature Ascher cites, who are not women, and who do not know New York City are still likely to understand and appreciate Ascher's main point.

The **inferences**, or conclusions, that readers might draw from Ascher's essay depend in part on the personal store of knowledge and ideas they bring to it. A reader with firsthand experience of poverty, for instance, might take issue with the author's assumptions and conclude that some observers fail to understand the root problems of homelessness. On the other hand, a lonely older woman might read the same essay, see something of herself in it, and decide to heed Ascher's advice to "find . . . a friend in [her] own voice" (20). And a reader familiar with *Walden* might recognize connections between Thoreau's and Ascher's philosophies and want to investigate them further. Your own interpretations, too, will vary, although to be reasonable they must draw on evidence and ideas from the work itself.

These notes on Ascher's essay show how a reader can arrive at a deeper, more personal understanding of a piece of writing by attentive, thoughtful analysis. Guided by the questions at the end of each essay and by your own sense of what works and why, you'll find similar lessons and pleasures in all of this book's readings.

Reading Visuals

Much of what you read will have a visual component—a photograph, perhaps, or a drawing, chart, table, or graph. Sometimes these **visuals** stand alone, as is the case in the ten chapter-opening images in Part Two, but often they contribute to the overall meaning and effect of a written work. Several of the essays in this book, in fact, include visuals: Jarrod Ballo's "Women and Children First" (p. 84) uses a line graph to explain a point, Amy Tan's "Pretty beyond Belief" (p. 116) includes a photograph of the author as a girl, David Brooks's "People Like Us" (p. 228) has a cartoon, Barbara Kingsolver's "Stalking the Vegetannual" (p. 258) starts with a drawing, Walter Mosley's "Get Happy" (p. 318) features a graphic icon, and Charlie LeDuff's "End of the Line" (p. 352) incorporates several photographs.

Like written texts, visual texts are composed. That is, the people who create them do with images what writers do with words: they come to the task with a purpose, an audience, and a message to convey. You can and should, therefore, "read" visuals actively. Don't simply glance over images or take them at face value. Instead, examine them closely and with a critical eye.

Reading visuals critically draws on the same skills you use for closely reading written works. The checklist for critical reading on page 8 can get you started. Determining who created an image, why, and for whom, for instance, will help you tease out details that you might have missed at first look.

▶ Photographs and Artwork

Examining each element of a visual composition—such as the placement and arrangement of objects, the focus, and the uses of color, light, and shadow—will give you a greater appreciation of its intent and overall effect. Notice what first captures your attention, where your eye is drawn, and how different parts of the image interact with one another to create a dominant impression. Finally, if the visual accompanies written text, such as an essay or advertisement, ask yourself what it contributes to the writer's meaning and purpose.

Consider, for example, one student's notes about a photograph of a homeless man in New York City (next page). The picture was taken by amateur photographer Colin Gregory Palmer and has been featured on the Web sites of several homeless advocacy groups.

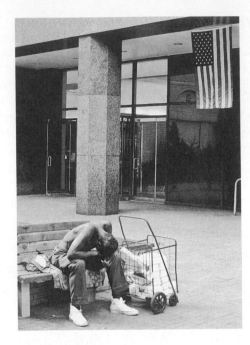

dark shadows
feel dangerous

relative position
of man and
flag = a comment
on government?

cold surfaces,
hard angles
dominate the
center

slumped over
and faceless
(shame? or
defeat?)

man stuffed
in corner —
seems powerless,
insignificant

shoes look
new — where
did they
come from?

▶ Infographics

Often, writers and speakers use visuals to make a point easier to comprehend. **Infographics** put information in visual forms, such as tables, charts, graphs, and maps. In popular periodicals and on Web sites, artists sometimes enhance data with pictures (see, for example, the illustrated pyramid chart on p. 178 and the census table on p. 208).

To read infographics critically, approach them as you would a written work (see the reading checklist on p. 8). First, identify who created the visual and try to determine what purpose it is meant to serve. Take care to read any title, label, or caption that accompanies the graphic; such information provides important context and clues to the creator's intentions. Then look at the parts of the graphic closely to take in their meanings, considering whether any information seems to be missing, inaccurate, or potentially misleading. Finally, draw inferences from the visual as a whole, looking for any new information and ideas it suggests to you.

For an example, take a close look at the two infographics on the next page. Both present information from the same government survey, and both use classification (see Chapter 10) to sort out categories of homeless people.

The table (fig. 1) was prepared by the US Department of Housing and Urban Development (HUD), a government agency responsible for (among other things) funding homeless shelters and support programs, referred to in the caption as "Continuums of Care," or CoCs. The data are presented in the agency's annual report summarizing information from those programs' applications for assistance; the purpose of the table might be to justify the department's spending, but also perhaps to suggest what kinds of people are most likely to become homeless.

The bar graph (fig. 2) was prepared by the National Alliance to End Homelessness (NAEH), a nonprofit organization that works to reform government policies. Using the same data provided in the HUD report, the NAEH translates the numbers into a more visually arresting graphic. The graph was published in the organization's annual report and distributed to the Alliance's member organizations; its purpose seems to be to inform interested parties and possibly to interpret the impact of assistance from agencies like HUD.

Both the table and the bar graph present similar information, but notice the differences. For one thing, they sort subpopulations into different categories: while the HUD table categorizes homeless individuals (minors, domestic violence victims, and so on), the primary focus in the NAEH graph is on family composition and living situation. Furthermore, the HUD table subcategorizes each group by whether or not they have shelter; the NAEH graph indicates only how many homeless people overall do or don't. In the two categories that appear in both visuals (veterans and chronically homeless), the numbers are the same; so it seems that the data is at least somewhat reliable, although the authors of both captions caution that it is not exact.

What can readers infer from these graphics? Close readers might be surprised by the information in the HUD table: the numbers suggest, for instance, that the majority of people seeking shelter are mentally ill or substance abusers (drug addicts and alcoholics), but they also show that quite a few homeless people are children, veterans, or medical patients. In the case of the NAEH bar graph, viewers can see at a glance that more homeless people live in shelters than on the street, and that only a small portion of the overall homeless population is chronic (that is, permanently without a home). Both infographics might lead readers to conclude that homelessness continues to be a significant problem in

TABLE 1　Summary of Homeless Persons by Subpopulations Reported

	Sheltered	Unsheltered	Total
Chronically Homeless	38,971	68,177	**107,148**
Severely Mentally Ill	70,884	44,480	**115,364**
Chronic Substance Abuse	87,630	56,616	**144,246**
Veterans	40,033	27,462	**67,495**
Persons with HIV/AIDS	9,698	3,523	**13,221**
Victims of Domestic Violence	53,055	20,025	**73,080**
Unaccompanied Youth (Under 18)	2,981	3,845	**6,826**

Important notes about this data: This report is based on point-in-time (PIT) information provided to HUD by Continuums of Care (CoCs) in the 2011 application for CoC Homeless Assistance Programs. CoCs are required to provide an unduplicated count of homeless persons according to HUD standards. HUD has not independently verified the information. The reader is therefore cautioned that since compliance with these standards may vary, the reliability and consistency of the homeless counts may also vary among CoCs.

Source: US Department of Housing and Urban Development. *HUD's 2011 Continuum of Care Homeless Assistance Programs Report.* Homeless Resource Exchange, n.d. Web.

Fig. 1. *A table.*

FIGURE 1　Homeless Population and Subpopulations, 2011

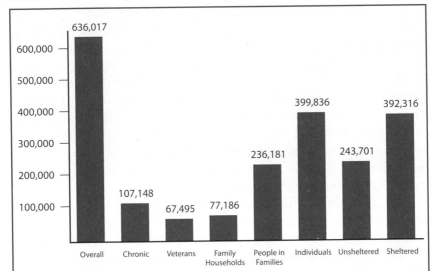

Note: Subpopulation data do not equal the overall homeless population number. This is because people could be counted as part of more than one subpopulation (e.g., a person could be an unsheltered, chronic, veteran individual). Further, family households are a separate measure as household is comprised of numerous people (e.g., at least one adult and at least one child).

Source: National Alliance to End Homelessness. *State of Homelessness 2012.* Washington, DC: NAEH, 2012. 8. Print.

Fig. 2. *A graph.*

the United States, or that the Box Man in Barbara Lazear Ascher's essay (p. 9) may not be representative of the general homeless population. Many other inferences are possible as well.

As the examples on the previous pages demonstrate, visual images can pack many layers of meaning into a condensed space. Learning to unpack those layers is a skill worth cultivating. (For advice on using visuals in your own writing, see p. 43.)

2

DEVELOPING AN ESSAY

▶

Analyzing a text as shown in the previous chapter is valuable in itself: it can be fun, and the process helps you better understand and appreciate whatever you read. But it can make you a better writer, too, by showing you how to read your own work critically, broadening the range of strategies available to you, and suggesting subjects for you to write about.

The reading selections collected in this book are accompanied by a range of materials designed to help you use your reading to write effectively. Brief commentaries direct your attention to details in the visuals that open Chapters 6–15. Each sample paragraph is annotated to help you see how the writer used a particular method to express an idea. And every essay and speech is introduced with information on the writer and the selection and followed by several questions that will help you read critically and examine the writing strategies that make the piece successful. Accompanying the questions are writing topics—ideas for you to adapt and develop into essays and presentations of your own. Some of these call for your analysis of the work; others lead you to examine your own experiences or outside sources in light of another writer's ideas. Chapters 6–15 each conclude with two additional sets of writing topics: one group provides a range of subjects for using the chapter's method of development; the other encourages you to focus on thematic connections in the chapter.

To help you develop your writing, this book also offers several tools that guide you through composing effective essays. This chapter and the next two (on revising and editing) offer specific ways to strengthen and clarify your work as you move through the **writing process**, the activities that contribute to a finished piece of writing. This process is presented here as a sequence of stages: analyzing the writing situation, generating ideas, focusing, shaping, revising, and editing. As you'll discover, these stages are actually somewhat arbitrary because writers rarely move straight through fixed steps. Instead, just as they do when thinking or talking, writers continually revisit covered territory, each time picking up more information or seeing new relationships, until their meaning is clear to themselves and can be made clear to readers. No two writers work in exactly the same way, either. Still, viewing writing in stages does help sort out its many activities so that you can develop the process that works best for you.

Complementing the general overview of the writing process in Part One are the more specific introductions to the methods of development in Part Two—narration, comparison and contrast, definition, and so on—and tips for preparing effective presentations in the Appendix. The method introductions follow the pattern set here by also moving through stages, but they take up particular concerns of the method, such as organizing a narrative or clarifying a definition. (See the Guide to the Elements of Writing at the back of the book for a list of the topics covered.)

Getting Started

Every writing situation involves several elements: you communicate a *thesis* (idea) to an *audience* of readers for a particular *purpose*. At first you may not be sure of your idea or your purpose. You may not know how you want to approach your readers, even when you know who they are. Your job in getting started, then, is to explore options and make choices.

▶ Considering Your Subject and Purpose

A **subject** for writing may arise from any source, including your own experience or reading, a suggestion in this book, or an assignment from your teacher. In the previous chapter, Barbara Lazear Ascher's essay on a homeless man demonstrates how an excellent subject can be found from observing one's surroundings. Whatever its source, the subject should be something you care enough about to explore deeply and to stamp with your own perspective.

This personal stamp comes from your **purpose**, your reason for writing. The purpose may be one of the following:

- To *persuade* readers to accept an idea or opinion or to take a certain action.

- To *explain* a subject so that readers understand it or see it in a new light.
- To *express* the thoughts and emotions triggered by a revealing or an instructive experience.
- To *entertain* readers with a humorous, exciting, or moving story.

A single essay may sometimes have more than one purpose: for instance, a writer might both explain what it's like to have a disability and try to persuade readers to respect special parking zones for people with disabilities. Your reasons for writing may be clear to you early on, arising out of the subject and its significance for you. But you may need to explore your subject for a while—even to the point of writing a draft—before you know what you want to do with it.

▶ Considering Your Audience

Either very early, when you first begin exploring your subject, or later, as a check on what you have generated, you may want to make a few notes on your anticipated **audience**. The notes are optional, but thinking about audience definitely is not. Your topic and purpose, as well as your thesis, supporting ideas, details and examples, organization, style, tone, and language—all should reflect your answers to the following questions:

- What impression do you want to make on readers?
- What do readers already know about your subject? What do they need to know?
- What are readers' likely expectations and assumptions about your subject?
- How can you build on readers' previous knowledge, expectations, and assumptions to bring them around to your view?

These considerations are crucial to achieve the fundamental purpose of all public writing and speaking: communication. Accordingly, they come up again and again in the chapter introductions and the questions after each essay.

▶ Generating Ideas

Ideas for your writing—whether your subject itself or the many smaller ideas and details that shape what you have to say about it—may come to you in a rush, or you may need to hunt for them. (You may also need to do some research to learn more about your subject or back up your ideas. See Chapter 5.) Writers use a variety of searching techniques, from jotting down thoughts while they pursue other activities to focusing on drafting for a set period of time. Here are a few techniques you might try.

Speaking and Listening

When you write, you join a conversation on a subject: you add your own thoughts to what other writers have said. So it makes sense that one of the best ways to generate ideas for writing is to talk with other people. Speaking and listening will give you new insights into a subject and reveal connections that you may not have found on your own. That's why much of your time in class will be spent discussing what you read. To get the most out of those conversations, follow these guidelines:

- *Be prepared.* Do the assigned reading and jot down your thoughts and questions before class. If you will be discussing one of the essays or speeches in this book, you can use the questions that accompany it to help prepare your notes.

- *Pay attention.* When somebody else is speaking, listen. Look at the speaker and focus on what he or she is saying. Don't interrupt, and don't let your mind wander.

- *Be polite.* Even if you disagree with people or detect flaws in their reasoning, respect their points of view. Ask questions, and try to express other speakers' thoughts in your own words to better understand them.

- *Build on one another's ideas.* The purpose of discussion is to discover new perspectives and to find common ground, so feel free to add your thoughts to what others have to say. Just make sure your points are relevant. Think before you speak, have evidence ready to support your view, and express yourself clearly and calmly.

As you discuss readings and exchange ideas with others, you'll almost certainly discover new ways of thinking about a subject. Write those ideas down. Later, you can explore them further using the other techniques described in this section.

Journal Writing

Many writers keep a **journal**, a record of thoughts and observations. Journal entries give you an opportunity to explore ideas just for yourself, free of concerns about readers who will judge what you say or how you say it. Regular journaling can also make you more comfortable with the act of writing and build your confidence. Indeed, writing teachers often require their students to keep journals or blogs for these reasons.

In a journal you can write about whatever interests, puzzles, or disturbs you. Here are just a few possible uses:

- Imitate a writer you admire, such as a poet or songwriter.
- Examine your reactions to a movie or television program.
- Analyze a relationship that's causing you problems.
- Confide your dreams and fears.
- Question a social or scientific phenomenon that you've never fully understood.

Any of this material could provide a seed for a writing assignment, but you can also use a journal deliberately to explore your responses to a reading in this book and other sources. The following journal entry by a student, Grace Patterson, shows such a response to Barbara Lazear Ascher's "The Box Man" (pp. 9–12):

> Ascher gives an odd view of homelessness—hadn't really occurred to me that the homeless man on the street might want to be there. Always assumed that no one would want to live in filthy clothes, without a roof. What is a home anyway—shelter? decor? a clothes closet? Can your body and few "possessions" = home?

Writing for herself, Patterson felt free to explore what was on her mind, without worrying about correctness and without trying to make it clear to outside readers what she means or why they should accept her views. Indeed, she didn't come to any conclusions herself, as the entry's final question makes clear. She did, however, begin to work out ideas that would serve as the foundation for a more considered critical response later on. (Further stages of Patterson's writing process appear throughout the rest of this chapter.)

Freewriting

To discover ideas for a particular assignment, you may find it useful to try **freewriting**, or writing without stopping for a set amount of time, usually five to ten minutes. In freewriting you push yourself to keep writing, following ideas wherever they lead, paying no attention to completeness or correctness or even sense. When she began composing an essay response to Barbara Lazear Ascher's "The Box Man," Grace Patterson produced this freewriting:

Something in Ascher's essay keeps nagging at me. Almost ticks me off. What she says about the Box Man is based on certain assumptions. Like she knows what he's been through, how he feels. Can he be as content as she says? What bothers me is, how much choice does the guy really have? Just becuz he manages to put a little dignity into his life on the street and refuses handouts — does that mean he chooses homelessness? Life in a shelter might be worse than life on the street.

Notice that this freewriting is rough: the tone is very informal, as if Patterson were speaking to herself; some thoughts are left dangling; some sentences are shapeless or incomplete; a word is misspelled (*becuz* for *because*). But none of this matters because the freewriting is just exploratory. Writing rapidly, without pausing to rethink or edit, actually pulled insights out of Patterson. She moved from being vaguely uneasy with Ascher's essay to generating an argument against it. Then, with a more definite focus, she could begin drafting in earnest.

Brainstorming

Another technique that helps to pull ideas from you is **brainstorming**, listing ideas without stopping to judge or change them. As in freewriting, write for five or ten minutes, jotting down everything that seems even remotely related to your subject. Don't stop to reread and rethink what you have written; just keep pulling and recording ideas, no matter how silly or dull or irrelevant they seem. When your time is up, look over the list to find the promising ideas and discard the rest. Depending on how promising the remaining ideas are, you can resume brainstorming, try freewriting about them, or begin a draft.

Using the Methods of Development

The ten methods of development discussed in Chapters 6–15 can also help you expand your thinking. Try asking the following questions to open up ideas about your subject:

- **Narration** (Chapter 6): What is the story in the subject? How did it happen?
- **Description** (Chapter 7): How does the subject look, sound, smell, taste, and feel?
- **Example** (Chapter 8): How can the subject be illustrated? What are instances of it?
- **Division or Analysis** (Chapter 9): What are the subject's parts, and what is their relationship or significance?

- **Classification** (Chapter 10): What groups or categories can the subject be sorted into?
- **Process Analysis** (Chapter 11): How does the subject work, or how does someone do it?
- **Comparison and Contrast** (Chapter 12): How is the subject similar to or different from something else?
- **Definition** (Chapter 13): What are the subject's characteristics and boundaries?
- **Cause-and-Effect Analysis** (Chapter 14): Why did the subject happen? What were or may be its consequences?
- **Argument and Persuasion** (Chapter 15): Why do I believe as I do about the subject? Why do others have different opinions? How can I convince others to accept my opinion or believe as I do?

Forming a Thesis

Have you ever read a newspaper or magazine article and wondered, "What's the point?" Whether consciously or not, we expect a writer to *have* a point, a central idea that he or she wants readers to accept. We expect that idea to determine the content of the work—so that everything relates to it—and we expect the content in turn to demonstrate or prove the idea.

Arriving at a main idea, or **thesis**, is thus an essential part of the writing process. Sometimes your thesis will occur to you at the moment you hit on your subject—for instance, if you think of writing about a new grading policy because you want to make a claim about its unfairness. More often, you will need to explore your subject for a while—even to the point of writing a draft or more—before you pin down just what you have to say. Even if your final thesis will take shape over time, however, it's a good idea to draft it early because it can help keep you focused as you generate more ideas, seek evidence, and organize your thoughts.

▶ Identifying Your Main Point

A thesis is distinct from the subject of an essay. The subject is what an essay is about; the thesis captures a writer's unique understanding of or opinion on that subject. In the case of "The Box Man," for example, the subject is homelessness, but Ascher's thesis—that one homeless man's quiet dignity should serve as a model for how the rest of us go about our lives—makes a strong point that readers may not have contemplated on their own. Student writer Grace Patterson takes the same subject—homelessness—but she makes a completely different point: that a homeless person's "choice" to live on the streets is not a choice at all.

The distinction between a subject and a thesis is evident throughout this book. Each chapter in Part Two focuses on a single subject—such as nature, popular culture, or food—yet the individual paragraphs and essays demonstrate the writers' unique perspectives on particular aspects of those general topics. The readings in Chapter 6, for instance, all center on the subject of childhood, but no two take the same approach. Michael Ondaatje writes to capture the mystery of a snake that seemed immortal; Donald Hall recalls the "bliss" of hurting a playmate; Frederick Douglass writes about the hardships of slavery to make a point about education; Maya Angelou recalls a thrilling incident to explain the hopes and dreams of a community; and Amy Tan considers the ways in which her mother's and grandmother's beauty shaped her self-perception.

To move from a general subject to a workable thesis for your own writing, keep narrowing your focus until you have something to say about a subject. For example, one student decided to write about family but quickly discovered that the topic is too broad to work with. She then narrowed the subject to adoptive families, but even that covered too much territory. As she consistently tightened her focus, she first thought to discuss adopted children who try to contact their birth parents, then considered explaining how adoptees can locate the necessary information, and finally decided to discuss how legal and other barriers can impede adoptees' efforts to find their birth parents. In a few steps, the writer turned a broad subject into a manageable idea worth pursuing. The process isn't always simple, but it is a necessary first step in finding a thesis.

▶ Drafting and Revising a Thesis Statement

Once you've narrowed your subject and have something to say about it, the best way to focus on your thesis is to write it out in a **thesis statement**: a claim that makes your point about the subject. In these two sentences from the end of "The Box Man" (p. 9), Barbara Lazear Ascher asserts the main idea of her essay:

> [We are] all outcasts from the dream of perfect understanding. We might as well draw the night around us and find solace there and a friend in our own voice.

Ascher's thesis statement, while poetic, nonetheless ties together all of the other ideas and details in her essay; it also reflects her purpose in writing the essay and focuses her readers on a single point. All effective thesis statements do this: they go beyond generalities or mere reports of fact to express the writer's opinion about the subject. Notice the differences in the following sentences Grace Patterson considered for her response to "The Box Man":

GENERAL STATEMENT   Homelessness is a serious problem in America.

STATEMENT OF FACT   Some homeless people avoid staying in temporary shelters.

EFFECTIVE THESIS   For homeless people in America today, there are no good choices.

The first sentence offers an opinion, but because it's a very broad claim that few would dispute, it fails to capture readers' interest or make a significant point. The second sentence merely expresses a fact, not a main idea worth developing in an essay. The final sentence, however, makes a strong claim about a narrow subject and gives readers an idea of what to expect from the rest of the essay.

Because the main point of an essay may change over the course of the writing process, your own thesis statement may also change, sometimes considerably. The following examples show how the student discussed earlier moved from an explanatory to a persuasive purpose between the early stages of the writing process and the final draft:

FIRST DRAFT   Adopted children can contact their birth parents, although sometimes the process is difficult.

SECOND DRAFT   Adopted children often need persistence to locate information about their birth parents.

FINAL DRAFT   Laws and traditions unfairly block adopted children from seeking information about their birth parents.

The first two sentences identify the subject of the essay, but they are broad and bland and neither clearly focuses on the writer's interest: the barriers to obtaining information. In contrast, the final sentence makes a definitive assertion and clearly conveys a persuasive purpose. Thus the sentence lets readers know what to expect: an argument that adopted children should be treated more fairly when they seek information about their birth parents. Readers will also expect some discussion of the "laws and traditions" that hamper adoptees' searches, what is "unfair" and "fair" in this situation, and what changes the author proposes.

Commonly in academic writing, the thesis statement comes near the beginning of an essay, sometimes in the first paragraph, where it serves as a promise to examine a particular subject from a particular perspective. But as Ascher demonstrates by stating her main idea at the end, the thesis statement may come elsewhere as long as it controls the whole essay. The thesis may even go unstated, as other essays in this book illustrate, but it still must govern every element of the work as if it were announced.

Organizing

Writers vary in the extent to which they arrange their material before they begin drafting, but most do establish some plan. A good time to do so is after you've explored your subject and developed a good stock of ideas about it. Before you begin drafting, you can look over what you've got and consider the best ways to organize it.

▶ Creating a Plan

A writing plan may consist of a list of key points, a fuller list including evidence and specifics as well, or even a detailed formal outline—whatever gives order to your ideas and provides some direction for your writing.

As you'll see in later chapters, many of the methods of development suggest specific structures, most notably description, narration, classification, process analysis, and comparison and contrast. But even when the organization is almost built into the method, you'll find that some subjects demand more thoughtful plans than others. You may be able to draft a straightforward narrative of a personal experience with very little advance planning. But a nonpersonal narrative, or even a personal one involving complex events and time shifts, may require more thought about arrangement.

Though some sort of plan is almost always useful when drafting, resist any temptation at this stage to pin down every detail in its proper place. A huge investment in planning can get in your way during drafting, making it difficult to respond to new ideas and even new directions that may prove fruitful.

▶ Thinking in Paragraphs

Most essays consist of three parts: an introduction and a conclusion (discussed in the next section) and the **body**, the most substantial and longest part, which develops the main idea or thesis.

As you explore your subject, you will generate ideas that directly support your thesis and come up with more specific examples, details, and other evidence to support these ideas. In the following outline of Grace Patterson's "A Rock and a Hard Place" (pp. 61–62), you can see how each supporting idea, or reason, helps to build the thesis:

THESIS   For homeless people in America today, there are no good choices.

REASON   A "good choice" is one made from a variety of options determined and narrowed down by the chooser.

REASON   Homeless people do not necessarily choose to live on the streets.

REASON   The streets are the only alternative to shelters, which are dangerous and dehumanizing.

Patterson uses specific evidence to develop each reason in a paragraph. In essence, the paragraphs are like mini-essays with their own main ideas and support. (See pp. 38–41 for more on paragraph structure.)

When you create a plan for your ideas, first identify your reasons, the main supports for your thesis. Use these as your starting points to work out your essay one chunk (or paragraph) at a time. You can sketch the supporting details and examples into your organizational plan, or you can wait until you begin drafting to get into the specifics.

▶ Considering the Introduction and Conclusion

You'll probably have to be drafting or revising before you'll know for sure how you want to begin and end your essay. Still, it can be helpful to consider the introduction and conclusion earlier, so you have a sense of how you might approach readers and what you might leave them with.

The basic opening and closing serve readers by demonstrating your interest in their needs and expectations:

- The **introduction** draws readers into the essay and focuses their attention on the main idea and purpose, often stated in a thesis sentence.

- The **conclusion** ties together the parts of the essay and provides a final impression for readers to take away with them.

These basic forms allow considerable room for variation. Especially as you are developing your writing skills, you will find it helpful to state your thesis sentence near the beginning of the essay; but sometimes you can place it effectively at the end, or you can let it direct what you say in the essay but never state it at all. One essay may need two paragraphs of introduction but only a one-sentence conclusion, whereas another essay may require no formal introduction but a lengthy conclusion. How you begin and end depends on your subject and purpose, the kind of essay you are writing, and the likely responses of your readers. Specific ideas for opening and closing essays are included in the "Organizing" section of each chapter of readings and in the Glossary under *introductions* and *conclusions*.

Drafting

However detailed your organizational plan is, you should not view it as a rigid taskmaster while you are drafting your essay. **Drafting** is the chance for you to give expression to your ideas, filling them out, finding relationships, drawing conclusions. If you are like most writers, you will discover much of what you have to say while forming your thoughts into sentences and paragraphs. In fact, if your subject is complex or difficult for you to write about, you may need several drafts just to work out your ideas and their relationships.

▶ Writing, Not Revising

Some writers draft rapidly, rarely looking up from the paper or keyboard. Others draft more in fits and starts, gazing out the window or doodling as much as writing. Any method that works is fine, but one method rarely works: collapsing drafting and revising into one stage, trying to do everything at once.

Write first; then revise. Concentrate on *what* you are saying, not on *how* you are saying it. You pressure yourself needlessly if you try to produce a well-developed, coherent, interesting, and grammatically correct paper in one sitting. You may have trouble getting words down because you're afraid to make mistakes, or you may be distracted by mistakes from exploring your ideas fully. Awkwardness, repetition, wrong words, grammatical errors, spelling mistakes—these and other more superficial concerns can be dealt with in a later draft. The same goes for considering your readers' needs: like many writers, you may find that attention to readers during the first draft inhibits the flow of ideas. If so, postpone that attention until the second or third draft.

If you experience writer's block or just don't know how to begin, start writing the part you're most comfortable with. Writing in paragraph chunks, as described on page 32, will also make drafting more manageable. You can start with your thesis sentence—or at least keep it in view—as a reminder of your purpose and main idea. But if you find yourself pulled away from the thesis by a new idea, let go and follow, at least for a while. If your purpose and main idea change as a result of such exploration, you can always revise your thesis accordingly.

▶ Grace Patterson's First Draft

Some exploratory work by the student Grace Patterson appears on pages 26 and 27. What follows is the first draft she then wrote on homelessness. The draft is very rough, with frequent repetitions, wandering paragraphs, and many other flaws. But such weaknesses are not important at this early stage. The draft gave Patterson the opportunity to discover what she had to say, explore her ideas, and link them in rough sequence.

Title?

In the essay, "The Box Man," Barbara Lazear Ascher says that a homeless man who has chosen solitude can show the rest of us how to "find . . . a friend in our own voice." Maybe. But her case depends on the Box Man's choice, her assumption that he *had* one.

Discussions of the homeless often use the word *choice*. Many people with enough money can accept the condition of the homeless in America when they tell themselves that many of the homeless chose their lives. That the streets are in fact what they want. But it's not fair to use the word *choice* here: the homeless don't get to choose their lives the way most of the rest of us do. For homeless people in America today, there are no good choices.

What do I mean by a "good choice"? One made from a variety of options determined and narrowed down by the chooser. There is plenty of room for the chooser to make a decision that he will be satisfied with. When I choose a career, I expect to make a good choice. There is plenty of interesting fields worth investigating, and there is lots of rewarding work to be done. It's a choice that opens the world up and showcases its possibilities. If it came time for me to choose a career, and the mayor of my town came around and told me that I had to choose between a life of cleaning public toilets and operating a jackhammer on a busy street corner, I would object. That's a lousy choice, and I wouldn't let anyone force me to make it.

When the mayor of New York tried to take the homeless off the streets, some of them didn't want to go. People assumed that the homeless people who did not want to get in the mayor's car for a ride to a city shelter *chose* to live on the street. But just because some homeless people chose the street over the generosity of the mayor does not necessarily mean that life on the streets is their ideal. We allow ourselves as many options as we can imagine, but we allow the homeless only two: go to a shelter, or stay where you are. Who narrowed down the options for the homeless? Who benefits if they go to a shelter? Who suffers if they don't?

Homeless people are not always better off in shelters. I had a conversation with a man who had lived on the streets for a long time. The man said that he had spent some time in those shelters for the homeless, and he told me what they were like. The shelters are crowded and dirty and people have to wait in long lines for everything. People are constantly being herded around and bossed around. It's dangerous — drug dealers, beatings, theft. Dehumanizing. It matches my picture of hell. From the sound of it, I couldn't spend two hours in a shelter, never mind a whole night. I value my peace of mind and my sleep too much, not to mention my freedom.

When homeless people sleep in the street, though, that makes the public uncomfortable. People with enough money wish the homeless would just disappear. They don't care where they go. Just out of sight. I've felt this way too but I'm as uneasy with that reaction as I am at the sight of a person sleeping on the sidewalk. And I tell myself that this is more than a question of my comfort. By and large I'm comfortable enough.

The homeless are in a difficult enough situation without having to take the blame for making the rest of us feel uncomfortable. If we cannot offer the homeless a good set of choices, the opportunity to choose lives that they will be truly satisfied with then the least we can do is stop dumping on them (?). They're caught between a rock and a hard place: there are not many places for them to go, and the places where they can go afford nothing but suffering.

3

REVISING

The previous chapter took you through the first-draft stage of the writing process, when you have a chance to work out your ideas without regard for what others may think. This chapter describes the crucial next stage, when you actively consider your readers: revising to focus and shape your meaning.

Revision means "re-seeing." Looking at your draft as your reader would, you cut, add, and reorganize until the ideas make sense on their own. Revision is not the same as editing. In revising, you make fundamental changes in content and structure. Editing comes later: once you're satisfied with the revised draft, you work on the sentences and words, attending to style, grammar, punctuation, and the like (see Chapter 4). The separation of these two stages is important because if you try to edit while you revise, you'll be likely to miss the big picture. You may also waste effort perfecting sentences you'll later decide to cut.

Reading Your Own Work Critically

Perhaps the biggest challenge of revision is reading your own work objectively, as a reader would. To gain something like a reader's critical distance from your draft, try one or more of the following techniques:

- *Put your first draft aside for at least a few hours—and preferably overnight—before attempting to revise it.* You may have further thoughts in the interval, and you will be able to see your work more objectively when you return to it.

- *Ask another person to read and comment on your draft.* Your teacher may ask you and your classmates to exchange drafts so that you can help each other revise. But even without such a procedure, you can benefit from others' responses. Keep an open mind to readers' comments, and ask questions when you need more information.

- *Make an outline of your draft by listing what you cover in each paragraph.* Such an outline can show gaps, overlaps, and problems in organization. (See also p. 31.)
- *Read the draft out loud.* Speaking the words and hearing them can help to create distance from your draft.
- *Imagine you are someone else*—a friend, perhaps, or a particular person in your intended audience—and read the draft through that person's eyes, as if for the first time.
- *Print a double-spaced copy of your draft.* It's much easier to read text on paper than on a computer screen, and you can spread out printed pages to see the whole paper at once. Once you've finished revising, transferring changes to the computer requires little effort.

Looking at the Whole Draft

Revision involves seeing your draft as a whole, focusing mainly on your purpose and thesis, the support for your thesis, and the movement among ideas. You want to determine what will work and what won't for readers—where the draft strays from your purpose, fails to develop your thesis, does not flow logically, or needs more details. (See the revision checklist on p. 45.) Besides rewriting, you may need to cut entire paragraphs, condense paragraphs into sentences, add passages of explanation, rearrange sections, or try a different approach.

▶ Purpose and Thesis

When drafting, you may lose sight of why you are writing or what your main point is. Both your purpose and your thesis may change as you work out your ideas, so that you start in one place and end somewhere else or even lose track of where you are.

Your first goal in revising, then, is to see that your essay is well focused. Readers should grasp a clear purpose right away, and they should find that you have achieved it at the end. They should see your main idea, your thesis, very early, usually by the end of the introduction, and they should think that you have proved or demonstrated the thesis when they reach the last paragraph.

Like many writers, you may sometimes start with one thesis and finish with another, in effect discovering what you think about a subject by writing about it. In many cases you'll need to rewrite your thesis statement to reflect what you actually wrote in your draft. Or you may need to upend your essay, plucking your thesis out of the conclusion and starting over with it, providing new reasons and details to develop it. You'll probably find the second draft much easier to write because you know better what you want to say, and the next round of revision after that will go even more smoothly.

▶ Unity

When a piece of writing has **unity**, all its parts are related: the sentences build the central idea of their paragraph, and the paragraphs build the central idea of the whole essay. Readers do not have to wonder what the essay is about or what a particular paragraph has to do with the rest of the piece.

Unity in Paragraphs

Earlier we saw how the body paragraphs of an essay are almost like mini-essays themselves, each developing an idea, or reason, that supports the thesis. (See p. 28.) In fact, a body paragraph should have its own thesis usually expressed in a **topic sentence** or sentences. The rest of the paragraph develops the topic with specifics.

In the following paragraph from the final draft of Grace Patterson's student essay "A Rock and a Hard Place" (pp. 61–62), the topic sentence is italicized:

> *The fact is that homeless people are not always better off in shelters.* I spoke recently with a man who had lived on the streets for a long time. He said that he had spent some time in shelters for the homeless, and he told me what they are like. They're dangerous and dehumanizing. Drug deals, beatings, and thefts are common. Because shelters are crowded, residents have to wait in long lines for everything; they also have to accept being constantly bossed around. No wonder some homeless people prefer the street: it affords some space to breathe, some independence, some peace for sleeping.

Notice that every sentence of this paragraph relates to the topic sentence. Patterson achieved this unity in revision (see pp. 46–47). In her first draft she focused the last sentences of this paragraph on herself rather than on the conditions of homeless shelters:

> It matches my picture of hell. From the sound of it, I couldn't spend two hours in a shelter, never mind a whole night. I value my peace of mind and my sleep too much, not to mention my freedom.

If you look back at the full paragraph above, you'll see that Patterson deleted these sentences and substituted a final one that focuses on the paragraph's topic, the conditions of the shelters for homeless people themselves.

Your topic sentences will not always fall at the very beginning of your paragraphs. Sometimes you'll need to create a transition from the preceding paragraph before stating the new paragraph's topic, or you'll build the paragraph to a topic sentence at the end, or you'll divide the statement between the beginning and the end. (Patterson's second paragraph, on p. 34, works this way, defining a good choice at the beginning and a bad choice at the end.) Sometimes, too, you'll write a paragraph with a topic but without a topic sentence. In all these cases, you'll need to have an idea for the paragraph and to unify the paragraph around that idea, so that all the specifics support and develop it.

Unity in Essays

Just as sentences must center on a paragraph's main idea, so paragraphs must center on an essay's main idea, or thesis. Readers who have to ask "What is the point?" or "Why am I reading this?" generally won't appreciate or accept the point.

Look at the outline of Grace Patterson's essay on page 30. Her thesis sentence states, "For homeless people in America today, there are no good choices," and each paragraph clearly develops this idea: what a good choice is, whether homeless people choose to live on the streets, and why shelters are not good alternatives to the streets. This unity is true of Patterson's revised draft but not of her first draft, where she drifted into considering how the homeless make other people uncomfortable. The topic could be interesting, but it blurred Patterson's focus on homeless people and their choices. Recognizing as much, Patterson deleted her entire second-to-last paragraph when she revised (see p. 47). Deleting this distracting passage also helped Patterson clarify her conclusion.

Like Patterson, you may be pulled in more than one direction while drafting, so that you digress from your thesis or pursue more than one thesis. Drafting and revising are your chances to find and then sharpen your focus. Revising for unity strengthens your thesis.

▶ Coherence

Writing is **coherent** when readers can follow it easily and can see how the parts relate to each other. The ideas develop in a clear sequence, the sentences and paragraphs connect logically, and the connections are clear and smooth. The writing flows.

Coherence in Paragraphs

Coherence starts as sentences build paragraphs. The example below, from the final draft of Grace Patterson's "A Rock and a Hard Place," shows several devices for achieving coherence in paragraphs:

- **Repetition and restatement** of key words (underlined twice in the example).
- **Pronouns** such as *they* and *them* that substitute for nouns such as *shelters* and *residents* (circled in the example).
- **Parallelism**, the use of similar grammatical structures for related ideas of the same importance (boxed in the example). See also pages 55 and 278–79.
- **Transitions** that clearly link the parts of sentences and whole sentences (underlined once in the example). Transitions may indicate time (*later, soon*), place (*nearby, farther away*), similarity (*also, likewise*), difference (*in contrast, instead*), and many other relationships. See the Glossary, page 467, for a list of transitions.

> The fact is that homeless people are not always better off in shelters. I spoke recently with a man who had lived on the streets for a long time. He said that he had spent some time in shelters for the homeless, and he told me what they are like. They're dangerous and dehumanizing. Drug deals, beatings, and thefts are common. Because shelters are crowded, residents have to wait in long lines for everything; they also have to accept being constantly bossed around. No wonder some homeless people prefer the street: it affords some space to breathe, some independence, some peace for sleeping.

Check all your paragraphs to be sure that each sentence connects with the one before it and that readers will see the connection without having to stop and reread. You may not need all the coherence devices

Patterson uses, or as many as she uses, but every paragraph you write will require some devices to stitch the sentences together.

Coherence in Essays

Reading a coherent essay, the audience does not have to ask "What does this have to do with the other paragraphs?" or "Where is the writer going here?" The connections are apparent, and the organization is clear and logical.

TRANSITIONS   Transitions link ideas between sentences and paragraphs. When two ideas are closely related, a simple word or phrase may be all that's needed to show the relationship. In each example below, the underlined transition opens the topic sentence of the paragraph:

> Moreover, the rising costs of health care have long outpaced inflation.
>
> However, some kinds of health-care plans have proved much more expensive than others.

When a paragraph is beginning a new part of the essay or otherwise changing direction, a sentence or more at the beginning will help explain the shift. In the next example, the first sentence summarizes the preceding paragraph, the second introduces the topic of the new paragraph, and the third gives the paragraph's topic sentence:

> Traditional health-care plans have thus become an unaffordable luxury for most individuals and businesses. The majority of those with health insurance now find themselves in so-called managed plans. Though they do vary, managed plans share at least two features: they pay full benefits only when the insured person consults an approved doctor, and they require prior approval for certain procedures.

Notice that underlined transitions provide further cues about the relationship of ideas.

ORGANIZATION   Just as important in achieving coherence is an overall **organization** that develops ideas in a clear sequence and directs readers in a familiar pattern:

- A **spatial** organization arranges information to parallel the way we scan people, objects, or places: top to bottom, left to right, front to back, near to far, or vice versa. This scheme is especially useful for a description (Chapter 7).

- A **chronological** organization arranges events or steps as they occurred in time, first to last. Such an arrangement usually organizes a narrative (Chapter 6) or a process analysis (Chapter 11) and may also help with a cause-and-effect analysis (Chapter 14).

- A **climactic** organization builds from least to most important, building to the most interesting example, the most telling point of comparison, the most significant argument. A climactic organization is most useful for writing examples (Chapter 8), a comparison (Chapter 12), or an argument (Chapter 15).

The introduction to each method of development in Chapters 6–15 gives detailed advice on organizing with these arrangements and variations on them.

When revising your draft for organization, try outlining it by jotting down the topic sentence of each paragraph and the key support for each topic. The exercise will give you some distance from your ideas and words, allowing you to see the structure like a skeleton. Will your readers grasp the logic of your arrangement? Will they see why you move from each idea to the next one? After checking the overall structure, be sure you've built in enough transitions between sentences and paragraphs to guide readers through your ideas.

▶ Development

When you **develop** an idea, you provide concrete and specific reasons, details, examples, facts, opinions, and other evidence to make the idea vivid and true in readers' minds. Readers will know only as much as you tell them about your thesis and its support. Gaps, vague statements, and unsupported conclusions will undermine your efforts to win their interest and agreement.

The following undeveloped paragraph barely outlines one type of friend:

> Buddies are the workhorses of the friendship world. They call you and listen. They accompany you. They help you and offer advice.

Contrast the preceding bare-bones adaptation with the actual paragraph written by Marion Winik in "What Are Friends For?" (p. 223):

> Buddies, for example, are the workhorses of the friendship world, the people out there on the front lines, defending you from loneliness and boredom. They call you up, they listen to your complaints, they celebrate your successes and curse your misfortunes, and you do the same for them in return. They hold out through innumerable crises before concluding that the person you're dating is no good, and even then understand if you ignore their good counsel. They accompany you to a movie with subtitles or to see the diving pig at Aquarena Springs. They feed your cat when you are out of

town and pick you up from the airport when you get back. They come over to help you decide what to wear on a date. Even if it is with that creep.

In the first sentence, Winik clarifies what she means when she says buddies are "workhorses" with general statements of what they do for friends. The rest of the paragraph expands on these statements with specific, vivid examples of individual acts of friendship, each time showing that such acts take effort.

Development begins in sentences, when you use the most concrete and specific words you can find to explain your meaning. (See p. 49.) At the level of the paragraph, these sentences develop the paragraph's topic. Then, at the level of the whole essay, these paragraphs develop the governing thesis.

Sometimes, you may discover that the most effective way to develop an idea is through **visuals**. For instance, if you support a point with numbers or statistics, presenting them in a chart or graph can make the information easier for readers to grasp. Similarly, a photograph may help to illustrate an idea or create an emotional response in your readers. If you decide to add a visual element to your draft, be sure that you have a purpose for using the image, that you provide a caption to clarify that purpose, and that you credit the source of the image. (For an effective use of a visual in a student essay, see Jarrod Ballo's "Women and Children First" on p. 84. For information on crediting visual sources, see p. 83.)

The key to adequate development is a good sense of your readers' needs for information and reasons. The list of questions on page 24 can help you estimate these needs as you start to write; reconsidering the questions when you revise can help you see where your draft may fail to address, say, readers' unfamiliarity with your subject or possible resistance to your thesis.

The introduction to each method of development in Chapters 6–15 includes specific advice for meeting readers' needs when using the method to develop paragraphs and essays. When you sense that a paragraph or section of your essay is thin but you don't know how to improve it, you can also try the discovery techniques given on pages 23–25 or ask the questions for all the methods of development on pages 27–28.

▶ Tone

The **tone** of writing is like the tone of voice in speech: it expresses the writer's attitude toward his or her subject and audience. In writing we express tone with word choice and sentence structure. Notice the marked differences in these two passages discussing the same information on the same subject:

> Voice mail can be convenient, sure, but for callers it's usually more trouble than it's worth. We waste time "listening to the following menu choices," when we just want the live person at the end. All too often, there isn't even such a person!
>
> For callers the occasional convenience of voice mail generally does not compensate for its inconveniences. Most callers would prefer to speak to a live operator but must wait through a series of choices to reach that person. Increasingly, companies with voice-mail systems do not offer live operators at all.

The first passage is informal, expresses clear annoyance, and with *we* includes the reader in that attitude. The second passage is more formal and more objective, reporting the situation without involving readers directly.

Tone can range from casual to urgent, humorous to serious, sad to elated, pleased to angry, personal to objective. The particular tone you choose for a piece of writing depends on your purpose and your audience. For most academic and business writing, you will be trying to explain or argue a point. Your readers will be interested more in the substance of your writing than in a startling tone, and indeed an approach that is too familiar or humorous or hostile could put them off.

Tone is something you want to evaluate in revision, along with whether you've achieved your purpose and whether you've developed your thesis adequately for your audience. But adjusting tone is largely a matter of replacing words and restructuring sentences, work that could distract you from an overall view of your essay. If you think your tone is off base, you may want to devote a separate phase of revision to it, after addressing unity, coherence, and the other matters discussed in this chapter.

For additional information, see "Focus on Tone" on pages 379–80. For advice on sentence structures and word choices, see Chapter 4 on editing.

Using a Revision Checklist

The checklist on the next page summarizes the advice on revision given in this chapter. Use the checklist to remind yourself what to look for in your first draft. But don't try to answer all the questions in a single read-

---

CHECKLIST FOR Revision

- What is your purpose in writing? Will it be clear to readers? Do you achieve it?

- What is your thesis? Where is it made clear to readers?

- How unified is your essay? How does each body paragraph support your thesis? (Look especially at your topic sentences.) How does each sentence in the body paragraph support the topic sentence of the paragraph?

- How coherent is your essay? Do repetition and restatement, pronouns, parallelism, and transitions link the sentences in paragraphs?

- Does the overall organization clarify the flow of ideas? How does your introduction work to draw readers in and preview your purpose and thesis? How does your conclusion work to pull the essay together and give readers a sense of completion?

- How well developed is your essay? Where might readers need more reasons and evidence to understand your ideas and find them convincing? Would visual images help?

- What is the tone of your essay? How is it appropriate for your purpose and your audience?

---

ing of the draft. Instead, take the questions one by one, rereading the whole draft for each. That way you'll be able to concentrate on each element with minimal distraction from the others.

Note that the introductions to the methods of development in Chapters 6–15 also have their own revision checklists. Combining this list with the one for the method you're using will produce a more targeted set of questions. (The Guide to the Elements of Writing in the back of the book will direct you to the discussion you want.)

▶ Grace Patterson's Revised Draft

Considering questions like those in the revision checklist led the student Grace Patterson to revise the rough draft we saw on pages 34–35.

Patterson's revision follows. Notice that she made substantial cuts, especially of digressions near the end of the draft. She also revamped the introduction, tightened many passages, improved the coherence of paragraphs, and wrote a wholly new conclusion to sharpen her point. She did not try to improve her style or fix errors at this stage, leaving these activities for later editing.

~~Title?~~ A Rock and a Hard Place

In the essay, "The Box Man," Barbara Lazear Ascher says that a homeless man who has chosen solitude can show the rest of us how to "find . . . a friend in our own voice." Maybe. But ~~her~~ Ascher's case depends on the Box Man's choice, her assumption that he *had* one.

Discussions of the homeless often use the word *choice*. Many ~~people with enough money can accept the condition of the homeless in America when they tell themselves~~ of us with homes would like to think that many of the homeless chose their lives. ~~That the streets are in fact what they want. But it's not fair to use the word *choice* here: the homeless don't get to choose their lives the way most of the rest of us do.~~ But ~~F~~for the homeless people in America today, there are no good choices.

What do I mean by a "good choice"? ~~One~~ A good choice is made from a variety of options determined and narrowed down by the chooser. There is plenty of room for the chooser to make a decision that he will be satisfied with. When I choose a career, I expect to make a good choice. There is plenty of interesting fields worth investigating, and there is lots of rewarding work to be done. ~~It's a choice that opens the world up and showcases its possibilities. If it came time for me to choose a career, and~~ However, if the mayor of my town came around and told me that I had to choose between a life of cleaning public toilets and operating a jackhammer on a busy street corner, I would object. That's a lousy choice, and I wouldn't let anyone force me to make it.

When the mayor of New York tried to take ~~the~~ homeless people off the streets, he likewise offered them a bad choice. ~~some of them didn't want to go. People assumed that the homeless people who did not want to~~ They could get in the mayor's car for a ride to a city shelter ~~chose to live~~ or they could stay on the street. ~~But just because some homeless people chose the street over the generosity of the mayor does not necessarily mean that life on the streets is their ideal.~~ People assumed that the homeless people who refused a ride to the shelter wanted to live on the street. But that assumption is not necessarily true. We allow ourselves as many options as we can imagine, but we allow the homeless only two~~:~~ ~~go to a shelter, or stay where you are. Who narrowed down the options~~ ~~for the homeless? Who benefits if they go to a shelter? Who suffers if~~ ~~they don't?~~, both unpleasant.

Homeless people are not always better off in shelters. I had a conversation with a man who had lived on the streets for a long time. ~~The man~~ He said that he had spent some time in those shelters for the homeless, and he told me what they were like. ~~The shelters are~~ ~~crowded and dirty and people have to wait in long lines for everything.~~ ~~People are constantly being herded around and~~ They're dangerous and dehumanizing. Drug dealing, beatings, and theft are common. The shelters are dirty and crowded, so that residents have to wait in long lines for everything and are constantly bossed around. ~~It's dangerous — drug~~ ~~dealers, beatings, theft. Dehumanizing. It matches my picture of hell.~~ ~~From the sound of it, I couldn't spend two hours in a shelter, never mind~~ ~~a whole night. I value my peace of mind and my sleep too much, not to~~ ~~mention my freedom and independence.~~ No wonder some homeless people prefer the street: some space to breathe, some independence, some peace for sleeping.

~~When homeless people sleep in the street, though, that makes the~~ ~~public uncomfortable. People with enough money wish the homeless~~ ~~would just disappear. They don't care where they go. Just out of sight. I've~~ ~~felt this way too but I'm as uneasy with that reaction as I am at the sight~~ ~~of a person sleeping on the sidewalk. And I tell myself that this is more~~ ~~than a question of my comfort. By and large I'm comfortable enough.~~

~~The homeless are in a difficult enough situation without having to~~ ~~take the blame for making the rest of us feel uncomfortable with our~~ ~~wealth. If we cannot offer the homeless a good set of choices, the oppor-~~ ~~tunity to choose lives that they will be truly satisfied with then the least~~ ~~we can do is stop dumping on them (?). They're caught between a rock~~ ~~and a hard place: there are not many places for them to go, and the places~~ ~~where they can go afford nothing but suffering.~~

Focusing on the supposed choices the homeless have may make us feel better, but it distracts attention from the kinds of choices that are really being denied the homeless. The options we take for granted — a job with decent pay, an affordable home — do not belong to the homeless. They're caught between no shelter at all and shelter that dehumanizes, between a rock and a hard place.

4

EDITING

The final stage of the writing process is **editing** to clarify and polish your work.

In editing you turn from global issues of purpose, thesis, unity, coherence, organization, development, and tone to more particular issues of sentences and words to ensure that your finished draft adheres to standard English grammar and usage. The written language of educated native speakers, **standard English** follows well-established expectations regarding sentence structure, punctuation, and vocabulary—the "rules" of writing—such as those addressed in this chapter.

Like revision, editing requires that you gain some distance from your work so that you can see it objectively. Try these techniques:

- Work on a clean copy of your revised draft. Edit on a printout rather than on the computer, because it's more difficult to spot errors on-screen.

- Read your revised draft aloud so that you can hear the words. But be sure to read what you have actually written, not what you may have intended to write but didn't.

- To catch errors, try reading your draft backward sentence by sentence. You'll be less likely to get caught up in the flow of your ideas and more likely to see your mistakes.

- Keep a list of problems that you tend to have or that others have pointed out in your previous writing. Add this personal checklist to the one on page 60.

Editing gets easier with practice. A "focus" box in each chapter of Part Two will give you an opportunity to try several key skills in context. You can also find interactive exercises for all of the topics discussed in this chapter by visiting Exercise Central at *bedfordstmartins.com/exercisecentral*.

Making Sentences Clear and Effective

Clear and effective sentences convey your meaning concisely and precisely. In editing, you want to ensure that readers will understand you easily, follow your ideas without difficulty, and stay interested in what you have to say.

▶ Clarity

The first goal of editing is to express your ideas as clearly as possible, without errors that might distract, confuse, or annoy readers. The guidelines here can help you catch some of the most common mistakes.

- *Make sure every sentence is complete.* A complete sentence has a subject and a verb and expresses a complete thought. In contrast, a **sentence fragment** is a word group that is punctuated like a sentence but is not complete: it lacks a subject, lacks a verb, or is just part of a thought. Experienced writers sometimes use fragments deliberately, but unless you're very sure of what you're doing, add the necessary verb or subject or attach the word group to a nearby sentence:

  FRAGMENT   The price of oil unpredictable and rising.

  COMPLETE   The price of oil is unpredictable and rising.

  FRAGMENT   Consumers are warming up to alternative heating systems. Such as heat pumps and solar panels.

  COMPLETE   Consumers are warming up to alternative heating systems, such as heat pumps and solar panels.

- *Use colons with caution.* A colon can help to introduce a list or a quotation, but the colon must be preceded by a complete sentence. If it is not, remove the colon (before a list), replace it with a comma (before a quotation), or rewrite the first part of the sentence:

  FRAGMENT   Three newer options include: wind turbines, outdoor furnaces, and pellet stoves.

  COMPLETE   Three newer options include wind turbines, outdoor furnaces, and pellet stoves.

  COMPLETE   Three newer options are becoming common: wind turbines, outdoor furnaces, and pellet stoves.

  FRAGMENT   Local homeowner Marisol Gutierrez says: "fossil fuels cost too much, both financially and environmentally."

COMPLETE   Local homeowner Marisol Gutierrez says, "fossil fuels cost too much, both financially and environmentally."

COMPLETE   Local homeowner Marisol Gutierrez <u>explained the appeal of such alternatives</u>: "fossil fuels cost too much, <u>both</u> financially and environmentally."

(For additional advice on using colons and introducing quotations, see pp. 69–72, "Focus on Sources" on p. 186, and "Focus on Punctuation" on p. 215.)

- *Keep independent clauses separated.* An **independent clause** can be punctuated like a sentence: it has a subject and a verb, and it expresses a complete thought. Two independent clauses in a row need a clear separation. If the clauses run together with no punctuation between them, they create a **run-on sentence**. If they run together with only a comma between them, they create a **comma splice**. You can correct these errors most easily by punctuating each clause as its own sentence, by putting a colon between them, by inserting a semicolon (and maybe a conjunctive adverb such as *therefore* or *moreover*), or by separating the clauses with a comma along with *and, but, or, nor, for, so,* or *yet*:

RUN-ON   Pellet stoves are especially popular suppliers can't keep up with demand.

COMMA SPLICE   Pellet stoves are especially popular, suppliers can't keep up with demand.

EDITED   Pellet stoves are especially popular. Suppliers can't keep up with demand.

EDITED   Pellet stoves are especially popular: suppliers can't keep up with demand.

EDITED   Pellet stoves are especially popular; therefore, suppliers can't keep up with demand.

EDITED   Pellet stoves are especially popular, and suppliers can't keep up with demand.

- *Match subjects and verbs.* Use singular verbs with singular subjects and plural verbs with plural subjects. Watch especially for the following situations.

When a group of words comes between the subject and the verb, be careful not to mistake a noun in that word group (such as *pellets* below) for the subject of the sentence:

MISMATCHED   The <u>use</u> of construction waste to manufacture wood pellets <u>contribute</u> to their appeal.

MATCHED   The use of construction waste to manufacture wood pellets contributes to their appeal.

When two subjects are joined by *and*, use a plural verb:

MISMATCHED   Low carbon emissions and the renewability of sawdust adds
to the belief that pellets are environmentally friendly.

MATCHED   Low carbon emissions and the renewability of sawdust add to
the belief that pellets are environmentally friendly.

- *Check that pronouns have clearly stated antecedents.* An **antecedent** is
  the noun to which a pronoun refers. Rewrite sentences in which
  the reference is vague or only implied:

VAGUE   Text messaging while driving is dangerous, but it doesn't deter
everyone.

CLEAR   Text messaging while driving is dangerous, but the risk doesn't
deter everyone.

IMPLIED   Despite numerous studies showing that distracted driving causes
accidents, they keep typing.

CLEAR   Despite numerous studies showing that distracted drivers cause
accidents, they keep typing.

- *Match pronouns and the words they refer to.* Singular nouns and pronouns take singular pronouns; plural nouns and pronouns take
  plural pronouns. The most common error occurs with singular
  indefinite pronouns such as *anybody, anyone, everyone, nobody,* and
  somebody. We often use these words to mean "many" or "all" and
  then mistakenly refer to them with plural pronouns:

MISMATCHED   Everyone must check in before they can vote.

MATCHED   Everyone must check in before he or she can vote.

MATCHED   All students must check in before they can vote.

- *Make sure that modifiers clearly modify the intended words.* A **modifier**
  is a word, phrase, or clause that describes another word (or words)
  in a sentence. Misplaced and dangling modifiers can be awkward or
  even unintentionally amusing:

MISPLACED   I watched as the snow swirled around my feet in amazement.

CLEAR   I watched in amazement as the snow swirled around my feet.

DANGLING   Enjoying the quiet of the forest, the crack of a hunter's rifle
startled me out of my reverie.

CLEAR   Enjoying the quiet of the forest, I was startled out of my reverie by
the crack of a hunter's rifle.

- *Be consistent.* Don't shift needlessly between the present tense and the past tense of verbs:

  INCONSISTENT   The coaster <u>rattles</u> so much it <u>shook</u> the platform.

  CONSISTENT   The coaster <u>rattled</u> so much it <u>shook</u> the platform.

  Don't shift needlessly among the first person (*I*, *we*), second person (*you*), and third person (*he, she, they*):

  INCONSISTENT   <u>We</u> were excited, but <u>you</u> tried to stay calm.

  CONSISTENT   <u>We</u> were excited, but <u>we</u> tried to stay calm.

  Don't shift needlessly between the active voice and the passive voice of verbs (see the next page for an explanation of voice):

  INCONSISTENT   The <u>ride attendant</u> <u>told</u> us to leave our belongings in the bins, and <u>we</u> <u>were advised</u> to remove our hats and sunglasses.

  CONSISTENT   The ride attendant told us to leave our belongings in the bins, and <u>she</u> <u>advised</u> us to remove our hats and sunglasses.

  (For more help avoiding shifts, see "Focus on Consistency" on p. 246.)

▶ Conciseness

In drafting, we often struggle with our ideas, making various attempts to express them. As a result, sentences may use more words than necessary to make their points. To edit for conciseness, focus on the following changes.

- *Put the main meaning of the sentence in its subject and verb.* Generally, the subject should name the actor, and the verb should describe what the actor does or is. Notice the difference in these two sentences (the subjects and verbs are underlined):

  WORDY   According to some experts, the <u>use</u> of calculators by students <u>is</u> sometimes why they fail to develop computational skills.

  CONCISE   According to some experts, <u>students</u> who use calculators sometimes <u>fail</u> to develop computational skills.

- *Prefer the active voice.* In the active voice, a verb describes the action done by the subject (*We <u>grilled</u> vegetables*), whereas in the passive voice, a verb describes the action done to the subject (*Vegetables <u>were grilled</u>*, or, adding who did the action, *Vegetables were grilled <u>by</u> <u>us</u>*). The active voice is usually more concise and more direct than the passive:

WORDY PASSIVE Calculators were withheld from some classrooms by school administrators, and the math performance of students with and without the machines was compared.

CONCISE ACTIVE School administrators withheld calculators from some classrooms and compared the math performance of students with and without the machines.

- *Delete repetition and padding.* Words that don't contribute to your meaning will interfere with readers' understanding and interest. Watch out for unneeded repetition or restatement:

WORDY Students in the schools should have ample practice in computational skills, skills such as long division and work with fractions.

CONCISE Students should have ample practice in computational skills, such as long division and work with fractions.

Avoid empty phrases that add no meaning:

WORDY The nature of calculators is such that they remove the drudgery from computation, but can also for all intents and purposes interfere with the development of important cognitive skills.

CONCISE Calculators remove the drudgery from computation, but can also interfere with the development of important cognitive skills.

(For more advice on reducing wordiness, see "Focus on Conciseness" on p. 336.)

▶ Emphasis

Once your sentences are as clear and concise as you can make them, you'll want to ensure that they give the appropriate emphasis to your ideas. Readers will look for the idea of a sentence in its subject and its verb, with modifiers clarifying or adding texture. You can emphasize important ideas by altering the structure of sentences and using punctuation for effect. Following are the most common techniques.

- *Use subordination to de-emphasize what's less important.* Subordination places minor information in words or word groups that modify the sentence's subject and verb:

UNEMPHATIC Computers can manipulate film and photographs, and we cannot trust these media to represent reality. [The sentence has two subject-verb structures (both underlined), and they seem equally important.]

EMPHATIC Because computers can manipulate film and photographs, we cannot trust these media to represent reality. [*Because* makes the first subject-verb group into a modifier, de-emphasizing the cause of the change and emphasizing the effect.]

- *Use coordination to balance equally important ideas.* Coordination emphasizes the equality of ideas by joining them with a comma and a coordinating conjunction (*and, but, or, nor, for, so,* or *yet*):

  UNEMPHATIC Two people may be complete strangers. A photograph can show them embracing.

  EMPHATIC Two people may be complete strangers, but a photograph can show them embracing.

- *Set off parenthetical and nonrestrictive elements.* If a modifier adds information to a sentence but is not essential to the meaning, separate it from the rest of the sentence with commas, dashes, or parentheses. Your choice of punctuation depends on how much emphasis you want to give the information:

  NONESSENTIAL Fashion magazines including *Vogue* and *GQ* have been accused of setting unrealistic beauty standards by altering photographs to hide models' flaws.

  UNEMPHATIC Fashion magazines (including *Vogue* and *GQ*) have been accused of setting unrealistic beauty standards by altering photographs to hide models' flaws.

  EMPHATIC Fashion magazines, including *Vogue* and *GQ*, have been accused of setting unrealistic beauty standards by altering photographs to hide models' flaws.

  MORE EMPHATIC Fashion magazines—including *Vogue* and *GQ*—have been accused of setting unrealistic beauty standards by altering photographs to hide models' flaws.

  Note: Do not use punctuation to set off words that are essential to the meaning of a sentence:

  ESSENTIAL The fashion magazines *Vogue* and *GQ* have been accused of setting unrealistic beauty standards by altering photographs to hide models' flaws.

  (For more information, see "Focus on Restrictive and Nonrestrictive Elements" on p. 305.)

- *Use the ends and beginnings of sentences to highlight ideas.* The end of a sentence is its most emphatic position, and the beginning is the next most emphatic. Placing the sentence's subject and verb in one of these positions draws readers' attention to them. In these sentences the core idea is underlined:

  UNEMPHATIC With computerized images, filmmakers can entertain us, placing historical figures alongside today's actors.

EMPHATIC   Filmmakers can entertain us with computerized images that place historical figures alongside today's actors.

MORE EMPHATIC   With computerized images that place historical figures alongside today's actors, filmmakers can entertain us.

- *Use short sentences to underscore points.* A very short sentence amid longer sentences will focus readers' attention on a key point:

UNEMPHATIC   Such images of historical figures and fictional characters have a disadvantage, however, in that they blur the boundaries of reality.

EMPHATIC   Such images of historical figures and fictional characters have a disadvantage, however. They blur the boundaries of reality.

▶ Parallelism

Parallelism is the use of similar grammatical structures for elements of similar importance, either within or among sentences:

PARALLELISM WITHIN A SENTENCE   Smoking can worsen heart disease and cause lung cancer.

PARALLELISM AMONG SENTENCES   Smoking has less well-known effects, too. It can cause gum disease. It can impair circulation of blood and other fluids. And it can reduce the body's supply of vitamins and minerals.

The second example shows how parallelism can relate sentences to improve paragraph coherence (see pp. 40–42).

To make the elements of a sentence parallel, repeat the forms of related words, phrases, and sentences:

NONPARALLEL   Harris expects dieters to give up bread, dairy, and eating meat.

PARALLEL   Harris expects dieters to give up bread, dairy, and meat.

NONPARALLEL   Harris emphasizes self-denial, but with Marconi's plan you can eat whatever you want in moderation.

PARALLEL   Harris emphasizes self-denial, but Marconi emphasizes moderation.

NONPARALLEL   If you want to lose weight quickly, choose the Harris diet. You'll have more success keeping the weight off if you choose the Marconi diet.

PARALLEL   If you want to lose weight quickly, choose the Harris diet. If you want to keep the weight off, choose the Marconi diet.

(For additional help with parallel structure, see "Focus on Parallelism" on p. 278).

▶ Variety

Variety in the structure and length of sentences helps keep readers alert and interested, but it also does more. By emphasizing important points and de-emphasizing less important points, varied sentences make your writing clearer and easier to follow.

Consider, for example, the two passages below. The first is adapted from "How Boys Become Men," an essay by Jon Katz. The second is the passage Katz actually wrote.

> UNVARIED   I was walking my dog last month past the playground near my house. I saw three boys encircling a fourth. They were laughing and pushing him. He was skinny and rumpled. He looked frightened. One boy knelt behind him. Another pushed him from the front. The trick was familiar to any former boy. The victim fell backward.

> VARIED   Last month, walking my dog past the playground near my house, I saw three boys encircling a fourth, laughing and pushing him. He was skinny and rumpled, and he looked frightened. One boy knelt behind him while another pushed him from the front, a trick familiar to any former boy. He fell backward.

Katz's actual sentences work much better to hold and direct our attention because he uses several techniques to achieve variety:

- *Vary the lengths of sentences.* The eight sentences in the unvaried adaptation range from four to thirteen words. Katz's four sentences range from three to twenty-two words, with the long first sentence setting the scene and the short final sentence creating a climax.

- *Vary the beginnings of sentences.* Every sentence in the unvaried adaptation begins with its subject (*I, I, They, He, One boy, Another, The trick, The victim*). Katz, in contrast, begins the first sentence with a transition and a dependent clause (*Last month, walking my dog past the playground near my house . . .*).

- *Vary the structure of sentences.* The sentences in the unvaried adaptation are all similar in structure, marching like soldiers down the page and making it difficult to pick out the important events of the story. Katz's version emphasizes the important events by making them the subjects and verbs of the sentences, turning the other information into modifying phrases and clauses that either precede or follow.

(For additional examples and practice, see "Focus on Sentence Variety" on p. 158).

Choosing Clear and Effective Words

The words you choose can have a dramatic effect on how readers understand your meaning, perceive your attitude, and respond to your thesis.

▶ Denotations and Connotations

The **denotation** of a word is its dictionary meaning, the literal sense without emotional overtones. A **connotation** is an emotional association the word produces in readers. Using incorrect or inappropriate words will confuse or annoy readers.

Using a word with the wrong denotation muddies meaning. Be especially careful to distinguish between words with similar sounds but different meanings, such as *to / too / two, their / there / they're, it's / its, lose / loose, sites / cites,* and *whether / weather*; and between words with related but distinct meanings, such as *reward / award* and *famous / infamous.* Keeping a list of the new words you acquire will help you build your vocabulary and improve your spelling.

Using words with strong connotations can shape readers' responses to your ideas. For example, consider the distinctions among *feeling, enthusiasm, passion,* and *mania.* Describing a group's *enthusiasm* for its cause is quite different from describing its *mania*: the latter connotes much more intensity, even irrationality. If your aim is to imply that the group's enthusiasm is excessive, and you think your readers will respond well to that characterization, then *mania* may be the appropriate word. But words can backfire if they set off inappropriate associations in readers.

Spell checkers and auto-correct functions can't catch words that are spelled correctly but used incorrectly. Consult a dictionary whenever you are unsure of a word's spelling or meaning. For connotations, you'll find a wide range of choices in a thesaurus, which lists words with similar meanings. A thesaurus doesn't provide definitions, however, so you'll need to check unfamiliar words in a dictionary.

▶ Concrete and Specific Words

Clear, exact writing balances abstract and general words, which provide outlines of ideas and things, with concrete and specific words, which limit and sharpen.

- **Abstract words** name ideas, qualities, attitudes, or states that we cannot perceive with our senses of sight, hearing, touch, smell, and taste: *liberty, hate, anxious, brave, idealistic.* **Concrete words**, in contrast, name objects, persons, places, or states that we can perceive with our senses: *newspaper, Mississippi River, red-faced, tangled, screeching, smoky, sweet.*

- **General words** name groups: *building, color, clothes.* **Specific words** name particular members of a group: *courthouse, red, boot-cut jeans.*

You need abstract and general words for broad statements that set the course for your writing, expressing concepts or referring to entire groups. But you also need concrete and specific words to make meaning precise and vivid by appealing to readers' senses and experiences:

> VAGUE The pollution was apparent in the odor and color of the stream.
>
> EXACT The stagnant stream smelled like rotten eggs and glowed a sickly yellowish green.

Concrete and specific language may seem essential only in descriptions like that of the polluted stream, but it is equally crucial in any other kind of writing. Readers can't be expected to understand or agree with general statements unless they know what evidence the statements are based on. The evidence is in the details, and the details are in concrete and specific words. (See also "Focus on Concrete and Specific Language" on p. 129.)

▶ Figures of Speech

You can make your writing concrete and specific, even lively and forceful, with **figures of speech**, expressions that imply meanings beyond or different from their literal meanings. Here are some of the most common figures.

- A **simile** compares two unlike things with the use of *like* or *as*: *The car spun around like a top. Coins as bright as sunshine lay glinting in the chest.*

- A **metaphor** also compares two unlike things, but more subtly, equating them without *like* or *as*: *The words shattered my fragile self-esteem. The laboratory was her prison, the beakers and test tubes her guards.*

- **Personification** is a simile or metaphor that attributes human qualities or powers to things or abstractions: *The breeze sighed and whis-*

pered in the grasses. The city squeezed me tightly at first but then relaxed its grip.

- **Hyperbole** is a deliberate overstatement or exaggeration: *The dentist filled the tooth with a bracelet's worth of silver. The children's noise shook the walls and rafters.*

By briefly translating experiences and qualities into vividly concrete images, figures of speech can be economical and powerful when used sparingly. Be careful not to combine them into confusing or absurd images, such as *The soccer players danced around the field like bulls ready for a fight.*

In trying for figures of speech, we sometimes resort to **clichés**, worn phrases that have lost their power: *ripe old age, hour of need, heavy as lead, thin as a rail, goes on forever.* If you have trouble recognizing clichés in your writing, be suspicious of any expression you have heard or read before. When you do find a cliché, cure it by substituting plain language (for instance, *seems endless* for *goes on forever*) or by substituting a fresh figure of speech (*thin as a sapling* for *thin as a rail*).

Using an Editing Checklist

The checklist on the next page summarizes the editing advice given in this chapter and adds a few other technical concerns as well. Some of the items will be more relevant for your writing than others: you may have little difficulty with variety in sentences, but may worry that your language is too general. Concentrate your editing efforts where they're needed most, and then survey your draft to check for other problems.

▶ Grace Patterson's Editing and Final Draft

The following paragraph comes from the edited draft of Grace Patterson's "A Rock and a Hard Place." Then Patterson's full final draft appears with notes in the margins highlighting its thesis, structure, and uses of the methods of development. If you compare the final version with the first draft on pages 34–35, you'll see clearly how Patterson's revising and editing transformed the essay from a rough exploration of ideas to a refined, and convincing, essay.

EDITED PARAGRAPH

~~What do I mean by a~~ A "good choice"~~?~~ ~~A good choice~~ is one made from a variety of options determined and narrowed down by the chooser. ~~There is plenty of room for the chooser to make a decision that he will~~ ~~be satisfied with.~~ When I choose a career, I expect to make a good choice. There ~~is plenty of~~ are many interesting fields ~~worth~~ to investigat~~e~~ing, and there is ~~lots of~~ much rewarding work to ~~be done~~ do. If the mayor of my town ~~came around and~~ suddenly told me that I ~~had~~ would have to choose between a ~~life~~ career of cleaning public toilets and one of operating a jackhammer on a busy street corner, I would object. That's a ~~lousy~~ *bad* choice~~., and I wouldn't let anyone force me to make it.~~

CHECKLIST FOR **Editing**

- Where do sentences need editing for grammar — so that, for instance, sentences are complete, subjects and verbs agree, pronouns are used correctly, modifiers make sense, and tense is consistent?

- Is each sentence as concise as it can be?

- How well have you used sentence structure, variety, parallelism, and other techniques to emphasize ideas and hold readers' interest?

- Have you used the right words? Where can you clarify meaning with concrete and specific words or with figures of speech?

- Do any sentences need editing for punctuation, such as for appropriate use of dashes and colons? Concentrate on finding and correcting errors that readers have pointed out in your work before.

- Where might spelling be a problem? Look up any word you're not absolutely sure of. (You'll still have to proofread a spell-checked paper; the programs don't catch everything.)

FINAL DRAFT

A Rock and a Hard Place

In the essay "The Box Man" Barbara Lazear Ascher says that a homeless man who has chosen solitude can show the rest of us how to "find . . . a friend in our own voice." Maybe he can. But Ascher's case depends on the Box Man's choice, her assumption that he *had* one. Discussions of homelessness often involve the word *choice*. Many of us with homes would like to think that homeless people chose their lives. But for homeless people in America today, there are no good choices.

A "good choice" is one made from a variety of options determined and narrowed down by the chooser. When I choose a career, I expect to make a good choice. There are many interesting fields to investigate, and there is much rewarding work to do. If the mayor of my town suddenly told me that I would have to choose between a career of cleaning public toilets and one of operating a jackhammer on a busy street corner, I would object. That's a *bad* choice.

When the mayor of New York tried to remove homeless people from the streets, he offered them a similarly bad choice. They could get in the mayor's car for a ride to a city shelter, or they could stay on the street. People assumed that the people who refused a ride to the shelter *wanted* to live on the street. But the assumption is not necessarily true. We allow ourselves as many options as we can imagine, but we allow homeless people only two, both unpleasant.

The fact is that homeless people are not always better off in shelters. I spoke recently with a man who had lived on the streets for a long time. He said that he had spent some time in homeless shelters, and he told me what they are like. They're dangerous and dehumanizing. Drug deals, beatings, and thefts are common. Because shelters are crowded, residents have to wait in long lines for everything; they also have to accept being constantly bossed around. No wonder some people prefer the street: it affords some space to breathe, some independence, some peace for sleeping.

Marginal annotations:

Introduction establishes point of contention with Ascher's essay

Thesis statement (see pp. 28–31)

Definition and comparison of *good choices* and *bad choices*

Examples

Application of definition to homeless people; analysis of choice offered

Cause-and-effect analysis: why homeless people avoid shelters

Description of shelter

Comparison of shelter and street

Focusing on the supposed choices homeless people have may make us feel better. But it distracts our attention from something more important than our comfort: the options we take for granted—a job with decent pay, an affordable home—are denied the homeless. These people are caught between no shelter at all and shelter that dehumanizes, between a rock and a hard place.

Conclusion: returns to good vs. bad choices

5

WORKING WITH SOURCES

Writing is a means of communicating, a conversation between writers and readers—and between writers and other writers. Finding out what others have said about a subject, or looking for information to support and develop a thesis, is a natural part of the composing process.

A **source** is any work that you draw on for ideas or evidence in the course of writing an essay or research paper. Whether you are analyzing or responding to an essay in this book or using research to support your interpretation of a subject, the guidelines in this chapter will help you use the work of others effectively in your own writing.

Writing about Readings

Many of the assignments that follow the readings in this book ask you to respond directly to an essay or to write about it in relation to one or more other essays—to analyze two writers' approaches, to compare several writers' ideas about a subject, or to use the ideas in one reading to investigate the meanings of another. The same will be true of much writing you do throughout school, whether you are examining literary works, lab experiments, case studies, historical documents, or news reports.

In some academic writing, you'll be able to use an idea in a selection as a springboard for an essay about your own opinions or experiences, as Grace Patterson does in "A Rock and a Hard Place," her response to Barbara Lazear Ascher's essay (p. 9). However, when academic writing requires you to write *about* one or more readings, you will analyze the material (see Chapter 1) and synthesize, or recombine, the elements of that analysis to form a new idea of your own (see pp. 68–72). Your goal is to think critically about what other writers have said and to reach your own conclusions.

When writing about a reading, refer to the writer's ideas directly and cite evidence from the text to support your conclusions; the questions that follow each selection in this book can help to guide your analysis. Use summary, paraphrase, and quotation (see pp. 68–71) to give readers a sense of the work, a clear picture of the elements that you are responding to, and a measured understanding of how those elements contribute to your thesis.

Researching a Topic

Often, when you draft an essay, you'll discover that you need more information to clarify part of your subject or to develop a few of your points more fully—for instance, when you need several examples to develop your draft, when you are troubled by conflicting assertions in essays you're comparing, or when you want expert opinion or facts to support your argument. A little outside material can contribute compelling and informative support for an essay.

Sometimes, however, you'll need to do more extensive research. Some of the writing suggestions in this book, for instance, ask you to conduct focused, short-term research in service of exploring new ideas for a brief essay; other times, you may need to look up information to guide your analysis of a work of literature or gather supporting evidence for a presentation. And sometimes, your teacher will assign a full-scale research paper that involves finding and using multiple sources to develop and support an original argument.

No matter the scale of a writing project, research takes time and requires careful thought. This section explains the basics of researching sources and using what you find responsibly and correctly.

▶ Asking Questions

Researching a topic provides an opportunity for you to build knowledge and to think critically about what you learn. The effort will be more productive if you start your search with a specific question (or questions) in mind. Such questions might be provided for you—as is the case with the research questions that follow many of the readings in this book—or you may need to ask them on your own. In that case, think about what interests or puzzles you about a subject. What do you know about it? What don't you know? What bothers you, confuses you, or intrigues you? Do you sense a problem in need of a solution, a source of disagreement among writers, a desire for more information?

The techniques for generating ideas and for narrowing a topic discussed on pages 24–28 and 28–31 can help you develop fruitful research questions. Whatever questions occur to you, focus on those you care about most, because you will spend significant time and effort exploring them.

▶ Finding Sources

Once you have a question in mind, you have two basic options for locating sources that can help you answer it: the library and the Internet. Although both can be good sources of information, usually you will find that printed sources and information located through a library's electronic research portals (such as subject directories and databases) are more trustworthy. Library resources are more likely to have gone through an editorial review process to ensure the information is accurate, reliable, and accepted by experts in the field.

When you're looking for sources, never be shy about asking librarians for help, but make a point of familiarizing yourself with the most useful research tools:

- *Library catalogs* offer a comprehensive listing of materials (books, magazines, newspapers, reference works, and the like) housed in a library. Most catalogs are computerized, which means you can plug in a search term—subject keyword, author, or title, for instance—and pull up a list of what the library has. Many school and local libraries also let you search the holdings of related libraries and arrange for interlibrary loan (allow plenty of time to arrange for transfers).

- *Periodical indexes* provide listings of the articles in thousands of magazines, scholarly journals, and newspapers. Electronic subscription services, such as EBSCO and ProQuest, often provide full-text copies of some of the articles located in a search; other times, you will need to use the information listed in the citation to track down the relevant issue on the library shelves.

- *Subject directories* organize material on the Web into categories. Although the open Internet can be less reliable than the library, a good directory is a helpful starting point because it can show the broad dimensions of a subject and lead to questions worth asking. The best are those compiled by librarians and teachers, particularly *ipl2.org* and directories created for individual schools (check your library's home page).

- *Online search engines*, such as *Google* and *Bing*, can locate information unavailable anywhere else—some government reports, for instance, many Web-only publications, or current data from research groups. Navigating the Internet effectively, however, takes effort. A single word plugged into a search box can easily bring up millions of results, with no indication of which ones are worthy of your time. To get the most out of a Web search, experiment with multiple keywords and use advanced search features to focus your hunt, narrowing results by kind of document (images, news, and so on), by type of site (government, educational, or commercial, for instance), by date, and by other parameters offered by the search engine. The more detailed the search terms, the more productive the results.

- *Wikis*, such as *Wikipedia* and *SourceWatch*, are collaborative documents hosted online; generally they are written by anonymous users and can be edited by anyone with an Internet connection and an opinion. You should never use a wiki as a source for a research paper: a post can look very different from day to day, and even hour to hour, making the information unpredictable and unreliable. All the same, *Wikipedia* can be a useful tool. Frequently it is a good place to start if you are generating ideas and looking for topics to explore. *Wikipedia* articles also tend to list sources at the bottom; those links are generally reliable (though you should judge for yourself) and could serve as valuable starting points for more involved research.

▶ Evaluating Sources

When you read a written work for an assignment, you read it critically, considering the author's intentions and analyzing the use of evidence (see Chapter 1). The same is true when you use sources to build and support your ideas. Drawing on reliable information and balancing varied opinions strengthens your essay.

Critical thinking becomes especially important when you are doing research. A quick search online, for instance, might bring up useful articles from quality publications, but it might also bring up personal blogs filled with unproven opinions, political arguments using fabricated statistics, stealth marketing sites that skew information to promote a product, and many other types of misinformation. Being able to determine what is credible or trustworthy thus becomes much more difficult and much more important.

You need not read everything you find closely. Instead, scan potential sources to see how well each one satisfies the following criteria.

- *Is the source relevant?* Keep your thesis in mind as you research, and use it to help you focus on sources that are directly related to your subject. If you are writing about the treatment of animals in the circus, for instance, your readers are not going to find information from an article on zoos convincing. With so many sources available, you can afford to be selective.

- *Are you looking at a primary or a secondary source?* A primary source is an original document written by a creator or an eyewitness: for instance, a short story, a lab report, or a speech delivered at an event. A secondary source is a writer's interpretation of a primary source or sources: a movie review, a summary of recent scientific discoveries, or a historian's explanation of an event. While secondary sources can be very helpful in obtaining factual data and general overviews of a subject, primary sources usually provide more valuable evidence for analysis.

- *How current is the information?* In most cases, the more recently your source was published or updated, the better. Know when a document was created and consider how its age affects its usefulness for your purposes.

- *What is the author's purpose?* Consider, for instance, whether a source is meant to provide information, argue a point, support a political view, or sell a product. In books, the preface and table of contents will often provide clues to the author's intentions. When you're looking at a periodical or a Web site, scanning the titles of nearby articles or checking the "About" page can give you a sense of the purpose of the material.

- *Is the author reliable?* Determine not only who wrote the material but also the writer's qualifications for writing on the subject, and look for any potential biases—especially in the case of online sources. Be wary of writers who use inflammatory or sensationalist language, and notice how they use evidence: reliable writers provide detailed support for their ideas, distinguish between facts and opinions, acknowledge opposing viewpoints, and cite their sources.

Once you've determined that a source is worth using, the checklist for critical reading on page 0 can help you to examine it more closely.

Synthesizing Source Material

When you bring information and ideas from outside sources into your writing, your goal is to develop and support an argument of your own making, not to report on what others have written. Always strive to maintain your voice. It can be tempting to string together facts and quotations from your sources and to think that they speak for themselves—or for you—but your own argument should always be the main event. Aim for **synthesis**, weaving the elements into a new whole: gather related information and ideas from your sources and summarize, paraphrase, and quote them to support your thesis.

▶ Summarizing

A **summary** is a condensed statement, *in your own words*, of the main meaning of a work. Summaries omit supporting details and examples to focus on the original author's thesis. You can find short summaries of essays throughout this book in the sections "A Note on Thematic Connections," which appear in Chapters 6–15. Here are two examples:

> Joan Didion's essay on a wind coming from the mountains above Los Angeles shows how an air current can transform a city (130–34).
>
> Kirk Johnson questions the common assumption that today's slang is contributing to a decline in the English language (167–70).

Notice that each summary names the author of the work being summarized and provides page numbers; it also refrains from using any of the original authors' language.

Summarizing is one of the most effective ways to bring the ideas of others into your writing without losing your voice or bogging down your essay with unnecessary details. Depending on the length of the original work and your reasons for using it, your summary might be a single sentence or paragraph; keep it as short as possible—generally no longer than 10 percent of the original. If you're responding to a short essay, for example, a handful of sentences will usually be enough to express its meaning.

▶ Paraphrasing

A **paraphrase** is a restatement, again *in your own words*, of a short passage from another writer's work. While summarizing makes it possible to explain someone else's main idea without repeating specifics, paraphrasing lets you incorporate important details that support your own main idea.

A paraphrase is about the same length as the original, but it does not use any of the other writer's unique words, phrasings, or sentence structures. Simply replacing a few words with synonyms won't suffice; in fact, that shortcut counts as plagiarism (see pp. 72–73). If you cannot avoid using some of the writer's language, put it in quotation marks:

> ORIGINAL PASSAGE   "Poverty is defined, in my system, by people not being able to cover the basic necessities in their lives. Indispensable medical care, nutrition, a place to live: all these essentials, for poor people, are often and classically beyond reach. If a poor person needs $10 a day to make ends meet, often he or she only makes eight and a half."
>
> —Walter Mosley, "Show Me the Money," p. 6.

> PARAPHRASE   As Walter Mosley sees it, poverty is a matter of inadequate resources. The poor have difficulty obtaining adequate health care, food, and shelter—things most of us take for granted—not because they have no income at all, but because the money they earn is not enough to cover these basic expenses (6).

> ORIGINAL PASSAGE   "Wealth, in my definition, is when money is no longer an issue or a question. Wealthy people don't know how much money they have or how much they make. Their worth is gauged in property, natural resources, and power, in doors they can go through and the way the law works."
>
> —Walter Mosley, "Show Me the Money," p. 6.

> PARAPHRASE   Wealth, in contrast, is defined by freedom. The rich don't have to worry about finances; indeed, their "property, natural resources, and power" represent social and legal privileges far more significant than freely available cash (Mosley 6).

Notice here, too, that a paraphrase identifies the original source and provides a page number. Even if the words are your own, the ideas are someone else's, and so they must be credited.

▶ Quoting

Sometimes a writer's or speaker's exact words will be so well phrased or so important to your own meaning that you will want to quote them.

When you are responding to or analyzing passages in a written work, such as an essay or a novel, direct **quotations** will be essential evidence as you develop your points. Even when you are borrowing ideas from other writers, however, quoting can be useful if the author's original wording makes a strong impression that you want to share with your readers.

Be sparing in your use of quotations. Limit yourself to those lines you're analyzing or responding to directly and perhaps a handful of choice passages that would lose their punch or meaning if you paraphrased them. Quoting others too often will make you vanish as a writer, leaving your readers to wonder what *you* have to say and why they should care.

When you do use a quotation, be careful to copy the original words and punctuation exactly, and to identify clearly the boundaries and source of the quotation:

- Put *quotation marks* around all quoted material shorter than four typed lines.

- Use *block quotations* for quoted passages longer than four typed lines. Introduce the quotation with a complete sentence followed by a colon, then start the quotation on a new line and indent the whole passage ten spaces or one inch. Don't use quotation marks; the indention shows that the material is quoted.

- *Cite the source of the quotation*, giving a page number as well as the author's name (see pp. 74–76). For short quotations, place a parenthetical citation after the final quotation mark and before the period. For block quotations, place a parenthetical citation after the final period.

You can make changes in quotations so that they fit the flow of your own sentences — say, by deleting a word or sentence that is not relevant to your purpose or by inserting a word or punctuation mark to clarify meaning. However, such changes must be obvious:

- Use an *ellipsis mark*, or three spaced periods (. . .), to show a deletion:

   Thomas De Zengotita believes that "in this virtual revolution, it's not workers against capitalists . . . , it's spectators against celebrities" (194).

- Use *brackets* ([ ]) around any change or addition you make:

   As Patricia Cline Cohen suggests, "the perplexity over [Robinson's] acquittal exposed to view the raw dynamics of class and sex privilege in American society" (365).

For examples of the use and formatting of quotations, see the sample research paper by Jarrod Ballo (p. 84).

▶ Integrating

When you incorporate material from outside sources, make a point to introduce every summary, paraphrase, or quotation and to specify why it's relevant to your thesis. At the same time, make it clear where your thoughts end and someone else's thoughts begin. Three techniques are especially helpful in giving your readers the necessary guidance.

- *Use signal phrases to introduce summaries, paraphrases, and quotations.* A signal phrase names the author of the borrowed material and thus provides a transition between your idea and someone else's. If the information is relevant, you might also explain why the author is an authoritative source or name the article or book you're referring to. Here are some examples of signal phrases:

  As physician Oliver Sacks points out in his book *The Mind's Eye*, . . .

  US Census Bureau data reveal . . .

  Not everyone agrees. Pat Mora, for example, insists that . . .

  In his trial summation, Darrow argued that nobody has control over his or her fate: . . .

  Note that a signal phrase followed by a colon must be a complete sentence. (See pp. 69 and 70.) Be careful, as well, to craft each signal phrase to reflect your reasons for including a source. Using the same phrase over and over (such as "According to _____") will frustrate your readers.

- *Generally, mark the end of borrowed material with a parenthetical citation identifying at least the page number of your source.* (See pp. 74–76.) In most cases, the citation is required—an exception would be a source lacking page or other reference numbers—and it makes clear that you've finished with the source and are returning to your own argument.

- *Follow up with a brief explanation of how the material supports your point.* To show that the borrowed material backs up your ideas, comment afterward on what it contributes to your essay. You might, for example, comment on the meaning of the borrowed material, dispute it, or summarize it in the context of a new idea. Such follow-ups are especially necessary after block quotations.

For examples of effective integration of source materials, see Jarrod Ballo's sample researched essay (p. 84).

Avoiding Plagiarism

Claiming credit for writing that you didn't compose yourself is **plagiarism**, a form of academic dishonesty that can carry serious consequences. Buying an essay online and submitting it as your own, copying a friend's essay and submitting it as your own, or copying a sentence from a source and including it as your own—these are most obvious forms of plagiarism. But plagiarism is often unintentional, caused not by deliberate cheating but by misunderstanding or sloppiness. Be aware of the rules and responsibilities that come with using the work of others in your writing.

- *Take careful notes.* No matter what your system for researching—formal note cards, dedicated notebooks, photocopies, electronic files—thorough and accurate records are essential. It's all too easy to forget, when you return to your notes, which words are your own and which ones are borrowed. If you copy down the exact words of a source, enclose them in quotation marks and make note of the source. If you paraphrase or summarize, make a note that the language is your own, and double-check that you haven't picked up any of the original phrasing. Always record full source information for any material you find, using the models on pages 73–83.

- *Use electronic sources with care.* Just because something appears on the Internet doesn't mean you're free to use it however you wish. Any language or idea you find, regardless of where you find it, must be credited to its source. Resist the urge to cut and paste snippets from online sources directly into your working draft: later on you won't be able to distinguish the borrowed text from your own words. Print electronic documents for your records, or save them as clearly labeled individual files.

- *Know the definition of* common knowledge. *Common knowledge* is information that is so widely known or broadly accepted that it can't be traced to a particular writer. Facts that you can find in multiple sources—the date of a historic event, the population of a major city—do not need to be credited as long as you state them in your own words. In contrast, original material that can be traced to a particular person—the lyrics to a song, an article on the Web—must be cited even if it has been distributed widely. Note that even if a piece of information is common knowledge, the wording of that information is not: put it in your own words.

- *Never include someone else's ideas in your writing without identifying the borrowed material and acknowledging its source.* Whether you quote directly or rephrase information in your own words, you must make it clear to readers when words and ideas are not your own. If you use another writer's exact words, enclose them in quotation marks and identify the source. If you summarize or paraphrase, clearly distinguish your ideas from the source author's with a signal phrase and a source citation. Then, at the end of your paper, list all your sources in a works cited list. (See the next section, "Documenting Sources in MLA style.")

When in doubt, err on the side of caution. It's better to have too much documentation in your essay than not enough.

Documenting Sources in MLA Style

The purpose of citing your sources is twofold: you acknowledge the sources that helped you, and you enable curious readers to verify your information by looking it up themselves.

In English classes, and in some other humanities classes as well, you will be expected to document your sources with the system outlined by the Modern Language Association in *MLA Handbook for Writers of Research Papers*, Seventh Edition (2009). MLA style calls for a brief parenthetical citation for each use of a source within the body of the essay and a comprehensive list of works cited at the end.

PARENTHETICAL TEXT CITATION

In the essay "The Box Man" Barbara Lazear Ascher says that a homeless man who has chosen solitude can show the rest of us how to "find . . . a friend in our own voice" (12).

ENTRY IN LIST OF WORKS CITED

Ascher, Barbara Lazear. "The Box Man." *Common Threads: Core Readings by Method and Theme.* Ed. Ellen Kuhl Repetto and Jane E. Aaron. Boston: Bedford, 2014. 9-12. Print.

▶ In-Text Citations

Citations within the body of your essay include just enough information for readers to recognize the boundaries of borrowed material and to locate the full citation in the works-cited list. Generally, they name the author of a source and the page number on which you found the information or idea cited.

Keep in-text citations unobtrusive by making them as brief as possible without sacrificing necessary information. The best way to do this is to name the author of the source in a signal phrase, limiting the parenthetical information to the page number. Otherwise, include the author's name in the parenthetical citation.

AUTHOR NAMED IN THE TEXT

Historian Thomas French notes that Mount Auburn Cemetery was a popular leisure destination for city residents (37).

AUTHOR NOT NAMED IN THE TEXT

Mount Auburn Cemetery was a popular leisure destination for city residents (French 37).

A WORK BY MULTIPLE AUTHORS

If a source has two or three authors, list all of their names.

Some of the most successful organized tours in New York bring visitors on guided walks or bus rides to locations featured in television shows (Espinosa and Herbst 228).

In the case of four or more authors, you may list all of the names or shorten the reference by naming the first author and following with "et al." (short for *et alia*, Latin for "and others"). Whichever option you choose, use the same format for your works-cited list. (See p. 76.)

As early as 1988, scholars cautioned against educators' dependence on computers, warning that technology is "accompanied by rapid change, instability, and general feelings of insecurity and isolation" (Ferrante, Hayman, Carlson, and Phillips 1).

As early as 1988, scholars cautioned against educators' dependence on computers, warning that technology is "accompanied by rapid change, instability, and general feelings of insecurity and isolation" (Ferrante et al. 1).

A WORK BY A CORPORATE OR GOVERNMENT AUTHOR

For works written in the name of an organization, company, or government that doesn't list individual authors, treat the name of the group as the author.

> Progressive neurological disorders damage the body in repeated but unpredictable intervals, forcing patients to adapt to new losses several times over (National Multiple Sclerosis Society 2).

TWO OR MORE WORKS BY THE SAME AUTHOR(S)

If your essay cites more than one work by the same author(s), include the title of the specific source within each citation. In the following examples, both works are by Fredey, who is named in the text.

> Maura Fredey notes that most of the nurses at the Boston Home have been on staff for more than five years, and many boast a quarter century or more of service ("21st Century" 26).

> The home's high level of care includes not only medical, dental, and vision treatments, says Fredey, but also round-the-clock nursing attention and extensive social and rehabilitative services ("Bridges" 13).

If the title is long, you may shorten it. (The complete titles for the articles cited above are "The 21st Century Home: How Technology Is Helping to Improve the Lives of Patients at the Boston Home" and "Bridges to Care: The Boston Home Reaches Out.")

A NOVEL

In addition to the page number, list the part or chapter cited; this helps readers locate the quotation in an edition different from the one you consulted.

> The newspaper reporters investigating the death of Mary Dalton in Richard Wright's *Native Son* are quick to recognize the similarities between her murder and that of Bobby Franks fifteen years earlier: "This is better than Loeb and Leopold," one of them remarks enthusiastically (214; bk. 2).

A PLAY

If a verse play (such as a work by William Shakespeare) is divided into parts, cite any part, act, scene, and line numbers, leaving out page numbers. For a prose play (such as Henrik Ibsen's *A Doll's House*), include the page number or numbers and a semicolon before the rest of the citation.

In Shakespeare's *The Tragedy of Macbeth*, a trio of witches famously chants, "Double, double toil and trouble; / Fire burn, and caldron bubble" (4.1.12–13).

A fight over money in the opening scene of Ibsen's *A Doll's House* reveals immediately that Nora and Torvald Helmer struggle for power in their marriage (7–12; act 1).

A POEM

Instead of pages, cite the line numbers of the material quoted. Include the word "line" or "lines" in the first citation; omit it in later references.

> Robert Frost's "Design" contrasts the deadliness of "a dimpled spider, fat and white" (line 1) with the curative powers of a "flower like froth" (7).

AN ANONYMOUS WORK

If no author is named, include the title within the parentheses. You may shorten the title if it is long.

> The population of Pass Christian, Mississippi, is less than a third of what it was before Hurricane Katrina ("New Town Crier" 22).

AN INDIRECT SOURCE

Use the abbreviation "qtd. in" (for "quoted in") to indicate that you did not consult the source directly but found it quoted in another source.

> As psychologist Robert Sternberg has pointed out, a high IQ does not guaran-tee success. Just as important is "knowing what to say to whom, knowing when to say it, and knowing how to say it for maximum effect" (qtd. in Gladwell 101).

AN ELECTRONIC SOURCE

Treat most electronic sources as you would any other source—cite the author's name if it is available, or cite the title if no author is named. For electronic sources that number paragraphs instead of pages, insert a comma between the author's name and the abbreviation "par." (for "paragraph"). If neither pages nor paragraphs are numbered, include the author's name only.

> At the time *Dr. Strangelove* was released, filmmakers had begun to believe that fictional portrayals of nuclear war were actually "contributing to the nuclear threat" by instilling fear in American audiences (Abbot, par. 35).

One teacher who successfully brought computers into his classroom argues that to use new technologies effectively, teachers need to become "side-by-side learners" with their students (Rogers).

▶ List of Works Cited

The works-cited list provides complete publication information for every source you refer to within your essay. Format the list as follows:

- Start the list on a new page following the conclusion to your essay.
- Center the title "Works Cited" (without quotation marks) at the top of the page.
- Double-space everything in the list.
- Alphabetize the entries by authors' last names. If a work doesn't have a listed author, alphabetize by title, ignoring the initial words *A*, *An*, and *The*.
- For each entry, align the first line with the left margin and indent subsequent lines five spaces or one-half inch.

The elements of individual entries will vary somewhat, as shown in the models in this section. The basic content and formatting rules, however, can be summarized in a few general guidelines:

- Start with the author's last name, followed by a comma and the author's first name. (For more than one author, list the names as they appear in the work, reversing only the first author's name.)
- Provide the full title of the work, with all major words capitalized. Italicize the titles of books, periodicals, whole Web sites, and longer creative works such as plays or television series; put quotation marks around the titles of book chapters, periodical articles, pages on Web sites, and short creative works such as stories, poems, and song titles.
- Include complete publication information. At a minimum this includes city of publication, publisher, and date (for books); date and inclusive page numbers (for periodicals); sponsor, date of publication, and access date (for Web sites); and medium of publication (print, Web, television, radio, DVD, CD, lecture, and so on).
- Separate the elements of an entry (author, title, publication information) with periods.

MLA does not require URLs for Web sources, but your teacher might. If so, place the URL at the end of the entry, enclosed in angle brackets and followed by a period (see p. 82 for an example). If you must break a long URL to fit, break it only after a slash and do not add a hyphen.

PRINT BOOKS

A BOOK BY ONE AUTHOR

Treuer, David. *Rez Life: An Indian's Journey through Reservation Life*. New York: Atlantic, 2012. Print.

A BOOK BY MULTIPLE AUTHORS

List all of the authors, or, if there are more than three, you may provide the first author's name followed by "et al." (Latin abbreviation for "and others"). Whichever option you choose, use the same format for your in-text citations. (See p. 74.)

Cooper, Martha, and Joseph Sciorra. *R.I.P.: Memorial Wall Art*. London: Thames, 1994. Print.

Ferrante, Reynolds, John Hayman, Mary Susan Carlson, and Harry Phillips. *Planning for Microcomputers in Higher Education: Strategies for the Next Generation*. Washington: Assn. for Study of Higher Educ., 1988. Print.

Ferrante, Reynolds, et al. *Planning for Microcomputers in Higher Education: Strategies for the Next Generation*. Washington: Assn. for Study of Higher Educ., 1988. Print.

A BOOK WITH AN AUTHOR AND AN EDITOR

Cather, Willa. *My Antonia*. Ed. Guy Reynolds. Boston: Bedford, 2013. Print.

A BOOK WITH A TRANSLATOR

Ovid. *Metamorphoses*. Trans. Z. Philip Ambrose. Newburyport: Focus, 2004. Print.

A BOOK BY A CORPORATE OR GOVERNMENT AUTHOR

For books written in the name of an organization, company, or government that doesn't list individual authors, treat the name of the group as the author.

United States. Dept. of Commerce. *Statistical Abstract of the United States 2012-2013: The National Data Book*. New York: Skyhorse, 2012. Print.

MORE THAN ONE WORK BY THE SAME AUTHOR(S)

Roach, Mary. *Packing for Mars: The Curious Science of Life in the Void*. New York:
    Norton, 2010.

---. *Spook: Science Tackles the Afterlife*. New York: Norton, 2005. Print.

EDITION OTHER THAN THE FIRST

Gonzales, Manuel G. *Mexicanos: A History of Mexicans in the United States*. 2nd ed.
    Bloomington: Indiana UP, 2009. Print.

AN ILLUSTRATED BOOK OR GRAPHIC NARRATIVE

For a book that contains both text and illustrations, begin the entry with
the name of the contributor whose work you are emphasizing (author,
editor, or illustrator), using the abbreviations "illus." for illustrator and
"ed." for editor. Treat a graphic narrative written and illustrated by the
same person as you would a book with one author.

Moser, Barry, illus. *Mark Twain's Book of Animals*. Ed. Shelley Fisher Fishkin. Berkeley:
    U of California P, 2010. Print.

Thompson, Craig. *Habibi*. New York: Pantheon, 2012. Print.

AN ANTHOLOGY

James, Rosemary, ed. *My New Orleans: Ballads to the Big Easy by Her Sons, Daughters,
    and Lovers*. New York: Touchstone, 2006. Print.

Cite an entire anthology only when you are referring to the editor's
material or cross-referencing multiple selections that appear within it,
as shown in the next model.

A SELECTION FROM AN ANTHOLOGY

List the work under the selection author's name. Include the page numbers for the entire selection after the publication date.

Peck, Cheryl. "Fatso." *Common Threads: Core Readings by Method and Theme*. Ed.
    Ellen Kuhl Repetto and Jane E. Aaron. Boston: Bedford, 2014. 289-93. Print.

If you are citing two or more selections from the same anthology, you
can avoid unnecessary repetition by listing the anthology in its own
entry and cross-referencing it in the selection entries. Put each entry in
its proper alphabetical place in the list of works cited, and include the
medium of publication only in the anthology entry.

Angelou, Maya. "Champion of the World." Repetto and Aaron 111-13.

King, Martin Luther, Jr. "I Have a Dream." Repetto and Aaron 449-53.

Repetto, Ellen Kuhl, and Jane E. Aaron, eds. *Common Threads: Core Readings by Method and Theme*. Boston: Bedford, 2014. Print.

A SECTION OF A BOOK

When referring to only part of a book (such as an introduction, fore-word, or a specific chapter), name the author and indicate the part of the book you are citing, with page numbers.

Schlosser, Eric. Foreword. *The Jungle*. By Upton Sinclair. New York: Penguin, 2006. vii-xv. Print.

Sedaris, David. "The Smoking Section." *When You Are Engulfed in Flames*. New York: Little, 2008. 240-323. Print.

A REFERENCE WORK

"Social Security." *The Encyclopedia Americana*. 2006 ed. Print.

PRINT OR ONLINE JOURNALS, MAGAZINES, AND NEWSPAPERS
The formats for articles in journals, magazines, and newspapers are similar whether the publication appears only in print, appears in print with additional online content, or appears only online. The key differences are (1) the inclusive page numbers for print articles and some online journal articles; (2) the sponsor or publisher of the site for online magazine and newspaper content; and (3) the date you consulted any online source.

AN ARTICLE IN A SCHOLARLY JOURNAL

Include the author's name, the article title, the volume and any issue number (separated by a period), the year, and the page numbers. If an online journal does not have number pages, use "n. pag." instead.

Sewald, Ronda L. "Forced Listening: The Contested Use of Loudspeakers for Commercial and Political Messages in the Public Soundscape." *American Quarterly* 63.3 (2011): 761-80. Print.

Singer, P. W. "Robots at War: The New Battlefield." *Wilson Quarterly* 33.1 (2009): n. pag. Web. 18 Oct. 2012.

AN ARTICLE IN A MONTHLY OR BIMONTHLY MAGAZINE

If you consult an online magazine or newspaper, including one that also has a print version, provide the publisher's or sponsor's name between the periodical title and the publication date. Use "N.p." if no publisher or sponsor is named.

Ballí, Cecilia. "Calderón's War: The Gruesome Legacy of Mexico's Antidrug Campaign." *Atlantic Monthly* Jan. 2012: 37-49. Print.

McConnico, Patricia Busa. "Being a Super Model." *Texas Monthly.com*. Texas Monthly, Sept. 2009. Web. 19 Mar. 2013.

AN ARTICLE IN A WEEKLY MAGAZINE

Walsh, Bryan. "Outsmarting the Surge." *Time.com*. Time Inc., 12 Nov. 2012. Web. 18 Nov. 2012.

Kapur, Akash. "The Shandy." *New Yorker*. 10 Oct. 2011: 72-79. Print.

AN ARTICLE IN AN ONLINE-ONLY MAGAZINE

Gerber, Eve. "Gender Debunked." *Salon.com*. Salon Media Group, 3 May 2012. Web. 6 May 2012.

AN ARTICLE IN A NEWSPAPER

Many print newspapers appear in more than one edition, so you need to specify which edition you used ("New York ed." in the model below). Give the section label as part of the page number when the newspaper does the same ("A1" in the model). Otherwise, give the section after the edition (for example, "Natl. ed., sec. 3: 7"). Cite an article that runs on nonconsecutive pages with the starting page number followed by a plus sign ("+"). For an article in an online newspaper, omit page numbers and add the site's sponsor or publisher and the date you accessed it.

Rodriguez, Gregory. "Answers Can Be Found in Questions." *Los Angeles Times*. Los Angeles Times, 29 June 2009. Web. 4 Dec. 2012.

Semple, Kirk. "Affluent, Born Abroad, and Choosing New York's Public Schools." *New York Times*, 15 Feb. 2012, New York ed.: A1+. Print.

A LETTER TO THE EDITOR

Wing, Joseph. Letter. *Washington Post*, 13 Feb. 2012: A16. Print.

AN UNSIGNED ARTICLE OR EDITORIAL

"It's Simple: Break the Law, Pay the Price." Editorial. *Eagle-Tribune*, 5 Feb. 2012: 8. Print.

"Teenagers' Argot: Purists May Disapprove, but Multi-Ethnic Dialects Are Spreading."
    Economist.com. Economist, 11 Feb. 2012. Web. 19 Oct. 2012.

AN ARTICLE IN AN ONLINE DATABASE

Cite a full-text source that you obtain through a database in much
the same way as a print article, but instead of ending with "Print" as
the medium, add the database name, the medium "Web," and your
access date.

Porco, Carolyn. "Adventures in Wonderland." *New Statesman*, 19 Dec. 2011: 34-37.
    Academic Search Premier. Web. 17 Apr. 2013.

OTHER ONLINE SOURCES

AN ENTIRE WEB SITE

Start with the author(s) or editor(s) of the site, followed by the site title
in italics, the name of the sponsoring organization or publisher, the date
of publication or most recent update, the medium, and the date you
visited the site. If any of this information is unavailable, include as much
as you can find. (Use "N.p." if there is no publisher or sponsor and
"n.d." if there is no date.)

Carson, Clayborne, ed. *The King Papers Project*. Martin Luther King, Jr., Research &
    Educ. Inst., Stanford U, n.d. Web. 9 Oct. 2012.
Songwriter's Resource Network. N.p., 2011. Web. 4 Mar. 2012.

A SHORT WORK FROM A WEB SITE

Include as much information from the entire Web site as you can find
(see above), as well as a title for the work. If your teacher requires a URL,
or if the page would be difficult to find without one, include it at the
end of the entry, enclosed in angle brackets.

Dryden-Edwards, Roxanne. "Obsessive-Compulsive Disorder." *MedicineNet*. WebMD,
    3 Sept. 2008. Web. 9 May 2013.
Mikkelson, Barbara. "Organ Nicked: Vegetable." *Urban Legends Reference Pages*.
    Barbara and David P. Mikkelson, 30 June 2011. Web. 4 Mar. 2013.
    <http://www.snopes.com/horrors/robbery/kidney2.asp>.

A BLOG ENTRY

Follow the preceding guidelines for a short work from a Web site. If an
entry is not titled, use "Online posting."

Boyle, Lili. "An American Girl in Cuba." *Huffington Post*. Huffingtonpost.com, 8 Feb.
    2012. Web. 15 Feb. 2012.

Doctorjudlth. Online posting. *Huffington Post*. Huffingtonpost.com, 8 Feb. 2012.
Web. 15 Feb. 2012.

AUDIO AND VISUAL SOURCES

A TELEVISION OR RADIO PROGRAM

Provide as much of the following as available: episode or segment title, program or series title, network, local station, broadcast date, and medium. Include the name of the director ("Dir."), performers ("Perf."), narrator ("Narr."), or host ("Host") if such information is significant.

"Play the Part." *This American Life*. Host Ira Glass. Natl. Public Radio. WBUR, Boston, 17 Feb. 2012. Radio.

"Extreme Cave Diving." *NOVA*. PBS. 15 Feb. 2012. Television.

A SOUND RECORDING

Vampire Weekend. "California English." *Contra*. XL, 2010. CD.

Zappa, Frank. *Ship Arriving Too Late to Save a Drowning Witch*. Barking Pumpkin, 1982. LP.

A FILM, VIDEO, OR DVD

Donnie Darko. Dir. Richard Kelly. Perf. Jake Gyllenhaal, Jena Malone, Drew Barrymore, Noah Wyle, Patrick Swayze, and Mary McDonnell. 2001. 20th Cent. Fox, 2004. DVD.

Mowry, Jonah. "What's Goin On." *YouTube*. YouTube, 10 Aug. 2010. Web. 5 Apr. 2013.

A PHOTOGRAPH OR OTHER WORK OF ART

For original works viewed in person, provide the artistic medium and the museum's or collection's name and location. For reproductions, omit the artistic medium, indicate where the original is located, and provide complete publication information for the source, including a page number if available.

Kandinsky, Wassily. *Improvisation No. 30 (Cannons)*. 1913. Oil on canvas. Art Inst. of Chicago.

Magritte, René. *The Human Condition II*. 1935. Coll. Madame E. Happé-Lorge, Brussels. *Surrealists and Surrealism*. Ed. Gaëtan Picon. New York: Rizzoli, 1983. 145. Print.

Riis, Jacob. *9 Boys Waist Deep in Country Stream*. N.d. Prints and Photographs Div., Lib. of Cong. *Jacob A. Riis Papers*. Web. 25 Apr. 2013.

AN ADVERTISEMENT

Honda CR-V. Advertisement. NBC. WNKY, Bowling Green, 5 Feb. 2012. Television.

Spiriva. Advertisement. *Reader's Digest* Mar. 2012: 32-35. Print.

OTHER SOURCES

E-MAIL

Jones, Liza. "Re: Question about Group Homes." Message to the author. 9 May
    2013. E-mail.

A PERSONAL INTERVIEW

Conti, Regina. Personal interview. 3 May 2013.

Sample Research Paper

The research paper here was written by Jarrod Ballo, a high school sopho-
more from New Hampshire. After reading Barbara Lazear Ascher's "The
Box Man" (p. 9), Ballo found himself thinking about a family friend who
had been forced to sleep in a car for a few weeks. His initial research question was a practical one: "Where can a newly homeless person turn for
help?" In the course of looking for answers, he discovered a fact that not
only surprised him but made him angry. The resulting research paper,
which took Ballo two months to complete, outlines the problem he
found and proposes a solution.

As you read, notice that Ballo goes beyond reporting facts and uses
what he learned to develop an argument of his own. Notice also how
he synthesizes information and ideas from sources to develop his thesis
without relying on those sources to speak for him. His essay isn't perfect,
but Ballo does an exemplary job of combining reasons and evidence to
support an argument while addressing opposing views convincingly
and fairly.

Jarrod Ballo

15 May 2012

Women and Children First

When most people think of homelessness they imagine someone like the character Barbara Lazear Ascher describes in "The Box Man"—an unemployed, mentally ill man who has been living on the streets for years. That old stereotype, however, is no longer true. In fact, working families now make up the largest segment of the homeless population in America, and their numbers are rising. Given the shift in the nature of homelessness, it is time to shift focus in looking for solutions. Public service agencies should concentrate on preventing family homelessness by helping people get back on their feet if they fall on hard times.

When Ascher wrote her essay, most people without a place to live were "chronically" homeless, defined as adult individuals "with severe disabilities and long homeless histories" (United States ii). Only a tiny fraction of homeless people were in families (Burge A1). Today, however, the National Alliance to End Homelessness (NAEH) reports that families represent 37% of the homeless overall, more than double the number of those categorized as chronic (7-8). Families also represent the fastest-growing portion of the homeless population. As figure 1 shows, while individual homelessness has dropped, family homelessness has increased dramatically in just three years. Typically, a homeless family consists of a single mother with two or three children in tow, and most of those children are younger than twelve (United States 20). Innocent kids, it turns out, are the real face of homelessness.

A lot of people assume that when families wind up homeless it must be the parents' fault—they were too irresponsible to hold down a job, or too lazy to look for one in the first place. Most homeless parents, however, do have jobs, sometimes two or three, but their incomes still fall below the poverty line (NAEH 24). Others believe that the parents are alcoholics or drug addicts, but homeless mothers rarely show signs of substance abuse (United States 18-19). The real cause of

---

Surprising fact grabs readers' attention and clearly introduces topic

Thesis statement makes an arguable claim

Reason: analysis of trends in homelessness

Quotation, paraphrase, and summary integrate evidence from three sources

Figure introduced in text

Follow-up comment explains significance of data

Reason: causes of family homelessness

Two opposing claims acknowledged and disputed

Figure 1   Change in Annual Sheltered Homeless Estimates by
Household Type from 2007 to 2010

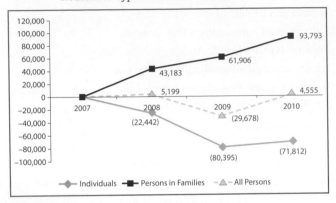

Bar graph presents numerical data in visual form

Line graph from United States, Dept. of Housing and Urban Dev.,
Office of Community Planning and Dev.; *The 2010 Annual Home-
less Assessment Report to Congress*; US Dept. of Housing and
Urban Dev., June 2011; 12; Web; 17 Mar. 2012.

Figure caption labels visual and credits source

homelessness for families comes down to financial emergencies:
unexpected layoffs, uninsured medical expenses, missed rent
payments, disasters such as fires (Kozol 5-11). Usually such
emergencies are temporary, but families have few resources for
dealing with them.

Citations for summaries identify all pages summarized

Besides living with family or friends or staying on the street,
what can a homeless family do? Traditionally, a patchwork
assistance system has provided three basic options: emergency
shelters, transitional housing units, and hotel vouchers (United
States 33). Each comes with limitations and obstacles, especially for families.

Reason: classification of shelter options

The first place a homeless family normally goes is an
emergency shelter. As one advocate describes them, shelters
provide a "definite place to get food and have a bed to sleep
in," but that's about it: residents must leave during the day and
return in time to check in for the next night (Karash). Another
advocate, Jonathan Kozol, points out that emergency shelters
can also be dangerous for women and children: shared sleeping
areas and bathrooms leave them vulnerable to theft and assault,
and expose them to prostitution and drugs. At the same time,
residents are deliberately treated poorly, on the theory that

Paraphrase integrates direct quotation

Concrete details support example

making shelters unpleasant will stop people from staying long (69, 111-12).

Transitional housing programs are slightly better. They offer private rooms, let people stay for up to two years, and usually provide social services to help families regroup (Culhane and Metraux 112). They have one big drawback, though: men and teenage boys are almost always excluded, so families may be forced to split up (Kozol 58-59). Transitional housing also involves interventions, such as job training and mental counseling, that are not only disruptive but also unnecessary for most residents (Culhane and Metraux 117). Families get hassled and treated like losers, when all they need is a place to stay.

Some cities provide hotel vouchers, paying market rates for families to stay in double rooms. While it might sound glamorous, hotel life is tough. As *Boston Globe* reporter Kathleen Burge reveals, participating hotels tend to be located in suburbs, forcing long commutes to work and to school. They offer no space for children to play, no room for privacy, and no kitchens; homeless "guests" are forced to live on fast food and cold cuts. Families may find themselves stuck in these conditions for months, even years, before they manage to find a better place to live (A14-A15). And the instability of temporary housing makes it difficult for them to transition out of homelessness, creating a vicious cycle that adds to public expense while solving nothing.

Solutions do exist, though. In 2009 Congress passed the Homeless Emergency Assistance and Rapid Transition to Housing, or HEARTH, act, which put a new emphasis on "permanent supportive housing" (United States 1). As Malcolm Gladwell explains in an influential article, chronically homeless people consume the majority of assistance funds even though they represent the smallest portion of the homeless population; the idea behind HEARTH is to put them in stable homes *before* addressing issues such as addiction, improving the chances for recovery and saving millions of dollars in the long run (101). Although it may seem unlikely for "disenfranchised people . . . to re-adapt to life on Main Street" (Karash), studies show that permanent supportive housing works. Most

---

Summaries of two sections separated by comma

Authors not named in signal phrase listed in parenthetical citation

Summaries and paraphrase integrate evidence from two sources

Signal phrase names author and gives credentials

Summary of newspaper article

Page numbers only because author (Burge) is named in signal phrase

Reason: example of solution for chronically homeless people

Definition outlines solution

Ellipses indicate words deleted from quotation; no page numbers in citation because online article doesn't have them states have seen promising results, with chronic homelessness dropping by as much as 69% in some areas (NAEH 16)—and public expenses dropping along with it.

As successful as HEARTH has been for individuals, it has left families in the cold. Permanent supportive housing, limited to people with disabilities, now accounts for more beds than any other shelter option (United States 1). If homeless families do manage to find a spot, one in five will find themselves stuck for a year or more (United States 24), simply because they can't find affordable housing or scrape together the costs of moving (NAEH 25-26). Yet public service agencies spend "$22,000 to $55,000 per family per stay"—more than enough to cover an entire year's rent for a decent apartment or a down payment on a house (Culhane and Metraux 117).

Reason: implications of chronic solution for families

Paraphrase integrates direct quotation

Rather than waste so much money on temporary shelter, agencies should apply the logic behind permanent supportive housing to families: get them into real homes first. In arguing this solution, sociologists Dennis Culhane and Stephen Metraux make an important point:

> Most homeless households need temporary, low-cost assistance with resolving a recent housing loss or other displacement, or with transitioning out of an institutional living environment. They do not necessarily need a shelter stay or a shelter stay of long duration. (112)

Block format for long quotation

The HEARTH act allows for this kind of help, providing rental subsidies and moving costs, but eligibility is very restricted and few families qualify (United States 55). Harsh limitations put parents in a difficult situation, mostly because opponents worry that handouts will encourage them to choose homelessness as a "lifestyle" (Karash). Such concerns, however, have been proven false. Most recipients of cash assistance needed help for less than three months, and almost all of them found independent housing and self-sufficiency within a year (United States 66).

Opposing claim acknowledged and disputed

Treating women and children in need as potential frauds only makes it more difficult for families to get their lives in order. Because most family homelessness is caused by short-term financial emergencies, most homeless families would be

Conclusion summarizes reasons, restates thesis, and offers solution

better off with short-term cash assistance. Shelters create obstacles to recovery, and they cost much more than putting people into stable homes. The success of permanent supportive housing for chronically homeless individuals has reduced costs and opened up more resources for homeless families, and that's where the money should go. By increasing access to rental assistance, we might even help families avoid homelessness in the first place.

Works Cited

Ascher, Barbara Lazear. "The Box Man." *Common Threads: Core Readings by Method and Theme*. Ed. Ellen Kuhl Repetto and Jane E. Aaron. Boston: Bedford, 2014. 9-12. Print.

Burge, Kathleen. "For Homeless Families, Hotel Is a Life in Limbo." *Boston Sunday Globe* 25 Mar. 2012: A1+. Print.

Culhane, Dennis P., and Stephen Metraux. "Rearranging the Deck Chairs or Reallocating the Lifeboats? Homelessness Assistance and its Alternatives." *Journal of the American Planning Association* 74.1 (2008): 111-121. *Academic Search Premier*. Web. 14 Apr. 2012.

Gladwell, Malcolm. "Million-Dollar Murray: Why Problems Like Homelessness May Be Easier to Solve Than to Manage." *New Yorker*. New Yorker Digital Edition, 13 Feb. 2006: 96-107. Web. 2 Apr. 2012.

Karash, Robert L. "Housing Lost, Housing Regained, Housing Kept." *Spare Change News*. Spare Change News, 25 Feb. 2010. Web. 14 Apr. 2012.

Kozol, Jonathan. *Rachel and Her Children: Homeless Families in America*. Rev. ed. New York: Three Rivers, 2006. Print.

National Alliance to End Homelessness. *The State of Homelessness in America: 2012*. *Library*. Natl. Alliance to End Homelessness, Jan. 2012. Web. 6 Feb. 2012.

United States. Dept. of Housing and Urban Dev. Office of Community Planning and Dev. *The 2010 Annual Homeless Assessment Report to Congress*. Dept. of Housing and Urban Dev., June 2011. Web. 17 Mar. 2012.

List of works cited starts on a new page

Selection from an anthology

Article in a print newspaper

Scholarly article in an online database

Article in a weekly magazine archived online

Article in an online newspaper

Book edition other than the first

Book by a corporate author

Book by a government author

PART TWO

SHORT ESSAYS BY METHOD AND THEME

THE RETURN

AFTER FOUR YEARS LIVING IN VIENNA, HERE I AM BACK IN TEHRAN. FROM THE MOMENT I ARRIVED AT MEHRABAD AIRPORT AND CAUGHT SIGHT OF THE FIRST CUSTOMS AGENT, I IMMEDIATELY FELT THE REPRESSIVE AIR OF MY COUNTRY.

DO YOU HAVE ANYTHING FORBIDDEN? FASHION MAGAZINES, TAPES, ALCOHOL, PORK ...

NO, SIR!

PLEASE FIX YOUR VEIL, MY SISTER!

YES, MY BROTHER.

NEXT! COME ON, SPEED IT UP!

BROTHER AND SISTER ARE THE TERMS USED IN IRAN BY THE REPRESENTATIVES OF THE LAW TO GIVE ORDERS TO PEOPLE, WITHOUT OFFENDING THEM.

THERE WERE PEOPLE EVERYWHERE. EACH PASSENGER WAS BEING MET BY A DOZEN PEOPLE. SUDDENLY, AMONGST THE CROWD, I SPOTTED MY PARENTS ...

...BUT IT WASN'T RECIPROCAL. OF COURSE IT MADE SENSE. ONE CHANGES MORE BETWEEN THE AGES OF FOURTEEN AND EIGHTEEN THAN BETWEEN THIRTY AND FORTY.

DAD!

EBI! LOOK! IT'S MARJI!

MARI..?

MY DARLING, MY DAUGHTER, OH MY! I DIDN'T RECOGNIZE YOU!

I KNEW THAT I HAD GROWN, BUT IT WAS ONLY ONCE I WAS IN THE ARMS OF MY FATHER THAT I REALLY FELT IT. HE, WHO HAD ALWAYS BEFORE APPEARED SO IMPOSING, WAS ABOUT THE SAME SIZE AS ME.

6

NARRATION

▶
GROWING UP

You narrate every time you tell a story about something that happened. **Narration** helps us make sense of events and share our experiences with others; consequently, it is one of the longest-standing and most essential methods of communicating. (As the writer Joan Didion famously put it, "We tell stories in order to live.") You can use narration to entertain friends by retelling an amusing or a scary experience, to explain a sequence of events in a history paper, to summarize a sales-clerk's actions in a letter complaining about bad customer service, or to persuade skeptics by means of several anecdotes that the lumber indus-try is sincere about restoring clear-cut forests. Storytelling is instinctive to the ways we think and speak; it's no surprise, then, that narration should figure into so much of what we read and write.

↰ Seeing Narration

Published in four volumes between 2000 and 2003, *The Complete Persepolis* is a memoir by Iranian graphic artist Marjane Satrapi. Part comic book, part autobiography, *Persepolis* tells a story of war and repres-sion through the eyes of a young girl. In 1979, when Satrapi was nine years old, revolutionaries overtook the Iranian government and installed a new regime determined to restructure the country's culture and poli-tics around strict interpretation of Islamic religious rule. As living amid the ongoing fighting became increasingly dangerous, Satrapi's parents shipped her off to Vienna, Austria, where she spent her high school years on her own. These panels from Satrapi's memoir narrate her return to her hometown of Tehran. What strikes you about the images and words? Consider, for instance, the darkness surrounding the crowds, the dialogue between Satrapi and the customs agent, and the way the teenager's and mother's heads are drawn to show movement. What do such details tell you about the artist's experience? What do they tell you about life in Iran?

Reading Narration

Narration relates a sequence of events that are linked in time. By arranging events in an orderly progression, a narrative illuminates the stages leading to a result. Sometimes the emphasis is on the story itself, as in fiction, biography, autobiography, some history, and much journalism. But often a narrative serves some larger point, as when a paragraph or a brief story about an innocent person's death helps to strengthen an argument for stricter handling of drunk drivers. When used as a primary means of developing an essay, such pointed narration usually relates a sequence of events that led to new knowledge or had a notable outcome. The point of the narrative—the idea the reader is to take away—then determines the selection of events, the amount of detail devoted to them, and their arrangement.

Though narration arranges events in time, narrative time is not real time. An important event may fill whole pages, even though it took only minutes to unfold; a less important event may be dealt with in a sentence, even though it lasted for hours. Suppose, for instance, that a writer wants to narrate the experience of being mugged to show how courage came unexpectedly to his aid. He might provide a slow-motion account of the few minutes' encounter with the muggers, including vivid details of the setting and of the attackers' appearance, a moment-by-moment replay of his emotions, and exact dialogue. At the same time, he might compress events that merely fill in background or link main events, such as how he got to the scene of the mugging or the follow-up questioning by a police detective. And he might entirely omit many events, such as a conversation overheard at the police station, that have no significance for his point.

The point of a narrative influences not only which events are covered and how fully but also how the events are arranged. There are several possibilities:

- A straight **chronological order** is most common because it relates events in the sequence of their actual occurrence. It is particularly useful for short narratives, for those in which the last event is the

most dramatic, or for those in which the events preceding and following the climax contribute to the point being made.

- The final event, such as a self-revelation, may come first, followed
  by an explanation of the events leading up to it.

- The entire story may be summarized first and then examined in
  detail.

- **Flashbacks**—shifts backward rather than forward in time—may
  recall events whose significance would not have been apparent earlier. Flashbacks are common in movies and fiction: a character in
  the midst of one scene mentally replays another.

In addition to providing a clear organization, writers also strive to
adopt a consistent **point of view**, a position relative to the events, conveyed in two main ways:

- Pronouns indicate the storyteller's place in the story: the first-person
  I if the narrator is a direct participant; the third-person *he, she, it,* or
  they if the writer is observing or reporting.

- Verb tense indicates the writer's relation in time to the sequence of
  events: present (*is, run*) or past (*was, ran*).

Combining the first-person pronoun with the present tense can create
great immediacy ("I feel the point of the knife in my back"). At the other
extreme, combining third-person pronouns with the past tense creates
more distance and objectivity ("He felt the point of the knife in his
back"). In between these extremes are combinations of first person with
past tense ("I felt . . .") or third person with present tense ("He feels . . .").
The choice depends on how involved the writer is in the events and on
his or her purpose.

Analyzing Narration in Paragraphs

Michael Ondaatje (born 1943) is a poet, fiction writer, essayist, and filmmaker. The
following paragraph is from *Running in the Family* (1982), Ondaatje's memoir of his
childhood in Ceylon, now called Sri Lanka, off the southern tip of India.

<u>After</u> my father died, a grey cobra came into the house.   Past tense

My stepmother loaded the gun and fired at point blank range.

The gun jammed. She stepped back and reloaded but <u>by then</u>   Chronological
order

the snake had slid out into the garden. <u>For the next month</u> this snake would often come into the house and <u>each time</u> the gun would misfire or jam, or my stepmother would miss at absurdly short range. The snake attacked no one and had a tendency to follow my younger sister Susan around. Other snakes entering the house were killed by the shotgun, lifted with a long stick and flicked into the bushes, but the old grey cobra led a charmed life. <u>Finally</u> one of the old workers at Rock Hill told my stepmother what had become obvious, that it was my father who had come to protect his family. <u>And in fact</u>, whether it was because the chicken farm closed down or because of my father's presence in the form of a snake, very few other snakes came into the house <u>again</u>.

Transitions (underlined)

Point of view: participant / observer

Purpose: to relate a colorful, mysterious story

Donald Hall (born 1928) served as poet laureate of the United States from 2006 to 2007. He is also an award-winning essayist, critic, playwright, and children's author. The following paragraph comes from his memoir *Unpacking the Boxes* (2008).

Memory is stronger when it recalls transgression. I played with a neighbor boy <u>while</u> a repairman worked on the kitchen refrigerator, which had a white coil at its top. The repairman's dented Model T, cut down to a pickup, stood beside the kitchen door on two narrow strips of breaking-apart cement. My playmate and I lifted chunks of concrete onto the pickup's bed. My mother, <u>peeking</u> out the screen door, issued a reprimand, <u>and</u> my friend and I set to undo the crime. I stood in the truck bed lifting chunks down to my accomplice, who wore an Indian headdress. I stood above the boy <u>looking down</u> on his head surrounded by feathers, <u>and</u> carefully dropped a large lump of concrete onto his skull. Oh, the bliss of targeting a head circled by feathers! He howled <u>and</u> ran home; I was sent to my room.

Chronological order

Past tense

Transitions (underlined)

Point of view: direct participant

Purpose: to express the joy of getting into trouble

Developing a Narrative Essay

▶ Getting Started

You'll find narration useful whenever relating a sequence of events can help you make a point, sometimes to support the thesis of a larger paper, sometimes as the thesis of a paper. If you're assigned a narrative essay, probe your own experiences for a situation such as an argument involving strong emotion, a humorous or embarrassing incident, a dramatic scene you witnessed, or a learning experience like a job. If you have the opportunity to do research, you might choose a topic dealing with the natural world (such as the Big Bang scenario for the origin of the universe) or an event in history or politics (such as how a local activist worked to close down an animal-research lab).

Explore your subject by listing all the events in sequence as they happened. At this stage you may find the traditional journalist's questions helpful:

- *Who* was involved?
- *What* happened?
- *When* did it happen?
- *Where* did it happen?
- *Why* did it happen?
- *How* did it happen?

These questions will lead you to examine your subject from all angles. Then you need to decide which events should be developed in great detail because they are central to your story; which merit compression because they merely contribute background or tie the main events together; and which should be omitted altogether because they are irrelevant to the story or might clutter your narrative.

While you are weighing the relative importance of events, consider also what your readers need to know to understand and appreciate your narrative:

- What information will help locate readers in the narrative's time and place?
- How will you expand and compress events to keep readers' attention?
- What details about people, places, and feelings will make the events vivid for readers?
- What is your attitude toward the subject—lighthearted, sarcastic, bitter, serious?—and how will you convey it to readers in your choice of events and details?
- What should your point of view be? Do you want to involve readers intimately by using the first person and the present tense? Or does that seem overdramatic, less appropriate than the more detached,

objective view that would be conveyed by the past tense or the third person or both?

▶ Forming a Thesis

Whatever your subject, you should have some point to make about it: Why was the incident or experience significant? What does it teach or illustrate? If you can, phrase this point in a sentence before you start to draft, like these, for instance:

> I used to think small-town life was boring, but one taste of the city made me appreciate the leisurely pace of home.

> A recent small earthquake demonstrated the hazards of inadequate civil defense measures.

Sometimes you may need to draft your story before the point of it becomes clear to you, especially if the experience had a personal impact or if the event was so recent that writing a draft will allow you to gain some perspective.

Whether to state your main point outright in your essay, as a thesis sentence, depends on the effect you want to have on readers. You might use your introduction to lead to a statement of your thesis so that readers will know from the start why you are telling them your story. Then again, to intensify the drama of your story, you might decide to withhold your thesis sentence for the conclusion or omit it altogether. Remember, though, that the thesis must be evident to readers even if it isn't stated: the narrative needs a point.

▶ Organizing

Narrative essays often begin without formal **introductions**, instead drawing the reader in with one of the more dramatic events in the sequence. But you may find an introduction useful to set the scene for your narrative, to summarize the events leading up to it, to establish the context for it, or to lead in to a thesis statement if you want readers to know the point of your story before they start reading it.

The arrangement of events in the **body** of your essay depends on the actual order in which they occurred and the point you want to make. To narrate a trip during which one thing after another went wrong, you might find a strict chronological order most effective. To narrate an earthquake that began and ended in an instant, you might sort simultaneous events into groups—say, what happened to buildings and what happened to people—or you might arrange a few people's experiences in order of increasing drama. To narrate an experience of city life, you might interweave events in the city with contrasting flashbacks to life in a small town, or you might start by relating one especially bad experience in the city, drop back to explain how you ended up in that situation, and then go on to tell what happened afterward. Narrative time can be manipulated in any number of ways, but your scheme should have a purpose that your readers can see, and you should stick to it.

Let the ending of your essay be determined by the effect you want to leave with readers. You can end with the last event in your sequence, or the one you have saved for last, if it reveals your point and provides a strong finish. Or you can summarize the aftermath of the story if it contributes to the point. You can also end with a formal **conclusion** that states your point—your thesis—explicitly. Such a conclusion is especially useful if your point unfolds gradually throughout the narrative and you want to emphasize it at the finish.

▶ Drafting

Drafting a narrative can be less of a struggle than drafting other kinds of papers, especially if you're close to the events and you use a straight chronological order. But the relative ease of storytelling can be misleading if it causes you to describe events too quickly or write without making a point. While drafting, be as specific as possible. Tell what the people in your narrative were wearing, what expressions their faces held, how they gestured, what they said. Specify the time of day, and describe the weather and the surroundings (buildings, vegetation, and the like). All these details may be familiar to you, but they won't be to your readers.

At the same time, try to remain open to what the story means to you, so that you can convey that meaning in your selection and description of events. If you know before you begin what your thesis is, let it guide you. But the first draft may turn out to be a search for your point, so that you'll need another draft to make it evident in the way you relate events.

In your draft you may want to experiment with **dialogue**—quotations of what participants said, in their words. Dialogue can add immediacy and realism as long as it advances the narrative and doesn't ramble beyond its usefulness. In reconstructing dialogue from memory, try to recall not only the actual words but also the sounds of speakers' voices and the expressions on their faces—information that will help you represent each speaker distinctly. And keep the dialogue natural sounding by using constructions typical of speech. For instance, most speakers prefer contractions such as *don't* and *shouldn't* to the longer forms *do not* and *should not*; and few speakers begin sentences with *although*, as in the formal-sounding "Although we could hear our mother's voice, we refused to answer her."

Whether you are relating events in strict chronological order or manipulating them for some effect, try to make their sequence in real time and the distance between them clear to readers. Instead of signaling sequence with the monotonous *and then . . . and then . . . and then* or *next . . . next . . . next*, use informative **transitions** that signal the order of events (*afterward, earlier*), the duration of events (*for an hour, in that time*), or the amount of time between events (*the next morning, a week later*). (See the Glossary under *transitions* for a list of such expressions.)

▶ Revising and Editing

When your draft is complete, revise and edit it by answering the following questions and considering the information in the focus box on the next page.

- *Is the point of your narrative clear, and does every event you relate contribute to it?* Whether or not you state your thesis, it should be obvious to readers. They should be able to see why you have lingered over some events and compressed others, and they should not be distracted by insignificant events and details.

- *Is your organization clear?* Be sure that your readers will understand any shifts backward or forward in time.

- *Have you used transitions to help readers follow the sequence of events?* Transitions such as *meanwhile* or *soon afterward* serve a dual purpose: they keep the reader on track, and they link sentences and paragraphs so that they flow smoothly. (For more information, see pp. 40 and 245 and the Glossary under *transitions*.)

- *If you have used dialogue, is it purposeful and natural?* Be sure all quoted speech moves the action ahead. And read all dialogue aloud to check that it sounds like something someone would actually say.

FOCUS ON **Verbs**

Narration depends heavily on verbs to clarify and enliven events. Weak verbs, such as forms of *make* and *be*, can sap the life from a story. Strong verbs sharpen meaning and engage readers:

WEAK   The wind made an awful noise.

STRONG The wind roared and shook the trees.

Verbs in the active voice (the subject does the action) usually pack more power than verbs in the passive voice (the subject is acted upon):

WEAK PASSIVE   Shelter was sought in the basement.

STRONG ACTIVE We sought shelter in the basement.

While strengthening your verbs, also ensure that they're consistent in tense. The tense you choose, present or past, should not shift:

INCONSISTENT As the water slowly rose, we held a conference to consider our options. It takes only a minute to decide to evacuate.

CONSISTENT   As the water slowly rose, we held a conference to consider our options. It took only a minute to decide to evacuate.

See page 52 for a discussion of passive versus active voice and page 55 for advice on avoiding shifts in tense.

Practice

Edit each of the following sentences to strengthen weak and passive verbs and to repair shifts in tense.

1. We went outside and looked around.
2. Broken tree limbs were all over the yard and in the street.
3. As we debated where to go, my father screams: "Sparky!" The dog was forgotten.
4. Frantic, my mother went to the basement and the door was jerked open.
5. A very wet but very happy dog came out and got in the car.

▸ For more practice editing for weak and passive verbs and avoiding shifts in tense, visit Exercise Central at bedfordstmartins.com/exercisecentral.

A Note on Thematic Connections

All the authors in this chapter saw reasons to articulate key events in their youths, and for that purpose narration is the obvious choice. In a graphic memoir, Marjane Satrapi pictures returning home after living abroad (p. 92). Michael Ondaatje, in a paragraph, recalls his stepmother's inability to kill a cobra, perhaps because it embodied his dead father (p. 95). Donald Hall, in another paragraph, remembers hurting a playmate without remorse (p. 96). Frederick Douglass's essay relates his efforts to become literate in a society that strongly discouraged his education (opposite), while Maya Angelou breathlessly re-creates the experience of listening to a boxing match on the radio (p. 111). And Amy Tan's narrative recounts choice moments of her family's history to explore her feelings about beauty (p. 116).

Frederick Douglass

One of the most influential public figures of the nineteenth century, Frederick Douglass (1818–95) lived his first twenty years as a slave. He was born on a plantation in eastern Maryland and grew up forced to do field labor in Talbot county and to work as a house servant and hired-out craftsman in Baltimore. After escaping to the North in the late 1830s, Douglass worked at odd jobs in New Bedford, Massachusetts, while immersing himself in both abolitionism, a movement to end slavery in the United States, and the emerging struggle for women's rights. By the time he published his first book of autobiography, *Narrative of the Life of Frederick Douglass, an American Slave* (1845), Douglass had developed international renown as a newspaper publisher and traveling orator. In all his speeches and written works—including "What to the Slave Is the Fourth of July?" (1852), *My Bondage and My Freedom* (1855), and *The Life and Times of Frederick Douglass* (1881)—Douglass drew on a powerful command of rhetoric to fight injustice of any kind and to shape the course of history.

Learning to Read and Write

A chapter in *Narrative of the Life of Frederick Douglass*, "Learning to Read and Write" is a compelling narrative about a period of intellectual and emotional discovery for a boy of twelve. As you read Douglass's account, notice how he uses a simple story about his personal experience to argue a complex point.

I lived in Master Hugh's family about seven years. During this time, I 1
succeeded in learning to read and write. In accomplishing this, I was
compelled to resort to various stratagems. I had no regular teacher. My
mistress, who had kindly commenced to instruct me, had, in compliance with the advice and direction of her husband, not only ceased to
instruct, but had set her face against my being instructed by any one
else. It is due, however, to my mistress to say of her, that she did not
adopt this course of treatment immediately. She at first lacked the
depravity indispensable to shutting me up in mental darkness. It was at
least necessary for her to have some training in the exercise of irresponsible power, to make her equal to the task of treating me as though I were
a brute.

My mistress was, as I have said, a kind and tender-hearted woman; 2
and in the simplicity of her soul she commenced, when I first went to
live with her, to treat me as she supposed one human being ought to
treat another. In entering upon the duties of a slaveholder, she did not
seem to perceive that I sustained to her the relation of a mere chattel,
and that for her to treat me as a human being was not only wrong, but

dangerously so. Slavery proved as injurious to her as it did to me. When I went there, she was a pious, warm, and tender-hearted woman. There was no sorrow or suffering for which she had not a tear. She had bread for the hungry, clothes for the naked, and comfort for every mourner that came within her reach. Slavery soon proved its ability to divest her of these heavenly qualities. Under its influence, the tender heart became stone, and the lamb-like disposition gave way to one of tiger-like fierceness. The first step in her downward course was in her ceasing to instruct me. She now commenced to practice her husband's precepts. She finally became even more violent in her opposition than her husband himself. She was not satisfied with simply doing as well as he had commanded; she seemed anxious to do better. Nothing seemed to make her more angry than to see me with a newspaper. She seemed to think that here lay the danger. I have had her rush at me with a face made all up of fury, and snatch from me a newspaper, in a manner that fully revealed her apprehension. She was an apt woman; and a little experience soon demonstrated, to her satisfaction, that education and slavery were incompatible with each other.

From this time I was most narrowly watched. If I was in a separate 3 room any considerable length of time, I was sure to be suspected of having a book, and was at once called to give an account of myself. All this, however, was too late. The first step had been taken. Mistress, in teaching me the alphabet, had given me the *inch*, and no precaution could prevent me from taking the *ell*.[1]

The plan which I adopted, and the one by which I was most suc- 4 cessful, was that of making friends of all the little white boys whom I met in the street. As many of these as I could, I converted into teachers. With their kindly aid, obtained at different times and in different places, I finally succeeded in learning to read. When I was sent of errands, I always took my book with me, and by going one part of my errand quickly, I found time to get a lesson before my return. I used also to carry bread with me, enough of which was always in the house, and to which I was always welcome; for I was much better off in this regard than many of the poor white children in our neighborhood. This bread I used to bestow upon the hungry little urchins, who, in return, would give me that more valuable bread of knowledge. I am strongly tempted to give the names of two or three of those little boys, as a testimonial of the gratitude and affection I bear them; but prudence forbids:—not that it

---

[1] An English unit of measurement, no longer used, equivalent to roughly 45 inches. [Editors' note.]

would injure me, but it might embarrass them; for it is almost an unpardonable offence to teach slaves to read in this Christian country. It is enough to say of the dear little fellows, that they lived on Philpot Street, very near Durgin and Bailey's ship-yard. I used to talk this matter of slavery over with them. I would sometimes say to them, I wished I could be as free as they would be when they got to be men. "You will be free as soon as you are twenty-one, *but I am a slave for life!* Have not I as good a right to be free as you have?" These words used to trouble them; they would express for me the liveliest sympathy, and console me with the hope that something would occur by which I might be free.

I was now about twelve years old, and the thought of being *a slave* 5 *for life* began to bear heavily upon my heart. Just about this time, I got hold of a book entitled "The Columbian Orator."[2] Every opportunity I got, I used to read this book. Among much of other interesting matter, I found in it a dialogue between a master and his slave. The slave was represented as having run away from his master three times. The dialogue represented the conversation which took place between them, when the slave was retaken the third time. In this dialogue, the whole argument in behalf of slavery was brought forward by the master, all of which was disposed of by the slave. The slave was made to say some very smart as well as impressive things in reply to his master—things which had the desired though unexpected effect; for the conversation resulted in the voluntary emancipation of the slave on the part of the master.

In the same book, I met with one of Sheridan's[3] mighty speeches on 6 and in behalf of Catholic emancipation. These were choice documents to me. I read them over and over again with unabated interest. They gave tongue to interesting thoughts of my own soul, which had frequently lashed through my mind, and died away for want of utterance. The moral which I gained from the dialogue was the power of truth over the conscience of even a slaveholder. What I got from Sheridan was a bold denunciation of slavery, and a powerful vindication of human rights. The reading of these documents enabled me to utter my thoughts, and to meet the arguments brought forward to sustain slavery; but while they relieved me of one difficulty, they brought on another even more painful than the one of which I was relieved. The more I read, the more

---

[2] An anthology of speeches, essays, and literature that was widely used as a textbook in the early nineteenth century. [Editors' note.]

[3] Richard Brinley Sheridan (1751–1816) was a playwright and outspoken member of the British House of Commons. Catholic emancipation, a push to expand legal protections for Great Britain's religious minority, was one of the many causes he championed. [Editors' note.]

I was led to abhor and detest my enslavers. I could regard them in no other light than a band of successful robbers, who had left their homes, and gone to Africa, and stolen us from our homes, and in a strange land reduced us to slavery. I loathed them as being the meanest as well as the most wicked of men. As I read and contemplated the subject, behold! that very discontentment which Master Hugh had predicted would follow my learning to read had already come, to torment and sting my soul to unutterable anguish. As I writhed under it, I would at times feel that learning to read had been a curse rather than a blessing. It had given me a view of my wretched condition, without the remedy. It opened my eyes to the horrible pit, but to no ladder upon which to get out. In moments of agony, I envied my fellow-slaves for their stupidity. I have often wished myself a beast. I preferred the condition of the meanest reptile to my own. Any thing, no matter what, to get rid of thinking! It was this everlasting thinking of my condition that tormented me. There was no getting rid of it. It was pressed upon me by every object within sight or hearing, animate or inanimate. The silver trump of freedom had roused my soul to eternal wakefulness. Freedom now appeared, to disappear no more forever. It was heard in every sound, and seen in every thing. It was ever present to torment me with a sense of my wretched condition. I saw nothing without seeing it, I heard nothing without hearing it, and felt nothing without feeling it. It looked from every star, it smiled in every calm, breathed in every wind, and moved in every storm.

I often found myself regretting my own existence, and wishing 7 myself dead; and but for the hope of being free, I have no doubt but that I should have killed myself, or done something for which I should have been killed. While in this state of mind, I was eager to hear any one speak of slavery. I was a ready listener. Every little while, I could hear something about the abolitionists. It was some time before I found what the word meant. It was always used in such connections as to make it an interesting word to me. If a slave ran away and succeeded in getting clear, or if a slave killed his master, set fire to a barn, or did any thing very wrong in the mind of a slaveholder, it was spoken of as the fruit of *abolition*. Hearing the word in this connection very often, I set about learning what it meant. The dictionary afforded me little or no help. I found it was "the act of abolishing"; but then I did not know what was to be abolished. Here I was perplexed. I did not dare to ask any one about its meaning, for I was satisfied that it was something they wanted me to know very little about. After a patient waiting, I got one of our city papers, containing an account of the number of petitions from the north, praying for the abolition of slavery in the District of Columbia, and of the slave trade between the States. From this time I understood the words *abolition* and *abolitionist*, and always drew near when that word was spoken, expecting to hear something of importance to myself and fellow-slaves. The light broke in upon me by degrees. I went one day down on the wharf of Mr. Waters; and seeing two Irishmen unloading a scow of stone, I went, unasked, and helped them. When we had finished, one of them came to me and asked me if I were a slave. I told him I was. He asked, "Are ye a slave for life?" I told him that I was. The good Irishman seemed to be deeply affected by the statement. He said to the other that it was a pity so fine a little fellow as myself should be a slave for life. He said it was a shame to hold me. They both advised me to run away to the north; that I should find friends there, and that I should be free. I pretended not to be interested in what they said, and treated them as if I did not understand them; for I feared they might be treacherous. White men have been known to encourage slaves to escape, and then, to get the reward, catch them and return them to their masters. I was afraid that these seemingly good men might use me so; but I nevertheless remembered their advice, and from that time I resolved to run away. I looked forward to a time at which it would be safe for me to escape. I was too young to think of doing so immediately; besides, I wished to learn how to write, as I might have occasion to write my own pass. I consoled myself with the hope that I should one day find a good chance. Meanwhile, I would learn to write.

The idea as to how I might learn to write was suggested to me by **8** being in Durgin and Bailey's ship-yard, and frequently seeing the ship carpenters, after hewing, and getting a piece of timber ready for use, write on the timber the name of that part of the ship for which it was intended. When a piece of timber was intended for the larboard side, it would be marked thus—"L." When a piece was for the starboard side, it would be marked thus—"S." A piece for the larboard side forward, would be marked thus—"L. F." When a piece was for starboard side forward, it would be marked thus—"S. F." For larboard aft, it would be marked thus—"L. A." For starboard aft, it would be marked thus— "S. A." I soon learned the names of these letters, and for what they were intended when placed upon a piece of timber in the ship-yard. I immediately commenced copying them, and in a short time was able to make the four letters named. After that, when I met with any boy who I knew could write, I would tell him I could write as well as he. The next word would be, "I don't believe you. Let me see you try it." I would then make the letters which I had been so fortunate as to learn, and ask him to beat that. In this way I got a good many lessons in writing, which it is quite possible I should never have gotten in any other way. During this time, my copy-book[4] was the board fence, brick wall, and pavement; my pen and ink was a lump of chalk. With these, I learned mainly how to write. I then commenced and continued copying the Italics in Webster's Spelling Book,[5] until I could make them all without looking on the book. By this time, my little Master Thomas had gone to school, and learned how to write, and had written over a number of copy-books. These had been brought home, and shown to some of our near neighbors, and then laid aside. My mistress used to go to class meeting at the Wilk Street meetinghouse every Monday afternoon, and leave me to take care of the house. When left thus, I used to spend the time in writing in the spaces left in Master Thomas's copy-book, copying what he had written. I continued to do this until I could write a hand very similar to that of Master Thomas. Thus, after a long, tedious effort for years, I finally succeeded in learning how to write.

Vocabulary

The following words might be new to you. Try to determine their meanings from the context of Douglass's essay, test your guesses in a dictionary, and then use each word in a sentence of your own.

depravity (1)	testimonial (4)	abhor (6)
sustained (2)	prudence (4)	animate (6)
chattel (2)	disposed (5)	inanimate (6)
pious (2)	emancipation (5, 6)	scow (7)
divest (2)	unabated (6)	treacherous (7)
disposition (2)	utterance (6)	hewing (8)
apt (2)	denunciation (6)	
urchins (4)	vindication (6)	

Key Ideas and Details

1. Douglass writes in the first paragraph that he "was compelled to resort to various stratagems," or tricks, to learn to read and write. What were those stratagems? Why was Douglass forced to use them?

2. Speaking of the mistress of the house, Douglass says, "Slavery proved as injurious to her as it did to me" (paragraph 2). What does he mean? What evidence does he provide to support his claim?

---

[4]A workbook containing samples of vocabulary and handwriting for students to practice by copying. [Editors' note.]

[5]A spelling textbook and workbook popular in early nineteenth-century grade school classrooms. [Editors' note.]

3. What is the main point of Douglass's narrative? Can you find a direct statement of his thesis in the essay?

Craft and Structure

1. LANGUAGE "Learning to Read and Write" includes several figures of speech, such as "shutting me up in mental darkness" (paragraph 1), a metaphor, and "lamb-like disposition" (2), a simile. Find two or three other figures of speech and analyze how each contributes to Douglass's meaning and helps convey his attitude toward his education. (If necessary, consult pages 58–59 for an explanation of common figures of speech.)

2. Douglass relates his childhood experience in a formal adult style, using many complex sentences and difficult words. What effect do you think he is trying to achieve with this style?

3. Where in his narrative does Douglass flash back in time to explain events, compress time by summarizing events, or jump ahead in time by omitting events? Where does he expand time by drawing moments out? How does each of these insertions and manipulations of time relate to Douglass's main point?

4. OTHER METHODS Douglass takes pains to explain his struggle to understand the meaning of the words *abolition* and *abolitionism* (paragraph 7). What does the definition (Chapter 13) contribute to the point of his essay?

Integration of Knowledge and Ideas

1. What does Douglass seem to assume about his readers' familiarity with, and attitudes toward, slavery? What details help him reinforce such attitudes?

2. How did the dialogues and speeches in "The Columbian Orator" change Douglass's perceptions of himself and his situation? To what use did he put the new knowledge and ideas he gained from his reading?

3. FOR DISCUSSION Why do you think Douglass wrote "Learning to Read and Write" as part of his autobiography fifteen years after the experience? Was his purpose simply to express feelings prompted by a significant accomplishment in his life? Did he want to criticize his mistress and other slaveholders? Did he want to explain something about slavery or argue a point about education? Something else? What passages support your answer?

Writing Topics

1. In teaching himself to read and write, Douglass went against the wishes of society and broke the rules of his household. When have you experienced a powerful desire to do something forbidden? Write a narrative essay about

a time when others encouraged or discouraged you from engaging in a particular behavior—perhaps against your true beliefs or values. What appeal did the behavior hold? What did you gain by conforming or rebelling? What did you lose? Use specific details to explain how and why the experience affected you.

2. Douglass worked hard to get an education that was otherwise denied him, yet he found that learning brought him both pleasure and pain. Consider your own experiences with reading and writing and compose an essay that explores the rewards and frustrations of your current English class. Do you find it worthwhile, tedious, enjoyable, pointless, something else? What do you expect to gain—or lose—from reading about new subjects or improving your writing skills? What could you do to take control of your own education and shape the future you want for yourself?

3. RESEARCH Although it was formally abolished in the United States at the end of the Civil War, the practice of slavery is still very much alive. Research recent forms of forced labor and human trafficking, either here or abroad, reading three to five articles on the subject (see pp. 65–66 for advice on conducting searches). Then prepare a presentation that reports your findings. Consider the following questions as you research: What form does modern slavery take? Where is it practiced? Who is affected? What can be done to stop it?

4. CONNECTIONS In telling of his own successful efforts to become literate, Douglass refutes nineteenth-century arguments that African Americans were inferior to white slaveholders. In "Champion of the World" (next page), Maya Angelou also tells a story to argue for equality among the two races, but she takes a very different approach. How does Douglass's experience differ from the one reported by Angelou? Write an essay analyzing what these narratives have in common and any significant differences between them.

Maya Angelou

Maya Angelou was born Marguerite Johnson in Saint Louis, Missouri, in 1928. Angelou's childhood was troubled — she was shuttled between the homes of her divorced parents and her grandmother, was raped as a young girl, and became an unwed mother as a teenager. She went on, however, to become a prolific writer whose work is filled with joy and hope. Though she is best known for her poetry, novels, and six-volume autobiography — beginning with *I Know Why the Caged Bird Sings* (1970) through *A Song Flung Up to Heaven* (2002) — Angelou has also worked in theater, film, and television. She appeared in off-Broadway plays, wrote and produced several television specials, costarred in the movie *How to Make an American Quilt* (1995), and directed the film *Down in the Delta* (1998). She has taught at the University of Kansas, Wichita State University, California State University at Sacramento, and Wake Forest University, where she is Reynolds Professor of American Studies.

Champion of the World

Rich in detail, this chapter from *I Know Why the Caged Bird Sings* captures the suspense of a memorable moment in Angelou's childhood — the night when African American boxer Joe Louis, the "Brown Bomber," defended his heavyweight title against a white contender. The narrative is set in her grandmother and Uncle Willie's store, where the community of Angelou's Arkansas hometown gathered to listen to the fight.

The last inch of space was filled, yet people continued to wedge themselves along the walls of the Store. Uncle Willie had turned the radio up to its last notch so that youngsters on the porch wouldn't miss a word. Women sat on kitchen chairs, dining-room chairs, stools, and upturned wooden boxes. Small children and babies perched on every lap available and men leaned on the shelves or on each other. 1

The apprehensive mood was shot through with shafts of gaiety, as a black sky is streaked with lightning. 2

"I ain't worried 'bout this fight. Joe's gonna whip that cracker like it's open season." 3

"He gone whip him till that white boy call him Momma." 4

At last the talking finished and the string-along songs about razor blades were over and the fight began. 5

"A quick jab to the head." In the Store the crowd grunted. "A left to the head and a right and another left." One of the listeners cackled like a hen and was quieted. 6

"They're in a clinch, Louis is trying to fight his way out." 7

Some bitter comedian on the porch said, "That white man don't 8
mind hugging that niggah now, I betcha."

"The referee is moving in to break them up, but Louis finally pushed 9
the contender away and it's an uppercut to the chin. The contender is
hanging on, now he's backing away. Louis catches him with a short left
to the jaw."

A tide of murmuring assent poured out the door and into the yard. 10

"Another left and another left. Louis is saving that mighty right . . ." 11
The mutter in the Store had grown into a baby roar and it was pierced
by the clang of a bell and the announcer's "That's the bell for round
three, ladies and gentlemen."

As I pushed my way into the Store I wondered if the announcer gave 12
any thought to the fact that he was addressing as "ladies and gentlemen" all the Negroes around the world who sat sweating and praying,
glued to their "Master's voice."[1]

There were only a few calls for RC Colas, Dr Peppers, and Hires root 13
beer. The real festivities would begin after the fight. Then even the old
Christian ladies who taught their children and tried themselves to practice turning the other cheek would buy soft drinks, and if the Brown
Bomber's victory was a particularly bloody one they would order peanut patties and Baby Ruths also.

Bailey and I laid the coins on top of the cash register. Uncle Willie 14
didn't allow us to ring up sales during a fight. It was too noisy and might
shake up the atmosphere. When the gong rang for the next round we
pushed through the near-sacred quiet to the herd of children outside.

"He's got Louis against the ropes and now it's a left to the body and 15
a right to the ribs. Another right to the body, it looks like it was low . . .
Yes, ladies and gentlemen, the referee is signaling but the contender
keeps raining the blows on Louis. It's another to the body, and it looks
like Louis is going down."

My race groaned. It was our people falling. It was another lynching, 16
yet another Black man hanging on a tree. One more woman ambushed
and raped. A Black boy whipped and maimed. It was hounds on the trail
of a man running through slimy swamps. It was a white woman slapping
her maid for being forgetful.

The men in the Store stood away from the walls and at attention. 17
Women greedily clutched the babes on their laps while on the porch

---

[1]"His master's voice," accompanied by a picture of a little dog listening to a
phonograph, was a familiar advertising slogan. (The picture still appears on some
RCA recordings.) [Editors' note.]

the shufflings and smiles, flirtings and pinching of a few minutes before were gone. This might be the end of the world. If Joe lost we were back in slavery and beyond help. It would all be true, the accusations that we were lower types of human beings. Only a little higher than apes. True that we were stupid and ugly and lazy and dirty and, unlucky and worst of all, that God Himself hated us and ordained us to be hewers of wood and drawers of water, forever and ever, world without end.

We didn't breathe. We didn't hope. We waited.   18

"He's off the ropes, ladies and gentlemen. He's moving towards the   19
center of the ring." There was no time to be relieved. The worst might still happen.

"And now it looks like Joe is mad. He's caught Carnera with a left   20
hook to the head and a right to the head. It's a left jab to the body and another left to the head. There's a left cross and a right to the head. The contender's right eye is bleeding and he can't seem to keep his block up. Louis is penetrating every block. The referee is moving in, but Louis sends a left to the body and it's an uppercut to the chin and the contender is dropping. He's on the canvas, ladies and gentlemen."

Babies slid to the floor as women stood up and men leaned toward   21
the radio.

"Here's the referee. He's counting. One, two, three, four, five, six,   22
seven . . . Is the contender trying to get up again?"

All the men in the store shouted, "NO."   23

"—eight, nine, ten." There were a few sounds from the audience, but   24
they seemed to be holding themselves in against tremendous pressure.

"The fight is all over, ladies and gentlemen. Let's get the microphone   25
over to the referee . . . Here he is. He's got the Brown Bomber's hand, he's holding it up . . . Here he is . . ."

Then the voice, husky and familiar, came to wash over us—"The   26
winnah, and still heavyweight champeen of the world . . . Joe Louis."

Champion of the world. A Black boy. Some Black mother's son. He   27
was the strongest man in the world. People drank Coca-Colas like ambrosia and ate candy bars like Christmas. Some of the men went behind the Store and poured white lightning in their soft-drink bottles, and a few of the bigger boys followed them. Those who were not chased away came back blowing their breath in front of themselves like proud smokers.

It would take an hour or more before the people would leave the   28
Store and head for home. Those who lived too far had made arrangements to stay in town. It wouldn't do for a Black man and his family to be caught on a lonely country road on a night when Joe Louis had proved that we were the strongest people in the world.

Vocabulary

If you do not know the meanings of the following words, try to guess them from the context of Angelou's essay. Test your guesses in a dictionary; then use each word in a sentence of your own.

apprehensive (2)	lynching (16)	ordained (17)
gaiety (2)	ambushed (16)	ambrosia (27)
assent (10)	maimed (16)	white lightning (27)

Key Ideas and Details

1. What connection does Angelou make between the outcome of the fight and the pride of African Americans? To what degree do you think the author's view is shared by the others in the store listening to the broadcast?

2. To what extent are the statements in paragraphs 16 and 17 to be taken literally? What function do they serve in Angelou's narrative?

Craft and Structure

1. LANGUAGE Describe Angelou's style. How does her use of nonstandard English contribute to her narrative? (For the definition of *nonstandard English*, consult the Glossary under *diction*.)

2. Comment on the irony in Angelou's final paragraph. (If necessary, consult the Glossary for the definition of *irony*.)

3. How does Angelou build up suspense in her account of the fight? At what point were you able to predict the winner?

4. OTHER METHODS Besides narration, Angelou also relies heavily on the method of description (Chapter 7). Analyze how narration depends on description in paragraph 27.

Integration of Knowledge and Ideas

1. What do you take to be the author's purpose in telling this story?

2. Primo Carnera was probably *not* the Brown Bomber's opponent on the night Maya Angelou recalls. Louis fought Carnera only once, on June 25, 1935, and it was not a title match; Angelou would have been no more than seven years old at the time. Does the author's apparent error detract from her story?

3. FOR DISCUSSION Angelou does not directly describe relations between African Americans and whites, yet her essay implies quite a lot. What you can infer from the exaggeration of paragraphs 16–17 and the obliqueness of paragraph 28? Focus on Angelou's details and the language she uses to present them.

Writing Topics

1. Consider groups that you belong to based on race, ethnic background, religion, sports, hobbies, politics, friendship, or any other ties. In a narrative, relate an incident that strengthened your sense of community with one of these groups. Make the event come alive for your readers with vivid details, dialogue, and tight sequencing of events.

2. Write an essay based on some childhood experience of your own, still vivid in your memory.

3. RESEARCH What did it mean in the 1930s for an African American to become a prominent and universally admired athlete? Find a book or two with some information on the career of Joe Louis, the history of boxing in general, or African American life in the early twentieth century. Take notes on your findings and report them to class.

4. CONNECTIONS Angelou's "Champion of the World" and the next essay, Amy Tan's "Pretty beyond Belief," both tell stories of children who felt like outsiders in predominantly white America. Compare and contrast the two writers' perceptions of what sets them apart from the dominant culture. How do their narratives reflect that sense of difference? Use specific examples from both essays as your evidence.

Amy Tan

Amy Tan was born in 1952 in Oakland, California, the daughter of Chinese immigrants. She grew up in northern California and majored in English and linguistics at San Jose State University, where she ultimately received a master's degree. Tan's first career was as a business writer, crafting corporate reports and executives' speeches. Dissatisfied with her work, she began writing fiction. Her first book, *The Joy Luck Club* (1989), a critical and popular success, is a series of interrelated stories about the bonds between immigrant Chinese mothers and their American-born daughters. Since *The Joy Luck Club*, she has written four more novels: *The Kitchen God's Wife* (1991), *The Hundred Secret Senses* (1995), *The Bonesetter's Daughter* (2001), and *Saving Fish from Drowning* (2005). She has also published a collection of essays, *The Opposite of Fate* (2003); a digital novella, *Rules for Virgins* (2011); and two books for children.

Pretty beyond Belief

In both her fiction and nonfiction, Tan often writes about the complexities of mother-daughter relationships. "Pretty beyond Belief," an essay from *The Opposite of Fate*, recounts episodes from her mother's and her grandmother's lives to explore the impacts they have had on hers.

I once asked my mother whether I was beautiful by Chinese standards. 1 I must have been twelve at the time, and I believed that I was not attractive according to an American aesthetic based on Marilyn Monroe as the ultimate sex goddess.

I remember that my mother carefully appraised my face before con- 2 cluding, "To Chinese person, you not beautiful. You plain."

I was unable to hide my hurt and disappointment. 3

"Why you want be beautiful?" my mother chided. "Pretty can be 4 bad luck, not just good." She should know, she said. She had been born a natural beauty. When she was four, people told her they had never seen a girl so lovely. "Everyone spoil me, the servants, my grandmother, my aunts, because I was pretty beyond belief."

By the time she was a teenager, she had the looks of a movie starlet: 5 a peach-shaped face, a nose that was rounded but not overly broad, tilted large eyes with double lids, a smile of small and perfect teeth. Her skin bore "no spots or dots," and she would often say to me, even into her seventies and eighties, "Feel. Still smooth and soft."

When she was nineteen, she married. She was innocent, she said, 6 and her husband was a bad man. The day before their wedding, he was with another woman. Later he openly brought his girlfriends home to humiliate her, to prove that her beauty and her pride were worth nothing. When she ran away with the man who would become my father, her husband had her jailed. The Shanghai tabloids covered her trial for months, and all the city girls admired her front-page photos. "They cried for me," she avowed. "They don't know me, but they thought I too pretty to have such bad life."

Beauty ruined her own mother as well. A rich man spotted my grand- 7 mother when she was newly widowed, strolling by a lakeside. "She was exquisite, like a fairy," my mother reported. The man forced the widow to become his concubine, thus consigning her to a life of disgrace. After she gave birth to his baby son, my grandmother killed herself by swallowing raw opium.

Although my mother chastised 8 my adolescent beauty, she sometimes lamented my lack of it. "Too bad you got your father's feet," she would say. She wondered why I had not inherited any of the good features of her face, and pointed out that my nostrils and lips were too coarse, my skin too dark. When I was nineteen, after a car accident left my nose and mouth askew, she told me she was sorry that she could not afford the plastic surgery to fix this, as well as my misshapen left

Glam shot of me at age twelve, with my cat Fufu.

ear. By then I didn't care that I would never meet my mother's standards of beauty. I had a boyfriend who loved me.

In the last years of my mother's life, when she had developed 9 Alzheimer's disease, she never forgot that she was a beauty. I could always make her giggle by telling her how pretty she was, how I wished I had been born with her good looks. She whispered back that some of the other women in the assisted-living residence were jealous of her for the same reason. But as she lost her ability to reason and remember, she also came to believe that my face had changed.

"You look like me," she said. I was moved to tears to hear her say 10 this. Time and age had allowed us to come closer. Now we had the same lines formed by cautious half-smiles. We had the same loss of fat above the innocent eye, the same crimped chin holding back what we really felt. My psyche had molded itself into my mother's face.

Since my mother died, I find myself looking into the mirror more 11 often than I did when I was twelve. How else is my face changing? If beauty is bad luck, why do I still want it? Why do I wish for reasons to be vain? Why do I long to look like my mother?

Vocabulary

If you do not know the following words, try to determine their meanings from the context of Tan's essay. Test your guesses in a dictionary; then use each word in a sentence of your own.

aesthetic (1)	exquisite (7)	lamented (8)
appraised (2)	concubine (7)	askew (8)
chided (4)	consigning (7)	psyche (10)
avowed (6)	chastised (8)	

Key Ideas and Details

1. "Pretty beyond Belief" does not include a thesis statement. Does the essay have a main point, and if so, what is it? How can you tell?

2. Why do you suppose the essay includes a photograph of the writer at age twelve? What does the picture contribute to Tan's meaning?

3. What evidence does Tan provide to support her mother's claim that "[p]retty can be bad luck, not just good" (paragraph 4)? To what extent does either woman believe that beauty is a negative quality?

Craft and Structure

1. LANGUAGE Tan switches point of view from first person (*I, me*) in paragraphs 1–3 to third person (*she, her*) in paragraphs 4–7 and back to first person in paragraphs 8–11. Why? Are these shifts purposeful or distracting? Why do you think so?

2. What effect does the writer achieve by quoting her mother at several points in the essay?

3. Analyze the organization of Tan's narrative. Why does it not follow strict chronological order?

4. OTHER METHODS Within her narrative about accepting her appearance, Tan tells two additional stories, about her mother and her grandmother. What is the focus of each of these examples (Chapter 8)? What do they contribute to Tan's story?

Integration of Knowledge and Ideas

1. For whom does Tan seem to be writing? What might be her reason for sharing such a personal story?

2. Reread paragraphs 6 and 7 closely. From the clues they provide, what conclusions can you draw about what life was like for women in China three or four generations ago?

3. FOR DISCUSSION Tan ends her essay with several unanswered questions. What is the purpose of such questions? Pick one question and, based on details from the body of the essay and the inferences to be made from them, propose an answer.

Writing Topics

1. In "Pretty beyond Belief," Tan suggests that beauty is subjective. Using visual evidence, write an essay or create a presentation about someone or something you consider beautiful but others do not. Your subject could be a person, a building, a work of art, an animal, a natural phenomenon, an object you hold dear. To prepare for your draft, list some of the criticisms that have been (or might be) leveled at your subject and explain why you disagree. Then counter the criticisms with your own perspective, using details from your own experience and observation.

2. Tan's essay illustrates mixed feelings not only about appearance but also about her relationship with her mother. In a brief essay, analyze how she conveys her sense of the mother-daughter relationship so that her emotions are concrete, not vague. Focus on her words and especially on their tone. (See pp. 43 and 379 for more on tone.)

3. RESEARCH Interview two or three older family members (parents, grandparents, aunts, or uncles) about an aspect of their childhoods that interests you. What memories stand out, and why are they significant? Following Tan's essay as a model, draft a brief family history based on what you learn about your relatives. You may need to conduct some additional research to provide context for their experiences (consult Chapter 5 for advice on finding and using sources).

4. CONNECTIONS Tan suggests that her dissatisfaction with her appearance stemmed from living in a culture that presented "Marilyn Monroe as the ultimate sex goddess" (paragraph 1). Similarly, Pat Mora, in "Great Expectations" (p. 199), worries about the impact of advertising messages aimed at young Latinas. Using these two essays and your own observations for evidence, write an essay that examines the influence of popular culture on self-image. To what extent do the visual images presented in movies, television, and advertising affect teenagers' perceptions of themselves and others?

WRITING WITH THE METHOD

NARRATION

Select one of the following topics, or any other topic they suggest, for an essay developed by narration. Be sure to choose a topic you care about so that narration is a means of communicating an idea, not an end in itself.

Friends and Relations

1. Seeking independence
2. A friend's generosity or sacrifice
3. A wedding or funeral
4. An incident from family legend

The World Around You

5. An interaction you witnessed on a bus
6. A storm, a flood, an earthquake, or another natural event
7. A neighborhood event, such as a block party or new construction
8. A school event, such as a meeting, demonstration, or celebration
9. A time when a poem, story, film, or song changed you

Lessons of Daily Life

10. An especially satisfying run, tennis match, bicycle race, or other sports experience
11. A time when you confronted authority
12. A time when you had to deliver bad news
13. A time when a long-anticipated possession proved disappointing
14. Your biggest social blunder

Firsts

15. Your first day of school, as a child or more recently
16. The first time you met someone who became important to you
17. The first performance you gave

Adventures

18. An episode of extrasensory perception
19. An intellectual journey: discovering a new idea, pursuing a subject, solving a mystery
20. A trip to an unfamiliar place

WRITING ABOUT THE THEME

RECALLING CHILDHOOD

1. The vulnerability of youth is a recurring theme in the essays and paragraphs in this chapter. Michael Ondaatje (p. 95), Frederick Douglass (p. 103), and Amy Tan (p. 116) all write in some way about psychological pain. After considering each writer's situation individually, write an essay analyzing the differences among these situations. Based on these narratives, which writers seem to have the most in common? Which of their responses seem unique to children? Which are most likely to be outgrown?

2. While growing up inevitably involves fear, disappointment, and pain, it usually brings moments of security and happiness as well. Michael Ondaatje clearly finds comfort in his dead father's reappearance as a cobra, Donald Hall (p. 96) relishes the joy of misbehaving, Maya Angelou (p. 111) is thrilled by tension, and Amy Tan believes that her childhood dissatisfactions with appearance strengthened her relationship with her mother. Write a narrative essay about a similarly mixed experience from your childhood, making sure to describe your feelings vividly so that your readers share them with you.

3. Life is full of epiphanies, or sudden moments of realization, insight, or understanding. But there is often a price to pay for epiphanies. Marjane Satrapi (p. 92), Frederick Douglass, and Amy Tan all experience such moments in their narratives. Satrapi is surprised to realize how much she changed while separated from her family. Douglass is enraged and frustrated when he comes to understand the injustice of slavery, and Tan is "moved to tears" when she recognizes that she is a lot like the mother she mourns. Write a narrative essay in which you tell of events leading to an epiphany that you have experienced. Make sure both the events themselves and the nature of the epiphany are vividly clear.

7

DESCRIPTION

▶

SENSING OUR NATURAL SURROUNDINGS

Whenever you use words to depict or re-create a scene, an object, a person, or a feeling, you use **description**. A mainstay of conversation between people, description is likely to figure in almost any writing situation: a text message may describe a friend's new spiky yellow hair; a laboratory report may describe the colors and odors of chemicals; a business memo may examine the tastes and textures of competitors' low-fat potato chips; an insurance claim may explain the condition of an apartment after a kitchen fire. Because the method builds detail and brings immediacy to a subject for readers, description is an important part of most essay writing as well.

Seeing Description

You've probably heard the phrase "can't see the forest for the trees." When focusing on the details of a situation, we often overlook the larger issues and miss the big picture. The goal of description, the subject of this chapter, is to reveal both the proverbial trees *and* the forest: to create an understanding of a subject by building up details that form a dominant impression. Look closely at this photograph by Ansel Adams (1902–84), a prominent nature photographer and environmentalist whose work helped to establish several American nature reserves and national parks. Taken in 1958 in the Sangre de Cristo Mountains north of Santa Fe, New Mexico, the photograph captures a stand of Aspen trees on a crisp autumn day. Adams once said of this picture, "I do not consider it a 'pretty' scene; for me it is cool and aloof and rather stately." Do you agree? Notice where the light falls and to what parts of the image your eyes are first drawn. Then shift your focus to those elements that are pushed to the background. How would you characterize the overall effect? What emotions does the image stir in your mind, and why?

Reading Description

Description draws on perceptions of the five senses—sight, sound, smell, taste, and touch—to communicate a particular experience of the world. A writer's purpose in writing and his or her involvement with the subject will largely determine how **objective** or **subjective** a description is:

- *Objective description* strives for precision, trying to convey the subject impersonally, without emotion. This is the kind of description required in scientific writing—for instance, a medical diagnosis or a report on an experiment in psychology—where cold facts and absence of feeling are essential for readers to judge the accuracy of procedures and results. It is also the method of news reports and reference works such as encyclopedias.

- *Subjective description*, in contrast, draws on emotions, giving an impression of the subject filtered through firsthand experience. Instead of withdrawing to the background, the writer invests feelings in the subject and lets those feelings determine which details he or she will describe and how he or she will describe them. State of mind—perhaps loneliness, anger, or joy—can be re-created by reference to sensory details such as numbness, heat, or sweetness.

In general, writers favor objective description when their purpose is explanation and subjective description when their purpose is self-expression or entertainment. But the categories are not exclusive, and most descriptive writing mixes the two. A news report on a tropical storm, for instance, might objectively describe bent and broken trees, fallen wires, and lashing rain, but the reporter might also interview a family to get a subjective impression of the storm's fearsomeness.

Whether objective or subjective or a mixture of the two, effective description requires a **dominant impression**—a central theme or idea that all of the details support. The dominant impression may be something a writer sees in the subject, such as the distractedness of city pedestrians or the expressiveness of an actor. Or it may derive from an emotional response to the subject, perhaps amusement (or despair) at the pedestrians' collisions, perhaps admiration (or disdain) for the actor's technique. Whatever its source, the dominant impression serves as a unifying principle that guides both the writer's selection of details and the reader's understanding of the subject.

One aid in creating a dominant impression is a consistent **point of view**, the position from which a writer approaches a subject. Point of view in description has two main elements:

- A real or imagined *physical* relation to the subject: a writer could view a mountain, for instance, from the bottom looking up, from fifteen miles away across a valley, or from an airplane passing overhead. The first two points of view are fixed because the writer remains in one position and scans the scene from there; the third is moving because the writer changes position.

- A *psychological* relation to the subject, a relation partly conveyed by pronouns. In subjective description, where feelings are part of the message, writers might use *I* and *you* freely to narrow the distance between themselves and the subject and between themselves and the reader. But in the most objective, impersonal description, writers will use *one* ("One can see the summit") or avoid self-reference altogether to appear distant from and unbiased toward the subject.

Once a physical and psychological point of view has been established, readers come to depend on it. Thus a sudden and inexplicable shift from one view to another—zooming in from fifteen miles away to the foot of a mountain, abandoning *I* for the more removed *one*—can disorient readers and distract them from the dominant impression.

Analyzing Description in Paragraphs

David Mura (born 1952) is a poet, essayist, and performance artist. This paragraph comes from his book *Turning Japanese* (1991), a memoir of his time in Japan as a *sansei*, or a third-generation Japanese American. Mura describes Tokyo during the rainy season.

And then the rains of June came, the typhoon season. Every day endless streaks of gray drilled down from the sky. A note held, passing from monotone into a deeper, more permanent dirge. The air itself seemed to liquefy, like the insides of a giant invisible jellyfish. In the streets the patter grew into pools, then rushes and torrents. Umbrellas floated,

Specific, concrete details (underlined once)

Figures of speech (underlined twice)

black bobbing circles, close as the wings of bats in under-
ground caves. In the empty lot across the street, the grass
turned a deep, tropical green; then the earth itself seemed to
bubble up in patches, foaming. In the country, square after
square of rice field filled to the brim and overflowed. In the
city, the city of labyrinths, the rain became another laby-
rinth, increased the density of inhabitants; everything seemed
thicker, moving underwater.

Point of view:
moving;
psychologically
somewhat distant

Dominant
impression:
overwhelming,
intense wetness

Diane Ackerman (born 1948) is a poet and essayist who writes extensively on the
natural world. The following paragraph comes from *A Natural History of the Senses*
(1991), a prose exploration of sight, hearing, touch, taste, and smell.

Pastel icebergs roamed around us, some tens of thousands of years old. Great pressure can push the air bubbles
out of the ice and compact it. Free of air bubbles, it reflects
light differently, as blue. The waters shivered with the goose-
flesh of small ice shards. Some icebergs glowed like dull pep-
permint in the sun—impurities trapped in the ice (phyto-
plankton and algae) tinted them green. Ethereal snow petrels
flew around the peaks of the icebergs, while the sun shone
through their translucent wings. White, silent, the birds
seemed to be pieces of ice flying with purpose and grace. As
they passed in front of an ice floe, they became invisible.
Glare transformed the landscape with such force that it
seemed like a pure color. When we went out in the inflatable
motorized rafts called Zodiacs to tour the iceberg orchards, I
grabbed a piece of glacial ice and held it to my ear, listening
to the bubbles cracking and popping as the air trapped inside
escaped. And that night, though exhausted from the day's
spectacles and doings, I lay in my narrow bunk, awake with
my eyes closed, while sun-struck icebergs drifted across the
insides of my lids, and the Antarctic peninsula revealed itself
slowly, mile by mile, in the small theater of my closed eyes.

Specific, concrete
details (under-
lined once)

Figures of speech
(underlined
twice)

Point of view:
fixed, then
moving; psycho-
logically close

Dominant
impression:
awesome, chilly
brightness

Developing a Descriptive Essay

▶ Getting Started

The subject for a descriptive essay may be any object, place, person, animal, or state of mind that you have observed closely enough or experienced sharply enough to invest with special significance. A chair, a tree,

a room, a shopping mall, a movie actor, an armadillo, a passerby on the street, a feeling of fear, a sense of achievement—anything you have a strong impression of can prompt effective description.

Observe your subject directly, if possible, or recall it as completely as you can. Jot down the details that seem to contribute most to the impression you're trying to convey. You needn't write the description of those details yet—that can wait for drafting—but you do want to capture the possibilities in your subject.

You should start to consider the needs and expectations of your readers early on. If the subject is something readers have never seen or felt before, you will need enough objective details to create a complete picture in their minds. A description of a friend, for example, might focus on his distinctive voice and laugh, but readers will also want to know something about his appearance. If the subject is essentially abstract, like an emotion, you will need details to make it concrete for readers. And if the subject is familiar to readers, as a shopping mall or an old spruce tree on the school grounds probably would be, you will want to skip obvious objective information in favor of fresh observations that will make readers see the subject anew.

▶ Forming a Thesis

When you have your subject, express in a sentence the dominant impression that you want to create for readers. The sentence will help keep you on track while you search for the sensory details that will make your description concrete and vivid. It should evoke a quality or an atmosphere or an effect, as these examples do:

> His fierce anger at the world shows in every word and gesture.
>
> The mall is a thoroughly unnatural place, like a space station in a science-fiction movie.

Such a sentence can serve as the thesis of your essay. You don't necessarily need to state it outright in your draft; sometimes you may prefer to let the details build to a conclusion. But the thesis should hover over the essay nonetheless, governing the selection of every detail and making itself as clear to readers as if it were stated.

▶ Organizing

Though the details of a subject may not occur to you in any particular order, you will need to arrange them so that readers are not confused by shifts among features. You can give readers a sense of the whole subject in the **introduction** to the essay: objective details of location or size or shape, the incident leading to a state of mind, or the reasons for describing a familiar object. In the introduction, also, you may want to state your thesis—the dominant impression you will create.

The organization of the **body** of the essay depends partly on point of view and partly on dominant impression. If you take a moving point of view—say, strolling down a city street—the details will probably arrange themselves for you. But a fixed point of view, scanning a subject from one position, requires your intervention. When the subject is a landscape, a person, or an object, you'll probably want to use a spatial organization: near to far, top to bottom, left to right, or vice versa. (See also p. 98.) Other subjects, such as a shopping mall, might be better treated in groups of features: shoppers, main concourses, insides of stores. Or a description of an emotional state might follow the chronological sequence of the event that aroused it (thus overlapping description and narration, the subject of the previous chapter). The choice of order itself is not important, as long as there *is* an order that channels readers' attention.

▶ Drafting

The challenge of drafting your description will be bringing the subject to life. Whether it is in front of you or in your mind, you may find it helpful to consider the subject one sense at a time—what you can see, hear, smell, touch, taste. Of course, not all senses will be applicable to all subjects; a chair, for instance, may not have a noticeable odor, and you're unlikely to know its taste. But proceeding sense by sense can help you uncover details, such as the smell of a tree or the sound of a person's voice, that you may have overlooked.

Examining one sense at a time is also one of the best ways to think of concrete words and figures of speech to represent sensations and feelings. For instance, does *acid* describe the taste of fear? Does an actor's voice suggest the buzz of a mosquito? Does a shopping mall sound like the monkey house at a zoo? In creating distinct physical sensations for readers, such representations make meaning inescapably clear. (See pp. 49–59 and the box on the next page for more on specific, concrete language and figures of speech.)

▶ Revising and Editing

When you are ready to revise and edit, use the following questions and the focus box on the next two pages as a guide.

■ *Have you created the dominant impression you intended to create?* Check that you have plenty of specific details and that each one helps to pin down one crucial feature of your subject. Cut irrelevant details that may have crept in. What counts is not the number of details but their quality and the strength of the impression they make.

■ *Are your point of view and organization clear and consistent?* Watch for confusing shifts from one vantage point or organizational scheme to another. Watch also for confusing and unnecessary shifts in pronouns, such as from *I* to *one* or vice versa (see pp. 49 and 52). Any shifts in point of view or organization should be clearly essential for your purpose and for the impression you want to create.

FOCUS ON Concrete and Specific Language

For readers to imagine your subject, you'll need to use concrete, specific language that appeals to their experiences and senses. (See p. 58 for the meanings of *concrete* and *specific*.) All of the writers in this chapter use highly descriptive words and phrases to bring their subjects to life:

> The Pacific turned ominously glossy during a Santa Ana period, and one woke in the night troubled not only by the peacocks screaming in the olive trees but by the eerie absence of surf.   — *Joan Didion*

> I find the latest Salsa Rio brand of Doritos, Big Gulp Grande cups, paper (or plastic or both) bowls with the slimy remains of what goes for cheese on nachos from the smiley-faced Good Time Store two blocks away, used napkins, orange burger pouches, the new glossy-clean plastic soda containers, waxy candy wrappers from Mounds and Mars and Milky Way.
> — *Dagoberto Gilb*

> Weasel! I'd never seen one wild before. He was ten inches long, thin as a curve, a muscled ribbon, brown as fruitwood, soft-furred, alert.
> — *Annie Dillard*

In contrast, the first sentence below shows a writer's first-draft attempt to describe something she saw. After editing, the second sentence is much more vivid.

VAGUE Beautiful, scented wildflowers were in the field.

CONCRETE AND SPECIFIC Backlighted by the sun and smelling faintly sweet, thousands of lavenders swayed in the wind.

The writer might also have used figures of speech (see p. 58) to show what she saw: for instance, describing the field as "a giant's bed covered in a quilt of lavender dots" (a metaphor) or describing the backlighted flowers as "glowing like tiny lavender lamps" (a simile).

When editing your description, keep a sharp eye out for vague words such as *delicious*, *handsome*, *loud*, and *short* that force readers to create their own impressions or, worse, leave them with no impression at all. Use details that call on readers' sensory experiences, say why delicious or why handsome, how loud or how short. When stuck for a word, conjure up your subject and see it, hear it, touch it, smell it, taste it.

Practice

In each of the following sentences, identify any vague or unclear words. Then use your imagination to replace them with concrete and specific language.

1. The swamp nearby is an interesting place.
2. Nature trails let people walk around.
3. On a recent visit I saw a lot of wildlife.
4. A big snake was on the path, so I left.
5. The Internet says the snake was harmless; now I can't wait to go back.

▶ For more practice editing for concrete and specific language, visit Exercise Central at bedfordstmartins.com/exercisecentral.

A Note on Thematic Connections

The writers represented in this chapter all set out to explore something in nature. They probably didn't decide consciously to use description, but turned to the method intuitively as they chose to record the perceptions of their senses. Ansel Adams's photograph spotlights the vulnerability of a sapling in a clutch of full-grown Aspen trees (p. 122). In a paragraph, David Mura captures the dense unpleasantness of a seemingly endless downpour (p. 125). In another paragraph, Diane Ackerman describes the sharp, lasting images of a sea of icebergs (p. 126). Joan Didion's essay on a wind coming from the mountains above Los Angeles shows how an air current can transform a city (opposite). Dagoberto Gilb's essay on a desert lawn examines the cultural tensions in a border town (p. 136). And Annie Dillard's philosophical essay (p. 141) contemplates the lessons to be learned from a thrilling encounter with a wild animal.

Joan Didion

One of America's leading nonfiction writers, Joan Didion brings a journalist's eye for detail and a terse, understated style to her explorations of modern American society. She was born in 1934 in Sacramento, a fifth-generation Californian, and graduated from the University of California at Berkeley in 1956. Her essays have been collected in *Slouching Towards Bethlehem* (1968), *The White Album* (1979), *Salvador* (1983), *Essays and Conversations* (1984), *Miami* (1987), *After Henry* (1992), *Political Fictions* (2001), *Fixed Ideas: America Since 9.11* (2003), and *We Tell Ourselves Stories in Order to Live* (2006). Didion has published five novels: *Run River* (1963), *Play It as It Lays* (1970), *A Book of Common Prayer* (1977), *Democracy* (1984), and *The Last Thing He Wanted* (1996). With her husband, the writer John Gregory Dunne, she wrote screenplays for movies, among them *Panic in Needle Park* (1971), *A Star Is Born* (1976), *True Confessions* (1981), and *Up Close and Personal* (1996). Didion's most recent books are memoirs of devastating loss: *The Year of Magical Thinking* (2005) recounts her emotional state in the wake of her husband's sudden death, and *Blue Nights* (2011) explores her feelings about losing their daughter to an extended illness not long afterward.

The Santa Ana

In this classic essay, Didion describes the violent effects of a hot, dry wind on her, on her neighbors, and on the entire city of Los Angeles. "The Santa Ana," from *Slouching Towards Bethlehem*, first appeared in the *Saturday Evening Post.*

There is something uneasy in the Los Angeles air this afternoon, some 1 unnatural stillness, some tension. What it means is that tonight a Santa Ana will begin to blow, a hot wind from the northeast whining down through the Cajon and San Gorgonio Passes, blowing up sandstorms out along Route 66, drying the hills and the nerves to the flash point. For a few days now we will see smoke back in the canyons, and hear sirens in the night. I have neither heard nor read that a Santa Ana is due, but I know it, and almost everyone I have seen today knows it too. We know it because we feel it. The baby frets. The maid sulks. I rekindle a waning argument with the telephone company, then cut my losses and lie down, given over to whatever it is in the air. To live with the Santa Ana is to accept, consciously or unconsciously, a deeply mechanistic view of human behavior.

I recall being told, when I first moved to Los Angeles and was living 2 on an isolated beach, that the Indians would throw themselves into the sea when the bad wind blew. I could see why. The Pacific turned ominously glossy during a Santa Ana period, and one woke in the night troubled not only by the peacocks screaming in the olive trees but by the eerie absence of surf. The heat was surreal. The sky had a yellow cast, the kind of light sometimes called "earthquake weather." My only neighbor would not come out of her house for days, and there were no lights at night, and her husband roamed the place with a machete. One day he would tell me that he had heard a trespasser, the next a rattlesnake.

"On nights like that," Raymond Chandler[1] once wrote about the   3 Santa Ana, "every booze party ends in a fight. Meek little wives feel the edge of the carving knife and study their husbands' necks. Anything can happen." That was the kind of wind it was. I did not know then that there was any basis for the effect it had on all of us, but it turns out to be another of those cases in which science bears out folk wisdom. The Santa Ana, which is named for one of the canyons it rushes through, is a *foehn* wind, like the *foehn* of Austria and Switzerland and the *hamsin* of Israel. There are a number of persistent malevolent winds, perhaps the best known of which are the mistral of France and the Mediterranean sirocco, but a *foehn* wind has distinct characteristics: it occurs on the leeward slope of a mountain range and, although the air begins as a cold mass, it is warmed as it comes down the mountain and appears finally as a hot dry wind. Whenever and wherever a *foehn* blows, doctors hear about headaches and nausea and allergies, about "nervousness," about "depression." In Los Angeles some teachers do not attempt to conduct formal classes during a Santa Ana, because the children become unmanageable. In Switzerland the suicide rate goes up during the *foehn*, and in the courts of some Swiss cantons the wind is considered a mitigating circumstance for crime. Surgeons are said to watch the wind, because blood does not clot normally during a *foehn*. A few years ago an Israeli physicist discovered that not only during such winds, but for the ten or twelve hours which precede them, the air carries an unusually high ratio of positive to negative ions. No one seems to know exactly why that should be; some talk about friction and others suggest solar disturbances. In any case the positive ions are there, and what an excess of positive ions does, in the simplest terms, is make people unhappy. One cannot get much more mechanistic than that.

Easterners commonly complain that there is no "weather" at all in   4 Southern California, that the days and the seasons slip by relentlessly, numbingly bland. That is quite misleading. In fact the climate is characterized by infrequent but violent extremes: two periods of torrential subtropical rains which continue for weeks and wash out the hills and

---

[1] Chandler (1888–1959) is best known for his detective novels featuring Philip Marlowe. [Editors' note.]

send subdivisions sliding toward the sea; about twenty scattered days a year of the Santa Ana, which, with its incendiary dryness, invariably means fire. At the first prediction of a Santa Ana, the Forest Service flies men and equipment from northern California into the southern forests, and the Los Angeles Fire Department cancels its ordinary non-firefighting routines. The Santa Ana caused Malibu to burn the way it did in 1956, and Bel Air in 1961, and Santa Barbara in 1964. In the winter of 1966–67 eleven men were killed fighting a Santa Ana fire that spread through the San Gabriel Mountains.

Just to watch the front-page news out of Los Angeles during a Santa   5 Ana is to get very close to what it is about the place. The longest single Santa Ana period in recent years was in 1957, and it lasted not the usual three or four days but fourteen days, from November 21 until December 4. On the first day 25,000 acres of the San Gabriel Mountains were burning, with gusts reaching 100 miles an hour. In town, the wind reached Force 12, or hurricane force, on the Beaufort Scale; oil derricks were toppled and people ordered off the downtown streets to avoid injury from flying objects. On November 22 the fire in the San Gabriels was out of control. On November 24 six people were killed in automobile accidents, and by the end of the week the Los Angeles *Times* was keeping a box score of traffic deaths. On November 26 a prominent Pasadena attorney, depressed about money, shot and killed his wife, their two sons, and himself. On November 27 a South Gate divorcée, twenty-two, was murdered and thrown from a moving car. On November 30 the San Gabriel fire was still out of control, and the wind in town was blowing eighty miles an hour. On the first day of December four people died violently, and on the third the wind began to break.

It is hard for people who have not lived in Los Angeles to realize   6 how radically the Santa Ana figures in the local imagination. The city burning is Los Angeles's deepest image of itself: Nathanael West perceived that, in *The Day of the Locust*; and at the time of the 1965 Watts riots what struck the imagination most indelibly were the fires.[2] For days one could drive the Harbor Freeway and see the city on fire, just as we had always known it would be in the end. Los Angeles weather is the weather of catastrophe, of apocalypse, and, just as the reliably long and bitter winters of New England determine the way life is lived there, so the violence and the unpredictability of the Santa Ana affect the

---

[2] *The Day of the Locust* (1939), a novel about Hollywood, ends in riot and fire. The August 1965 disturbances in the Watts neighborhood of Los Angeles resulted in millions of dollars in damage from fires. [Editors' note.]

entire quality of life in Los Angeles, accentuate its impermanence, its unreliability. The wind shows us how close to the edge we are.

Vocabulary

Based on their context in the essay, try to determine the meanings of any of the following words that you don't know. Test your guesses in a dictionary; then try out your knowledge of each word by using it in a sentence of your own.

flash point (1)	leeward (3)	indelibly (6)
mechanistic (1)	cantons (3)	apocalypse (6)
ominously (2)	mitigating (3)	accentuate (6)
machete (2)	incendiary (4)	
malevolent (3)	derricks (5)	

Key Ideas and Details

1. Does Didion describe purely for the sake of describing, or does she have a thesis she wants to convey? If so, where does she most explicitly state this thesis?

2. What is the dominant impression Didion creates of the Santa Ana wind? What effect does it have on residents of Los Angeles?

3. How might Didion's last sentence have multiple meanings?

Craft and Structure

1. LANGUAGE What is the effect of the vivid imagery in paragraph 2? In what way is this imagery "surreal" (fantastic or dreamlike)?

2. Didion alternates between passages of mostly objective and mostly subjective description. Trace this movement throughout the essay. What does Didion achieve by using the first-person (*I* and *we*) point of view when she does?

3. What is the function of the quotation from Raymond Chandler at the beginning of paragraph 3? How does it serve as a transition?

4. OTHER METHODS The essay is full of examples (Chapter 8) of the wind's effects on human beings. How do these examples help Didion achieve her purpose?

Integration of Knowledge and Ideas

1. Why do you think Didion felt compelled to write about the Santa Ana? Consider whether she might have had a dual purpose. What details in the essay lead you to your conclusion?

2. What kind of audience is Didion writing for? Primarily people from Los Angeles? How do you know? Does Didion identify herself as an Angelena?

3. FOR DISCUSSION Explain what Didion means by a "mechanistic view of human behavior" (paragraph 1). What would the opposite of such a view of human behavior be?

Writing Topics

1. Using Didion's essay as a model, write a descriptive essay about something that annoys, frightens, or even crazes you and others. Your subject could be a natural phenomenon, such as a full moon, a dark sky, or a heat wave, or something else: bumper-to-bumper traffic, long lines at the post office, complicated voice-mail menus that come to dead ends. You may use examples from your own experience and observation, from experiences you have read or heard about, or, like Didion, from both sources.

2. Didion perceives the Santa Ana as a cultural phenomenon that affects the attitudes, relationships, and activities of Los Angeles residents "just as the reliably long and bitter winters of New England determine the way life is lived there" (paragraph 6). Consider a place you know well and write an essay or create a presentation that describes how some aspect of the climate or weather affects "the way life is lived," not only during a particular event or season but throughout the year.

3. RESEARCH Didion tries to explain the Santa Ana phenomenon scientifically in paragraph 3 as having something to do with an excess of positive ions in the air. But she admits that nobody knows why there are more positive than negative ions or why that fact should translate into human unhappiness. To what extent do you think our moods can be explained by science? Are our emotions simply the byproducts of brain chemistry, as some scientists would suggest? Choose an emotion, such as loneliness, anxiety, or joy, and find an article that tries to explain it in scientific terms. In a brief essay, summarize the writer's claims and explain why you agree or disagree with them.

4. CONNECTIONS Both Didion and Dagoberto Gilb, in "My Landlady's Yard" (next page), describe desert conditions in the American West. Compare the way Gilb describes the effects of "West Texas wind" in paragraphs 3 and 6 of his essay to Didion's description, in paragraph 2, of the effects of the Santa Ana winds. How does each writer combine striking images and original figures of speech to convey a strong sense of mood and a feeling in the reader that he or she is there? Do you think one author's description is more successful than the other's? Why?

Dagoberto Gilb

A fiction writer and essayist, Dagoberto Gilb was born in 1950 in Los Angeles. After enrolling in junior college with some doubts about his academic ability, Gilb "just went nuts over books" and earned advanced degrees in philosophy and religion from the University of California at Santa Barbara. He had difficulty finding work after college and for fifteen years scraped together a living with irregular construction jobs while keeping a journal on the side. The son of a Mexican mother and a German American father, Gilb celebrates his *mestizaje* (mixed) culture and often examines the experiences and perspectives of working-class Latinos in his work. He has published a collection of essays, *Gritos* (2003); two novels, *The Last Known Residence of Mickey Acuña* (1994) and *The Flowers* (2008); and four collections of short stories, *Winners on the Pass Line* (1985), *The Magic of Blood* (1993), *Woodcuts of Women* (2001), and *Before the End, After the Beginning* (2011). Gilb has received many honors and prizes, including the Hemingway Foundation / PEN Award, a *New York Times* notable book designation, and a Guggenheim Fellowship. He currently directs the Center for Mexican American Literature and Culture at the University of Houston–Victoria, where he is also the artist-in-residence.

My Landlady's Yard

Gilb's writing can be both deceptively simple and deliberately provocative. In the following piece, first published in the *Texas Observer* and later reprinted as the opening essay in *Gritos*, he finds surprising meanings in the seeming futility of yard work.

It's been a very dry season here. Not enough rain. And the sun's begin-   1
ning to feel closer. Which, of course, explains why this is called the desert. Why the kinds of plants that do well enough in the region — creosote, mesquite, ocotillo, yucca — aren't what you'd consider lush, tropical blooms. All that's obvious, right? To you, I'm sure, it's obvious, and to me it is, too, but not to my landlady. My landlady doesn't think of this rock house I rent in central El Paso as being in the desert. To her, it's the big city. She's from the country, from a ranch probably just like the one she now calls home, a few miles up the paved highway in Chaparral, New Mexico, where the roads are graded dirt. She must still see the house as she did when she lived here as a young wife and mother, as part of the city's peaceful suburbs, which it certainly was thirty years ago. She probably planted the shrubs and evergreens that snuggle the walls of the house now, probably seeded the back- and front-yard grass herself. And she wants those Yankee plants and that imported grass to continue to thrive as they would in all other American, nondesert neigh-

borhoods, even if these West Texas suburbs moved on to the east and west many years ago, even if the population has quadrupled and water is more scarce, and expensive, than back then.

So I go ahead and drag around a green hose despite my perception 2 that *gold*, colorless and liquid, is pouring out onto this desert, an offering as unquenchable and ruthless as to any Aztec deity (don't water a couple of days and watch how fast it dries away). Superstitions, if you don't mind my calling them that, die hard, and property values are dependent on shared impressions. I'm not ready to rent and load another U-Haul truck.

With my thumb over the brass fitting and squeezed against the 3 water, I use the digits on my other hand to pluck up loose garbage. You've heard, maybe, of West Texas wind. That explains why so much of it lands here on my front yard, but also a high school is my backyard: the school's rear exit is only a dirt alley and fence away from my garage, and teenagers pass by in the morning, during lunch, and when school lets out. I find the latest Salsa Rio brand of Doritos, Big Gulp Grande cups, paper (or plastic or both) bowls with the slimy remains of what goes for cheese on nachos from the smiley-faced Good Time Store two blocks away, used napkins, orange burger pouches, the new glossy-clean plastic soda containers, waxy candy wrappers from Mounds and Mars and Milky Way. Also beer cans and bottles, grocery-store bags both plastic and paper, and fragments from everything else (believe me) possible.

I'm betting you think I'm not too happy about accumulating such 4 evidence. You're right. But I'm not mentioning it to complain. I want the image of all the trash, as well as the one of me spraying precious water onto this dusty alkaline soil, to get your attention. Because both stand for the odd way we live and think out here, a few hundred miles (at least) from everyplace else in the United States.

My green grass in the desert, for instance. My landlady wants thick, 5 luxuriant grass because that's the way of this side of the border, and this side is undeniably better, whatever misconception of place and history and natural resources the desire for that image depends on. It's not just her, and it's not just lawns. Take another example: a year ago about this time, police cars squealed onto the asphalt handball and basketball courts on the other side of the school fence to regain control of a hundred or so students lumped around a fight, most of them watching, some swinging baseball bats. What happened? According to the local newspaper, the fight broke out between a group of black students, all of them dependents of Fort Bliss military personnel (as their jargon has it), and a group of Hispanic students. "Hispanic" is the current media term for those of descent from South of the Border. Even around here. Which is the point: that even in this town—the other side of the concrete river considered the official land of Spanish-language history and culture—the latest minority-language terminology is used to describe its historic, multigenerational majority population. With the exception of one high school on the more affluent west side of town, Anglos are the overwhelming minority; at the high school behind my backyard the ratio must be ten to one. Though Mexico has been the mother of this region, and remains so, it's the language and understanding of The North that labels the account of the school incident: "Hispanic" students, black dependents of GIs.

If green grass is the aspiration, the realization of an American fantasy, then the trash is from the past, the husks of a frontier mentality that it took to be here, and stay, in the first place. Trash blowing by, snared by limbs and curbs and fences, is a display of what was the attitude of the West. The endlessness of its range. The ultimate principle of every man, woman, animal, and thing for itself. The meanness required to survive. The wild joy that could abandon rules. The immediacy of life. Or the stupidity of the non-Indian hunter eating one meal, then leaving behind the carcass. Except that vultures and coyotes and finally ants used to clean that mess up. The remains of the modernized hunt don't balance well in nature or its hybrid shrubs, do not biodegrade. And there are a lot more hunters than before.   6

Trash contradicts the well-tended lawn. And in my neighborhood, not all is Saint Augustine or Bermuda.[1] Hardy weeds sprout and grow tall everywhere, gray-green century plants shoot stalks beside many homes. El Paso is still crossing cultures and times, the wind blows often, particularly this time of year, the sun will be getting bigger, but the pretty nights cool things off here on the desert. Let me admit this: I'd like it if grass grew well in my backyard. What I've got is patchy at best, and neglected, the brown dirt is a stronger color than the green. So the other day, I soaked that hard soil, dug it up, threw seed grown and packaged in Missouri, covered it with peat humus from Menard, Texas, and I'm waiting.   7

Vocabulary

If you're unsure of any of the following words, try to determine their meanings from the context of Gilb's essay. Then look them up to see if you were right and use each word in a sentence of your own.

---

[1] Varieties of cultivated grass. [Editors' note.]

lush (1)	digits (3)	husks (6)
graded (1)	alkaline (4)	snared (6)
Yankee (1)	luxuriant (5)	hardy (7)
unquenchable (2)	misconception (5)	peat humus (7)
deity (2)	aspiration (6)	

Key Ideas and Details

1. Gilb starts his essay with the observation that grass cannot thrive in the desert and that watering is a waste of both money and natural resources. So why does he try to grow a lawn?

2. What dominant impression of his yard does Gilb create?

3. In his conclusion Gilb writes, "What I've got is patchy at best, and neglected, the brown dirt is a stronger color than the green" (paragraph 7). What does he mean? Is he talking about the yard, or something else?

Craft and Structure

1. LANGUAGE Gilb's essay includes many sentence fragments (for an explanation of *sentence fragments*, see the Glossary and pp. 49–50). Identify at least two examples. Is this sloppy writing, or does Gilb break the rules of sentence grammar for a purpose? What do Gilb's fragments contribute to (or take away from) his essay? Explain your answer.

2. How many of the five senses does Gilb appeal to in his description? Find words or phrases that seem especially precise in conveying sensory impressions, and explain their effect.

3. What relation does Gilb take toward his subject? How does his point of view direct the organization of details?

4. OTHER METHODS Gilb uses several methods of development in addition to description—for instance, paragraphs 2–6 use division (Chapter 9) to analyze the political and cultural meanings of green grass in the desert, and paragraph 3 gives several examples (Chapter 8) of the garbage that litters the yard. Most notably, paragraph 5 uses definition (Chapter 13) to explore the Texas media's use of the term *Hispanic*. Why is the label so important to Gilb?

Integration of Knowledge and Ideas

1. In describing the plot of land that surrounds his home, Gilb shifts the possessive pronoun from *my landlady's* yard in the title to *my* backyard in the conclusion. What does this shift reveal about Gilb's reasons for writing about his home?

2. This piece was originally written for a regional magazine that often covers political issues. What, then, could Gilb assume about his audience? How are those assumptions reflected in his essay? (You might want to take a look at an issue of the *Texas Observer* or the magazine's Web site, *texasobserver.org*, for more clues.)

3. FOR DISCUSSION Gilb writes about his yard to make a point about something else entirely: cultural tensions in a border town. How does grass in this essay function as a symbol? (If necessary, see *symbol* in the Glossary.)

Writing Topics

1. To keep our living spaces comfortable, we all have to perform tasks that can feel tedious or even pointless. What household chore do you dislike (or enjoy) the most? Why? Write an essay or prepare a speech that describes the chore and how you feel about doing it. Try to make the task as vivid as possible. If you choose to make a speech, you might use visual aids or music to enhance your description.

2. In paragraph 5, Gilb characterizes his landlady's attitude as the belief that the American "side of the border . . . is undeniably better" than the Mexican side. Does he agree with her? Write an essay that identifies and analyzes Gilb's position on the issue of cultural assimilation in American border towns, paying close attention to each of his examples and explaining how he reaches his conclusions.

3. Our dreams for the future are often influenced by the family, community, or larger culture in which we grew up. Think of a personal goal that seems to have come at least partly from other people. In an essay describe the goal and your feelings about it, and explain the origins of your feelings as best you can.

4. CONNECTIONS Both Gilb and Lars Eighner, in "Dumpster Diving" (p. 253), write about trash, Gilb from the perspective of a renter forced to clean litter off his lawn and Eighner from the perspective of a homeless person who has learned to survive on what others throw away. Compare and contrast what trash means to them. How do their respective points of view affect their experiences and attitudes? Be sure to include examples from both essays to support your comparison.

Annie Dillard

A poet and essayist, Annie Dillard (born 1945) is part naturalist, part mystic. Growing up in Pittsburgh, she was an independent child given to exploration and reading. After graduating from Hollins College in the Blue Ridge Mountains of Virginia, Dillard settled in the area to investigate her natural surroundings and to write. Dillard demonstrated her intense, passionate involvement with the world of nature and the world of the mind early in her career with *Pilgrim at Tinker Creek* (1974), a series of related essays that earned her a Pulitzer Prize. Dillard's output since then has spanned several genres, including poetry in volumes such as *Tickets for a Prayer Wheel* (1974) and *Mornings Like This* (1995); essays collected in *Teaching a Stone to Talk* (1982), *The Writing Life* (1989), and *For the Time Being* (1999); literary criticism in *Living by Fiction* (1982) and *Encounters with Chinese Writers* (1984); and, most recently, a novel, *The Maytrees* (2007). In 1999 she was inducted into the American Academy of Arts and Letters. Dillard lives in North Carolina and is professor emeritus at Wesleyan University.

Living Like Weasels

In almost all of her writing, Dillard's enthusiasm for life in its many forms colors both her experiences and the ideas they inspire. "Living Like Weasels," from *Teaching a Stone to Talk*, describes a few moments of glorious excitement to share an unexpected life lesson.

A weasel is wild. Who knows what he thinks? He sleeps in his under- 1
ground den, his tail draped over his nose. Sometimes he lives in his den for two days without leaving. Outside, he stalks rabbits, mice, muskrats, and birds, killing more bodies than he can eat warm, and often dragging the carcasses home. Obedient to instinct, he bites his prey at the neck, either splitting the jugular vein at the throat or crunching the brain at the base of the skull, and he does not let go. One naturalist refused to kill a weasel who was socketed into his hand deeply as a rattlesnake. The man could in no way pry the tiny weasel off, and he had to walk half a mile to water, the weasel dangling from his palm, and soak him off like a stubborn label.

And once, says Ernest Thompson Seton[1] — once, a man shot an 2
eagle out of the sky. He examined the eagle and found the dry skull of a weasel fixed by the jaws to his throat. The supposition is that the eagle had pounced on the weasel and the weasel swiveled and bit as instinct

---

[1] A founding chair of the Boy Scouts of America, Ernest Thompson Seton (1860–1946) was a British wildlife illustrator, naturalist, and writer. [Editors' note.]

taught him, tooth to neck, and nearly won. I would like to have seen that eagle from the air a few weeks or months before he was shot. Was the whole weasel still attached to his feathered throat, a fur pendant? Or did the eagle eat what he could reach, gutting the living weasel with his talons before his breast, bending his beak, cleaning the beautiful airborne bones?

I have been reading about weasels because I saw one last week. I 3
startled a weasel who startled me, and we exchanged a long glance.

Near my house in Virginia is a pond—Hollins Pond. It covers two 4
acres of bottomland near Tinker Creek with six inches of water and six thousand lily pads. There is a fifty-five mph highway at one end of the pond, and a nesting pair of wood ducks at the other. Under every bush is a muskrat hole or a beer can. The far end is an alternating series of fields and woods, fields and woods, threaded everywhere with motorcycle tracks—in whose bare clay wild turtles lay eggs.

One evening last week at sunset, I walked to the pond and sat on 5
a downed log near the shore. I was watching the lily pads at my feet tremble and part over the thrusting path of a carp. A yellow warbler appeared to my right and flew behind me. It caught my eye; I swiveled around—and the next instant, inexplicably, I was looking down at a weasel, who was looking up at me.

Weasel! I'd never seen one wild before. He was ten inches long, thin 6
as a curve, a muscled ribbon, brown as fruitwood, soft-furred, alert. His face was fierce, small and pointed as a lizard's; he would have made a good arrowhead. There was just a dot of chin, maybe two brown hairs' worth, and then the pure white fur began that spread down his underside. He had two black eyes I didn't see, any more than you see a window.

The weasel was stunned into stillness as he was emerging from 7
beneath an enormous shaggy wild rose bush four feet away. I was stunned into stillness twisted backward on the tree trunk. Our eyes locked, and someone threw away the key.

Our look was as if two lovers, or deadly enemies, met unexpectedly 8
on an overgrown path when each had been thinking of something else: a clearing blow to the gut. It was also a bright blow to the brain, or a sudden beating of brains, with all the charge and intimate grate of rubbed balloons. It emptied our lungs. It felled the forest, moved the fields, and drained the pond; the world dismantled and tumbled into that black hole of eyes. If you and I looked at each other that way, our skulls would split and drop to our shoulders. But we don't. We keep our skulls.

He disappeared. This was only last week, and already I don't remem- 9
ber what shattered the enchantment. I think I blinked, I think I retrieved
my brain from the weasel's brain, and tried to memorize what I was
seeing, and the weasel felt the yank of separation, the careening splashdown into real life and the urgent current of instinct. He vanished under
the wild rose. I waited motionless, my mind suddenly full of data and
my spirit with pleadings, but he didn't return.

Please do not tell me about "approach-avoidance conflicts." I tell 10
you I've been in that weasel's brain for sixty seconds, and he was in
mine. Brains are private places, muttering through unique and secret
tapes—but the weasel and I both plugged into another tape simultaneously, for a sweet and shocking time. Can I help it if it was a blank?

What goes on in his brain the rest of the time? What does a weasel 11
think about? He won't say. His journal is tracks in clay, a spray of feathers, mouse blood and bone: uncollected, unconnected, loose-leaf, and
blown.

I would like to learn, or remember, how to live. I come to Hollins 12
Pond not so much to learn how to live as, frankly, to forget about it. That
is, I don't think I can learn from a wild animal how to live in particular—
shall I suck warm blood, hold my tail high, walk with my footprints
precisely over the prints of my hands?—but I might learn something
of mindlessness, something of purity of living in the physical senses and
the dignity of living without bias or motive. The weasel lives in necessity and we live in choice, hating necessity and dying at the last ignobly in its talons. I would like to live as I should, as the weasel lives as he
should. And I suspect that for me the way is like the weasel's: open to
time and death painlessly, noticing everything, remembering nothing,
choosing the given with a fierce and pointed will.

I missed my chance. I should have gone for the throat. I should have 13
lunged for that streak of white under the weasel's chin and held on,
held on through mud and into the wild rose, held on for a dearer life.
We could live under the wild rose wild as weasels, mute and uncomprehending. I could very calmly go wild. I could live two days in the den,
curled, leaning on mouse fur, sniffing bird bones, blinking, licking,
breathing musk, my hair tangled in the roots of grasses. Down is a good
place to go, where the mind is single. Down is out, out of your ever-
loving mind and back to your careless senses. I remember muteness as
a prolonged and giddy fast, where every moment is a feast of utterance
received. Time and events are merely poured, unremarked, and ingested

directly, like blood pulsed into my gut through a jugular vein. Could two live that way? Could two live under the wild rose, and explore by the pond, so that the smooth mind of each is as everywhere present to the other, and as received and as unchallenged, as falling snow?

We could, you know. We can live any way we want. People take   14
vows of poverty, chastity, and obedience—even of silence—by choice. The thing is to stalk your calling in a certain skilled and supple way, to locate the most tender and live spot and plug into that pulse. This is yielding, not fighting. A weasel doesn't "attack" anything; a weasel lives as he's meant to, yielding at every moment to the perfect freedom of single necessity.

I think it would be well, and proper, and obedient, and pure, to grasp   15
your one necessity and not let it go, to dangle from it limp wherever it takes you. Then even death, where you're going no matter how you live, cannot you part. Seize it and let it seize you up aloft even, till your eyes burn out and drop; let your musky flesh fall off in shreds, and let your very bones unhinge and scatter, loosened over fields, over fields and woods, lightly, thoughtless, from any height at all, from as high as eagles.

Vocabulary

If you do not know the meanings of the following words, try to guess them from the context of Dillard's essay. Test your guesses in a dictionary; then use each word in a sentence of your own.

carcasses (1)	thrusting (5)	ignobly (12)
socketed (1)	inexplicably (5)	musk (13)
supposition (2)	grate (8)	utterance (13)
bottomland (4)	enchantment (9)	supple (14)

Key Ideas and Details

1. What lesson does Dillard take from her encounter with the weasel? Where is her point explicitly revealed?

2. What dominant impression of a weasel does Dillard create? What is her attitude toward this animal? What words and passages support your answer?

3. Examine Dillard's description of looking at the weasel in paragraph 8 alone. Does she mean for readers to take her statements here literally? What is their effect?

Craft and Structure

1. LANGUAGE Dillard re-creates her impressions with concrete words that appeal to readers' senses. Look, for instance, at the verbs "stalks," "killing," "dragging," "bites," "splitting," and "crunching" in paragraph 1. Locate ten or twelve other examples of concrete language. What sense or senses does each one appeal to?

2. Locate several examples of objective description and several of subjective description in Dillard's essay. What does each type of description contribute to the essay? What about her purpose leads Dillard to rely chiefly on subjective description?

3. Explain how the last paragraph relates to the first two. What is the effect of connecting the introduction and conclusion as Dillard does?

4. OTHER METHODS Dillard makes extensive use of comparison and contrast (Chapter 12). Locate examples of this method and analyze what they contribute to the essay as a whole.

Integration of Knowledge and Ideas

1. How does Dillard use information gained from reading to develop a new idea of her own?

2. What seems to be Dillard's purpose: to encourage readers to behave like animals? to entertain readers with vivid descriptions of wildlife? to share a moment of personal discovery? to do something else? What passages support your interpretation?

3. FOR DISCUSSION In paragraph 12 Dillard writes, "I don't think I can learn from a wild animal how to live in particular . . . but I might learn something of mindlessness, something of purity of living in the physical senses and the dignity of living without bias or motive." What exactly is Dillard saying about the relationship between thinking and living well? Do you think she is recommending "mindlessness" as a means to happiness? Why, or why not?

Writing Topics

1. Prepare a descriptive speech or write a descriptive essay about a time you were surprised to see a wild animal. Was it exciting? scary? How did the animal react to the encounter? Use the first-person *I*, strong verbs, and plenty of descriptive details to render vividly the event and its effects on you and the animal. If you wish, you may incorporate information about the animal gleaned from your reading, as Dillard does in her essay.

2. In her concluding paragraphs (13–15), Dillard argues that we might be happier if we lived in necessity rather than thought. What is *your* "one necessity"? Do you agree with Dillard that the purpose of life is to focus on that one thing and yield to it? Why, or why not? Write a short personal essay that contemplates what you want from life and explains how you intend to achieve your goals.

3. RESEARCH "Please do not tell me about 'approach-avoidance conflicts,'" Dillard writes in paragraph 10. What does she mean? Find a definition of the term, either on the Web or in a psychology reference, and analyze how this concept informs Dillard's essay as a whole.

4. CONNECTIONS Annie Dillard and Barbara Kingsolver ("Stalking the Vegetannual," p. 258) share an exuberant attitude toward nature, at least toward the small portions they describe in their essays. But Dillard focuses on a concrete, specific object, while Kingsolver focuses on a general process. Write an essay examining the effects each essay has on readers, and why. What techniques does each writer use to create these effects?

WRITING WITH THE METHOD

DESCRIPTION

Select one of the following topics, or any topic they suggest, for an essay developed by description. Be sure to choose a topic you care about so that description is a means of communicating an idea, not an end in itself.

People

1. An exceptionally neat or messy person
2. A person whose appearance and mannerisms are at odds with his or her real self
3. A person you admire or respect
4. An irritating child
5. A person who intimidates you (teacher, salesperson, doctor, police officer, fellow student)

Places and Scenes

6. A shopping mall, yard sale, or flea market
7. A frightening place
8. A prison cell, police station, or courtroom
9. Your home
10. The devastation caused by a natural disaster
11. A scene of environmental destruction
12. The scene at a concert (rock, rap, country, folk, classical, jazz)

Animals and Things

13. Birds at a bird feeder
14. A work of art
15. A pet or an animal in a zoo
16. A prized possession
17. The look and taste of a favorite or detested food

Sensations

18. Waiting for important news
19. Being freed of some restraint

20. Sunday afternoon

21. Writing

22. Skating, running, bodysurfing, skydiving, or some other activity

23. Extreme hunger, thirst, cold, heat, or fatigue

WRITING ABOUT THE THEME

SENSING OUR NATURAL SURROUNDINGS

1. Although we tend to think of nature as unspoiled wilderness, some of the authors in this chapter recognize that the natural world can be difficult to cope with. Joan Didion's description of the Santa Ana wind (p. 131) and David Mura's description of rain (p. 125) are most notable in this respect, but Dagoberto Gilb's examination of the allure of a green lawn (p. 136) emphasizes the desert's hostility to plant life, and Annie Dillard's assessment of weasels (p. 141) dwells on their inherently violent nature. Even Ansel Adams characterizes the trees in his photograph (p. 122) as "cool and aloof." Write a descriptive essay about a natural environment that is special to you, emphasizing its blemishes rather than its beauty.

2. All of the writers in this chapter demonstrate strong feelings for the place, thing, or phenomenon they describe, but the writers vary considerably in the ways they express their feelings. For example, Joan Didion's own discomfort in the Santa Ana colors all of her perceptions, whereas Annie Dillard's description of a weasel mixes fear and awe. Write an essay analyzing the tone of these and the other selections in this chapter: David Mura's paragraph on typhoons, Diane Ackerman's paragraph on icebergs (p. 126), and Dagoberto Gilb's "My Landlady's Yard." Discuss which pieces you find most effective and why.

3. Each writer in this chapter vividly describes a specific place or thing that represents some larger, abstract concept: for example, Dagoberto Gilb's backyard represents cultural conflict, Annie Dillard's weasel represents instinct, and Diane Ackerman's icebergs represent the awesomeness of nature. Think of a specific, tangible place or thing in your life that represents some larger abstract idea and write a descriptive essay exploring this relationship.

8

EXAMPLE

▶

USING LANGUAGE

An **example** represents a general group or an abstract concept or quality. Quentin Tarantino is an example from the group of movie directors. A friend's texting at 2:00 a.m. is an example of her inconsiderateness—or desperation. We habitually use examples to bring broad ideas down to specifics so that others will take an interest in them and understand them. You might use examples to entertain friends with the idea that you're accident prone, to persuade family members that a sibling is showing self-destructive behavior that requires intervention, to demonstrate to voters that your school's athletic department deserves a budget increase, or to convince your employer that a new manager's scheduling practices are unreasonable. Examples are so central to human communication, in fact, that you will find them in nearly everything you read and use them in nearly everything you write.

 Seeing Examples

Many people have grammar and usage pet peeves—common errors in spelling, punctuation, and the like that they find especially annoying. For blogger Bethany Keeley, unnecessary quotation marks are the most irritating offenders. Noticing mistakes in signs both handwritten and professional on school grounds, office buildings, and other public places, she started taking photographs and uploading them to her Web site. The effort quickly gained a following, and now Keeley's friends and fans regularly send her photographs of examples they find from around the world. In each of the five signs on the facing page, quotation marks are used incorrectly, usually revealing the signmakers' misguided attempts to give emphasis. But every one of them commits other language errors

151

as well. Can you find them? Look for misspellings, commonly misused words, misplaced commas, unnecessary capitalization, incorrect pluralization, double negatives, and faulty comparisons. How do the mistakes affect the signs' meanings and their creators' credibility? Why do such errors matter?

Reading Examples

The chief purpose of examples is to make the general specific and the abstract concrete. Since these operations are among the most basic in writing, it is easy to see why illustration or exemplification (the use of example) is among the most common methods of writing. Examples appear frequently in essays developed by other methods. In fact, as diverse as they are, all the essays in this book employ examples for clarity, support, and liveliness. If the writers had not used examples, we might have only a vague sense of their meaning or, worse, might supply mistaken meanings from our own experiences.

While nearly indispensable in any kind of writing, exemplification may also serve as the dominant method of developing an essay. When a writer's primary goal is to convince readers of the truth of a general statement—whether a personal observation or a controversial assertion—using examples is a natural choice. Any of the following **generalizations**, for instance, might form the central assertion of an essay developed by example:

- Generalizations about trends: "Electronic books are forcing the publishing industry to rethink the way it does business."
- Generalizations about events: "Some fans at the championship game were more competitive than the players."
- Generalizations about institutions: "A mental hospital is no place for the mentally ill."
- Generalizations about behaviors: "The personalities of parents are sometimes visited on their children."
- Generalizations about rituals: "A funeral benefits the dead person's family and friends."

How many examples are necessary to support a generalization? That depends on a writer's subject, purpose, and intended audience. Two basic patterns are possible:

- A single *extended example* of several paragraphs or several pages fills in needed background and gives the reader a complete view of the subject from one angle. For instance, the purpose of a funeral might be made clear with a narrative and descriptive account of a particular funeral, the family and friends who attended it, and the benefits they derived from it.

- *Multiple examples*, from a few to dozens, illustrate the range covered by the generalization. The competitiveness of a team's fans might be captured with three or four examples. But supporting the generalization about mental hospitals might demand many examples of patients whose illnesses worsened in the hospital or (from a different angle) many examples of hospital practices that actually harm patients.

Sometimes a generalization merits support from both an extended example and several briefer examples, a combination that provides depth along with range. For instance, half the essay on mental hospitals might be devoted to one patient's experiences and the other half to brief summaries of others' experiences.

When you read essays developed by illustration and exemplification, pay attention to how writers use examples to develop a point. Rarely will a simple list do an idea justice. Effective writers, you will see, not only provide examples but also explain how those examples support their ideas.

Analyzing Examples in Paragraphs

Richard Rodriguez (born 1944) entered school speaking essentially no English and left it with a PhD in English literature. Raised in California by Mexican immigrants, Rodriguez is a lecturer and writer who frequently addresses issues that affect Spanish-speaking Americans. The following paragraph is adapted from his essay "Aria: A Memoir of a Bilingual Childhood," an argument against bilingual education.

But it was one thing for *me* to speak English with difficulty. It was more troubling for me to hear my parents speak in public: their high-whining vowels and guttural consonants; their sentences that got stuck with "eh" and "ah" sounds; the confused syntax; the hesitant rhythm of sounds so different from the way *gringos* spoke. . . . There were many times like the night at a brightly lit gasoline station (a blaring white

Generalization and topic sentence (underlined)

memory) when I stood uneasily, hearing my father. He was talking to a teenaged attendant. I do not recall what they were saying, but I cannot forget the sounds my father made as he spoke. At one point his words slid together to form one word— sounds as confused as the threads of blue and green oil in the puddle next to my shoes. His voice rushed through what he had left to say. And, toward the end, reached falsetto notes, appealing to his listener's understanding. I looked away to the lights of passing automobiles. I tried not to hear anymore. But I heard only too well the calm, easy tones in the attendant's reply. Shortly afterward, walking toward home with my father, I shivered when he put his hand on my shoulder. The very first chance that I got, I evaded his grasp and ran on ahead into the dark, skipping with feigned boyish exuberance.

Single detailed example

William Lutz (born 1940) is an expert on doublespeak, which he defines as "language that conceals or manipulates thought. It makes the bad seem good, the negative appear positive, the unpleasant appear attractive or at least tolerable." In this paragraph from his book *Doublespeak* (1989), Lutz illustrates one use of this deceptive language.

Because it avoids or shifts responsibility, doublespeak is particularly effective in explaining or at least glossing over accidents. An air force colonel in charge of safety wrote in a letter that rocket boosters weighing more than 300,000 pounds "have an explosive force upon surface impact that is sufficient to exceed the accepted overpressure threshold of physiological damage for exposed personnel." In English: if a 300,000-pound booster rocket falls on you, you probably won't survive. In 1985 three American soldiers were killed and sixteen were injured when the first stage of a Pershing II missile they were unloading suddenly ignited. There was no explosion, said Major Michael Griffen, but rather "an unplanned rapid ignition of solid fuel."

Generalization and topic sentence (underlined)

Two examples

Developing an Essay by Example

▶ Getting Started

You need examples whenever your experiences, observations, or reading lead you to make a general statement; the examples give readers evidence for the statement so that they see its truth. An appropriate subject for an example paper is likely to be a general idea you have formed about people, things, the media, or any other feature of your life. Say, for instance, that you have noticed while watching television that many shows aimed at teenagers deal with sensitive topics such as drug abuse, domestic violence, or chronic illness. There is a promising subject: teen dramas that address controversial social issues.

After choosing a subject, you should make a list of all the relevant examples that occur to you. This stage may take some thought and even some further reading or observation. When you're making this list, focus on identifying as many examples as you can, but keep your intended readers at the front of your mind: what do they already know about your subject, and what do they need to know to accept your view of it?

▶ Forming a Thesis

Having several examples of a subject is a good starting place, but you will also need a thesis that ties the examples together and gives them a point. A clear thesis is crucial for an example paper because without it readers can only guess what your illustrations are intended to show.

To move from a general subject toward a workable thesis, try making a generalization based on what you know of individual examples:

> Some teen dramas do a surprisingly good job of dramatizing and explaining difficult social issues.
>
> Some teen dramas trivialize difficult social issues in a quest for higher ratings.

Either of these statements could serve as the thesis of an essay, the point you want readers to take away from your examples.

Avoid the temptation to start with a broad statement and then try to drum up a few examples to prove it. A thesis such as "Teenagers do poorly in school because they watch too much television" would require factual support gained from research, not the lone example of your brother. If your brother performs poorly in school and you attribute his performance to his television habits, then narrow your thesis so that it accurately reflects your evidence—perhaps "In the case of my brother, at least, the more time spent watching television the poorer the grades."

After arriving at your thesis, you should narrow your list of examples down to those that are most significant, adding new ones as necessary to persuade readers of your point. For instance, in illustrating the social value of teen dramas for readers who believe television is worthless or even harmful, you might concentrate on the programs or individual episodes that are most relevant to readers' lives, providing enough detail about each to make readers see the relevance.

▶ Organizing

Most example essays open with an **introduction** that engages readers' attention and gives them some context to relate to. You might begin the paper on teen dramas, for instance, by briefly narrating the plot of one episode. The opening should lead into your thesis sentence so that readers know what to expect from the rest of the essay.

Organizing the **body** of the essay may not be difficult if you use a single example, for the example itself may suggest a distinct method of development (such as narration) and thus an arrangement. But an essay using multiple examples usually requires close attention to arrangement so that readers experience not a list but a pattern. Consider these guidelines:

- With a limited number of examples—say, four or five—use a climactic organization (p. 42), arranging examples in order of increasing importance, interest, or complexity. Then the strongest and most detailed example provides a dramatic finish.

- With many examples—ten or more—find some likenesses among them that will allow you to treat them in groups. For instance, instead of covering fourteen teen dramas in a shapeless list, you might group them by subject into shows dealing with family relations, those dealing with illness, and the like. (This is the method of classification, discussed in Chapter 10.) Covering each group in a separate paragraph or two would avoid the awkward string of choppy paragraphs that might result from covering each example independently. And arranging the groups themselves in order of increasing interest or importance would further structure your presentation.

To conclude your essay, you may want to summarize by elaborating on the generalization of your thesis now that you have supported it. But the essay may not require a **conclusion** at all if you believe your final example emphasizes your point and provides a strong finish.

▶ Drafting

While you draft your essay, remember that your examples must be plentiful and specific enough to support your generalization. If you use fifteen different examples, their range should allow you to treat each one briefly, in one or two sentences. But if you use only three examples, say, you will have to describe each one in sufficient detail to make up for their small number. And obviously, if you use only a single example, you must be as specific as possible so that readers see clearly how it illustrates your generalization.

▶ Revising and Editing

To be sure you've met the expectations that most readers hold for examples, revise and edit your draft by considering the following questions and the information in the focus box on the next two pages.

- *Is your generalization fully supported by your examples?* If not, you may need to narrow your thesis statement or add more evidence to prove your point.

- *Are all examples, or parts of a single example, obviously relevant to your generalization?* Be careful not to get sidetracked by interesting but unrelated information.

- *Are the examples specific?* Examples bring a generalization down to earth only if they are well detailed. For an essay on the social value of teen dramas, for instance, simply naming representative programs and their subjects would not demonstrate their social value. Each drama would need a plot or character summary that shows how the program fits and illustrates the generalization.

- *Do the examples, or the parts of a single example, cover all the territory mapped out by your generalization?* To support your generalization, you need to present a range of instances that fairly represents the whole. An essay would be misleading if it failed to acknowledge that not *all* teen dramas have social value. It would also be misleading if it presented several shows as representative examples of socially valuable teen programming when in fact they were the *only* instances of such television.

FOCUS ON **Sentence Variety**

While accumulating examples and detailing them during drafting — both essential tasks for a successful essay — you may find yourself writing strings of similar sentences:

> **UNVARIED**   One example of a teen drama that deals with chronic illness is *Rockingham Place*. Another example is *The Beating Heart*. Another is *Tree of Life*. These three shows treat misunderstood or little-known diseases in a way that increases the viewer's sympathy and understanding. The characters in *Rockingham Place* include a little boy who suffers from cystic fibrosis. *The Beating Heart* features a mother of four who is weakening from multiple sclerosis. *Tree of Life* deals with brothers who are both struggling with muscular dystrophy. All these dramas show complex, struggling human beings caught blamelessly in desperate circumstances.

The writer of this paragraph was clearly pushing to add examples and to expand them, but the resulting passage needs editing so that the writer's labor isn't so obvious and the sentences are more varied and interesting. Following is the same paragraph edited for sentence variety:

> **VARIED**   Three teen dramas dealing with chronic illness are *Rockingham Place*, *The Beating Heart*, and *Tree of Life*. In these shows people with little-known or misunderstood diseases become subjects for the viewer's sympathy and understanding. A little boy suffering from cystic fibrosis, a mother of four weakening from multiple sclerosis, a pair of brothers struggling with muscular dystrophy — these complex, struggling human beings are caught blamelessly in desperate circumstances.

As you review your draft, be alert to repetitive sentence structures and look for opportunities to change them: try coordinating and subordinating ideas, varying the beginnings and endings of sentences, shortening some and lengthening others, and so on. Editing for sentence variety will ensure that your writing is more interesting and flows more smoothly. For more on sentence variety, see pages 32 and 56.

Practice

Edit the sentences in the paragraph on the next page so that their structures are varied and the most important ideas are emphasized. Focus on combining sentences, adjusting their lengths, and reversing the order of ideas within them.

The language used in teen dramas is often graphic. This is especially true for shows on cable. The teenage characters use swear words frequently. The adult characters discuss bodily functions and organ failures in disgusting detail. Yet such language seems appropriate given the context of these characters' struggles with illness. The language also reveals the characters' frustrations. The Federal Communications Commission puts strict limits on the words characters can use on network programs. The Federal Communications Commission does not put limits on the words characters can use on cable programs. The cable programs are more engaging because the language is more realistic.

▸ For more practice editing for sentence variety, visit Exercise Central at bedfordstmartins.com/exercisecentral.

A Note on Thematic Connections

The authors represented in this chapter all have something to say about language—how we learn it, use it, abuse it, or change from it. Their ideas probably came to them through examples as they read, talked, and listened, so naturally they use examples to demonstrate those ideas. On her blog, Bethany Keeley posts multiple examples of inappropriate punctuation to express frustration with usage errors (p. 150). In one paragraph, Richard Rodriguez draws on a single example to show the embarrassment he felt at his father's limited English abilities (p. 153). In another, William Lutz uses two examples to illustrate how evasive doublespeak can be (p. 154). In an essay, David Sedaris uses humor to explore the difficulties of learning a second language (p. 160). Kirk Johnson questions the common assumption that slang is contributing to a decline in the English language (p. 167). And Anita Jain finds unexpected meaning in her father's use of pronouns (p. 172).

David Sedaris

David Sedaris's hilarious yet often touching autobiographical essays have earned him both popular and critical acclaim; in 2001 he received the Thurber Prize for American Humor and was named Humorist of the Year by *Time* magazine. Born in 1957, Sedaris grew up in North Carolina and attended the School of the Art Institute of Chicago, where he taught writing for several years before moving to New York City. Working odd jobs during the day and writing about them at night, Sedaris cata-pulted to near-overnight success in 1993 after reading on National Public Radio a piece about working as a department-store Christmas elf. Since then, he has been a frequent contributor to the *New Yorker, Esquire,* and public radio's *Morning Edition* and *This American Life.* In 1994 Sedaris published his first collection of essays, *Barrel Fever,* followed by *Naked* (1996), *Holidays on Ice* (1997), *Me Talk Pretty One Day* (2000), *Dress Your Family in Corduroy and Denim* (2004), and *When You Are Engulfed in Flames* (2008). His most recent book is *Squirrel Seeks Chipmunk* (2010), a collection of original fables about animals.

Me Talk Pretty One Day

Sedaris alternates his time between New York, Paris, and rural France. In this title essay from *Me Talk Pretty One Day,* he launches his trademark wit at a favorite target: the French language. Learning to speak a new language, he shows, involves a mixture of humiliations and triumphs.

At the age of forty-one, I am returning to school and have to think of myself as what my French textbook calls "a true debutant." After pay-ing my tuition, I was issued a student ID, which allows me a discounted entry fee at movie theaters, puppet shows, and Festyland, a far-flung amusement park that advertises with billboards picturing a cartoon stegosaurus sitting in a canoe and eating what appears to be a ham sandwich.

I've moved to Paris with hopes of learning the language. My school is an easy ten-minute walk from my apartment, and on the first day of class I arrived early, watching as the returning students greeted one another in the school lobby. Vacations were recounted, and questions were raised concerning mutual friends with names like Kang and Vlatnya. Regardless of their nationalities, everyone spoke in what sounded to me like excellent French. Some accents were better than others, but the students exhibited an ease and confidence I found intimidating. As an added discomfort, they were all young, attractive, and well dressed, causing me to feel not unlike Pa Kettle[1] trapped backstage after a fashion show.

The first day of class was nerve-racking because I knew I'd be expected 3 to perform. That's the way they do it here—it's everybody into the language pool, sink or swim. The teacher marched in, deeply tanned from a recent vacation, and proceeded to rattle off a series of administrative announcements. I've spent quite a few summers in Normandy, and I took a month-long French class before leaving New York. I'm not completely in the dark, yet I understood only half of what this woman was saying.

"If you have not *meimslsxp* or *lgpdmurct* by this time, then you 4 should not be in this room. Has everyone *apzkiubjxow*? Everyone? Good, we shall begin." She spread out her lesson plan and sighed, saying, "All right, then, who knows the alphabet?"

It was startling because (a) I hadn't been asked that question in a 5 while and (b) I realized, while laughing, that I myself did *not* know the alphabet. They're the same letters, but in France they're pronounced differently. I knew the shape of the alphabet but had no idea what it actually sounded like.

"Ahh." The teacher went to the board and sketched the letter *a*. "Do 6 we have anyone in the room whose first name commences with an *ahh*?"

Two Polish Annas raised their hands, and the teacher instructed 7 them to present themselves by stating their names, nationalities, occupations, and a brief list of things they liked and disliked in this world. The first Anna hailed from an industrial town outside of Warsaw and had front teeth the size of tombstones. She worked as a seamstress, enjoyed quiet times with friends, and hated the mosquito.

"Oh, really," the teacher said. "How very interesting. I thought that 8 everyone loved the mosquito, but here, in front of all the world, you claim to detest him. How is it that we've been blessed with someone as unique and original as you? Tell us, please."

The seamstress did not understand what was being said but knew 9 that this was an occasion for shame. Her rabbity mouth huffed for breath, and she stared down at her lap as though the appropriate comeback were stitched somewhere alongside the zipper of her slacks.

The second Anna learned from the first and claimed to love sunshine 10 and detest lies. It sounded like a translation of one of those Playmate of the Month data sheets, the answers always written in the same loopy

---

[1] A fictional hillbilly character featured in a series of books and movies in the 1940s and '50s. [Editors' note.]

handwriting: "Turn-ons: Mom's famous five-alarm chili! Turnoffs: inse-curity and guys who come on too strong!!!!"

The two Polish Annas surely had clear notions of what they loved **11** and hated, but like the rest of us, they were limited in terms of vocabu-lary, and this made them appear less than sophisticated. The teacher forged on, and we learned that Carlos, the Argentine bandonion[2] player, loved wine, music, and, in his words, "making sex with the womens of the world." Next came a beautiful young Yugoslav[3] who identified herself as an optimist, saying that she loved everything that life had to offer.

The teacher licked her lips, revealing a hint of the saucebox we **12** would later come to know. She crouched low for her attack, placed her hands on the young woman's desk, and leaned close, saying, "Oh yeah? And do you love your little war?"

While the optimist struggled to defend herself, I scrambled to think **13** of an answer to what had obviously become a trick question. How often is one asked what he loves in this world? More to the point, how often is one asked and then publicly ridiculed for his answer? I recalled my mother, flushed with wine, pounding the tabletop late one night, say-ing, "Love? I love a good steak cooked rare. I love my cat, and I love . . . ." My sisters and I leaned forward, waiting to hear our names. "Tums," our mother said. "I love Tums."

The teacher killed some time accusing the Yugoslavian girl of master- **14** minding a program of genocide, and I jotted frantic notes in the mar-gins of my pad. While I can honestly say that I love leafing through medical textbooks devoted to severe dermatological conditions, the hobby is beyond the reach of my French vocabulary, and acting it out would only have invited controversy.

When called upon, I delivered an effortless list of things that I **15** detest: blood sausage, intestinal pâtés, brain pudding. I'd learned these words the hard way. Having given it some thought, I then declared my love for IBM typewriters, the French word for *bruise*, and my electric floor waxer. It was a short list, but still I managed to mispronounce *IBM* and assign the wrong gender to both the floor waxer and the typewriter.[4]

---

[2] A South American musical instrument, similar to a small accordion. [Editors' note.]

[3] A native of Yugoslavia, a former communist country in Eastern Europe divided after several wars into Bosnia and Herzegovina, Croatia, Kosovo, Macedonia, Montenegro, Serbia, and Slovenia. [Editors' note.]

[4] In French, nouns are considered either male or female. Masculine nouns are pre-ceded by the article *le*; feminine nouns are preceded by *la*. As is the case with English pronouns and antecedents, French nouns must agree in gender with the pronouns and adjectives used to describe them. [Editors' note.]

The teacher's reaction led me to believe that these mistakes were capital crimes in the country of France.

"Were you always this *palicmkrexis*?" she asked. "Even a *fiuscrzsa* 16 *ticiwelmun* knows that a typewriter is feminine."

I absorbed as much of her abuse as I could understand, thinking— 17 but not saying—that I find it ridiculous to assign a gender to an inanimate object incapable of disrobing and making an occasional fool of itself. Why refer to Lady Crack Pipe or Good Sir Dishrag when these things could never live up to all that their sex implied?

The teacher proceeded to belittle everyone from German Eva, who 18 hated laziness, to Japanese Yukari, who loved paintbrushes and soap. Italian, Thai, Dutch, Korean, and Chinese—we all left class foolishly believing that the worst was over. She'd shaken us up a little, but surely that was just an act designed to weed out the deadweight. We didn't know it then, but the coming months would teach us what it was like to spend time in the presence of a wild animal, something completely unpredictable. Her temperament was not based on a series of good and bad days but, rather, good and bad moments. We soon learned to dodge chalk and protect our heads and stomachs whenever she approached us with a question. She hadn't yet punched anyone, but it seemed wise to protect ourselves against the inevitable.

Though we were forbidden to speak anything but French, the teacher 19 would occasionally use us to practice any of her five fluent languages.

"I hate you," she said to me one afternoon. Her English was flaw- 20 less. "I really, really hate you." Call me sensitive, but I couldn't help but take it personally.

After being singled out as a lazy *kfdtinvfm*, I took to spending four 21 hours a night on my homework, putting in even more time whenever we were assigned an essay. I suppose I could have gotten by with less, but I was determined to create some sort of identity for myself: David the hard worker, David the cut-up. We'd have one of those "complete this sentence" exercises, and I'd fool with the thing for hours, invariably settling on something like "A quick run around the lake? I'd love to! Just give me a moment while I strap on my wooden leg." The teacher, through word and action, conveyed the message that if this was my idea of an identity, she wanted nothing to do with it.

My fear and discomfort crept beyond the borders of the classroom 22 and accompanied me out onto the wide boulevards. Stopping for a coffee, asking directions, depositing money in my bank account: these things were out of the question, as they involved having to speak. Before beginning school, there'd been no shutting me up, but now I was convinced that everything I said was wrong. When the phone rang, I ignored it. If someone asked me a question, I pretended to be deaf. I knew my fear was getting the best of me when I started wondering why they don't sell cuts of meat in vending machines.

My only comfort was the knowledge that I was not alone. Huddled   23
in the hallways and making the most of our pathetic French, my fellow students and I engaged in the sort of conversation commonly overheard in refugee camps.

"Sometime me cry alone at night."   24

"That be common for I, also, but be more strong, you. Much work   25
and someday you talk pretty. People start love you soon. Maybe tomorrow, okay."

Unlike the French class I had taken in New York, here there was no   26
sense of competition. When the teacher poked a shy Korean in the eyelid with a freshly sharpened pencil, we took no comfort in the fact that, unlike Hyeyoon Cho, we all knew the irregular past tense of the verb *to defeat*. In all fairness, the teacher hadn't meant to stab the girl, but neither did she spend much time apologizing, saying only, "Well, you should have been *vkkdyo* more *kdeynfulh*."

Over time it became impossible to believe that any of us would ever   27
improve. Fall arrived and it rained every day, meaning we would now be scolded for the water dripping from our coats and umbrellas. It was mid-October when the teacher singled me out, saying, "Every day spent with you is like having a cesarean section." And it struck me that, for the first time since arriving in France, I could understand every word that someone was saying.

Understanding doesn't mean that you can suddenly speak the lan-   28
guage. Far from it. It's a small step, nothing more, yet its rewards are intoxicating and deceptive. The teacher continued her diatribe and I settled back, bathing in the subtle beauty of each new curse and insult.

"You exhaust me with your foolishness and reward my efforts with   29
nothing but pain, do you understand me?"

The world opened up, and it was with great joy that I responded,   30
"I know the thing that you speak exact now. Talk me more, you, plus, please, plus."

Vocabulary

If you are not familiar with the following words, try to determine their meanings from the context of Sedaris's essay. Test your guesses in a dictionary; then use each word in a sentence of your own.

debutant (1)	genocide (14)	belittle (18)
hailed (7)	dermatological (14)	temperament (18)
detest (8)	capital (15)	inevitable (18)
saucebox (12)	inanimate (17)	invariably (21)
flushed (13)	disrobing (17)	diatribe (28)

Key Ideas and Details

1. Why do Sedaris and the other students have difficulty expressing their likes and dislikes in class?

2. Sedaris devotes the majority of his essay to enumerating the humiliations and frustrations he experienced as a student, but his feelings change markedly toward the end. What causes his shift in attitude?

3. How does Sedaris characterize his classmates? his teacher? Does he mean for readers to take his examples literally? How can you tell?

4. In your own words, explain Sedaris's thesis. Where does he state it explicitly?

Craft and Structure

1. LANGUAGE Analyze the structures and lengths of sentences in paragraph 2. What strategies does Sedaris use to achieve variety?

2. What is the effect of the nonsense words, such as *meimslxsp* and *lgpdmurct* (paragraph 4), that Sedaris sprinkles through his essay? Why doesn't he simply repeat the French words or their English translations instead?

3. Which paragraphs fall into the introduction, body, and conclusion of Sedaris's essay? What function does each part serve?

4. OTHER METHODS "Me Talk Pretty One Day" relies on narration (Chapter 6) as much as it does example. How does Sedaris use dialogue to move his story forward?

Integration of Knowledge and Ideas

1. It can be painful to recall a difficult experience in your life, yet Sedaris chooses to do so. What do you believe is his purpose in recording these episodes from his French class: to understand his experience? to mock his classmates? to express his frustrations? to argue a point about learning? to do something else?

2. What do Sedaris's examples reveal about his attitude toward his teacher and her methods? Does he feel anger? bitterness? shame? appreciation? amusement? Why do you think so?

3. FOR DISCUSSION What impression of himself does Sedaris create? How seriously does he expect readers to take him? What words and passages support your answer?

Writing Topics

1. When he attended a French class in Paris, David Sedaris discovered the difficulties of acquiring a new language and with it some new attitudes about learning. Write an essay about new languages and attitudes you have encountered in high school. Have you been confronted with different kinds of people (teachers, other students) from the ones you knew before? Have you had difficulty understanding some words people use? Have you found yourself embracing ideas you never thought you would or speaking differently? Have others noticed a change in you that you may not have been aware of? Have you noticed changes in your friends? Focus on a particular kind of obstacle or change, using specific examples to share this experience with readers.

2. If you are studying or have learned a second language, write an essay in which you explain the difficulty of learning it. Draw your examples not just from the new language's grammar and vocabulary but from its underlying logic and attitudes. For instance, does one speak to older people differently in the new language? make requests differently? describe love or art differently? What do you expect to gain—or lose—from acquiring a new language? If you like, try to achieve humor in your essay by imitating Sedaris's style.

3. RESEARCH Sedaris jokes that he and other students "engaged in the sort of conversation commonly overhead in refugee camps" (paragraph 23), but many of the students in his class in fact moved from countries ravaged by war. Poland, for instance, was for many years occupied by Nazi Germany and populated with concentration camps; the former Yugoslavia endured decades of civil war and genocide. Choose one of the students Sedaris mentions and research the background from which he or she came. Then share your findings with the class.

4. CONNECTIONS Like Sedaris, Richard Rodriguez (p. 153) relates an experience of discomfort with hearing a new language. But while Sedaris focuses on his own trouble understanding French, Rodriguez emphasizes the awkwardness of listening to his father attempt to speak English. Write an essay analyzing what the two writers' examples have in common and any significant differences between them. How do their competing perspectives inform each other's experiences?

Kirk Johnson

Kirk Johnson was born in Salt Lake City, Utah. A Pulitzer-nominated writer for the *New York Times* and an endurance runner, Johnson has written a book entitled *To the Edge: A Man, Death Valley, and the Mystery of Endurance* (2001). He lives in northern New Jersey.

Today's Kids Are, Like, Killing the English Language

In "Today's Kids Are, Like, Killing the English Language," which first appeared in the *New York Times*, Johnson takes a long look at the changes occurring in, like, the vocabulary of younger generations. Contrary to common opinion, Johnson contends that these changes are neither superficial nor dangerous.

As a father of two preteen boys, I have in the last year or so become a   1 huge fan of the word *duh*. This is a word much maligned by educators, linguistic Brahmins[1] and purists, but they are all quite wrong.

Duh has elegance. *Duh* has shades of meaning, even sophistication.   2 *Duh* and its perfectly paired linguistic partner, *yeah, right*, are the ideal terms to usher in the millennium and the information age, and to highlight the differences from the stolid old twentieth century.

Even my sons might stop me at this point and quash my hyperbole   3 with a quickly dispensed, "Yeah, right, Dad." But hear me out: I have become convinced that *duh* and *yeah, right* have arisen to fill a void in the language because the world has changed. Fewer questions these days can effectively be answered with *yes* or *no*, while at the same time, a tidal surge of hype and mindless blather threatens to overwhelm old-fashioned conversation. *Duh* and *yeah, right* are the cure.

Good old *yes* and *no* were fine for their time—the archaic, black-   4 and-white era of late industrialism that I was born into in the 1950s. The *yes*-or-*no* combo was hard and fast and most of all simple: it belonged to the Manichean[2] red-or-dead mentality of the cold war, to manufacturing, to *Father Knows Best* and *It's a Wonderful Life*.

The information-age future that my eleven-year-old twins own   5 is more complicated than *yes* or *no*. It's more subtle and supple, more loaded with content and hype and media manipulation than my childhood—or any adult's, living or dead—ever was.

---

[1] *Brahmins* are members of an elite, sophisticated group. [Editors' note.]

[2] *Manichean* means dualistic. Manicheism is the belief that the world consists of dual oppositions, such as good and evil. [Editors' note.]

And *duh*, whatever else it may be, is drenched with content. Between   6
them, *duh* and *yeah, right* are capable of dividing all language and thought
into an exquisitely differentiated universe. Every statement and every
question can be positioned on a gray scale of understatement or overstatement, stupidity or insightfulness, information saturation or yawning emptiness.

And in an era when plain speech has become endangered by the   7
pressures of political correctness, *duh* and *yeah, right* are matchless tools
of savvy, winking sarcasm and skepticism: caustic without being con-
frontational, incisive without being quite specific.

With *duh*, you can convey a response, throw in a whole basket full   8
of auxiliary commentary about the question or the statement you're
responding to, and insult the speaker all at once! As in this hypothetical
exchange:

> Parent: Good morning, son, it's a beautiful day.
> Eleven-year-old boy: Duh.

And there is a kind of esthetic balance as well. *Yeah, right* is the yin   9
to *duh*'s yang, the antithesis to *duh*'s empathetic thesis. Where *duh* is
assertive and edgy, a perfect tool for undercutting mindless understatement or insulting repetition, *yeah, right* is laid back, a surfer's cool kind
of response to anything overwrought or oversold.

New York, for example, is *duh* territory, while Los Angeles is *yeah,*   10
right. Television commercials can be rendered harmless and inert by
simply saying, "yeah, right," upon their conclusion. Local television
news reports are helped out with a sprinkling of well-placed *duh*s, at
moments of stunning obviousness. And almost any politician's speech
cries out for heaping helpings of both at various moments.

Adolescent terms like *like*, by contrast, scare me to death. While I   11
have become convinced through observation and personal experimen-
tation that just about any adult of even modest intelligence can figure
out how to use *duh* and *yeah, right* properly, *like* is different. *Like* is hard.
Like is, like, dangerous.

Marcel Danesi, a professor of linguistics and semiotics at the Univer-   12
sity of Toronto who has studied the language of youth and who coined
the term "pubilect" to describe the dialect of pubescence, said he believes
like is in fact altering the structure of the English language, making it
more fluid in construction, more like Italian or some other Romance
language than good old hard-and-fast Anglo-Saxon. Insert *like* in the
middle of a sentence, he said, and a statement can be turned into a
question, a question into an exclamation, an exclamation into a quiet
meditation.

Consider these hypothetical expressions: "If you're having broccoli 13
for dinner, Mr. Johnson, I'm, like, out of here!" and "I was, like, no way!"
and perhaps most startlingly, "He was, like, duh!"

In the broccoli case, *like* softens the sentence. It's less harsh and con- 14
frontational than saying flatly that the serving of an unpalatable vegetable would require a fleeing of the premises.

In the second instance, *like* functions as a kind of a verbal quotation 15
mark, an announcement that what follows, "no way," is to be heard
differently. The quote itself can then be loaded up with any variety of
intonation—irony, sarcasm, even self-deprecation—all depending on
the delivery.

In the third example—"He was, like, duh!"—*like* becomes a crucial 16
helping verb for *duh*, a verbal springboard. (Try saying the sentence without *like* and it becomes almost incomprehensible.)

But *like* and *duh* and *yeah, right*, aside from their purely linguistic 17
virtues, are also in many ways the perfect words to convey the sense of
reflected reality that is part of the age we live in. Image manipulation,
superficiality, and shallow media culture are, for better or worse, the
backdrop of adolescent life.

Adults of the *yes*-or-*no* era could perhaps grow up firm in their 18
knowledge of what things "are," but in the Age of *Duh*, with images
reflected back from every angle at every waking moment, kids swim in
a sea of what things are "like." Distinguishing what is from what merely
seems to be is a required skill of an eleven-year-old today; *like* reflects
modern life, and *duh* and *yeah, right* are the tools with which such a life
can be negotiated and mastered.

But there is a concealed paradox in the Age of *Duh*. The infor- 19
mation overload on which it is based is built around the computer,
and the computer is, of course, built around—that's right—the good
old *yes*-or-*no* binary code: billions of microcircuits all blinking on or
off, black or white, current in or current out. Those computers were
designed by minds schooled and steeped in the world of *yes* or *no*, and
perhaps it is not too much of a stretch to imagine my sons' generation,
shaped by the broader view of *duh*, finding another path: binary code
with attitude. Besides, most computers I know already seem to have an
attitude. Incorporating a little *duh* would at least give them a sense of
humor.

Vocabulary

If you are uncertain of the meanings of any of the words listed below, try to
guess them from the context of Johnson's essay. Then look them up to see how

close your definitions were to those in the dictionary. Test out the new words by using each of them in a sentence.

hyperbole (3)	esthetic (9)	unpalatable (14)
hype (3)	antithesis (9)	self-deprecation (15)
blather (3)	overwrought (9)	springboard (16)
caustic (7)	semiotics (12)	backdrop (17)
incisive (7)	confrontational (14)	steeped (19)

Key Ideas and Details

1. What is Johnson's main point? Identify the sentence that you believe best demonstrates his main idea.

2. Which slang terms does Johnson single out, and what do they contribute to the main point of his essay?

3. What is a paradox? What is the "paradox" that Johnson refers to in his last paragraph?

Craft and Structure

1. LANGUAGE How does the author attempt to make his ideas accessible while also maintaining his sophistication? In your opinion, is this essay difficult to read, easy to read, or something in between? Why?

2. Examine the quotations that Johnson offers as examples of *duh* and *yeah, right* and *like*. How well do they, along with Johnson's explanations of them, convey the meanings of the expressions? Are there places where you would like to see more examples?

3. Weigh the evidence that Johnson gives to support his opinions. Which evidence is personal, and which is not? Are both the personal and the non-personal equally effective? Why, or why not?

4. OTHER METHODS Johnson's example essay is also a model of definition (Chapter 13) because he establishes the meanings of three slang terms. What are the meanings of *duh* and *yeah, right* and *like*? How is each distinct from the others?

Integration of Knowledge and Ideas

1. Do you think Johnson wants to provoke, educate, or entertain us? Or does he want to do all of these things? What evidence can you provide for your answer?

2. What clues can you find that this essay was originally published in the *New York Times*? For instance, what does Johnson seem to assume about his

readers—that they're teenagers? adults? linguists? parents? Does he assume that they speak the slang he analyzes or that they approve of it? Provide examples from the essay to support your answers.

3. FOR DISCUSSION Johnson establishes his viewpoint in the first few paragraphs. What objections does he anticipate? How does he respond to them? How convinced are you by his response?

Writing Topics

1. Think of one or more expressions that you use when speaking with friends or family but that you might not use in writing an essay—private code words that you use only with certain people or slang expressions such as *duh*, *like*, and *yeah*, *right*, the subjects of Johnson's essay. Using specific examples, write an essay about the expression or expressions you use with friends or family and what those expressions mean to you. What shades of meaning do the expressions have? What situations do you use them in? How do others react to them?

2. You may not agree with Johnson's opinion that certain slang expressions are ideal for our modern world and actually enrich our language. Write a speech or essay in which you consider the opposite view: that English is actually being harmed by terms such as *duh* and *yeah*, *right* and *like*. You may use examples from Johnson's essay or others of your own, but be sure to support your case.

3. Many English speakers use words from other languages, nonstandard forms such as *ain't* or *can't hardly*, or slang such as *duh* or *yeah*, *right*—and many listeners find the language richer for these additions. Yet not all ways of speaking gain equal acceptance. Write an essay in which you examine how negative stereotyping may use the language of a particular group—an accent, say, or certain slang expressions—against the members of that group. In stereotyping, what connections are drawn between the language and the perceived or imagined qualities of its speakers? What purpose might such stereotyping serve for those who do it? What effect might it have on them?

4. CONNECTIONS Both Johnson and William Lutz, in a paragraph from *Doublespeak* (p. 154), discuss language use among a particular group. Johnson explains how his preteen sons and their friends use certain slang expressions to reflect the reality of the world around them. Lutz, in contrast, shows how carefully chosen terminology used by the military can actually obscure meaning. Write an essay in which you examine a form of double-speak, jargon, or slang, such as the language of teachers, journalists, or college students. Does the language used clarify or confuse reality?

Anita Jain

Anita Jain was born in 1972 in New Delhi, India, and grew up in the United States, living in eleven different school districts before her family made a permanent home in the Sacramento, California, area. Jain is a successful financial reporter who has worked out of Mexico City, London, Singapore, New York, and New Delhi. She is also the author of a best-selling memoir, *Marrying Anita* (2008), that details her frustrations with American dating norms and her experience of returning to India to seek a husband through traditional means such as arranged marriage. Jain now lives in New Delhi, a city she found unexpectedly modern and cosmopolitan.

A Nameless Respect

In "A Nameless Respect" (Editors' title), an excerpt from *Marrying Anita*, Jain takes a careful look at the way her parents address each other. Her father, she discovers, has found a subtle way to accord his wife a measure of equality traditionally denied Indian women of her generation.

My father's interests tend toward daytime talk shows and his latest cash-   1
generating shenanigans, which at this moment is day trading. But while he may not be highbrow in his pursuits or refined in his habits, a distinct nobility of mind and dignity of character underlie his ideas and actions regarding gender relations.

Disgusted with the poor treatment of women he observed growing   2
up in 1940s India, my father became an ardent feminist. He was hardly poised to become one, born into a lower-middle-class family of seven brothers and one sister in Meerut, an industrial town two hours outside of Delhi. It was a town earlier immortalized in history as the one whose hotheads gave India its first insurrection against imperial rule, the 1857 mutiny against the British. Although my paternal grandfather ensured that all his children received a proper education—all of them went on to study engineering—I suspect the Hindi-language public schools my father and his siblings attended may have given short shrift to ideas stemming from the Enlightenment such as equality, justice, and liberty. Given a background destined to turn a man into a brute, or at least one not especially attuned to his feminine side, my father managed to chart a personal philosophy predicated on the belief that women are equal to men and should be treated so accordingly, every day, in every conversation.

As in many languages other than English, there are several ways   3
to say "you" in Hindi. (The English language is veritably impoverished when it comes to the second-person pronoun, our default for the second-

person plural across the vast English-speaking world being the inelegant "you guys.") There is the formal *aap* that is used for elders and unfamiliar people, the familiar *tum* used with friends and siblings, and beneath that, the somewhat rough-hewn *tu*, which can be deployed with affection, as parents do with their children or between close friends, but can also be crude, unrefined, and imperious when directed at servants or underlings.

My mother, in accordance with her generation and small-town 4 middle-class manners, was expected to address my father with the formal *aap*. In my mother's era, it was also considered disrespectful for a woman to utter her husband's name, as in "Rajiv, dinner's ready!" or "Amit, what a day I had today," or even when referring to him in the third person ("Ashok and I would like our son to be a doctor."). To this day, I have never heard my mother mouth my father's name, Naresh. When calling out to him, she says, "Listen up!" or "Do you hear?" When referring to him in conversation with other Indians, she just uses "he." To avoid confusing non-Indians who would not understand her delicacy, she will say "My husband." As a childish prank, I used to try to trick her and get her to voice his name by asking her the correct pronunciation or employing some other ruse, but she would always manage to get around repeating his name.

In every conversation in the forty years my parents have been mar- 5 ried, my father also addresses my mother as *aap* and has similarly never uttered her name, Santosh. When conversing with others, he will refer to her as "she" much as she does with him. I've never actually seen any other Indian man do this. Other uncles address their wives with the middle form *tum*, or even the boorish *tu*, while most often wives reply with *aap*. I've also seen many couples of my parents' generation, having perhaps established a good rapport or being from a more modern background, address each other equally with *tum* as well as refer to each other by name. Indeed this is what modern couples do now and what I would expect to do when speaking Hindi with a partner. If my father had simply done what most men of his generation did and employed the middle form of *you*, it hardly would mark him as a discourteous or ill-mannered husband, and I daresay many men in the West would do the same. But my father believed that if women were equal to men, then certainly one should start at the beginning, as it were: linguistic parity.

I still marvel at the depth of principle and reserve of restraint that 6 would keep a man from ever letting his wife's name slip, even after forty years. For a woman, of course, it's hardly unusual to fathom that she would continue to use the respectful form when addressing her husband, seeing as females in all societies have been inculcated to behave in

a manner that is seen as befitting their gender. But for a man in a traditional society, it is nothing short of extraordinary.

Vocabulary

If you are uncertain of the meanings of any of the words listed below, try to
guess them from the context of Jain's essay. Then look them up to see how
close your definitions were to those in the dictionary. Test out the new words
by using each of them in a sentence.

shenanigans (1)	veritably (3)	boorish (5)
ardent (2)	deployed (3)	rapport (5)
insurrection (2)	imperious (3)	parity (5)
imperial (2)	accordance (4)	fathom (6)
predicated (2)	ruse (4)	inculcated (6)

Key Ideas and Details

1. What is Jain's thesis? Identify the sentence that you believe best demonstrates her main idea.
2. What pronouns does Jain discuss, and why is her father's use of one of them
   so extraordinary to her?
3. Why have Jain's mother and father never referred to each other by name?
   Consider each parent individually.

Craft and Structure

1. LANGUAGE How would you characterize Jain's tone in this essay—for
   instance, sarcastic, argumentative, admiring, humorous, serious, flippant,
   ambivalent, irritated, confused, enthusiastic? Give examples to support
   your analysis.
2. Why do you think that Jain does not give examples of her parents' uses of
   language until halfway through the essay? Does this delay make the essay
   weaker or more interesting for you?
3. OTHER METHODS Where in this essay can you find an instance of classification (Chapter 10)? How is this classification central to Jain's subject and
   purpose?

Integration of Knowledge and Ideas

1. "A Nameless Respect" expresses the author's admiration for her father. Is
   Jain's praise weakened by her references to his shortcomings in the first
   paragraph? Why, or why not?

2. What assumptions does Jain seem to make about her readers—their gender or age, their marital status, their attitudes toward traditional gender roles, their knowledge of Indian culture and history, and so on?

3. FOR DISCUSSION Jain does not specify what she means by "the poor treatment of women . . . in 1940s India" (paragraph 2). Is it fair for her to expect that readers will understand the generalization? Does she offer clarification anywhere else in the essay?

Writing Topics

1. With Jain's essay as a model, write an essay of your own that uses examples to explain why you admire another person. You might write about a parent, as Jain does, or about anyone who has had a positive influence on you.

2. Think of a traditional form of politeness that some people now object to. Examples might include holding a door open, addressing a customer as *ma'am*, or offering to help an older person cross the street. Why do some people interpret such behaviors as common courtesy, while others consider them rude or insulting? Using specific examples, create a video presentation arguing that your chosen form of politeness has outlived its usefulness. As you draft your script, consider these questions: Under what circumstances did the courtesy originate, and why was it considered polite? What has changed to render it objectionable to some people? Are they right to object? Is there some other behavior that should take its place?

3. RESEARCH In her conclusion, Jain comments that "females in all societies have been inculcated to behave in a manner that is seen as befitting their gender" (paragraph 6). She seems to believe, in other words, that women everywhere willingly adhere to rigidly defined gender roles. What do you think of this assertion? Can you think of examples that contradict it? Research gender roles in one or more countries other than the United States and India and use what you find to write an essay that examines Jain's assumption. Whether you agree with her or not, offer plenty of evidence to support your conclusions.

4. CONNECTIONS In "I Want a Wife" (p. 308), Judy Brady also writes about what was expected of wives forty years ago. Read her essay and consider what she might think of Naresh Jain's effort to treat his wife as an equal. Would "linguistic parity" be enough for Brady? What aspects of the Jains' marriage might she criticize? What aspects might she applaud?

WRITING WITH THE METHOD

EXAMPLE

Select one of the following statements and agree or disagree with it in an essay developed by example. The statement you choose should concern a topic you care about so that the example or examples are a means of communicating an idea, not an end in themselves.

Family

1. In happy families, talk is the main activity.
2. Grandparents relate more closely to their grandchildren than to their children.
3. Sooner or later, children take on the personalities of their parents.

Behavior and Personality

4. Rudeness is on the rise.
5. Facial expressions often communicate what words cannot say.
6. Our natural surroundings contribute to our happiness or unhappiness.

Education

7. The best classes are the difficult ones.
8. Education is an easy way to get ahead in life.
9. Students at schools with enforced dress codes behave better than students at schools without such codes.

Politics and Social Issues

10. Talk radio can influence public policy.
11. Drug or alcohol addiction is not restricted just to "bad" people.
12. Unemployment is hardest on teenagers.
13. The best popular musicians treat social and political issues in their songs.

Rules for Living

14. Murphy's Law: If anything can go wrong, it will go wrong, and at the worst possible moment.
15. With enough motivation, a person can accomplish anything.
16. Lying may be justified by the circumstances.

WRITING ABOUT THE THEME

USING LANGUAGE

1. Richard Rodriguez (p. 153), William Lutz (p. 154), Kirk Johnson (p. 167), and Anita Jain (p. 172) discuss the power of language with a good deal of respect. Rodriguez refers to its cultural implications, Lutz to its effectiveness "in explaining . . . accidents," and Jain to its effect on intimate relationships. Think of a time when you were in some way profoundly affected by language, and write an essay about this experience. Provide as many examples as necessary to illustrate both the language that affected you and how it made you feel.

2. Bethany Keeley (p. 150), Kirk Johnson, David Sedaris (p. 160), and Anita Jain all examine forms of language that do not obey traditional rules and are considered incorrect by some people. As you see it, what are the advantages and disadvantages of using nonstandard language when speaking and writing? How effective are these forms of language as ways to communicate? Write an essay answering these questions, using examples from the selections and your own experience.

3. As Anita Jain points out, the English language has only one form of the second-person pronoun *you*. Jain characterizes this quality as a weakness but then goes on to suggest ways in which different levels of the pronoun's formality in Hindi can be used to reinforce inequality. Focusing on a single example, write an essay about the influence of language on culture, and vice versa. How might multiple forms of the pronoun *you*, for instance, reflect social hierarchies? How do usage errors on public signs (see Keeley) affect the relationship between the signs' creators and their audiences? How does doublespeak (see Lutz) serve to obscure reality? What does lack of fluency in the dominant language do to a person's self-esteem (Rodriguez, Sedaris)? How does assigning gender to nouns (see Sedaris) affect perception of their meaning? Other examples may come to mind; write about what interests you most.

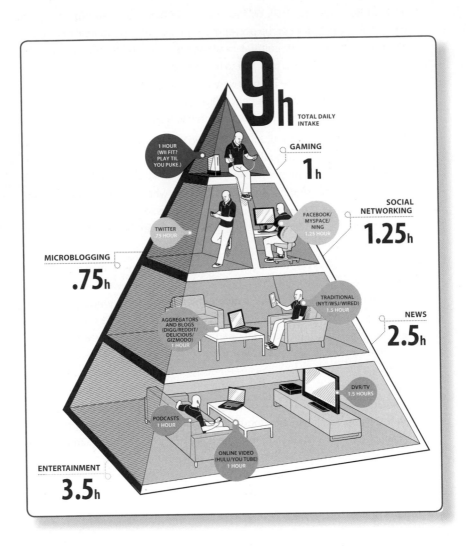

9h TOTAL DAILY INTAKE

GAMING
1h

1 HOUR (WII FIT? PLAY TIL YOU PUKE.)

SOCIAL NETWORKING
1.25h

FACEBOOK/ MYSPACE/ NING
1.25 HOUR

TWITTER
.75 HOUR

MICROBLOGGING
.75h

TRADITIONAL (NYT/WSJ/WIRED)
1.5 HOUR

NEWS
2.5h

AGGREGATORS AND BLOGS (DIGG/REDDIT/ DELICIOUS/ GIZMODO)
1 HOUR

DVR/TV
1.5 HOURS

PODCASTS
1 HOUR

ENTERTAINMENT
3.5h

ONLINE VIDEO (HULU/YOU TUBE)
1 HOUR

9

DIVISION OR ANALYSIS

▶

LOOKING AT POPULAR CULTURE

Division and **analysis** are interchangeable terms for the same method. *Division* comes from a Latin word meaning "to force asunder or separate." *Analysis* comes from a Greek word meaning "to undo." Using this method, we separate a whole into its elements, examine the relations of the elements to one another and to the whole, and reassemble the elements into a new whole informed by the examination.

Analysis (as we will call it) is the foundation of **critical thinking**, the ability to see beneath the surface of things, images, events, and ideas; to uncover and test assumptions; to see the importance of context; and to draw and support independent conclusions. The method, then, is essential to academic learning, whether in discussing literature, solving a math problem, or interpreting a historical event. It is also fundamental in the workplace, from choosing a career to making sense of market research. Analysis even informs and enriches life outside of school or work, whether we ponder our relationships with others, decide whether a movie was worthwhile, evaluate an advertiser's messages, or determine whether a new video game system is worth buying.

Seeing Division or Analysis

This illustrated pyramid chart from an article in *Wired* magazine takes a typical day and breaks it down by the time readers might spend consuming five distinct elements of popular media, with specific examples of each. "When you add it all up," writes Steven Leckart, "the average American spends roughly nine hours a day glued to some kind of screen, and like your diet, quality is as important as quantity. Here are *Wired*'s suggested servings for optimal media health." Why do you suppose he and illustrator Jason Lee chose a pyramid format to represent the magazine's suggestions rather than, say, a pie chart or bar graph? Do the suggestions seem reasonable to you? How accurately do they represent your own relationship to electronic media? (What kinds of screen time are left out, for instance?) If you were to chart one of your days using the criteria in this graphic, what would it look like?

Reading Division or Analysis

At its most helpful, division or analysis peers inside an object, institution, work of art, policy, or any other whole. It identifies the parts, examines how the parts relate, and leads to a conclusion about the meaning, significance, or value of the whole. The subject of any analysis is usually singular—a freestanding, coherent unit, such as a bicycle or a poem, with its own unique constitution of elements. (In contrast, classification, the subject of the next chapter, usually starts with a plural subject, such as bicycles or the poems of the Civil War, and groups them according to their shared features.) A writer chooses the subject and with it a **principle of analysis**, a framework that determines how the subject will be divided and thus what elements are relevant to the discussion.

Sometimes the principle of analysis is self-evident, especially when the subject is an object, such as a bicycle or a camera, that can be "undone" in only a limited number of ways. Most of the time, however, the principle depends on the writer's view of the whole. In academic disciplines, distinctive principles are part of what each field is about and are often the subject of debate within the field. In art, for instance, some critics see a painting primarily as a visual object and concentrate on its composition, color, line, and other formal qualities; other critics see a painting primarily as a social object and concentrate on its content and context (cultural, economic, political, and so on). Both groups use a principle of analysis that is a well-established way of looking at a painting, yet each group finds different elements and thus meaning in a work.

Writers have a great deal of flexibility in choosing a principle of analysis, but the principle also must meet certain requirements: it should be appropriate for the subject and the field or discipline; it should be significant; and it should be applied thoroughly and consistently. Analysis is not done for its own sake but for a larger goal of illuminating the subject, perhaps concluding something about it, perhaps evaluating it. But even when the method leads to evaluation—a judgment of the subject's value—the analysis should represent the subject as it actually is, in all its fullness and complexity, from the writer's unique perspective.

Analyzing Division or Analysis in Paragraphs

Jon Pareles (born 1953) is the chief critic of popular music for the *New York Times*. The following paragraph comes from "Gather No Moss, Take No Prisoners, but Be Cool," a review of a concert by the guitarist Keith Richards.

<u>Mr. Richards shows off by not showing off</u>. He uses rhythm chords as a goad, not a metronome, slipping them in just ahead of a beat or skipping them entirely. The distilled twang of his tone has been imitated all over rock, but far fewer guitarists have learned his guerrilla timing, his coiled silences. When he switches to lead guitar, Mr. Richards goes not for long lines, but for serrated riffing, zinging out three or four notes again and again in various permutations, wringing from them the essence of the blues. The phrasing is poised and suspenseful, but it also carries a salutary rock attitude: that less is more, especially when delivered with utter confidence.

Principle of analysis (topic sentence underlined): elements of "not showing off"

1. Chords as goad (or prod)

2. Timing

3. Silences

4. Riffing (or repeating variations of rhythms)

5. Confident, less-is-more attitude

Luci Tapahonso (born 1953) is a poet and teacher. This paragraph is from her essay "The Way It Is," which appears in *Sign Language*, a book of photographs (by Skeet McAuley) of life on the reservation for some Navajo and Apache Indians.

It is rare and, indeed, very exciting to see an Indian person in a commercial advertisement. Word travels fast when that happens. Nunzio's Pizza in Albuquerque, New Mexico, ran commercials featuring Jose Rey Toledo of Jemez Pueblo talking about his "native land—Italy" while wearing typical Pueblo attire—jewelry, moccasins, and hair tied in a chongo. Because of the ironic humor, because Indian grandfathers specialize in playing tricks and jokes on their grandchildren, and because Jose Rey Toledo is a respected and well-known elder in the Indian communities, word of this commercial spread fast among Indians in New Mexico. It was the cause of recognition and celebration of sorts on the reservations and in the pueblos. His portrayal was not in the categories which the media usually associate with Indians but as a typical sight in

Principle of analysis: elements of the commercial that appealed to Indians

1. Rarity of an Indian in a commercial

2. Indian dress

3. Indian humor

4. Indian tradition

5. Respected Indian spokesperson

6. Realism

the Southwest. It showed Indians as we live today—enjoying pizza as one of our favorite foods, including humor and fun as part of our daily lives, and recognizing the importance of preserving traditional knowledge.

Topic sentence (underlined) summarizes elements.

Developing an Essay by Division or Analysis

▶ Getting Started

Analysis is one of the most readily available methods for developing a subject: almost anything whole can be separated into its elements, from a lemon to a play by Shakespeare to an economic theory. In school and at work, many assignments will demand analysis with a verb such as *analyze, criticize, discuss, evaluate, interpret,* or *review.* If you need to develop your own subject for analysis, think of something whose meaning or significance puzzles or intrigues you and whose parts you can distinguish and relate to the whole—for instance, an object such as a machine, an artwork such as a poem, a media product such as a news broadcast, an institution such as a hospital, a relationship such as stepparenting, or a social issue such as sheltering the homeless.

Dissect your subject, looking at the actual physical thing if possible, imagining it in your mind if necessary. Make detailed notes of all the elements you see, their distinguishing features, and how those features work together. In analyzing someone's creation, tease out the creator's influences, assumptions, intentions, conclusions, and evidence. You may have to go outside the work for some of this information—researching an author's background, for instance, to uncover the biases that may underlie his or her opinions. Even if you do not use all this information in your final draft, it will help you see the elements and help keep your analysis true to the subject.

If you begin by seeking meaning or significance in a subject, you will be more likely to find a workable principle of analysis and less likely to waste time on a hollow exercise. Each question below suggests a distinct approach to the subject's elements—a distinct principle of analysis— that makes it easier to isolate the elements and see their connections.

To what extent is an enormously complex hospital a community in itself?

What is the function of the front-page headlines in the local tabloid newspaper?

Why did a certain movie have such a powerful effect on you and your friends?

▶ Forming a Thesis

A clear, informative thesis is crucial in division or analysis because readers need to know the purpose and structure of your analysis to follow
your points. If your exploratory question proves helpful as you gather
ideas, you can also use it to draft a thesis sentence (or sentences): answer
the question in such a way that you state your opinion about your subject and reveal your principle of analysis.

> QUESTION   To what extent is an enormously complex hospital a community
> in itself?
>
> THESIS SENTENCE   The hospital includes such a wide range of personnel and
> services that it resembles a good-size town.

> QUESTION   What is the function of the front-page headlines in the local
> tabloid newspaper?
>
> THESIS SENTENCE   The newspaper's front-page headlines routinely appeal to
> readers' fear of crime, anger at criminals, and sympathy for victims.

> QUESTION   Why did a certain movie have such a powerful effect on you and
> your friends?
>
> THESIS SENTENCE   The film is a unique and important statement of the pri-
> vate terrors of adolescence.

Note that all three thesis sentences imply an explanatory purpose—an
effort to understand something and share that understanding with the
reader. The third thesis sentence, however, suggests a persuasive purpose as well: the writer hopes that readers will accept her evaluation of
the film.

A well-focused thesis sentence benefits not only your readers but
also you as writer because it gives you a yardstick to judge the completeness, consistency, and supportiveness of your analysis. Don't be discouraged, though, if your thesis sentence doesn't come to you until *after*
you've written a first draft and had a chance to focus your ideas. Writing about your subject may be the best way for you to find its meaning
and significance.

▶ Organizing

In the **introduction** to your essay, let readers know why you are bothering to analyze your subject: Why is the subject significant? How might
the essay relate to the experiences of readers or be useful to them? A
subject unfamiliar to readers might be summarized or described, or part
of it (an anecdote or a quotation, say) might be used to grab readers'

interest. A familiar subject might be introduced with a surprising fact or an unusual perspective. An evaluative analysis might open with an opposing viewpoint.

In the body of the essay, you'll need to explain your principle of analysis. The arrangement of elements and analysis should suit your subject and purpose: you can describe the elements and then offer your analysis, or you can introduce and analyze elements one by one. You can arrange the elements themselves from least to most important, least to most complex, most to least familiar, spatially, or chronologically. Devote as much space to each element as it demands: there is no requirement that all elements be given equal space and emphasis if their complexity or your framework dictates otherwise.

Most analysis essays need a **conclusion** that reassembles the elements, returning readers to a sense of the whole subject. The conclusion can restate the thesis, summarize what the essay has contributed, consider the influence of the subject or its place in a larger picture, or (especially in an evaluation) assess the effectiveness or worth of the subject.

▶ Drafting

If your subject or your view of it is complex, you may need at least two rough drafts of an analysis essay—one to work out what you think and one to clarify your principle, cover each element, and support your points with concrete details and vivid examples (including quotations if the subject is a written work). Plan on two drafts if you're uncertain of your thesis when you begin; you'll save time in the long run by attending to one goal at a time. Especially because the analysis essay says something about the subject by explaining its structure, you need to have a clear picture of the whole and relate each part to it.

As you draft, be sure to consider your readers' needs as well as the needs of your subject and your own framework:

- If the subject is unfamiliar to your readers, you'll need to carefully explain your principle of analysis, define all specialized terms, distinguish parts from one another, and provide ample illustrations.

- If the subject is familiar to readers, your principle of analysis may not require much justification (as long as it's clear), but your details and examples must be vivid and convincing.

- If readers may dispute your way of looking at your subject, be careful to justify as well as explain your principle of analysis.

Whether readers are familiar with your subject or not, always account for any evidence that may seem not to support your opinion—either by showing why, in fact, the evidence is supportive or explaining why it is unimportant. (If contrary evidence cannot be refuted, you may have to rethink your approach.)

▶ Revising and Editing

When you revise and edit your essay, use the following questions and the focus box on the next page to uncover any weaknesses remaining in your analysis.

- *Is your principle of analysis clear?* The significance of your analysis and your view of the subject should be apparent throughout your essay.

- *Is your analysis complete?* Have you identified all elements according to your principle of analysis and determined their relations to one another and to the whole? If you have omitted some elements from your discussion, will the reason for their omission be clear to readers?

- *Is your analysis consistent?* Is your principle of analysis applied consistently to the entire subject? Do all elements reflect the same principle, and are they clearly separate rather than overlapping? You may find it helpful to check your draft against your list of elements or to outline the draft itself.

- *Is your analysis well supported?* Is the thesis supported by clear assertions about parts of the subject, and are the assertions supported by concrete, specific evidence (sensory details, facts, quotations, and so on)? Do not rely on your readers to prove your thesis.

- *Is your analysis coherent?* To help readers keep your analysis straight, rely on the techniques of paragraph coherence discussed on pages 40–41, especially on transitions and on repitition. Transitions, like those listed in the Glossary, act as signposts to tell readers where you, and they, are headed. And repitition, or restatement, of labels for your principle of analysis or for individual elements makes clear the topic of each sentence.

- *Is your analysis true to the subject?* Is your thesis unforced, your analysis fair? Is your new whole (your reassembly of the elements) faithful to the original?

FOCUS ON **Sources**

When you examine a subject for an analysis, you can help readers to better understand your perception of it by integrating quotations, paraphrases, and summaries into your writing. As you do so, however, be careful to avoid plagiarism, the error of presenting other writers' words or ideas as if they were your own.

Especially if your subject is a written work, including quotations as evidence can be essential to supporting the points you wish to make. In "Great Expectations" (p. 199) for example, Pat Mora quotes advertising messages aimed at Mexican Americans (following convention, she italicizes Spanish words):

> QUOTATIONS They speak to us *en español. "Ven es la hora de Miller."* Coors tells us, *"Celebre! Cinco de mayo."* Canadian Club says, *"¡Qué pareja! Canadian Club y tu!"* Xerox tells us that its Hispana employees are *"especial."*

When you quote another person's words, you must clearly indicate that those words are not your own. Surround direct quotations with quotation marks, and identify the source by naming the author and providing a page number (if one is available) in parentheses.

> PLAGIARIZED Advertisers speak to us *en español.*

> CORRECTED Pat Mora writes that advertisers "speak to us *en español"* (200).

If you want to share an idea or information you found in a source but the exact words are not important to your analysis, put the meaning in your own words. Use summary to condense the main idea of a longer work into a sentence or two, or use paraphrase to restate a point in a new way. Mora does both in her essay:

> SUMMARY In her documentary *A Famine Within,* Katherine Gilday skillfully reveals our obsession with The Body, the difficulty we have accepting and loving ourselves, our imperfect selves.

> PARAPHRASE Fashion models are often role models, says Gilday.

As with quotations, when you summarize or paraphrase you must make it clear that the idea is not your own, even if the words are. Name the source, as Mora does, and if it has page numbers, cite them in parentheses (Mora does not because her source is a film). Be careful not to repeat any of the original words, phrases, or sentence structures:

ORIGINAL PASSAGE People who stop for a hamburger — at a Wendy's, a Harvey's, a McDonald's, or a Burger King — know exactly what the building that houses the establishment should look like; architectural variations merely ring changes on rigidly imposed themes.
— Margaret Visser, "The Ritual of Fast Food," p. 189

PLAGIARIZED People who eat at a place like Wendy's, Harvey's, McDonald's, or Burger King expect to find themselves in a building that looks familiar (Visser 189).

CORRECTED Customers at fast-food restaurants expect to find themselves in familiar surroundings (Visser 189).

PLAGIARIZED According to Margaret Visser, when a restaurant does vary from the norm, the differences simply reflect adaptations of strictly enforced rules (189).

CORRECTED According to Margaret Visser, when a restaurant does vary from the norm, the general appearance is still recognizable to regular patrons (189).

See pages 68–72 for more advice on integrating sources and avoiding plagiarism.

Practice

The sentences below all quote, summarize, or paraphrase paragraph 3 from Thomas de Zengotita's essay "*American Idol* Worship" (p. 194). Using the original passage on page 195 as a reference, identify instances of plagiarism and correct them.

1. Thomas de Zengotita claims that most people name pop music performers as their heroes.

2. Nobody, he points out, thinks of role models in the old-fashioned statesman, warrior, genius, artist kind of way (195).

3. People involved with students are particularly worried (de Zengotita 195).

4. According to de Zengotita, however, efforts to rekindle an aura of greatness for historical figures are doomed to failure.

5. Citizens of the modern world are more likely to admire people they know, he says (195).

▶ For more practice integrating sources and avoiding plagiarism, visit Exercise Central at bedfordstmartins.com/exercisecentral.

A Note on Thematic Connections

Because popular culture is everywhere, and everywhere taken for granted, it is a tempting and challenging target for writers. Having chosen to write critically about a cheering, intriguing, or disturbing aspect of popular culture, all the authors represented in this chapter naturally pursued the method of division or analysis. The pyramid chart from *Wired* magazine divides a day into recommended time spent with various elements of electronic media (p. 178).The paragraph by Jon Pareles dissects the unique playing style of the rock guitarist Keith Richards (p. 181). The other paragraph, by Luci Tapahonso, analyzes a pizza commercial that especially appealed to Native Americans (p. 181). Margaret Visser's essay considers what besides food we buy when we visit McDonald's (opposite). Thomas de Zengotita's essay examines the television show *American Idol* to determine what makes it so irresistible to viewers (p. 194). And Pat Mora's essay asks how advertising messages shape Latinas' self-perception and future potential (p. 199).

Margaret Visser

Born in 1940 in South Africa, Margaret Visser was raised in Zambia and lived in England, France, Iraq, and the United States before settling in Toronto, Ontario. (She is a naturalized citizen of Canada.) Visser was educated at the University of Toronto, where she earned a PhD in classics in 1980. She taught classics at York University in Toronto and has published articles in scholarly and popular periodicals. Visser also appears on television and radio, discussing her discoveries about the history and social mythology of everyday life. "The extent to which we take everyday objects for granted," she says, "is the precise extent to which they govern and inform our lives." Five of Visser's books illuminate this important territory: *Much Depends on Dinner* (1986), *The Rituals of Dinner* (1991), *The Way We Are* (1994), *The Geometry of Love* (2001), and *The Gift of Thanks* (2008).

The Ritual of Fast Food

In this excerpt from *The Rituals of Dinner*, an investigation of table manners, Visser analyzes the fast-food restaurant. What do we seek when we visit such a place? How does the management oblige us? Success hinges on predictability.

An early precursor of the restaurant meal was dinner served to the public at fixed times and prices at an eating house or tavern. Such a meal was called, because of its predetermined aspects, an "ordinary," and the place where it was eaten came to be called an "ordinary," too. When a huge modern business conglomerate offers fast food to travelers on the highway, it knows that its customers are likely to desire No Surprises. They are hungry, tired, and not in a celebratory mood; they are happy to pay—provided that the price looks easily manageable—for the safely predictable, the convenient, the fast and ordinary.

Ornamental formalities are pruned away (tables and chairs are bolted to the floor, for instance, and "cutlery" is either nonexistent or not worth stealing); but rituals, in the sense of behavior and expectations that conform to preordained rules, still inform the proceedings. People who stop for a hamburger—at a Wendy's, a Harvey's, a McDonald's, or a Burger King—know exactly what the building that houses the establishment should look like; architectural variations merely ring changes on rigidly imposed themes. People want, perhaps even need, to *recognize* their chain store, to feel that they know it and its food in advance. Such an outlet is designed to be a "home away from home," on the highway, or anywhere in the city, or for Americans abroad.

Words and actions are officially laid down, learned by the staff from   3
handbooks and teaching sessions, and then picked up by customers in
the course of regular visits. Things have to be called by their correct
names ("Big Mac," "large fries"); the McDonald's rubric in 1978 required
servers to ask "Will that be with cheese, sir?" "Will there be any fries
today, sir?" and to close the transaction with "Have a nice day." The staff
wear distinctive garments; menus are always the same, and even placed
in the same spot in every outlet in the chain; prices are low and predictable; and the theme of cleanliness is proclaimed and tirelessly reiterated.
The company attempts also to play the role of a lovable host, kind and
concerned, even parental: it knows that blunt and direct confrontation
with a huge faceless corporation makes us suspicious, and even badly
behaved. So it stresses its love of children, its nostalgia for cozy warmth
and for the past (cottage roofs, warm earth tones), or its clean, brisk
modernity (glass walls, smooth surfaces, red trim). It responds to social
concerns—when they are insistent enough, sufficiently widely held, and
therefore "correct." McDonald's for example, is at present busy showing
how much it cares about the environment.

Fast-food chains know that they are ordinary. They *want* to be ordi-   4
nary, and for people to think of them as almost inseparable from the
idea of everyday food consumed outside the home. They are happy to
allow their customers time off for feasts—on Thanksgiving, Christmas,
and so on—to which they do not cater. Even those comparatively rare
holiday times, however, are turned to a profit, because the companies
know that their favorite customers—law-abiding families—are at home
together then, watching television, where carefully placed commercials
will spread the word concerning new fast-food products, and re-imprint
the image of the various chain stores for later, when the long stretches
of ordinary times return.

Families are the customers the fast-food chains want: solid citizens   5
in groups of several at a time, the adults hovering over their children,
teaching them the goodness of hamburgers, anxious to bring them up
to behave typically and correctly. Customers usually maintain a clean,
restrained, considerate, and competent demeanor as they swiftly, grate-
fully, and informally eat. Fast-food operators have recently faced the
alarming realization that crack addicts, craving salt and fat, have spread
the word among their number that French fries deliver these substances
easily, ubiquitously, cheaply, and at all hours. Dope addicts at family
"ordinaries"! The unacceptability of such a thought was neatly captured
by a news story in *The Economist* (1990) that spelled out the words a
fast-food proprietor can least afford to hear from his faithful customers,

the participants in his polite and practiced rituals: the title of the story was "Come on Mabel, let's leave." The plan to counter this threat included increasing the intensity of the lighting in fast-food establishments—drug addicts, apparently, prefer to eat in the dark.

The formality of eating at a restaurant belonging to a fast-food 6 chain depends upon the fierce regularity of its product, its simple but carefully observed rituals, and its environment. Supplying a hamburger that adheres to perfect standards of shape, weight, temperature, and consistency, together with selections from a pre-set list of trimmings, to a customer with fiendishly precise expectations is an enormously complex feat. The technology involved in performing it has been learned through the expenditure of huge sums on research, and after decades of experience—not to mention the vast political and economic ramifications involved in maintaining the supplies of cheap beef and cheap buns. But these costs and complexities are, with tremendous care, hidden from view. We know of course that, say, a Big Mac is a cultural construct: the careful control expended upon it is one of the things we are buying. But McDonald's manages—it must do so if it is to succeed in being ordinary—to provide a "casual" eating experience. Convenient, innocent simplicity is what the technology, the ruthless politics, and the elaborate organization serve to the customer.

Vocabulary

If any of the following words are new to you, try to guess their meanings from the context of Visser's essay. Test your guesses in a dictionary, and then use each new word in a sentence or two.

precursor (1)	reiterated (3)	proprietor (5)
conglomerate (1)	cater (4)	expenditure (6)
pruned (2)	hovering (5)	ramifications (6)
preordained (2)	demeanor (5)	
rubric (3)	ubiquitously (5)	

Key Ideas and Details

1. In paragraph 6 Visser writes, "Supplying a hamburger that adheres to perfect standards of shape, weight, temperature, and consistency . . . to a customer with fiendishly precise expectations is an enormously complex feat." How does this statement illustrate Visser's main idea?

2. What do you think Visser means by the statement that "a Big Mac is a cultural construct" (paragraph 6)?

Craft and Structure

1. LANGUAGE What is Visser's tone? How seriously does she take her subject?

2. Into what elements does Visser divide the fast-food restaurant? Be specific, supporting your answer with examples from the text.

3. How does Visser's analysis, breaking the fast-food experience down into its elements, help her give readers a fresh understanding of her subject?

4. OTHER METHODS In paragraph 5 Visser uses cause-and-effect analysis (Chapter 14) to explain both why crack addicts began to frequent chain restaurants and why these restaurants couldn't risk including addicts among their clientele. What does this cause-and-effect analysis add to the analysis of fast-food restaurants? How would addicts, whose money is presumably as good as anyone else's, interfere with the operation of these restaurants?

Integration of Knowledge and Ideas

1. What is Visser's purpose in writing this essay: to propose more interesting surroundings and menus at fast-food restaurants? to argue that the patrons of these establishments are too demanding? to explain how these chains manage to satisfy so many customers? something else?

2. Whom does Visser seem to imagine as her audience? Is she writing for sociologists? for managers at corporations such as McDonald's and Burger King? for diners who patronize fast-food restaurants? What evidence in the essay supports your answer?

3. FOR DISCUSSION According to Visser, people who patronize fast-food restaurants "want, perhaps even need, to *recognize* their chain store" (paragraph 2); they are looking for "the safely predictable, the convenient, the fast and ordinary" (1). Find other instances in the essay where Visser describes the people who eat in these restaurants. What portrait emerges of these customers? How does this portrait contribute to Visser's overall message?

Writing Topics

1. What kinds of junk food do you regularly consume? Think about when and where and why you eat it, and then write an essay in which you analyze your behavior as a consumer of junk food. Make a list of all the elements that constitute this activity and the setting in which it occurs. In your essay, examine each element to show what it contributes to the whole. Be sure your principle of analysis is clear to readers.

2. All of us have probably experienced a particular moment (or perhaps many moments) when we were willing to dine out on anything *but* fast food.

What, at these moments, do you think we are seeking? Following Visser's example, write a presentation analyzing the "culture" of a particular *non-chain* restaurant. How does the management deliver what the customer wants?

3. RESEARCH In her last paragraph, Visser writes that the "costs and complexities" of providing "a 'casual' eating experience" in a fast-food restaurant are "hidden from view." Does this seem appropriate to you, or would you rather know what the corporation feeding you puts into its operation, such as the "economic ramifications involved in maintaining the supplies of cheap beef and cheap buns" (paragraph 6)? Find some articles and books that examine the fast-food industry and write an essay exploring the issues this question raises for you.

4. CONNECTIONS Visser writes that fast-food chains adhere to "rituals" meant to give patrons a comforting sense of a "home away from home" (paragraph 2). Firoozeh Dumas, in "Sweet, Sour, and Resentful" (p. 248) also examines the ritual of serving meals—in her case, to recent immigrants seeking a sense of home in a new country. What importance does each writer assign to ritual in our daily lives? to food? to home? What do they see as the benefits and disadvantages of ritual in a culturally diverse world?

Thomas de Zengotita

A contributing editor for *Harper's Magazine*, Thomas de Zengotita (born 1943) earned a PhD in anthropology from Columbia University in 1985 and teaches at both the Dalton School (a private preparatory school in New York City) and New York University. His essays have appeared in the *Nation*, *Shout Magazine*, the scholarly journal *Cultural Anthropology*, and the *Huffington Post*. De Zengotita's interest in the influences of mass media led him to develop the analytic concept of *mediation*, which theorizes that every aspect of our consciousness is filtered through what we see and hear in popular culture. He elaborates on this central idea of his critical work in *Mediated: How the Media Shapes Your World and the Way You Live in It* (2005), his widely acclaimed first book.

American Idol Worship

A major tenet of de Zengotita's theory of mediation is that the media flatter audiences by suggesting that popular culture is ultimately about the people who consume it. (As he explains it, contemporary media offer "a place where everything is addressed to us, everything is for us, and nothing is beyond us anymore.") In this essay, written in 2006 and published in both the *Los Angeles Times* and the *Christian Science Monitor*, de Zengotita examines how this flattery works in one of the most popular media productions going — the television show *American Idol*.

When the ratings numbers came in after last week's Grammy Awards, the news wasn't good for the professionals. A show that features amateurs had attracted a far bigger audience than had one with the likes of Madonna, Coldplay, and U2. . . . *American Idol* drew almost twice as many viewers as the awards show. What's going on here? Why does this reality show consistently attract the weekly attention of close to 35 million viewers?   1

It's a nexus of factors shaping the "virtual revolution" unfolding all around us, on so many fronts. Think chat rooms, *MySpace.com*, blogs, life journals illustrated with photos snapped by cell phones, flash-mobbing, marathon running, focus groups, talk radio, e-mails to news shows, camcorders, sponsored sports teams for tots — and every garage band in town with its own CD. What do all these platforms have in common? They are all devoted to otherwise anonymous people who don't want to be mere spectators. In this virtual revolution, it's not workers against capitalists — that's so nineteenth century. In our mediated world, it's spectators against celebrities, with spectators demanding a share of the last scarce resource in the overdeveloped world — attention. The *American Idol* format combines essential elements of this revolution.   2

Have you followed the ruckus over why people don't have heroes **3** anymore—in the old-fashioned statesman, warrior, genius, artist kind of way? People concerned with education are especially alarmed. They invest a lot of energy in trying to rekindle an aura of greatness around the Founding Fathers. But it's hopeless. Ask natural-born citizens of the mediated world who their heroes are, and their answers fall into one of two categories: somebody in their personal lives or performers—above all, pop music performers.

The "everyday hero" answer reflects the virtual revolution, but what **4** about performers? Why are they so important to their fans? Because, in concert especially, these new kinds of heroes create an experience of belonging that their fans would otherwise never know, living as they do in a marketplace of lifestyles that can make one's existence feel optional. That's why there's a religious quality to a concert when the star meets the audience's awesome expectations and creates, in song and persona, a moment in which each individual feels personally understood and, at the same time, fused with other fans in a larger common identity. "Performer heroes" are, in the end, all about us. They don't summon us to serve a cause—other than the one of being who we are. So, naturally, they have been leaders of the virtual revolution. From their perch on high, they make us the focus of attention.

American Idol takes the next step. It unites both aspects of the **5** relationship—in the climactic final rounds, a fan becomes an idol; the ultimate dream of our age comes true before our eyes and in our hearts.

That's mediational magic. **6**

And don't forget the power of music. *American Idol* wouldn't be **7** what it is if, say, amateur actors were auditioning. You can disagree with someone about movie stars and TV shows and still be friends. But you can't be friends with someone who loves the latest boy band, in a totally unironic way, if you are into Gillian Welch. That's because tastes in pop music go right to the core of who you are, with a depth and immediacy no other art form can match. Music takes hold of you on levels deeper than articulated meaning. That's why words, sustained by music, have such power. There is nothing like a song for expressing who we are.

That brings us to the early rounds of *American Idol*, in which contes- **8** tants are chosen for the final competition in Hollywood. The conventional wisdom is that they're an exercise in public humiliation, long a staple of reality TV. That's not wrong, as far as it goes, but it isn't just any old humiliation exercise—it is the most excruciating form of voluntary personal humiliation the human condition allows for because it involves the most revealing kind of performance there is, this side of pornography. During this phase of the show, the audience, knowing it will eventually fuse in a positive way with a finalist idol, gets to be in the most popular clique on the planet, rendering snarky judgments on one of the most embarrassing pools of losers ever assembled.

American Idol gives you so many ways to feel good about yourself.   9
No wonder it's a hit.   10

Vocabulary

Try to guess the meanings of any of the following words that you are unsure of, based on their context in de Zengotita's essay. Test your guesses in a dictionary, and then use each word in a sentence of your own.

nexus (2)	persona (4)	excruciating (8)
ruckus (3)	climactic (5)	clique (8)
rekindle (3)	unironic (7)	snarky (8)
aura (3)	articulated (7)	

Key Ideas and Details

1. What is de Zengotita's thesis? Where does he state it explicitly? Summarize the central meaning of de Zengotita's analysis in a sentence or two of your own.

2. According to de Zengotita, what elements define the "virtual revolution" (paragraph 2)? How does *American Idol* bring together these elements to create an irresistible media experience?

3. What do you think de Zengotita means when he writes, "*American Idol* . . . unites both aspects of the relationship—in the climactic final rounds, a fan becomes an idol; the ultimate dream of our age comes true before our eyes and in our hearts. . . . That's mediational magic" (paragraphs 5 and 6)? According to de Zengotita, how does *American Idol* transform both the contestants and the audience?

Craft and Structure

1. LANGUAGE This essay combines loose, informal language—"What's going on here?" (paragraph 1) and "that's so nineteenth century" (2)—with scholarly vocabulary to explore a complex idea. What do you suppose is the author's purpose in employing these different levels of diction? What is the effect on you as a reader? (If necessary, see *diction* in the Glossary.)

2. What is de Zengotita's principle of analysis, and what elements of *American Idol* does he analyze? How does he reassemble these elements into a new whole? Support your answer with evidence from the essay.

3. De Zengotita begins his essay by contrasting *American Idol*'s ratings with those for the Grammy Awards. How does beginning with this comparison foreshadow the conclusions he draws about the implications of the "virtual revolution" in popular culture?

4. OTHER METHODS In addition to division, de Zengotita uses cause-and-effect analysis (Chapter 14) to show how *American Idol*'s individual elements explain its popularity. What does this cause-and-effect analysis add to the analysis of *American Idol*? What would be lost without it?

Integration of Knowledge and Ideas

1. What do you think was de Zengotita's purpose in writing this essay? Does he want to shock, inform, persuade, or entertain his readers? something else? What evidence from the text supports your viewpoint?

2. What assumptions does de Zengotita make about his audience? Does he assume that his readers are familiar with *American Idol*? with his theory of *mediation*? How familiar would readers have to be with the show (or the author's theory) to understand de Zengotita's analysis?

3. FOR DISCUSSION De Zengotita's immediate subject of analysis is *American Idol*, but he's also using the show to examine a wider phenomenon. What is that wider phenomenon? How does the author's analysis of *American Idol* explain it?

Writing Topics

1. Write an essay or create a presentation in which you describe your favorite TV show and explain what makes it so enjoyable for you. Just as de Zengotita took *American Idol* apart to understand its popularity, explain what elements contribute to the appeal of the show you selected. Does its appeal rest mostly on the actors involved, the places depicted, the story line, or other features? Does it make you think about who you are as a person or change your view of the world? If it is merely good "entertainment," describe what makes it so.

2. American television programs are watched all over the world: *Baywatch*, for example, is one of the most popular shows in Germany, and *Desperate Housewives* is popular in China. Many global viewers say they watch the programming to improve their English language skills or to learn about American culture. But what are they learning? Write an essay that focuses on a particular type of show—network news, for example, or medical dramas—and explores how a non-American viewer might interpret it. Does the program provide an accurate depiction of life in the United States, or does it distort reality?

3. RESEARCH Although the idea of *mediation* may seem complicated, it boils down to a relatively simple concept: de Zengotita believes that popular culture influences the way we perceive the world and ourselves. What do you think of this notion? Do the media control how you think, or can you pick and choose among their offerings without being affected in any meaningful way? Find more information on de Zengotita's theory and write an essay that uses the concept of mediation to explore your relationship with an aspect of popular culture of your choosing (for example, you might examine how a fashion or lifestyle magazine has changed the way you look at yourself, or describe how a song changed your attitude toward a problem you were facing). Or, if you don't accept the concept of mediation, write an essay that uses examples from your own experience to explain why you disagree with de Zengotita.

4. CONNECTIONS Like de Zengotita, Margaret Visser, in "The Ritual of Fast Food" (p. 189), writes seriously about a subject that some people would consider unworthy of serious attention. How informative and useful do you find such analyses of popular culture? Where does each essay tell us something significant about ourselves, or, in contrast, where does it fail in trying to make the trivial seem important? Is popular culture—magazines, television, Hollywood movies, *YouTube* videos, self-help books, toys, fast-food restaurants, music—best looked at critically, best ignored, or best simply enjoyed, do you think? Explain your answers in an essay, using plenty of examples to support your thesis.

Pat Mora

A poet, speaker, and literacy advocate, Pat Mora was born in 1942 in El Paso, Texas, and grew up in a bilingual family of Mexican heritage. She received a bachelor's degree from Texas Western College and a master's degree from the University of Texas, El Paso. Mora taught high school and college English for several years and worked as a college administrator and museum director at the University of New Mexico for nearly a decade before turning her focus to writing. "Like many Chicana writers," she says, she "was motivated to write because . . . our voices were absent from what is labeled American literature." In addition to voicing herself in two dozen books of poetry, Mora has written several illustrated books for children, the memoir *House of Houses* (1997), and a volume of literary and cultural criticism, *Nepantla: Essays from the Land in the Middle* (1993). She is also the founder of El Día de los Niños / El Día de los Libros (Childen's Day / Book Day), a nationwide family literacy project. She lives in Santa Fe, New Mexico, and Cincinnati, Ohio.

Great Expectations

In this extract from *Nepantla* (the book's title is a Mexican Indian word meaning "place in the middle"), Mora analyzes the overarching message sent to young Latinas by advertisers. When girls take such messages at face value, Mora worries, they help the advertiser but hurt themselves.

Latinas are labeled a *double minority*. The words are depressing. They 1
don't quite sound like "twice-blessed." Little wonder that most Latinas, whether in the Southwest or elsewhere in this country, don't dwell on this uncomfortable term. Anyway, who has time? We often are too busy playing the game of Great Expectations.

Most humans play some form of this game; most of us strive to 2
fulfill the dreams that our society, our family, and our self have for us. Latinas, though, confront some unique challenges, and we often receive little support in fulfilling our potential.

In the eighties this country began to hear a Latin beat. Generations 3
of determined women and men had questioned discriminatory hiring and promotion practices, immigration laws, inadequate health-care systems, biased arts council panels, and had endured meeting after meeting requesting and ultimately demanding equal opportunities for our people. Singers, writers, and artists had worked to capture the vigor of *lo mejicano*.[1] Their works are more and more visible. And demographics

---

[1] Spanish: *Mexicanness*. [Editors' note.]

conspire with us. These populations shifts, combined with historic equity struggles, mean we live in a society that finds it grudgingly necessary to notice our community. We can't ignore even this luke-warm willingness to respond to the needs of Latinos, whether by politicians, corporations, or federal or state agencies, because we know the grim statistics on wages and education for US Latinos.

Ah, but our millions have billions to spend. Hundreds of millions   4
are targeted by advertisers, who now like us and suddenly care deeply about our needs. Unlike those enmeshed in the political machinations of English Only,[2] advertisers are happy to be bilingual. Well, their messages are. They speak to us *en español*.[3] "*Ven es la hora de Miller.*"[4] Coors tells us, "*Celebre! Cinco de mayo.*"[5] Canadian Club says, "*¡Qué pareja! Canadian Club y tu!*"[6] Xerox tells us that its Hispana employees are "*especial.*"[7]

Advertisers track our values and thus our buying habits. Their analy-   5
ses confirm the conclusions of psychologists and sociologists: we are loyal: to our families, the Spanish language, this country. Advertisers like loyalty, which they hope translates to brand-name loyalty. For those to whom English is a new language, brand names probably do bring a sense of security and predictability in the cacophony of strange noises. I remember that when my grandmother, who never spoke or wanted to speak English though all three of her children were born here, had a headache, only Bayer would do. She trusted the symbol on that small, pain-easing white circle.

Politicians, of course, are busy courting our loyalty too, because we   6
are a young segment of an aging population. No more will candidates bite into a *tamal*[8] with corn husk in place. Media visibility, the occasional Latina actor, the occasional Latino family in a commercial, can in an odd way foster a sense of group identity, even though cultural sym-

---

[2] A movement to make English the official language of the United States, proposing that all official government documents and business be written and conducted solely in English. [Editors' note.]

[3] Spanish: *in Spanish.* [Editors' note.]

[4] Spanish: "*It's Miller time.*" [Editors' note.]

[5] Spanish: "*Celebrate! The fifth of May.*" Cinco de Mayo, a commemoration of the Mexican army's 1862 victory over the French in the Battle of Puebla during the Franco-Mexican war (1862–67), is a minor holiday in Mexico. [Editors' note.]

[6] Spanish: "*What a pair!* Canadian Club *and you.*" Canadian Club is a brand of whiskey. [Editors' note.]

[7] Spanish: "*special.*" [Editors' note.]

[8] Cornmeal dough stuffed with ground meat or sweet filling and steamed in a corn husk. [Editors' note.]

bols are usually being appropriated, used. Our growing population makes it less threatening to delve into our cultural past, for what we discover suddenly interests people—perhaps because it is trendy, but the information nourishes us.

Such targeted marketing doesn't change the reality that this country often views us as either fiery, and thus less rational, less than intellectual; or as docile, and thus less than effective, less than assertive. A woman named María might be considered as a candidate for a position as a domestic worker or secretary, but it is unlikely that she will seriously be considered as a candidate for senator. Yet. How easy is it, then, for a Latina to deal with a society that finds her dark eyes and hair attractive, but that is a bit surprised to see her aggressively pursuing a goal, striving to become an architect or veterinarian or literary critic? T'ain't easy.   7

And then there are our families. Intense emotional ties. Our parents, siblings, and relatives are a source of indescribable strength. Perhaps because marriage traditionally has been so important in our culture, men and our families often equate an attractive physical appearance with true womanhood. Many a *tía* or *abuelita*[9] at home wants her niece to pursue a career, preferably in teaching or nursing, but *Tía* is secretly hoping—and probably praying—that we'll receive both a degree and a marriage proposal. She loves us and longs for some fine, respectful, hard-working man who will protect this vulnerable single woman from financial worries and the world's indifference.   8

Our parents also may do some frowning. How happy will they be at the news that we're considering joining the space program or applying for graduate school in another state? Frowns may really multiply once we're married with a family and announce that we need to begin traveling. Their frowns will say, "Neglect your children and husband? What kind of a woman are you?" Often their concern is genuine, and it is not easy to help them see that their desire to protect can be an unacknowledged desire to control.   9

Hard choices. We know women are socialized to please. How does a bright, talented Latina weather her family's displeasure when she works long hours rather than visiting regularly with sisters and cousins? *Tía*'s frowns have a way of giving us tired blood.   10

And what about the woman who gazes back in the mirror? What Great Expectations does she have for us? Chances are she wants us to   11

---

[9] *Tía* is Spanish for *aunt. Abuelita* means *grandmother.* [Editors' note.]

look energetic, to excel in our chosen work, to struggle against injustice, to be a loving and respectful daughter, niece. Chances are she will never be quite satisfied with our efforts. She will be pressuring us, often relentlessly, to try harder, to produce better work. She can be our harshest critic. Convincing her to wink back at us occasionally may be a lifelong challenge.

The Latina who completes her college education—a small percent- 12 age of us—may indeed now have more opportunities, whether for employment or for service on panels, committees, and boards, which is appropriate. As double minorities committed to societal change, though, we find ourselves working doubly hard, struggling to prove to others that women like us are not a risk. We often feel tired, alone.

Alone, yet emeshed in family responsibilities, concerned about 13 our parents and siblings, about our children. And we worry about our national family or community as we hear the statistics about our growing Latina population. If Latinas have families—and fewer of us are marrying—they tend to be larger than the average, and more and more we head these families alone, often in poverty. Although we have high participation in the work force, we tend to be clerical or service workers. Our median income remains below that of Anglos. How well prepared are we for these challenges? How are we assisting other women to plan for the future, to have realistic expectations? Too many of us don't finish high school, too many of us who complete community college programs don't transfer to four-year institutions, too many of us are denied the opportunity to attend colleges away from home, too many of us are not encouraged fully to develop our talents.

As we mother, teach, write, mentor the next generation of women, 14 we need to examine the lives of women in this country, our lives, not as we might want them to be, but as they are. It's difficult to change what we don't understand. What do we know about ourselves and about the women who will appear in our offices and classrooms? What do we know about our inside lives, the inside lives of the female middle class? Most women in the United States are not reading professional journals in their apartments or houses today. We ingest pollutants—toxic ideas and attitudes—while we watch movies and television or read steamy novels or relax with women's magazines. Women in this country continue to devour novels about women who find comfort in the image of being swept off tiny feet by determined, hard-muscled men.

We turn slick, musk-scented magazine pages that promise The Secrets 15 of Skin Polish, 9 Ways to Prevent Wrinkles, Beauty from Head to Toe. For the price of the magazine, we are lured to believe that we can transform our flabby egos and disappointing bodies into the confident creatures who gaze boldly, sirens who beckon us to become perfect, smiling decorations. Listen to the bait. We are promised that we can be glamorous, attractive, radiant, exhilarating, classic, breathtaking, dazzling, legendary, mysterious. Similar magazines from Mexico promise that we can be *sensual, increíble, sexy, elegante, bella, enigmática.*[10] We're taught the world over that it's our job to be pretty. Too often do we brood when we're five or eighty-five about our exteriors, peer in annoyance at our hips (too wide), noses (too long), lips (too thin). Some of us stop eating or eat until we're sick. We bare our unsatisfactory bodies so they can be reshaped, be made more loveable by surgeons who can mold us into beauty and happiness. How much time we spend looking the part, a part we didn't write.

In her documentary *A Famine Within*, Katherine Gilday skillfully 16 reveals our obsession with The Body, the difficulty we have accepting and loving ourselves, our imperfect selves. She shows how we are bombarded with images of women who seldom look like the women in our lives or in our mirror. Our shapes and the shapes of our mothers are steadily described as inferior, proof of our lack of self-control. We define others by their contours, equate thinness with morality. The young women Gilday interviews visibly struggle for words ugly enough to describe their reaction to being overweight. To be fat is to be "grotesque." Fashion models are often role models, says Gilday. Decorative, silent women.

Driving down the freeway, we see, "You've Come a Long Way, 17 Baby."[11] Baby? The woman smiling at us casually holding a cigarette is young, sleek, glamorous. Success is being defined for us as eternal youth, a carefree life, trendy clothes, and getting to do what men do—in this case, savor a health hazard. We want to define ourselves in broader and richer terms than that, but how do we help young women, all young women, to perceive such manipulation and to wrench their lives free from images that bind?

---

[10] Spanish: *sensual, incredible, sexy, elegant, beautiful, mysterious.* [Editors' note.]
[11] An advertising slogan for Virginia Slims, a brand of cigarettes targeted at women. [Editors' note.]

Vocabulary

If you are not familiar with any of the following words, try to determine their meanings from the context of Mora's essay. Test your guesses in a dictionary, and then use each word in a sentence of your own.

vigor (3)	machinations (4)	docile (7)
demographics (3)	cacophony (5)	median (13)
conspire (3)	courting (6)	sirens (15)
equity (3)	appropriated (6)	bombarded (16)
enmeshed (4)	delve (6)	

Key Ideas and Details

1. Why are Latinas "labeled a *double minority*" (paragraph 1)? What makes the label significant to Mora?

2. "We often are too busy playing the game of Great Expectations," Mora writes in her first paragraph. What does she mean? What does the "game" consist of, and what is its goal? Why is winning more difficult for Latinas?

3. What is wrong, in Mora's opinion, with media portrayals that depict Latinas as either "fiery" or "docile" (paragraph 7)?

4. Mora's essay does not contain a direct thesis statement, but her main idea is clear. Express the point of her analysis in your own words.

Craft and Structure

1. LANGUAGE A poet, Mora enlivens her prose with figures of speech. Find several examples of metaphors and personifications and comment on their effectiveness. (See p. 58 for more on figures of speech.)

2. According to Mora, what have advertisers learned about Latino values? How does she use those values to organize her essay?

3. What elements of popular culture does Mora examine? What principle of analysis does she use to reassemble those elements into a new whole?

4. OTHER METHODS Mora's essay relies heavily on cause-and-effect analysis to examine the impact of popular culture on Latina women (paragraph 14). If media messages promoting loyalty and beauty are the cause, what does Mora believe are the effects?

Integration of Knowledge and Ideas

1. For whom is Mora writing? How can you tell?

2. In paragraph 16, Mora summarizes the content of a documentary film. What is the subject of the film? How does citing it contribute to or support Mora's analysis?

3. FOR DISCUSSION What kind of future does Mora envision for young Latinas? How does she propose they achieve such goals?

Writing Topics

1. Toward the end of her essay, Mora suggests that the images in fashion magazines make Latinas feel inadequate—a response that some say is the direct result of advertising practices that create insecurities for all types of people in order to exploit them. Choose an example of advertising that you think appeals to a real or invented insecurity to sell a product, and analyze its message in a brief essay or presentation. Are the advertiser's techniques effective? ethical? entertaining? Be sure to identify a principle of analysis for your response and to support your argument with details from the advertisement.

2. This essay was written two decades ago. To what extent do Mora's concerns and criticisms still hold true? Select two or three of her statements and think of some contemporary examples that either support or undermine her claims. For instance, how visible are the works of Latino "[s]ingers, writers, and artists" (paragraph 3) today? Do you know of any Latina politicians or professionals (7)? Write an essay of your own responding to Mora's essay. Be sure to include examples to support your view.

3. RESEARCH Mora mentions demographics and the "grim statistics on wages and education for US Latinos" in paragraphs 3 and 13 but doesn't specify the numbers. Go the Web site of the Pew Hispanic Center (*pewhispanic.org*) and search the research group's data sets and statistical portraits for recent information on these subjects. For instance, what percentage of the US population identifies as Latino? How many Latino men and women finish high school? college? How do their earnings compare with the national average? How many Latino families are headed by married couples? How many of them live in poverty? Create a table or graph to report your findings.

4. CONNECTIONS Mora writes of familial disapproval of married Latina women who pursue educations and careers. How does this pressure relate to the marital roles that Judy Brady focuses on in her essay "I Want a Wife" (p. 308)? Write an essay analyzing these writers' attitudes toward tradition and feminism. How much do Mora and Brady seem to have in common? Use evidence from both essays to support your response.

WRITING WITH THE METHOD

DIVISION OR ANALYSIS

Select one of the following topics, or any other topic they suggest, for an essay developed by analysis. Be sure to choose a topic you care about so that analysis is a means of communicating an idea, not an end in itself.

People, Animals, and Objects

1. The personality of a friend or relative
2. An animal such as a cat, dog, horse, cow, spider, or bat
3. A machine or an appliance such as a car engine, harvesting combine, laptop computer, hair dryer, toaster, or sewing machine
4. A nonmotorized vehicle such as a skateboard, in-line skate, bicycle, or snowboard
5. A building such as a hospital, theater, or sports arena

Ideas

6. The perfect city
7. The perfect crime
8. A theory or concept in a field such as biology, mathematics, or astronomy
9. The evidence in a political argument (written, spoken, or reported in the news)
10. A well-rounded education

Aspects of Culture

11. A style of dress or "look," such as that associated with the typical business-person, bodybuilder, rap musician, or outdoors enthusiast
12. A typical hero or villain in science fiction, romance novels, war movies, or movies or novels about adolescents
13. A television or film comedy
14. A literary work: short story, novel, poem, essay
15. A visual work: painting, sculpture, building
16. A musical work: song, concerto, symphony, opera
17. A performance: sports, acting, dance, music, speech
18. The slang of a particular group or occupation

WRITING ABOUT THE THEME

LOOKING AT POPULAR CULTURE

1. The essays by Margaret Visser (p. 189), Thomas de Zengotita (p. 194), and Pat Mora (p. 199) all include the theme that what you see — whether in fast-food restaurants, entertainment, or advertising — is not all you get. Think of something you have used, seen, or otherwise experienced that made you suspect a hidden message or agenda. Consider, for example, a childhood toy, a popular breakfast cereal, a political speech, a magazine, a textbook, a video game, a movie, or a visit to a theme park. Using the essays in this chapter as models, write an analysis of your subject, making sure to divide it into distinct elements and to conclude it by reassembling those elements into a new whole.

2. Luci Tapahanso (p. 181) and Pat Mora both analyze advertising aimed at minority groups. Mora calls for an awakening to negative "images that bind" Mexican American girls and young women. Tapahanso, in contrast, thinks that Native Americans found cause for celebration in a positive commercial that "showed Indians as we live today." What do you think of niche advertising? Is Mora's concern justified, or are the ads she singles out unusual? How common are ads like the one Tapahanso analyzes? Consider ads you've seen or pay close attention to the ads as you're watching television or surfing the Internet over a week or so. Then write an essay addressing whether advertisers seem to treat the differences among people fairly or to exploit those differences. Are there notable exceptions in either case?

3. Thomas de Zengotita argues that popular culture is moving in a new direction that shifts power to the audience. How do de Zengotita's observations affect your reading of the other selections in this chapter? For instance, do interactive media like those dissected in *Wired* magazine (p. 178) give readers more or less control over the information they consume? Does Jon Pareles (p. 181) present Keith Richards as an "everyday hero" or a "performer hero"? Did Native American viewers appreciate the advertisement described by Luci Tapahanso because it made them the center of attention? Are people drawn to fast-food restaurants because they crave the comfort of familiarity, as Margaret Visser suggests? How does de Zengotita's idea that the media is ultimately about its consumers resonate with Pat Mora's concerns about the effects of advertisements, novels, and magazines on Latinas' perceptions of themselves? Write an essay using de Zengotita's concept of mediation to explain the appeal (or lack of appeal) of one or several of the popular culture examples in this chapter. Quote de Zengotita's analysis and passages from other writers as necessary, being sure to use proper citation format (see pp. 73–82) to acknowledge your sources.

NATIONAL POPULATION BY RACE
UNITED STATES: 2010

PERCENT OF POPULATION	CHANGE 2000-2010
White alone 72.4%	5.7% ⬆
Black or African American alone 12.6%	12.3% ⬆
American Indian and Alaska Native alone 0.9%	18.4% ⬆
Asian alone 4.8%	43.3% ⬆
Native Hawaiian and Other Pacific Islander alone 0.2%	35.4% ⬆
Some Other Race alone 6.2%	24.4% ⬆
Two or More Races 2.9%	32.0% ⬆

NATIONAL POPULATION BY HISPANIC OR LATINO ORIGIN
UNITED STATES: 2010

PERCENT OF POPULATION	CHANGE 2000-2010
Hispanic or Latino 16.3%	43.0% ⬆
Not Hispanic or Latino 83.7%	4.9% ⬆

10

CLASSIFICATION

▶
SORTING FRIENDS AND NEIGHBORS

We classify when we sort things into groups: kinds of cars, styles of writing, types of customers. Because it creates order, **classification** helps us make sense of our experiences and our surroundings. With it, we see the correspondences among like things and distinguish them from unlike things, similarities and distinctions that can be especially helpful when making a decision or encouraging others to see things from a new perspective. You use classification when you prioritize your to-do list, sort your laundry, or organize your music collection; you might also draw on the method to choose among types of smartphone apps, to rearrange supplies in your work space, or to argue at a club meeting that some types of volunteer projects are more valuable than others. Because classification helps us name things, remember them, and discuss them with others, it is also a useful method for developing and sharing ideas in writing.

 ## Seeing Classification

Once every ten years, the federal government undertakes the enormous project of conducting a census, or count, of the country's population. Using mail-in questionnaires and door-to-door interviews, the US Census Bureau attempts to get a snapshot of the American population, looking at how people fall into categories such as job types, family structures, and housing arrangements. The latest census raised some controversy: for the first time, the 2010 questionnaire allowed respondents to identify as multiracial; the questions also distinguished between race (white, black, and so forth) and ethnicity (Hispanic / Latino or not). The graphic shown here reports the results of the race and ethnicity questions. Examine both the percentages reported and the categories themselves. How diverse is the American population? Which groups are largest, and smallest? Which groups represent the fastest-growing portions of the population as a whole? Why do you suppose Hispanic or Latino origin was not grouped as a racial category? How does the distinction between race and ethnicity reflect perceptions of multiculturalism in the United States? Is the mixture shown in the table similar to the diversity you see in your neighborhood?

Reading Classification

Writers classify primarily to explain a pattern in a subject that might not have been noticed before: a sportswriter, for instance, might observe that great basketball defenders tend to fall into one of three groups based on their style of play: the shot blockers, the stealers, and the brawlers. Sometimes, writers also classify to persuade readers that one group is superior: that same sportswriter might argue that shot blockers are the most effective defenders because they not only create turnovers like the stealers do, but they also intimidate the opponent like the brawlers do.

Classification involves a three-step process:

1. Separate things into their elements, using the method of division or analysis (previous chapter).
2. Isolate the similarities among the elements.
3. Group or classify the things based on those similarities, matching like with like.

A familiar example of classification — at least in its broad outlines — is the scientific system of ordering all living things into categories. The primary groups are the animals and the plants. Then each divides into subclasses, each of which in turn divides into smaller subclasses, and so on. The diagram below shows the subclasses for one larger class, the chordates (animals with spines).

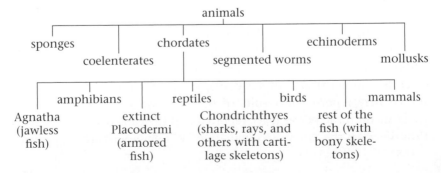

All the members of the overall group—the animals—share at least one characteristic: the need to obtain food instead of manufacturing it, as all the plants do. The animals in each subcategory also share at least one characteristic: some chordates may be jawless, for instance, or have cartilage skeletons. The animals in each subcategory are also independent of one another, and none of them is essential to the existence of the category; indeed, as the extinct armored fish indicate, a category continues to exist as a slot even when no representatives fill it at the moment.

The number of groups in a classification scheme depends entirely on the basis for establishing the classes in the first place. There are two systems:

- In a *complex classification* like that used for the animal kingdom, each individual fits firmly into one class because of at least one distinguishing feature shared with all members of that class but not with any members of any other classes. All the fishes classified as Chondrichthyes have cartilage skeletons, but none of the jawless fishes do.

- In a *binary or two-part classification*, two classes are set up, often one with a certain characteristic and one without it. For instance, fish could be classified into those with bony skeletons and those without them. A binary scheme is useful to emphasize the possession of a particular characteristic, but it is limited if it specifies nothing about the members of the "other" class except that they lack the trait. (An old joke claims that there are two kinds of people in the world—those who classify and all others.)

Sorting items demands a **principle of classification** that determines the groups by distinguishing them. The principle in sorting the animals, for instance, is their anatomy—the structure of their bodies. Principles for sorting a year's movies might be genre (action-adventure, comedy, drama); place of origin (domestic, foreign); or cost of production (low-budget, medium-budget, high-budget). The choice of a principle of classification depends on the writer's main interest in the subject.

Although a writer may emphasize one class over the others, the classification itself must be complete and consistent. A classification of movies by genre would be incomplete if it omitted comedies. It would be inconsistent if it included action-adventures, comedies, dramas, low-budget films, and foreign films: such a system mixes *three* principles (genre, cost, origin); it omits whole classes (what about high-budget domestic dramas?); and it overlaps other classes (a low-budget foreign action-adventure would fit in three different groups).

Analyzing Classification in Paragraphs

Nelson George (born 1957) is a filmmaker, television producer, journalist, novelist, and noted historian and critic of African American music. This paragraph is from "Strangers on His Street," a memoir of the changes in his New York City neighborhood, first published in the *New York Times* in 2009.

When I moved to the neighborhood, a significant number of white home owners were living on the glorious brownstone "South" streets like Oxford, Porter, and Elliot, but <u>their presence was dwarfed by two kinds of black folks.</u> First, there were the working-class people who drank at Frank's bar on Fulton Street, ate Sunday brunch at Two Steps Down on Dekalb Avenue, and avoided eye contact with the minorleague clockers selling crack cocaine and marijuana outside a bodega on Lafayette near Fort Greene Place. Then there were aspiring young black artists like me . . . a wave of young writers, designers, cartoonists, dancers, actors, and musicians who gave parties, walked the streets, and worked hard at becoming good and famous. A few did both. But in the last half-dozen years, many of my contemporaries have departed. . . . Black artists still live in Fort Greene, but they are only a piece of the neighborhood's color palette.

> Principle of classification (topic sentence underlined): black residents of the Fort Greene neighborhood
>
> 1. Working-class people: focused on daily life
>
> 2. Artists: focused on future success

Luis Alberto Urrea (born 1955) is an award-winning poet, fiction writer, essayist, and investigative journalist whose work often focuses on the lives of impoverished Mexicans. In the following passage from "Night Shift," a 2012 essay about his former job as a campground janitor, Urrea classifies temporary neighbors in a California motor-home park.

The better sections of the campground were reserved for the RVs and fifth wheels. They had nice fat pullouts with room for an extra car or pickup, a little grass so they could unfurl their awnings and set up their lawn chairs. Electric and sewer hookups. It was deluxe, as far as blacktop roughing it went. The smaller RVs, Class 1 and shorter, got tawdrier, smaller parking slots. Yellower grass in narrower strips. Fewer oleanders. Farther from the golf course. And the suckers who came with tents—who should have had the smarts to head up to the Cuyamaca Mountains and at least hear a blue jay—why, they

> Principle of classification: equipment ownership
>
> 1. Large RVs: given "deluxe" accommodations
>
> 2. Small RVs: provided with "tawdrier" spaces
>
> 3. Tents: pushed aside to an undesirable area

were crammed over on the far side, near the beach, but also near the adjacent trailer park with its . . . nocturnal Bachman Turner Overdrive recitals. Stray cats from the trailer park cruised our property, but there wasn't any policy about them. They kept rodents under control and might have even dissuaded the skunks, which really enjoyed the French fries and Sno Balls scattered around the trailers.

Developing an Essay by Classification

▶ Getting Started

Classification essays are often assigned in school: you might be asked to explain the major branches of government for a civics class, for instance, or to categorize personality types in a business class. When you need to develop your own subject for a classification essay, think of one large class of things whose members you've noticed fall into subclasses, such as different types of study habits, marching band performers, or charity fund-raising requests. Be sure that your general subject forms a class in its own right—that all its members share at least one important quality. Then look for your principle of classification, the quality or qualities that distinguish some members from others. One such principle for charity fund-raising requests might be the different methods of delivery, such as telephone calls, rallies, social gatherings, advertisements, and social media campaigns.

While generating ideas for your classification, keep track of them in a list, diagram, or outline to ensure that your principle is applied thoroughly (all classes) and consistently (each class relating to the principle). Fill in the list, diagram, or outline with the distinguishing features of each class and with examples that will clarify your scheme.

▶ Forming a Thesis

You will want to state your principle of classification in a thesis sentence so that you know where you're going and your readers know where you're taking them. Be sure the sentence also conveys a *reason* for the classification so that the essay does not become a dull list of categories. The following draft thesis sentence is mechanical; the revision is more interesting.

DRAFT THESIS SENTENCE   Charity fund-raising requests are delivered in many ways.

REVISED THESIS SENTENCE   Of the many ways to deliver charity fund-raising requests, the three that rely on personal contact are generally the most effective.

(Note that the revised thesis sentence implies a further classification based on whether the appeals involve personal contact.)

▶ Organizing

The **introduction** to a classification essay should make clear why the classification is worthwhile: What situation prompted the essay? What do readers already know about the subject? What use might they make of the information you will provide? Unless your principle of classification is self-evident, you may want to explain it briefly—though save extensive explanation for the body of the essay.

In the body of the essay, the classes may be arranged in order of decreasing familiarity or increasing importance or size—whatever pattern provides the emphasis you want and clarifies your scheme for readers. You should at least mention each class, but some classes may demand considerable space and detail.

A classification essay often ends with a **conclusion** that restores the wholeness of the subject. Among other uses, the conclusion might summarize the classes, comment on the significance of one particular class in relation to the whole, or point out a new understanding of the whole subject gained from the classification.

▶ Drafting

For the first draft of your classification, your main goal will be to establish your scheme: spelling out the purpose and principle of classification and defining the groups so that they are complete and consistent, covering the subject without mixing principles or overlapping. The more you've been able to plan your scheme, the less difficult the draft will be. If you can also fill in the examples and other details needed to develop the groups, do so.

Be sure to consider your readers' needs as you draft. For a subject familiar to readers, such as study habits, you probably wouldn't need to justify your principle of classification, but you would need to enliven the classes themselves with vivid examples. For an unfamiliar subject, in contrast, you might need to take considerable care in explaining the principle of classification as well as in detailing the classes.

▶ Revising and Editing

The following questions and the information in the focus box below can help you revise and edit your classification.

- *Will readers see the purpose of your classification?* Let readers know early why you are bothering to classify your subject, and keep this purpose evident throughout the essay.

- *Is your classification complete?* Your principle of classification should create categories that encompass every representative of the general subject. If some representatives will not fit the scheme, you may have to create a new category or revise the existing categories to include them.

- *Is your classification consistent?* Consistency is essential to save readers from confusion or irritation. Make sure all the classes reflect the same principle and that they do not overlap. Remedy flaws by adjusting the classes or creating new ones.

- *Are your paragraphs fully developed?* It's not unusual to get so focused on identifying and sorting categories during the draft stage that you neglect the details. In that case, you'll need to go back and provide examples, comparisons, and other particulars to make the groups clear. (For more on developing paragraphs through specifics, see pp. 22–34.)

FOCUS ON **Punctuation**

A crucial aim of revising a classification essay is clarifying how your examples and details fit with your principle of classification. To help readers visualize your categories and the elements within them, try using punctuation — especially colons — for clarity and effect.

Previewing the categories you will discuss by listing them in your thesis statement can help readers follow your classification. Introduce the list with a colon, being careful that all the items in the list are parallel in form (see pp. 55 and 278) and separated by commas:

UNCLEAR   The most effective fund-raising requests rely on personal contact with friends and acquaintances: telephone calls, social gatherings and rallying.

CLEAR   The most effective fund-raising requests rely on personal contact with friends and acquaintances: telephone calls, social gatherings, and rallies.

You can also use a colon to introduce a quotation. Remember to surround direct quotations with quotation marks and to cite the source:

Marion Winik points out that family members aren't necessarily friends: "Most of them are people you just got stuck with, and though you love them, you may not have very much in common" (223).

See pages 69–71 for more information about punctuating and citing quotations.

Finally, colons can create emphasis by connecting two related independent clauses. David Brooks uses this technique toward the end of his essay "People Like Us" (p. 228):

It might also be a good idea to make national service a rite of passage for young people in this country: it would take them out of their narrow neighborhood segment and thrust them in with people unlike themselves.

Whether you use a colon to introduce a list or quotation or to link independent clauses, the colon must be preceded by a complete sentence. Make sure the clause before the colon has a subject and a verb and expresses a complete thought. If it does not, remove the colon or rewrite the first part of the sentence.

FRAGMENT   Volunteer organizations have turned to social networks to raise funds, especially: *Facebook, Twitter,* and *LinkedIn.*

COMPLETE   Volunteer organizations have turned to social networks to raise funds, especially *Facebook, Twitter,* and *LinkedIn.*

COMPLETE   Volunteer organizations have turned to three social networks in particular to raise funds: *Facebook, Twitter,* and *LinkedIn.*

For more on sentence fragments and how to correct them, see page 49.

Practice

Edit each of the following sentences for incorrect or ineffective use of colons, commas, and quotation marks.

1. One charity that has succeeded at raising money online is the Avon Walk for Breast Cancer. The group has more than 40,000 *Facebook* fans and 11,000 *Twitter* followers.

2. The New York chapter's Web site explains: Social networking is . . . the fastest way to spread the word on the Internet.

3. The organization suggests three specific ways walkers can seek donations. Join the Avon Walk for Breast Cancer *Facebook* group, blogging their reasons for walking on *MySpace* and broadcast their progress on *Twitter*.

4. Such tactics, however, can backfire for several reasons. Friends quickly become irritated by requests for money, nagging reminders and feeling guilty.

5. As Brandon Griggs complains about *Facebook* users who constantly boast about their activities or ask friends to support their causes: "You probably mean well, but stop. Just stop" (000).

▶ For more practice editing for punctuation, visit Exercise Central at bedfordstmartins.com/exercisecentral.

A Note on Thematic Connections

Writers classify people more than any other subject, perhaps because the method gives order and even humor to our relationships with each other. The authors in this chapter explore the connections and distinctions that give people a sense of where they fit in with friends and neighbors. In a bar graph, the US Census Bureau categorizes residents of the United States by race and by cultural origin (p. 208). In a paragraph, Nelson George identifies two types of black residents in his neighborhood, workers and artists (p. 212). Also in a paragraph, Luis Alberto Urrea sorts campers at an RV park by their assigned parking spaces (p. 212). Brandon Griggs's essay identifies a dozen irritating behaviors among *Facebook* friends (next page). Marion Winik's essay categorizes her friends into nine groups (p. 223). And David Brooks's essay examines different kinds of neighborhoods to argue that American society isn't as diverse as we like to think (p. 228).

Brandon Griggs

Brandon Griggs (born 1960) is a journalist who writes about culture and technology. He graduated from Tufts University in 1982 and studied at Columbia University's Graduate School of Journalism under a fellowship with the National Arts Journalism Program. Griggs held a staff writing position as the "Culture Vulture" for the *Salt Lake Tribune* for fifteen years before taking his current position as senior technology producer for *CNN.com*. He is the author of *Utah Curiosities: Quirky Characters, Roadside Oddities and Other Offbeat Stuff* (2008), a guide to the state's peculiar legends and unconventional tourist attractions.

The Most Annoying Facebookers

In this article for *CNN.com*, Griggs draws on his personal experience and his sense of humor to call attention to behaviors that are guaranteed to alienate anyone's network of friends.

Facebook, for better or worse, is like being at a big party with all your 1 friends, family, acquaintances, and coworkers. There are lots of fun, interesting people you're happy to talk to when they stroll up. Then there are the other people, the ones who make you cringe when you see them coming. This article is about those people.

Sure, *Facebook* can be a great tool for keeping up with folks who are 2 important to you. Take the status update, the 160-character message that users post in response to the question, "What's on your mind?" An artful, witty, or newsy status update is a pleasure—a real-time, tiny window into a friend's life.

But far more posts read like navel-gazing diary entries, or worse, 3 spam. A recent study categorized 40% of *Twitter* tweets as "pointless babble," and it wouldn't be surprising if updates on *Facebook*, still a fast-growing social network, break down in a similar way.

Combine dull status updates with shameless self-promoters, "friend- 4 padders," and that friend of a friend who sends you quizzes every day, and *Facebook* becomes a daily reminder of why some people can get on your nerves.

Here are twelve of the most annoying types of *Facebook* users: 5

The Let-Me-Tell-You-Every-Detail-of-My-Day Bore. "I'm waking 6 up." "I had Wheaties for breakfast." "I'm bored at work." "I'm stuck in traffic." You're kidding! How fascinating! No moment is too mundane for some people to broadcast unsolicited to the world. Just because you have 432 *Facebook* friends doesn't mean we all want to know when you're waiting for the bus.

The Self-Promoter. OK, so we've probably all posted at least once 7 about some achievement. And sure, maybe your friends really do want to read the fascinating article you wrote about beet farming. But when almost EVERY update is a link to your blog, your poetry reading, your 10k results, or your art show, you sound like a bragger or a self-centered careerist.

The Friend-Padder. The average *Facebook* user has 120 friends on 8 the site. Schmoozers and social butterflies—you know, the ones who make lifelong pals on the subway—might reasonably have 300 or 400. But 1,000 "friends"? Unless you're George Clooney or just won the lottery, no one has that many. That's just showing off.

The Town Crier. "Michael Jackson is dead!!!" You heard it from me 9 first! Me, and the 213,000 other people who all saw it on TMZ. These Matt Drudge[1] wannabes are the reason many of us learn of breaking news not from TV or news sites but from online social networks. In their rush to trumpet the news, these people also spread rumors, half-truths, and innuendo. No, Jeff Goldblum did not plunge to his death from a New Zealand cliff.

The TMIer. "Brad is heading to Walgreens to buy something for 10 these pesky hemorrhoids." Boundaries of privacy and decorum don't seem to exist for these too-much-information updaters, who unabashedly offer up details about their sex lives, marital troubles, and bodily functions. Thanks for sharing.

The Bad Grammarian. "So sad about Fara Fauset but Im so gladd its 11 friday yippe." Yes, I know the punctuation rules are different in the digital world. And, no, no one likes a spelling-Nazi schoolmarm. But you sound like a moron.

The Sympathy-Baiter. "Barbara is feeling sad today." "Man, am I 12 glad that's over." "Jim could really use some good news about now." Like anglers hunting for fish, these sad sacks cast out their hooks—baited with vague tales of woe—in the hopes of landing concerned responses. Genuine bad news is one thing, but these manipulative posts are just pleas for attention.

The Lurker. The Peeping Toms of *Facebook*, these voyeurs are too 13 cautious, or maybe too lazy, to update their status or write on your wall.

---

[1] Creator and editor of the *Drudge Report*, an online news and gossip site. [Editors' note.]

But once in a while, you'll be talking to them and they'll mention something you posted, so you know they're on your page, hiding in the shadows. It's just a little creepy.

The Crank. These curmudgeons, like the trolls who spew hate in   14
blog comments, never met something they couldn't complain about. "Carl isn't really that impressed with idiots who don't realize how idiotic they are." (Actual status update.) Keep spreading the love.

The Paparazzo. Ever visit your *Facebook* page and discover that some-   15
one's posted a photo of you from last weekend's party—a photo you didn't authorize and haven't even seen? You'd really rather not have to explain to your mom why you were leering like a drunken hyena. . . .

The Obscurist. "If not now then when?" "You'll see . . ." "Grist for   16
the mill." "John is, small world." "Dave thought he was immune, but no. No, he is not." (Actual status updates, all.) Sorry, but you're not being mysterious—just nonsensical.

The Chronic Inviter. "Support my cause." "Sign my petition." "Play   17
Mafia Wars with me." "Which 'Star Trek' character are you?" "Here are the 'Top 5 cars I have personally owned.'" "Here are '25 Things about Me.'" "Here's a drink." "What drink are you?" "We're related!" "I took the 'What President Are You?' quiz and found out I'm Millard Fillmore! What president are you?"

You probably mean well, but stop. Just stop. I don't care what presi-   18
dent I am—can't we simply be friends? Now excuse me while I go post the link to this story on my *Facebook* page.

Vocabulary

Try to determine the meanings of any of the following words that are unfamiliar to you. Test your guesses in a dictionary, and then come up with sentences using each new word.

mundane (6)	unabashedly (10)	curmudgeons (14)
unsolicited (6)	anglers (12)	paparazzo (15)
innuendo (9)	voyeurs (13)	chronic (17)
decorum (10)		

Key Ideas and Details

1. Does Griggs have a thesis? Where in the essay does he make his point clear?

2. If Griggs's subject is *Facebook*, why does he mention a study of *Twitter* in his introduction (paragraph 3)? What do that study's findings have to do with his thesis?

Craft and Structure

1. LANGUAGE Find three places where Griggs uses hyperbole (see p. 59 for a definition). What effect does this figure of speech have in this essay?

2. Consider the labels Griggs devises for each category. What connotations do these words and phrases have? How do they contribute to his overall point? (If necessary, see p. 57 on connotation.)

3. What is the one quality that all members of Griggs's subject share, and what principle of classification does he use to sort them?

4. OTHER METHODS In addition to classification, Griggs relies heavily on example (Chapter 8) to make his point. Why do you think he uses so many direct quotations from *Facebook* status updates? What would the essay lose if Griggs didn't provide these examples?

Integration of Knowledge and Ideas

1. How can we tell that Griggs intends to entertain with his essay? Do you detect any other purpose?

2. In which category or categories of *Facebook* users, if any, does Griggs place himself? How can you tell?

3. FOR DISCUSSION What assumptions does Griggs make about the readers of his essay? Are the assumptions correct in your case?

Writing Topics

1. Do you have a *Facebook* account? A *Twitter* following? A *Pinterest* board? Write a response to Griggs's essay. Does it amuse you? anger you? embarrass you? make you feel something else? Does it make you want to change your habits when writing posts? Do you find Griggs's categories, examples, and conclusions fair? Why, or why not? Support your response with details from Griggs's essay and examples from your own experience.

2. Using Griggs's essay as a model, write an essay that classifies a group of people (teachers, bosses, or drivers, for example) for the purpose of getting readers to examine their own behaviors. Sort your subject into classes according to a consistent principle, and provide plenty of details to clarify the classes you decide on. In your essay, be sure to explain to your readers why the classification should persuade them to change their ways.

3. RESEARCH In questioning how anyone could have 1,000 friends, Griggs reveals an assumption that online friendship is nothing more than a digital extension of real-world friendship. Do you agree, or is the definition of *friend* unique to each context? How do online communities function differently

than face-to-face communities do, and what distinct purposes are served by each? Write an essay answering these questions. As evidence for your response, find and use expert opinion to support your ideas.

4. CONNECTIONS In *"American Idol* Worship" (p. 194), Thomas de Zengotita asserts that social networking sites are "devoted to otherwise anonymous people who don't want to be mere spectators." Read or reread de Zengotita's essay and write an essay of your own that applies his principle of analysis to the *Facebook* behaviors Griggs complains about. In what way does social networking belong to the "virtual revolution" that de Zengotita describes? Why might a person share too much information, for instance, or fish for sympathy? In what ways does posting on *Facebook* help people feel good about themselves?

Marion Winik

Marion Winik was born in New York City in 1958. She graduated from Brown University and earned a master's degree in fine arts from Brooklyn College. Perhaps best known as a commentator for National Public Radio's *All Things Considered*, Winik regularly publishes pieces in print periodicals such as *Parenting, Cosmopolitan, Ladies Home Journal*, and *Reader's Digest*. Her books include *Telling: Confessions, Concessions, and Other Flashes of Light* (1994), an essay collection; *First Comes Love* (1997), a memoir about life with her gay husband, who died of AIDS in 1994; *The Lunch Box Chronicles* (1998), a look at single parenthood; *Above Us Only Sky* (2005), a series of musings on "family and friendship and faith"; and *The Glen Rock Book of the Dead* (2008), memorial portraits of people who have touched her life. Winik is also the author of two books of poetry. She teaches writing at the University of Baltimore.

What Are Friends For?

In "What Are Friends For?" Winik locates various kinds of friends, from "Faraway" to "Hero" to "Friends You Love to Hate." The essay appears in Winik's essay collection *Telling*.

I was thinking about how everybody can't be everything to each other, but some people can be something to each other, thank God, from the ones whose shoulder you cry on to the ones whose half-slips you borrow to the nameless ones you chat with in the grocery line.

Buddies, for example, are the workhorses of the friendship world, the people out there on the front lines, defending you from loneliness and boredom. They call you up, they listen to your complaints, they celebrate your successes and curse your misfortunes, and you do the same for them in return. They hold out through innumerable crises before concluding that the person you're dating is no good, and even then understand if you ignore their good counsel. They accompany you to a movie with subtitles or to see the diving pig at Aquarena Springs. They feed your cat when you are out of town and pick you up from the airport when you get back. They come over to help you decide what to wear on a date. Even if it is with that creep.

What about family members? Most of them are people you just got stuck with, and though you love them, you may not have very much in common. But there is that rare exception, the Relative Friend. It is your cousin, your brother, maybe even your aunt. The two of you share the same views of the other family members. Meg never should have divorced Martin. He was the best thing that ever happened to her. You can confirm each other's memories of things that happened a long time ago. Don't you remember when Uncle Hank and Daddy had that awful fight in the middle of Thanksgiving dinner? Grandma always hated Grandpa's stamp collection; she probably left the windows open during the hurricane on purpose.

While so many family relationships are tinged with guilt and obli- 4
gation, a relationship with a Relative Friend is relatively worry free. You don't even have to hide your vices from this delightful person. . . .

Then there is that special guy at work. Like all the other people at 5
the job site, at first he's just part of the scenery. But gradually he starts to stand out from the crowd. Your friendship is cemented by jokes about coworkers and thoughtful favors around the office. Did you see Ryan's hair? Want half my bagel? Soon you know the names of his turtles, what he did last Friday night, exactly which model CD player he wants for his birthday. His handwriting is as familiar to you as your own.

Though you invite each other to parties, you somehow don't quite 6
fit into each other's outside lives. For this reason, the friendship may not survive a job change. Company gossip, once an infallible source of entertainment, soon awkwardly accentuates the distance between you. But wait. Like School Friends, Work Friends share certain memories which acquire a nostalgic glow after about a decade.

A Faraway Friend is someone you grew up with or went to school 7
with or lived in the same town as until one of you moved away. Without a Faraway Friend, you would never get any mail addressed in handwriting. A Faraway Friend calls late at night, invites you to her wedding, always says she is coming to visit but rarely shows up. An actual visit from a Faraway Friend is a cause for celebration. . . .

Faraway Friends go through phases of intense communication, 8
then may be out of touch for many months. Either way, the connection is always there. A conversation with your Faraway Friend always helps to put your life in perspective: when you feel you've hit a dead end, come to a confusing fork in the road, or gotten lost in some crackerbox sub-division of your life, the advice of the Faraway Friend—who has the big picture, who is so well acquainted with the route that brought you to this place—is indispensable.

Another useful function of the Faraway Friend is to help you remem- 9
ber things from a long time ago, like the name of your seventh-grade history teacher, what was in that really good stir-fry, or exactly what happened that night on the boat with the guys from Florida.

Ah, the Former Friend. A sad thing. At best a wistful memory, at 10
worst a dangerous enemy who is in possession of many of your deepest

secrets. But what was it that drove you apart? A misunderstanding, a betrayed confidence, an unrepaid loan, an ill-conceived flirtation. A poor choice of spouse can do in a friendship just like that. Going into business together can be a serious mistake. Time, money, distance, cult religions: all noted friendship killers. . . .

And lest we forget, there are the Friends You Love to Hate. They call 11 at inopportune times. They say stupid things. They butt in, they boss you around, they embarrass you in public. They invite themselves over. They take advantage. You've done the best you can, but they need professional help. On top of all this, they love you to death and are convinced they're your best friend on the planet.

So why do you continue to be involved with these people? Why do 12 you tolerate them? On the contrary, the real question is, What would you do without them? Without Friends You Love to Hate, there would be nothing to talk about with your other friends. Their problems and their irritating stunts provide a reliable source of conversation for everyone they know. What's more, Friends You Love to Hate make you feel good about yourself, since you are obviously in so much better shape than they are. No matter what these people do, you will never get rid of them. As much as they need you, you need them too.

At the other end of the spectrum are Hero Friends. These people are 13 better than the rest of us, that's all there is to it. Their career is something you wanted to be when you grew up—painter, forest ranger, tireless doer of good. They have beautiful homes filled with special handmade things presented to them by villagers in the remote areas they have visited in their extensive travels. Yet they are modest. They never gossip. They are always helping others, especially those who have suffered a death in the family or an illness. You would think people like this would just make you sick, but somehow they don't.

A New Friend is a tonic unlike any other. Say you meet her at a party. 14 In your bowling league. At a Japanese conversation class, perhaps. Wherever, whenever, there's that spark of recognition. The first time you talk, you can't believe how much you have in common. Suddenly, your life story is interesting again, your insights fresh, your opinion valued. Your various shortcomings are as yet completely invisible.

It's almost like falling in love. 15

Vocabulary

Try to guess the meanings of the following words from their context in Winik's essay. Look up the words in a dictionary to check your guesses. Then use each word in a sentence of your own.

counsel (2)	nostalgic (6)	lest (11)
tinged (4)	crackerbox (8)	inopportune (11)
cemented (5)	wistful (10)	butt in (11)
infallible (6)	ill-conceived (10)	tonic (14)

Key Ideas and Details

1. What is Winik's thesis? How does it relate to the question she poses in the title?

2. What label does Winik assign to each category of friend that she establishes? What functions does each group fulfill?

3. Winik concludes her essay by describing the experience of meeting a New Friend (paragraphs 14–15). How is a New Friend different from other types of friends, and why does Winik compare this experience with falling in love?

Craft and Structure

1. LANGUAGE Winik sometimes repeats actual lines from conversation without quotation marks. For example, in paragraph 3 she writes, "The two of you share the same views of the other family members. Meg should never have divorced Martin. He was the best thing that ever happened to her." She also uses occasional sentence fragments, such as "Even if it is with that creep" (2). Why do you think she chooses to break some rules of writing? What is the effect of her choices?

2. In paragraph 3, Winik asks, "What about family members?" as a transition to the category of Relative Friends. Study how she moves from one category to another in the rest of the essay. Are her transitions appropriate and effective? Why, or why not?

3. What is Winik's principle of classification? Does she group her friends based on differences among them independent of her or on differences in their relationships with her? Why do you think she just mentions but doesn't explain School Friends (paragraph 6)? Do you understand what she means by this category? Is it a flaw in the essay that Winik does not explain the category?

4. OTHER METHODS How does Winik use definition (Chapter 13) to differentiate her categories of friends? Where in the essay does she seem to take the most care with definition? Why do you think she gives more attention to some categories than to others?

Integration of Knowledge and Ideas

1. Winik begins her essay by saying, "I was thinking about . . ." (paragraph 1). What does this introductory sentence reveal about her purpose?

2. Is the essay addressed to both male and female readers? In your opinion, is it accessible to both sexes? Why, or why not? According to the information presented in this essay, does Winik believe that friends can be of either sex?

3. FOR DISCUSSION Winik uses several metaphors in the essay—for example, "Buddies . . . are the workhorses of the friendship world" (paragraph 2). Find other examples of metaphor. What do they contribute to the essay? (If necessary, review *metaphor* in the Glossary.)

Writing Topics

1. Draw up a list of your friends. Include people you see on a regular basis and others you haven't seen for a while. Can you sort them into categories— for instance, by the places you see them, the things you discuss with them, the ways they make you feel, or their importance to you? Write an essay about one of these categories of friends—for example, friends you study with, childhood friends, or friends you confide in. Using the method of classification, examine the *functions* this category of friends performs. What activities do you do with them that you don't do with others? What do you talk about? How relaxed or tense, happy or irritated, do they make you feel? Why are they significant to you? For each function, provide plenty of examples for readers.

2. Winik uses classification to explore friendship. Use the same method to develop your own essay about people with whom you do *not* get along. What categories do they fall into—for example, are some gossipy, others arrogant, still others unreliable? (Detail the categories with plenty of examples.) What does your dislike of these types of people ultimately reveal about you and your values?

3. Closeness with another person can often bring both joys and difficulties. And sometimes, as Winik points out, friendships end. Write an essay about a relationship you have lost. Describe the ups and downs of this relationship, from feelings of support and happiness to moments of conflict and anger. How did the relationship end, and how do you feel about the loss? Would you like to reconnect with the person, or do you feel that you're better off without him or her? Why?

4. CONNECTIONS Winik and Suzanne Britt, in "Neat People vs. Sloppy People" (p. 280), use similar means to achieve humorous effects. Write an essay in which you compare and contrast the tone, style, and use of language in each essay. How does each writer make readers laugh? Is one more successful than the other, and why?

David Brooks

A distinguished journalist, political analyst, and moderate conservative, David Brooks has engaged readers across the political spectrum for three decades. He was born in 1961 in Toronto, Ontario, grew up in New York City and a Philadelphia suburb, and graduated from the University of Chicago in 1983. He began his journalism career as a police reporter for the Chicago City News Bureau, and in 1984 he moved to the *Washington Times*, writing editorials and movie reviews. Brooks has since worked as an international reporter and contributing editor for the *Wall Street Journal*, the *Weekly Standard*, *Newsweek*, and the *Atlantic*. In 2003 he launched a regular column for the *New York Times*, now appearing twice weekly on the op-ed page. He is the editor of the anthology *Backward and Upward: The New Conservative Writing* (1996) and the author of three books of what he calls "comic sociology" — *Bobos in Paradise: The New Upper Class and How They Got There* (2000), *On Paradise Drive: How We Live Now (and Always Have) in the Future Tense* (2004), and *The Social Animal: The Hidden Sources of Love, Character, and Achievement* (2011). Brooks is a media personality as well, regularly appearing as a commentator on the NPR program *All Things Considered* and the PBS show *NewsHour*.

People Like Us

The United States is often described as a multicultural "melting pot," in which people with diverse backgrounds come together and form a shared American identity. Taking a close look at the populations of several US cities, towns, and universities, Brooks disputes this notion. "People Like Us" first appeared in the *Atlantic* in 2003.

Maybe it's time to admit the obvious. We don't really care about diversity all that much in America, even though we talk about it a great deal. Maybe somewhere in this country there is a truly diverse neighborhood in which a black Pentecostal minister lives next to a white anti-globalization activist, who lives next to an Asian short-order cook, who lives next to a professional golfer, who lives next to a postmodern-literature professor and a cardiovascular surgeon. But I have never been to or heard of that neighborhood. Instead, what I have seen all around the country is people making strenuous efforts to group themselves with people who are basically like themselves. 1

Human beings are capable of drawing amazingly subtle social distinctions and then shaping their lives around them. In the Washington, DC, area Democratic lawyers tend to live in suburban Maryland, and Republican lawyers tend to live in suburban Virginia. If you asked a Democratic lawyer to move from her $750,000 house in Bethesda, 2

Maryland, to a $750,000 house in Great Falls, Virginia, she'd look at you as if you had just asked her to buy a pickup truck with a gun rack and to shove chewing tobacco in her kid's mouth. In Manhattan the owner of a $3 million SoHo loft would feel out of place moving into a $3 million Fifth Avenue apartment. A West Hollywood interior decorator would feel dislocated if you asked him to move to Orange County. In Georgia a barista from Athens would probably not fit in serving coffee in Americus.

It is a common complaint that every place is starting to look the same. But in the information age, the late writer James Chapin[1] once told me, every place becomes more like itself. People are less often tied down to factories and mills, and they can search for places to live on the basis of cultural affinity. Once they find a town in which people share their values, they flock there, and reinforce whatever was distinctive about the town in the first place. Once Boulder, Colorado, became known as congenial to politically progressive mountain bikers, half the politically progressive mountain bikers in the country (it seems) moved there; they made the place so culturally pure that it has become practically a parody of itself.

But people love it. Make no mistake—we are increasing our happiness by segmenting off so rigorously. We are finding places where we are comfortable and where we feel we can flourish. But the choices we make toward that end lead to the very opposite of diversity. The United States might be a diverse nation when considered as a whole, but block by block and institution by institution it is a relatively homogeneous nation.

When we use the word "diversity" today we usually mean racial integration. But even here our good intentions seem to have run into the brick wall of human nature. Over the past generation reformers have tried heroically, and in many cases successfully, to end housing discrimination. But recent patterns aren't encouraging: according to an analysis of the 2000 census data, the 1990s saw only a slight increase in the racial integration of neighborhoods in the United States. The number of middle-class and upper-middle-class African American families is rising, but for whatever reasons—racism, psychological comfort—these families tend to congregate in predominantly black neighborhoods.

In fact, evidence suggests that some neighborhoods become more segregated over time. New suburbs in Arizona and Nevada, for example,

---

[1]A progressive democrat, Professor Chapin (1942–2002) was a political analyst, a writer for United Press International, and an author of history textbooks. [Editors' note.]

start out reasonably well integrated. These neighborhoods don't yet have reputations, so people choose their houses for other, mostly economic reasons. But as neighborhoods age, they develop personalities (that's where the Asians live, and that's where the Hispanics live), and segmentation occurs. It could be that in a few years the new suburbs in the Southwest will be nearly as segregated as the established ones in the Northeast and the Midwest.

Even though race and ethnicity run deep in American society, we   7 should in theory be able to find areas that are at least culturally diverse. But here, too, people show few signs of being truly interested in building diverse communities. If you run a retail company and you're thinking of opening new stores, you can choose among dozens of consulting firms that are quite effective at locating your potential customers. They can do this because people with similar tastes and preferences tend to congregate by ZIP code.

The most famous of these precision marketing firms is Claritas, which   8 breaks down the US population into sixty-two psycho-demographic clusters, based on such factors as how much money people make, what they like to read and watch, and what products they have bought in the past. For example, the "suburban sprawl" cluster is composed of young families making about $41,000 a year and living in fast-growing places such as Burnsville, Minnesota, and Bensalem, Pennsylvania. These people are almost twice as likely as other Americans to have three-way calling. They are two and a half times as likely to buy Light n' Lively Kid Yogurt. Members of the "towns & gowns" cluster are recent college graduates in places such as Berkeley, California, and Gainesville, Florida. They are big consumers of DoveBars and *Saturday Night Live*. They tend to drive small foreign cars and to read *Rolling Stone* and *Scientific American*.

Looking through the market research, one can sometimes be amazed   9 by how efficiently people cluster—and by how predictable we all are. If you wanted to sell imported wine, obviously you would have to find places where rich people live. But did you know that the sixteen counties with the greatest proportion of imported-wine drinkers are all in the same three metropolitan areas (New York, San Francisco, and Washington, DC)? If you tried to open a motor-home dealership in Montgomery County, Pennsylvania, you'd probably go broke, because people in this ring of the Philadelphia suburbs think RVs are kind of uncool. But if you traveled just a short way north, to Monroe County, Pennsylvania, you would find yourself in the fifth motor-home-friendliest county in America.

Resources for Teaching

COMMON THREADS

THREADS

Core Readings by Method and Theme

ELLEN KUHL REPETTO

RESOURCES FOR TEACHING

COMMON THREADS

Core Readings by Method and Theme

Ellen Kuhl Repetto

Bedford / St. Martin's
Boston ■ New York

For information, write: Bedford/St. Martin's, 75 Arlington Street, Boston, MA 02116   (617-399-4000)

ISBN 978-1-4576-4760-4

PREFACE

This manual has five parts, all intended to help you take maximum advantage of *Common Threads* as a classroom text. Part I discusses the content and possible classroom uses of the book's five introductory chapters, each element of the editorial apparatus in the chapters of readings, and the appendix of historic speeches. Part II discusses additional course materials with which *Common Threads* might be combined. Part III offers answers to the practice exercises in the reading chapters as well as teaching suggestions, a content quiz, and a vocabulary quiz for every essay and speech, along with lists of thematically related works of literature and possible answers to the critical reading questions following each selection. Part IV offers suggestions for integrating nonfiction into a Common Core curriculum, with sample lesson units. Finally, Part V presents a correlation chart that indicates how the materials in *Common Threads* align with each strand of the Common Core State Standards for grades 9 and 10.

Many thanks to Emily Richardson, of Naperville North High School in Illinois, for Part IV of this manual, "Integrating *Common Threads* into a Common Core Curriculum," and for her creative ideas for combining the individual essays and speeches in the reader with literary works and longer informational texts. Her assistance has been invaluable.

CONTENTS

Contents

PART IV Integrating *Common Threads* into a Common Core Curriculum   157
—*Emily Richardson, Naperville North High School*

PART V *Common Threads* and the Common Core State Standards   168

I
USING *COMMON THREADS*

The structure of *Common Threads* is uncomplicated: five introductory chapters coach students on reading, writing, revising, editing, and working with sources; ten thematically organized chapters explain and illustrate ten rhetorical methods of development; an appendix offers a collection of historic speeches and guidelines for speaking and listening effectively; and a glossary defines key writing terms.

Five Introductory Chapters on Reading and Writing

You may wish to discuss these chapters explicitly in class, adapting all or parts of them to your lesson plans, or you may find the chapters self-explanatory enough simply to ask students to read them on their own. Either way, these chapters lay useful groundwork for a reading and writing course. They explain and illustrate how critical reading is linked to good writing, how to read a text critically, how to work productively through the initial stages of writing, how to revise and edit one's own drafts, and how to use evidence and sources to bolster a thesis.

Reading (Chapter 1)

The introduction to reading addresses the key skills needed to read nonfiction texts, both written and visual, actively and critically.

A highlight of the chapter is the extended discussion of Barbara Lazear Ascher's essay "The Box Man," showing how a critical reader might approach an essay and what conclusions might result. This discussion is organized around generalized versions of the questions that appear after each essay in Chapters 6–15. These questions—divided into the Common Core categories of Vocabulary, Key Ideas and Details, Craft and Structure, and Integration of Knowledge and Ideas—invite students to consider the elements an author calls upon in constructing an essay. By observing how a critical reader might answer these questions for Ascher's essay, students have an opportunity to see what kinds of answers they might provide to the questions following the other essays in the book—and, more significant, to begin honing their own skills as critical readers.

Ascher's essay combines many of the methods of development (definition, example, description, and so on), thus providing an overview of the methods treated separately in the subsequent chapters. At the same time, the discussion of Ascher's essay introduces a point assumed throughout *Common Threads*: writers rarely use a single method alone, but rather gain shape, texture, and clarity for their writing by applying whatever method is best suited to a particular point or purpose.

To engage students actively in writing from the start, you might ask them to do some prewriting as preparation for reading the Ascher essay. Possible questions: What's the difference between solitude and loneliness? What kind of people would you describe as lonely? solitary? Or, to move in another direction: What is your impression of the homeless? Do you think some people choose to be homeless? Can one find dignity in such a situation? After reading Ascher's essay, students could compare their responses with hers and with one another's. They may see Ascher's as more complete and insightful than their own, and they will probably note that she presents her characters quite vividly, perhaps even prompting some students to recall similar characters in their own experiences. This comparison would provide a useful springboard to a discussion of the writer's task—and to Chapter 2.

A brief discussion of reading visuals helps students understand how to apply critical reading skills to the images they might come across in their reading or daily life, such as photographs, paintings, or drawings. A sample annotated photograph and interpretive comments on two infographics continue Part One's homelessness theme and show students how critical readings of different kinds of images might work. Because students tend to respond well to images, and to discover in the process that they already possess some critical reading faculties that can be applied to written texts, every chapter in Part Two opens with a visual, such as a cartoon, a graph, or a poster. The book also includes several essays with visual components: Jarrod Ballo's "Women and Children First" incorporates a line graph (Chapter 5), Amy Tan's "Pretty beyond Belief" has a photograph of the author as a girl (Chapter 6), David Brooks's "People Like Us" includes a political cartoon (Chapter 10), Barbara Kingsolver's "Stalking the Vegetannual" (Chapter 11) is illustrated with a line drawing, Walter Mosley's "Get Happy" features a graphic icon (Chapter 13), and Charlie LeDuff's "End of the Line" (Chapter 14) is accompanied by images from a related photo essay.

Developing an Essay (Chapter 2)

This chapter provides an overview and illustrations of the discovery and drafting process, detailing the basic concepts, terms, and stages that are used in the introductions to the rhetorical methods.

The introduction to the writing process focuses on the work in progress of a student, Grace Patterson, as she develops a response to Ascher's "The Box Man." Chapter 2 includes Patterson's journal writing (p. 26) and freewriting (p. 27), along with her complete first draft (p. 34). If your class does peer editing, you might ask students to comment on the draft as a beginning exercise. In discussing their own and their classmates' comments, they will come to see what kinds of responses are appropriate and how best to phrase them.

Revising (Chapter 3)

Continuing the introduction to the writing process, this chapter covers the crucial stages of revision, aiming to help students with questions they may have while revising. Concise text and specific examples explain each element of writing, and a boxed checklist guides students through rethinking their own work. Then, in the introduction to each rhetorical method, a more specific revision checklist appears to help students assess their drafts.

Editing (Chapter 4)

This chapter on editing discusses grammatical errors and stylistic choices, each illustrated with clearly marked examples.

The chapter focuses on the most common writing problems that students are likely to encounter, such as sentence fragments, comma splices, and word choice. The content is not, of course, comparable to a handbook in scope or detail, but it should provide just enough to help students who struggle to recognize or correct sentence-level errors; it also suggests realistic techniques for student writers to polish their style, such as by using parallel structure and streamlining sentences for clarity and emphasis.

To further aid students in recognizing potential problems and opportunities, a "Focus" box in the introduction to each rhetorical chapter calls out an element of editing especially relevant to the method—for instance, verbs in narration, punctuation in classification, and consistency in process analysis. Each of these boxes features a practice exercise; students can find additional opportunities to practice their grammar and punctuation skills for free at Exercise Central (*bedfordstmartins.com/rewriting2e*). All discussions of the elements of writing—in Chapters 2, 3, and 4 and in the method introductions—are indexed inside the book's back cover so that students know just where to go for help.

Working with Sources (Chapter 5)

The overarching assumption of this chapter is that students will be drawing on the readings in this book and ideas gathered from research to support their own ideas in short essays, rather than developing formal research or term papers. Accordingly, the emphasis is on synthesizing outside materials to develop an original idea, with a focus on summarizing, paraphrasing, quoting, integrating sources, and avoiding plagiarism. The chapter also offers a few pointers on finding and evaluating sources in the library and on the Web, along with several MLA documentation models—in-text and works cited—for the types of sources students are most likely to use.

The chapter culminates in an annotated sample student essay that both demonstrates how sources can be used to develop a student's own argument and illustrates the most important mechanical aspects of documented writing. It is a brief essay, but it effectively shows how sources can add to a thesis without overwhelming a student's voice.

Taking advantage of this coverage, most of the essays and speeches in *Common Threads* include a suggested writing topic that asks students to conduct some research on a subject as they respond to readings and develop their ideas.

Ten Chapters on the Methods of Development
Chapter Introductions

Though brief, *Common Threads* anticipates many student questions about the use of the methods of development; hence you can ask students to read the chapter introductions independently, reserving class time to discuss the chapter's theme or the application of the writing principles.

The introductions to Chapters 6–15 all proceed in the same way. The opening section, "Seeing _____," discusses the visual chapter opener and asks students to analyze it and begin to think critically about the chapter theme. "Reading _____," discusses the purposes for which the method is suited and provides essential concepts and definitions while showing students what elements to look for when reading paragraphs and essays that use the method. The next section, "Analyzing _____ in Paragraphs," annotates two paragraphs that illustrate the method. As noted above, a "Focus" box in each chapter emphasizes a particular element that students should be aware of when editing, whether it is concrete and specific language in description or parallelism in comparison and contrast, and provides exercises to help students master the concept. (Answers to the exercises are provided in Part III of this manual, at the beginning of each readings chapter.) Finally, "A Note on Thematic Connections" highlights the common topic of the chapter's selections.

The two annotated paragraphs in each introduction allow students to study the method in brief, uncomplicated examples before moving on to complete essays. If you discuss the methods of development in class, the annotated paragraphs can serve as concrete illustrations of each method's special concerns. In addition, the paragraphs can serve as models for students to follow in writing paragraphs of their own (perhaps drawing on the list of topics at the end of each chapter) before they move on to more complex, essay-length applications of the method.

Chapter 15, "Argument and Persuasion: Debating Law and Order," is slightly different from the chapters before it. Because argumentation is so central to the Common Core State Standards, this chapter introduction is more extensive than the others, with detailed discussions of the elements of argument; ethical, emotional, and rational appeals; and common logical fallacies. The chapter also offers four extra essays that argue opposing viewpoints on texting while driving and on Internet privacy.

The Essays

The thirty-four essays in Part Two of *Common Threads* satisfy several criteria. Most important, they are interesting, and they plainly illustrate the rhetorical methods. The essays are also short, averaging two to four pages, so students will find them approachable and imitable; yet they are substantial enough for sharpening reading skills and encouraging lively discussion. A few longer essays provide transition to more challenging academic work.

Though organized as a rhetorical reader, *Common Threads* also offers a parallel thematic approach: the visual, paragraphs, and essays in each chapter relate in subject as well as form. Thus, for example, Chapter 7's descriptive selections all deal with the subject of nature, and Chapter 13's definition essays all address what happiness means. The themes make it easy to identify nonfiction readings that connect with a core work of literature. If you teach Harper Lee's *To Kill a Mockingbird*, for instance, you could focus on the novel's theme of lost innocence with the paragraphs and essays in Chapter 6, "Narration: Growing Up"; on issues of race with the selections in Chapter 12, "Comparison and Contrast: Examining Stereotypes"; or on questions of justice with the works in Chapter 15, "Argument and Persuasion: Debating Law and Order." (Detailed suggestions for integrating the essays in *Common Threads* with commonly taught works of literature are provided in Part IV of this manual; see pp. 157–167.)

Alternatively, you might have students read two or three of a chapter's essays and then discuss in class their theme as an entry to a discussion of the rhetorical approach. Or you could focus discussion on just the theme in preparation for reading a literary work. As noted later, a "Connections" writing topic for each essay and a set of thematic topics for each chapter help students perceive and write about the thematic links both within and among chapters.

Biographical and Essay Headnotes

The preface to each essay establishes a context for the essay, offering background on the writer's expertise in his or her subject and providing information about his or her intended audience. Students are often inclined to skip such sections, so it may be worthwhile to point out how helpful the headnotes can be for analyzing the essays along with the discussion questions.

Critical Reading Questions

The questions following each essay help students analyze and evaluate the essay, either on their own or in group or class discussions. The questions are organized in four groups — Vocabulary, Key Ideas and Details, Craft and Structure, and Integration of Knowledge and Ideas — that align with the Common Core State Standards and lead students to examine the essay with an increasingly broad focus. As mentioned earlier, the groups of questions correspond to those following Ascher's essay in the chapter on reading (Chapter 1). Possible answers to the questions are provided in this manual (see Part III).

Writing Topics

At least four writing topics follow each essay. Some relate to the essay's content; some suggest a subject compatible with the method introduced in the chapter; some ask students to do research on a subject raised by the essay. And a final topic, labeled "Connections," encourages students to tease out thematic or rhetorical links between the essay and either a sample paragraph or another essay or speech in the book.

In addition to the topics following each essay, every chapter ends with two sets of supplementary writing suggestions. The first set, "Writing with the Method," includes many possibilities for applying the chapter's method of development. The second set, "Writing about the Theme," includes three detailed ideas for drawing on the chapter's resources to explore its topic.

Appendix of Historic Speeches

To help teachers implement the Common Core emphases on foundational American documents and on speaking and listening, *Common Threads* concludes with an Appendix of Historic Speeches.

The section begins with advice on reading and listening to speeches, then helps students plan, structure, integrate multimedia into, and rehearse their own oral presentations. This brief but comprehensive instruction is followed by five classic speeches that span American history, each touching on the question of liberty. Like the essays, the speeches are accompanied by thorough editorial support: headnotes introducing both the speakers and their speeches, gloss notes explaining allusions and historic contexts, and complete sets of critical reading questions and suggested writing topics.

Glossary

This section provides definitions of terms used in the text. Because most entries include page references to longer text discussions, the glossary can serve as an index as well as a freestanding quick reference. In some cases, the glossary offers specific aids—such as options for essay introductions and conclusions, with cross-references to the book's essays—that could serve as the basis of class discussion.

II
COMBINING *COMMON THREADS* WITH OTHER MATERIALS

Because of its thematic approach and brevity, *Common Threads* can easily be combined with other classroom materials and approaches. Teachers can successfully integrate the reader with literary works, grammar textbooks, library research, current newspaper and magazine articles, and the writing of their own students.

Literature

You may want to pair *Common Threads* with individual works of literature or with an anthology, using the chapter introductions and the essay models to guide students as they construct their own essays in response to literature.

The discussions of description (Chapter 7) and narration (Chapter 6) may help students analyze the descriptive and narrative passages they encounter in short stories or novels; and you may want to discuss the similarities and differences between fictional and nonfictional description and narration. Using these methods, students could experiment with either fiction or nonfiction (or both, contrasting in a class discussion the problems they encountered with each). You can also emphasize that much writing about literature relies heavily on example (Chapter 8), comparison and contrast (Chapter 12), cause-and-effect analysis (Chapter 14), and argument and persuasion (Chapter 15); and you can tailor assignments in which students use these methods to explain, analyze, or evaluate the readings in the literature anthology.

We offer detailed suggestions for combining *Common Threads* with popularly taught works of literature and longer nonfiction titles in Part IV of this manual (see pp. 157–167). Some teachers may wish to use those suggestions as they stand; others might take them as inspiration for integrating informational and argumentative texts with the literary works that are already part of their curricula.

Grammar Textbooks

Given its coverage of the writing process, *Common Threads* can easily complement a handbook or a workbook. The reader can inspire writing assignments and guide students through the stages of drafting, revising, and editing. For more detailed discussion of their specific problems—such as paragraph coherence, clear sentences, or word choice—and for help with grammar and punctuation, students can consult the other textbook.

Research Tools

You may wish to help prepare students for academic writing by asking them to use outside sources in at least some of their writing. Many of the essays and themes in *Common Threads* invite further investigation. Frequent suggestions for research writing ask students to consult a dictionary, an encyclopedia, or a book or article found through the library catalog or the Internet. When possible, specific sources are suggested in the entries in this manual. The assignments are limited so that students can quickly find and read the other sources, using most of their time to construct their essays.

If you incorporate research into the course, you may wish to spend a class period or two introducing students to the library and its basic reference tools. You may also teach formats for documentation of sources, such as the MLA system discussed in Chapter 5.

Reading from Current Sources

One advantage of a brief collection like *Common Threads* is that you can supplement the paragraphs and essays with topical articles on the book's themes or examples of the methods of development, or both. Op-ed pieces, essays in *Time* and *Newsweek*, popular blogs, articles in the school paper or the local paper, letters to the editor—all of these are good sources. Students are often surprised to see how the "textbook" methods abound in current periodicals, and at the same time they often respond well to the immediacy of last week's or yesterday's news items. In small groups or in the class as a whole, students can analyze the structure of these samples using questions like those first presented in Chapter 1 on reading. Outside readings can also serve as the basis for in-class writing topics. For instance, Brandon Griggs's "The Most Annoying Facebookers" might be compared with another article on the virtues or vices of social networking.

You can also encourage students to look for thematic connections or applications of the methods and bring them to class. For instance, students may watch for ways they use the methods in their own lives: comparing and contrasting in order to buy a new smartphone; analyzing causes and effects in order to uncover the reasons for an unexpectedly high or low grade. Or students may examine television programs, films, magazines, and other sources for ideas to support the readings' or the class's approach to a chapter topic such as using language or eating well. And, of course, students can watch for the methods in the readings, lectures, and exams of their other courses: the descriptive lab report in biology, the cause-and-effect analysis in history, and so on.

Student Writing

Like many teachers, you may rely on students' own writing to provide the substance of some class discussion. Given drafts of student papers to read, students may work in small groups or in pairs, using the method of careful reading and analysis recommended in Chapter 1. Then, using as a model the comments on Grace Patterson's drafts in Chapters 2 and 3, students can evaluate their peers' writing, making specific recommendations for improving each draft. When the paper employs a particular method of development, students may tailor their recommendations by referring to the chapter introduction to that method. To instruct students in this kind of peer-editing procedure—or instead of the small-group work—you may want to go over a sample student essay with the whole class.

In addition to responding to the essays in the reader, students may respond, in writing, to one another's essays. Especially for topics in argument and persuasion (Chapter 15), you can circulate one or two provocative student essays and ask the class to write arguments countering (or reinforcing) the arguments in those essays. Or students can exchange their own argumentative essays blindly and then write an essay in response to the one they receive. Knowing that someone will be responding to their essays invites students to formulate their arguments specifically and persuasively—perhaps more so than if they were writing just for you.

III
NOTES ON THE READINGS IN *COMMON THREADS*

Chapter 6

Narration

Growing Up

Focus on Verbs

Answers will vary. Possible edits are provided below.

1. We staggered outside and surveyed the damage.

2. Broken tree limbs littered the yard and blocked the street.

3. As we debated where to go, my father screamed: "Sparky!" We forgot the dog.

4. Frantic, my mother sprinted to the basement and jerked the door open.

5. A very wet but very happy dog bolted out and jumped in the car.

Frederick Douglass
Learning to Read and Write (p. 103)

Students can usually understand and identify with Douglass's childhood emotions, for nearly everyone can recall an experience of determined rule-breaking or frustrated learning. Those points of connection, suggested in the first two writing topics, can provide a starting place for discussion of the essay.

Although the Common Core State Standards gauge the reading level of *Narrative of the Life of Frederick Douglass* at high-end grade 8, the historical context, the use of memoir as argument, and the vocabulary and syntax will likely pose a challenge to some high school students. Should they struggle, the best approach might be to focus them on the obstacles Douglass himself faced in learning to read and write, demonstrating that effort and determination can pay off for anyone.

Related Texts

Pulled from one of the most important personal narratives in American history, Douglass's essay has strong thematic links with just about any work touching on slavery, the US Civil War, race relations, or oppression. The former slave's perspectives on the corruptions of power and the impacts of education could enhance students' appreciation of the following works in particular.

Chinua Achebe, *Things Fall Apart*

Louisa May Alcott, *Little Women*

Isabel Allende, *The House of the Spirits*

Maya Angelou, *I Know Why the Caged Bird Sings* (see "Champion of the World," p. 111)

Suzanne Collins, *The Hunger Games*

Khaled Hosseini, *The Kite Runner*

Martin Luther King, Jr., "I Have a Dream" (p. 449)

Harper Lee, *To Kill a Mockingbird*

Abraham Lincoln, "Gettysburg Address" (p. 446)

Toni Morrison, *Beloved*

George Orwell, *1984*

Sophocles, *Oedipus Rex*

Harriet Beecher Stowe, *Uncle Tom's Cabin*

Sojourner Truth, "Ain't I a Woman?" (p. 443)

Mark Twain, *The Adventures of Huckleberry Finn*

Alice Walker, *The Color Purple*

Elie Wiesel, "Hope, Despair, and Memory"

Elie Wiesel, *Night*

Richard Wright, *Black Boy*

Content Quiz

1. Who taught Douglass to read?
   [Initially his mistress taught him the alphabet, and then he learned from boys in the neighborhood. Ultimately, he taught himself.]

2. What was the effect of Douglass learning how to read?
   [The more he read, the more he hated his situation.]

3. Once he learned how to read, what did Douglass realize he would prefer to be?
    [Illiterate and thus ignorant of his oppression. He specifically says that he'd rather be a reptile or dead.]

4. What important word puzzles Douglass?
    [*Abolition.*]

5. Where did Douglass learn to read?
    [The shipyard.]

Vocabulary Quiz

1. *Chattel* (paragraph 2) is closest in meaning to
    a. cattle   b. property   c. child
    [b. property]

2. *Divest* (2) is closest in meaning to
    a. give   b. inspire   c. take away
    [c. take away]

3. *Urchins* (4) is closest in meaning to
    a. barnacles   b. rascals   c. criminals
    [b. rascals]

4. *Denunciation* (6) is closest in meaning to
    a. condemnation   b. ruination   c. preparation
    [a. condemnation]

5. *Abhor* (6) is closest in meaning to
    a. hate   b. pity   c. love
    [a. hate]

Answers
Key Ideas and Details

1. Douglass was forced to find creative ways to learn because the master of the house insisted that his wife stop teaching the child, out of concern that literacy would render him dangerously dissatisfied with his position and therefore unfit as a slave. He outlines several of the tricks he used: for reading, he befriended hungry boys and exchanged food for lessons (paragraph 4), he read extensively and repeatedly (5–6), he listened attentively (7), and looked up words he didn't know (7); for writing, he copied letters he observed in the shipyard (8), goaded boys into revealing new letters by pretending he knew more than they did (8), and practiced writing in discarded used workbooks (8).

2. Douglass is saying that slavery dehumanizes both slaves and slaveholders. To support the claim in the case of slaves, he refers to himself as a "brute" (paragraph 1) and "a mere chattel" (2) who, after becoming educated, often

12

would have preferred to return to his previous state as "a beast" or "the meanest reptile" (6). In the case of slaveholders, he describes a marked shift in the mistress's demeanor from that of a "pious, warm, and tender-hearted woman" to that of a "violent," "angry," tormentor beset with "tiger-like fierceness" and "apprehension" (2).

3. Douglass's point is that literacy empowers and that knowledge is the key to freedom—precisely why cultural norms discouraged or forbade educating slaves. The closest to a direct thesis statement appears at the end of paragraph 2: ". . . education and slavery were incompatible with each other."

Craft and Structure

1. Some metaphors: "the tender heart became stone" (paragraph 2); "Mistress . . . had given me the *inch*, and no precaution could prevent me from taking the *ell*" (3); "bread of knowledge" (4); "They gave tongue to the interesting thoughts of my own soul, which had frequently lashed through my mind, and died away for want of utterance" (5); "It opened my mind to the horrible pit, but no ladder upon which to get out" (6); "silver trump of freedom" (6); "The light broke in upon me by degrees" (7). Some similes: "tiger-like fierceness" (2);"as the fruit of *abolition*" (7). Some personifications: "Slavery soon proved its ability" (2); "It looked from every star, it smiled in every calm, breathed in every wind, and moved in every storm" (6). Douglass's plentiful figures of speech demonstrate his deep love of language and the positive results of his self-directed education.

2. Douglass's language helps to prove his intelligence for readers who may have assumed that African Americans, especially those held as slaves, lacked the mental capacity to function on their own. By extension, his formal style serves as a counterargument to those who, at the time, cited inferiority as a justification for slavery.

3. Examples of flashbacks in Douglass's narrative: the mistress's earlier willingness to teach him (paragraph 1); her transition from kindness to cruelty (2). Examples of compression of time: several years of self-study retold in just one paragraph (4); the slow discovery of the meaning of *abolition* (7). Examples of omitted events: Douglass's activities as a house servant; the gap between the dockworkers' advice and Douglass's eventual escape (8). Examples of expanded time: Douglass's emotional response to reading (6); his conversation with the dockworkers (7). By condensing or omitting some events, Douglass keeps the narrative moving and emphasizes the crucial moments of insight resulting from his effort. These moments are drawn out in a way that makes us sympathize with Douglass's predicament, understand his reason for defiance, and share his sense of agony and determination.

4. The definition is important because Douglass's purpose in writing was to support the abolitionism movement. By revealing the difficulty he had understanding the meaning of the word, Douglass lets readers see the issue through the eyes of an uneducated slave who may not be aware of the possibilities.

Integration of Knowledge and Ideas

1. Douglass seems to assume that the bulk of his readers are aware of the abuses inherent in slavery and that they oppose the institution in principle, although he also offers up details meant to reinforce their opposition and to sway the minds of readers who may not object to slavery or fully understand its effects. While leaving out details concerning forced labor or physical abuse in this chapter (and in fact suggesting in paragraph 6 that he was better off than many poor white children), he provides several examples of his struggles and emotional turmoil—particularly in paragraphs 6–7—and of free people's empathy for him, such as the boys who "would express . . . the liveliest sympathy" (4) and the Irishmen who "seemed to be deeply affected" by his status as a "slave for life" (7).

2. The material he read, especially the one dialogue between master and slave (paragraph 5) and the emancipation speech by Sheridan (6) taught Douglass new ways of looking at his life by articulating antislavery arguments for him, shaping his thoughts, and showing him that freedom was a possibility. Although he reports that the new knowledge caused him anger and frustration, it also spurred him to learn more and to work toward his own emancipation by developing his literacy.

3. Clearly, the learning experience was a significant one for Douglass (paragraph 7), and that fact alone could explain his including a chapter on it in his autobiography. He is certainly critical of his mistress and other slaveholders, although as an adult he seems to understand that they were caught up in an "injurious" (2) system that diminished them as much as it did him. But his emphasis on emancipation (5–6) and abolitionism (7) points to the main purpose of the essay: to underscore the role literacy plays in fighting oppression and to argue that "education and slavery were incompatible with each other" (2). Douglass may also have wanted to illustrate the point at which a child learns to rely on himself or herself, not on others, for knowledge.

Maya Angelou
Champion of the World (p. 111)

A story within a story, Maya Angelou's suspenseful narrative invites attention to both its method and its matter. Inside the story of what happens in the general store (told in the first person, as Angelou looks back to her childhood), we follow the story of the Louis-Carnera fight. Suspense builds from the beginning, in the introductory glimpse of the people crowding in eagerly, in the "apprehensive mood" compared to a sky "streaked with lightning" (paragraph 2), and in the scraps of conversation. Larger events of the history of civil rights form a background to this narrative—for example, the fact that African Americans were not safe at night, although we learn this only at the end of the story.

You might begin by asking students what they know of the career of Joe Louis. (In some classes no one may know of him.) Starting with the suggestions in Writing Topic 3, you could break the class into groups of three or four and have them research what it meant in the 1930s for an African American to become a prominent and universally admired athlete. (A good starting point might be the first chapter of *Manliness and Civilization* by Gail Bederman [U of Chicago P, 1995] or the third chapter of *Gender and Jim Crow* by Glenda Elizabeth Gilmore [U of North Carolina P, 1996].) Assign each group its own contextual category: Louis's career overall; other firsthand reminiscences of boxing in the 1930s; African American life in the 1930s. Each group could then present its findings for five to ten minutes, ending with a whole-class discussion of Angelou's memoir. (Note: If this sort of background research is something you'd like to have students do fairly regularly, you might consider rotating the responsibility so that just one group works and reports on any given essay.)

Related Texts

Chinua Achebe, *Things Fall Apart*

Suzanne Collins, *The Hunger Games*

Frederick Douglass, *Narrative of the Life of Frederick Douglass* (see "Learning to Read and Write," p. 103)

Martin Luther King, Jr., "I Have a Dream" (p. 449)

Harper Lee, *To Kill a Mockingbird*

William Shakespeare, *Othello*

John Steinbeck, *The Grapes of Wrath*

Alice Walker, *The Color Purple*

Tennessee Williams, *The Glass Menagerie*

Richard Wright, *Black Boy*

Content Quiz

1. Where does Angelou's story take place?
    [Uncle Willie's store.]

2. What famous boxer do the people gather to watch?
    [Joe Louis.]

3. What is the boxer's nickname?
    [The Brown Bomber.]

4. How do the youngsters celebrate the victory?
    [Drinking soft drinks and eating candy bars.]

5. According to Angelou, what did the victory prove?
    [That African Americans "were the strongest people in the world."]

Vocabulary Quiz

1. *Gaiety* (paragraph 2) is closest in meaning to
   a. festiveness   b. nervousness   c. hatred
   [a. festiveness]

2. *Assent* (10) is closest in meaning to
   a. agreement   b. gibberish   c. loud
   [a. agreement]

3. *Maimed* (16) is closest in meaning to
   a. silenced   b. shaved   c. wounded
   [c. wounded]

4. *Ordained* (17) is closest in meaning to
   a. restrained   b. penalized   c. chosen
   [c. chosen]

5. *Ambrosia* (27) is closest in meaning to
   a. food of the gods   b. water   c. elephant
   [a. food of the gods]

Answers
Key Ideas and Details

1–2. As Angelou indicates in much of her story, and especially in paragraphs 16 and 17, the pride of the race depends on the fight. Not only pride but a whole future rides on the outcome: "If Joe lost we were back in slavery. . . ." Everyone in the store believes this, but the author's view is not so simple. Obviously she doesn't share the notion that if Joe Louis lost it would be clear that "God Himself hated us"; she is exaggerating the assumptions of the people in the store to emphasize the ideological importance of the fight.

Craft and Structure

1. Nonstandard English here makes the people gathered in the store come alive for us. (This story offers a great opportunity to point out the occasional high value of nonstandard English. The comments in paragraphs 4 and 8 are so well put that they're hard to forget.)

2. Students who sense the irony will probably express it in any of several ways. Some will say that despite all the hopes and dreams bound up in the fight, Louis's victory hasn't delivered his people. Maybe Louis is the strongest man in the ring, but African Americans in rural Arkansas are still vulnerable. Angelou's irony in the final line is so strong that it is practically sarcasm. Isn't there a suggestion, too, that on this particular night some whites, resenting the Louis victory, will be out to punish any African Americans they can find alone or in small numbers?

3.   From paragraph 1 we feel anticipation and a tension that mounts to a crisis in paragraph 15, when the contender rains blows on Louis and staggers him. Short, punchy sentences add speed and force to Angelou's account: "We didn't breathe. We didn't hope. We waited" (paragraph 18—incidentally, a good example of parallelism). The whole device of telling the story of the fight through a radio announcer's spiel is particularly effective because, as Angelou makes clear, the listeners in the store hang onto the announcer's every word. Using radio as a medium in storytelling can increase suspense by leaving much to the imagination.

Anyone familiar with the history of boxing will predict the winner as soon as the name of Joe Louis emerges; others may not be sure until Louis rallies in paragraph 20.

4.   The descriptive details in paragraph 27—drinking Coke "like ambrosia," eating candy "like Christmas," boys "blowing their breath in front of themselves like proud smokers"—move the story ahead and re-create the special joy and pride of the occasion.

Integration of Knowledge and Ideas

1.   Like the rest of the autobiography from which this selection is taken, "Champion of the World" seems written for a dual purpose: to recall vivid and significant moments of the author's life and to reveal the ironic situation of African Americans in America in the 1930s: able to become world champions but not able to walk a country road at night. This irony is given great weight by being placed at the end the story.

2.   The error makes untrue a small corner of the story (and might distract people who recognize it), but the fact that Angelou mixed up Louis's fights does not discredit what she reports experiencing.

3.   The hyperboles and ironies in paragraphs 16–17 and 28 reveal that African Americans in the early twentieth century were under tremendous physical threat and misplaced hostility, especially in the South. In just a few sentences Angelou invokes the lynchings that often took place, the rapes endured by women, the assaults on boys (often accused of wanting to rape white women), the mobs that chased after black males, and the corporal punishments routinely meted out to house servants. In the last paragraph of her essay she implies that such attacks stemmed from white insecurities about their relative position of power.

Amy Tan
Pretty beyond Belief (p. 116)

Deceptively simple, "Pretty beyond Belief" is a triple narrative that explores themes of beauty, self-esteem, ethnicity, family, gender, and truth—all in under two pages. Although it's shorter than the other essays in this chapter, it's also more complex. Tan's thesis is unstated, her ideas are sophisticated and impressionistic, and her organization is intricate.

Teenage girls will likely respond strongly to Tan's essay; boys may need a little encouragement to take her ideas seriously. You might want to spend some time with your students analyzing the way Tan weaves together her own experience with the stories and words of others not only to give her narrative immediacy and to highlight different perceptions of beauty but also to persuade readers that childish perceptions of race are more fragile and vulnerable than adult ones.

Related Texts

Tan's personal reflections on the mother-daughter relationship in this essay offer an obvious foil to the fictional relationships in *The Joy Luck Club*. In addition to the essays highlighted in the "connections" question following "Pretty beyond Belief," literary works that focus on beauty or on parent-child relationships include the following.

Isabel Allende, *The House of the Spirits*

Julia Álvarez, "Against Cinderella"

Julia Álvarez, *How the Garcia Girls Lost Their Accents*

Sandra Cisneros, "Bien Pretty"

Sandra Cisneros, *The House on Mango Street*

Judith Ortiz Cofer, *The Meaning of Consuelo*

Jamaica Kincaid, "Girl"

Toni Morrison, *The Bluest Eye*

Tillie Olsen, "I Stand Here Ironing"

Marge Piercy, "Barbie Doll"

William Shakespeare, *Othello*

Amy Tan, *The Joy Luck Club*

Kurt Vonnegut, Jr., "Harrison Bergeron"

Alice Walker, *The Color Purple*

Scott Westerfeld, *Pretties*

Content Quiz

1. Tan's mother thinks that being pretty can be what?
   ["Bad luck."]

2. What is Tan's mother still proud of well into her 70s and 80s?
   [Her skin: "Still smooth and soft."]

3. Why was Tan's mother featured in the Shanghai tabloids?
   [She was jailed for leaving her former husband and running away with the man who would become her husband and Tan's father.]

4. How did Tan's grandmother kill herself?
   [By swallowing raw opium.]

5. What makes Tan's mother begin to think that she and her daughter look alike?
   [Alzheimer's disease.]

Vocabulary Quiz

1. *Appraised* (paragraph 2) is closest in meaning to
   a. summarized   b. assessed   c. touched
   [b. assessed]

2. *Chided* (4) is closest in meaning to
   a. complained   b. scolded   c. demanded
   [b. scolded]

3. *Avowed* (6) is closest in meaning to
   a. bragged   b. affirmed   c. promised
   [b. affirmed]

4. *Consigning* (7) is closest in meaning to
   a. advancing   b. imprisoning   c. handing over
   [c. handing over]

5. *Askew* (8) is closest in meaning to
   a. absent   b. scarred   c. crooked
   [c. crooked]

Answers
Key Ideas and Details

1. The essay seems to have two interlocking points: that beauty is subjective, and that having it does not guarantee a happy life. Or, as Tan's mother put it, "Pretty can be bad luck, not just good" (paragraph 4).

2. The photograph shows readers what the insecure girl actually looked like. Many readers might comment that although Tan might have been a little awkward, she was in fact (and still is) quite pretty, an irony that underscores her point that perceptions of beauty or lack thereof are influenced by culture and context.

3. Tan provides brief narratives of the negative consequences her mother and grandmother experienced as a result of their attractiveness. Her mother, she reports, was punished for her beauty by her first husband (paragraph 6), and her grandmother was abducted and forced into a nonconsensual sexual relationship (7). And yet neither Tan nor her mother fully reject the appeal of beauty: the mother boasts about her prettiness (4–5, 6, 9) and criticizes Tan's lack of it (2, 8), and the daughter acknowledges, with a strong sense of ambivalence, that she still wishes to be beautiful (11). Students might

note, as well, that in using the phrase "pretty beyond belief" as her title, Tan implies that she doesn't necessarily believe her mother's claims.

Craft and Structure

1. Tan shifts point of view to reflect the alternating focus of her narrative: the paragraphs about herself are in the first person; the ones about her mother and grandmother are in the third person.

2. As it always does, the dialogue creates immediacy. It also creates a vivid and multi-layered impression of Tan's immigrant mother, whose English is less than perfect but whose sense of pride is strong.

3. Tan opens with a memory from her childhood (paragraphs 1–4), jumps back in time to relate incidents from her mother's (5–6) and grandmother's (7) lives, returns to her own childhood and teenage years (8), then jumps forward to the end of her mother's life (9–10) and the present (11). This organization allows her to open with the question she means to explore, provide background information to explain her mother's comments, then return to her question and the new ones it has opened for her — a complexity that would not be possible with straight chronology.

4. Both mini-narratives provide examples of hardships experienced by beautiful women. They provide a backstory to explain Tan's family history and provide context for her own mixed feelings about appearance; they also serve to support her mother's assertion that beauty brings misfortune (4).

Integration of Knowledge and Ideas

1. Tan seems to be writing mostly for herself. The essay is a highly personal and introspective rumination on her self-esteem and her relationship with her mother; her purpose seems to be to understand her own feelings and find peace with her mother's death. At the same time, her subjects — beauty, maturity, and loss — are largely universal, easily understood by girls and women especially. Male readers may be less receptive to her ideas, but can still appreciate the mixed emotions and the insights to be gained from a female perspective.

2. Readers can draw several inferences from the details in Tan's stories about her mother and grandmother: for instance, that Chinese women in the early to mid twentieth century had little or no rights or protections from abuse, that adultery was a crime for women (but apparently not for men), that divorce was unavailable, that abduction and rape were acceptable, and that honor was so important in the culture that a woman might rather die than be shamed. Although students might not realize that Tan is describing pre-communist China or be aware of the high rates of Chinese emigration in the 1950s, they might also conclude that such oppressive conditions could explain why her mother came to the United States.

3. Tan's questions are rhetorical, meant to probe further thinking. Although she doesn't give answers, the essay suggests some possibilities: her face is

aging, of course, and possibly softening; she may still want beauty because she wishes to be like her mother; she wants reasons to be vain because her plainness, or her family history, has humbled her; she wants to look like her mother because she misses her. Students might well suggest other answers. Encourage them to explore multiple possibilities and support their thoughts with details from the essay.

Chapter 7

Description
Sensing Our Natural Surroundings

Focus on Concrete and Specific Language

Vague and unclear words are underlined. Students' revisions will vary; possible rewrites are provided under each original sentence.

1. The swamp nearby is an interesting place.
   Soggy, overgrown, and buggy, the marshland preserve in the Salem Town Forest nonetheless enchants visitors.

2. Nature trails let people walk around.
   A marked system of groomed dirt paths, raised wooden walkways, and improvised rock bridges invite residents to explore the deepest recesses of the preserve without getting wet or losing their way.

3. On a recent visit I saw a lot of wildlife.
   While exploring the northwest corner of the park last Saturday afternoon, I was thrilled when a small red fox jumped out of the brush and pounced on an unsuspecting chipmunk ten yards in front of me.

4. A big snake was on the path, so I left.
   Half a mile further, I stopped in my tracks. Coiled in a thick, glistening rope in the center of the path, a four-foot-long water snake seemed to be eyeing me hungrily. Not wanting to meet the chipmunk's unhappy fate, I spun around and sprinted my way back to the parking lot.

5. The Internet says the snake was harmless; now I can't wait to go back.
   The New Hampshire Department of Fish and Game reports on its Web site that Northern water snakes are neither poisonous nor aggressive, so I'm going to return to the preserve this weekend for a fresh dose of thrills.

Joan Didion
The Santa Ana (p. 131)

Joan Didion's piece is an excellent example of descriptive writing. Her colorful yet unsettling images appeal to the senses—sight, sound, taste, and touch. Didion's precision permits the reader to share her sensual impressions with the "persistent [and] malevolent" (paragraph 3) Santa Ana wind. Perhaps the most interesting question to begin discussion with your students is whether Didion admires the destructive force she writes about. Because it may remind them of one, Didion's essay could start a discussion about a "phenomenon" that drives students crazy where they live, leading into questions 1 and 2 under "Writing Topics."

Related Texts

Didion considers how external forces can affect human perception and behavior. The following literary works do the same.

Khaled Hosseini, *The Kite Runner*

Henrik Ibsen, *A Doll's House*

William Shakespeare, *A Midsummer Night's Dream*

Mary Shelley, *Frankenstein*

Sophocles, *Oedipus Rex*

Johann Wolfgang von Goethe, *Faust*

Elie Wiesel, *Night*

Content Quiz

1. Where does the Santa Ana come from?
    [From the northeast, down mountains and through canyons.]

2. Has Didion lived in Los Angeles all her life?
    [No: "when I first moved to Los Angeles"]

3. What color is the sky right before the Santa Ana comes?
    [Yellow.]

4. What are the two extremes of weather in Southern California?
    [The rainy season and the dry season of the Santa Ana.]

5. How long does the Santa Ana usually last?
    [Three or four days.]

Vocabulary Quiz

1. *Mechanistic* (paragraph 1) is closest in meaning to
    a. conniving b. determined c. complex
    [b. determined]

2. *Malevolent* (3) is closest in meaning to
    a. evil b. powerful c. dangerous
    [a. evil]

3. *Mitigating* (3) is closest in meaning to
    a. aggravating b. circumstantial c. excusing
    [c. excusing]

23

4. *Incendiary* (4) is closest in meaning to
   a. inflammatory   b. insensitive   c. windy
   [a. inflammatory]

5. *Apocalypse* (6) is closest in meaning to
   a. draught   b. end of the world   c. winter
   [b. end of the world]

Answers
Key Ideas and Details

1. Didion's statement of thesis is found in paragraph 6: "[T]he violence and the unpredictability of the Santa Ana affect the entire quality of life in Los Angeles, accentuate its impermanence, its unreliability. The wind shows us how close to the edge we are."

2. The wind leaves the city dry, hot, and still. It makes people a little crazy, "drying the hills and the nerves to the flash point" (paragraph 1). "The baby frets, the maid sulks" (1). It makes Didion testy and argumentative, causing her to "rekindle a waning argument with the telephone company" (1). Indians used to throw themselves into the sea when the Santa Ana came. Didion's neighbor holes up inside, and the neighbor's husband runs around with a machete. People go to their doctors complaining of "headaches and nausea and allergies, about 'nervousness,' about 'depression'" (3). Schoolchildren become unmanageable. People have even committed murder.

3. The last sentence could be read both literally (Los Angeles is on the edge of the continent) and figuratively (life in Los Angeles pushes residents to the edge of sanity).

Craft and Structure

1. The colorful images (the glossy ocean, screaming peacocks in trees, the yellow sky) bring the effects of the Santa Ana to life and make them memorable. The imagery is surreal because it's jarring, otherworldly.

2. Paragraphs 1 and 2 are mostly subjective: Didion describes the first signs of a Santa Ana coming on as she is writing, then goes on to describe its effects on herself and on her neighbors. Paragraphs 3–5 are most objective, based on literary and journalistic sources: Didion situates the Santa Ana in the context of other malevolent winds throughout the world, attempts a scientific explanation for its effects, discusses the two violent seasons in Los Angeles, and recounts a particularly devastating Santa Ana in 1957. Paragraph 6 returns to a subjective point of view: Didion suggests that the Santa Ana is emblematic of life in Southern California. The first person makes the description more personal and intimate, helping us feel the effects of the Santa Ana as though we were there.

3. The quotation helps move the essay from examples based on Didion's personal experience to examples she has heard or read about.

4.   Didion's description relies on concrete examples because what she's trying to describe is essentially intangible. Her examples are colorful and memorable and paint a vivid portrait for the outsider of what it's like to live with such a malign phenomenon.

Integration of Knowledge and Ideas

1.   The essay uses the Santa Ana to make a larger point about the craziness of life in Los Angeles. Didion seems to be responding to the problem she states in paragraph 6: "It is hard for people who have not lived in Los Angeles to realize how radically the Santa Ana figures in the local imagination." At the same time there is a self-expressive element to the essay: such a potent force begs to be written about and affords Didion the opportunity to explore its dramatic effects on herself and her surroundings.

2.   Didion is writing for the outsider as well: "It is hard for people who have not lived in Los Angeles to realize how radically the Santa Ana figures in the local imagination" (paragraph 6). We know she is from the city because the essay is written from a personal, insider's point of view, and she uses the first person: "when I first moved to Los Angeles" (2); "just as we had always known it would be in the end" (6).

3.   A mechanistic view holds that human behavior is entirely controlled by outside forces (in this case, a force of nature). The opposite view would be that humans act of their own account, that they have free will.

Dagoberto Gilb
My Landlady's Yard (p. 136)

Gilb's essay uses a description of a barren desert lawn to explore issues of immigration and assimilation without ever explicitly naming either as his subject. But even if students miss Gilb's deeper point, "My Landlady's Yard" offers a promising subject for writing: those immediate surroundings that we all too often take for granted. Gilb's relationship with the landscape is unusually intimate: he finds meaning in details that most other observers would overlook, from the general dustiness of El Paso down to the brand names of discarded wrappers scattered around his yard. Gilb's perceptions are highly personal, and his descriptions more impressionistic than precise, yet he succeeds in creating a pervasive sense of melancholy and hope that his readers can easily appreciate.

You might want to ask students to try applying Gilb's strategy to a description of their own homes, relying on mood rather than precision to create a dominant impression. Alternatively, if you think your students are up to it, you could explore with the class how the author uses description of a mundane subject to make a point about something else altogether.

Related Texts

In addition to any of Gilb's fiction, works that consider issues of cultural assimilation include the following.

Chinua Achebe, *Things Fall Apart*

Sherman Alexie, *The Absolutely True Diary of a Part-Time Indian*

Julia Álvarez, *How the Garcia Girls Lost Their Accents*

Gloria Anzaldua, *Borderlands: La Frontera*

Sandra Cisneros, *The House on Mango Street*

F. Scott Fitzgerald, *The Great Gatsby*

Khaled Hosseini, *The Kite Runner*

Richard Rodriguez, *Hunger of Memory* (see p. 153)

Anzia Yezierska, *Bread Givers*

Content Quiz

1. Where is Gilb's rental house located?
    [El Paso, Texas]

2. What kind of plants grow well in the desert?
    [Gilb names four: creosote, mesquite, ocotillo, and yucca.]

3. What kind of plants did the landlady plant in the yard?
    ["Yankee plants and . . . imported grass" better suited to nondesert climates.]

4. What cultural institution is located in the author's backyard?
    [The local high school.]

5. Who makes up the majority of El Paso's population?
    [Mexican immigrants and their descendants, or, as the local media refers to them, "Hispanics."]

Vocabulary Quiz

1. *Lush* (paragraph 1) is closest in meaning to
    a. drunk   b. colorful   c. plentiful
    [c. plentiful]

2. *Digits* (3) is closest in meaning to
    a. numbers   b. fingers   c. scars
    [b. fingers]

3. *Misconception* (5) is closest in meaning to
    a. knowledge   b. mistake   c. creation
    [b. mistake]

4. *Aspiration* (6) is closest in meaning to
    a. goal   b. sweat   c. breath
    [a. goal]

5. *Husks* (6) is closest in meaning to
    a. dogs   b. seeds   c. shells
    [c. shells]

Answers
Key Ideas and Details

1. On the surface, Gilb waters the lawn because his landlady expects him to, and he doesn't want to give her a reason to evict him. On a deeper level, he tends the grass because he, too, would like a green suburban lawn. (On an even deeper level, Gilb is using the grass as a symbol for himself: he does the work because he wants to survive. See question 1 under "Integration of Knowledge and Ideas.")

2. The yard Gilb describes is dusty, neglected, and strewn with litter, but it also shows signs of effort and hope.

3. By the end of the essay (paragraph 7), close readers will have caught on to Gilb's use of symbolism. If Gilb is writing about his own cultural ambivalence as a Mexican American, the sentence captures his main point perfectly: he may be trying to assimilate, but the process is incomplete (or "patchy, at best"), and he's not sure that he should be making the effort. Ultimately, his "Mexican" self ("the brown dirt") still dominates over his "American" self (the "green").

Craft and Structure

1. Although readers may reasonably object to Gilb's casual way with his sentences and argue that the grammar flaws weaken his credibility as a writer, he is using fragments and run-ons to approximate a spoken voice. The author is trying to establish a connection with his readers by assuming a conversational style, encouraging readers to imagine that he is talking with them, perhaps over the fence, in a neighborly way. This point of view helps to temper the controversial argument he is making under the surface of his words. At the same time, the chatty tone may cause less discerning readers to miss the larger point of his essay entirely.

2. Gilb appeals to four of the five senses: sight ("[t]rash blowing by, snared by limbs and curbs and fences" [paragraph 6]); touch ("[w]ith my thumb over the brass fitting and squeezed against the water" [3]); taste ("the slimy remains of what goes for cheese on nachos" [3]); and sound ("police cars squealed" [5]). Although he doesn't directly invoke smell, some sensitive readers may even get a sense of it in his depictions of the area's unyielding dryness.

3. Gilb takes a psychological point of view but builds his description around the process of tending to the grass in front of and back of his house.

4. The label is important to Gilb because it gets at the crux of his argument. The culturally dominant "Anglo" population sees the numerically dominant Mexican American population solely in terms of "otherness"—focusing on language but ignoring a shared history and culture that is only superficially divided by a political border. The label allows the Anglo community to define members of the majority community as minorities.

Integration of Knowledge and Ideas

1. Gilb's shift in possessive pronouns is part of his assimilation argument. He is saying (again, very subtly) that the work he does to maintain and improve the house and yard will eventually make the property his own (as he already considers it by the end of the essay). In many ways, that property is a metaphor for the United States as a whole: Gilb is pressing readers to accept Mexican Americans as full participants in American culture.

2. Gilb can assume that his readers are intimately familiar with the desert landscape he describes, so he doesn't need to describe the general landscape in much detail. (Notice, for instance, that he rattles off the names of desert plants without bothering to explain what they are.) Instead, he focuses on the details that his readers may not know: the specific kinds of trash he finds in the yard, for instance. Because the *Texas Observer* devotes many pages to politics and tends to take a liberal stance, Gilb can also assume that his readers will be well versed in the cultural and political tensions surrounding immigration issues. He doesn't feel a need to make his argument explicit because he can count on readers to pick up his subtler meanings without much effort. For readers unfamiliar with Texas and its politics, of course, this assumption could pose problems.

3. Gilb uses grass to symbolize Mexican immigrants and their descendants in the Southwest, particularly El Paso. The first clue appears in the introduction: both the plants and the people are "imported" (paragraph 1). Once students see this connection, the essay will take on levels of meaning that many may have missed. Gilb describes the grass in an effort to discuss assimilation without diving into the contentiousness of the current debate over immigration. Students may notice several parallels between the grass and the Mexican community in Texas: both have trouble thriving in the American desert; both seem out of place; both require an extraordinary amount of care to survive. Yet Gilb—a Mexican American himself—embraces the ideals of the dominant culture (symbolized by his landlady) and is determined to thrive in the harsh environment, even if he's not convinced that he should.

Annie Dillard
Living Like Weasels (p. 141)

Students should enjoy Dillard's dramatic renderings of her surprise encounter with a wild animal, even if some express frustration at the more complex philosophical elements of her prose. Dillard is at her descriptive and narrative best here, capturing a feeling of joy at embracing the violent rhythms of nature. Vivid, convincing detail is, of course, the key to making a description compelling, and only through careful word choice will students be able to re-create their feelings as effectively as Dillard does. The essay provides rich opportunity to discuss how figurative and concrete language operate: see question 3 under "Key Ideas and Details" and question 4 under "Craft and Structure."

Related Texts

Elizabeth Bishop, "The Fish"

The Epic of Gilgamesh

William Golding, *Lord of the Flies*

Franz Kafka, "The Metamorphosis"

Harper Lee, *To Kill a Mockingbird*

George Orwell, *Animal Farm*

Edgar Allan Poe, "The Raven"

John Steinbeck, *Of Mice and Men*

Henry David Thoreau, *Walden, Or Life in the Woods*

Mark Twain, *The Adventures of Huckleberry Finn*

Content Quiz

1. Where does Dillard's encounter with the weasel take place?
    [Hollins Pond, a body of water near Tinker Creek and Dillard's home in Virginia.]

2. What weasel behaviors does the author seem to fixate on?
    [The way they hunt (by biting their prey at the neck).]

3. To what animal does Dillard compare a weasel's face?
    [A lizard.]

4. Who is Ernest Thompson Seton?
    [The American author and naturalist whose descriptions of weasels Dillard cites.]

5. What does Dillard recommend the reader should "grasp" as the weasel does?
    [Necessity.]

Vocabulary Quiz

1. *Supposition* (paragraph 2) is closest in meaning to
    a. assumption   b. remark   c. question
    [a. assumption]

2. *Inexplicably* (5) is closest in meaning to
    a. excitedly   b. mysteriously   c. brazenly
    [b. mysteriously]

3. *Ignobly* (12) is closest in meaning to
    a. graphically   b. honorably   c. miserably
    [c. miserably]

4. *Utterance* (13) is closest in meaning to
    a. speech   b. silence   c. frustration
    [a. speech]

5. *Supple* (14) is closest in meaning to
    a. fuzzy   b. adaptable   c. resistant
    [b. adaptable]

Answers
Key Ideas and Details

1. "The thing is to stalk your calling in a certain skilled and supple way, to locate the most tender and live spot and plug into that pulse" (paragraph 14). The lesson, in other words, is that the trick to living well is to yield to instinct rather than intellect, or that the unbridled, unfettered impulses of nature are more rewarding and more satisfying than the restraints of logic and civilization. Some students may notice the irony that Dillard reaches this conclusion through careful philosophical thought.

2. The dominant impression is one of vicious fearsomeness, which the writer clearly reveres and aspires to. Every passage describing weasels in general and Dillard's weasel in particular (paragraphs 1–2, 6–11, 13, 15) revels in graphic descriptions of violent carnage, such as "either splitting the jugular vein at the throat or crunching the brain at the base of the skull" (1), "fixed by the jaws to his throat" (2), "a bright blow to the brain" (8), "a spray of feathers, mouse blood and bone" (11), and "I should have gone for the throat" (13).

3. Paragraph 8 is pure figure of speech, overlapping simile ("as if two lovers . . . ,"), metaphor ("a clearing blow to the gut," "a bright blow to the brain," "a sudden beating of brains," "all the charge and intimate grate of rubbed balloons"), personification ("If you and I looked at each other that way"), and most notably, hyperbole ("It felled the forest, moved the fields, and drained the pond; the world dismantled and tumbled into that black hole of eyes," "our skulls would split"). Not meant literally at all, the pas-

sage nonetheless perfectly captures Dillard's exhilaration at the encounter and highlights the moment of her epiphany.

Craft and Structure

1. Nearly every word in Dillard's essay is concrete, specific, and evocative. Students should have no trouble finding examples. Here is a partial list of words and phrases they might identify. *Sight*: "pounced" (paragraph 2), "six thousand lily pads" (4), "brown as fruitwood" (6), "two black eyes I didn't see, any more than you see a window" (6), "enormous shaggy wild rose bush" (7), "blinking" (13). *Hearing*: "threaded everywhere with motorcycle tracks" (4), "yellow warbler" (5), "stunned into stillness" (7), "shattered" (9), "splashdown" (9), "muttering" (10), "mute and uncomprehending" (13). *Touch*: "socketed into his hand" (1), "soak him off like a stubborn label" (1), "dry skull" (2), "fixed by the jaws to his throat" (2), "feathered throat" (2), "swiveled and bit" (2), "soft-furred" (6), "yank" (9), "leaning on mouse fur" (13). *Smell*: "wild rose" (13), "sniffing bird bones" (13), "breathing musk" (13). *Taste*: "did the eagle eat what he could reach, gutting the living weasel with his talons . . . ?" (2), "sweet" (10), "suck warm blood" (12), "licking" (13), "prolonged and giddy fast" (13).

2. The first five paragraphs are mostly objective description and help to establish the basic facts of weasels and their habitat. The rest of the essay is highly subjective, even visceral, creating the very sense of enthrallment and emotional connection with nature to which Dillard aspires.

3. You may want to spend some time in class having students analyze the imagery of the last paragraph in relation to the first two. Dillard masterfully reworks each disturbing image gleaned from her reading into rapturous images that affirm life and death in all their glory. The technique of circling back to the beginning not only gives the essay a satisfying unity, but in this case also emphasizes the cyclical nature of life.

4. Paragraph 4 compares the natural and manmade elements of Hollins Pond, paragraphs 9–11 compare the weasel's brain with Dillard's, and paragraph 12 compares animal necessity and human choice. The comparisons emphasize the similarities and differences between wild animals and human beings and help Dillard make her point that the similarities would be better embraced than overcome.

Integration of Knowledge and Ideas

1. The two opening paragraphs summarize information Dillard found after a chance encounter with a weasel inspired her to research the animal (paragraph 3). It's unclear whether she refers to one source (Seton) or two (Seton and "one naturalist"), but students should grasp that learning new information raised new questions for Dillard. The essay represents her attempt to answer them, shaping her thoughts into a new idea—that she would like to live as a weasel does—in the process. By the end of the essay, she has synthesized the information from her sources into a whole new personal meaning.

2. Dillard has several overlapping purposes in this essay. Definitely she means to share a personal revelation and to entertain readers in the process, but more so she hopes to encourage readers to adopt a purposeful "mindlessness," to embrace their animal natures and let their instincts shape their choices.

3. Mindlessness is not per se a means to happiness — total abandon to instinct and desire, to the point of "living without bias or motive," is. Being open to this kind of abandon may well lead to mindlessness, but it's the *abandon* rather than the mindlessness that leads to happiness.

Chapter 8

Example

Using Language

Focus on Sentence Variety

Answers will vary. Possible edits are provided below.

    The language used in teen dramas is often graphic. This is especially true for shows on cable: teenage characters swear frequently, and adult characters often discuss bodily functions and organ failures in disgusting detail. Such language seems appropriate given the context of these characters' struggles and frustrations with illness. Because the Federal Communications Commission puts strict limits on the words characters can use on network television but not on cable, the cable programs are more realistic and engaging.

David Sedaris
Me Talk Pretty One Day (p. 160)

In this direct, personal essay, humorist David Sedaris uses exaggerated examples to explore the frustrations of learning a new language by fits and starts. The essay provides a likely occasion for class discussion of the value of education and the reasons for persevering through failure. It is also almost guaranteed to get a laugh from students, many of whom have likely struggled through similar difficulties and feelings of inadequacy in their own foreign language classes.

    Sedaris's essay beautifully surmounts a central difficulty in essays developed by example: how to weave together many examples without sounding monotonous. He avoids tedium through sentence variety and also by varying the way he presents his examples: he paraphrases some of his classmates' and teacher's comments and quotes others directly; he treats some examples briefly and lingers over others; he groups those having to do with likes and dislikes into a separate class. Students often overlook the importance of variety — or, if they are aware that their writing lacks it, don't quite know how to remedy the problem. Sedaris's essay provides a useful model. (Question 1 under "Craft and Structure" focuses their attention on this point.)

    Sedaris's reading of *Me Talk Pretty One Day*, from which this essay comes, is available on CD or MP3. Students may enjoy his distinctive delivery, familiar to anyone who has heard him on National Public Radio.

Related Texts

Works touching on abusive authority figures, refugees, or the frustrations and rewards of learning include the ones listed here.

Sherman Alexie, *The Absolutely True Diary of a Part-Time Indian*

Toni Cade Bambara, "The Lesson"

Suzanne Collins, *The Hunger Games*

Frederick Douglass, *Narrative of the Life of Frederick Douglass* (see "Learning to Read and Write," p. 103)

William Golding, *Lord of the Flies*

Khaled Hosseini, *The Kite Runner*

Henrik Ibsen, *A Doll's House*

John Knowles, *A Separate Peace*

Harper Lee, *To Kill a Mockingbird*

Greg Mortenson and David Oliver Relin, *Three Cups of Tea*

J. K. Rowling, *Harry Potter* series

J. D. Salinger, *The Catcher in the Rye*

William Shakespeare, *A Midsummer Night's Dream*

Sophocles, *Oedipus Rex*

Robert Louis Stevenson, *Dr. Jekyll and Mr. Hyde*

Mark Twain, *The Adventures of Huckleberry Finn*

Content Quiz

1. Why did Sedaris move to Paris?
    [To learn French.]

2. What was the subject of the first lesson in the author's French class?
    [The alphabet.]

3. What do "vkkdyo," "kdeynfulh," "meimslsxp," and "kfdtinvfm" represent to Sedaris?
    [French words he does not understand.]

4. What were the students asked to list about themselves in way of introduction to their classmates?
    [Name, nationality, occupation, and likes and dislikes.]

5. At the end of the essay, what does the author discover he has accomplished?
    [He can understand what his teacher is saying.]

Vocabulary Quiz

1. *Detest* (paragraph 8) is closest in meaning to
   a. hate   b. protest   c. taste
   [a. hate]

2. *Genocide* (14) is closest in meaning to
   a. punishment   b. jail   c. murder
   [c. murder]

3. *Inanimate* (17) is closest in meaning to
   a. physical   b. nonliving   c. expensive
   [b. nonliving]

4. *Belittle* (18) is closest in meaning to
   a. small   b. insult   c. amuse
   [b. insult]

5. *Invariably* (21) is closest in meaning to
   a. consistently   b. uniquely   c. often
   [a. consistently]

Answers
Key Ideas and Details

1. Sedaris gives two reasons for the students' difficulties. To begin with, "they were limited in terms of vocabulary" (paragraph 11). And the teacher's hostile, sarcastic responses to their answers intimidated them from speaking freely.

2. About halfway through the term, Sedaris discovers that he's learned enough French to "understand every word" of one his teacher's insults (paragraph 27). After months of hard work and perceived failure, he has gained a renewed sense of possibility, even though his final sentence makes it clear that his speaking abilities are still a work in progress.

3. Sedaris describes his classmates as a motley group of immigrants from a wide range of countries who are "all young, attractive, and well dressed" and speak French better than he does (paragraph 2). He portrays the teacher as an angry, abusive villain bent on humiliating her students. Although he quotes her and the students frequently, he freely admits that he "understood only half of what this woman was saying" (3) and reveals through quotations that his classmates' French is not as good as he first imagined; furthermore, his examples are so over the top and clearly exaggerated for comic effect (especially the stabbing in paragraph 26) that readers know not to take them at face value.

4. Sedaris's thesis would seem to be that learning is difficult but worthwhile. He states this most clearly in his conclusion: "Understanding . . . [is] a small

step, nothing more, yet its rewards are intoxicating and deceptive" (paragraph 28).

Craft and Structure

1. The sentences in paragraph 2 range in length from ten to thirty-three words. Some begin with the subject ("I've moved . . . ," "My school is . . ."), others begin with transitional and modifying phrases ("Regardless of their nationalities . . . ," "Some accents were better than others . . . ," "As an added discomfort . . ."). One sentence ("Vacations were recounted . . .") is in the passive voice to emphasize the author's own sense of nonparticipation. The second sentence coordinates three separate ideas, and the last two sentences use subordinate clauses.

2. The words are completely foreign and unpronounceable for both Sedaris and his readers. In using them, he recreates the incomprehension he experienced. He can't repeat or translate the French words because he didn't recognize them or understand their meaning.

3. The introduction consists of paragraphs 1–3: these provide the background for Sedaris's experience and his reasons for taking the class. In the body of the essay (4–26), Sedaris gives examples that illustrate his main idea, showing how difficult and awkward his learning process was. Paragraphs 27–30 serve as the conclusion, sharing the author's epiphany and expressing the main point of the essay.

4. By quoting his classmates, Sedaris chronicles their struggles to speak French. But by quoting his teacher's insults, he shows his own progression as a student. Riddled with nonsense words (see "Craft and Structure" question 2) at first, her statements grow increasingly abusive — and yet more fully understood — over time.

Integration of Knowledge and Ideas

1. Sedaris's purpose is to entertain, as evidenced by his humor throughout.

2. Sedaris's feelings appear to be mixed. It's clear throughout that he doesn't like the teacher and that he felt humiliated by her at every turn, and yet he seems to find her approach amusing for its bizarreness; he also reveals an admiration for the "subtle beauty" (paragraph 28) of her cruelties. Ultimately, her unorthodox teaching method worked for him, which gave him "great joy" (30) and an eagerness to continue learning from her.

3. As he does in most of his writing, Sedaris portrays himself as an oddball character who shouldn't be taken too seriously. Raised by a mother who purportedly prefers antacids to her children (paragraph 13), he enjoys "leafing through medical textbooks devoted to severe dermatological conditions" (14) and expresses a fondness for "IBM typewriters, the French word for *bruise*, and [his] electric floor waxer" (15). Considering himself a "hard worker" and a "cut-up" (21), he nonetheless reveals a somewhat twisted imagination and determined irreverence in completing his homework (21).

Kirk Johnson
Today's Kids Are, Like, Killing the English Language (p. 167)

Students might be surprised to find Johnson, a writer and father, proclaim with thinly veiled humor that "*Duh* has elegance. *Duh* has shades of meaning, even sophistication" (paragraph 2). These unorthodox views are bound to inspire debate about the way young people express themselves and the impact their slang has on older generations. An interesting class discussion might revolve around the compilation of a "master list" of slang expressions that students commonly use and an objective, academic study of the function of these terms. Johnson's essay asks us to think about the role of language in conveying identity and in communicating with others.

Related Texts

The works listed below touch on Johnson's themes of adolescence or subversive uses of language.

Sherman Alexie, *The Absolutely True Diary of a Part-Time Indian*

Suzanne Collins, *The Hunger Games*

William Golding, *Lord of the Flies*

Khaled Hosseini, *The Kite Runner*

John Knowles, *A Separate Peace*

Harper Lee, *To Kill a Mockingbird*

George Orwell, *1984*

J. K. Rowling, *Harry Potter* series

J. D. Salinger, *The Catcher in the Rye*

William Shakespeare, *Romeo and Juliet*

Mark Twain, *The Adventures of Huckleberry Finn*

Scott Westerfeld, *Pretties*

Markus Zusak, *The Book Thief*

Content Quiz

1. When was the author born?
    [The 1950s.]

2. Which two cities do *duh* and *yeah, right* represent?
    [New York and Los Angeles.]

3. Who is Marcel Danesi?
    [Professor of linguistics and semiotics, who coined the term "pubilect."]

4. In the sentence "He was, like, duh!" what is the function of the word *like*?
   [It is a "crucial helping verb . . . , a verbal springboard."]

5. Why does the computer represent the paradox of the age?
   [It is built around a binary code of black and white, but the information it transmits represents the gray scale of modern life.]

Vocabulary Quiz

1. *Hyperbole* (paragraph 3) is closest in meaning to
   a. understatement   b. exaggeration   c. sarcasm
   [b. exaggeration]

2. *Incisive* (7) is closest in meaning to
   a. complaining   b. sharp   c. indirect
   [b. sharp]

3. *Overwrought* (9) is closest in meaning to
   a. overstressed   b. unintended   c. fascinating
   [a. overstressed]

4. *Unpalatable* (14) is closest in meaning to
   a. uninteresting   b. unpleasant   c. unavailable
   [b. unpleasant]

5. *Steeped* (19) is closest in meaning to
   a. saturated   b. devoid   c. related
   [a. saturated]

Answers
Key Ideas and Details

1. Johnson's main point is that slang terms, although commonly decried as a deterioration in language use, in fact reflect the times and convey a wide array of meanings. He states that terms such as *duh* and *yeah, right* are "the ideal terms to usher in the millennium and the information age, and to highlight the differences from the stolid old twentieth century" (paragraph 2).

2. Johnson focuses first on the paired terms *duh* and *yeah, right*. They reflect opposite attitudes and replace the black-and-white, right-and-wrong approach of past generations. He also gives special attention to *like*, while admitting that its uses are more difficult to pinpoint. The variety of the first two expressions and the ambivalence of the third powerfully represent the complexity of the modern world.

3. Although *duh* and *yeah, right* spring from a desire to think more flexibly, they also reflect a world governed by yes-or-no, binary-based computers.

Craft and Structure

1. The quoted examples and colloquial language (for example, "Good old *yes* and *no*" [paragraph 4] and "throw in a whole basket" [8]) keep the essay easygoing and accessible. The more precise, formal language (for example, "exquisitely differentiated universe" [6] and "*Yeah, right* is . . . the antithesis to *duh*'s empathetic thesis" [9]) conveys a serious purpose and also helps to pin down meaning more exactly. Students who have difficulty with the more formal vocabulary may be engaged enough by the examples and colloquialisms (and the subject itself) to explore and master the passages they didn't initially understand.

2. The examples are so interesting that more would be welcome, but there seem to be enough to get Johnson's points across. We see the difference between *duh* and *yeah, right* in the paragraphs of contrast (8–10). And *like* comes through clearly in the three very different examples in paragraphs 13 and 16.

3. Johnson's experiences with his sons both prompted the essay and support it. They also add immediacy and humor. But Johnson also strengthens his opinions with more objective evidence, such as historical references (paragraph 3), serious analysis of his examples (for instance, paragraph 14), and perhaps most impressively, the opinion of an expert (12). Students may find the mixture of personal and objective evidence more convincing than either alone.

4. In Johnson's definitions, *duh* "undercut[s] mindless understatement or insulting repetition," and *yeah, right* responds coolly to overstatement (paragraph 9); the more complex *like* softens statements, serves as quotation marks around often ironic quotations, serves as a helping verb, and distinguishes what seems to be from what is. Summarizing, Johnson says, "[L]*ike* reflects modern life, and *duh* and *yeah, right* are the tools with which such a life can be negotiated and mastered" (18).

Integration of Knowledge and Ideas

1. The author appears to write for a variety of reasons. On the one hand, opening with "they are all quite wrong" (paragraph 1) and "hear me out" (3) and his detailed analyses of meaning indicate an explanatory and persuasive purpose. On the other hand, his examples and many of his statements are clearly intended to amuse—for instance, "almost any politician's speech cries out for heaping helpings of both [*duh* and *yeah, right*] at various moments" (paragraph 10).

2. Johnson addresses readers who, like *The New York Times* audience, are adults and probably parents: he is bringing them news of young people's language and analyzing it at a level of detail that would be unnecessary for the young people who use it (and would not be tolerated by them, as Johnson asserts of his own sons). The audience is a general one, not a group of linguistic specialists, or Johnson would surely present his argument in a more academic manner by, for instance, citing more than a single scholar.

3.   The author evidently expects disagreement from the "educators, linguistic Brahmins and purists" (paragraph 1) with whom he disagrees, and he expects dismissal from his own sons. He responds by asking readers to hear him out and then by presenting a reasoned, well-supported case for his view. Students' own responses will vary. The most interesting may come from those who use the terms that Johnson analyzes.

Anita Jain

A Nameless Respect (p. 172)

In writing about her parents' relationship, Jain touches on a subject most students have strong feelings about. Some will likely be less admiring of their own fathers or mothers, but all should be able to appreciate why Jain is impressed with her father and how his example has influenced her own expectations for marriage.

Jain's essay could open up class discussion about gender roles and how they have changed over the last half century or so. As an assignment, you might ask students to research "the poor treatment of women . . . in 1940s India" that Jain mentions in paragraph 2 but doesn't explain. They will surely be shocked by the rapes, kidnappings, and mutilations that Jain is alluding to—and very possibly outraged that she seems to minimize what her father was rebelling against.

Related Texts

As "A Nameless Respect" does, these works look at marriage or gender equity.

Jane Austen, *Pride and Prejudice*

Kate Chopin, *The Awakening*

F. Scott Fitzgerald, *The Great Gatsby*

Charlotte Perkins Gilman, "The Yellow Wallpaper"

Nathaniel Hawthorne, *The Scarlet Letter*

Henrik Ibsen, *A Doll's House*

Arthur Miller, *The Crucible*

William Shakespeare, *Othello*

William Shakespeare, *Romeo and Juliet*

Amy Tan, *The Joy Luck Club*

Tennessee Williams, *The Glass Menagerie*

Content Quiz

1.   What current financial activity occupies Jain's father? [Day trading.]

2. Where did Jain's parents grow up?
   [India.]

3. What do the terms *aap*, *tum*, and *tu* mean?
   [They are Hindi words for *you*. *Aap* is formal and used as an indication of respect; *tum* is familiar, used when talking to those with whom someone has close relationships such as friends or siblings; *tu* is informal and is most often applied when talking to children or servants.]

4. Have Jain's parents ever addressed each other by name?
   [No—at least not in the time they've been married.]

5. What did Jain's father and all six of her uncles study in college?
   [Engineering.]

Vocabulary Quiz

1. *Shenanigans* (paragraph 1) is closest in meaning to
   a. clovers   b. blankets   c. mischief
   [c. mischief]

2. *Insurrection* (2) is closest in meaning to
   a. stitches   b. rebellion   c. construction
   [b. rebellion]

3. *Ruse* (4) is closest in meaning to
   a. flower   b. trick   c. simmer
   [b. trick]

4. *Rapport* (5) is closest in meaning to
   a. connection   b. worry   c. building
   [a. connection]

5. *Parity* (5) is closest in meaning to
   a. healthy   b. quantity   c. equality
   [c. equality]

Answers
Key Ideas and Details

1. Jain's main point, expressed most clearly in the last sentence of paragraph 2 and in the essay's conclusion, is that her father not only developed but also expressed a feminist attitude that was unheard of for men of his generation and background. Less obvious, but apparent in Jain's tone, is that she admires her father for bucking tradition and treating his wife as an equal—and will expect the same of any man she might marry.

2. Jain focuses on three forms of the second-person pronoun in Hindi: *aap*, *tum*, and *tu*. Although all three translate as *you*, she explains that they denote different levels of formality and that their uses are determined by cultural and

social hierarchies. Traditionally, Indian wives would be expected to address their husbands with the high-formal *aap*, while husbands would address their wives with the mid-level *tum* or the informal *tu*, usages that indicated men's superior position in society and marriage as well as women's subordinate status. For Jain's father to use *aap* with her mother indicates both his rejection of traditional gender roles and his deep respect for his wife, whom he considers his equal.

3. Jain's mother refrains from using her husband's first name in compliance with tradition. Her father, on the other hand, refrains from using his wife's first name in defiance of tradition.

Craft and Structure

1. Jain's tone is highly admiring and infused with awe, but there is also an element of flippancy that suggests some ambivalence toward her father's solution. She achieves this tone primarily by mixing colloquial and formal language, often in the same breath. For instance, she refers to "hotheads [who] gave India its first insurrection against imperial rule" (paragraph 2) and expresses amazement "at the depth of principle and reserve of restraint that would keep a man from ever letting his wife's name slip" (6). The mix of academic and casual language reinforces the contrast between her parents' traditional formality and her own generation's tendency toward more easygoing forms of communication; by using both kinds of vocabulary, Jain also suggests that her preference lies somewhere in the middle. Readers may suspect that Jain would have preferred that her parents both use more familiar forms of address and refer to each other by name.

2. The first half of the essay is devoted to providing historical, cultural, and linguistic background. Jain's father's determination to treat his wife as an equal, and the language choices he makes, would not seem unusual without the contrast of history and tradition.

3. Paragraph 3 classifies the Hindi words for *you*. If readers didn't know that each one expressed a different level of formality and implied a particular kind of relationship among speakers, they wouldn't understand what is so compelling to Jain about her father's use of the formal *aap* to address her mother.

Integration of Knowledge and Ideas

1. Jain's mention of her father's flaws actually strengthens her praise, for several reasons: it conveys a child's embarrassment of parents' quirks; it injects a feeling of clear-eyed realism, mitigating sentimentality; and it intensifies, through contrast, the "nobility of mind and dignity of character" (paragraph 1) exemplified by her father's feminism.

2. *Marrying Anita* was written for general readers. All the same, Jain seems to imagine an audience composed primarily of unmarried women who share her values and frustrations, as well as her ambivalence toward tradition.

She assumes some familiarity with Indian culture and history but provides just enough detail to fill in readers who may know little or nothing.

3. The lack of examples to back up this generalization seems to be a weakness in Jain's essay. Although she offers some clues, mostly in the subservience of women implied by conventions of personal address, she leaves it to readers to fill in the blanks. Use any confusion or frustration among your students as an opportunity to discuss the importance of providing examples to make the general specific.

Chapter 9
Division or Analysis
Looking at Popular Culture

Focus on Sources

Answers will vary. Suggested edits are provided below.

1. Thomas de Zengotita claims that most people name musicians as their heroes (193).

2. Nobody, he points out, thinks of role models "in the old-fashioned statesman, warrior, genius, artist kind of way" (193).

3. Teachers find this state of affairs troubling (de Zengotita, 193).

4. According to de Zengotita, however, efforts "to rekindle an aura of greatness" for historical figures are doomed to failure (193).

5. Today's youth are more likely to admire people they know, he says (193).

Margaret Visser
The Ritual of Fast Food (p. 189)

Visser's essay focuses on an experience many students probably take for granted: eating at a fast-food restaurant. Her assumption that most fast-food customers never stop to think about this ritual resembles the underlying assumptions of de Zengotita (p. 192) and Mora (p. 197) that readers haven't really analyzed television or advertisements. Students may wonder, Why *not* take fast-food meals for granted? Visser suggests some reasons in her last paragraph. Questions 2 and 3 under "Craft and Structure" are intended to help students begin thinking about this issue, as are the second and fourth "Writing Topics."

Related Texts

Many nonfiction books and novels examine the food industry or rituals of eating, including the ones below.

Chinua Achebe, *Things Fall Apart*

Laura Esquivel, *Like Water for Chocolate*

Jonathan Safran Foer, *Eating Animals*

Barbara Kingsolver, *Animal, Vegetable, Miracle* (see "Stalking the Vegetannual," p. 258)

Mark Kurlansky, *Cod: A Biography of the Fish That Changed the World*

Michael Pollan, *The Omnivore's Dilemma*

Eric Schlosser, *Fast Food Nation*

Upton Sinclair, *The Jungle*

Morgan Spurlock, *Supersize Me* (documentary film)

Content Quiz

1. What is an "ordinary"?
    [A term referring both to a dinner served to the public at a fixed time and
    price and to the eating house or tavern in which it was served.]

2. Who are the customers the fast-food chains want?
    [Families.]

3. Who comes to fast-food restaurants craving the salt and fat in French fries?
    [Crack addicts.]

4. What does the formality of eating at a fast-food chain depend on?
    ["The fierce regularity of its product, its simple but carefully observed ritu-
    als, and its environment."]

5. When we buy a Big Mac, what more than the food are we purchasing?
    [The careful control expended on it.]

Vocabulary Quiz

1. *Precursor* (paragraph 1) is closest in meaning to
    a. example   b. forerunner   c. legacy
    [b. forerunner]

2. *Conglomerate* (1) is closest in meaning to
    a. diversified company   b. monopoly   c. restaurant
    [a. diversified company]

3. *Rubric* (3) is closest in meaning to
    a. philosophy   b. training   c. set of rules
    [c. set of rules]

4. *Ubiquitously* (5) is closest in meaning to
    a. everywhere   b. mechanically   c. worldwide
    [a. everywhere]

5. *Ramifications* (6) is closest in meaning to
    a. costs   b. consequences   c. faults
    [b. consequences]

Answers
Key Ideas and Details

1. This sentence provides a good illustration of Visser's main idea: that the apparently informal, comfortable, and predictable fast-food restaurant is actually the result of a tremendous amount of money, research, time, effort, and ingenuity. In short, it is not really quick or easy at all; it only appears that way to the patron.

2. A "cultural construct" is a concept created from elements of the culture. A Big Mac is not just a hamburger; when you buy one, you are also buying a whole set of cultural expectations about its appearance, size, shape, temperature, texture, taste, and how quickly it will be served. These expectations are unconscious and pervasive.

Craft and Structure

1. Visser seems to take her subject quite seriously. She writes with the formality and detached objectivity of the anthropologist: "rituals, in the sense of behavior and expectations that conform to preordained rules, still inform the proceedings" (paragraph 2); "architectural variations merely ring changes on rigidly imposed themes" (2); "The staff wear distinctive garments" (3); "in groups of several at a time, the adults hovering over their children" (5). Nevertheless, she is writing for a general audience, and her language is not stuffy or academic.

2. Visser divides the restaurant into four elements: the environment, its rituals, its customers, and its products. The environment encompasses the restaurant's architecture (customers "know exactly what the building that houses the establishment should look like" [paragraph 2]); interior decor ("cottage roofs, warm earth tones" or "glass walls, smooth surfaces, red trim" [3]); and a predictable ambience ("distinctive garments" and menus "in the same spot" and featuring the same content "in every outlet" [3]). Rituals include the employees' use of standard language and the "time off for [holiday] feasts" (4). The restaurant's ideal customers are families, who "maintain a clean, restrained, considerate, and competent demeanor" (5). Finally, the restaurant's product must adhere to standards of "fierce regularity" (6).

3. By breaking the fast-food experience into elements, Visser reveals how these chains and their customers thrive by following certain common rituals—rituals the chains are probably more aware of than their customers are. In paragraph 2, Visser writes that these rituals "inform the proceedings"; she then goes on to illustrate the rituals in paragraphs 2–5.

4. Although it is not, of course, true that all crack addicts necessarily look different from everyone else in a fast-food establishment, the restaurants can't afford to be tolerant. Filthy or crazy or violent crack addicts would violate the code of the "clean, restrained, considerate, and competent demeanor"

(paragraph 5) expected of restaurant patrons. This, in turn, would drive "desirable" customers out the door.

Integration of Knowledge and Ideas

1. Visser's purpose is explanatory.

2. Visser seems to imagine a general audience rather than a professional one. Her essay includes little, if any, sociological terminology, and the people who run the chains already know the information Visser presents. (Since Visser mentions their handbooks and teaching sessions in paragraph 2, she has apparently had access to their inside information.) Visser assumes that her readers take fast-food establishments for granted, that they are oblivious to the "costs and complexities" (paragraph 6) of the fast-food experience, which is of course precisely what the restaurants themselves want their customers to be.

3. Other instances: the company "knows that blunt and direct confrontation with a huge faceless corporation makes us suspicious, and even badly behaved" (paragraph 3); customers are "watching television, where carefully placed commercials will . . . re-imprint the image of the various chain stores for later" (4); "adults hovering over their children, teaching them the goodness of hamburgers, anxious to bring them up to behave typically and correctly. Customers usually maintain a clean, restrained, considerate, and competent demeanor" (5). The portrait that emerges is not flattering. Customers come off as childlike, susceptible, passive, malleable. This picture is an integral part of the "casual" eating experience Visser describes: if the customers did not play these roles, the whole system would collapse.

Thomas de Zengotita
American Idol Worship (p. 194)

De Zengotita's essay focuses on a popular culture phenomenon that many students enjoy but probably have not thought about critically: the reality show *American Idol*. De Zengotita suggests some reasons for examining it more closely in his second and third paragraphs: the "virtual revolution" epitomized by *American Idol* affects our perceptions not only of the world around us but of ourselves as well.

The concept of "mediation" may prove challenging to some of your students, but most of them, having grown up thoroughly immersed in popular culture and implicitly trained to question its messages, will probably grasp the idea intuitively right away. Try not to let them get caught up in the jargon of de Zengotita's scholarly theorizing: the complexities of mediational theory are not essential to understanding his analysis of *American Idol*. If students are interested, however, the author's book *Mediated: How the Media Shapes Your World and the Way You Live in It* (2005) is a relatively accessible and consistently fascinating read. The introductory chapter, in particular, does a good job of explaining the basics of the author's conceptual framework.

Related Texts

De Zengotita's analysis would enhance students' understanding of any literature that addresses hero worship or the influences of culture on self-perception, such as these.

Sherman Alexie, *The Absolutely True Diary of a Part-Time Indian*

Ray Bradbury, *Fahrenheit 451*

Kate Chopin, *The Awakening*

Sandra Cisneros, *The House on Mango Street*

Charles Dickens, *Oliver Twist*

The Epic of Gilgamesh

Aldous Huxley, *Brave New World*

Harper Lee, *To Kill a Mockingbird*

George Orwell, *1984*

Sophocles, *Oedipus Rex*

Percy Bysshe Shelley, "Ozymandias"

Robert Louis Stevenson, *Dr. Jekyll and Mr. Hyde*

Scott Westerfeld, *Pretties*

Markus Zusak, *The Book Thief*

Content Quiz

1. How many people watch *American Idol*?
   [The show has nearly 35 million viewers every week.]

2. What is the "virtual revolution"?
   [It's the recent phenomenon in which regular people produce and distribute their own forms of entertainment, such as blogs, podcasts, chat room posts, *YouTube* videos, and the like.]

3. Whom do most people identify as their heroes?
   [According to de Zengotita, most people would name somebody from their own lives or a performer/entertainer from popular culture.]

4. Why do musicians wield so much influence in contemporary culture?
   [De Zengotita offers two reasons: (1) they "create an experience of belonging that their fans would otherwise never know" by making "us the focus of attention," and (2) music is a profoundly personal and very powerful medium.]

5.   What makes the humiliation of *American Idol* contestants unique?
     [Unlike contestants on other reality shows, *American Idol* hopefuls are performing music, which, because it is so personal, leaves the performer psychically exposed and tremendously vulnerable.]

Vocabulary Quiz

1.   *Nexus* (paragraph 2) is closest in meaning to
     a. vanity   b. combination   c. height
     [b. combination]

2.   *Ruckus* (3) is closest in meaning to
     a. commotion   b. fistfight   c. explanation
     [a. commotion]

3.   *Aura* (3) is closest in meaning to
     a. light   b. quality   c. crown
     [b. quality]

4.   *Unironic* (7) is closest in meaning to
     a. predictable   b. sincere   c. self-conscious
     [b. sincere]

5.   *Articulated* (7) is closest in meaning to
     a. literal   b. implied   c. spoken
     [c. spoken]

Answers
Key Ideas and Details

1.   De Zengotita's thesis can be found in the first and last lines of paragraph 2. The reasons behind *American Idol*'s popularity, he asserts, lie in "a nexus of factors shaping the 'virtual revolution' unfolding all around us. . . . The *American Idol* format combines essential elements of this revolution." He repeats his thesis in the last two one-sentence paragraphs: "*American Idol* gives you so many ways to feel good about yourself. No wonder it's a hit."

2.   For de Zengotita, the "virtual revolution" is marked by the audience's unwillingness to be "mere spectators" (paragraph 2) of the media. Recent technologies—notably, Internet file-sharing venues and the accessibility of digital photography and recording—make it easy for regular people to create and distribute their own media productions. *American Idol* takes the democratic impulse of the virtual revolution and repackages it for audience members, who in turn get to feel as if they had a hand in creating not only the show but also the individual "idols" themselves.

3.   Students may struggle with this concept at first, but it's actually pretty simple. The central conceit of *American Idol* is that it turns everyday people— the fans—into musical heroes. The people watching the show are encouraged to imagine themselves as contestants, and they are given the voting

49

power to decide which contestants will win, so they form a double identity in which they have the ability to transform themselves into superstars. Stardom is the ultimate fantasy for people immersed in a popular culture that repeatedly tells them they're the center of the media universe, hence the "magic" of the show.

Craft and Structure

1. Your students may be relieved to know that several reviewers of *Mediated* complained about de Zengotita's predilection for mixing colloquial and scholarly language. He attempts to make complex ideas more accessible and "hip" by speaking the language of his high school students—hoping both to draw in readers who would normally avoid academic or philosophical subjects and to present himself as a savvy participant in media culture (rather than as an objective or disconnected academic observer). The effect depends on each reader's attitude. Some readers find it jarring and distracting to the point of invalidating de Zengotita's authority as a writer; others find it a reassuring source of the kind of performer-audience fusion that de Zengotita writes about.

2. De Zengotita is interested in the elements of *American Idol* that draw on the "'virtual revolution' unfolding all around us" (paragraph 2). Those elements, as he sees them, are the show's appeal to the "everyday hero" (3), its creation of "performer heroes" (4), the "power of music" in general (7), and the program's infamous exploitation of the contestants' "voluntary personal humiliation" (8). All of these elements combine to make "you . . . feel good about yourself" (9).

3. De Zengotita finds it striking that "a show that features amateurs" (paragraph 1) is more popular than one that features professional musicians, but younger readers in particular won't be surprised by the discrepancy. And that is the essence of the author's point: just as the Grammy Awards and *American Idol* compete for viewership, the current media landscape as a whole pits "spectators against celebrities" (2) in a bid for attention. The spectators are winning, de Zengotita argues, because the deck is stacked in their favor. If the major function of popular culture is to make the spectator feel good, as the author believes, any program that directly involves the spectator in the spectacle is going to win.

4. The cause-and-effect component allows de Zengotita to anticipate and answer the question so often raised by division or analysis: so what? The author could have analyzed the elements of the show without examining the reasons for (and the implications of) its popularity, but the exercise would have seemed empty to most readers. Certainly, it wouldn't have satisfied de Zengotita, whose long-abiding interest in the media's effect on individual consciousness was his reason for examining the show in the first place.

Integration of Knowledge and Ideas

1. De Zengotita sets out to explain why *American Idol* is popular. His primary purpose is, therefore, explanatory. But in encouraging his readers to examine the show closely, he's also trying to persuade them to develop a critical understanding of their own relationships with the "mediated world," as he describes it. By breaking a popular reality show down into its component parts, he forces us to look more closely at why it appeals to us. And by taking a critical rather than a personal stance toward his subject, the author attempts to exempt himself from the mediating influences he analyzes. How successful he is in that effort is open to debate.

2. De Zengotita assumes that he is addressing people who have seen *American Idol* and enjoyed it, but who have not thought fully about the show's implications. At the same time, the author is careful to describe individual elements of the show in enough detail so that the rare reader who has not seen it would probably have no trouble following his analysis.

    The question of being well versed in de Zengotita's *mediation* theory is a little trickier. Certainly, if readers are well versed in the concept of *mediation* as he defines it, it will help them follow his analysis of *American Idol*. All the same, perceptive readers should be able to grasp the basic idea — that popular culture influences how we perceive ourselves — from the context of the essay. Even if *mediation* means nothing to readers, however, de Zengotita's analysis of *American Idol* is developed thoroughly enough to make sense on its own merit and to open a few eyes to a new way of looking at the show.

3. In de Zengotita's assessment, the unprecedented popularity of *American Idol* epitomizes the implications of the "virtual revolution" for consumers and producers of media products. Any of the examples the author cites in paragraph 2 — chat rooms, live journals, etc. — could serve to illustrate his point that new technologies and platforms are profoundly transforming the ways we interact with the media. But *American Idol* is so popular and its influence is so wide-reaching, that it's an ideal subject for his analysis.

Pat Mora

Great Expectations (p. 199)

Pat Mora is best known for her young-adult poetry and children's books, but she is also an astute literary and cultural critic with a sincere concern for the well-being of her primary readers, as this essay shows.

Mora's feminist analysis of advertising and media messages aimed at young women of Mexican American heritage is rich, intriguing, and complex. If students have difficulty following her line of thought, you might want to spend some time in class analyzing the essay's organization, a task suggested in "Craft and Structure" question 2. Class discussion would also be enriched by asking students to find and share examples of Spanish-language advertising in current newspapers, magazines, and television, attempting to apply Mora's principle of analysis to what they bring to class.

Related Texts

"Great Expectations" (editors' title) would be a fitting companion to any of Mora's poetry. In "Desert Women," the lengthy critical essay from which this selection is excerpted, Mora cites several of her own and others' poems that illustrate or complicate her central ideas about Latina feminism:

Julia Álvarez, "Against Cinderella"

Sandra Cisneros, "Bien Pretty"

Margarita Cota-Cárdenas, "*Justo Será*"

Emma Lazarus, "The New Colossus"

Pat Mora, "Desert Women"

Pat Mora, "Legal Alien"

Pat Mora, "Withdrawal Symptoms"

Other related works of literature include (naturally) Charles Dickens's *Great Expectations*, feminist poetry, and Latina fiction:

Julia Álvarez, *How the Garcia Girls Lost Their Accents*

Sandra Cisneros, *The House on Mango Street*

Judith Ortiz Cofer, *The Meaning of Consuelo*

Laura Esquivel, *Like Water for Chocolate*

Marge Piercy, "Barbie Doll"

Content Quiz

1. What two groups of people, according to the author, appeal to the loyalty of Latinas?
   [Advertisers and politicians.]

2. Why are Latinas deemed "double minorities"?
   [They are women, and they are Hispanic.]

3. According to the author, what two conflicting adjectives do Americans often use to describe Latinas?
   [*Fiery* and *docile*.]

4. Name at least three of the six "Great Expectations" held for Latinas in America.
   [Loyalty, family values, marriage, ambition, education, and employment.]

5. What is a *Tía*?
   [An aunt.]

Vocabulary Quiz

1. *Vigor* (paragraph 3) is closest in meaning to
   a. energy   b. lethargy   c. essence
   [a. energy]

2. *Machinations* (4) is closest in meaning to
   a. industries   b. logistics   c. conspiracies
   [c. conspiracies]

3. *Cacophony* (5) is closest in meaning to
   a. unpleasantness   b. combination   c. harmony
   [a. unpleasantness]

4. *Docile* (7) is closest in meaning to
   a. intelligent   b. submissive   c. strong
   [b. submissive]

5. *Bombarded* (16) is closest in meaning to
   a. enraptured   b. attacked   c. engaged
   [b. attacked]

Answers
Key Ideas and Details

1. Latinas are neither white nor male, so their minority status and, thus, their disadvantages in American society are compounded. Mora finds that "depressing" (paragraph 1), both because Latinas tend not to think about their position and because it forces them to "confront some unique challenges, [with] little support in fulfilling [their] potential" (2). At the same time, "double minorities committed to societal change . . . find [themselves] working doubly hard, struggling to prove to others that women like [them] are not a risk" (12). Such efforts, Mora says, are exhausting and alienating.

2. The "game" is, essentially, a process of overcoming obstacles in pursuit of success. What defines success, however, and how likely we are to achieve it are shaped by the influences of family and society. Mora argues that achieving success is more of a challenge for Latinas because expectations have been set low and obstacles are more numerous. Discouraged from pursuing educations or professional careers, they are pressured by relatives to focus on family, limited by employment opportunities "to be clerical or service workers" (paragraph 13), and "taught the world over that it's [their] job to be pretty" (15). Mora wants better for them. (Students who have read Dickens's *Great Expectations* may catch the implied comparison with the orphaned Pip, who starts out disadvantaged but rises to success because a mysterious benefactor both expects him to and provides the means to do so.)

3. Such portrayals are inaccurate stereotypes. Both limit opportunities for a Latina woman: If she's "fiery," she's not taken seriously; if she's "docile,"

she's taken advantage of. Overcoming either assumption, as Mora puts it, "T'aint easy" (paragraph 7).

4. Mora's thesis is that media messages emphasizing traditional values such as loyalty, femininity, and beauty limit Latinas' potential to become successful, productive members of society. She wants educators in particular to teach girls to recognize and reject such messages so that they can "wrench their lives free from images that bind" (paragraph 17).

Craft and Structure

1. Metaphors: "the game of Great Expectations" (paragraph 1), "In the eighties this country began to hear a Latin beat" (3), "cacophony of strange noises" (5), "the information nourishes us" (6), "We ingest pollutants" (14), "devour novels" (14), "sirens who beckon us" (15), "decorations" (15), "How much time we spend looking the part, a part we didn't write" (15). Personifications: "demographics conspire with us" (3), "the woman who gazes back in the mirror" (11), "magazine pages that promise" (15), "flabby egos" (15), "images that bind" (17).

2. After establishing her subject and providing background information about Latino demographics in her introduction (paragraphs 1–4), Mora identifies the most important value in paragraph 5: "we are loyal: to our families, the Spanish language, this country." She then traces several forms of that loyalty in the body of her essay: "brand-name loyalty" (5), cultural loyalty that leads to "a sense of group identity" to which politicians appeal (6), and family loyalty that pressures women to marry and raise children rather than pursue their own dreams (8–13). Her analysis then shifts to focus on how media manipulations of such loyalties affect Latinas (14–16) before invoking an implied loyalty to children and concluding with a call for change.

3. Mora looks at advertising (paragraphs 4–6, 15), traditions (8–13), movies and television and novels (14), and women's magazines (14–15). Her principle of analysis centers on the messages sent to Latinas in particular, which allows her to conclude that such cultural elements, if consumed uncritically, conspire to keep such women from realizing their potential.

4. Such messages set low expectations for Latina women, damage their self-esteem, lead many into poverty, lead others to eating disorders, and discourage all from achieving their full potential as human beings.

Integration of Knowledge and Ideas

1. Mora's intended audience consists of her peers: Latinas in general and educators in particular. The use of *we*, *our*, and *us* throughout, along with the untranslated Spanish, reveal Mora's assumption that her readers are Spanish-speaking women. And she appeals directly to educators in paragraph 14: "As we mother, teach, write, mentor the next generation of women, we need to examine the lives of women in this country . . . What do we know about ourselves and about the women who will appear in our offices and classrooms?"

2.   Although Mora doesn't say so explicitly, Gilday's documentary would appear to be about eating disorders among girls. She cites the film partly to show that she is not alone in her concerns, but more so because in documenting the negative physical and psychological effects of images of women in advertising, the film provides evidence for Mora's claim that images used in advertising hurt women.

3.   Mora looks to a day when Latinas can "fulfill the dreams that our society, our family, and our self have for us" (paragraph 2), the twist being that she'd like those dreams to aim higher and include college educations and personally satisfying professional careers. To that end, she wants adult women to set the bar higher, to teach girls and young women to recognize the obstacles placed before them, to offer them encouragement, and to help them resist the "manipulation" (17) exacted by limiting media messages.

Chapter 10

Classification
Sorting Friends and Neighbors

Focus on Punctuation

Answers will vary. Possible edits are provided below.

1. One charity that has succeeded at raising money online is the Avon Walk for Breast Cancer: the group has more than 40,000 *Facebook* fans and 11,000 *Twitter* followers.

2. The New York chapter explains the appeal of online fundraising on its Web site: "Social networking is . . . the fastest way to spread the word on the Internet."

3. The organization suggests three specific ways walkers can seek donations: joining the Avon Walk for Breast Cancer group on *Facebook*, blogging their reasons for walking on *MySpace*, and broadcasting their progress on *Twitter*.

4. Such tactics, however, can backfire for several reasons: friends quickly become irritated by requests for money, nagging reminders, and feelings of guilt.

5. Brandon Griggs, for example, complains about *Facebook* users who constantly boast about their activities or ask friends to support their causes: "You probably mean well, but stop. Just stop," he pleads (219).

Brandon Griggs
The Most Annoying Facebookers (p. 218)

With the continuing popularity of social networking, Griggs's essay should be compelling to students, most of whom will undoubtedly recognize themselves (and their friends) in at least one of the groups he identifies. It's likely that all of your students spend time on *Facebook*; if some don't, consider starting a class discussion about why some people are resistant to the trend. What are the advantages and disadvantages of social networking? Why do some people embrace it so wholeheartedly, while others find it pointless—or even dangerous?

Related Texts

Although Grigg's primary focus is the *Facebook* phenomenon, his concept of bad behaviors of so-called friends relates to any work that involves more traditional social networks and troubled friendships in general, such as these.

Sherman Alexie, *The Absolutely True Diary of a Part-Time Indian*

Suzanne Collins, *The Hunger Games*

F. Scott Fitzgerald, *The Great Gatsby*

William Golding, *Lord of the Flies*

Khaled Hosseini, *The Kite Runner*

John Knowles, *A Separate Peace*

Harper Lee, *To Kill a Mockingbird*

George Orwell, *Animal Farm*

J. K. Rowling, *Harry Potter* series

J. D. Salinger, *The Catcher in the Rye*

John Steinbeck, *Of Mice and Men*

Edith Wharton, *The Age of Innocence*

Content Quiz

1. To what does the author compare *Facebook*?
   [It's "like being at a big party with all your friends, family, acquaintances, and coworkers."]

2. How did a recent study describe a significant percentage of *Twitter* posts?
   ["As pointless babble."]

3. How many *Facebook* friends does the average user have?
   [120.]

4. Did Jeff Goldblum "plunge to his death from a New Zealand cliff"?
   [No.]

5. Which category of *Facebook* users does Griggs describe as "just a little creepy"?
   [The Lurker.]

Vocabulary Quiz

1. *Mundane* (paragraph 6) is closest in meaning to
   a. weekly   b. unimportant   c. incorrect
   [b. unimportant]

2.   *Innuendo* (9) is closest in meaning to
     a. suggestion   b. perfection   c. opposite
     [a. suggestion]

3.   *Unabashedly* (10) is closest in meaning to
     a. argumentatively   b. harmlessly   c. shamelessly
     [c. shamelessly]

4.   *Anglers* (12) is closest in meaning to
     a. fishers   b. mathematicians   c. liars
     [a. fishers]

5.   *Chronic* (17) is closest in meaning to
     a. pleasant   b. constant   c. coughing
     [b. constant]

Answers
Key Ideas and Details

1.   Griggs's thesis is simple and can be found in paragraphs 4 and 5: "...
     Facebook becomes a daily reminder of why some people can get on your
     nerves" and "Here are twelve of the most annoying types of *Facebook* users."

2.   The study of *Twitter* tweets, supposedly an academic source, found that
     40% of them are "pointless babble." He mentions this because *Twitter* and
     Facebook have similar functions and because the findings help him estab-
     lish, in a relatively objective way, the truth of his complaint that too many
     Facebook updates are also pointless.

Craft and Structure

1.   Nearly every one of Griggs's quotations can be read as hyperbole, particu-
     larly the ones that he insists are real examples. (Students might rightfully
     object that they've seen the exact same or very similar posts from their own
     Facebook friends; the hyperbole lies in the accumulation of examples.) The
     exaggerations establish Griggs's comic tone of exasperation.

2.   Griggs's labels for his categories all carry negative connotations as unde-
     sirable personality traits. By attaching harsh judgment to every category of
     status update he lists, Griggs makes clear to readers that they should not
     be indulging in such behaviors if they want to keep their friends.

3.   Griggs identifies his group, their shared characteristic, and his principle of
     classification in paragraph 2: "Sure, *Facebook* can be a great tool for keeping
     up with folks who are important to you. Take the status update. . . ."

4.   The examples make it clear how Griggs forms his classes, provide a sense
     of recognition, help prove his point, and contribute to the essay's humor.
     Without them, his essay would be nothing more than a list of insulting
     labels, and his categories would make no sense.

Integration of Knowledge and Ideas

1. The entire essay is tongue-in-cheek. Griggs's humor grows above all out of hyperbole (see question 1 under "Craft and Structure"), with examples of posts that are so outrageous he sometimes feels a need to emphasize that he's not making them up. To achieve comic effect, he also uses a consistently deadpan style, as well as sarcasm. As funny as his examples can be, however, Griggs clearly has another purpose for sharing them. He wants readers to find themselves in at least one of the categories, and he wants them to change: "You probably mean well, but stop. Just stop" (paragraph 18).

2. The author seems to hold himself above the behaviors he criticizes, implying but not stating outright, that his own status updates are of the type he describes in paragraph 2: "artful, witty, or newsy . . . a real-time, tiny window into a friend's life." His concluding sentence, however, suggests that Griggs may sometimes be a "Self-Promoter."

3. Griggs assumes, probably rightly, that all or most CNN.com readers will have firsthand experience with *Facebook* and that most have been guilty (at one time or another) of the behaviors he criticizes. Even if some readers are blameless in that regard, however, they've probably seen posts of the type he describes and shared in his annoyance and frustration. For readers who are not personally familiar with *Facebook*, Griggs offers enough examples to give a flavor of the kinds of things people share with their online friends.

Marion Winik
What Are Friends For? (p. 223)

Winik's essay deals with the topic of friendship, a concept that arouses an immediate and profound emotional response. She uses the method of classification to help her account for the complexity of experiences that we share with all those whom we regard as our "friends." Class discussion could begin by eliciting information about students' friends and proceed to differentiate the varying relationships that develop among individuals and groups.

Winik also relies on definition as a way to name the groups she is classifying. This technique can be quite useful to students in their own writing, and classroom discussion might revolve around how to combine classification and definition effectively.

Related Texts

Sherman Alexie, *The Absolutely True Diary of a Part-Time Indian*

Charles Dickens, *Oliver Twist*

F. Scott Fitzgerald, *The Great Gatsby*

The Epic of Gilgamesh

William Golding, *Lord of the Flies*

Khaled Hosseini, *The Kite Runner*

John Knowles, *A Separate Peace*

J. K. Rowling, *Harry Potter* series

J. D. Salinger, *The Catcher in the Rye*

John Steinbeck, *Of Mice and Men*

Mark Twain, *The Adventures of Huckleberry Finn*

Content Quiz

1. Who are the "workhorses of the friendship world"?
   ["Buddies."]

2. What does Winik think about a relative who is also a friend?
   [She describes this person as "the rare exception" but says that a relationship with a "Relative Friend" is comparatively worry-free.]

3. With what kind of friend might you share big celebrations?
   [A "Faraway Friend."]

4. Is it good or bad to have a "Former Friend"?
   [It could be both. Winik describes this friend as "[a]t best a wistful memory, at worst a dangerous enemy."]

5. Which kind of friend is on the other end of the spectrum from the "Friends You Love to Hate"?
   [The "Hero Friend."]

Vocabulary Quiz

1. *Counsel* (paragraph 2) is closest in meaning to
   a. advice   b. stories   c. conversation
   [a. advice]

2. *Infallible* (6) is closest in meaning to
   a. undependable   b. reliable   c. unflinching
   [b. reliable]

3. *Wistful* (10) is closest in meaning to
   a. unrelenting   b. nostalgic   c. profound
   [b. nostalgic]

4. *Lest* (11) is closest in meaning to
   a. indeed   b. in fact   c. in case
   [c. in case]

5. *Inopportune* (11) is closest in meaning to
    a. optimal   b. suitable   c. inconvenient
    [c. inconvenient]

Answers
Key Ideas and Details

1. Winik's thesis is that different people fulfill different functions for each other. In her first sentence, she states clearly, "[E]verybody can't be everything to each other, but some people can be something to each other." In showing what people can be to each other, the rest of the essay answers the title question, "What Are Friends For?"

2. There are nine categories of friends, according to Winik, and they all fulfill different functions. Buddies, described as the "workhorses of the friendship world" (paragraph 2), perform myriad important and insignificant tasks. Relative Friends offer insights into family affairs. Work Friends are vital at work but do not function outside the workplace. They resemble School Friends in eventually providing nostalgic memories. Faraway Friends offer a map of your past. Former Friends are either sad memories or dangerous enemies. Friends You Love to Hate are people you can gossip about. Hero Friends somehow do not annoy you because they really are perfect. New Friends are a pleasure, a "tonic unlike any other" (14).

3. New Friends are different from other kinds of friends in that they do not know you well enough to judge you: Winik remarks, "Your various shortcomings are as yet completely invisible" (paragraph 14). Finding a New Friend is like falling in love because it has the same freshness and unspoiled romantic glow.

Craft and Structure

1. The other instances of dialogue appear later in paragraph 3 and in this passage from paragraph 5: "Your friendship is cemented by jokes about coworkers and thoughtful favors around the office. Did you see Ryan's hair? Want half my bagel?" These unmarked lines of dialogue intensify the informal, conversational tone of the piece. Omitted words, incomplete sentences, and and other rule bending also add to the impression that Winik is engaging in a conversation with the reader, since they are more typical of oral rather than written style.

2. Winik makes few explicit transitions between categories besides those in paragraphs 3, 5, 11, and 13. Some of her moves are rather abrupt, such as those in paragraphs 7, 10, and 14. Some students may prefer a more guided approach. Others may find Winik's approach appropriate for her casual, informal tone.

3. Winik establishes these groups based not on inherent differences between her friends but on the role that each type of friend plays for her. For example,

the Work Friend is important to her because together they can make jokes about coworkers (paragraphs 5, 6). As for why Winik gives short shrift to School Friends (simply comparing them to Work Friends), perhaps she thinks the category is one all readers will have experience with and thus understand. Some students may question the lack of development of the category, even in an informal classification like Winik's.

4. Winik takes the most care to define Buddies (paragraph 2), Relative Friends (3, 4), Work Friends (5, 6), Faraway Friends (7–9), Friends You Love to Hate (11, 12), and possibly Hero Friends (13). These, presumably, are the categories she finds most important or most problematic (needing the most explanation). Winik elaborates on the titles she assigns to the groups by giving specific definitions. For example, we might initially confuse Faraway Friends with Former Friends. However, the definitions of these friends (7, 10) clearly differentiate between the two categories.

Integration of Knowledge and Ideas

1. The opening sentence implies that Winik intends the essay not to be taken as gospel: she's just thinking, reminiscing about her own friendships, sharing ideas, not especially trying to win readers over to her opinion. "I was thinking" (paragraph 1) is typical of conversation and establishes the conversational tone of the essay.

2. While this essay is written from a decidedly female viewpoint (for instance, the first paragraph mentions the friends "whose half-slips you borrow"), Winik's examples make clear that at least two categories—Relative Friends (paragraph 3) and Work Friends (5)—can be of either sex. Perhaps the others can, too. This openness may make the essay more accessible to both male and female readers, although some students may not agree that the two sexes can be more than casual friends.

3. Other metaphors include the description of the Work Friend as initially "just part of the scenery" (paragraph 5) and eventually sharing memories with "a nostalgic glow" (6). In an extended metaphor on Faraway Friends, Winik likens them to guides when "you've hit a dead end, come to a confusing fork in the road, or gotten lost in some crackerbox sub-division of your life"—guides who have "the big picture," who know "the route that brought you to this place" (8). These and other metaphors convey meaning vividly and economically by calling on readers' associations.

David Brooks
People Like Us (p. 228)

In many ways an essay about the drawbacks of classifying, "People Like Us" uses classification to argue some controversial points: that multiculturalism is a flawed concept, and that elite liberals are out of touch with the majority of the American population. Depending on their backgrounds, students may find Brooks's essay enlightening, or they may cite their own communities to dispute his claims—a good starting point for discussion, suggested by the first writing topic.

Charles Murray, one of the authors of *The Bell Curve* (which Brooks cites in paragraph 11), expands on Brooks's concerns about liberal isolation in his 2012 book *Coming Apart: The State of White America, 1960–2010*. After discussing his thesis during an interview on *PBS Newshour*, Murray created an interactive, annotated quiz—"How Thick Is Your Bubble?"—to measure elites' awareness of mainstream culture (*pbs.org/newshour/rundown/2012/03/white-educated-and-wealthy-congratulations-you-live-in-a-bubble.html*). Having students take the quiz and discuss their results would be an interesting and entertaining way to examine some of the assumptions that underlie both his and Brooks's arguments.

Related Texts

Just about any work of literature that examines diversity and community, such as those listed here, would be well complemented by Brooks's essay.

Chinua Achebe, *Things Fall Apart*

Sherman Alexie, *The Absolutely True Diary of a Part-Time Indian*

Sandra Cisneros, *The House on Mango Street*

Khaled Hosseini, *The Kite Runner*

Harper Lee, *To Kill a Mockingbird*

William Shakespeare, *Othello*

John Steinbeck, *The Grapes of Wrath*

Amy Tan, *The Joy Luck Club*

Elie Wiesel, *Night*

Content Quiz

1. What does Brooks blame for the segmentation of America?
    [Human nature.]

2. Name three factors the market research firm Claritas uses to classify the US population into "psycho-demographic clusters."
    [Income, interests, and consumer habits.]

3. According to Brooks, do American college professors tend to be politically liberal or politically conservative?
    [Liberal.]

4. At the time Brooks wrote this essay, what percentage of Americans were evangelical Christians?
    [40.]

5. How does the author recommend that Americans make their lives more diverse?
[Experience a range of different institutions and environments, encourage young people to do national service, and encourage adults to venture outside of familiar circles.]

Vocabulary Quiz

1. *Strenuous* (paragraph 1) is closest in meaning to
   a. strong   b. defiant   c. ironic
   [a. strong]

2. *Congenial* (3) is closest in meaning to
   a. sticky   b. friendly   c. hostile
   [b. friendly]

3. *Homogeneous* (4) is closest in meaning to
   a. segregated   b. similar   c. eclectic
   [b. similar]

4. *Mores* (13) is closest in meaning to
   a. additional   b. restrictions   c. customs
   [c. customs]

5. *Renounce* (15) is closest in meaning to
   a. quit   b. speak   c. balance
   [a. quit]

Answers
Key Ideas and Details

1. Brooks withholds his thesis for the conclusion: "It's probably better to think about diverse lives, not diverse institutions. Human beings, if they are to live well, will have to move through a series of institutions and environments, which may be individually homogenous but, taken together, will offer diverse experiences" (paragraph 18). His point is that while diversity is a noble goal, it cannot be—nor should it be—achieved in geographical clusters such as neighborhoods and workplaces. Instead, he'd like to see people seek out diversity through their experiences, reaching out to interact with and understand people who are different than themselves.

2. As Brooks suggests elsewhere in the essay, psycho-demographics is a marketing tool used to identify groups of "people with similar tastes and preferences" (paragraph 7). He invokes the concept to make his point that diversity can be measured in a seemingly infinite number of ways—not just by "race and ethnicity" (6). He then supports this point with multiple examples of varying tastes and preferences, from the "suburban sprawl" and "towns & gowns" clusters identified by the marketing firm Claritas (8), to "imported-wine drinkers" and motor-home aficionados (9), pop culture

consumers (10), ivy-league graduates (11–13), and Republicans and evangelical Christians (13–14).

3. Brooks points out that self-segregation enables people to build communities of like-minded people (paragraph 3), which makes them happy and enables them to "flourish" (4). But the resulting insularity limits employment opportunities (14), promotes inequality (15), and fosters divisiveness (16).

Craft and Structure

1. Brooks's metaphors include "people . . . tied down to factories and mills" (paragraph 3), "the brick wall of human nature" (5), "building diverse communities" (7), "sings the diversity anthem" (13), "to hammer diversity into every neighborhood" (17), and "the iron curtains that now separate the nation's various cultural zones" (18)—the last a reference to the Cold War between the US and Soviet Russia that students are likely to miss. The most effective metaphors emphasize construction and barriers of some sort, reinforcing Brooks's point that Americans deliberately separate themselves from others.

2. The tone is calm, civil, and even-handed. As a conservative addressing liberals whose thought and attitudes he hopes to change, Brooks has to take a reasonable tone to avoid alienating readers.

3. Brooks's classification scheme is complex. He considers racial diversity (paragraphs 5–6), cultural diversity (7–14), intellectual diversity (11–13), and political and religious diversity (13–14, 16). Although his categories do overlap, seemingly breaking the rules of effective classification, the overlapping categories are part of his point that diversity is a fluid concept subject to interpretation.

4. Brooks compares and contrasts people in different regions of Washington, DC, Manhattan, California, and Georgia (paragraph 2); "suburban sprawl" and "towns & gowns" psycho-demographic clusters (8); motor-home popularity in two Pennsylvania counties (9); news, entertainment, and worship preferences (10); the distribution of Democrats, Republicans, and evangelical Christians in the general population and in elite universities (13); and university professors and conservatives (14 and the cartoon). In each case, the comparison and contrast helps to clarify the distinctions between different types of people.

Integration of Knowledge and Ideas

1. As paragraphs 11–13 in particular make clear, Brooks addresses his argument to highly educated, affluent, liberal readers. He assumes that they, or their friends, have attended elite universities. He also assumes that they "live in a coastal, socially liberal neighborhood" (18), and that they value diversity even as they fail to be "in touch with the broad diversity of American life" (19).

2. The cartoon illustrates the comparison Brooks makes in paragraph 14. Some students may object to the negative stereotypes it presents, but they're the point of both Brooks's words and Brodner's drawing: each image captures the assumptions that elite liberals and regular conservatives make about each other.

3. "People Like Us" is a model of synthesis. Citing ideas and statistics from a personal interview (paragraph 3), the US Census (5), the marketing firm Claritas (8–9), the book *The Bell Curve* (11), and a study conducted by the Center for the Study of Popular Culture and the American Enterprise Unit (13), Brooks avoids direct quotation completely, instead using summary, paraphrase, and follow-up comments to build a new idea of his own. (If students question why the essay has no works-cited list, you may want to explain that like most magazine writers, Brooks does not follow MLA style. He is careful, all the same, to identify ideas and information that are drawn from sources, even if readers would have a hard time tracking down those sources for themselves.)

Chapter 11

Process Analysis
Eating Well

Focus on Consistency

Answers will vary. The sentences below have been edited back to Fischetti's original language.

1. Water molecules exist in most foods. They have positive and negative charge at opposite "ends."

2. The electric field of a microwave orients the positive ends in one direction, but the field reverses 4.9 billion times a second, causing the molecules to turn back and forth. As they turn, they bump, creating friction that produces heat.

3. Ceramic and glass containers are water-free and thus remain cool, although hot food might heat them through conduction.

4. Can't the microwaves fly through the window and harm our bodies—especially our eyes? [Note that Fischetti shifts between third and first person here. A better revision might be: . . . *harm people's bodies—especially their eyes?*]

5. No. The waves reflect off a metal screen embedded in the glass.

Firoozeh Dumas
Sweet, Sour, and Resentful (p. 248)

Popular humorist Firoozeh Dumas has made it her mission to humanize Iranian people in the American consciousness, a mission that seems especially important in the context of political unrest and wars in the Middle East, nuclear proliferation, and terrorism.

Students may not be familiar with the Iranian revolution to which Dumas refers or with the ensuing exodus of Iranian families to America and Americans' distrust of them in the 1970s and 1980s. The third writing topic encourages students to research this background, but you may also want to give students the basic outline of events: In the late 1970s, fundamentalist Muslims fostered political and religious unrest in the country, culminating in a coup and the exile of

American-backed Shah Reza Pahlavi. In his place, revolutionaries installed Ayatollah Ruhollah Khomeini, who was determined to jettison Western influence and restructure Iranian culture and politics around strict interpretation of Islamic religious rule. In 1979, Khomeini supporters captured fifty-three Americans at the US embassy in Tehran, precipitating a hostage crisis that lasted 444 days and ended in a botched rescue attempt and embarrassment for the Carter administration; the hostages were released upon Ronald Reagan's inauguration in 1981. (During the same period, Iran was attacked by Iraq, leading to a brutal war that lasted until 1988.) Backlash against Iranians in the United States—the vast majority of whom had fled the violence and repression in their country—was severe and included general hostility, physical attacks, and demands for universal deportation.

Related Texts

Because Dumas's writing resonates so well with teenagers, many teachers assign one of her two complete essay collections: *Funny in Farsi* and *Laughing without an Accent*. Relevant works of fiction include the following.

Chinua Achebe, *Things Fall Apart*

Laura Esquivel, *Like Water for Chocolate*

F. Scott Fitzgerald, *The Great Gatsby*

Khaled Hosseini, *The Kite Runner*

Marjane Satrapi, *Persepolis* (see p. 93)

Anzia Yezierska, *Bread Givers*

Markus Zusak, *The Book Thief*

Content Quiz

1. Where was the author born?
    [Abadan, Iran.]

2. How often did the Dumas family host dinner guests in their small condo?
    [Every week.]

3. In the author's culture, what dish is the litmus test of a cook's ability?
    [Rice.]

4. Why is 1979 a particularly significant year to Dumas and her family?
    [It was the year of the Iranian Revolution, and also the year that many of her Iranian family and friends fled to join her family in America.]

5. What were the author's two contributions to her mother's meal preparations?
    [Chopping the stems of grape leaves and announcing that dinner was ready.]

Vocabulary Quiz

1. *Ubiquitous* (paragraph 1) is closest in meaning to
    a. isolated   b. everywhere   c. enormous
    [b. everywhere]

2. *Quintessential* (1) is closest in meaning to
    a. ideal   b. theoretical   c. irregular
    [a. ideal]

3. *Persian* (4) is closest in meaning to
    a. Iranian   b. cat   c. rug
    [a. Iranian]

4. *Pith* (8) is closest in meaning to
    a. attitude   b. stem   c. sadness
    [b. stem]

5. *Lavished* (11) is closest in meaning to
    a. experienced   b. refused   c. offered
    [c. offered]

Answers
Key Ideas and Details

1. The dinners provided an opportunity to orient recent Iranian immigrants to life in California; they also allowed the hosts to share "the hospitality that Iranians so cherish" (paragraph 3) as well as stay connected to their roots. For both the hosts and the guests, the elaborate and traditional Persian meals helped to maintain a sense of community; they also served as a bittersweet "reminder of the life [they] had left behind" (10).

2. "As I watched my mother experience the same draining routine week after week, I decided that tradition is good only if it brings joy to all involved. . . . Sometimes, even our most cherished beliefs must evolve" (paragraph 12).

3. Dumas suggests potluck, or requiring guests to contribute to the meals by bringing food with them. Based on the way Dumas characterizes her (traditional, diplomatic, judgmental of inadequate or lazy cooks, perfectionist, and controlling), it seems unlikely that her mother would have relinquished the role of hostess, no matter how much it strained her. However, Dumas does relate the process in the past tense, so it's possible that her mother did, indeed, scale back her efforts—or that the number of guests dwindled after the first wave of Iranian immigration in the late 1970s and early 1980s.

Craft and Structure

1. Dumas provides the Persian names for most of the dishes her mother prepared and served to guests every week. In doing so, she emphasizes the sense of home those meals provided for both her family and their guests.

She ensures that American readers will understand the meaning by renaming each dish in an appositive phrase, such as "*fesenjan*, pomegranate stew with ground walnuts" (paragraph 4) or "*qormeh sabzi*, herb stew" (6).

2. The introductory paragraphs establish the context behind the elaborate weekly meals: the guests who came to the author's parents' condo every weekend were reluctant immigrants, possibly even refugees, displaced from their "real home" (paragraph 1) by war. At the same time, the introduction indicates the parallels between Iranian culture and American culture to help make Iranians seem less "foreign" to readers — one of the Dumas's overriding goals as a writer.

3. Although Dumas identifies "the first step" as "preparing the herbs" (paragraph 6), the process actually began with her father taking phone calls and extending invitations to near strangers. Next came menu planning (on Mondays) and softening the neighbors with gifts of food (4), followed by Tuesday shopping trips that usually ended in frustration. With all ingredients corralled, by midweek the author's parents began the simultaneous tasks of chopping by hand and frying herbs and onions (6); mixing, cooking, and rolling the contents of stuffed grape leaves (7); and preparing home-made yogurt and other side dishes (8). The guests would arrive on the weekends, at which time Dumas's mother cooked and drained the rice. The meals would then be served "buffet-style" (10) and consumed in a matter of minutes (11). The final step was "fielding thank-you phone calls from . . . guests" (12) and extending more invitations. With several overlapping stages occurring over the course of a week, Dumas ensures coherence by providing clear time-markers and transitions throughout her analysis, then circling back to the first stage in her conclusion, implying that the process never ended.

4. By comparing bucolic local market days in Abadan with frustrating car-dependent shopping trips in California, Dumas harkens back to her introduction and underscores her point that adjusting to life in the United States was challenging and unpleasant for Iranian immigrants. At the same time, she emphasizes how much additional trouble her mother went to in order to give her guests a taste of home.

Integration of Knowledge and Ideas

1. Dumas wants to share a belief that she developed as a witness to her mother's exhaustion and resentment — the importance of adapting tradition and beliefs when circumstances demand it. To some extent, she is also relating the impetus behind her own assimilation to American culture.

2. "Sweet, Sour, and Resentful" was first published in the now-defunct *Gourmet*, an upscale magazine for "foodies" (paragraph 5) that often featured complicated recipes and travel essays. Dumas could reasonably assume, then, that her readers held a strong interest in food and culture. Most readers of the magazine would have had some experience preparing elaborate dishes, hunting down elusive ingredients, and hosting large gath-

erings themselves, so it's likely they could empathize with the difficulties and stresses the author's mother endured—if not, perhaps, her resentment.

3. In its literal sense, a "litmus test" is a chemical process that measures the pH level of a substance to determine where it falls within a range of base to acid; colloquially, the phrase refers to a basis for making a judgment. Dumas uses the term in its colloquial meaning, but notice the echo of "sweet" (base) and "sour" (acidic) with the title and the concept's effectiveness in evoking her mother's bitterness about performing her tasks.

4. Dumas tempers the implied criticism of her parents' and guests' behavior with several self-deprecating remarks, which is where most of her humor lies. Throughout the essay, she portrays her young self as baffled, awkward, and inept. You might ask students how the writer's attitude toward her parents would have come across without the mocking comments about her own abilities.

Lars Eighner
Dumpster Diving (p. 253)

Eighner's essay is a wonderful model of a process analysis written for a larger purpose. While he does want to explain to his readers what it's like to be a scavenger, he is equally interested in sharing the lessons he has learned from scavenging and challenging the stereotypes of scavengers many people hold. You might begin discussion of this essay by asking students to jot down all the words and phrases they would have used to describe scavengers *before* they read this essay. After reading "Dumpster Diving," which words and phrases would they drop? Are there any they would add?

Related Texts

Horatio Alger, *Ragged Dick*

Toni Cade Bambara, "The Lesson"

Suzanne Collins, *The Hunger Games*

Charles Dickens, *Oliver Twist*

Barbara Ehrenreich, *Nickel and Dimed: On (Not) Getting By in America*

F. Scott Fitzgerald, *The Great Gatsby*

William Golding, *Lord of the Flies*

Khaled Hosseini, *The Kite Runner*

William Shakespeare, *Macbeth*

William Shakespeare, *Othello*

David K. Shipler, *The Working Poor: Invisible in America*

John Steinbeck, *The Grapes of Wrath*

Mark Twain, *The Adventures of Huckleberry Finn*

Jeanette Walls, *The Glass Castle*

Elie Wiesel, *Night*

Content Quiz

1. When did Eighner start dumpster diving?
   ["About a year before [he] became homeless."]

2. According to Eighner, what emotions does someone who is new at scavenging feel?
   [Disgust and self-loathing.]

3. When looking for food in dumpsters, what does Eighner consider one of his favorite finds?
   [Yogurt.]

4. About how often does Eighner get dysentery?
   [At least once a month.]

5. What "two rather deep lessons" has Eighner learned from his experiences as a dumpster diver?
   ["The first is to take what I can use and let the rest go. . . . The second . . . is the transience of material being." The lessons might be paraphrased as *hoarding is bad and nothing lasts forever*.]

Vocabulary Quiz

1. *Refuse* (paragraph 3) is closest in meaning to
   a. material   b. garbage   c. shame
   [b. garbage]

2. *Niche* (3) is closest in meaning to
   a. specialty   b. cut   c. shelf
   [a. specialty]

3. *Qualms* (10) is closest in meaning to
   a. oysters   b. shoes   c. concerns
   [c. concerns]

4. *Transience* (14) is closest in meaning to
   a. temporary   b. homeless   c. invisible
   [a. temporary]

5. *Bauble* (16) is closest in meaning to
   a. talk   b. trinket   c. soap
   [b. trinket]

Answers
Key Ideas and Details

1. Eighner is sorry for "the rat-race millions who have confounded their selves with the objects they grasp and who nightly scavenge the cable channels for they know not what" (paragraph 16)—in other words, for all who are preoccupied with material goods and wealth because they believe these things will make them happy. Dumpster diving has taught him the true value of material goods and how misguided is our culture's emphasis on them as a means to happiness.

2. Eighner keeps only "items of relatively immediate utility" (paragraph 7). An item's value rests entirely on whether or not he can use it or make it useful (see paragraph 13).

Craft and Structure

1. This formal style may be startling at first, since many of us do not expect street people to be educated, much less dignified. Eighner's dignity, however, is precisely what this language expresses. Some other examples: "I find from the experience of scavenging two rather deep lessons" (paragraph 13); "however fine or rare it may be" (13), "the transience of material being" (14); "desire to grab for the gaudy bauble has been largely sated" (16).

2. Eighner's tone is simultaneously matter of fact and proud. His matter-of-fact, realistic attitude shows up in other statements: "I like the frankness of the word *scavenging*" (paragraph 3), and "most divers come to realize that they must restrict themselves to items of relatively immediate utility" (7). But he is also proud of the fact that he's good at what he does, which is revealed in "I think it a sound and honorable niche" (3) and the fact that he considers himself a professional (9).

3. During the first stage, the scavenger "is ashamed of being seen" (paragraph 5). During the second stage, the scavenger begins to find things that "look and smell brand-new" or are in "perfect working order"; he "begins to understand" that people throw away "a lot of perfectly good stuff" (6). He enters the third stage when he learns to restrict himself to "items of relatively immediate utility" (7). Some scavengers never make it that far, however. Once they realize how much is there for the taking, they "may become lost and never recover . . . trying to acquire everything they touch" (7). The implication is that they become obsessed with collecting things and unable to pursue other aims, while those scavengers who *don't* get stuck can use scavenging as a means, not an end.

4. Eighner reserves the word *foraging* for foods that grow naturally and that he can collect when they are in season. *Scavenging* refers specifically to living off the refuse of others. This definition establishes that Eighner is intelligent, articulate, and forthright and therefore gives him both credibility and authority with his readers.

Integration of Knowledge and Ideas

1. Eighner's phrase "I prefer" clearly asserts that he has the ability to exercise choice, both over his vocabulary and over his life. His focus on fine points of meaning reveal him to be intelligent and articulate, while his reference to foraging shows that he is resourceful and capable. Many of us have preconceived notions of scavengers as helpless, pathetic, desperate, and perhaps even mentally ill. But Eighner presents himself in such a way that this is clearly not the case.

2. Eighner assumes that most of his readers don't know how much perfectly good food is thrown away; listing what he finds brings this point home. Eighner also assumes that his audience perceives scavengers as dirty and indiscriminate, so he takes a great deal of care to present the process of scavenging for food as one guided by common sense and hygienic concerns.

3. Answers will vary.

Barbara Kingsolver
Stalking the Vegetannual (p. 258)

Kingsolver's essay focuses on an experience many readers probably take for granted: eating fresh produce regardless of the season. Her assertion that most grocery shoppers never stop to think about the origin of the fruits and vegetables on display at the supermarket may raise objections from environmentally conscious students. Many others, however, are likely to be shocked into a new kind of awareness: How *do* those bananas get here?

Kingsolver also shows students that process analysis need not be a dull series of directions and demonstrates how the method can be used to explain and support a strongly held belief. It may be worth pointing out to your class that only the first half of the essay illustrates process analysis per se (see question 4 under "Craft and Structure"); Kingsolver uses the method to establish the relevance of her subject and to educate readers about a basic botanical fact, then builds on the implications of her process analysis in the remaining paragraphs to make an impassioned argument for cultural and social change.

Related Texts

Laura Esquivel, *Like Water for Chocolate*

F. Scott Fitzgerald, *The Great Gatsby*

Jonathan Safran Foer, *Eating Animals*

Mark Kurlansky, *Cod: A Biography of the Fish That Changed the World*

Michael Pollan, *The Omnivore's Dilemma*

Eric Schlosser, *Fast Food Nation*

Upton Sinclair, *The Jungle*

Henry David Thoreau, *Walden, Or Life in the Woods*

Content Quiz

1. What are angiosperms?
   [*Angiosperm* is the botanical term for a flowering plant.]

2. Put the following stages of plant life in the correct order: green fruits, flowers, hard fruits, leaves, ripe fruits, buds.
   ["Leaves, buds, flowers, green fruits, ripe fruits, hard fruits."]

3. What is "the trademark fruit of late October"?
   [The pumpkin.]

4. How many calories of fuel are expended to ship one calorie of fruit from California to New York?
   [Approximately 87.]

5. According to Kingsolver, what are three "debts that will be paid by our children" for our habit of eating out-of-season produce?
   ["Extinctions, economic unravelings, and global climate change."]

Vocabulary Quiz

1. *Terrestrial* (paragraph 2) is closest in meaning to
   a. alien   b. land-based   c. fenced in
   [b. land-based]

2. *Predestined* (6) is closest in meaning to
   a. fated   b. prevented   c. religious
   [a. fated]

3. *Fretting* (8) is closest in meaning to
   a. musical   b. different   c. worrying
   [c. worrying]

4. *Untallied* (11) is closest in meaning to
   a. not counted   b. not known   c. not important
   [a. not counted]

5. *Quixotic* (14) is closest in meaning to
   a. Spanish   b. impractical   c. rural
   [b. impractical]

Answers
Key Ideas and Details

1. A *vegetannual* is the imaginary plant Kingsolver invokes to teach readers how to recognize which vegetables are in season at any given time of year.

Helping readers "picture a season of foods unfolding as if from one single plant," she explains that the vegetannual "bears over the course of one growing season a cornucopia of all the different vegetable products we can harvest" (paragraph 4). Each stage of the plant's life represents a general class of vegetables, and each class is edible in turn over the course of a year: "First, the leaves.... Then more mature heads of leaves and flower heads.... Then tender young fruit-set.... Then more mature, colorfully ripened fruits.... Then the large, hard-shelled fruits with developed seeds inside ... ," ending with the "root crops" (5). The carefully constructed metaphor helps her explain and reinforce the main idea of her essay: that indulging in off-season vegetables is unnatural and unwise.

2. The verb *stalking* refers, of course, to pursuit, but it also suggests the noun *stalk*, or the stem that supports a plant's growth. The play on words hints that Kingsolver is interested in both reaching and supporting a new understanding of vegetables. The title is also an obscure allusion to Euell Gibbons' classic book on food and the environment *Stalking the Wild Asparagus*.

3. She is saying that the year-round availability of most produce is unnatural and wrong. Regularly indulging in off-season fruits and vegetables is "outrageous" because the habit has environmental and economic consequences (discussed in paragraphs 11 and 12, and alluded to in 16)—not to mention that the foods taste better at the peak of freshness (14–16).

Craft and Structure

1. By giving annual plants human characteristics and desires, Kingsolver injects her subject with some personality and helps make an abstract concept livelier and easier to grasp. She also demonstrates that she has a sense of humor. All the same, some students may object that the paragraph comes off as juvenile, overly cute, or condescending.

2. The drawing is a pictorial representation of the process Kingsolver analyzes in paragraphs 3–6. The image reinforces her point that every plant must follow the same process, "[n]o variations ... allowed" (paragraph 3).

3. Kingsolver explains the process quite clearly. The main stages of plant growth are fertilization and seed (paragraph 3), followed by shoots, "leaves, buds, flowers, green fruits, ripe fruits, hard fruits," and back again to seed (4, 6).

4. Kingsolver follows the process analysis proper with an unsettling example of an unseasonal meal (paragraph 10), a brief consideration of the environmental and economic effects of shipping foods long distances (11–12), and an attempt to convert readers to local eating (13–16). The second half of the essay extends Kingsolver's process analysis and gives it a broader significance.

Integration of Knowledge and Ideas

1. With this essay, Kingsolver is asking readers to recognize that their eating habits have damaging consequences. More to the point, she wants readers

to change those habits. Opening with her call to action would have put readers on the defensive, defeating her purpose.

2. Kingsolver seems to imagine an audience of "[w]ell-heeled North American epicures" (paragraph 9). She assumes, in other words, that her readers are relatively affluent, that they eat for recreation and pleasure as much as for sustenance, and that they feel entitled to immediate gratification of their food desires.

3. Kingsolver's style in this essay is usually informal, even conversational, as in "For the life of them, they can't do it differently" (paragraph 6). But often she uses advanced vocabulary and sometimes seems to imitate the technical, impersonal style of scientists, as in "Flowering plants, known botanically as angiosperms, evolved from ancestors similar to our modern-day conifers" (2). The colloquial language keeps the essay easygoing and accessible. The more precise, formal language conveys a serious purpose and also helps to pin down concepts more exactly. Students who have difficulty with the more formal vocabulary may be engaged enough by the colloquialisms (and the subject itself) to explore and master the passages they didn't initially understand.

Chapter 12

Comparison and Contrast
Examining Stereotypes

Focus on Parallelism

Answers will vary. Possible edits are provided below.

1. Most people would rather get a tooth pulled than speak in public.

2. The most popular country songs feature interesting characters and inspiring story lines.

3. My sister wants to be a police officer, but my brother wants to be a nurse.

4. The city offers three kinds of public transportation: buses, trains, and trams.

5. Where will we go? What will we do? Who will join us?

Suzanne Britt
Neat People vs. Sloppy People (p. 280)

Whatever Suzanne Britt believes, she believes wholeheartedly. Then she merrily sets out to convince her readers that she's right. A danger in teaching this essay, perhaps, is that students without Britt's skill may be inspired to emulate her slapdash unreasonableness without quite achieving the desired effect. Some inspired students, though, just might surprise you with the delightful writing they can produce.

Small groups can be useful for helping students through the brainstorming part of writing an essay. Students might appreciate having time to talk about the points of comparison they have listed in preparing to write an essay for either of the first two writing suggestions. Group members can help each other expand their lists and find the details that will bring these points to life.

Related Texts

Sherman Alexie, *The Absolutely True Diary of a Part-Time Indian*

Henrik Ibsen, *A Doll's House*

John Knowles, *A Separate Peace*

Harper Lee, *To Kill a Mockingbird*

William Shakespeare, *Macbeth*

John Steinbeck, *Of Mice and Men*

Content Quiz

1. Whom does Britt describe as lazy and mean: neat people or sloppy people?
[Neat people.]

2. What explanation does the author give for people who are sloppy?
[Britt cites their moral superiority and perfectionism: "Sloppy people carry in their mind's eye a heavenly vision, a precise plan, that is so stupendous, so perfect, it can't be achieved in this world or the next."]

3. What is "the only messy thing in a neat person's house"?
[The trash can.]

4. What "two unvarying principles" does the author claim neat people live by?
["Never handle anything twice, and throw everything away."]

5. According to Britt, why would neat people sell a dog?
["[T]oo many fleas."]

Vocabulary Quiz

1. *Rectitude* (paragraph 2) is closest in meaning to
a. stiffness   b. formality   c. integrity
[c. integrity]

2. *Métier* (3) is closest in meaning to
a. specialty   b. curse   c. fate
[a. specialty]

3. *Accumulate* (4) is closest in meaning to
a. gather   b. climate   c. discard
[a. gather]

4. *Scrupulously* (5) is closest in meaning to
a. fastidiously   b. wastefully   c. conscientiously
[c. conscientiously]

5. *Salvaging* (9) is closest in meaning to
a. ruining   b. saving   c. hiding
[b. saving]

Answers
Key Ideas and Details

1. Whoever said it failed to perceive Britt's humor.

2. "As always" means what it says. Yes, Britt is saying—with tongue only partially in cheek—the distinctions among people are moral.

Craft and Structure

1. The word is not to be understood literally, but humorously, as are *rectitude*, *stupendous* (paragraph 2), *excavation* (5), and *vicious* (9). Students may argue for one or two others that they perceive are not to be taken literally.

2. Britt constantly clarifies her subjects by repeating *sloppy people* and *neat people*.

3. Britt finds no similarities at all between the two. Had she mentioned any, her essay would be less exaggerated and would therefore lose some of its force. Writers who aren't exaggerating might give short shrift to similarities, too, if they are obvious or irrelevant.

4. The examples do specify the kinds of behavior Britt has in mind, but they are themselves generalizations about the two kinds of people. They illustrate behavior but not particular persons.

Integration of Knowledge and Ideas

1. Britt is writing to an audience of both neat and sloppy people. Although she criticizes neat people, readers who perceive her humor are unlikely to be offended. The essay probably will amuse students, no matter what category they fit into.

2. These broad statements are generalizations because they make conclusive assertions on the basis of some evidence—although, of course, Britt is deliberately exaggerating whatever evidence she has. By using so many generalizations, Britt compounds the outrageous nature of her essay. Her humor derives from her being unfair to neat people and finding no fault at all with their opposites.

3. Mostly, she writes to amuse and entertain. Britt is hardly impartial. It's easy to see that her sympathies lie with sloppy people and that she considers herself one of them.

Leanita McClain
The Middle-Class Black's Burden (p. 284)

McClain's essay addresses the significant issues of race and class relations both thoughtfully and uncompromisingly. Positioning herself among middle-class African Americans, McClain directly confronts the mistaken assumptions she faces among both other African Americans and middle-class white Americans.

Throughout her essay, McClain poses some rather difficult rhetorical questions, such as "I have made it, but where?" (paragraph 9) and "How can they be sincere about respecting me, yet hold my fellows in contempt?" (16). You might direct students' attention to these questions: What does McClain hope to gain with them?

Related Texts

Chinua Achebe, *Things Fall Apart*

Sherman Alexie, *The Absolutely True Diary of a Part-Time Indian*

Jane Austen, *Pride and Prejudice*

Toni Cade Bambara, "The Lesson"

Ralph Ellison, *Invisible Man*

Lorraine Hansberry, *A Raisin in the Sun*

Khaled Hosseini, *The Kite Runner*

Langston Hughes, "Harlem: A Dream Deferred"

Harper Lee, *To Kill a Mockingbird*

Toni Morrison, *Beloved*

Toni Morrison, *The Bluest Eye*

William Shakespeare, *Othello*

Robert Louis Stevenson, *Dr. Jekyll and Mr. Hyde*

Mark Twain, *The Adventures of Huckleberry Finn*

Alice Walker, "Everyday Use"

Alice Walker, "Women"

Richard Wright, *Black Boy*

Markus Zusak, *The Book Thief*

Content Quiz

1. What has McClain "had it" with?
    ["[B]eing patted on the head by white hands and slapped in the face by black hands for [her] success."]

2. What do other African Americans call middle-class African Americans like McClain?
    ["Oreos . . . black on the outside, white within."]

3. What has happened to some of McClain's childhood friends?
    [Old classmate waits on her table, girl she played with has five children and is on welfare, boy from church is imprisoned for murder, pal died of drug overdose.]

4. What is McClain's relationship to the middle class?
    [She is "uncomfortably" in it.]

5. What is it that blacks and whites will not believe about McClain?
    ["Whites won't believe I remain culturally different; blacks won't believe I remain culturally the same."]

Vocabulary Quiz

1. *Proverbial* (paragraph 2) is closest in meaning to
   a. desired   b. commonly expressed   c. everywhere evident
   [b. commonly expressed]

2. *Berate* (3) is closest in meaning to
   a. scold   b. punish   c. frown at
   [a. scold]

3. *Nemesis* (11) is closest in meaning to
   a. friend   b. rival   c. source of harm
   [c. source of harm]

4. *Vernacular* (12) is closest in meaning to
   a. idiom   b. rule   c. advice
   [a. idiom]

5. *Assuage* (13) is closest in meaning to
   a. inflame   b. erase   c. calm
   [c. calm]

Answers
Key Ideas and Details

1. "Incongruities" (paragraph 6) are inconsistencies (Latin *in-*, "not," and *congruere*, "to agree"). As a middle-class African American, McClain feels that she fits well in neither the predominantly white middle class nor the angry and fear-ridden African American community. Her examples include being called an "Oreo" (3), a trip to Paris back-to-back with a backcountry funeral (6), and an aunt who cleans for one of her neighbors (6). See also paragraphs 10, 13, and 14.

2. Paragraph 1 sums up the "middle-class black's burden" and states McClain's main idea—that she's "had it with being patted on the head by white hands and slapped in the face by black hands for my success." McClain does not use "patted" and "slapped" literally, of course; they are metaphors for her experiences. Whites pat her on the head by applauding her for succeeding when they might not have expected her to; blacks slap her by berating her for her success and insisting that she has forsaken her people.

3. McClain's "ancestors" are, of course, slaves and the oppressed African Americans who descended from them. "The purposeless present" of her contemporaries presumably refers to the endemic poverty and social problems of many present-day African Americans (paragraph 8).

Craft and Structure

1. Parallelism reinforces McClain's comparisons because similar grammatical structures encompass contrasting ideas. Other examples: "patted on the

head . . . and slapped in the face" (paragraph 1); "I have overcome . . . , but I have not overcome" (11); "Life is easier, being black is not" (11); "I know how tenuous my grip on one way of life is, and how strangling the grip of the other way of life can be" (14).

2. McClain is comparing her feelings among and misjudgment by African Americans and whites. Her points of comparison include life goals (paragraph 2), respect for roots (3, 4, 19, 20), congruence (5, 6), racism (9–12, 15, 16, 18), and tokenism (13).

3. In paragraph 6, McClain shifts from her life among other African Americans to her life among whites. The paragraph merges the two worlds.

4. Other clarifying expressions: "too" (paragraph 5), "however" (8), "still" (9), "yet" (11), "two worlds" (13), "each world" (14), "but" (16), "As for" (19), "nor" (20).

5. Description, narration, and example all appear in paragraphs 5 and 6. The entire essay analyzes the causes and effects of McClain's "burden" as a middle-class African American; specific instances appear in paragraphs 5 and 20.

Integration of Knowledge and Ideas

1. McClain is trying to communicate the burden she feels and ultimately to promote change: "We [middle-class blacks] know the black and white worlds can meld, that there can be a better world" (paragraph 4); "Racism still dogs my people" (9); "Inasmuch as we all suffer for every one left behind, we all gain for every one who conquers the hurdle" (20).

2. McClain addresses both whites and blacks, trying to educate members of both worlds about the prejudice she experiences and convince both to change their attitudes and behavior.

3. McClain's tone is angry, her language strong and uncompromising: "who has had it" (paragraph 1), "pencil pushing" (2), "antiquated ideology" (3), "wretched past . . . purposeless present" (8), "hollow victory" (10), "simplistic reproach" (11), "transparent deceptions . . . bitter hopelessness" (14), "lulled themselves" (15), "freak" (16), "No" (19), "drowning" (20). Some students will find her moral outrage appropriate given the gravity of her subject and what is at stake: the state of race relations in America. Others may wish she had tempered her anger.

Cheryl Peck
Fatso (p. 289)

Peck's essay, both ironic and angry, addresses a heated topic: obesity. Though not specifically about the public health and political issues that comprise the current obesity debate, the essay does succeed in raising many issues and attitudes involved in it. As a large woman herself, Peck identifies several types of hostility and discrimination that overweight people face every day. She directly compares others' perceptions of her with her own perception of herself, finding disturbing similarities in the negative attitudes about "people of substance" on both sides. At the same time, she obliquely compares sizism with racism, a connection that some readers will appreciate and others will undoubtedly reject outright. Currently or formerly overweight students are sure to see themselves in some of her examples, but so might those who are "normal" weight or underweight; most readers will find her essay quite moving regardless of where they fit on the spectrum.

Students who connect with Peck's writing will undoubtedly enjoy her essay collections *Fat Girls and Lawn Chairs* (2004) and *Revenge of the Paste Eaters* (2005). Both books are filled with personal reflections and funny stories that resonate with readers regardless of their backgrounds. It's worth reminding students that although Peck has published two books, she is not a professional writer. She worked full-time in a welfare office until she retired and writes primarily for her own satisfaction. Yet she has developed both a strong style and a wide audience, a source of inspiration for other aspiring writers.

Related Texts

Peck's ruminations on appearance, discrimination, and self-loathing might resonate with any of the following works.

Chinua Achebe, *Things Fall Apart*

Sherman Alexie, *The Absolutely True Diary of a Part-Time Indian*

Toni Cade Bambara, "The Lesson"

Sandra Cisneros, "Bien Pretty"

Stephen Crane, *The Red Badge of Courage*

William Golding, *Lord of the Flies*

Khaled Hosseini, *The Kite Runner*

Henrik Ibsen, *A Doll's House*

Marge Piercy, "Barbie Doll"

John Steinbeck, *The Grapes of Wrath*

Scott Westerfeld, *Pretties*

Markus Zusak, *The Book Thief*

Content Quiz

1. What hurtful comment did a stranger make to a large man who was eating an elephant ear at a fair?
    ["You don't need to eat that."]

2. Why have people told Peck that she doesn't have any experience with discrimination?
    [Because she is white and middle class.]

3. What did a salesperson suggest that Peck could wear on her large feet?
    [Shoe boxes.]

4. What were some of Peck's nicknames in school?
    [She was called "fatso," "lardbucket," and "Bismarck."]

5. What unsolicited information did a stranger give Peck in the street?
    [She told Peck about a weight-loss program that worked for her "second cousin in Tulsa."]

Vocabulary Quiz

1. *Register* (paragraph 1) is closest in meaning to
    a. understand   b. repeat   c. weigh
    [a. understand]

2. *Debilitate* (3) is closest in meaning to
    a. energize   b. repair   c. cripple
    [c. cripple]

3. *Crude* (5, 9) is closest in meaning to
    a. raw   b. tactless   c. simple
    [b. tactless]

4. *Asexual* (8) is closest in meaning to
    a. gay   b. promiscuous   c. gender neutral
    [c. gender neutral]

5. *Demeanor* (9) is closest in meaning to
    a. attitude   b. cruelty   c. language
    [a. attitude]

Answers
Key Ideas and Details

1. Peck does not mean any of her "I have never" statements literally. Each example is drawn from her personal experience, as her references to specific incidents—such the shoe store clerk's rude joke (paragraph 4), the grade school nicknames (5), or the hurtful letter she read in a magazine (6)—make

clear. She is being bitterly ironic to underscore the difference between what people assume about her and what is actually true.

2. She is angry—an emotion Peck (again, ironically) denies in her last paragraph—not only because others have treated her badly but also because she has internalized many of the negative stereotypes applied to obese people and often treats herself as poorly as others do.

3. The title serves a couple of functions. It has a shock value that draws readers in more effectively than, say, "Obesity" would. At the same time, it recalls the name-calling that Peck experienced as a child and predicts the self-loathing that is a major theme of her essay. It could also serve as a verbalization of the prejudice that she describes in her introduction and responds to in the body of her comparison.

Craft and Structure

1. Peck's repeated invocation of the phrase "I have never" (as well as its variations) gives the essay coherence as well as a rhythm that is difficult to resist. At the same time, the parallelism created by her usage emphasizes that each incident she describes is equally important and on a par with the racial discrimination she discusses in paragraph 3.

2. This essay is based primarily on a point-by-point contrast between Peck's life as it is and her life as she imagines it would be if she were smaller. At the same time, she compares what others assume about her with how she sees herself. Her major points of comparison include interpersonal relationships (paragraphs 5, 9, 11), media representations (6), and self-esteem (7, 8, 10). Peck also suggests an implicit comparison between racism and sizism (3), but she uses that to bolster her main point, not as the focus of the essay itself.

3. The comparison begins in Peck's discussion of racial discrimination in the third paragraph, but she deliberately waits until the fourth paragraph to make it clear that she is writing a comparison and contrast essay. On the first reading of paragraph 3, most readers will assume that she is writing from a somewhat detached point of view, interpreting her "I have never" statements literally. When Peck shifts to an obviously personal example of discrimination in paragraph 4 ("My feelings were not hurt"), however, she makes it clear that the types of racial discrimination outlined in the previous paragraph are actually meant to serve as examples of the discrimination she has experienced as a large woman.

4. Although she is writing about sizism in general, Peck uses profoundly personal examples to make her point. Some of the more notable examples include her humiliation in the shoe store (paragraph 4), her sexual awkwardness (8), and her encounter with the woman who suggested a weight-loss program (9). Obesity is a charged topic in contemporary America. By exposing her vulnerabilities in such a raw manner, Peck makes the subject personal and tries to form a bond with her readers, which increases her

chances of success in making readers sympathetic to the difficulties and social stigmas that overweight people face.

Integration of Knowledge and Ideas

1. Peck is writing primarily to judgmental thin people—specifically, she is responding to the person who made the hurtful comment to her friend at a fair and to the people who have told her that because she is a "middle-class white person" she has "no idea what it is like to be discriminated against" (paragraph 3). At the same time, however, because Peck is very forthright in counting herself among those who stereotype overweight people, we can also conclude that she is writing a cautionary tale for others who have internalized society's negative assessments of fat people.

2. Peck is trying to teach her readers not to discriminate against people of size by revealing the pain caused by snap judgments and insensitive comments. She underscores the importance of her message by implicitly comparing sizism to racism early in her essay (paragraph 3): both forms of discrimination, she insists, are equally hurtful. Peck acknowledges, however, that her lesson is a difficult one to learn. At three hundred pounds, she has caught herself making negative assumptions about other overweight people.

3. Answers will vary.

Chapter 13

Definition

Pursuing Happiness

Focus on Restrictive and Nonrestrictive Elements

Answers will vary. Suggested edits are provided below.

1. Studies by psychologist Dacher Keltner have shown that maintaining a positive attitude can increase a person's chances for success.

2. But other scientists, such as Barbara Ehrenreich, question the findings of positive psychologists. [Parentheses or dashes would also be acceptable.]

3. Ehrenreich—a trained biologist who studies culture—argues that a focus on positive thinking can have negative consequences. [Parentheses or commas would also be acceptable.]

4. She cites the example of customer service representatives, who are often told that they need to stay upbeat if they want to keep their jobs. [A dash would also be acceptable.]

5. Employees forced to hide their true emotions can become physically ill from the stress caused by lying.

Judy Brady
I Want a Wife (p. 308)

Dating from the early 1970s, "I Want a Wife" is one of the most frequently taught essays in recent memory. Brady's definition uses carefully selected examples to present an angry statement about a wife's place in the home and in society.

Some students may initially misunderstand the essay and think that Brady really does want a slave of her own. Other students may see the essay as excessively hostile toward wives, husbands, and marriage. And still other students may find Brady's sense of oppression somewhat passé, not as much of an issue now as it was in the less liberated early 1970s. Class discussion may be guided by the questions under "Integration of Knowledge and Ideas" and by the second and third writing topics.

Related Texts

As "I Want a Wife" does, these works look at marriage or gender equity.

Jane Austen, *Pride and Prejudice*

Kate Chopin, *The Awakening*

F. Scott Fitzgerald, *The Great Gatsby*

Charlotte Perkins Gilman, "The Yellow Wallpaper"

Nathaniel Hawthorne, *The Scarlet Letter*

Henrik Ibsen, *A Doll's House*

Anita Jain, *Marrying Anita* (see "A Nameless Respect," p. 172)

Arthur Miller, *The Crucible*

William Shakespeare, *Othello*

William Shakespeare, *Romeo and Juliet*

Amy Tan, *The Joy Luck Club*

Alice Walker, "Women"

Jeanette Walls, *The Glass Castle*

Tennessee Williams, *The Glass Menagerie*

Content Quiz

1. With whom does the child of Brady's recently divorced male friend live?
   [The child's mother.]

2. Why does Brady want to go back to school?
   [So she can become economically independent and support herself and her family.]

3. Why should a wife go on family vacations?
   [To continue caring for her partner and for the children.]

4. According to Brady's definition, which partner in a marriage must arrange social gatherings?
   [The wife.]

5. What should the first wife do if a new wife is taken?
   ["Take the children and be solely responsible for them."]

Vocabulary Quiz

1. *Incidentally* (paragraph 1) is closest in meaning to
   a. angrily   b. logically   c. accidentally
   [c. accidentally]

2.   *Nurturant* (3) is closest in meaning to
     a. compassionate   b. gentle   c. nourishing
     [c. nourishing]

3.   *Mended* (3, 4) is closest in meaning to
     a. broken   b. repaired   c. updated
     [b. repaired]

4.   *Hors d'oeuvres* (6) is closest in meaning to
     a. appetizers   b. cocktails   c. napkins
     [a. appetizers]

5.   *Replenished* (6) is closest in meaning to
     a. removed   b. refilled   c. rewashed
     [b. refilled]

Answers
Key Ideas and Details

1.   A wife is a person whose entire function is the selfless serving of others, especially the husband.

2.   The wife's chief responsibilities are to work when doing so is beneficial to the spouse, to care for the children, to care for the house and to cook, to meet the spouse's needs, and to arrange and run social events. The wife's behavior should be entirely selfless. The spouse's responsibilities are to attend school and study and eventually to support dependents "if need be" (paragraph 3)—but nothing is required or contributed at home. The spouse's behavior may be entirely selfish.

Craft and Structure

1.   Use of the phrase "my wife" emphasizes the spouse's depersonalization and possession of the wife. At the same time, the phrase allows Brady to avoid expressing a wish for another woman, which might be more distracting than the occasionally awkward sentences now in the essay.

2.   The repetition portrays the spouse as childish, demanding, and selfish.

3.   Paragraph 1 suggests that the author is defined by society according to her role as a wife. Paragraph 2 presents a man who seems to view a wife's role just as Brady goes on to define it: he is divorced; he has left his child to his wife; and he wants "a wife"—as if anyone might do. The question at the end of the introduction leads into the definition; once the earlier question is answered, the final rhetorical question opens up the divorced man's wish and Brady's wish to everyone.

4.   With classification, Brady makes the definition more manageable. She classifies the wife's responsibilities into financial support and child care (paragraph 3), housekeeping and cooking (4), emotional support (5), and social

organization (6). The categories are increasingly personal and intrusive, thus emphasizing the exploitation of women in marriage.

Integration of Knowledge and Ideas

1. Brady's purpose is to attack society's—and men's—attitudes toward the role of wife. She presents a deliberately one-sided definition, exaggerating to achieve this purpose.

2. Brady seems to assume that her readers are mostly women who will understand and appreciate her anger. Her perspective seems to be that of a middle-class woman in her twenties or early thirties: the wife works to put the spouse through school; the children are relatively young; the family lives in a house; and the couple has an active social life.

3. Answers will vary widely.

Pico Iyer
The Joy of Less (p. 312)

Even if they resist Pico Iyer's definition of happiness, students immersed in our material culture will surely benefit from exposure to his impassioned argument that chasing after money and luxury can bring more emotional harm than good. A good way to begin discussion might be to ask students about their own ambitions in life, as suggested in the first writing topic: What do they think will make them happy as adults, and why do they think so?

Rich in literary and philosophical references, Iyer's essay also offers an opportunity to discuss how reading and incorporating the works of others can add depth and complexity to a writer's ideas: See question 3 under "Integration of Knowledge and Ideas."

Related Texts

"The Joy of Less" has strong thematic connections to several of the works in *Common Threads*. One such link is suggested in the "Connections" question that follows the essay, but with its focus on wealth, aspiration, and happiness, Iyer's work could also be taught in conjunction with Pat Mora's "Great Expectations" (p. 199), Lars Eighner's "Dumpster Diving" (p. 253), Leanita McClain's "The Middle-Class Black's Burden" (p. 284), or any of the essays in this chapter and the next chapter, "Cause-and-Effect Analysis: Investigating the Working World."

Related works include the many titles and authors Iyer mentions in his essay as well as the following.

Chinua Achebe, *Things Fall Apart*

Jane Austen, *Pride and Prejudice*

Toni Cade Bambara, "The Lesson"

F. Scott Fitzgerald, *The Great Gatsby*

The Epic of Gilgamesh

O. Henry, "The Gift of the Magi"

Khaled Hosseini, *The Kite Runner*

Henrik Ibsen, *A Doll's House*

Arthur Miller, *Death of a Salesman*

John Steinbeck, *The Grapes of Wrath*

François-Marie Arouet de Voltaire, *Candide, Or the Optimist*

Jeanette Walls, *The Glass Castle*

Content Quiz

1. Where does Iyer live?
   [Near Kyoto, Japan.]

2. What does Iyer do for a living?
   [Write.]

3. What Shakespearean play includes the line "There is nothing either good or bad but thinking makes it so"?
   [*Hamlet*.]

4. Why was Iyer "always to remain unsatisfied" with his job in New York?
   [Because there was always some higher position to struggle for.]

5. What are the benefits of not owning a car?
   [One less thing to "think or worry about" and the opportunity to take "daily walks around the neighborhood."]

Vocabulary Quiz

1. *Mired* (paragraph 2) is closest in meaning to
   a. stuck   b. involved   c. interested
   [a. stuck]

2. *Renunciation* (4) is closest in meaning to
   a. intellectualism   b. self-denial   c. sarcasm
   [b. self-denial]

3. *Precarious* (7) is closest in meaning to
   a. ridiculous   b. uncertain   c. inspired
   [b. uncertain]

4. *Austerity* (7) is closest in meaning to
   a. creativity   b. adventurousness   c. simplicity
   [c. simplicity]

5. *Resplendent* (7) is closest in meaning to
    a. glorious   b. consuming   c. arduous
    [a. glorious]

Answers
Key Ideas and Details

1. Iyer's personal definition of *happiness* is most succinctly expressed in paragraph 4: for him, it's a state of "peace of mind or absorption"—that is, having the freedom to fully immerse himself in the activities he enjoys.

2. The point of Iyer's essay is stated in his introduction and reiterated in his conclusion: "happiness lies less in our circumstances than in what we make of them, in every sense" (paragraph 2); "happiness comes from matching your wants to your needs" (8). He is trying to persuade readers that money is not essential to well-being; in fact, he suggests, the blind pursuit of material wealth can present obstacles to true happiness.

3. Iyer presents these examples as evidence for his claim that money doesn't necessarily "buy happiness" (paragraph 2).

Craft and Structure

1. Iyer addresses readers directly in his conclusion, encouraging them to apply what he has learned about himself to their own lives. He seems to believe that at least some of them share his preferences but haven't learned how to follow them.

2. The examples that open Iyer's essay cite the words and attitudes of three writers who expressed joy and contentment with their lives, even though each one could be considered to have suffered greatly. The irony of each writer's perspective previews and helps to prove his thesis that happiness is shaped by attitude rather than by situation.

3. The expressions of uncertainty seem to accomplish several purposes. Rhetorically, they introduce topics that Iyer goes on to explore. They suggest that Iyer is not claiming special expertise—that he's no more an expert than readers are, just someone observing and thinking. But since it turns out he has quite a bit to say on each topic, students may find his expressions of uncertainty somewhat insincere.

4. After listing the many things he doesn't have—"I have no bicycle, no car, no television I can understand, no media" (paragraph 3)—Iyer explains that not having such things creates some inconvenience and isolation, but also frees him from worry and allows him to focus on simpler joys, such as "adventure" (4), interacting with loved ones (4, 5), reading for pleasure (5, 7), and listening to music (7).

Integration of Knowledge and Ideas

1. Iyer wrote this essay as a blog post for the *New York Times*, a daily news-paper read largely by educated, middle-class and upper-middle-class pro-fessionals. He assumes familiarity with New York City, as his references to Rockefeller Center and Park Avenue show, and he assumes familiarity with the works of literature and philosophy he cites, but even more so, he assumes that his readers value wealth, technology, and career advancement. At the same time, he assumes that his readers have been personally affected by the stock market losses that occurred shortly before he wrote the essay, "con-demned to a simplicity they never needed or wanted" (paragraph 6).

2. Iyer recognizes that his scaled-back lifestyle is probably too extreme for most people, and he acknowledges that his approach to making a living is risky. He seems to want to reassure readers, most of whom had likely been nega-tively affected by the economic downturn, that getting by with less is not only a possibility but an opportunity. On some level, his essay is a an attempt to persuade readers to reassess their lives—to stop "running to stand still" (paragraph 8) and figure out what they truly need to be happy.

3. Iyer is a deeply intellectual person who tells readers that he finds his joy in reading and culture. Accordingly, he cites several works of literature and philosophy to develop his own ideas: Etty Hillesum's holocaust diary, Ralph Waldo Emerson's "Immortality," and the poetry of Issa (paragraph 1); Shakespeare's *Hamlet* (2); P.G. Wodehouse's stories, Henry David Thoreau's *Walden*, and Henry James's *Portrait of a Lady* (5); Zeno of Elea's arrow para-dox (6); and John le Carré's novels (7). By drawing on examples from a diverse variety of writers (a twentieth-century Dutch journal keeper, a nineteenth-century American transcendentalist, an eighteenth-century Japa-nese poet, a sixteenth-century English playwright, a nineteenth-century English humorist, another nineteenth-century American transcendentalist, a nineteenth-century American novelist, an ancient Greek philosopher, and a twenty-first-century spy thriller), Iyer demonstrates his love of literature and intellectualism while supporting his points with a broad historical rep-resentation of human thought. Students may report frustration that read-ers do need at least some familiarity with the works he cites to understand their full impact on his meaning—for instance, they may not recognize that Iyer's own thinking is transcendental, or that le Carré's novels are escapist—but Iyer offers just enough detail in each case to get his point across. (And the gloss notes provided with the essay should help students grasp the deeper implications.)

Walter Mosley
Get Happy (p. 318)

Mosley's essay is more challenging than the other essays in the chapter, but it should capture students' interest because it touches on a subject that affects everyone at some point: unhappiness. Whether students approach his definition from the belief that happiness comes from within or from a conviction that others are mostly to blame for our unhappiness, Mosley's proposal is likely to come as a surprise—especially for readers who haven't given much thought to what happiness is or where it comes from.

Some students will surely be put off by Mosley's strong language, while others may embrace the writer's socialist perspective. Such political divisions could lead to compelling (if contentious) classroom debate, provided you set some ground rules for mutual respect and thoughtful deliberation. Alternatively, you might focus on how Mosley structures his argument, noting how half of his essay sets up his reasons for claiming that Americans are unhappy (paragraphs 2–9) and the other half explains his proposal for helping them (10–16). Mosley uses definition to advance a serious (and controversial) argument, not as an end in itself.

Related Texts

Mosley's interest in the role of the government and the causes of unhappiness might illuminate students' appreciation of any of the following works.

Chinua Achebe, *Things Fall Apart*

Sherman Alexie, *The Absolutely True Diary of a Part-Time Indian*

Ray Bradbury, *Fahrenheit 451*

Kate Chopin, *The Awakening*

Suzanne Collins, *The Hunger Games*

Henrik Ibsen, *A Doll's House*

Thomas Jefferson, Declaration of Independence

Martin Luther King, Jr., "I Have a Dream" (p. 449)

George Orwell, *1984*

J. D. Salinger, *The Catcher in the Rye*

Mary Shelley, *Frankenstein*

Sophocles, *Oedipus Rex*

John Steinbeck, *The Grapes of Wrath*

Robert Louis Stevenson, *Dr. Jekyll and Mr. Hyde*

François-Marie Arouet de Voltaire, *Candide, Or the Optimist*

Jeanette Walls, *The Glass Castle*

Tennessee Williams, *The Glass Menagerie*

Content Quiz

1. What foundational American document does Mosley quote in his introduction and reference throughout the essay?
    [The Declaration of Independence.]

2. Identify at least two of the six causes of unhappiness Mosley names. [Schools, jobs, un(der)employment, illness, politicians, and corporations.]

3. How long does it take for the "sum total of our knowledge" to double? [A year, if that.]

4. Does Mosley believe that money can buy justice? [No.]

5. What does Mosley propose to cure the happiness problem in America? [A "government department . . . designed to monitor, propagate, and ensure the happiness of" all Americans.]

Vocabulary Quiz

1. *Subsequent* (paragraph 2) is closest in meaning to
    a. unique   b. resulting   c. exclusive
    [b. resulting]

2. *Rampant* (3) is closest in meaning to
    a. unrestrained   b. negligent   c. careful
    [a. unrestrained]

3. *Aberrant* (4) is closest in meaning to
    a. impressionable   b. wrong   c. depressed
    [b. wrong]

4. *Malaise* (9) is closest in meaning to
    a. restlessness   b. righteousness   c. illness
    [c. illness]

5. *Propagate* (11) is closest in meaning to
    a. enact   b. regulate   c. increase
    [c. increase]

Answers
Key Ideas and Details

1. Mosley's thesis, which he uses as a transition between his definition and his proposal, appears in the middle of his essay. "One cure" for American unhappiness, he says, "is the institution of a government department that has as its only priority the happiness of all Americans" (paragraph 10).

2. Happiness, to Mosley, seems to be "a state of mind" (paragraph 6) based on a sense of freedom and security. The questions he asks toward the end of his essay hint at his idea of the sources of "a contented existence" (15): food security, good health, family, education, investment, and support.

3. Students may have difficulty with this statement and with Mosley's assertion that "the quote above says (and does not say)" it. They will need to

infer, first, that neither black slaves nor white women enjoyed full citizenship rights in the early republic: the former were not considered fully human; the latter could not vote or hold property (see Frederick Douglass's "Learning to Read and Write," p. 103, and Elizabeth Cady Stanton's "Seneca Falls Convention Keynote Address," p. 437). And they will then need to work out Mosley's implication that today even white men have lost the freedoms promised in the Declaration of Independence — a point he examines in the body of his essay.

4. Mosley blames corporations (paragraphs 2–3, 9), politicians (2–3, 9), and the media (3–6, 10) for making Americans unhappy. He reasons that because "the Declaration of Independence says that the pursuit of happiness is an 'unalienable right,'" the government accepted from the start a "responsibility to ensure that all Americans . . . are given a clear path toward that pursuit" (12). Just as "[l]ife and liberty are addressed to one degree or another by our executive, legislative and judicial branches" (1), he argues, the government should use its power to curb the institutions that impede happiness through their actions and messages.

Craft and Structure

1. Examples of similes include "prisonlike schools" (paragraph 2), "like employees" (3), "like a pampered foot into a sheepskin slipper" (8), "[o]ur world is more like the tropics" (13). Examples of metaphors include "scare the votes out of us" (2), "cut loose" (3), "drags us down" (3), "the seat of our discontent, a throne of nails under a crown of thorns" (4), "money cannot buy happiness" (5), "bedrock of justice" (5), "labor camps of American and international capitalism" (10), "first blush" (11), "a clear path" (12), "rocky roadway through a barren landscape" (13), "a lush forest of fast-growing knowledge" (13), "the path must be cleared" (13), "clear the path" (14), "tame the shadowy government" (14), "our own path" (15), "all paths" (16). Mosley's figures of speech clarify his points without distracting readers from his message. The extended path-through-the-jungle metaphor, in particular, makes the otherwise abstract concept of information overload concrete and vividly describes the function he imagines for an agency dedicated to ensuring citizens' happiness.

2. The epigraph introduces Mosley's topic. It also provides textual evidence to support his argument that the American government is responsible for enabling its citizens' happiness; Mosley refers back to it in paragraphs 1, 2, 7, 10, 12, 14, and 16.

3. The first half of Mosley's essay presents his definition of unhappiness and examines its sources; the second half takes off from the definition to present a proposal for ensuring that Americans can pursue happiness effectively.

4. Mosley acknowledges that some readers are "happy, content, satisfied and generally pleased with the potentials presented to [them] and others" (paragraph 8). He also acknowledges that others might feel that individuals are "responsible for [their] own happiness" or that government should not be

given additional powers (11). In describing such readers as "pampered" (8) recipients of "the good fortune to be born at the right moment, in the right place" (9), he suggests that those who disagree with his assessments are unusually privileged and lacking in compassion for the "many of us" who have not been so lucky.

Integration of Knowledge and Ideas

1. He does seem to believe in his proposal, yes. "Life and liberty are addressed to one degree or another by our executive, legislative and judicial branches," he says, "but our potential for happiness has lagged far behind" (paragraph 1). Although Mosley acknowledges that his proposal "might seem . . . frivolous" or overreaching (11), he explains that his idea is to create a government department devoted to studying the "possibilities for happiness" (12) and influencing the policies and actions of "the other branches of government" (14), not necessarily to enforce them itself. But because he offers almost no details concerning what functions such a department would serve or how it might be structured, his purpose appears more to be to open "a dialogue" (14) and to encourage readers to examine the questions he poses.

2. As explained in the headnote preceding the essay, Mosley wrote this for the *Nation*, a progressive magazine with a strong political focus and a well-educated, high-income subscriber base. According to the magazine's own demographic profiles, more than three-quarters of its readers hold a college degree, more than half hold a graduate degree, nearly half earn $75,000 or more a year, and the vast majority are employed in a professional or managerial position. Mosley knows this about his readers, but despite their relative affluence, he tries to shake them out of the belief that they are happy, at least partly by his continual use of the first person plural (*we, us*) to refer to unhappy citizens, and also by his characterization (in paragraphs 8–9) of happy readers as out of touch with the majority of Americans.

3. The image superimposes the iconic 1970s smiley face over a facsimile of the Declaration of Independence. It's mostly decorative, and some readers may feel that it trivializes Mosley's ideas. But it does manage to reinterpret the crux of Mosley's argument into a simple visual representation.

4. Mosley offers multiple, overlapping reasons supporting this claim in the first half of his essay. Americans, he says, "lack . . . freedom and the . . . potential for happiness" (paragraph 2). They have no financial security (2, 3, 5); they have no reliable access to truth (3); their health is at risk (2, 3); they have "empty and impossible" dreams fueled by the media and consumerism (4–5); they have no guarantee of justice (5); they are overwhelmed by the pace of expanding knowledge and changing lifestyles (6–7); and they lack intimate connections (7). "[M]any of us," he concludes, "suffer under a corporatized bureaucracy where homelessness, illiteracy, poverty, malnourishment (both physical and spiritual) and an unrelenting malaise are not only possible but likely" (9).

Chapter 14
Cause-and-Effect Analysis
Investigating the Working World

Focus on Conciseness

Answers will vary. Suggested edits are provided below.

1. Verbal harassment sometimes leads to physical abuse.

2. Many companies report incidents of employees shoving, even hitting, coworkers.

3. Some researchers say that workplace harassment stems from schoolyard bullying.

4. They believe that teenage bullies become adult bullies.

5. Regardless of the cause, employers must find a way to prevent harassment.

Dana Thomas
The Fake Trade (p. 339)

With this compelling and alarming analysis of causes and effects, Thomas is sure to surprise readers who have never given a second thought to the cheap knock-offs and questionable merchandise we've all seen at flea markets, dollar stores, and big-box discounters. Even if students recognize a fake when they see one, most have probably not considered where counterfeit goods come from or how they might contribute to such horrors as human trafficking and slave labor.

Related Texts

Thomas's muckraking article could be taught together with book-length examples of the genre, such as Upton Sinclair's *The Jungle* and Eric Schlosser's *Fast Food Nation*. At the same time, her focus on luxury goods and her exposé of human trafficking operations would nicely complement works that examine privilege, oppression, or the unintended consequences of "victimless crimes," such as these.

Chinua Achebe, *Things Fall Apart*

Toni Cade Bambara, "The Lesson"

Suzanne Collins, *The Hunger Games*

Frederick Douglass, *Narrative of the Life of Frederick Douglass* (see "Learning to Read and Write," p. 103)

F. Scott Fitzgerald, *The Great Gatsby*

Khaled Hosseini, *The Kite Runner*

George Orwell, *Animal Farm*

George Orwell, "Shooting an Elephant"

Jonathan Swift, "A Modest Proposal"

Content Quiz

1. What kind of handbag did the little girl at the lemonade stand have?
    [An imitation Louis Vuitton Murakami pouch.]

2. What kinds of merchandise are counterfeited?
    ["Everything." Thomas gives as examples handbags, luxury cars, medicine, health and beauty aids, perfume, and brakes.]

3. Why do people buy counterfeit goods?
    [Because they believe counterfeiting is a "victimless crime."]

4. Identify at least two methods counterfeiters use to smuggle items into the United States.
    [They once packed counterfeit items with legal merchandise; now they might ship raw materials for manufacturing or finishing in the United States, ship generic items and add labels when they get here, hide brand labels under generic ones, or create the appearance of legitimacy by applying for a trademark for a slightly altered logo (knowing that it will be denied but slipping past customs in the process).]

5. What major US retailer did Fendi sue in 2006 for selling counterfeits?
    [Wal-Mart Stores, Inc.]

Vocabulary Quiz

1. *Ingesting* (paragraph 6) is closest in meaning to
    a. saving   b. swallowing   c. carrying
    [b. swallowing]

2. *Syndicates* (8) is closest in meaning to
    a. organizations   b. channels   c. fakes
    [a. organizations]

3. *Clandestine* (8) is closest in meaning to
    a. flaming   b. illegal   c. hidden
    [c. hidden]

4. *Invariably* (8) is closest in meaning to
   a. angrily   b. lie   c. always
   [c. always]

5. *Pretense* (13) is closest in meaning to
   a. appearance   b. before   c. proof
   [a. appearance]

Answers
Key Ideas and Details

1. Most simply, *counterfeit* means "fake" and *legitimate* means "real." But Thomas may intend for the words' connotations to resonate. The word *counterfeit* seems somehow less judgmental than *fake*, and it carries a sheen of objectivity that obscures the full reality of its meaning; the usage echoes consumers' misguided belief that fake goods don't hurt anybody. At the same time, the word *legitimate* conveys a much stronger sense of moral judgment than *real* does. By juxtaposing the two words so often—and by reinforcing the connotations with the synonyms *fake*, *pirated*, *real*, and *genuine*—Thomas underscores her point that counterfeit goods are not equivalent to their legitimate counterparts and that they are far from harmless, no matter what readers might think.

2. A "victimless crime" is an illegal activity that doesn't hurt anybody; some people use the concept to justify breaking laws that seem pointless or irrelevant to them. Clearly, Thomas does not believe that counterfeiting falls into this category. She mentions the idea because her purpose in writing the essay is to counter the widely held assumption that buying counterfeit products causes no harm.

3. As Thomas explains it, the market for counterfeit goods exists because of the law of supply and demand. Consumers "keep happily buying fakes" because they're less expensive than legitimate brands and because buyers don't think they're causing any harm (paragraph 7). For counterfeit operations, the practice is enormously profitable, accounting for "approximately $600 billion annually" (5) and allowing individual counterfeiters to earn "millions" (14) at a time. The consequences of participating in this market, however, include lost business and lost jobs in the United States (5); unsafe and even deadly products (6); and support for "international crime syndicates that deal in money laundering, human trafficking, and child labor" (8).

Craft and Structure

1. Thomas's tone is both balanced and urgent—a good choice considering her purpose. She cultivates the sense of balance by relying on quotations, facts, and examples from her sources, hovering in the background as an objective reporter through most of the essay. But at the same time, Thomas paints a disturbing picture and (toward the end) addresses readers directly,

emphasizing the horrors of counterfeiting and pleading with readers to not be involved with it.

2. Because the organization of this essay is complex (see the next question), Thomas is careful to mark transitions among her supporting points. Paragraph transitions include "Though the fashion business has" (paragraph 5), "One of the primary reasons" (7), "But the reality is" (8), "a decade ago" (9), "As long as there is a demand, however" (10), "But as fashion companies grew wise" (11), "Another" (12, 13), "By the time the brand realizes what's going on" (14), "Well" (16), "Of course" (19), and "Most important" (20).

3. As is often the case with cause-and-effect analyses, the organization of this essay is somewhat complex. Thomas opens with a narrative about an encounter with a little girl (paragraphs 1–4) then moves to a brief overview of the counterfeit industry (6) and examples of counterfeit goods (6). She then digs in to the heart of her cause-and-effect analysis, considering why people buy fakes and what happens when they do (7–8). Next, she acknowledges that crackdowns have had some success (9), explains how the "supply chain" once worked (10), and describes current practices (11–14). She follows that with tips on how to recognize counterfeits and ensure that one's purchases are legitimate (15–19). She concludes by returning to her opening anecdote and issuing a call to action, imploring readers to share their new awareness and to "stop buying the stuff" (20). This approach allows Thomas to pull readers in, establish the significance of her subject, surprise readers with new and potentially upsetting information, explain how and why authorities are trying to stop counterfeiting, and persuade readers that they must become part of the solution.

4. Thomas's examples (paragraphs 6, 9) and process analyses (10–14) should shock and frighten most readers. Both strategies offer an effective way to get readers' attention and make them care about the subject.

Integration of Knowledge and Ideas

1. Thomas's relatively objective reportorial approach to exposing the realities of counterfeiting suggests that she wants to educate readers. At the same time, however, she clearly wants to persuade readers to stop buying fake goods. Her purpose is most evident in paragraph 8, where she outlines the horrors associated with the counterfeit market and cites other readers' and listeners' decisions to "never knowingly buy another fake good"; in paragraphs 15–19, where she explains how to recognize counterfeits; and in her conclusion, where she issues a call to action imploring readers to "spread the word" and "just stop buying the stuff" (paragraph 20).

2. Students may need to be reminded that "The Fake Trade" was first published in *Harper's Bazaar*, an upscale fashion magazine for women. Thomas's use of handbags as a recurring example makes clear that her intended audience is female, and her references to luxury brand names and boutique shopping suggest that her readers are fashion conscious and relatively affluent.

3. Thomas explains that she said nothing to the girl because "[i]t wasn't her fault her family had given it to her" (paragraph 20). She doesn't want to make a child feel bad, a reasonable and compassionate decision. But students may well object that the child could have asked (even begged) for the cartoon-inspired handbag, that preteens are prime targets of fashion merchandising and can be alarmingly brand conscious, and that a girl of that age is old enough to understand what Thomas chose not to tell her.

4. The author alludes to published studies in paragraphs 5 and 6 and cites two directly in paragraph 7; she also refers to a Web resource in paragraph 18. She quotes some of the experts she interviewed—two lawyers and a law enforcement agent—in paragraphs 6, 12, 13, and 17. Her personal experience comes into play in paragraphs 1–4, 8, 9, and 20. The evidence from sources helps establish the validity of her concern, confirms that what she says is true, and lends her an air of authority. Her personal anecdotes enliven the essay and help make the subject more concrete for readers; they also ensure that Thomas doesn't lose her voice to her sources.

Ellen Goodman
The Company Man (p. 347)

Written as a parable, Ellen Goodman's classic essay is a warning to Type A personalities. The moral of her story is simple—don't work too hard—but her technique is complex. Goodman deftly combines irony, repetition, and pathos to create a portrait of a universal everyman and family made deeply unhappy by workplace success.

"The Company Man" is often anthologized, usually as a model of definition (as the fourth question under "Craft and Structure" suggests). As a cause-and-effect analysis, however, Goodman's essay offers an excellent opportunity to discuss the differences between immediate and remote causes: see the first question under "Key Ideas and Details." Perhaps more significant, it offers an opportunity to examine students' assumptions about what their careers might entail and to consider how they could forge a track that takes their personal values fully into account as they think about their futures.

Related Texts

Goodman's essay complements other texts that focus on work, death, or grief, such as these.

Kate Chopin, *The Awakening*

Emily Dickinson, "Because I Could Not Stop for Death"

Emily Dickinson, "We Grow Accustomed to the Dark"

Arthur Miller, *Death of a Salesman*

George Orwell, "Shooting an Elephant"

Edgar Allan Poe, "The Raven"

William Shakespeare, *Hamlet*

William Shakespeare, *Macbeth*

Sophocles, *Oedipus Rex*

John Steinbeck, *The Grapes of Wrath*

Dylan Thomas, "Do Not Go Gentle into that Good Night"

Tennessee Williams, *The Glass Menagerie*

Markus Zusak, *The Book Thief*

Content Quiz

1. When did Phil die?
   ["3:00 a.m. Sunday morning."]

2. With which of his children was Phil closest?
   [His youngest son.]

3. What did Phil typically eat for lunch?
   [Egg salad sandwiches.]

4. Why did Phil's widow need to stay on good terms with the president of his company?
   [She would need him to help her with her finances.]

5. How many of Phil's employees will be considered for his job?
   [Three.]

Vocabulary Quiz

1. *Precisely* (paragraph 1) is closest in meaning to
   a. exactly   b. tragically   c. abruptly
   [a. exactly]

2. *Coronary* (2) is closest in meaning to
   a. heart   b. crown   c. glow
   [a. heart]

3. *Conceivably* (3) is closest in meaning to
   a. hopefully   b. possibly   c. obviously
   [b. possibly]

4. *Discreetly* (16) is closest in meaning to
   a. brazenly   b. kindly   c. cautiously
   [c. cautiously]

5. *Inquiries* (16) is closest in meaning to
    a. questions   b. assumptions   c. notes
    [a. questions]

Answers
Key Ideas and Details

1. The obituary attributes Phil's death to an immediate cause—a "coronary thrombosis" (paragraph 2), or heart attack. But Goodman blames his death on remote causes—a lifetime of overwork, unhealthy habits, worry, and isolation.

2. Goodman implies that Phil was a workaholic not only because of his "Type A" personality (paragraphs 2, 14), but also because of the pressures put on him by corporate culture. Wanting to be one of the "Important People" (4) and carrying the heavy workload of supervising some sixty employees (6), he was competing with two other vice-presidents for a promotion that we learn will go to whoever's "been working the hardest" (16).

3. Goodman's essay is a cautionary tale about working too hard. Her point, it seems, is that to sacrifice all of one's family and personal life to a job is a tragic mistake.

4. "The Company Man" is filled with numbers. Beyond those mentioned in the question, she cites "3:00 a.m. Sunday morning" (paragraphs 1, 3, 15), "one of three" who might be promoted to president (3), "six days a week, five of them until eight or nine at night" (4), "four-day week" (4), "twenty or twenty-five pounds" overweight (4), "maybe sixty" employees (6), "[t]hree of them" in line for Phil's job (6), "Helen, forty-eight years old" (7), the daughter who is "twenty-four" (10), the son who is "twenty" (11), "the last two years" of worry (11), "the sixty-year-old company president" (13), "the forty-eight-year-old widow" (13), "the fifty-one-year-old deceased" (13), "5:00 p.m. the afternoon of the funeral" (16), and "[o]ne of three men" (16) who could replace Phil. The essay reads like an actuarial table and suggests that businesses see workers as numbers, not human beings.

Craft and Structure

1. The quotations, too, are ironic. Those from the obituary—"extracurricular interests" (paragraph 4), "survivors" (7), and "dearly beloved" (9)—read like scare quotes and suggest how empty Phil's life turned out to be. Those from people speaking at his funeral underscore his family's emotional detachment and his employer's lack of concern.

2. The cause, of course, is workaholism (some students might identify it as pressure to work hard). The effects are several: social isolation (paragraph 4), poor physical health (4), estrangement from family (7–12), emotional damage to loved ones (7–12), financial damage to loved ones (7, 13), worry and stress (11, 14), and, ultimately, premature death.

105

3. Goodman's essay is full of repetition. In addition to the opening line, which implies that Phil was working when anybody else would be asleep, she repeats variations on "the obituary didn't say that" (paragraphs 2, 6); "of course" (2, 4, 16); "coronary thrombosis" and "heart attack" (2, 14); "Type A" (2, 14); "one of three" people in line for two different promotions (3, 6, 16); and the notion that Phil will be missed (7, 8, 13). The repetitions suggest the inevitability of his early death, hint at the meaninglessness of his work, and give the essay unity.

4. A "Type A" personality is someone who is driven, aggressive, status conscious, prone to working long hours, and (according to some theories) susceptible to heart disease. Goodman clarifies the personality traits at several points in the essay. She uses synonyms to define "Type A" as "workaholic" (paragraph 2) and "heart-attack natural" (14). She stresses his position as a vice-president (3), his desire to be one of the "Important People," and his view of golf as work (4) to reveal the emphasis he put on status. She stresses his late nights and six-day workweek (4–5) to show his tendency to put in long hours. She provides examples of his two sons—the older one who seems to have inherited the personality and the younger one who caused Phil worry because he didn't—to contrast Type A with the more easygoing Type B (9, 11). And she informs readers that Phil did, indeed, suffer a heart attack in the end (2, 14).

Integration of Knowledge and Ideas

1. Goodman's purpose is to nudge readers to examine their own lives—to think for more than just "five or ten minutes about" the lessons in her parable (paragraph 2). She wants them to rethink their attitudes toward work and upward mobility and strive instead for a healthy balance between their jobs and their personal lives. As the headnote preceding the essay explains, Goodman was writing to a general national audience of newspaper readers. But this essay seems to be aimed squarely at Phil's peers: adult male workaholics who may be headed down the same path he took.

2. Phil devoted himself to and sacrificed his life for a company that didn't care. At the same time, the conclusion implies that the man who takes his job will suffer the same fate.

3. Phil's job is unimportant, in both the specific and general senses: His work is meaningless to his life and to his employer, and describing it would distract from readers' understanding of the story. Other missing details include Phil's last name and his children's names, the name of the company president, where the characters live and work, what his wife's former office job entailed, and what his older son does as a "hard-working executive in a manufacturing firm down South" (paragraph 9). Goodman leaves out such details because she intends for her main character to serve as an everyman—someone in whom readers might recognize themselves or people they know.

Charlie LeDuff
End of the Line (p. 352)

LeDuff's dark look at the demise of a General Motors factory town is sure to elicit a strong response from students, many of whose families may have had experience with recessionary job loss. There is much to respond to in this essay, not only LeDuff's pessimistic and brooding viewpoint, but also the things he leaves unsaid or merely hinted at (see, for instance, question 2 under "Craft and Structure," as well as the third writing suggestion). Although the writer strives for an objective tone, students may sense judgment—of General Motors, of the federal government, or of the laid-off factory workers and their neighbors. Encourage them to tease out and debate the fairness of these judgments. Who, in the end, holds the blame for what happened in Janesville, Wisconsin?

Students interested in seeing Danny Wilcox Frazier's full photo essay can find it on the magazine's Web site (*motherjones.com/photoessays/2009/08/end-line*).

Related Texts

Chinua Achebe, *Things Fall Apart*

Sherman Alexie, *The Absolutely True Diary of a Part-Time Indian*

Isabel Allende, *The House of the Spirits*

Emily Dickinson, "We Grow Accustomed to the Dark"

F. Scott Fitzgerald, *The Great Gatsby*

Michael Moore, *Roger and Me* (documentary film)

George Orwell, *Animal Farm*

John Steinbeck, *The Grapes of Wrath*

Elie Wiesel, *Night*

Tennessee Williams, *The Glass Menagerie*

Content Quiz

1. Where is the Janesville assembly plant located?
   [In Wisconsin, "off Interstate 90 between the electric lights of Chicago [Illinois] and the sedate streets of Madison."]

2. When did the General Motors factory open, and when did it close?
   [It opened in 1919 and closed on December 23, 2008.]

3. What happened to the strip club that used to operate across the street from the factory?
   [The building is now being used for Alcoholics Anonymous meetings.]

4. Who is Pragnesh Patel?
   [He is the owner of a struggling motel in Janesville.]

5. To what city does LeDuff compare Janesville?
    [Detroit.]

Vocabulary Quiz

1. *Components* (paragraph 12) is closest in meaning to
    a. drums   b. parts   c. tickets
    [b. parts]

2. *Obsolescence* (14) is closest in meaning to
    a. uselessness   b. mistake   c. depression
    [a. uselessness]

3. *Wake* (19) is closest in meaning to
    a. wave   b. presence   c. funeral
    [c. funeral]

4. *Jilted* (21) is closest in meaning to
    a. limp   b. married   c. rejected
    [c. rejected]

5. *Monotony* (26) is closest in meaning to
    a. boredom   b. rhythm   c. faithfulness
    [a. boredom]

Answers
Key Ideas and Details

1. The mention of funerals sets up the central metaphor of LeDuff's essay. His trip to Janesville is the equivalent of attending a funeral because the GM plant closing has pretty much killed the town. In many ways, LeDuff presents what has happened to the people of Janesville as a metaphor for what is happening, and may continue to happen, across the country.

2. LeDuff doesn't hold out a lot of hope for Janesville. His conviction that the town is forever ruined is hinted at in several parts of the essay, particularly in his repeated allusions to death, funerals, and wakes (paragraphs 1, 19, 21, 26) but most clearly in his conclusion (27), where he writes, "Wind, solar, electric—that's the future, Washington says. But you get a pain-in-the-throat feeling that it is not the future. Not really."

3. What Pragnesh Patel means is that American employers will continue to outsource jobs to less affluent countries (like his native India), where workers are eager to accept low wages that would be insufficient to support a family in the United States. By extension, he is suggesting that American standards of living will inevitably be lowered by the global competition for work, no matter what new opportunities may arise. The idea both captures and reinforces LeDuff's pessimism about the future for American workers and communities.

Craft and Structure

1. Students should quickly discover that it is almost impossible to edit out LeDuff's sentence fragments without rewriting the paragraphs completely, removing all traces of the author's voice and meaning in the process. By expressing only partial, unfinished thoughts, the fragments help to build a mood that is overwhelmingly lethargic and hopeless.

2. Like the residents of Janesville themselves, LeDuff isn't interested in causes. As far as they (and he) are concerned, it doesn't matter *why* GM failed or *why* so many are out of work; what matters is that people are hurting and don't know what they'll do to make things better. The dismissal of causes re-creates for readers a sense of the fatalism and helplessness felt by the subjects of LeDuff's essay.

3. The quotations from residents allow LeDuff to describe their despair as objectively and dispassionately as possible. By letting those workers speak for themselves and express their own ambivalence, LeDuff is able to elicit empathy for them.

4. The photographs might best be described as haunting. Each one is deep in shadow, both ominous and depressing. At the same time, people are absent from all but one image, and even that one shows a lone man whose back is to the camera. Taken together, they visually reinforce LeDuff's depiction of a ghost town that is little more than a shell: no longer a vibrant community of hard-working people, but a place of loneliness, desolation, and gloom.

5. The writer switches between the past and the present throughout the essay to stress that Janesville and its residents have changed, and for the worse, in the few months since General Motors pulled out of town. He also compares the town to the infamously downtrodden Detroit ("a little Detroit in the making" [paragraphs 1, 20]) to warn that things could get even worse for the people of Janesville (and the rest of the country) than they already are.

Integration of Knowledge and Ideas

1. As he suggests in paragraph 4, LeDuff wrote "End of the Line" in response to the traumatic bankruptcy and federal takeover of General Motors. Rather than explore the company's problems or the government's response, however, he chooses to focus on the effects on laid-off employees and their community in a one-factory town.

2. LeDuff assumes that his readers have at least some knowledge of company towns, of the history of General Motors, and of the company's role in American politics and the economy. All the same, he is careful to explain references that may not be obvious to the uninitiated. For instance, he counts the population of Janesville; pinpoints the town's location on a mental map; describes its streets, buildings, and residents in some detail;

and distinguishes company towns from industry towns (20). He also gives a quick overview of GM's history (3) and describes physical artifacts from the plant's distant past (7, 13) to help readers grasp both what it once was and what it has become.

3.   Answers will vary.

Chapter 15

Argument and Persuasion
Debating Law and Order

Focus on Tone

Answers will vary. Possible revisions are provided below.

1. Federal law requires school districts to accommodate students with special needs.

2. The Individuals with Disabilities Education Act gives students with learning disabilities a right to the extra attention they need to obtain a good education.

3. Administrators should acknowledge that the current learning-disabled policies were influenced by budget issues.

4. A group of parents persuaded the school board that funding the integration of special-needs students would unfairly divert money from programs they felt were more important.

5. While any budget cut is unfortunate, segregating students with learning disabilities from the rest of the student population is a form of discrimination that our school should not allow.

Anna Quindlen
The *C* Word in the Hallways (p. 382)

The subject of student violence is a sensitive one, particularly for students who may have had a personal connection to an incident, as well as for those who worry about the possibility of a shooting at their own school. All the same, Quindlen's essay offers an excellent opportunity to discuss the effectiveness of using emotional appeals in argument.

One way to initiate discussion might be to ask how much has changed since Quindlen wrote this essay. Teachers and administrators have indeed started paying more attention to students' mental health, but some might argue that the increased scrutiny has caused more problems than it has solved. Others might reply that mental illness is just as stigmatized—if not more so—than it was in 1999. Still others might point out that despite the media frenzies that accompany each new shooting, the problem (as devastating as it is) is neither as new nor as widespread as news reports imply.

Related Texts

Sherman Alexie, *The Absolutely True Diary of a Part-Time Indian*

Jimmy Santiago Baca, *Stories from the Edge*

The Bad Seed (movie)

Kate Chopin, *The Awakening*

Suzanne Collins, *The Hunger Games*

The Epic of Gilgamesh

Charlotte Perkins Gilman, "The Yellow Wallpaper"

William Golding, *Lord of the Flies*

Khaled Hosseini, *The Kite Runner*

Shirley Jackson, "The Lottery"

Harper Lee, *To Kill a Mockingbird*

J. D. Salinger, *The Catcher in the Rye*

William Shakespeare, *Macbeth*

William Shakespeare, *Othello*

William Shakespeare, *Romeo and Juliet*

Sophocles, *Oedipus Rex*

Robert Louis Stevenson, *Dr. Jekyll and Mr. Hyde*

Amy Tan, *The Joy Luck Club*

Jeanette Walls, *The Glass Castle*

Elie Wiesel, *Night*

William Butler Yeats, "The Second Coming"

Content Quiz

1. What is a "psychological autopsy"?
   [It's the process by which doctors try to identify the reasons for a teenager's suicide or homicide.]

2. Who were Kip Kinkel and Sam Manzie?
   [Both were seventeen-year-olds who committed murders: Kinkel killed his parents and two classmates; Manzie killed an eleven-year-old boy.]

3. What ending did film censors insist be added to the 1956 movie *The Bad Seed*?
   [They forced the producers to add a scene in which the fictional father spanked the lead character as punishment for her killing spree.]

4. With what weapon did Kip Kinkel kill his father?
    [With the same gun (a Glock) that his father bought for him as an alternative to therapy.]

5. According to Quindlen, how many mentally ill children do not get psychological treatment?
    [Two-thirds of the total, which is estimated at six million.]

Vocabulary Quiz

1. *Ludicrous* (paragraph 4) is closest in meaning to
    a. laughable   b. cautious   c. thoughtful
    [a. laughable]

2. *Loll* (7) is closest in meaning to
    a. fight   b. droop   c. enjoy
    [b. droop]

3. *Utilitarian* (7) is closest in meaning to
    a. psychological   b. practical   c. financial
    [b. practical]

4. *Derision* (9) is closest in meaning to
    a. approval   b. support   c. ridicule
    [c. ridicule]

5. *Psychotropic* (10) is closest in meaning to
    a. mind-altering   b. recreational   c. legal
    [a. mind-altering]

Answers
Key Ideas and Details

1. The author's thesis is stated in the introduction: "Yet one solution continues to elude us, and that is ending the ignorance about mental health, and moving it from the margins of care and into the mainstream where it belongs. As surely as any vaccine, this would save lives" (paragraph 2). In other words, Quindlen believes that if American culture destigmatized mental illness and became more willing to treat it like any other illness, fewer troubled teenagers would kill themselves or others.

2. Quindlen focuses her essay on relatively targeted teen killings, using as her primary examples Kip Kinkel (who killed his parents and two Oregon classmates in November 1999) and Sam Manzie (who killed a young boy in his New Jersey home the same month), both of whom were sentenced to life in prison when they were seventeen years old. As she sees it, both boys were mentally ill. She further suggests that Kinkel's father aided and abetted his actions by buying him a gun and that Manzie was the victim of a pedophile.

113

3. She is implying that our culture encourages boys to use violence to solve their problems, a point she reinforces later when she remarks that "talk therapy, or even heartfelt talk, is somehow sissified, weak" (paragraph 9).

Craft and Structure

1. After asserting that "mental illness is an illness, not a character flaw" (paragraph 10), Quindlen creates an emphatic rhythm by ending three of the last four sentences with the same phrase: insurance providers, hospitals and schools, and parents "should act like it." She then uses a variation of this phrase ("will believe it") to argue that her solution will work.

2. Quindlen's argument is highly emotional. She sets the tone with her opening observation that the phrase "psychological autopsy" is "the saddest" one she's "read in a long time" (paragraph 1). Just a few examples of emotional appeal in her essay include her reference to "black-bordered photographs in yearbooks and murder suspects with acne problems" (2), her comment that "So many [lives] have already been lost" (3), her depiction of Manzie's father trying to navigate the insurance system (6), her chilling allusion to lobotomies (7), her acknowledgment that her argument has an element of the "[w]arm fuzzies" to it (7), her question of "how we would respond if two-thirds of America's babies were not being immunized" (8), and the "what if" scenario of her conclusion.

3. She tackles opposing viewpoints in paragraph 4, with her reference to the "ludicrous" solution to child homicides epitomized in the movie *The Bad Seed*, and in paragraphs 5 and 6, in which she acknowledges that Kinkel and Manzie did receive mental health care (but insists that it was inadequate). Although her discussion of the boys' treatment does seem balanced and reasonable, students may rightly object that in relying on a movie that is over fifty years old to characterize those who disagree with her perspective, Quindlen is unfairly depicting her opponents as almost comically irrational.

4. Quindlen's examples of teenage killers (paragraph 3) and ineffective responses (4) establish the urgency of the problem and the need for a better solution. The paragraphs of comparison and contrast explaining the boys' treatment (5, 6) emphasize the inadequacy of contemporary mental health interventions. The essay as a whole could be read as a cause-and-effect analysis, but the dangerous relationship between current attitudes and teenage boys' violence is articulated most clearly in paragraphs 8 and 9.

Integration of Knowledge and Ideas

1. Her reference to "we parents" in paragraph 10 suggests that Quindlen is writing primarily to parents of teenagers, hoping to urge them to take their children's problems more seriously. By extension, her conclusion hints that she also imagines representatives of insurance providers, hospitals, and schools among her readers.

2. The omission will almost certainly trouble, or at least puzzle, some readers, but there are reasonable explanations for Quindlen's decision not to

include the Columbine tragedy in her discussion. On the surface, her essay is a response to two very specific incidents that took place at around the same time. On a deeper level, however, it may be that the scale of Columbine is just too overwhelming to contemplate in a brief essay, that Quindlen doesn't put Harris and Klebold in the same category of untreated mental illness in which she places Kinkel and Manzie, or that she doesn't see fit to try to excuse their behavior—or to blame the massacre on society. (Such an attempt would probably have alienated readers.)

3. Depending on readers' knowledge of Shakespeare's play and Yeats's poem, these quick allusions pack a lot of meaning. *Romeo and Juliet*, of course, is largely a story about teenagers who get caught up in circumstances that were not of their making. "The Second Coming" describes the end of the world as the arrival of a terrible beast that destroys the innocent. Many high school students will have at least a passing familiarity with the play; you may want to bring a copy of the poem to class and share it with students.

Wilbert Rideau
Why Prisons Don't Work (p. 387)

Rideau's essay is serious and his proposal controversial, but his argument is relatively easy to follow. Taking as his premise the idea that society is right to want to protect itself from crime, he skillfully establishes several reasons for his titular assertion that prisons don't work: tough sentencing hasn't reduced violent crime, the threat of jail has not stopped people from committing crimes, long prison terms harden criminals instead of reforming them, even the worst crime—murder—is usually an isolated mistake, and prisoners simply need more support to rise above their weaknesses. At each step of his argument, Rideau manages to knock down a common assumption without alienating his readers. If nothing else, he is a master at building common ground.

What is perhaps most instructive in Rideau's essay is that even a convicted killer arguing for prison reform can establish a strong ethical appeal. The author's personal history might offer a good opening for a class discussion (see question 2 under "Integration of Knowledge and Ideas"). How do Rideau's circumstances affect his credibility? How successfully does he overcome this potential problem? How can students apply the same strategies to their own arguments?

Related Texts

Chinua Achebe, *Things Fall Apart*

Jimmy Santiago Baca, *Stories from the Edge*

Ray Bradbury, *Fahrenheit 451*

Kate Chopin, *The Awakening*

Suzanne Collins, *The Hunger Games*

Fyodor Dostoevsky, *Crime and Punishment*

Shirley Jackson, "The Lottery"

Martin Luther King, Jr., "Letter from Birmingham Jail"

John Knowles, *A Separate Peace*

Harper Lee, *To Kill a Mockingbird*

George Orwell, *1984*

George Orwell, "Shooting an Elephant"

Reginald Rose, *Twelve Angry Men*

William Shakespeare, *Othello*

Mark Twain, *The Adventures of Huckleberry Finn*

Richard Wright, *Native Son*

Content Quiz

1. Where was the author imprisoned, and for what?
   [He was at Louisiana State Penitentiary for murder.]

2. What did prison authorities in Louisiana take from an inmate in solitary confinement as punishment?
   [His underwear.]

3. What American state has the highest murder rate?
   [Louisiana.]

4. What category of prisoners work in the home of Louisiana's governor?
   [Murderers.]

5. Who, according to the author, is "the most dangerous criminal"?
   [The person "who has not yet killed but has a history of escalating offenses."]

Vocabulary Quiz

1. *Consigned* (paragraph 1) is closest in meaning to
   a. sold   b. committed   c. resigned
   [b. committed]

2. *Vies* (2) is closest in meaning to
   a. sins   b. competes   c. fails
   [b. competes]

3. *Incorrigible* (3) is closest in meaning to
   a. unreformable   b. violent   c. tricky
   [a. unreformable]

4. *Abhors* (3) is closest in meaning to
   a. hates   b. imprisons   c. releases
   [a. hates]

5. *Escalating* (5) is closest in meaning to
    a. driving   b. petty   c. increasing
    [c. increasing]

Answers
Key Ideas and Details

1. Rideau asserts his central assumption in paragraph 1. Prisons, he says, exist "so politicians can sell the illusion that permanently exiling people to prison will make society safe." In other words, the purpose of prison is to protect society. He refers again to this assumption in paragraphs 3 ("If getting tough resulted in public safety") and 4 ("Prison has a role in public safety"). Corollary to the goal of public safety are the intent of rehabilitating criminals (6) and the belief that the threat of jail is a deterrent to crime (7).

2. Put simply, prisons don't work because they don't accomplish what Rideau sees as their primary goal: they don't make society safe from crime. They don't deter people from committing crimes (paragraph 3), they hold people who no longer pose a threat to society (4, 5), and they don't do enough to rehabilitate those inmates who will ultimately be released (6, 7). Rideau's thesis might be summed up in a sentence from the middle of the essay: "Prison, like the police and the courts, has a minimal impact on crime because it is a response after the fact, a mop-up operation" (3).

3. The author believes that society should focus on prevention rather than punishment. He offers his proposal in his conclusion, where he insists that "Our youngsters must be taught to respect the humanity of others and to handle disputes without violence. . . . As a community, we must address the adverse life circumstances that spawn criminality" (paragraph 7). Some readers may notice an implication here that social inequities (especially poverty) are the real cause of crime.

Craft and Structure

1. His point is that most new inmates are stupid, immature kids rather than hardened, calculating criminals. By repeating the words "unskilled," "impulsive," and "uneducated" misfits, as well as variations on them — "dumb," "failures," "rejects" — several times in his opening paragraph, he emphasizes the need to educate potential criminals and make them productive members of society *before* they get into trouble.

2. Rideau's inductive reasoning is drawn from his experiences as a prisoner at Louisiana State Penitentiary. He provides examples of fellow prisoners' experiences and attitudes to generalize about inmates at other prisons. Similarly, he describes the failures of Louisiana's penal system to draw a conclusion about the effectiveness of prison in general. His deductive reasoning can be summarized in the following syllogism:

    MAJOR PREMISE: Prisons rely on deterrence, rehabilitation, and punishment to protect society.

MINOR PREMISE: Most criminals do not think about the possibility of jail when they commit their crimes, prisons don't rehabilitate inmates, and punishment happens after the fact.

CONCLUSION: Therefore, prisons don't protect society.

Some students may notice that Rideau's entire argument rests on the assumption that prisons are meant to protect society — an assertion that is not universally agreed upon. If one assumes that prisons are meant solely to punish, for instance, Rideau's argument falls apart.

3. "Ever see a dog chase its tail?" (paragraph 8) is a rhetorical question. It summarizes Rideau's main point (that current prison laws are based on faulty circular logic) with a compelling visual image; it also highlights his frustration.

4. Louisiana has enacted some of the most stringent sentencing guidelines in the country, raising mandatory sentences and restricting parole, yet the state still "has the highest murder rate" (paragraph 3) in the country. Rideau believes that the laws have failed because people don't think rationally when they're committing a crime. Rather, they're so caught up in desperate circumstances that any potential consequences are irrelevant at the time. He uses the example of Louisiana to emphasize his point that prison is not a deterrent to crime.

Integration of Knowledge and Ideas

1. It's a little difficult to gauge Rideau's purpose, but an astute reader might conclude that he wants to persuade politicians to change their "tough on crime" approach and refocus their efforts on measures that are more likely to prevent crime in the first place. It is conceivable that an opinion essay in a publication such as *Time* might play a small part in legislative change. Readers of such publications include policymakers, to be sure, but, more important, major news magazines influence public opinion, which in turn influences political opinion and action.

2. Most readers can be expected to doubt Rideau's objectivity. After all, how seriously can we take an admitted killer's claim that a life sentence is an ineffective way to protect society? Rideau's credibility is helped by his willingness to acknowledge his status as a lifer from the start. And in some ways, he turns his credibility problem to his advantage, most notably by sharing his firsthand knowledge of the prison population and of the effects that long sentences have on inmates, as well as by using his personal experience to bring in compelling examples (such as the prisoner whose underwear was taken away in paragraph 2). He wisely uses the expert testimony of a prison warden (5) to echo his claims, and he makes a point of introducing statistical and factual evidence to support individual points. Rideau also works to build common ground with his readers by acknowledging the validity of opposing viewpoints (see the next question).

3. Rideau anticipates that many readers will object to his argument, so he establishes common ground at every opportunity. Nearly every paragraph identifies an opposing viewpoint and attempts to discredit it. He begins paragraph 2, for instance, by describing the prevailing "tough on crime" ideology, then shows how one state (Louisiana) has taken that ideology too far. In the next paragraph (3), he accepts the need for public safety but argues that "getting tough" hasn't worked. In paragraphs 4–6, he acknowledges some valid uses of prisons, including temporary confinement and rehabilitation through education, but he insists that such uses should be limited or improved. And in his conclusion, he stresses that he shares with readers the desire to "curb crime" (7), offering his own solution to the problem.

Marie Myung-Ok Lee
I Was an Anchor Baby (p. 392)

Lee's essay deftly addresses what is possibly the most contentious topic among the selections in *Common Threads*: illegal immigration. Writing from a calm yet earnest point of view shortly after House Republican Jon Kyle of Arizona called for a congressional hearing on the issue of birthright citizenship, the author provides a very personal perspective on what has become a very public and increasingly heated issue. In reminding readers of the history of immigration laws, Lee deftly sidesteps the more controversial elements of the debate by reframing its terms. As she puts it at the beginning of the essay, birthright citizenship does "nothing to resolve [illegal] parents' situation; if anything, it only add[s] to their stress" (paragraph 3). And in the end, she stresses, the issue is about "American family" values (15). Some students will agree wholeheartedly, of course, while others might reject Lee's angle altogether.

A good place to begin a discussion of Lee's topic would be to focus on students' own immigration histories, exploring where their families came from and sharing stories they may have heard from relatives before delving into what could easily become a heated argument about immigration and legal status. Regardless of where students stand on the issue, they should come to recognize that the debate has a human component that is often overlooked.

Related Texts

Lee's essay would surely go well with her own novels for young adults. Just about any work of fiction that touches on the immigrant experience, especially as it affects families, would also be a good match, as would these.

Julia Álvarez, *How the Garcia Girls Lost Their Accents*

Gloria Anzaldua, *Borderlands: La Frontera*

Sandra Cisneros, *The House on Mango Street*

Stephen Crane, *The Red Badge of Courage*

The Epic of Gilgamesh

Henrik Ibsen, *A Doll's House*

M*A*S*H (movie)

Richard Rodriguez, *Hunger of Memory* (see p. 153)

Sophocles, *Oedipus Rex*

John Steinbeck, *The Grapes of Wrath*

Amy Tan, *The Joy Luck Club*

Robert Louis Stevenson, *Dr. Jekyll and Mr. Hyde*

Richard Wright, *Black Boy*

Content Quiz

1. From what country did Lee's parents come to the United States?
    [Korea.]

2. What does Lee's father do for work?
    [He is an anesthesiologist.]

3. What two laws made Lee's parents illegal immigrants?
    [The Chinese Exclusion Act of 1882 and the Immigration and Naturaliza-
    tion Act of 1924.]

4. How were Lee's parents saved from deportation?
    [The residents of the author's home town of Hibbing, Minnesota, signed a
    petition to allow them to stay, and the local representative in Congress
    granted them status as "permanent alien residents."]

5. Who signed the 1965 immigration law that enabled Lee's parents to apply
    for citizenship?
    [President Lyndon Johnson.]

Vocabulary Quiz

1. *Invoked* (paragraph 2) is closest in meaning to
    a. coined   b. used   c. forced
    [b. used]

2. *Liaison* (4) is closest in meaning to
    a. soldier   b. communicator   c. offender
    [b. communicator]

3. *Eschewed* (8) is closest in meaning to
    a. avoided   b. honored   c. coveted
    [a. avoided]

4. *Fathom* (11) is closest in meaning to
    a. accept   b. understand   c. dispute
    [b. understand]

5. *Entitled* (13) is closest in meaning to
    a. encouraged   b. excited   c. allowed
    [c. allowed]

Answers
Key Ideas and Details

1. Lee's purpose and main idea are evident throughout the essay, but her major claim is stated at the end of her introduction: "The words [anchor baby] suggest that having a child in America confers some kind of legal protection on illegal parents. . . . But in reality, merely having a baby on American soil doesn't change the parents' status" (paragraphs 2–3). She wants readers to reject arguments for repealing the Fourteenth Amendment; by extension, she also wants them to have a greater appreciation for the contributions immigrants make to American society, legal or not.

2. As Lee explains, an anesthesiologist "administer[s] anesthesia" (paragraph 4). The definition isn't especially helpful, but students should be able to infer that anesthesiologists are doctors who use drugs to manage patients' pain during surgery. Lee suggests that most doctors don't want to do the work because it involves "long hours," stress, and constant vigilance (5–6).

3. Lee's parents were refugees from the Korean War (paragraphs 1, 4). They came to United States at the encouragement of American doctors so that her father could "continue his education" (4) and overstayed their student visas (1). They did not apply for citizenship because they were ineligible to do so: laws banned Asian immigration (7–8). Although a town-wide petition succeeded in granting her parents permanent residency (12–13), it was only when President Johnson "signed a new immigration act" (15) that they were eligible to apply. They immediately did, successfully passed the exams, and "finally" became "an American family" (15).

Craft and Structure

1. An "anchor baby" is a child of non-US citizens granted American citizenship by virtue of having been born in the United States. In the minds of immigration opponents, such children provide incentive for illegal immigration by giving parents a reason to stay in the country and potential sponsorship for their own citizenship applications. To Lee, it's a racial slur. Like many members of minorities do, she reclaims the term and gives it a new, more positive definition: "we anchored my father to this place where his skills were so needed" (paragraph 13).

2. Lee draws on her family's and friends' experiences to support her argument: she asserts that her parents were invited to study and work in the United States (paragraphs 4–5); that "peculiar laws rather than criminal intent . . . made [her] parents outlaws at the time of [her] birth" (7); that the families of her "immigrant and second-generation friends" had similar experiences (10); that American citizens benefit from the work she and her father have done (11–13); and that her "father worked at a job that other Americans did not

121

want to do" (14). The argument is inductive: what was true for her parents, Lee implies, is true for most immigrant parents of American children.

3.   Lee briefly describes the opposing argument in her introduction, summarizing the effort "to repeal [the Fourteenth] amendment" as a mistaken belief that birthright citizenship benefits illegal immigrants and characterizing her opponents' attitudes as "pejorative" (paragraph 2). The rest of her essay presents her counterargument. While Lee certainly comes across as fair and reasonable, some readers might object that she does not fully address the arguments for repeal, focusing only on the "anchor baby" aspect and ignoring other points.

4.   Paragraphs 3–6, 9, and 12–15 narrate the family history. Lee gives examples of laws banning Asian immigration in paragraphs 7–8 and 15. In paragraphs 8–10, 12–13, and 15, she details how those laws affected her family and friends. By mixing personal examples with national trends, she emphasizes the human aspect of an issue that might otherwise seem abstract.

Integration of Knowledge and Ideas

1.   Lee is writing for a general audience of *Los Angeles Times* readers, but she seems to direct her argument specifically at those who might be sympathetic to arguments that the Fourteenth Amendment encourages or enables illegal immigration. She assumes, first, that her readers value American citizenship. Several other assumptions are apparent in the focus of her subclaims: that readers value medical expertise and hard work (paragraphs 4–5, 14), that they respect the law (7–10), that they're unfamiliar with legal history (7–8, 15), that they mistrust immigrants (7, 11), and that they put a strong emphasis on family (1, 15) and community (12–13).

2.   Lee is sharing a personal experience, to be sure, especially with her emphasis on her family's story. But her purpose is ultimately more serious. She wants to reveal what she sees as the misinformation and faulty assumptions underlying arguments for amending the US Constitution, and to persuade readers to reject "calls to repeal [the Fourteenth] Amendment" (paragraph 2) on the grounds that repeal would be harmful to immigrants and citizens alike.

3.   In addition to the personal experience and observations she uses throughout, Lee supports her argument with historical facts (paragraphs 7–8, 15), with the opinion of a "Korean American . . . academic who has written groundbreaking books and nurtured a generation of scholars" (10), published research concluding that "immigrants, legal and not, are more law-abiding than the rest of the populace, and possibly more patriotic" (10), and with the expert opinion of a president calling Asian immigration bans "a cruel and enduring wrong in the conduct of the American nation" (15). How convincing her evidence is will vary from student to student; some may catch that the studies Lee mentions in paragraph 10 are unattributed and therefore may question the validity of her generalization.

REGULATING TECHNOLOGY: DISTRACTED DRIVING

As new technologies emerge, new issues inevitably develop around them. The four essays that close this chapter function as a casebook of legal arguments on related topics. The first two, by Carolyn McCarthy and Radley Balko, debate the necessity of laws against using mobile technologies behind the wheel; the second two, by Nicholas Carr and Jim Harper, examine recent calls for rules preventing businesses and government agencies from recording data on Internet usage.

If ever there was an issue guaranteed to grab high school students' attention, texting and driving would probably be it. Published together in *US News Digital Weekly*, Carolyn McCarthy's and Radley Balko's essays work as a set of paired readings that take opposing positions on the same controversial issue: driving while distracted. While McCarthy feels strongly that new laws are needed to stop a dangerous practice, Balko insists that legislation is both unnecessary and unenforceable.

Carolyn McCarthy
Should Text Messaging While Driving Be Banned? Yes. (p. 398)

McCarthy's essay is an impassioned and highly earnest plea to save lives by enacting laws to stop distracted driving. Many students will likely resist her argument, believing that drivers can easily handle the distractions of mobile technologies behind the wheel; indeed, a shocking percentage of teen drivers admit to regularly engaging in the behavior McCarthy wants to ban.

Class discussion might naturally revolve around distracted driving itself or the social problems (and benefits) brought about by mobile technologies. The essay also invites further research into the evolution of driving policies and restrictions (see the third writing topic for a starting point).

Related Texts

The works suggested below address accidents or government intrusions.

Ray Bradbury, *Fahrenheit 451*

Anthony Burgess, *A Clockwork Orange*

F. Scott Fitzgerald, *The Great Gatsby*

Robert Frost, "Out, Out"

Aldus Huxley, *Brave New World*

Flannery O'Connor, "A Good Man Is Hard to Find"

George Orwell, *1984*

Content Quiz

1. Of what political group is McCarthy a member?
   [Congress.]

2. What does the ALERT Drivers Act propose to make illegal?
   [The act would ban "writing, sending, or reading text messages while operating a moving vehicle."]

3. Under the terms of McCarthy's proposal, what would states lose if they fail
   to comply with minimum standards?
   [Federal highway funding.]

4. To what dangerous behavior did *Car and Driver* magazine compare texting
   while driving?
   [Drunk driving.]

5. Prior to her political career, what was McCarthy's profession?
   [She was a nurse.]

Vocabulary Quiz

1. *Proponents* (paragraph 1) is closest in meaning to
   a. supporters   b. enemies   c. lawmakers
   [a. supporters]

2. *Adept* (4) is closest in meaning to
   a. skilled   b. scholarly   c. sluggish
   [a. skilled]

3. *Novice* (6) is closest in meaning to
   a. expert   b. beginner   c. guide
   [b. beginner]

4. *Vetting* (8) is closest in meaning to
   a. developing   b. evaluating   c. brainstorming
   [b. evaluating]

5. *Prudent* (9) is closest in meaning to
   a. strict   b. innocent   c. careful
   [c. careful]

Answers
Key Ideas and Details

1. McCarthy's thesis is that because distracted driving causes accidents (paragraph 1), texting while driving should be illegal. Since "only a handful of
   states ban texting and driving" (3), she proposes a nationwide ban to establish consistent laws that will "encourage people to stop" (10) engaging in the
   practice.

2. McCarthy is alarmed because as mobile devices become more common, so do the risks of automobile accidents, causing "unsafe and potentially fatal scenarios on the roadways" (paragraph 2). She blames "[i]nconsistent laws across our country [that] serve only to confuse drivers and embolden those who text and drive" (9) for enabling dangerous driver behavior.

3. As McCarthy explains in paragraph 3, the bill "would set in place guidelines that would lead to a nationwide ban on writing, sending, or reading text messages while operating a moving vehicle." She elaborates on the details in paragraph 5: the bill would set "minimum . . . standards" for safety rules, allowing states to "establish stricter standards as they see fit," and it would exempt "hands-free and voice-activated technologies." The bill seems to leave it to individual states to figure out how to enforce the rules, but it would penalize states that fail to participate by reducing the federal funds they currently receive.

Craft and Structure

1. McCarthy's tone seems almost motherly in its preachiness. Her use of chiding phrases such as "common-sense" (paragraph 2), "I was shocked to learn" (3), and "no excuse" (4) help to establish this tone, as does her closing emphasis on her identity as a "mother [and] nurse for over thirty years" (11). Some teenagers may be put off by her earnestness, interpreting her concerns as meddling, judgmental, or simply out of touch; while others might find her attitude comforting.

2. Examples of *emotional appeals*: the opening two paragraphs; the comparisons between distracted and drunk driving (paragraphs 5, 7); the claim that "90% of adults believe texting while driving should be illegal" (6); the expressions of thanks to Ray LaHood and President Barack Obama (8). Examples of *ethical appeals*: McCarthy's presentation of herself as a congresswoman (2), mother, and nurse (11); her acknowledgment that she relies on mobile technologies herself (4); her reasonable tone (throughout). Examples of *rational appeals*: statistical evidence (e.g., 6, 7); the entire structure of the argument, using deductive reasoning to make her case. Students' judgments of these appeals will of course vary widely depending on their knowledge and beliefs.

3. McCarthy mentions one opposing view — the problem of enforcement — in paragraphs 1 and 8, but she doesn't address it in any detail. The omission of conflicting arguments may present a problem for some readers, especially if they read McCarthy's essay in conjunction with Balko's (p. 403), which examines the enforceability issue thoroughly.

4. Paragraphs 2, 6, and 7 draw a connection between driver texting and fatal highway accidents; paragraph 10 asserts that laws influence human behavior. The negative effects of texting while driving form the crux of McCarthy's argument that the behavior should be made illegal.

Integration of Knowledge and Ideas

1. Answers will vary. On the one hand, McCarthy insists that her purpose is not motivated by politics, that her "agenda . . . rises above political ideology" (paragraph 6). Her views are obviously sincere, and she makes a point of stressing that she "seek[s] common ground on issues that . . . will make our country stronger and safer" (2). On the other hand, she *is* a professional politician attempting to pass a congressional act, and she names other political figures who agree with her. Even her writing for a national rather than local New York audience might be seen as politically motivated.

2. McCarthy seems to expect that many if not most readers will agree with her. In presenting the risks of texting while driving as a problem that "should come as no surprise to the American public" (paragraph 2), McCarthy's opening paragraphs make a nationwide ban seem just and fair: who wouldn't want to prevent fatal accidents? Presumably to avoid alienating readers with too much emotion, McCarthy also presents herself in these paragraphs as authoritative and coolly rational, establishing her position as a "member of Congress" (2) and commenting on her desire to "pass comprehensive, common-sense legislation that will benefit average Americans" (2).

3. Her evidence includes personal observations of "extended national coverage" (paragraph 3) of distracted driving and the appeal of mobile technologies (4), as well as the expert opinions of both the United States Secretary of Transportation and the president, but she relies most heavily on statistics drawn from a "CBS News/*New York Times* poll" (6), an academic study (7), and a study by *Car and Driver* magazine. Although opinion polls tend not to carry much weight, McCarthy's sources are generally considered respectable, so most students should find her evidence reliable; that a driving enthusiasts' magazine warns of the risks of distractions should be particularly convincing.

Radley Balko

Should Text Messaging While Driving Be Banned? No. (p. 403)

Published as a debate with McCarthy in *US News Digital Weekly*, Balko's essay responds directly to McCarthy's proposal and extends his argument to apply to any calls for new laws in response to new worries. In the course of arguing against texting bans, Balko questions the validity of the premises on which McCarthy bases her own argument: that mobile technologies have led to an increase in traffic accidents, and that enacting laws against using those technologies will have any effect.

Class discussion might start with consideration of Balko's tone (see the first question under "Craft and Structure"). Do students find the writer's heavy sarcasm effective and appropriate, given his subject and purpose, or could such openly expressed hostility make readers resistant to his argument? Why?

Related Texts

The works suggested below address accidents or government intrusions.

Ray Bradbury, *Fahrenheit 451*

Anthony Burgess, *A Clockwork Orange*

F. Scott Fitzgerald, *The Great Gatsby*

Robert Frost, "Out, Out"

Aldus Huxley, *Brave New World*

Flannery O'Connor, "A Good Man Is Hard to Find"

George Orwell, *1984*

Content Quiz

1. What does TOBAL stand for?
    ["There Oughtta Be a Law."]

2. How much did the number of cell phone subscriptions change between 1995 and 2009?
    [It increased by eight times.]

3. Has the number of fatal traffic accidents increased or decreased since 1995?
    [It has decreased.]

4. What does Maryland's texting ban permit drivers to do with their phones?
    [To read text messages.]

5. According to Balko, what are the only two things bans on texting will accomplish?
    ["They'll give police officers another reason to pull people over, and they'll bring in revenue for the municipalities that aggressively enforce them."]

Vocabulary Quiz

1. *Wrenching* (paragraph 2) is closest in meaning to
    a. interesting   b. absurd   c. upsetting
    [c. upsetting]

2. *Scrawl* (2) is closest in meaning to
    a. write   b. publish   c. discount
    [a. write]

3. *Penumbra* (3) is closest in meaning to
    a. exception   b. shadow   c. law
    [c. law]

4. *Arbitrarily* (10) is closest in meaning to
   a. rightfully   b. unreasonably   c. strictly
   [b. unreasonably]

5. *Revenue* (11) is closest in meaning to
   a. income   b. fame   c. entertainment
   [a. income]

Answers
Key Ideas and Details

1. Balko states his thesis at the end of his introduction: "I will argue that we need to get over the idea that we can solve every bad habit with a new law. We can't, and this issue illustrates why" (paragraph 3). He reiterates his point in his conclusion: "the one thing these bans aren't likely to do is make the roads much safer. And if they won't accomplish that, there's no reason to enact them" (11). The thesis denies McCarthy's claim that laws against texting while driving will make the roadways safer by deterring the behavior.

2. "TOBAL," as Balko explains in paragraph 2, "is short for 'There Oughtta Be a Law.'" "TOBAL-itis" (1) is a knee-jerk overreaction to an overhyped problem, a demand for new laws that in effect are merely symbolic because they neither address a real problem nor offer a workable solution; they merely create a feeling that something has been done about it. McCarthy's proposal represents an instance of this kind of reaction because, Balko argues in paragraphs 4–7, texting while driving does not in fact make the roadways more dangerous; at the same time, because laws against the habit are unenforceable (see next question), they actually create new problems.

3. Sending text messages accounts for just one of the many driver distractions caused by mobile phone technology. Laws such as the one McCarthy proposes permit drivers to look at screens and to make calls; police would be unable to tell which activity a driver is engaging in. Even if the laws were written to prohibit any use of cellphones by drivers, plenty of other distractions remain; again, determining which technology a driver is using and how is next to impossible (paragraphs 8–9).

Craft and Structure

1. Other examples of irony: "Wrenching anecdotes about the effect of some alleged new trend make national news. A panic takes root in the media. Earnest editorialists scrawl urgent pleas for action. Politicians grandstand" (paragraph 2); "I'm not going to defend the act of clumsily thumbing out an e-mail while guiding a two-ton, gasoline-loaded missile down the highway at 70 miles per hour" (3); "our highways are awash in BlackBerry-spilled blood" (4); "Strayer would have a point if he were looking at the right statistics" (6); "Unless a motorist is blatantly typing away at eye level . . ." (8); "Shiny objects? Pretty girls in the passenger seat?" (9). The irony, which often veers into sarcasm, conveys Balko's hostility toward texting-ban proponents and helps to keep readers interested. Readers who agree with Balko

may appreciate the irony. Those who don't are likely to find it flippant and inappropriate.

2. *Rational appeals*: like McCarthy, Balko uses statistics and other evidence to support his argument (e.g., paragraphs 4, 6, 8), and he uses deductive reasoning to point out the logical flaws in proponents' arguments (e.g., 4–6; see next question). *Emotional appeals*: the image of blood-soaked highways (4); the allusions to children, food, and music (7); the series of rhetorical questions in paragraph 9; the suggestion that bans will "give police officers another reason to pull people over" (11).

3. The faulty syllogism:

   MAJOR PREMISE: Texting while driving causes accidents.

   MINOR PREMISE: Laws against texting will prevent accidents.

   CONCLUSION: Texting while driving should be illegal.

   Balko claims that neither premise is valid: the increase in texting while driving has not, he argues, increased the number of accidents (paragraphs 4–6), and unenforceable laws cannot influence drivers' actions (7–9).

4. Other distractions include children, food and drink, and radios (paragraph 7); digital screens on phones and GPS devices (7); printed maps and directions (7); ringing phones (8); navigation systems (9); "shiny objects" (9); passengers; Web browsing (10); and hands-free devices (10). His point is that texting is hardly the only distraction drivers face and that banning merely one of many distractions is arbitrary and futile.

Integration of Knowledge and Ideas

1. Balko ridicules his opponents and questions their motives in paragraphs 2, 5–6, 9, and 10. The approach grabs readers' attention and makes the author's own points seem more reasoned by comparison, although many readers are likely to find his tone over the top.

2. Balko seems to address readers who might have been influenced by McCarthy's argument, not the strong supporters but those on more neutral ground. He apparently hopes to get readers to regard the actual consequences of a texting ban as more significant than abstract theorizing and, from there, see such bans as unnecessary and potentially threatening to civil liberties. Students' responses to Balko, as to McCarthy, will depend on their openness to his arguments.

3. McCarthy's account is sparse; she simply asserts that "actions that lead to diverting one's eyes from the roadway and hands from the steering wheel can, and often do, lead to roadway accidents" (paragraph 6), citing two studies to support her claim. Balko gives a detailed account of statistics and analyzes them to counter McCarthy's claim with his own assertion, that even if texting drivers "pose a threat" (4), increased cellphone use cannot be blamed for an increase in accidents. Balko's details involve readers more deeply in understanding the risks and hence may incline them to reject the

major premise in McCarthy's proposal—a necessary first step to getting them to oppose laws against texting.

REGULATING TECHNOLOGY: INTERNET PRIVACY

Nicholas Carr
Tracking Is an Assault on Liberty (p. 408)

Students may be surprised to learn how much information is gathered about them on the Web, and what could be done with that information; although having grown up online as they have, many may not see why they should care. Carr tries to make readers care about the issue by revealing surprising facts to support his argument: that by failing to safeguard their privacy, Americans risk losing civil liberties.

You might want to start discussion by asking students about their personal experiences with targeted online advertising (see the first writing topic). How open are they about sharing personal information online? Have they noticed any ads on their computers that seemed eerily connected to something they had posted or researched? Do they find such customized marketing helpful or creepy, and why?

Related Texts

The connections question following "Tracking Is an Assault on Liberty" directs students to the other half of the Internet privacy debate (Jim Harper, p. 415), but in addressing concerns about liberty and the pursuit of happiness, Carr's essay would also make a good companion to any of the essays in Chapter 13 and to any of the speeches in the Appendix. It also invites comparison to dystopian fiction, such as these works.

Anthony Burgess, *A Clockwork Orange*

Suzanne Collins, *The Hunger Games*

Aldus Huxley, *Brave New World*

George Orwell, *1984*

Kurt Vonnegut, Jr., *Slaughterhouse-Five*

Content Quiz

1. What "tradeoff has always been part of our lives as consumers and citizens"? ["To have goods, services and promotions tailored to our personal circumstances and desires, we need to divulge information about ourselves to corporations, governments or other outsiders."]

2. From what retail Web site did Tom Owad collect the data for his experiment on Internet privacy? [Amazon.com.]

3. Researchers at the University of Minnesota found that what three pieces of information can be used to identify most American Internet users by name? ["ZIP Code, birthday and gender."]

4. Who benefits from loss of individual privacy on the Internet? [Internet companies, as well as "crooks, con men and creeps."]

5. What, according to Carr, is "the greatest danger posed by the continuing erosion of personal privacy"? [That it might "lead us as a society to devalue the concept of privacy, to see it as outdated and unimportant."]

Vocabulary Quiz

1. *Surreptitious* (paragraph 1) is closest in meaning to
   a. blatant   b. constant   c. sneaky
   [c. sneaky]

2. *Divulge* (2) is closest in meaning to
   a. request   b. reveal   c. omit
   [b. reveal]

3. *Peccadilloes* (4) is closest in meaning to
   a. fish   b. misbehaviors   c. fears
   [b. misbehaviors]

4. *Seclusion* (4) is closest in meaning to
   a. alone   b. separation   c. open
   [a. alone]

5. *Purloined* (13) is closest in meaning to
   a. stolen   b. profitable   c. famous
   [a. stolen]

Answers
Key Ideas and Details

1. The problem, for Carr, is the "surreptitious collection of personal information" (paragraph 1) online by companies and government agencies, a practice that he believes not only poses practical dangers to individual Web users (13, 15–16, and 18) but also threatens their liberties and "pursuit of happiness" (19). He suggests two mostly undeveloped solutions: individual Web users should be more cautious about sharing information (14), and "software makers and site operators" should offer more control and transparency to users who wish to safeguard their information (17). Implied, but not stated outright, is that regulations should require such controls and transparency of technology providers.

2. Information might be disclosed voluntarily by individual users (paragraph 3) and through shopping hubs (4, 6, 11), social networking sites (11), and

131

"location-tracking services like *Foursquare*" (11), often with the false assumption that such sharing is anonymous or forgetfulness of how public such services are (4). Perhaps more worrisome to Carr is the growth of data tracking software (5) and the ease with which researchers can analyze disparate bits of supposedly anonymous cookies and data, not only to identify individual users (6–10), but also to anticipate and manipulate their behaviors (15–16).

3. Carr lists three distinct dangers. The first is practical: criminals can access and analyze data as easily as anybody else can, running the risk that Web users will be subjected to cons, theft, stalking, and the like (paragraph 13). The second is the problem of "manipulation" (15), Carr's concern that personalized marketing will influence people's knowledge and behaviors in ways they don't necessarily recognize (15–16). The final danger is more theoretical: Carr worries that as privacy continues to be lost, society will cease to value it, leading individuals to feel constantly monitored and forever on guard, and therefore less free (18).

Craft and Structure

1. Carr accepts that some loss of privacy online is inevitable and even desirable (paragraph 2), but he worries that Internet exposure is moving beyond individual users' control, creating "real dangers" for them and for society in general (12). His tone, while balanced, is one of deep concern and mild alarm; some readers might even characterize it as paranoid.

2. By acknowledging tracking's practical benefits before raising concerns about its personal and political dangers, Carr simultaneously addresses an opposing viewpoint and enhances his ethical appeal by establishing himself as a reasonable observer.

3. Carr's argument appeals to both reason and emotion. The closest reasoning appears in paragraphs 5–12, where the author draws on published research and expert opinion to forge a connection between new technologies and loss of privacy. He appeals to emotion throughout, but especially when discussing the dangers of exposure (13–16) and the potential tragic effects on "life and liberty" (18–19).

4. Carr warns that Americans' ability to protect their rights is threatened by the devaluation of privacy in an online culture that assumes "privacy is . . . just a screen we hide behind when we do something naughty or embarrassing" (paragraph 18). Privacy is more than that, he insists: it is a "boundary" (19) between ourselves and others, and it provides a sense of individuality that is "intrinsic to the concept of liberty" (18). The less privacy we have as individuals, he argues, the more we resign ourselves to the possibility of corporate and government manipulation. The definition allows him to state his conviction that privacy is a foundational American right and to explain how it protects civil liberties.

Integration of Knowledge and Ideas

1. Carr's purpose is to sound an alarm, to warn readers that their privacy is at risk and to persuade them to care about it. He is careful to establish the existence of a problem and to examine its scope, but he has little to say in the way of proposing solutions.

2. Earl Warren was Chief Justice of the US Supreme Court from 1953–69; Tom Owad is a computer consultant and experimental researcher; Scott McNealy is the former chief executive of Sun Microsystems, an information technology company; Eric Schmidt heads *Google*; and Bruce Schneier is a computer security expert. By quoting and paraphrasing expert opinion on both sides of the issue, Carr enhances his credibility while offering reliable evidence to support his ideas.

3. Carr seems to imagine that the more advertisers (and presumably, governments) know about individual consumers, the more they'll be able to direct those individuals' choices through subliminal mind control, subtly altering messages and available information to influence people's thoughts and behaviors. Many students, fully confident in their own free will, will likely dismiss his concerns as overblown, maybe even a little ridiculous. Others more skilled at critical media consumption may find that his concerns do ring true.

Jim Harper
Web Users Get as Much as They Give (p. 415)

In a pointed response to Nicholas Carr's argument for safeguarding privacy online, Jim Harper shifts the focus of the debate to business and commerce. In today's "information economy" (paragraph 1), he insists, personal information is a commodity that has monetary value for businesses and consumers alike. Whether your students agree with him or not will be a matter of both personal perspective and their evaluation of his argumentative technique. For some readers, the essay will smack of pro-business bias; others will surely find it very persuasive.

You might want to start a discussion by asking students about their positions on recent calls for privacy legislation. (The fourth writing prompt asks them to write on this topic.) Do they favor tighter restrictions on data tracking, do they think that individual Web users are responsible for protecting their privacy, do they think that information should be freely shared, or do they view privacy as a nonissue? Why?

Related Texts

Anthony Burgess, *A Clockwork Orange*

Suzanne Collins, *The Hunger Games*

Aldus Huxley, *Brave New World*

George Orwell, *1984*

Kurt Vonnegut, Jr., *Slaughterhouse-Five*

Content Quiz

1. What is the main difference between the Internet and television, as Harper sees it?
    [The Internet is "interactive," while television is "static."]

2. Why doesn't it make sense for an advertising network to sell the information it collects about Web users?
    ["If an ad network sold personal and contact info, it would undercut its advertising business and its own profitability."]

3. Where do "*Google*[,] *Facebook, Yahoo!*, MSN and thousands of blogs, news sites, and comment boards" get the money to provide free services to Internet users?
    [From paid advertising that uses personal data to target individual users.]

4. Do the default settings in Microsoft's Web browser Internet Explorer safeguard privacy?
    [No.]

5. What, according to Harper, is the only way to balance our privacy interests with our consumer interests?
    [Education.]

Vocabulary Quiz

1. *Gleaned* (paragraph 1) is closest in meaning to
    a. gathered   b. neatened   c. glowing
    [a. gathered]

2. *Commerce* (1) is closest in meaning to
    a. friendship   b. typical   c. business
    [c. business]

3. *Stratify* (6) is closest in meaning to
    a. separate   b. strengthen   c. organize
    [a. separate]

4. *Dubious* (10) is closest in meaning to
    a. intensive   b. questionable   c. deterring
    [b. questionable]

5. *Converge* (14) is closest in meaning to
    a. disagree   b. lean   c. come together
    [c. come together]

Answers
Key Ideas and Details

1. Harper's thesis is best summed up in his title: "Web Users Get as Much as They Give." The trade in personal data drives Internet commerce (advertising especially) and makes it possible for sites to produce and distribute free content; if Web users restrict access to their information, businesses will have less incentive, and fewer resources, to give anything in return.

2. Cookies are small files downloaded to Web users' computers by the sites they visit. Those files then send information from browsers' computers back to the sites, as well as to third parties, enabling site producers to "customize a visitor's experience" (paragraph 5). Most sites share aggregate data with advertising networks, which use demographics and individual visitors' interests and habits to personalize marketing messages. As far as Harper is concerned, this data mining and sharing is a good thing, because it increases profitability for businesses and enables them to provide free services and content to consumers.

3. He places the blame on the average American for failing to use the privacy tools that are available, and for failing to understand how the "information economy" (paragraph 1) works. His solution is to use those tools to control the spread of personal information, as well as to be willing to give up a certain amount of privacy in exchange for the services and materials provided online.

Craft and Structure

1. The mixed metaphors of Harper's first paragraph (surfing, gleaning, gears, and fuel, all at once) might make students' heads spin, but in general Harper uses figures of speech, especially personifications of businesses and technologies, to establish a friendly and reassuring (if sometimes condescending) tone. Other examples include the simile "[c]ookies are a surreptitious threat to privacy the way smoking is a surreptitious threat to health" (paragraph 7); the metaphors "eyeballs" (5), "hold businesses' feet to the fire" (11), "fade from view" (11), "passion play" (12); and the personifications throughout, such as "[a] network . . . will recognize a browser" (5), "enabling the ad network to get a sense of that person's interests" (5), "if the engineers' plan had won the day" (12), and "this is not to say that businesses don't want personal information—they do" (13).

2. Harper previews the organization of his argument with the series of questions he asks in paragraph 2: "Who is gathering this information? What are they doing with it? How might this harm me? How do I stop it?" A rough outline:

   a. Web sites and advertising networks gather Internet users' information (paragraph 5).

b. They use this information to personalize Web content and target advertising to individual interests, not to discriminate against people or harm them in any way (5).

c. Cookies and tracking in general have been in use for a long time; expressing concern about them is disingenuous and beside the point (6–7).

d. Trying to stop data tracking would harm both businesses and consumers (8–10).

e. It is not the government's job to protect privacy (11).

All but point *e* counter points Carr makes, although Harper's emphasis is decidedly different: while Carr's focus is on individual liberties, Harper's focus is on business and commerce. He does not directly address Carr's arguments about manipulation and potential loss of personal freedoms. Harper concentrates on issues of free trade.

3. Harper is attempting to establish ethical appeal by disclosing that he is one of those Web producers who relies on data tracking to generate advertising revenue and produce new content for viewers; in other words, he attempts to show readers that he knows what he's talking about. At the same time, by mentioning that his site monitors the government, he implies that the government can't be trusted to protect privacy. Although some readers might feel that Harper's admission increases his credibility, others might find that it reveals a conflict of interest.

4. Harper believes strongly that tighter privacy regulations would hurt business and consumers. "If Web users supply less information to the Web," he claims, "the Web will supply less information to them" (paragraph 9). Businesses would have less opportunity to grow and innovate (10), and consumers' interests would be both misinterpreted and thwarted (11), limiting their access to "free content, custom Web experiences, convenience and so on" (13).

Integration of Knowledge and Ideas

1. Harper's purpose is twofold: He wants to educate readers about the workings of the "internet economy" (paragraph 1); he also wants to persuade them to allow their own data to be tracked because such tracking, as he sees it, is for their benefit. Whether he succeeds in persuading readers will depend on their individual perspectives and concerns about business and privacy.

2. The *Wall Street Journal* is a business newspaper with a conservative slant; Harper assumes that his readers are affluent, influential professionals whose primary interest is making money. As businesspeople, Harper's readers may have a vested interest in Web commerce especially, and so are likely to be biased in favor of his claims. Harper also assumes that his readers— business professionals or not—are consumers who enjoy the free content and services provided online and expect unfettered access to such products. Students will likely fit the latter assumption, if not the former.

3. Harper offers two examples: the Federal Trade Commission's failed bid ten years ago "for power to regulate the Internet for privacy's sake" (paragraphs 10–11), and Microsoft engineers' recent attempt to tighten the privacy settings on Internet Explorer (12). In both cases, Harper argues that had the efforts succeeded, businesses would have been harmed and consumers would have been given less "access to free content" (12): *Google*, he claims, would not have grown to the powerhouse it is today (10), and Microsoft would have been accused of damaging "interactivity and the advertising business model" (12). The implication is that any efforts to protect privacy are ultimately counterproductive.

Appendix of Historic Speeches

Patrick Henry
Speech to the Second Virginia Convention
(p. 432)

"[G]ive me liberty or give me death!" Many students will be familiar with the famous closing line of Henry's impassioned argument, if not the context behind it. Although the Common Core State Standards list this speech as a foundational American document for the 9th and 10th grades, students are likely to find its language and syntax difficult. You may need to spend a fair amount of class time simply reviewing vocabulary and parsing the meanings of such phrases as "in proportion to the magnitude of the subject ought to be the freedom of the debate" (paragraph 1). With careful study, however, students should come to recognize and appreciate the finely honed rhetorical devices that drive the success of Henry's speech, as suggested in the second writing topic.

As with most speeches, Henry's is more effective when heard rather than read. Many contemporary actors have interpreted the speech. In addition to several middling performances uploaded to *YouTube*, available multimedia include an audio recording by Richard Schumann for Colonial Williamsburg (*history.org/almanack/life/politics/giveme.cfm*) and *Liberty or Death*, an hour-long documentary reenactment produced by PBS for the St. John's Church Foundation and available for purchase at *historicstjohnschurch.org/hist_giftshop.php*.

Related Texts
Henry's speech reflects both Enlightenment thinking and issues of colonialism, as do the works listed below.

> Chinua Achebe, *Things Fall Apart*
>
> Isabel Allende, *The House of the Spirits*
>
> Homer, *The Odyssey*
>
> Victor Hugo, *Les Misérables*
>
> Thomas Jefferson, Declaration of Independence
>
> Henry Wadsworth Longfellow, "Paul Revere's Ride"
>
> Mary Shelley, *Frankenstein*
>
> François-Marie Arouet de Voltaire, *Candide, Or the Optimist*
>
> William Wordsworth, "The World Is Too Much with Us"

Content Quiz

1. What reason does Henry give to explain his motives for speaking?
   [Failing to voice his opinion, Henry says, would be an act of treason toward his country and of disloyalty to God.]

2. Whose "fleets and armies" were assembling on American shores?
   [Great Britain's.]

3. For how many years had Americans been attempting to negotiate with the British ministry and Parliament?
   [Ten.]

4. Which war is Henry arguing for?
   [The American Revolution.]

5. At the time of this speech, where had fighting already broken out?
   [Boston.]

Vocabulary Quiz

1. *Revere* (paragraph 1) is closest in meaning to
   a. worship   b. patriot   c. distrust
   [a. worship]

2. *Arduous* (2) is closest in meaning to
   a. hopeless   b. difficult   c. stupid
   [b. difficult]

3. *Remonstrances* (3) is closest in meaning to
   a. complaints   b. advances   c. letters
   [a. complaints]

4. *Supplications* (paragraph 3) is closest in meaning to
   a. aggressions   b. pleadings   c. gifts
   [b. pleadings]

5. *Irresolution* (4) is closest in meaning to
   a. action   b. poverty   c. indecision
   [c. indecision]

Answers
Key Ideas and Details

1. The question before the Virginia House of Burgesses is whether the militia should take up arms in preparation for war with Great Britain. Henry's answer is a resounding *yes*.

2. Henry presents his major reasons in paragraph 3. The British government, he says, has ignored the colonists' petitions (for relief from recent taxes and

regulations), while building up "fleets and armies" on American shores (3). The presence of those military forces, Henry claims, proves that Great Britain intends to fight the colonists and "force [them] to submission" (3). Negotiations have failed "for the last ten years," leading to "additional violence and insult" (3) from the King of England. The only option left to the colonists, Henry insists, is war.

3. For Henry, life without freedom is itself a form of dying. By limiting the choices (attuned students might recognize the either/or fallacy), he forces his audience to accept his conclusion that war is inevitable.

Craft and Structure

1. In examining Henry's metaphors, most educators focus on the two highlighted in the question for students. His use of slavery to depict the colonists' status as mere property without rights (and subject to abuse) is the most fully developed metaphor, introduced in the first paragraph and brought up repeatedly: Henry warns that armies "are sent over to bind and rivet upon us those chains which the British ministry have been so long forging" (paragraph 3), reminds his audience that "we wish to be free" (3), imagines a time when "our enemies shall have bound us hand and foot" (4), insists that "[o]ur chains are forged" and "clanking . . . on the plains of Boston" (4), and suggests that "peace" would have "to be purchased at the price of chains and slavery" (5). Students may note the unintended irony of invoking slavery as an intolerable state given that many colonial leaders—including Henry—were slaveholders at the time. You may need to explain that many colonists did not consider African slaves fully human, which in their minds justified the institution and at the same time underscores Henry's argument that Parliament was mistreating its North American subjects.

    Henry's "lamp" metaphor is less developed, but it pervades a good portion of the speech. He introduces it subtly in paragraph 1, when he acknowledges that "different men often see the same subject in different lights," then presents it most forcefully in paragraph 3: "I have but one lamp by which my feet are guided, and that is the lamp of experience." He returns to the idea when he says that his compatriots have "held the subject up in every light of which it is capable" without finding a solution (3). Essentially, Henry equates knowledge of the past with guiding vision, and he intends to impart the relevant knowledge to his audience.

    Other extended metaphors include—but are not limited to—loyalty to God (introduced in paragraph 1), "illusions of hope" (2), the mythical siren (2), "betrayed" love (3), and "the storm which is now coming on" (3).

2. Because of the formal writing and speaking style of Henry's era, students may have trouble recognizing that he establishes a real sense of intimacy here. In part because this is an audience of peers, he can refer to his intention to "speak forth my sentiments freely and without reserve" (paragraph 1). Three particular techniques Henry uses to establish a connection with his audience are to refer directly to the "very worthy" (1) and "wise" (2) "gentlemen" (1, 3, 5) in the room (especially Peyton Randolph, whom he addresses as "Mr. President" or "Sir" in every paragraph), to speak in the third-person

we and *us* throughout, and to ask direct questions (in paragraphs 2, 3, 4, and particularly 5).

3. Although he hints at opposing views with each point in his reasoning in paragraph 3, Henry fully addresses potential counterarguments in paragraphs 4 and 5: some opponents argue that the colonists lack the military strength to fight, but Henry counters that "millions of people" are ready and willing to defend themselves (4); others counsel patience and continued negotiation, but Henry counters that the war is already under way (5).

Integration of Knowledge and Ideas

1. The speech is a call to arms. Henry wants his fellow legislators to prepare for war.

2. Many members of Henry's audience were opposed to American independence and argued for peaceful negotiation with Parliament (it may be necessary to remind students that the colonists were English citizens, and many of them strongly identified as royal subjects). By stressing his respect for the "patriotism, as well as the abilities" of his listeners, he establishes his credibility and reasonableness before announcing that he intends to "speak forth [his] sentiments freely and without reserve" (paragraph 1).

3. Throughout his speech, Henry poses questions to identify and undermine prevailing counterarguments to his claims—in each case, his answer is a form of "no." (At the same time, such questions involve the audience directly; see question 2 under "Craft and Structure.") The cascade of rhetorical questions in the conclusion engages listeners' emotions and builds to a climax that's difficult to resist.

Elizabeth Cady Stanton
Seneca Falls Convention Keynote Address
(p. 437)

As Stanton's speech suggests, early women's rights activism was about far more than suffrage. Antebellum women were victimized by a political and legal culture that not only stripped them of their autonomy but also rendered them, as Stanton put it in her autobiography, "civilly dead." Married women could not own property, which created practical problems; they also could not enter into contracts, which created civic problems. Laws rendered women *subjects* of the American government, rather than *citizens*. From this perspective, women needed the intervention of activists and politicians to rescue them from the indignities and disadvantages of their position and to endow them with the same political and economic rights and privileges enjoyed by men. Indeed, the early women's rights movement centered on a new notion of "co-equality," a theory that postulated that women and men were both different and the same—that although women did indeed have (and should have) a different social position than men, they were endowed with comparable rights by nature and by divine law.

Despite Stanton's protest to the contrary, you might want to tell students that she did indeed advocate clothing reform. Stanton (along with Lucretia Mott and Susan B. Anthony) was one of many women who adopted Amelia Bloomer's signature "costume" of baggy pantaloons topped with a relatively simple dress—the "loose, flowing garments" she mentions in paragraph 2—and argued the benefits of giving up restrictive garments such as corsets and heavy, long skirts. She ultimately abandoned the clothing cause because, as her introduction to this speech suggests, it distracted from more pressing concerns.

Related Texts

Louisa May Alcott, *Little Women*

Kate Chopin, "The Story of an Hour"

Emily Dickinson, "We Grow Accustomed to the Dark"

Ralph Waldo Emerson, "Self-Reliance"

Charlotte Perkins Gilman, "The Yellow Wallpaper"

Nathaniel Hawthorne, *The Blithedale Romance*

Nathaniel Hawthorne, *The Scarlet Letter*

Henrik Ibsen, *A Doll's House*

Thomas Jefferson, Declaration of Independence

William Shakespeare, *The Taming of the Shrew*

George Bernard Shaw, *Pygmalion*

Harriet Beecher Stowe, *Uncle Tom's Cabin*

Henry David Thoreau, *Walden, Or Life in the Woods*

Alice Walker, *The Color Purple*

Alice Walker, "Women"

Content Quiz

1. What was the purpose of the Seneca Falls Convention?
    [To discuss and advocate for women's rights: "We have met here today to discuss our rights and wrongs, civil and political, and not, as some have supposed, to go into the detail of social life alone."]

2. To what kinds of laws does Stanton object?
    [Those that give husbands ownership of their wives' earnings, possessions, and children, as well as those that deny women the right to vote.]

3. In what ways, according to Stanton, are women superior to men?
    [Women are morally purer, more merciful and loving, and more tender and sympathetic than men.]

4. To what historical figure does Stanton compare the women of her country and era?
    [Joan of Arc.]

5. What does Stanton want for women?
    ["Equality of Rights."]

Vocabulary Quiz

1. *Tacitly* (paragraph 2) is closest in meaning to
    a. silently   b. begrudgingly   c. boldly
    [a. silently]

2. *Chastise* (4) is closest in meaning to
    a. reward   b. punish   c. divorce
    [b. punish]

3. *Abominations* (8) is closest in meaning to
    a. insults   b. mistakes   c. horrors
    [c. horrors]

4. *Caprice* (12) is closest in meaning to
    a. pants   b. impulse   c. hatred
    [b. impulse]

5. *Rend* (14) is closest in meaning to
    a. rip   b. borrow   c. shield
    [a. rip]

Answers
Key Ideas and Details

1. After outlining the issues that will be the focus of the convention as a whole, Stanton states the thesis of her keynote speech in paragraph 4: "we now demand our right to vote. . . ." (Some students may identify the first sentence of the same paragraph as her thesis, but that expresses the purpose of the convention, not of her speech; see question 1 under "Integration of Knowledge and Ideas.")

2. She offers three broad reasons: first, women have no say in the laws that hurt them (4), and because "no just government can be formed without the consent of the governed" (7), those laws are unjust (a syllogism); second, the right to vote is guaranteed to all US citizens by the Constitution, a claim she supports with additional reasoning and evidence in paragraphs 5–6; and third, denying full citizenship to women will have a degrading effect on future generations of men, a claim whose reasoning she outlines in paragraphs 8–12 (see question 4 under "Craft and Structure").

3. In distinguishing between equality of sexes and equality of rights, Stanton raises and dismisses an argument that was used against woman suffrage.

She seems to accept claims that women are inferior to men, a concession meant to build common ground with opponents. Any such weaknesses, however, are irrelevant, Stanton insists, because physical, intellectual, and moral fitness have no bearing on rights: if lesser men are allowed to vote, she argues, so should women be granted the privilege.

Craft and Structure

1. Students should be quick to notice the most important repetition: "This right no one pretends to deny" (paragraph 5), followed by "The right is ours" (opening both 6 and 7); the words "right," "rights," and "righteousness" appear repeatedly throughout the speech (1, 4–8, 13–14). Stanton repeats, as well, the importance of the "consent of the governed" (4, 7). Parallelism also abounds. A few examples: "rights and wrongs, civil and political" (1); "how long . . . , how short . . . , how high . . . , how tight . . ." (3); "Have it, we must. Use it, we will" (7); "some new element, some purifying power, some spirit of mercy and love" (9). As repetition and parallel structure always do in speaking, the devices give Stanton's ideas emphasis and coherence while helping listeners to follow her points.

2. Students should be able to infer that a major argument against women's rights at the time centered on issues of dress—based on flawed assumptions that the goal of the movement was to "clothe every woman in male attire" (paragraph 1). In effect, Stanton opens her argument by naming and dismissing a prevailing counterargument, freeing her to focus on more important issues. At the same time, she engages her listeners with humor, wryly suggesting that given their own "philosophical experiments" (3) with fashion, the "leading men" (2) at the time were just as frivolous and vain as they accused women of being.

3. Whether this particular comment qualifies as ad hominem is open to debate: although Stanton resorts to name-calling, she makes a valid point that less-than-admirable men are permitted the rights denied to women. Other attacks include Stanton's depiction of opponents as hypocritical, overdressed dandies (paragraphs 2–3); her characterization of the drunk Irishman and "tiny, weak, ill-shaped stripling" allowed to vote (4); and the "idiotic laugh" of reformers waging pointless battles (8). Stanton's attacks reflect her anger at the legal status of women; they also hold listeners' attention and allow her to poke fun at opponents while echoing the "contempt and ridicule" (13) that they have lobbed at women's rights activists. Because of the formal writing and speaking style of Stanton's era, students may have trouble recognizing that she establishes a real sense of humor and connection with her audience of educated, middle-class reformers, many of whom openly expressed condescension toward immigrants and uneducated workers, if not necessarily themselves. The same strategies used today would undoubtedly be off-putting if not downright offensive.

4. Stanton traces a cause-and-effect relationship between women's legal status and "a kind of moral stagnation" (8) affecting the country as a whole. Although women were involved in several reform movements of the

period (including the pacifist, abolitionist, moral purity, temperance, vegetarian, and religious movements she mentions in paragraph 8), their efforts were ineffective because they were legally powerless to effect change. Women, Stanton suggests, are morally superior beings (9), but because they have no voice and no rights in society, they are unable to properly raise their sons to be upstanding "scholars and saints" (11)—resulting in a nation of "foolish" men and the degradation of the human race (12). Students may not recognize Stanton's references to republican motherhood (the idea that women's contribution to society and politics would best be channeled through the raising of virtuous sons), but her strategy here was one commonly used by women's rights activists of the time. By focusing on maternal values to stress the importance of rights, she couches the issue as one that affects men as strongly as it does women.

Integration of Knowledge and Ideas

1. Stanton's speech has two interlocking purposes: first, to introduce and frame the conversation that will take place at the first women's rights convention in America; and second, to present her argument for woman suffrage. Her purpose is most clearly stated in paragraph 4: "we are assembled to protest against a form of government existing without the consent of the governed—to declare our right to be free as man is free, to be represented in the government which we are taxed to support, to have such disgraceful laws . . . erased from our statute books. . . . And, strange as it may seem to many, we now demand our right to vote according to the declaration of the government under which we live."

2. Stanton is speaking to a largely sympathetic audience of male and female reformers who cared enough about the issue of women's rights to attend a convention on the subject. Through most of the address she speaks in the first person plural, indicating that she counts her listeners among those who share her situation and her views. But as the references to "you" and "leading men" in paragraphs 2, 3, and 11 suggest, she anticipates that some of the people in her audience, powerful men especially, will be hostile to her claims.

3. Stanton's most powerful metaphor may be in the battle-in-the-storm imagery of the final paragraph, concluding with a waving banner proclaiming "Equality of Rights"; it emphasizes her attitude toward women's rights as a righteous, "holy" war that will end in victory. Many (but not all) of Stanton's metaphors are religious in tone, stressing the same idea. These include the "sins . . . dragged naked before the people" (paragraph 8); the "tide of vice" (8); the "battlements of righteousness" (8); "the coming of some new element, some purifying power, some spirit of mercy and love" (9); the "fountains of life . . . poisoned at their source" (10); "mothers . . . ground to powder between the upper and nether millstone of tyranny and lust" (11, an allusion to Sodom and Gomorrah); "the sins of the fathers" (12); "woman all have fallen" (12); and the divine "voices" visited upon Joan of Arc and Stanton's contemporaries (13).

Sojourner Truth
Ain't I a Woman? (p. 443)

As Sojourner Truth's speech suggests, abolitionism had a strong influence on the development of women's activism in the mid-nineteenth century. While arguing that slavery violated every principle of republican ideology, women noted quickly the close parallels between the status of slaves and their own position in society. Neither slaves nor women had any representation in the government that oppressed them; neither had a legal right to their bodies and both were vulnerable to physical abuse; both were economically dependent on their oppressors. But although the women's rights movement emerged from the antislavery movement, reformers in both camps tended to ignore the needs (and humanity) of African American women. In a pointed, impassioned address to those reformers, Truth demands—and gets—their attention.

Several popular actresses and writers have performed "Ain't I a Woman?" including Alfre Woodard, Cicely Tyson, and Alice Walker. All are available on *YouTube*. Be sure to view at least one version with your students; comparing interpretations can help them to understand the role of vocal delivery in effective speaking.

Related Texts

Louisa May Alcott, *Little Women*

Maya Angelou, *I Know Why the Caged Bird Sings* (see "Champion of the World," p. 111)

Frederick Douglass, *Narrative of the Life of Frederick Douglass* (see "Learning to Read and Write," p. 103)

Charlotte Perkins Gilman, "The Yellow Wallpaper"

Nathaniel Hawthorne, *The Blithedale Romance*

Harriet Jacobs, *Incidents in the Life of a Slave Girl*

Martin Luther King, Jr., "I Have a Dream" (p. 449)

Abraham Lincoln, "Gettysburg Address" (p. 446)

Leanita McClain, "The Middle-Class Black's Burden" (p. 284)

Toni Morrison, *Beloved*

Harriet Beecher Stowe, *Uncle Tom's Cabin*

Mark Twain, *The Adventures of Huckleberry Finn*

Alice Walker, *The Color Purple*

Alice Walker, "Women"

Phillis Wheatley, "On Being Brought from Africa to America"

Content Quiz

1. Which two groups, at the time of this speech, were fighting for their rights?
   [Slaves and women.]

2. According to a member of Truth's audience, who "need to be helped into carriages, and lifted over ditches, and to have the best place everywhere"?
   [Women.]

3. What kind of labor has Truth done?
   [Hard, physical field work. As a former slave, she has "ploughed and planted, and gathered [crops] into barns."]

4. What happened to most of Truth's children?
   [They were sold into slavery.]

5. What two reasons did the men in Truth's audience give for denying women rights?
   [That women lack intellect, and that they are inferior because they are not the gender of Christ.]

Vocabulary Quiz

1. *Kilter* (paragraph 1) is closest in meaning to
   a. discomfort   b. excitement   c. order
   [c. order]

2. *'Twixt* (1) is closest in meaning to
   a. between   b. twisted   c. because
   [a. between]

3. *Carriages* (2) is closest in meaning to
   a. cribs   b. vehicles   c. jobs
   [b. vehicles]

4. *Mean* (3) is closest in meaning to
   a. stingy   b. able   c. angry
   [a. stingy]

5. *Obliged* (6) is closest in meaning to
   a. owed   b. sorry   c. thankful
   [c. thankful]

Answers
Key Ideas and Details

1. Truth uses the verb *head* colloquially, meaning to lead or outdo. Her point is that in her labor and physical strength, she has proven herself equal to men, if not superior.

2. "And now they is asking to do it [turn the world right side up again], the men better let them" (paragraph 5). The main message of Truth's speech is a demand that men accept, even support, women's push for equal rights. She withholds her demand to the end because it makes for a powerful conclusion and also because to have opened with it would have created resistance among her listeners, who had already shown the previous day that they were unreceptive to the idea of women's rights.

Craft and Structure

1. In a time when speakers used highly formal language, Truth's informal colloquialisms let her stand out and capture listeners' attention. They also underscore Truth's humanity and create immediacy between her and her audience. Students who compare this version of her speech with the original reported version (see Writing Topic 3) will probably find that the nonstandard diction is indeed more effective than more formal language, although some may feel that Frances Gage's insertion of stereotypically Southern black idioms is insulting.

2. The most significant repetition, of course, is "Ain't I a woman?" (paragraph 2)—asked four times, each instance more emphatic than the last. The point of her rhetorical question is that African American women deserve the same rights as white women and men. Truth also asks "Where did your Christ come from?" twice in a row (4), stressing her point about women's divinity and God-given rights.

3. Truth's speech follows a simple point/counterpoint arrangement, naming and refuting each of her opponents' claims and ending with her strongest argument.

4. As Truth's characterizations of women who "need to be helped into carriages" and given "the best place everywhere" (paragraph 2) suggest, her audience seems to define *woman* as privileged and helpless; her point that she has "borne thirteen children" (2) suggests that her listeners define women primarily by their role as mothers; and her comment that "intellect" has nothing "to do with women's rights or negroes' rights" (3) implies that her listeners question women's intelligence. As a former slave who has done hard physical labor and a mother who has lost her children to slavery (2), Truth sees womanhood differently: for her, it's a matter of gender and nothing more.

Integration of Knowledge and Ideas

1. Truth spoke because she felt compelled to respond to arguments against women's rights—the "racket" (paragraph 1)—that had been voiced by men in the audience. By identifying the individuals whose arguments she refutes and addressing them directly—"That man over there" (2) and "that little man in black there" (4)—she forces them to listen to what she has to say.

2. Truth stresses that she is a woman because women's rights reformers and their opponents tended not to put African American women in the same

category as middle-class white women. She makes the distinction evident in her observation that "the negroes of the South and the women at the North" (paragraph 1) represented two distinct movements, and in her separation of "women's rights or negroes' rights" (3). As both an abolitionist and a women's rights activist, Truth wants her listeners to understand that black women are doubly disadvantaged and want the same rights being sought by white women and by black men.

3.   Truth identifies three arguments against women's rights: that women are weak (paragraph 2), that they lack intelligence (3), and that religious tradition relegates them to lesser status (4–5). She swiftly turns each of those claims on its head, countering that she is strong (2), that "intellect" is irrelevant (3), and that religious tradition credits women with divinity and power (4–5).

Abraham Lincoln
Gettysburg Address (p. 446)

Lincoln's speech provides an example of the effective use of rhetorical devices to transform formal persuasive speaking into a graceful, moving public statement. Teachers may find that they need to coach students through this selection; for instance, the context of the Civil War and the losses at the battle of Gettysburg may need some clarification before the class can fully understand Lincoln's argument.

The Library of Congress Web site offers historical background, multiple drafts, and rich multimedia to enhance teaching of Lincoln's address (*myloc.gov/Exhibitions/gettysburgaddress/Pages/default.aspx*). Audio recordings of readings by famous performers and political figures (such as Johnny Cash, Sam Waterston, and Colin Powell) are available at the American Rhetoric Online Speech Bank (*americanrhetoric.com/speeches/gettysburgaddress.htm*).

Related Texts

Louisa May Alcott, *Little Women*

Ishmael Beah, *A Long Way Gone*

Stephen Crane, *The Red Badge of Courage*

Emily Dickinson, "Hope is the thing with feathers"

John Donne, "Death Be Not Proud"

Frederick Douglass, *Narrative of the Life of Frederick Douglass* (see "Learning to Read and Write," p. 103)

Khaled Hosseini, *The Kite Runner*

Harriet Jacobs, *Incidents in the Life of a Slave Girl*

Martin Luther King, Jr., "I Have a Dream" (p. 449)

Abraham Lincoln, Emancipation Proclamation

Toni Morrison, *Beloved*

Tim O'Brien, *The Things They Carried*

Harriet Beecher Stowe, *Uncle Tom's Cabin*

Sojourner Truth, "Ain't I a Woman?" (p. 443)

Mark Twain, *The Adventures of Huckleberry Finn*

Content Quiz

1. What year does Lincoln refer to as "Four score and seven years ago"?
   [1776.]

2. For what occasion did Lincoln give this speech?
   [The dedication ceremony for the Soldiers National Cemetery at Gettysburg.]

3. Who already consecrated the ground Lincoln wishes to dedicate?
   [The men who fought there.]

4. What was the "great task remaining for" Lincoln and his audience?
   [To win the Civil War and ensure that "government of the people, by the people, for the people, shall not perish from the earth."]

5. On what two principles, according to Lincoln, was America founded?
   [It was "conceived in Liberty, and dedicated to the proposition that all men are created equal."]

Vocabulary Quiz

1. *Proposition* (paragraph 1) is closest in meaning to
   a. theory   b. hope   c. guess
   [a. theory]

2. *Consecrate* (3) is closest in meaning to
   a. repossess   b. bless   c. release
   [b. bless]

3. *Hallow* (3) is closest in meaning to
   a. empty   b. holy   c. autumn
   [b. holy]

4. *Detract* (3) is closest in meaning to
   a. demand   b. increase   c. weaken
   [c. weaken]

5. *Perish* (3) is closest in meaning to
   a. die   b. rise   c. explode
   [a. die]

Answers
Key Ideas and Details

1. The blood of the soldiers has already made the site holy and infused it with more significance than words can. Lincoln is saying that the dedication is a merely symbolic gesture, and a somewhat feeble one at that.

2. Lincoln wants his listeners, all supporters of the Union cause, to dedicate themselves to the preservation of a unified nation and its founding ideals, particularly "the proposition that all men are created equal" (paragraph 1).

Craft and Structure

1. Nearly every sentence of the speech uses parallel structure. A few examples: "conceived in liberty, and dedicated to the proposition . . ." (paragraph 1); "so conceived and so dedicated" (2); "those who here gave their lives that the nation might live" (2); "we can not dedicate—we can not consecrate— we can not hallow" (3); "The world will little note, nor long remember what we say here, but it can never forget what they did here" (3); "that from these honored dead . . . that we here highly resolve . . . that this nation . . . and that government . . ." (3); and "of the people, by the people, for the people" (3). The parallelism creates a strong sense of rhythm, emphasizes the importance of Lincoln's ideas, and gives the speech unity and coherence.

2. For a speech of so few words, the density of Lincoln's repetitions and restatements is remarkable. He says *we* and *our* ten times, *here* five times, *nation* five times, *dedicated* five times and *devotion* (a synonym for *dedicated*) twice, variations of *live* and *dead* four times each (*perish* in paragraph 3 is another restatement), *conceived* twice (*birth* in paragraph 3 is a restatement, or synonym), *consecrate* twice (plus its synonym *hallow*), and *people* thrice. Taken together, the repeated words all emphasize the importance of actively pursuing the Union's survival.

3. Lincoln uses a straightforward and simple chronological organization. He begins with the past in the first paragraph, moves to the present in the second, and concludes with the future.

4. Lincoln suggests that the war is a struggle for liberty and equality, "testing" (paragraph 2) the intentions of the founding fathers. He doesn't name slavery as the "cause" (3) outright, but he implies it. His desired results are "a new birth of freedom" (3)—elimination of slavery—and the country's (the Union's) survival.

Integration of Knowledge and Ideas

1. On its face, the "Gettysburg Address" is a eulogy, an expression of respect for and gratitude to the dead. But Lincoln's purpose is also highly persuasive: he used the occasion to make a political argument for supporting the Union cause (see the second writing topic).

2.   Lincoln's appeals are highly emotional. He rightly assumes that his listeners are opposed to slavery on moral grounds and that they value the founding ideals of liberty and equality; he alludes to those values most strongly in the opening and concluding sentences (see the next question). He also makes reference to his listeners' religious values, especially with the words *consecrate, hallow,* and *devotion* (paragraph 3) and with the phrase "this nation, under God" (3).

3.   He is alluding, of course, to the Declaration of Independence, written 87 years earlier in 1776 (students may need to be prodded to do the math to figure it out; you might also want to read the relevant portions of the Declaration in class as a supplementary lesson). By framing his speech with a founding document, he reminds listeners of the values on which the country was built and stresses the need to honor them.

Martin Luther King, Jr.
I Have a Dream (p. 449)

King's inspirational speech offers an excellent opportunity to explore the use and effectiveness of emotional appeals (see questions 2 and 3 under "Integration of Knowledge and Ideas"). It also, of course, provides a context for discussing the improvements or lack of improvements in African American civil rights over the past three decades.

As effective as it is in print, the speech was even more effective in King's original delivery. A recording or film of his delivery—sonorous and movingly cadenced—can help students appreciate why the speech is so memorable. It can also encourage comparison between written and spoken persuasion: What are the strengths and weaknesses of each form?

Related Texts

Maya Angelou, *I Know Why the Caged Bird Sings* (see "Champion of the World," p. 111)

Toni Cade Bambara, "The Lesson"

David Brooks, "People Like Us" (p. 228)

Frederick Douglass, *Narrative of the Life of Frederick Douglass* (see "Learning to Read and Write," p. 103)

Ralph Ellison, *Invisible Man*

Lorraine Hansberry, *A Raisin in the Sun*

Langston Hughes, "Harlem: A Dream Deferred"

Zora Neal Hurston, *Their Eyes Were Watching God*

Harriet Jacobs, *Incidents in the Life of a Slave Girl*

Thomas Jefferson, Declaration of Independence

Jamaica Kincaid, "Girl"

Martin Luther King, Jr., "Letter from Birmingham Jail"

Harper Lee, *To Kill a Mockingbird*

Abraham Lincoln, Emancipation Proclamation

Abraham Lincoln, "Gettysburg Address" (p. 446)

James McBride, *The Color of Water*

Toni Morrison, *Beloved*

Toni Morrison, *The Bluest Eye*

Walter Mosley, "Get Happy" (p. 318)

Wilbert Rideau, "Why Prisons Don't Work" (p. 387)

Harriet Beecher Stowe, *Uncle Tom's Cabin*

Sojourner Truth, "Ain't I a Woman?" (p. 443)

Mark Twain, *The Adventures of Huckleberry Finn*

Alice Walker, *The Color Purple*

Alice Walker, "Everyday Use"

Phillis Wheatley, "On Being Brought from Africa to America"

August Wilson, *Fences*

Richard Wright, *Black Boy*

Richard Wright, *Native Son*

Content Quiz

1. What was the promise of the Emancipation Proclamation? In King's opinion, has that promise been fulfilled?
   [Lincoln's proclamation ended slavery. But King points out that African Americans are still "crippled by the manacles of segregation and the chains of discrimination."]

2. When does King want justice and equality for African Americans?
   ["*Now.*"]

3. How does King urge his followers to behave as they "conduct our struggle"?
   [Peacefully and nonviolently, with "dignity and discipline."]

4. King lists several injustices suffered by African Americans. Identify at least two.
   [Among the injustices King cites are segregation, discrimination, poverty, police brutality, separate facilities, ghettoization, and inability to vote.]

5. What does King dream of?
   [Full freedom and equality for all African Americans.]

Vocabulary Quiz

1. *Languishing* (paragraph 2) is closest in meaning to
   a. scheming   b. suffering   c. hiding
   [b. suffering]

2. *Inextricably* (6) is closest in meaning to
   a. unavoidably   b. recently   c. fortunately
   [a. unavoidably]

3. *Interposition* (16) is closest in meaning to
   a. location   b. sarcasm   c. authority
   [c. authority]

4. *Prodigious* (21) is closest in meaning to
   a. many   b. beautiful   c. enormous
   [c. enormous]

5. *Hamlet* (23) is closest in meaning to
   a. stage   b. village   c. pig
   [b. village]

Answers
Key Ideas and Details

1. African Americans, along with white people who support them, must continue to strive nonviolently for freedom, justice, and equality.

2. The nation's African Americans are oppressed by segregation and discrimination—isolated in poverty, subject to police brutality and harassment, denied access to public places, denied the vote.

3. Violence would deprive the civil rights movement of "dignity and discipline," and it would lose supporters (paragraph 6). Those who have been jailed or beaten should view their suffering as "creative" and have "faith that unearned suffering is redemptive" (8).

4. King dreams of brotherhood, equality, freedom, justice, and peace. By alluding to the American dream, he reminds his audience that none of these components of the dream are a reality for African Americans.

Craft and Structure

1. Throughout the speech, King's metaphors depict oppression as low, hot, dry, and dark: "the flames of withering injustice," "the long night of captivity" (paragraph 1); "the dark and desolate valley of segregation" (4); "This sweltering summer of the Negro's legitimate discontent" (5); "a desert state

sweltering with the heat of injustice and oppression" (13). In contrast, King depicts freedom and equality as elevated, cool, moist, and light: "a joyous daybreak" (1); "the sunlit path of racial justice" (4); "an invigorating autumn of freedom and equality," "the bright day of justice" (5); "justice rolls down like waters" (7); "an oasis of freedom and justice" (13); "From every mountainside, Let freedom ring" (20–22).

2. King first establishes the common ground with his listeners (paragraphs 3–5); then urges them to continue struggling nonviolently, whatever the emotional or physical costs (6–9); and finally creates a picture of the better world they can help achieve with their action (10–23). Thus he builds to an inspirational crescendo.

3. Other examples of repetition: "one hundred years later" (paragraph 2), "*now*" (4), "We can never be satisfied" (7), "Let freedom ring" (20–23). Other examples of parallelism: "a lonely island of poverty in the midst of a vast ocean of material prosperity" (2), "from the dark and desolate valley of segregation to the sunlit path of racial justice" (4), "their destiny is tied up with our destiny and their freedom is inextricably bound to our freedom" (6), "will not be judged by the color of their skin but by the content of their character" (14), "to work together, to pray together, to struggle together, to go to jail together, to stand up for freedom together" (19). The repetition and parallelism, suggesting an incantation or hymn, make an almost religious appeal to listeners and thus reinforce King's inspirational purpose.

4. The Declaration of Independence created a bank of justice with "vaults of opportunity" (paragraph 4) and issued a note to all Americans that promised "life, liberty, and the pursuit of happiness" (3). But the check issued to African Americans bounced, despite the fact that the bank had ample funds of freedom and justice. Most students will presumably find the comparison both clever and effective: it presents the plight of African Americans in terms readily understandable to everyone, while suggesting that the nation's unshared wealth consists of freedom and justice as well as money.

Integration of Knowledge and Ideas

1. King wanted to inspire his listeners to continue their struggle nonviolently — while also sending a message to the nation about the movement's determination to achieve its goals. Thus he emphasizes why the struggle is important (paragraphs 1–4); warns of the movement's seriousness (5); urges nonviolence (6); urges struggle until the goals are won, whatever the hardships (7–9); and details a dream of a different America (10–23).

2. King is primarily addressing people who, like him, want equality for African Americans and are willing to work for it. He assumes that the audience agrees with him in paragraphs 1–5 and 10–23; but in paragraphs 6–9, he addresses listeners' impatience, frustration, fatigue, and fear.

3. King's listeners are already convinced of the need for change; they do not require a rational argument. Emotional appeals are particularly effective in

inspiring an audience to act. King appeals to pride and dignity in para-graphs 6–9; to his listeners' religious beliefs in paragraphs 8, 18–19, and 23; and to their patriotism in paragraphs 1, 3, 11, and 20–22.

4. In paragraphs 5 and 7, King lets doubters and opponents know that the struggle will not stop until the goals of freedom, equality, and justice are fully achieved.

IV
INTEGRATING *COMMON THREADS* INTO A COMMON CORE CURRICULUM

—*Emily Richardson, Naperville North High School*

One concern teachers may have about implementing the Common Core State Standards (CCSS) is the question of how to handle the pronounced new emphasis on nonfiction. Many schools are deeply committed to the classics and wish to continue the traditional approach of teaching English under broad course titles such as "World Literature," "British Literature," and "American Literature." Teachers don't want to lose the works of literature they value and feel are pivotal to high school. They don't have to.

Intended as a supplemental resource rather than a primary textbook, *Common Threads* provides a variety of options. Those teaching a literature-based curriculum can select individual essays that implicitly relate to core pieces of fiction, as described below, or teachers can use selected chapters to teach close reading and different methods of writing, like classification, description, and comparison and contrast. The book is designed to let teachers pick and choose materials as they see fit, helping them to adapt their curricula to Common Core criteria.

To seamlessly implement a Common Core curriculum, the key may be to supplement favorite literary texts with relevant pieces of nonfiction. Instead of reading *To Kill a Mockingbird* merely as a study of literature, for instance, teachers can incorporate essays that relate to Harper Lee's themes for deeper student appreciation of the novel (see below). Using nonfiction to complement fiction will help students to better understand the core literary texts, as it allows them to examine the issues and themes presented in a novel, play, story, or poem from different perspectives. As a result, the study of core texts becomes a study of ideas and arguments about society, life, humanity, truth, and other universal themes.

The units suggested here are meant to help facilitate implementation of the CCSS. Each centers on one core piece of fiction and highlights essays in *Common Threads* that might be used to support it. The first group is thematic, approaching texts in the 9–10 grade level in regard to major ideas or concepts to be studied. The second is based on a chronological World Literature curriculum. The third is organized by writing skill. All of them are designed to offer inspiration and ideas, not rigid lesson plans or strict roadmaps.

As much as the CCSS place an emphasis on informational and argumentative writing, they stress the importance of teaching works at appropriate levels of complexity for each grade level. Fiction as well as nonfiction should meet three key components of complexity: qualitative dimensions (such as level of meaning), quantitative dimensions (such as Lexile scores), and reader/task considerations (the way in which a reader responds to a text). The texts suggested in each unit are titles either suggested in the Common Core list of exemplar texts in Appendix B of the CCSS or given Lexile scores that meet the levels recommended for grades 9 and 10.

The essays suggested in these syllabi do not always have a literal, explicit connection to the core pieces of fiction for each unit. In many cases, they hit on larger, more implicit themes or arguments. Consider having students study the nonfiction pieces trying to identify what the writers are ultimately trying to suggest. Then, have students determine what each supplemental piece elucidates about the core text. Sometimes the arguments might differ, sometimes the content might appear completely unrelated; however, with careful reading and critical thinking, all of the supplemental pieces can clarify concepts in the core texts.

Thematic Units

The units below are provided primarily as a guide. (Few high-school classrooms could adequately complete six core texts in one year.) Depending on curriculum, student ability, and grade level, the selections might be condensed, expanded, reordered, or simply used as inspiration when constructing a curriculum.

Coming of Age

This unit focuses on the development of the individual and how a young person comes into knowledge of self through a major event.

To Kill a Mockingbird, a Common Core exemplar text for grades 9–10, was selected as the core work of literature because of its strong moral message and the awareness it brings to racial and ethical dilemmas; it also one of the most frequently taught novels in American high schools.

Frederick Douglass's "Learning to Read and Write" offers another perspective on the ways in which race and self-awareness are interwoven. Toward the final third of the novel, students should be able to study Douglass's piece and discuss the types of knowledge the characters in *To Kill a Mockingbird* attain on their journey to adulthood. Scout's and Jem's experiences offer clear parallels to Douglass's plight. Students should also be able to see connections between Lee's novel and Maya Angelou's "Champion of the World." While an obvious comparison can be found between Joe Louis and Tom Robinson, some may even find Atticus Finch comparable to the famous boxer.

Core Text
Harper Lee, *To Kill a Mockingbird*

Suggested Supplemental Texts
Frederick Douglass, "Learning to Read and Write"
Maya Angelou, "Champion of the World"

Additional Suggestions
Martin Luther King, Jr., "I Have a Dream"

Wilbert Rideau, "Why Prisons Don't Work"
Leanita McClain, "The Middle-Class Black's Burden"
David Brooks, "People Like Us"

Perspectives on Happiness

While there are countless texts that could contribute to a discussion of the nature and importance of happiness, *A Doll's House*, which the CCSS offers as a complex text meeting the 9–10 grade level band, explores the concept of happiness within a marriage. Ibsen's main character, Nora, evaluates her conception of happiness through her relationships with others and their perception of her.

Both Judy Brady's "I Want a Wife" and Anita Jain's "A Nameless Respect" add insight into Nora's experiences, as well as the nature of happiness and self. While both essays focus primarily on the social and cultural aspects of marriage, they offer interesting comparisons to the ways in which identity and environment influence a relationship.

Teachers can also turn to Chapter 13 of *Common Threads*, "Definition: Pursuing Happiness," for additional resources and teaching strategies.

Core Text
Henrick Ibsen, *A Doll's House*

Suggested Supplemental Texts
Judy Brady, "I Want a Wife"
Anita Jain, "A Nameless Respect"

Additional Suggestions
Walter Mosley, "Get Happy"
Pico Iyer, "The Joy of Less"

Conceptions of Power

Power is a universal theme. This particular unit is focused on the nature of power and how one gains and wields it.

Shakespeare's *Othello* is often seen in tenth grade curricula. The play's complexity is in the language: the story is fairly easy to follow, allowing students of varying abilities an appropriate challenge. The struggle for power plays out between the characters Othello and Iago: the former has power and the latter is determined to gain it at all costs.

Both supplemental texts explore the notion of power and how it is obtained or used. In "Why Prisons Don't Work," Wilbert Rideau considers the power that society assumes in reforming criminals through prison. Suggesting that power is innate and that reform comes from within, Rideau's essay provides insight into the character of Othello and the way in which his power shifts and evolves through the influence of others. In "Dumpster Diving," Lars Eighner examines the values placed on material goods and presents an argument about want versus need, neatly capturing the central conflict between Iago and Othello. After reading his essay, students might examine what Eighner's message suggests about Iago's quest for power.

159

Core Text
>William Shakespeare, *Othello*

Suggested Supplemental Texts
>Wilbert Rideau, "Why Prisons Don't Work"
>Lars Eighner, "Dumpster Diving"

Additional Suggestions
>Leanita McClain, "The Middle-Class Black's Burden"
>Maya Angelou, "Champion of the World"
>Pat Mora, "Great Expectations"
>Amy Tan, "Pretty Beyond Belief"

Social Change

While this unit's core text, *The Grapes of Wrath*, has a low Lexile score, the CCSS suggest it for grades 9 and 10—probably because of its complex themes, such as the various ways social change impacts the individual. Throughout the novel, the reader observes the Joad family facing struggles and tragedy with dignity.

Two good supplemental texts would be "The Joy of Less" and "Living Like Weasels." Both essays have direct ties to the novel because they both present speakers who search to find meaning and happiness while living, as Dillard puts it, "in necessity."

Core Text
>John Steinbeck, *The Grapes of Wrath*

Suggested Supplemental Texts
>Pico Iyer, "The Joy of Less"
>Annie Dillard, "Living Like Weasels"

Additional Suggestions
>Lars Eighner, "Dumpster Diving"
>David Brooks, "People Like Us"
>Walter Mosley, "Get Happy"

Knowledge of Self

Sophocles' *Oedipus Rex*, suggested for grades 9 and 10 by the CCSS, is a title rich in character development. The play follows Oedipus's quest for self-awareness, which he believes can be found only by uncovering his past. His journey is similar in theme to Marie Myung-Ok Lee's "I Was an Anchor Baby." In this contemporary essay, Lee evaluates history to explain what was necessary to establish her family as American citizens. She explores the uneasiness she felt about her own identity because her parents were considered illegal aliens. While the situations are different, both "I Was an Anchor Baby" and *Oedipus Rex* tackle notions of forming an identity through knowledge of parents.

Core Text
>Sophocles, *Oedipus Rex*

Suggested Supplemental Text
> Marie Myung-Ok Lee, "I Was an Anchor Baby"

Additional Suggestions
> Walter Mosley, "Get Happy"
> Frederick Douglass, "Learning to Read and Write"
> Ellen Goodman, "The Company Man"
> Anna Quindlen, "The C Word in the Hallways"

Control and Rebellion

George Orwell's *1984*, commonly taught in grades 9 or 10, explores the notions of privacy, freedom, and rebellion. Similarly, Nicholas Carr's "Tracking Is an Assault on Liberty" and Jim Harper's "Web Users Get as Much as They Give" compare and contrast the dichotomy between privacy and freedom—in their case, online. Both essays update Orwell's concerns and facilitate discussion on the nature of external control and the ways in which it influences individuals.

Core Text
> George Orwell, *1984*

Suggested Supplemental Texts
> Nicholas Carr, "Tracking Is an Assault on Liberty"
> Jim Harper, "Web Users Get as Much as They Give"

Additional Suggestions
> Walter Rideau, "Why Prisons Don't Work"

World Literature

World Literature is a common course title in the ninth and tenth grades. While the curricula for the course vary greatly from school to school, a few core pieces are popular with teachers. Traditionally a World Literature course represents a variety of cultures and themes, often organized chronologically with an emphasis on world events. For schools reluctant to abandon their current curricula, these suggested units maintain the chronological approach while highlighting ways in which the course can be revised to include more nonfiction and meet Common Core criteria.

The Epic of Gilgamesh

Depending on which excerpts of *The Epic of Gilgamesh* are taught, two key essays from *Common Threads* can effectively supplement the text.

If students are reading about the friendship between Gilgamesh and Enkidu, they will be able to make connections to Marion Winik's "What Are Friends For?" After studying this essay, students will be better able to explore the nature of the friendship between Gilgamesh and Enkidu and how the friendship impacts Gilgamesh's journey.

If students are focusing more on Gilgamesh's grief after Enkidu's death, a nice supplement is "The C Word in the Hallways," by Anna Quindlen. On the surface this essay is about mental illness and teen homicides, but on further inspection, it becomes apparent that Quindlen is making an argument about the nature of the individual and how people are affected in instances of tragedy. Her essay could elicit a discussion about the extent to which Enkidu's death affects Gilgamesh's world view.

Core Text
　　Selections from *The Epic of Gilgamesh*

Suggested Supplemental Texts
　　Marion Winik, "What Are Friends For?"
　　Anna Quindlen, "The C Word in the Hallways"

Additional Suggestions
　　Annie Dillard, "Living Like Weasels"
　　Pico Iyer, "The Joy of Less"

Macbeth

When teaching *Macbeth*, a play suggested for grades 9–10 by the CCSS, many teachers focus on the nature of power and how the quest for power often results in loss of self. Ellen Goodman's "The Company Man" is a natural choice for a supplement. While the types of work examined in these texts are very different, Goodman contributes a fresh perspective to Shakespeare's themes of power and self. Analyzing Goodman's position on what causes Phil's death could lead students to examine Shakespeare's argument and consider the extent to which Macbeth allows Lady Macbeth to affect him.

Core Text
　　William Shakespeare, *Macbeth*

Suggested Supplemental Text
　　Ellen Goodman, "The Company Man"

Additional Suggestions
　　Pico Iyer, "The Joy of Less"
　　Lars Eighner, "Dumpster Diving"
　　Anna Quindlen, "The C Word in the Hallways"

Night

When studying *Night*, by Elie Wiesel, students come to recognize how external factors impact the individual. Wiesel's speaker is restricted by elements he is unable to control or predict. While there is a difference in the elements involved, the underlying argument of *Night* is similar to that of Joan Didion's "The Santa Ana." An excellent introduction to *Night*, students will better understand the speaker's internal struggle through a study of Didion's struggle with malevolent winds.

Core Text
　　Elie Wiesel, *Night*

Suggested Supplemental Text
　　Joan Didion, "The Santa Ana"

Additional Suggestions
> Charlie LeDuff, "End of the Line"
> Frederick Douglass, "Learning to Read and Write"
> Maya Angelou, "Champion of the World"
> Marie Myung-Ok Lee, "I Was an Anchor Baby"

Things Fall Apart

Chinua Achebe's *Things Fall Apart* is taught often, likely because the novel so beautifully captures the human condition and multiple universal themes ranging from family to power to shame.

Several of the essays in *Common Threads* could supplement study of Achebe's novel, depending on the themes addressed in class. One excellent resource is "People Like Us," by David Brooks. This essay encourages students to reevaluate pleas for diversity in America, much as the novel causes students to reevaluate the impact of British colonialism and missionary work on the small Nigerian community of Igbo. For another kind of connection, try Frederick Douglass's "Learning to Read and Write," which presents a former slave's view of how power is obtained through knowledge. Students can analyze the extent to which Douglass's quest for learning mirrors Okonkwo's shifts in understanding throughout the novel.

Core Text
> Chinua Achebe, *Things Fall Apart*

Suggested Supplemental Texts
> David Brooks, "People Like Us"
> Frederick Douglass, "Learning to Read and Write"

Additional Suggestions
> Maya Angelou, "Champion of the World"
> Dagoberto Gilb, "My Landlady's Yard"
> Firoozeh Dumas, "Sweet, Sour, and Resentful"
> Charlie LeDuff, "End of the Line"
> Patrick Henry, "Speech to the Second Virginia Convention"

The Kite Runner

Khaled Hosseini's *The Kite Runner*, a novel many students find engaging, achieves complexity through its various shifts in setting and time.

When studying the childhood of Amir and Hassan, you might provide students with "Today's Kids Are, Like, Killing the English Language," by Kirk Johnson. Although Johnson's explicit argument concerns the speech habits of children, students should be able to draw parallels between subversive uses of language and the decisions Amir makes as a young boy. By the middle of the novel, students will recognize the guilt that plagues Amir. To better understand the nature and root of that guilt, partner this section with Cheryl Peck's "Fatso," an essay that explores how the perceptions of others impact conceptions of self. Her perspective should help students analyze the shifts Amir has undergone since the beginning of the novel.

Core Text
> Khaled Hosseini, *The Kite Runner*

Suggested Supplemental Texts
> Kirk Johnson, "Today's Kids Are, Like, Killing the English Language"
> Cheryl Peck, "Fatso"

Additional Suggestions
> Marion Winik, "What Are Friends For?"
> Leanita McClain, "The Middle-Class Black's Burden"
> Firoozeh Dumas, "Sweet, Sour, and Resentful"
> Anna Quindlen, "The C Word in the Hallways"

Writing Skills

Another way to implement the Common Core is to organize units around the writing standards themselves, focusing on the products students will create and giving them the opportunity to study the key skills emphasized in each strand with professional models of good writing. The essays and chapter instructions in *Common Threads* will make learning meaningful because students have concrete and tangible models to emulate, instead of abstract concepts to figure out. Such an approach also gives students a greater understanding of the expectations for their work because they will be able to develop skills in practice, not in isolation.

The CCSS focus on three different types of writing (argumentative, expository, and narrative), which form the basis of the units suggested below.

Argumentative Writing

The crux of argumentative writing, according to the CCSS, is to persuade readers to accept a specific argument or point, enacting a relationship between writer and audience. Argument, according to the CCSS, "is a reasoned, logical way of demonstrating that the writer's position, belief, or conclusion is valid" (Appendix A, 23). Literary interpretations are considered arguments as well. Student writers must learn to defend an interpretation or idea by logically developing a claim and supporting it with original and sound reasons and examples.

The core texts suggested below range from fiction to memoir and biography to argumentative nonfiction to show a range of options. Regardless of the genre, students should look past the narrative to analyze how the author explores multiple perspectives and persuades the reader. The supplemental pieces listed provide other persuasive angles on the issues dealt with in the core texts.

Text Clusters
> George Orwell, *1984*
>> Nicholas Carr, "Tracking Is an Assault on Liberty"
>> Jim Harper, "Web Users Get as Much as They Give"
> Alex Kotlowitz, *There Are No Children Here*
>> Leanita McClain, "The Middle-Class Black's Burden"
>> Wilbert Rideau, "Why Prisons Don't Work"

Barbara Ehrenreich, *Nickel and Dimed: On (Not) Getting by in America*
Ellen Goodman, "The Company Man"
Charlie Le Duff, "End of the Line"

Working with any of these clusters, ask students to compose their own argumentative essays that provide an interpretation of one of the core texts or an issue related to it. (Specific writing prompts can be found in the questions following the supplementary essays and at the end of each chapter in *Common Threads*.) Regardless of the assignment, in following with the CCSS description of the argumentative essay, encourage students to explore both sides of an issue or multiple perspectives surrounding a topic. Students must also demonstrate awareness of audience and determine which strategies will most effectively persuade the reader.

Expository Writing

Unlike an argumentative essay, which seeks to convince or persuade, an expository essay seeks to inform or to explain. So, instead of arguing a point that might not otherwise be accepted, the writer seeks to help readers better understand a concept. The CCSS suggest that "to produce this kind of writing, students draw from what they already know . . . and answer questions about why or how" (Appendix A, 23). To be successful, students producing this type of writing will explain why something is true or explore the effect of it being true. They will still be defending a thesis, but their purpose is to deepen the reader's knowledge about the subject, perhaps by explaining why it occurs, the extent to which it can be seen, its effects, or and what deeper conclusions it might suggest.

Because there are so many different expository methods to draw on, it would be difficult (and most likely impossible) to incorporate all of them into a single cohesive unit, or even to cover all of them adequately in a term. You might, instead, select those methods that will benefit your students, considering individual abilities and needs and the goals of the class. This is probably the most natural way to use *Common Threads*, considering its rhetorical and thematic organization.

Each chapter's theme demonstrates how multiple writers can use the same method to different ends, but another way to approach the methods is to examine the ways in which different strategies can be applied to the same general topic. The clusters below show how such an approach might work, by centering around a general theme and touching briefly on each method.

Identity

In this unit, students look at how our identities are shaped, whether by learning a skill like Douglass and Sedaris, by contemplating self like Dillard and Iyer, or by some other influence.

Core Text	Jon Krakauer, *Into the Wild* or Richard Wright, *Black Boy*
Narration	Frederick Douglass, "Learning to Read and Write"
Description	Annie Dillard, "Living Like Weasels"

165

Example	David Sedaris, "Me Talk Pretty One Day"
Division or Analysis	Pat Mora, "Great Expectations"
Classification	David Brooks, "People Like Us"
Process Analysis	Firoozeh Dumas, "Sweet, Sour, and Resentful"
Comparison and Contrast	Leanita McClain, "The Middle-Class Black's Burden"
Definition	Pico Iyer, "The Joy of Less"
Cause-and-Effect Analysis	Ellen Goodman, "The Company Man"

American Popular Culture

In this unit, students investigate American popular culture, from its foods and foibles to its heroes and habits.

Core Text	Eric Schlosser, *Fast Food Nation*
Narration	Maya Angelou, "Champion of the World"
Description	Dagoberto Gilb, "My Landlady's Yard"
Example	Kirk Johnson, "Today's Kids Are, Like, Killing the English Language"
Division or Analysis	Margaret Visser, "The Ritual of Fast Food" (or any essay in Chapter 9)
Classification	Brandon Griggs, "The Most Annoying Facebookers"
Process Analysis	Lars Eighner, "Dumpster Diving"
Comparison and Contrast	Cheryl Peck, "Fatso"
Definition	Pico Iyer, "The Joy of Less"
Cause-and-Effect Analysis	Dana Thomas, "The Fake Trade"

Narrative Writing

The CCSS stress that "[n]arrative writing conveys experiences, either real or imaginary, and uses time as its deep structure" (Appendix A, 23), with the intent to meet the same goals as argumentative and informational writing (to convince or persuade and to explain) or simply to entertain. Narrative writing includes the fictional and factual stories and anecdotes we are most familiar with, as well as any type of writing that conveys an experience—like a memoir or autobiography. Narratives might be told for their own sake or incorporated into informational and argumentative works for color and evidence. Regardless of the form, to be successful at narrative writing, students have to fully develop characters and make decisions about what details are crucial to the understanding of the story. Depending on age, ability, and school, teachers might create assignments that move beyond merely telling a story to increasing complexity and depth.

166

Chapter 6 of *Common Threads* provides ample instruction in narration. Suggested here is a progression of narrative texts that reveal the range of this method and the purposes for which it might be used—to entertain, to inform, and to persuade.

Core Text

> Jeannette Walls, *The Glass Castle* or Barbara Ehrenreich, *Nickel and Dimed: On (Not) Getting by in America*

Supplemental Texts

> David Sedaris, "Me Talk Pretty One Day" (entertain)
> Frederick Douglass, "Learning to Read and Write" (inform)
> Wilbert Rideau, "Why Prisons Don't Work" (persuade)

V
COMMON THREADS AND THE COMMON CORE STATE STANDARDS

Writing Standards 9th–10th Grade	Common Threads
Text Types and Purposes	
1. Write arguments to support claims in an analysis of substantive topics or texts, using valid reasoning and relevant and sufficient evidence. a. Introduce precise claim(s), distinguish the claim(s) from alternate or opposing claims, and create an organization that establishes clear relationships among claim(s), counterclaims, reasons, and evidence.	Ch. 15 Argument and Persuasion Forming a Thesis 28–31; Purpose and Thesis 37–38; Sample Research Paper 84–89; The Elements of Argument 366–67; Forming a Thesis (Argument Essay) 375–76; Revising and Editing (an Argument) 378; Writing Topic #1 396; Writing with the Method (Argument) 421; Writing about the Theme (Debating Law and Order) 422–23
b. Develop claim(s) and counterclaims fairly, supplying evidence for each while pointing out the strengths and limitations of both in a manner that anticipates the audience's knowledge level and concerns.	Organizing 31–33; Unity and Coherence 38–42; Development 42–43; Checklist for Revision 45; Organizing (an Argument) 376–77
c. Use words, phrases, and clauses to link the major sections of the text, create cohesion, and clarify the relationships between claim(s) and reasons, between reasons and evidence, and between claim(s) and counterclaims.	Unity and Coherence 38–42; Development 42–43; Quoting 69–70; Integrating 71-72
d. Establish and maintain a formal style and objective tone while attending to the norms and conventions of the discipline in which they are writing.	Ch. 3 Revising; Ch. 4 Editing; Tone 43–44; Focus on Tone 379–80

Writing Standards 9th–10th Grade	Common Threads
Text Types and Purposes (continued)	
e. Provide a concluding statement or section that follows from and supports the argument presented.	Considering the Introduction and Conclusion 32–33; Checklist for Revision 45; Sample Essay Conclusion 47; Sample Research Essay Conclusion 88; Organizing (an Argument) 376–77; Structuring (Speech) 427–29
2. Write informative/explanatory texts to examine and convey complex ideas, concepts, and information clearly and accurately through the effective selection, organization, and analysis of content.	Ch. 7 Description; Ch. 8 Example; Ch. 9 Division or Analysis; Ch. 10 Classification; Ch. 11 Process Analysis; Ch. 12 Comparison and Contrast; Ch. 13 Definition; Ch. 14 Cause-and-Effect Analysis
a. Introduce a topic; organize complex ideas, concepts, and information to make important connections and distinctions; include formatting (e.g., headings), graphics (e.g., figures, tables), and multimedia when useful to aiding comprehension.	Organizing 31–33; Considering the Introduction and Conclusion 32–33; Purpose and Thesis 37–38; Unity and Coherence 38–42; Development 42–43; Checklist for Revision 45; Organizing (Example) 156; Organizing (Analysis) 183–84; Organizing (Classification) 214; Organizing (Process Analysis) 244; Organizing (Comparison and Contrast) 275–76; Organizing (Definition) 302–03; Organizing (Cause and Effect) 334–35; The Elements of Argument 366–67; Forming a Thesis (Argument Essay) 375–76; Revising and Editing (an Argument)378; Organizing (an Argument) 376–77; Structuring (Speech) 427–29 Reading Visuals 17–21; Sample Research Paper 83–89; Integrating Multimedia 429–30
b. Develop the topic with well-chosen, relevant, and sufficient facts, extended definitions, concrete details, quotations, or other information and examples appropriate to the audience's knowledge of the topic.	Development 42; Synthesizing Source Material 68–72; Focus on Concrete and Specific Language 129; Ch. 8 Example; Ch. 13 Definition; Developing an Argumentative and Persuasive Essay 374–78

169

Writing Standards 9th–10th Grade	Common Threads
Text Types and Purposes (continued)	
c. Use appropriate and varied transitions to link the major sections of the text, create cohesion, and clarify the relationships among complex ideas and concepts.	Unity and Coherence 38–42; Development 42–43; Checklist for Revision 45
d. Use precise language and domain-specific vocabulary to manage the complexity of the topic.	Ch. 4 Editing; Focus on Verbs 101; Drafting (Cause and Effect) 335; Revising and Editing (Cause and Effect) 335–36; Focus on Conciseness 336–37
e. Establish and maintain a formal style and objective tone while attending to the norms and conventions of the discipline in which they are writing.	Ch. 3 Revising; Ch. 4 Editing; Revising and Editing (Description) 128–129; Revising and Editing (Example) 157; Revising and Editing (Division or Analysis) 185; Revising and Editing (Classification) 215; Revising and Editing (Process Analysis) 245; Revising and Editing (Comparison and Contrast) 277; Revising and Editing (Definition) 304; Revising and Editing (Cause and Effect) 335–36
f. Provide a concluding statement or section that follows from and supports the information or explanation presented (e.g., articulating implications or the significance of the topic).	Organizing (Example) 156; Organizing (Division or Analysis) 183–84; Organizing (Classification) 214; Organizing (Process Analysis) 244; Organizing (Comparison and Contrast) 275–76; Organizing (Definition) 302–03; Organizing (Cause and Effect) 334–35
3. Write narratives to develop real or imagined experiences or events using effective technique, well-chosen details, and well-structured event sequences. a. Engage and orient the reader by setting out a problem, situation, or observation, establishing one or multiple point(s) of view, and introducing a narrator and/or characters;	Ch. 6 Narration; Ch. 7 Description Getting Started (Narration) 96–98; Forming a Thesis (Narration) 98; Organizing (Narration) 98–99; Drafting (Narration) 99–100; Revising and Editing (Narration) 100

Writing Standards 9th–10th Grade	Common Threads
Text Types and Purposes (continued)	
create a smooth progression of experiences or events.	
b. Use narrative techniques, such as dialogue, pacing, description, reflection, and multiple plot lines, to develop experiences, events, and/or characters.	Getting Started (Narration) 96–98; Forming a Thesis (Narration) 98; Organizing (Narration) 98–99; Drafting (Narration) 99–100; Revising and Editing (Narration) 100; Developing a Descriptive Essay 126–129
c. Use a variety of techniques to sequence events so that they build on one another to create a coherent whole.	Organizing (Narration) 98–99; Drafting (Narration) 99–100
d. Use precise words and phrases, telling details, and sensory language to convey a vivid picture of the experiences, events, setting, and/or characters.	Revising and Editing (Narration) 100; Focus on Verbs 101; Revising and Editing (Description) 129; Focus on Concrete and Specific Language 129–130
e. Provide a conclusion that follows from and reflects on what is experienced, observed, or resolved over the course of the narrative.	Organizing (Narration) 98–99; Organizing (Description) 127–128
Production and Distribution of Writing	
4. Produce clear and coherent writing in which the development, organization, and style are appropriate to task, purpose, and audience. (Grade-specific expectations for writing types are defined in standards 1–3 above.)	Ch. 2 Developing an Essay; Ch. 3 Revising; Ch. 4 Editing; Ch. 5 Working with Sources; Developing a Narrative Essay 96–100; Developing a Descriptive Essay 126–129; Developing an Essay by Example 154–157; Developing an Essay by Division or Analysis 182–85; Developing an Essay by Classification 213–15; Developing an Essay by Process Analysis 242–45; Developing an Essay by Comparison and Contrast 273–77; Developing an Essay by Definition 301–04; Developing an Essay by Cause and Effect 332–36; Developing an Argumentative and Persuasive Essay 374–78

Writing Standards 9th–10th Grade	Common Threads
Production and Distribution of Writing (continued)	
5. Develop and strengthen writing as needed by planning, revising, editing, rewriting, or trying a new approach, focusing on addressing what is most significant for a specific purpose and audience. (Editing for conventions should demonstrate command of Language standards 1–3 up to and including grades 9–10 on page 54.)	Ch. 2 Developing an Essay; Ch. 3 Revising; Ch. 4 Editing; Ch. 5 Working with Sources; Developing a Narrative Essay 96–100; Developing a Descriptive Essay 126–129; Developing an Essay by Example 154–157; Developing an Essay by Division or Analysis 182–85; Developing an Essay by Classification 213–15; Developing an Essay by Process Analysis 242–45; Developing an Essay by Comparison and Contrast 273–77; Developing an Essay by Definition 301–04; Developing an Essay by Cause and Effect 332–36; Developing an Argumentative and Persuasive Essay 374–78
6. Use technology, including the Internet, to produce, publish, and update individual or shared writing products, taking advantage of technology's capacity to link to other information and to display information flexibly and dynamically.	The many writing and research prompts in the book can be addressed through the traditional essay format, or written and published by more contemporary means as the teacher sees fit.
Research to Build and Present Knowledge	
7. Conduct short as well as more sustained research projects to answer a question (including a self-generated question) or solve a problem; narrow or broaden the inquiry when appropriate; synthesize multiple sources on the subject, demonstrating understanding of the subject under investigation.	Ch. 5 Working with Sources; Writing Topics (Research) pp. 110, 115, 119, 135, 146, 166, 175, 193, 198, 205, 221–22, 235, 252, 256, 264, 293, 311, 316, 323, 345, 350, 386, 391, 396, 402, 414, 420
8. Gather relevant information from multiple authoritative print and digital sources, using advanced searches effectively; assess the usefulness of each source in answering the research question; integrate infor-	Researching a Topic 64–68; Synthesizing Source Materials 68–72; Avoiding Plagiarism 72–73; Documenting Sources in MLA Style 73–83

Writing Standards 9th–10th Grade	Common Threads
Research to Build and Present Knowledge (continued)	
mation into the text selectively to maintain the flow of ideas, avoiding plagiarism and following a standard format for citation.	
9. Draw evidence from literary or informational texts to support analysis, reflection, and research.	Researching a Topic 64–68; Synthesizing Source Materials 68–72; Revising and Editing (Example) 157; Each reading is followed by text-based questions and writing topics that require students to draw evidence from informational texts in order to support their analysis, reflection, and research. There are no literary pieces in the book. The Teacher's Manual recommends literary texts that connect to the informational texts in this book. There are some writing topics that ask students to draw connections between literature and informational texts, for instance, Writing with the Method (Ch. 9, Division or Analysis) #14; Writing about the Theme (Ch. 9, Division or Analysis) #1; Writing Topic #2 391

Reading Standards for Informational Text 9th–10th Grade	Common Threads
Key Ideas and Details	
1. Cite strong and thorough textual evidence to support analysis of what the text says explicitly as well as inferences drawn from the text.	Each reading is followed by Key Ideas and Details questions that focus on these skills. Some specific examples follow: Explicit: Key Ideas and Details Questions 134 #1, 165 #2, 196 #2, 234 #3, 255 #2, 282 #2, 321 #2, 344 #3, 389 #1, 435 #1

Reading Standards for Informational Text 9th–10th Grade	Common Threads
Key Ideas and Details (continued)	
	Implicit: Key Ideas and Details Questions 134 #3, 174 #3, 191 #2, 226 #3, 251 #1, 287 #3, 315 #3, 344 #2, 385 #3, 441 #3
2. Determine a central idea of a text and analyze its development over the course of the text, including how it emerges and is shaped and refined by specific details; provide an objective summary of the text.	Each reading is followed by Key Ideas and Details questions that focus on this skill. Some specific examples follow: 118 #1, 144 #2, 165 #4, 204 #4, 226 #1, 255 #1, 287 #2, 321 #1, 349 #3, 389 #2, 444 #2
3. Analyze how the author unfolds an analysis or series of ideas or events, including the order in which the points are made, how they are introduced and developed, and the connections that are drawn between them.	Each reading is followed by Craft and Structure questions that focus on this skill. Some specific examples follow: 109 #3, 114 #3, 118 #3, 139 #3, 165 #3, 194 #2, 202 #2, 225 #2, 251 #2, 264 #4, 287 #3, 292 #3, 310 #3, 315 #2, 322 #3, 344 #2
Craft and Structure	
4. Determine the meaning of words and phrases as they are used in a text, including figurative, connotative, and technical meanings; analyze the cumulative impact of specific word choices on meaning and tone (e.g., how the language of a court opinion differs from that of a newspaper).	Each reading is followed by Vocabulary questions with words taken from the readings. Questions on figurative language, connotation, and the impact of word choices on meaning and tone can be found under the heading Craft and Structure, for instance: 114 #1, 145 #2, 165 #2, 196 #1, 234 #1, 263–64 #1, 282 #1, 321 #1, 344 #1, 389 #1, 444 #1.
5. Analyze in detail how an author's ideas or claims are developed and refined by particular sentences, paragraphs, or larger portions of a text (e.g., a section or chapter).	Opportunities for analysis of syntax, structure, and meaning can be found in the Craft and Structure questions that follow each reading, for instance: 109 #1, 145 #3, 165 #3, 197 #3, 226 #3, 255-56 #3, 287 #1, 322 #3, 359 #1, 395 #2, 444 #3.

Reading Standards for Informational Text 9th–10th Grade	Common Threads
Craft and Structure (continued)	
6. Determine an author's point of view or purpose in a text and analyze how an author uses rhetoric to advance that point of view or purpose.	Questions on purpose, point of view, and how an author uses rhetorical devices to persuade are found in the Craft and Structure questions that follow each reading, for instance: 109 #3, 139 #3, 170 #3, 192 #3 & #4, 234 #4, 263–64 #3, 292 #3, 315 #2, 344 #4, 401#3 & #4, 447 #2.
Integration of Knowledge and Ideas	
7. Analyze various accounts of a subject told in different mediums (e.g., a person's life story in both print and multimedia), determining which details are emphasized in each account.	Visual texts thematically linked to the readings in the chapter appear at the beginning of each chapter of readings. Each chapter includes a Seeing the Method section that asks students to analyze those images, for instance, Seeing Narration 93; Seeing Description 123; Seeing Examples 151; Seeing Division or Analysis 179–80; Seeing Classification 209–10; Seeing Process Analysis 239-40; Seeing Comparison and Contrast 269–70; Seeing Definition 297–98; Seeing Cause and Effect 327–28; Seeing Argument and Persuasion 365–66. Questions connecting these visuals to the readings in the chapter appear in the Writing about the Theme section at the very end of each chapter. Various essays throughout the book also include visual texts, including: Tan 117, Brooks 228, Kingsolver 258, Mosley 318, LeDuff 352.
8. Delineate and evaluate the argument and specific claims in a text, assessing whether the reasoning is valid and the evidence is relevant and sufficient; identify false statements and fallacious reasoning.	Integration of Knowledge and Ideas questions, particularly in Ch. 15, cover these topics, for instance: 385 #2; 390 #2; 395–96 #3; 401–02 #3; 413 #3; 419–20 #2.

Reading Standards for Informational Text 9th–10th Grade	Common Threads
Integration of Knowledge and Ideas (continued)	
9. Analyze seminal U.S. documents of historical and literary significance (e.g., Washington's Farewell Address, the Gettysburg Address, Roosevelt's Four Freedoms speech, King's "Letter from Birmingham Jail"), including how they address related themes and concepts.	See selections from Frederick Douglass 103, Patrick Henry 432, Elizabeth Cady Stanton 437, Sojourner Truth 443, Abraham Lincoln 446, and Martin Luther King, Jr. 449. See also the discussion of Roosevelt's Four Freedoms speech in Seeing Comparison and Contrast 270.

Speaking and Listening Standards for 9th–10th Grade	Common Threads
Comprehension and Collaboration	
1. Initiate and participate effectively in a range of collaborative discussions (one-on-one, in groups, and teacher-led) with diverse partners on grades 9–10 topics, texts, and issues, building on others' ideas and expressing their own clearly and persuasively. a. Come to discussions prepared, having read and researched material under study; explicitly draw on that preparation by referring to evidence from texts and other research on the topic or issue to stimulate a thoughtful, well-reasoned exchange of ideas. b. Work with peers to set rules for collegial discussions and decision-making (e.g., informal consensus, taking votes on key issues, presentation of alternate views), clear goals and deadlines, and individual roles as needed.	Speaking and Listening 25; questions marked For Discussion throughout the book provide opportunities for text-based conversations, see for instance 109, 135, 166, 192, 221, 256, 283, 311, 344, 385, 436

Speaking and Listening Standards for 9th–10th Grade	Common Threads
Comprehension and Collaboration (continued)	
c. Propel conversations by posing and responding to questions that relate the current discussion to broader themes or larger ideas; actively incorporate others into the discussion; and clarify, verify, or challenge ideas and conclusions.	
d. Respond thoughtfully to diverse perspectives, summarize points of agreement and disagreement, and, when warranted, qualify or justify their own views and understanding and make new connections in light of the evidence and reasoning presented.	
2. Integrate multiple sources of information presented in diverse media or formats (e.g., visually, quantitatively, orally), evaluating the credibility and accuracy of each source.	Reading Visuals 17–21, Evaluating Sources 66–68, Synthesizing Source Material 68–72, Integrating Multimedia 429–30
3. Evaluate a speaker's point of view, reasoning, and use of evidence and rhetoric, identifying any fallacious reasoning or exaggerated or distorted evidence.	Reading and Listening to Speeches 424–25; Reading Argument and Persuasion 366–73; Writing Topics 436 #2, 442 #1, 448 #1
Presentation of Knowledge and Ideas	
4. Present information, findings, and supporting evidence clearly, concisely, and logically such that listeners can follow the line of reasoning and the organization, development, substance, and style are appropriate to purpose, audience, and task.	Keys to Effective Speaking— Planning 426, Structuring 427–29, Integrating Multimedia 429–30, Rehearsing 430–31 Writing topics throughout the book suggest presentation projects. See, for instance, 110 #3, 115 #3, 135 #2, 166 #3, 171 #2, 190 #2, 234 #2, 252 #1, 293 #2, 316 #3, 345 #3, 396 #2
5. Make strategic use of digital media (e.g., textual, graphical, audio, visual, and interactive elements) in	Integrating Multimedia 429–30

Speaking and Listening Standards for 9th–10th Grade	Common Threads
Presentation of Knowledge and Ideas (continued)	
presentations to enhance understanding of findings, reasoning, and evidence and to add interest.	
6. Adapt speech to a variety of contexts and tasks, demonstrating command of formal English when indicated or appropriate. (See grades 9–10 Language standards 1 and 3 on page 54 for specific expectations.)	Keys to Effective Speaking 425–31; Ch. 4 Editing

Language Standards 9th–10th Grade	Common Threads
Conventions of Standard English	
1. Demonstrate command of the conventions of standard English grammar and usage when writing or speaking. a. Use parallel structure.	Parallelism 55; Focus on Parallelism 278; Craft and Structure 287 #1, 385 #1, 441 #1, 447 #1, 453 #3
b. Use various types of phrases (noun, verb, adjectival, adverbial, participial, prepositional, absolute) and clauses (independent, dependent; noun, relative, adverbial) to convey specific meanings and add variety and interest to writing or presentations.	Clarity 49–52; Conciseness 52–53; Emphasis 53–55; Variety 56; Checklist for Editing 60; Focus on Sentence Variety 158–159; Focus on Restrictive and Nonrestrictive Elements 305
2. Demonstrate command of the conventions of standard English capitalization, punctuation, and spelling when writing. a. Use a semicolon (and perhaps a conjunctive adverb) to link two or more closely related independent clauses. b. Use a colon to introduce a list or quotation. c. Spell correctly.	Ch. 4 Editing; Focus on Punctuation 215–16

Language Standards 9th–10th Grade	Common Threads
Knowledge of Language	
3. Apply knowledge of language to understand how language functions in different contexts, to make effective choices for meaning or style, and to comprehend more fully when reading or listening. a. Write and edit work so that it conforms to the guidelines in a style manual (e.g., MLA Handbook, Turabian's Manual for Writers) appropriate for the discipline and writing type.	Ch. 4 Editing; Focus on Tone 379–80; Each reading includes a question in the Craft and Structure questions marked Language that addresses these issues, for instance: 114 #1, 139 #1, 170 #1, 196 #1, 226 #1, 255 #1, 282 #1, 322 #1, 359 #1, 395 #1, 444 #1. Documenting Sources in MLA Style 73–83
Vocabulary Acquisition and Use	
4. Determine or clarify the meaning of unknown and multiple-meaning words and phrases based on grades 9–10 reading and content, choosing flexibly from a range of strategies. a. Use context (e.g., the overall meaning of a sentence, paragraph, or text; a word's position or function in a sentence) as a clue to the meaning of a word or phrase. b. Identify and correctly use patterns of word changes that indicate different meanings or parts of speech (e.g., analyze, analysis, analytical; advocate, advocacy). c. Consult general and specialized reference materials (e.g., dictionaries, glossaries, thesauruses), both print and digital, to find the pronunciation of a word or determine or clarify its precise meaning, its part of speech, or its etymology. d. Verify the preliminary determination of the meaning of a word or phrase (e.g., by checking the inferred meaning in context or in a dictionary).	Reading Critically 5–7; Checklist for Critical Reading 8. Each reading is followed by Vocabulary questions that challenge comprehension and prompt students to consult context and reference materials, for instance: 114, 134, 164–165, 196, 225–26, 255, 282, 321, 359, 395, 447.

Language Standards 9th–10th Grade	Common Threads
Vocabulary Acquisition and Use (continued)	
5. Demonstrate understanding of figurative language, word relationships, and nuances in word meanings. a. Interpret figures of speech (e.g., euphemism, oxymoron) in context and analyze their role in the text.	Figures of Speech 58-59. Throughout the book, Craft and Structure questions marked Language ask students to analyze the meaning and effect of figurative language, for instance: 109 #1, 204 #1, 234 #1, 263 #1, 322 #1, 419 #1.
b. Analyze nuances in the meaning of words with similar denotations.	Each reading is followed by Vocabulary questions that challenge comprehension and prompt students to consult context and reference materials, for instance: 114, 134, 164–65, 196, 225–26, 255, 282, 321, 359, 395, 447.
6. Acquire and use accurately general academic and domain-specific words and phrases, sufficient for reading, writing, speaking, and listening at the college and career readiness level; demonstrate independence in gathering vocabulary knowledge when considering a word or phrase important to comprehension or expression.	Each reading is followed by Vocabulary questions that challenge comprehension and prompt students to consult context and reference materials, for instance: 114, 134, 164–65, 196, 225–26, 255, 282, 321, 359, 395, 447.

Geography is not the only way we find ourselves divided from   10
people unlike us. Some of us watch Fox News, while others listen to
NPR. Some like David Letterman, and others—typically in less urban
neighborhoods—like Jay Leno. Some go to charismatic churches; some
go to mainstream churches. Americans tend more and more often to
marry people with education levels similar to their own, and to befriend
people with backgrounds similar to their own.

My favorite illustration of this latter pattern comes from the first,   11
noncontroversial chapter of *The Bell Curve*.[2] Think of your twelve closest
friends, Richard J. Herrnstein and Charles Murray write. If you had chosen them randomly from the American population, the odds that half
of your twelve closest friends would be college graduates would be six
in a thousand. The odds that half of the twelve would have advanced
degrees would be less than one in a million. Have any of your twelve
closest friends graduated from Harvard, Stanford, Yale, Princeton, Caltech,
MIT, Duke, Dartmouth, Cornell, Columbia, Chicago, or Brown? If you
chose your friends randomly from the American population, the odds
against your having four or more friends from those schools would be
more than a billion to one.

Many of us live in absurdly unlikely groupings, because we have   12
organized our lives that way.

It's striking that the institutions that talk the most about diversity   13
often practice it the least. For example, no group of people sings the
diversity anthem more frequently and fervently than administrators at
just such elite universities. But elite universities are amazingly undiverse
in their values, politics, and mores. Professors in particular are drawn
from a rather narrow segment of the population. If faculties reflected the
general population, 32% of professors would be registered Democrats
and 31% would be registered Republicans. Forty percent would be evangelical Christians. But a recent study of several universities by the conservative Center for the Study of Popular Culture and the American
Enterprise Institute found that roughly 90% of those professors in the
arts and sciences who had registered with a political party had registered
Democratic. Fifty-seven professors at Brown were found on the voter-
registration rolls. Of those, fifty-four were Democrats. Of the forty-two

---

[2] Published in 1994, the book uses statistical analysis to argue that IQ is inherited
and to warn that the American population will become less intelligent (and less
affluent) if college graduates continue having fewer children than less educated people
do—both controversial claims that upset many readers. [Editors' note.]

professors in the English, history, sociology, and political-science departments, all were Democrats. The results at Harvard, Penn State, Maryland,
and the University of California at Santa Barbara were similar to the
results at Brown.

What we are looking at here is human nature. People want to be 14
around others who are roughly like themselves. That's called community. It probably would be psychologically difficult for most Brown professors to share an office with someone who was pro-life, a member of
the National Rifle Association, or an evangelical Christian. It's likely that
hiring committees would subtly—even unconsciously—screen out any
such people they encountered. Republicans and evangelical Christians
have sensed that they are not welcome at places like Brown, so they don't
even consider working there. In fact, any registered Republican who
contemplates a career in academia these days is both a hero and a fool.
So, in a semi-self-selective pattern, brainy people with generally liberal
social mores flow to academia, and brainy people with generally conservative mores flow elsewhere.

The dream of diversity is like the dream of equality. Both are based 15
on ideals we celebrate even as we undermine them daily. (How many
times have you seen someone renounce a high-paying job or pull his
child from an elite college on the grounds that these things are bad for

equality?) On the one hand, the situation is appalling. It is appalling that Americans know so little about one another. It is appalling that many of us are so narrow-minded that we can't tolerate a few people with ideas significantly different from our own. It's appalling that evangelical Christians are practically absent from entire professions, such as academia, the media, and filmmaking. It's appalling that people should be content to cut themselves off from everyone unlike themselves.

The segmentation of society means that often we don't even have **16** arguments across the political divide. Within their little validating communities, liberals and conservatives circulate half-truths about the supposed awfulness of the other side. These distortions are believed because it feels good to believe them.

On the other hand, there are limits to how diverse any community **17** can or should be. I've come to think that it is not useful to try to hammer diversity into every neighborhood and institution in the United States. Sure, Augusta National[3] should probably admit women, and university sociology departments should probably hire a conservative or two. It would be nice if all neighborhoods had a good mixture of ethnicities. But human nature being what it is, most places and institutions are going to remain culturally homogeneous.

It's probably better to think about diverse lives, not diverse institu- **18** tions. Human beings, if they are to live well, will have to move through a series of institutions and environments, which may be individually homogeneous but, taken together, will offer diverse experiences. It might also be a good idea to make national service a rite of passage for young people in this country: it would take them out of their narrow neighborhood segment and thrust them in with people unlike themselves. Finally, it's probably important for adults to get out of their own familiar circles. If you live in a coastal, socially liberal neighborhood, maybe you should take out a subscription to *The Door*, the evangelical humor magazine; or maybe you should visit Branson, Missouri.[4] Maybe you should stop in at a megachurch. Sure, it would be superficial familiarity, but it beats the iron curtains that now separate the nation's various cultural zones.

Look around at your daily life. Are you really in touch with the broad **19** diversity of American life? Do you care?

---

[3] Located in Georgia, the private Augusta National Golf Club hosts the prestigious annual Masters tournament; until August 2012, it excluded women from membership. [Editors' note.]

[4] A tourist destination that features amusement parks, wax museums and similar attractions, and more than fifty theaters and music venues showcasing country-and-western acts and pop stars from the 1950s, '60s, and '70s. [Editors' note.]

Vocabulary

If you do not know the meanings of the following words, try to guess them from the context of Brooks's essay. Test your guesses in a dictionary, and then try to use each word in a sentence of your own.

Pentecostal (1)	congenial (3)	metropolitan (9)
globalization (1)	progressive (3)	charismatic (10)
postmodern (1)	segementing (4)	latter (11)
cardiovascular (1)	rigorously (4)	mores (13)
strenuous (1)	homogenous (4)	evangelical (13)
dislocated (2)	integration (5)	academia (14)
barista (2)	congregate (5)	renounce (15)
affinity (3)	demographic (8)	validating (16)

Key Ideas and Details

1. Can you find a statement of Brooks's thesis anywhere in his essay? Try to express the author's main idea in your own words.

2. What are "psycho-demographic clusters" (paragraph 8)? What do they have to do with Brooks's thesis?

3. What useful purposes are served by segregation, according to Brooks? What are the negative consequences of people choosing to live in areas where the neighbors are similar?

Craft and Structure

1. LANGUAGE Point out several metaphors in the essay. What effect do they have? (If necessary, see p. 58 and *figures of speech* in the Glossary for an explanation of *metaphor*.)

2. How would you characterize Brooks's tone? Why is the tone crucial in helping him achieve his purpose for writing?

3. What kinds of diversity does Brooks consider in his classification? Diagram or outline his categories. Do any of them overlap?

4. OTHER METHODS At several points in his essay, Brooks uses comparison and contrast (Chapter 12) to shape his ideas. Locate two or three uses of this method and explain what they contribute to the author's point.

Integration of Knowledge and Ideas

1. Does Brooks make any assumptions about his audience? Where does he give the clearest indication of the type of person he imagines reading his essay?

2. How does the cartoon by Steve Brodner (p. 232) relate to Brooks's essay? Why do you suppose the *Atlantic* included it with the article?

3. FOR DISCUSSION Examine the examples and details Brooks uses to develop his classification and be prepared to discuss them in class. Where did this information come from? What sources does Brooks cite, and what evidence does he draw from them? How does he use the evidence he cites?

Writing Topics

1. How accurately do Brooks's classifications represent your experience? Are all the people in your neighborhood alike—economically, racially, academically, and so forth? Write an essay that responds to Brooks, answering the two questions he poses in his final paragraph: "Are you really in touch with the broad diversity of American life? Do you care?"

2. Brooks encourages readers to seek out diversity in their experiences by interacting with people who are not like them—to find a way to connect with strangers. With a team of three or four classmates, create a ten-minute video presentation that demonstrates what, in your view, is the appropriate way to interact (or not interact) with a stranger. Ignore situations that might be risky, such as deserted nighttime streets or strangers who seem threatening. Think instead of a safe situation, such as a long line at the grocery store or coffee shop or the waiting room of a doctor's office. What are your "rules" for initiating conversation and for responding to a stranger's overtures? What informs your rules: experience? personality? upbringing? How can your audience apply your rules to make diverse acquaintances in their own lives?

3. RESEARCH Brooks notes in paragraph 5 that "according to an analysis of the 2000 census data, the 1990s saw only a slight increase in the racial integration of neighborhoods in the United States." Visit the Web site for the 2010 census (*census.gov*) and find more recent information on racial integration in your local area. Between 2000 and 2010, how has the shape of your community changed? Is it more diverse, or less, than it was a decade ago? Write an essay analyzing the state of diversity in your community, considering how recent changes have affected the ways people relate to each other.

4. CONNECTIONS In paragraph 5, Brooks writes, "The number of middle-class and upper-middle-class African American families is rising, but for whatever reasons—racism, psychological comfort—these families tend to congregate in predominantly black neighborhoods." Read "The Middle-Class Black's Burden" by Leanita McClain (p. 284). How might she explain the reasons for this phenomenon to Brooks?

WRITING WITH THE METHOD

CLASSIFICATION

Select one of the following topics, or any other topic they suggest, for an essay developed by classification. Be sure to choose a topic you care about so that classification is a means of communicating an idea, not an end in itself.

People

1. Boring people
2. Laundromat users
3. Teachers or students
4. Parents or children

Psychology and Behavior

5. Ways of punishing misbehavior
6. Obsessions
7. Diets
8. Dreams

Things

9. Buildings in town
10. Junk foods
11. Computer games
12. Trucks

Sports and Performance

13. Types of sports
14. Styles of baseball pitching, tennis serving, or another sports skill
15. Styles of dance, guitar playing, acting, or another performance art

Media

16. Talk-show hosts
17. Blogs
18. Sports announcers
19. Magazines or newspapers

WRITING ABOUT THE THEME

SORTING GROUP IDENTITIES

1. Write a brief essay in which you classify students at your school or a rival school. You may devise your own classification system, if you wish, or you might try adapting the categories of one of the other writers in this chapter to this subject. For instance, what racial and ethnic origins (p. 208) do you see represented among your peers? Are some students workers and some dreamers, like the people in Nelson George's (p. 212) neighborhood? Do they exhibit, in person, any of the characteristics that Brandon Griggs complains about in "The Most Annoying Facebookers" (p. 218)? Do they, like the subjects of David Brooks's "People Like Us," fit into a particular "psycho-demographic cluster" (p. 228)? Have you developed friendships in school similar to any of the types Marion Winik describes in "What Are Friends For?" (p. 223)?

2. Brandon Griggs and Marion Winik both classify and label people with some intention to amuse readers. However, as David Brooks suggests, not all labels used to classify people are harmless. Consider, for example, labels based on race or gender. Write an essay in which you discuss both the benefits and the costs of assigning labels to people — for those using the labels, for those being labeled, and for society as a whole. Give plenty of specific examples.

3. Groups of people often form distinct communities, such as the neighborhoods David Brooks examines, the artists on Nelson George's block, or the campers at Luis Alberto Urrea's RV park (p. 212). Write an essay in which you offer your definition of *community*. Consider not only what constitutes a group identity but also why people might seek (or reject) a connection with others. What do communities offer their members, and what do they demand of individuals in return?

Microwaves

Waveguide

Cooling fan

Antenna

Magnetron

Capacitor

Diode

Transformer

Transformer, diode, and capacitor raise household electricity from 120 to 3,000 volts or more and deliver it through a wire to a magnetron. The magnetron generates microwaves, sent by an antenna through a waveguide into the cooking chamber, where the waves reflect off metal walls. A platter rotates food through the waves for uniform heating. Models without a platter have a small spinning blade (*not shown*) at the end of the guide to thoroughly distribute the microwaves.

11

PROCESS ANALYSIS

EATING WELL

Game rules, repair manuals, cookbooks, science textbooks—these and many other familiar works are essentially process analyses. They explain how to do something (play Monopoly, patch a hole in the wall), how to make something (an omelet), or how something happens (how hormones affect behavior, how a computer stores and retrieves data). That is, they explain a sequence of actions with a specified result (the **process**) by dividing it into its steps (the **analysis**). You might use process analysis to explain how a hybrid engine saves gas or how a student organization can influence cafeteria menus. You also use process analysis when you want to teach someone how to do something, such as create a Web page or follow a new interviewing procedure.

Process analysis overlaps several other writing methods discussed in this book. The analysis component is the method examined in Chapter 9—dividing a thing or concept into its elements. And we analyze a process much as we analyze causes and effects (Chapter 14), except that cause-and-effect analysis asks *why* something happens or *why* it has certain results, whereas process analysis asks *how*. Process analysis also overlaps narration (Chapter 6), for the steps involved are almost always presented in chronological sequence. But narration recounts a unique sequence of events with a unique result, whereas process analysis explains a series of steps with the same predictable result. You might narrate a particularly exciting baseball game, for instance, but you would analyze the process—the rules—of any baseball game.

 ## Seeing Process Analysis

The drawing on the facing page was created as an illustration for "How the Microwave Works," an article by science writer Mark Fischetti in the magazine *Scientific American*. In the article, Fischetti explains that microwave ovens cook foods by using electromagnetic energy to heat the water molecules inside them. The image here shows a cross section of a microwave oven. Examine the labels that identify the mechanical components in the microwave and explain what some of them do, as well as the wavy lines representing the motion of microwaves. How does the illustration explain the process of microwave cooking? What sequence of steps does it show? How does the caption reinforce and clarify the information in the picture? Do the words and image together succeed in helping you understand how a microwave oven works? To what extent would your understanding be affected if one or the other were not provided?

Reading Process Analysis

Almost always, the purpose of process analysis is to explain, but sometimes a parallel purpose is to prove something about a process or to evaluate it: a writer may want to show how easy it is to change a tire, for instance, or urge aspiring marathon runners to follow a training regimen on the grounds of its safety and effectiveness.

Processes occur in several varieties, including mechanical (a car engine), natural (cell division), psychological (retrieval of memories), and political (the electoral process). Process analyses generally fall into one of two types:

- A *directive* process analysis tells how to do or make something: bake a cake, tune a guitar, negotiate a deal, write a process analysis. It outlines the steps in the process completely so that the reader who follows them can achieve the specified result. Generally, a directive process analysis addresses the reader directly, using the second-person *you* ("You should think of negotiation as collaboration rather than competition") or the imperative (commanding) mood of verbs ("Add one egg yolk and stir vigorously"). (See also p. 241.)

- An *explanatory* process analysis provides the information necessary for readers to understand the process, but more to satisfy their curiosity than to teach them how to perform it. It may address the reader directly, but the third-person *he, she, it*, and *they* are more common.

Whether directive or explanatory, process analyses usually follow a chronological sequence. Most processes can be divided into phases or stages, and these in turn can be divided into steps. The stages of changing a tire, for instance, may be jacking up the car, removing the flat, putting on the spare, and lowering the car. The steps within, say, jacking up the car may be setting the emergency brake, blocking the other wheels, loosening the lug nuts, positioning the jack, and raising the car. Following a chronological order, a writer covers the stages in sequence and, within each stage, covers the steps in sequence.

To ensure that the reader can duplicate the process or understand how it unfolds, a process analysis must fully detail each step and specify the reasons for it. In addition, the writer must ensure that the reader grasps the sequence of steps, their duration, and where they occur. To this end, transitional expressions that signal time and place—such as *after five minutes, meanwhile, to the left,* and *below*—can be invaluable.

Though a chronological sequence is usual for process analysis, the sequence may be interrupted or modified to suit the material. A writer may need to pause in a sequence to provide definitions of specialized terms or to explain why a step is necessary or how it relates to the preceding and following steps. Instructions on how to change a tire, for instance, might stop briefly to explain that the lug nuts should be loosened slightly *before* the car is jacked up to prevent the wheel from spinning once the weight is off the tire.

Analyzing Processes in Paragraphs

L. Rust Hills (1924–2008) was a fiction editor, writing teacher, and writer. This paragraph comes from "How to Eat an Ice-Cream Cone," which appears in his book *How to Do Things Right* (1972).

In trying to make wise and correct decisions about the ice-cream cone in your hand, you should always keep the objectives in mind. The main objective, of course, is to get the cone under control. Secondarily, one will want to eat the cone calmly and with pleasure. Real pleasure lies not simply in eating the cone but in eating it *right*. Let us assume that you have darted to your open space and made your necessary emergency repairs. The cone is still dangerous—still, so to speak, "live." But you can now proceed with it in an orderly fashion. First, revolve the cone through the full three hundred and sixty degrees, snapping at the loose gobs of ice cream; turn the cone by moving the thumb away from you

Directive process analysis: tells how to eat an ice-cream cone

Goals of the process

Transitions signal sequence, time, and place (underlined)

Process divided into three distinct steps

and the forefinger toward you, so the cone moves counter-
clockwise. Then with the cone still "wound," which will
require the wrist to be bent at the full right angle toward you,
apply pressure with the mouth and tongue to accomplish
overall realignment, straightening and settling the whole
mess. Then, unwinding the cone back through the full three
hundred and sixty degrees, remove any trickles of ice cream.
From here on, some supplementary repairs may be necessary,
but the cone is now defused.

Test for correct
performance of
step

Reason for step

Result of the
process

Jane E. Brody (born 1941) is a nutritionist whose weekly column, "Personal Health," has been syndicated in more than one hundred newspapers for three decades. This paragraph is from her guide to sensible eating, *Jane Brody's Nutrition Book* (1981).

When you think about it, it's impossible to lose—as
many . . . diets suggest—10 pounds of *fat* in ten days, even
on a total fast. A pound of body fat represents 3,500 calories.
To lose 1 pound of fat, you must expend 3,500 more calories
than you consume. Let's say you weigh 170 pounds and, as a
moderately active person, you burn 2,500 calories a day. If
your diet contains only 1,500 calories, you'd have an energy
deficit of 1,000 calories a day. In a week's time that would add
up to a 7,000-calorie deficit, or 2 pounds of real fat. In ten
days, the accumulated deficit would represent nearly 3 pounds
of lost body fat. Even if you ate nothing at all for ten days
and maintained your usual level of activity, your caloric deficit would add up to 25,000 calories (2,500 calories a day
times 10). At 3,500 calories per pound of fat, that's still only
7 pounds of lost fat. So if you want to lose fat, which is all
you should want to lose, the loss must be gradual—at most a
pound or two a week.

Explanatory pro-
cess analysis: tells
how weight loss
happens

Process divided
into steps

Transitions
(underlined)
signal sequence

Goal of process

Developing an Essay by Process Analysis

▶ Getting Started

You'll find yourself writing process analyses for your courses in school (for instance, assessing how nitrogen affects soil chemistry), at work (explaining how a new procedure will shorten checkout lines), or in life outside work (giving written instructions to a pet sitter). To find a subject when an assignment doesn't make one obvious, examine your interests or hobbies or think of something whose workings you'd like to research and understand better. Explore the subject by listing chronologically all the necessary stages and steps.

Remember your readers while you are generating ideas. Consider how much background information they need, where specialized terms must be defined, and where examples must be given. Especially if you are providing instructions, consider what special equipment readers will need, what hitches they may encounter, and what the interim results should be. To build a table, for instance, what tools would readers need? What should they do if the table wobbles even after the corners are braced? What should the table feel like after the first sanding or the first varnishing?

▶ Forming a Thesis

While you are exploring your subject, decide on the point of your process analysis and express it in a thesis sentence that will guide your writing and tell your readers what to expect. The simplest thesis states what the process is and outlines its basic stages:

> Building a table is a three-stage process of cutting, assembling, and finishing.

But you can increase your readers' interest in the process by also conveying your reason for writing about it. You might assert that a seemingly difficult process is actually quite simple, or vice versa:

> Changing a tire does not require a mechanic's skill or strength; on the contrary, a ten-year-old child can do it.

> Windsurfing may look easy, but it demands the knowledge of an experienced sailor and the balance of an acrobat.

You might show how the process demonstrates a more general principle:

> The process of getting a bill through Congress illustrates majority rule at work.

Or you might assert that a process is inefficient or unfair:

> The state's outdated licensing procedure forces new drivers to waste hours standing in line.

Regardless of how you structure your thesis sentence, try to make it clear that your process analysis has a point. Usually you will want to include a direct statement of your thesis in your introduction so that readers know what you're writing about and why the process should matter to them.

▶ Organizing

Many successful process analyses begin with an overview of the process to which readers can relate each step. In such an **introduction** you can lead up to your thesis sentence by specifying when or where the process occurs, why it is useful or interesting or controversial, what its result is, and the like. Especially if you are providing instructions, you can also use the introduction (perhaps a separate paragraph) to provide essential background information, such as the materials readers will need.

After the introduction, you should present the stages distinctly, perhaps one or two paragraphs for each, and usually in chronological order. Within each stage, also chronologically, you then cover the necessary steps. This chronological sequence helps readers see how a process unfolds or how to perform it themselves. Try not to deviate from it unless you have good reason to — perhaps because your process requires you to group simultaneous steps or your readers need definitions of terms, reasons for steps, connections between separated steps, and other explanations.

A process essay may end simply with the result. But your **conclusion** might contain a summary of the major stages, a comment on the significance or usefulness of the process, or a recommendation for changing a process you have criticized. For a directive process essay, you might state the standards by which readers can measure their success or give an idea of how much practice may be necessary to master the process.

▶ Drafting

While drafting your process analysis, concentrate on getting in as many details as you can: every step, how each relates to the one before and after, how each contributes to the result. In revising you can always delete unnecessary details and digressions if they seem cumbersome, but in the first draft it's better to overexplain than underexplain.

Drafting a process analysis is a good occasion to practice a straightforward, concise writing style, for clarity is more important than originality of expression. Stick to plain language and uncomplicated sentences. If you want to dress up your style a bit, you can always do so after you have made yourself clear.

▶ Revising and Editing

When you've finished your draft, ask a friend to read it. If you have explained a process, he or she should be able to understand it. If you have given directions, he or she should be able to follow them, or imagine following them. Then examine the draft yourself against the following questions and the information in the focus box on the next two pages.

- *Have you adhered to a chronological sequence?* Unless there is a compelling and clear reason to use some other arrangement, the stages and steps of your analysis should proceed in chronological order. If you had to depart from that order—to define or explain or to sort out simultaneous steps—the reasons should be clear to your readers.

- *Have you included all necessary steps and omitted any unnecessary digressions?* The explanation should be as complete as possible but not cluttered with information, however interesting, that contributes nothing to the readers' understanding of the process.

- *Have you accurately gauged your readers' need for information?* You don't want to bore readers with explanations and details they don't need. But erring in the other direction is even worse, for your essay will achieve little if readers cannot understand it.

- *Have you shown readers how each step fits into the whole process and relates to the other steps?* If your analysis seems to break down into a multitude of isolated steps, you may need to organize them more clearly into stages.

- *Have you used plenty of informative transitions?* Transitions such as *at the same time* and *on the other side of the machine* indicate when steps start and stop, how long they last, and where they occur. (A list of such expressions appears in the Glossary under *transitions*.) The expressions should be as informative as possible; signals such as *first . . . second . . . third . . . fourteenth* and *next . . . next* do not help indicate movement in space or lapses in time, and they quickly grow tiresome.

FOCUS ON **Consistency**

While drafting a process analysis, you may start off with subjects or verbs in one form and then shift to another form because the original choice feels awkward. In directive analyses, shifts occur most often with the subjects *a person* or *one*:

> INCONSISTENT To keep the car from rolling while changing the tire, one should first set the car's emergency brake. Then you should block the other three tires with objects like rocks or chunks of wood.

To repair the inconsistency here, you could stick with *one* for the subject (*one should block*), but that usually sounds stiff. It's better to revise the earlier subjects to be *you*:

> CONSISTENT To keep the car from rolling while changing the tire, you should first set the car's emergency brake. Then you should block the other three tires with objects like rocks or chunks of wood.

Sometimes, writers try to avoid *one* or *a person* or even *you* by using passive verbs that don't require actors:

> INCONSISTENT To keep the car from rolling while changing the tire, you should first set the car's emergency brake. . . . Before the car is raised, the lug nuts of the wheel should be loosened. . . .

But the passive voice is wordy and potentially confusing, especially when directions should be making it clear who does what. (See p. 101 for more on passive verbs.)

The easiest solution to the problem of inconsistent subjects and passive voice is to use the imperative, or commanding, form of verbs, in which *you* is understood as the subject:

> CONSISTENT To keep the car from rolling while changing the tire, first set the car's emergency brake. Then block the other three tires with objects like rocks or chunks of wood.

In informative analyses, passive verbs may be necessary if you don't know who the actor is or want to emphasize the action over the actor. But identifying the actor is generally clearer and more concise:

> CONSISTENT A mechanic always loosens the lug nuts of the wheel before raising the car.

Imperative and active verbs should be consistent, too. Don't shift back and forth between *block* and *you should block* or between *is raised* and *loosens*.

See pages 50–52 for more on shifts and how to avoid them.

Practice

The sentences below are adapted from Mark Fischetti's article "How the Microwave Works" (see the illustration on p. 238). Edit them to repair shifts in subject, verb, and voice. Aim for clearly identified subjects and active verbs in each.

1. One can find water molecules in most foods. They have positive and negative charge at opposite "ends."

2. The electric field of a microwave orients the positive ends in one direction, but the field is reversed 4.9 billion times a second, so you cause the molecules to turn back and forth. As they turn, they are bumped, creating friction that produces heat.

3. Ceramic and glass containers are water-free and thus remain cool, although one might heat them through conduction from hot food.

4. Can't the microwaves fly through the window and harm your body — especially our eyes?

5. No. The waves are reflected off a metal screen embedded in the glass.

▶ For more practice editing for shifts, visit Exercise Central at bedfordstmartins.com/exercisecentral.

A Note on Thematic Connections

The authors represented in this chapter set out to examine the steps involved in maintaining a healthy relationship with food, and for that purpose process analysis is the natural choice of method. With an illustration, Mark Fischetti shows how microwave ovens use electromagnetic energy to heat our meals (p. 238). In paragraphs, L. Rust Hills provides meticulous instructions for eating an ice-cream cone without making a mess (p. 241), while Jane E. Brody explains to dieters how calories translate into pounds (p. 242). Firoozeh Dumas, in an essay, examines the weekly routines her family endured as dinner hosts to recent immigrants (next page). Lars Eighner's essay details an eating strategy of the homeless and very poor: scavenging in trash bins (p. 253). And in an excerpt from a book that has helped to promote the local foods movement, Barbara Kingsolver creates an imaginary plant to explain the seasonality of produce (p. 258).

Firoozeh Dumas

Born in 1966 in Abadan, Iran, and raised there until her family emigrated in 1972, Firoozeh Dumas has lived in northern California most of her life. After marrying a French immigrant she met while both were students at the University of California at Berkeley, Dumas took up writing about her unusual childhood and quirky family as a way to share stories with her children. The unanticipated result was a best-selling collection of essays: *Funny in Farsi: A Memoir of Growing Up Iranian in America* (2003). Dumas decided to make a career of writing and has since published a second book, *Laughing Without an Accent: Adventures of an Iranian American, at Home and Abroad* (2008), as well as essays in *New York Times Magazine*, the *Los Angeles Times*, the *Wall Street Journal*, the *San Francisco Chronicle*, and *Good Housekeeping*. She also lectures and is an occasional guest on National Public Radio.

Sweet, Sour, and Resentful

Dumas writes, she has said, in part to dispel American fears of Iranian people by revealing their "shared humanity." She does just that in this essay, written for *Gourmet* magazine, by taking a humorous look at the elaborate weekly dinner parties her family hosted when she was a child.

My mother's main ingredient in cooking was resentment—not that I 1 can blame her. In 1979, my family was living temporarily in Newport Beach, California. Our real home was in Abadan, a city in the southwest of Iran. Despite its desert location and ubiquitous refineries, Abadan was the quintessential small town. Everybody's father (including my own) worked for the National Iranian Oil Company, and almost all the moms stayed home. The employees' kids attended the same schools. No one locked their doors. Whenever I hear John Mellencamp's "Small Town," I think of Abadan, although I'm guessing John Mellencamp was thinking of somewhere else when he wrote that song.

By the time of the Iranian revolution, we had adjusted to life in 2 California. We said "Hello" and "Have a nice day" to perfect strangers, wore flip-flops, and grilled cheeseburgers next to our kebabs. We never understood why Americans put ice in tea or bought shampoo that smelled like strawberries, but other than that, America felt like home.

When the revolution happened, thousands left Iran for Southern 3 California. Since we were one of the few Iranian families already there, our phone did not stop ringing. Relatives, friends, friends of relatives, friends of friends, and people whose connection we never quite figured out called us with questions about settling into this new land. Displaying the hospitality that Iranians so cherish, my father extended a dinner invitation to everyone who called. As a result, we found ourselves feeding dozens of people every weekend.

The marathon started on Monday, with my mother planning the 4 menu while letting us know that she was already tired. Fortunately, our rice dishes were made to be shared; our dilemma, however, was space. Our condo was small. Our guests squeezed onto the sofa, sat on the floor, or overflowed onto the patio. We eventually had to explain to our American neighbors why there were so many cars parked in front of our place every weekend. My mother, her diplomatic skills in full swing, had me deliver plates of Persian food, decorated with radish roses and mint sprigs, to them. In time, we learned not to share *fesenjan*, pomegranate stew with ground walnuts. "Yes, now that you mention it, it does look like mud, but it's really good," I'd explain, convincing no one.

Because my mother did not drive, my father took her to buy ingredi- 5 ents every Tuesday after work. In Abadan, my mother and I had started most days in the market, going from vendor to vendor looking for herbs, vegetables, and fruits. The fish came from the Karun and Arvand (Shatt al Arab) rivers, the *lavash* and the *sangak* breads were freshly baked, and the chickens were still alive. We were locavores by necessity and foodies without knowing it. In America, I learned that the time my parents spent shopping was in direct correlation to the degree of my mother's bad mood. An extra-long trip meant that my mother could not find everything she needed, a point she would make loud and clear when she got home: "Why don't they let fruit ripen here?" "Why are the chickens so huge and flavorless?" "I couldn't find fresh herbs." "My feet hurt." "How am I supposed to get everything done?"

The first step was preparing the herbs. My mother insisted that the 6 parsley, cilantro, and chives for *qormeh sabzi*, herb stew, had to be finely chopped by hand. The food processor, she explained, squished them. As she and my father sat across the table wielding huge knives, they argued incessantly. My father did his best to help her. It wasn't enough. As soon as the mountain of herbs was chopped, my mother started frying them. At any given time, my mother was also frying onions. Every few days, while my father was watching the six o'clock news, my mother would hand him a dozen onions, a cutting board, and a knife. No words were exchanged. Much to my father's relief, I once volunteered for this task, but apparently my slices were neither thin enough nor even. It took my father's precision as an engineer to slice correctly.

While all four burners were in use, my mother mixed the ground   7
beef, rice, split peas, scallions, and herbs for stuffed grape leaves. I chopped
the stems of the grape leaves. I had tried stuffing them once, but my rolls,
deemed not tight enough, were promptly unrolled and then rerolled by
my mother.

In between cooking, my mother made yogurt — the thick, sour   8
variety that we couldn't find in America. She soaked walnuts and almonds
in water to plump them up; fried eggplants for *kashk-e bademjan*, a popular appetizer with garlic, turmeric, mint, and whey; made *torshi-e limo*, a
sour lemon condiment; and slivered orange peels. I had been fired from
this task also, having left on far too much pith.

By the time our guests arrived, my mother was exhausted. But, the   9
work was not finished. Rice, the foundation of the Persian meal, the litmus test of the cook's ability, cannot be prepared ahead of time. To wit,
one day in Abadan, the phone rang when my mother was about to drain
the rice. During the time it took her to answer the phone and tell her
sister that she would call her back, the rice overcooked. Almost forty
years later, I still remember my mother's disappointment and her explaining to my father that her sister had time to talk because my aunt's maid
did all the cooking. My aunt did not even drain her own rice.

We certainly did not have a table big enough to set, so we simply   10
stacked dishes and utensils, buffet-style. As the guest list grew, we added
paper plates and plastic utensils. It was always my job to announce that
dinner was ready. As people entered the dining room, they gasped at the
sight of my mother's table. Her *zereshk polow*, barberry rice, made many
emotional. There are no fresh barberries in America (my mother had
brought dried berries from Iran in her suitcase), and the sight of that
dish, with its distinct deep red hue, was a reminder of the life our guests
had left behind.

Our dinners took days to cook and disappeared in twenty minutes.   11
As our guests heaped their plates and looked for a place to sit, they lavished praise on my mother, who, according to tradition, deflected it all.
"It's nothing," she said. "I wish I could've done more." When they told
her how lucky she was to have me to help her, my mother politely nod-
ded, while my father added, "Firoozeh's good at math."

On Sundays, my mother lay on the sofa, her swollen feel elevated,   12
fielding thank-you phone calls from our guests. She had the same conversation a dozen times; each one ended with, "Of course you can give
our name to your cousins." As I watched my mother experience the same
draining routine week after week, I decided that tradition is good only

if it brings joy to all involved. This includes the hostess. Sometimes, even our most cherished beliefs must evolve. Evolution, thy name is potluck.

Vocabulary

If you do not know any of following words, try to determine their meanings from their context in Dumas's essay. Then look them up in a dictionary, and use each one in a sentence of your own:

ubiquitous (1)	locavores (5)	lavished (11)
quintessential (1)	correlation (5)	deflected (11)
Persian (4)	pith (8)	potluck (12)

Key Ideas and Details

1. Why were weekend dinners so important to the author's parents and their guests? Consider not just the meals themselves but the larger context that prompted them.

2. In which sentence or sentences does Dumas state her thesis most directly?

3. What solution to her mother's exhausting role as hostess does Dumas propose in paragraph 12? Do you think her mother would have agreed to it? Why, or why not?

Craft and Structure

1. LANGUAGE Where in the essay does Dumas use Persian words? What is their effect?

2. Why does Dumas begin her essay with an overview of life in Abadan and an allusion to the Iranian revolution (paragraphs 1–3)? What purpose does this opening serve?

3. What steps does Dumas identify in the process of hosting Iranian guests every weekend? How does she ensure that her analysis has coherence? (For a definition of *coherence*, see the Glossary.)

4. OTHER METHODS What role does comparison and contrast play in paragraph 5?

Integration of Knowledge and Ideas

1. What would you say is Dumas's purpose in this essay? Is it primarily to entertain readers by describing her family's weekly routine, or does she seem to have another purpose in mind?

2. How does Dumas seem to imagine her audience? To what extent could she assume that readers would appreciate her mother's situation?

3. In paragraph 9, Dumas says that rice is "the litmus test" for Iranian cooks. What does she mean? What is a litmus test, and how does the phrase connect to the focus (and title) of Dumas's essay?

4. FOR DISCUSSION What impression of herself does Dumas create in this essay? What adjectives would you use to describe the writer as she reveals herself on the page? Cite specific language from the essay to support your analysis.

Writing Topics

1. Think of some rituals that are important to your family—for instance, a holiday celebration, a vacation activity, a way of decompressing after a stressful week. Choose one such ritual and prepare a visually rich presentation that explains it to outsiders. Focus on the details and steps of the ritual itself as well as on the significance it has for you and for other members of your family.

2. Dumas writes about the struggle to adjust to mainstream American culture while maintaining ethnic ties. Based on "Sweet, Sour, and Resentful" and your own observations, write an essay that considers one aspect of the immigrant experience in the United States, such as the challenges of assimilation, the effects of prejudice, or the role of family ties and cultural loyalty.

3. RESEARCH Find some information on the influx of Iranian families into California during the 1970s. What prompted this migration? What quality of life did newcomers face on arrival? What tensions did their arrival create? In an essay, consider these questions and others your research may lead you to. You may prefer to focus on a different migration—such as those during the nineteenth and twentieth centuries of Irish to the eastern United States, Chinese to the western United States, or African Americans from southern to northern states.

4. CONNECTIONS "We were locavores by necessity and foodies without knowing it," Dumas writes in paragraph 5. What does she mean? Read Barbara Kingsolver's "Stalking the Vegetannual" (p. 258), which looks at locavores and epicures in more detail. Using both essays for evidence, write an essay that examines the cultural reasons for importing food from other countries. Why, for instance, does Kingsolver believe that Americans consume fruits and vegetables that were grown thousands of miles away? Why was it so important for the Dumas family to obtain ingredients from Iran? What objections did Dumas's mother have to the foods available in California? What are the benefits and drawbacks of globally available food?

Lars Eighner

An essayist and fiction writer, Lars Eighner was born in 1948 in Corpus Christi, Texas, and attended the University of Texas at Austin. He has contributed essays and stories to *Threepenny Review* and several men's magazines. His novels and volumes of stories include *Bayou Boys and Other Stories* (1985), *American Prelude* (1994), *Whispered in the Dark* (1995), and *Pawn to Queen Four* (1995). In 1988 Eighner became homeless after losing a job he had held for ten years as an attendant in a mental hospital. His memoir about living on the streets, *Travels with Lizbeth* (1993), was critically acclaimed and sold enough copies to get him back on his feet. He now lives in Austin.

Dumpster Diving

This essay from the *Utne Reader* was abridged from a prize-winning piece published in *Threepenny Review* and later included in *Travels with Lizbeth*. Eighner explains a process that you probably do not want to learn: how to subsist on what you can scavenge from trash. But, as Eighner observes, scavenging has lessons to teach about value.

I began Dumpster diving about a year before I became homeless. 1

I prefer the term *scavenging*. I have heard people, evidently meaning 2 to be polite, use the word *foraging*, but I prefer to reserve that word for gathering nuts and berries and such, which I also do, according to the season and opportunity.

I like the frankness of the word *scavenging*. I live from the refuse 3 of others. I am a scavenger. I think it a sound and honorable niche, although if I could I would naturally prefer to live the comfortable consumer life, perhaps—and only perhaps—as a slightly less wasteful consumer owing to what I have learned as a scavenger.

Except for jeans, all my clothes come from Dumpsters. Boom boxes, 4 candles, bedding, toilet paper, medicine, books, a typewriter, . . . coins sometimes amounting to many dollars: all came from Dumpsters. And yes, I eat from Dumpsters, too.

There is a predictable series of stages that a person goes through in 5 learning to scavenge. At first the new scavenger is filled with disgust and self-loathing. He is ashamed of being seen.

This stage passes with experience. The scavenger finds a pair of run- 6 ning shoes that fit and look and smell brand-new. He finds a pocket calculator in perfect working order. He finds pristine ice cream, still frozen, more than he can eat or keep. He begins to understand: people do throw away perfectly good stuff, a lot of perfectly good stuff.

At this stage he may become lost and never recover. All the Dump- 7
ster divers I have known come to the point of trying to acquire everything they touch. Why not take it, they reason, it is all free. This is, of
course, hopeless, and most divers come to realize that they must restrict
themselves to items of relatively immediate utility.

The finding of objects is becoming something of an urban art. Even 8
respectable, employed people will sometimes find something tempting
sticking out of a Dumpster or standing beside one. Quite a number of
people, not all of them of the bohemian type, are willing to brag that
they found this or that piece in the trash.

But eating from Dumpsters is the thing that separates the dilettanti 9
from the professionals. Eating safely involves three principles: using
the senses and common sense to evaluate the condition of the found
materials; knowing the Dumpsters of a given area and checking them
regularly; and seeking always to answer the question "Why was this
discarded?"

Yet perfectly good food can be found in Dumpsters. Canned goods, 10
for example, turn up fairly often in the Dumpsters I frequent. I also have
few qualms about dry goods such as crackers, cookies, cereal, chips, and
pasta if they are free of visible contaminants and still dry and crisp. Raw
fruits and vegetables with intact skins seem perfectly safe to me, exclud-
ing, of course, the obviously rotten. Many are discarded for minor imper-
fections that can be pared away.

A typical discard is a half jar of peanut butter—though nonorganic 11
peanut butter does not require refrigeration and is unlikely to spoil in
any reasonable time. One of my favorite finds is yogurt—often discarded,
still sealed, when the expiration date has passed—because it will keep for
several days, even in warm weather.

No matter how careful I am I still get dysentery at least once a 12
month, oftener in warm weather. I do not want to paint too romantic
a picture. Dumpster diving has serious drawbacks as a way of life.

I find from the experience of scavenging two rather deep lessons. 13
The first is to take what I can use and let the rest go. I have come to
think that there is no value in the abstract. A thing I cannot use or make
useful, perhaps by trading, has no value, however fine or rare it may be.

The second lesson is the transience of material being. I do not sup- 14
pose that ideas are immortal, but certainly they are longer-lived than
material objects.

The things I find in Dumpsters, the love letters and rag dolls of so 15
many lives, remind me of this lesson. Now I hardly pick up a thing
without envisioning the time I will cast it away. This, I think, is a healthy

state of mind. Almost everything I have now has already been cast out at least once, proving that what I own is valueless to someone.

I find that my desire to grab for the gaudy bauble has been largely   16
sated. I think this is an attitude I share with the very wealthy—we both know there is plenty more where whatever we have came from. Between us are the rat-race millions who have confounded their selves with the objects they grasp and who nightly scavenge the cable channels for they know not what.

I am sorry for them.   17

Vocabulary

If you do not know the meanings of the following words, try to guess them from their context in Eighner's essay. Then look them up in a dictionary, and use each one in a sentence of your own:

scavenging (2)	qualms (10)	bauble (16)
foraging (2)	contaminants (10)	sated (16)
refuse (3)	dysentery (12)	confounded (16)
niche (3)	transience (14)	
dilettanti (9)	gaudy (16)	

Key Ideas and Details

1. Eighner ends his essay with the statement "I am sorry for them." Whom is he sorry for, and why? How does this statement relate to the main point of Eighner's essay?

2. How does Eighner decide what to keep when he digs through Dumpsters? How does he decide a thing's value? What evidence in the essay supports your answer?

Craft and Structure

1. LANGUAGE Eighner's style is often formal: consider the word choice and order in such phrases as "I think it a sound and honorable niche" (paragraph 3) and "who nightly scavenge the cable channels for they know not what" (16). Find at least three other instances of formal style. What is the effect of this language, and how does it further Eighner's purpose? (If necessary, consult *style* in the Glossary.)

2. Eighner says of his life as a scavenger, "I do not want to paint too romantic a picture. Dumpster diving has serious drawbacks as a way of life" (paragraph 12). How would you characterize the tone of this statement? Where else in the essay do you find this tone?

3. Eighner identifies three main stages "a person goes through in learning to scavenge" (paragraph 5). What are these stages, and do all scavengers experience each one? Support your answer with evidence from the essay.

4. OTHER METHODS In paragraph 2 Eighner uses definition (Chapter 13) to distinguish *foraging* from *scavenging*. What distinction does he make? How does it relate to the overall meaning of the essay?

Integration of Knowledge and Ideas

1. How does paragraph 2 reveal that Eighner's purpose is not simply to explain how to scavenge but also to persuade his readers to examine any stereotypes they may hold about scavengers?

2. In paragraphs 10 and 11 Eighner goes into considerable detail about the food he finds in Dumpsters. Why do you think he does this?

3. FOR DISCUSSION Eighner writes that since he became a scavenger he hardly "pick[s] up a thing without envisioning the time I will cast it away. This, I think, is a healthy state of mind" (paragraph 15). Do you agree? What associations do you have with material objects that cause you to support or deny Eighner's claim? Prepare to argue either for or against Eighner's position, making sure to provide your own illustrations to support your opinion.

Writing Topics

1. Eighner writes that he and the very wealthy share the attitude that "there is plenty more where whatever we have came from" (paragraph 16). In your experience, how true is this statement? Do you agree that one needs to be very poor or very rich to feel this way? Is this state of mind a response to the amount of money one has, or can it be developed independently, regardless of one's wealth or lack of it? Write an essay describing how you think people arrive at a belief that "there is plenty more" available of whatever it is they have.

2. Eighner attempts to teach his readers how to scavenge, certainly, but he also attempts to persuade readers to examine their stereotypes about the homeless. Write an essay in which you examine your stereotypes about homeless people. Describe both personal encounters and media images, and discuss how these experiences led to your beliefs. Finally, consider the extent to which "Dumpster Diving" changed your perspective.

3. RESEARCH Do you regard waste and pollution as critical problems? Do you believe that the government is taking adequate steps to protect the environment? Do you believe that the actions of individuals can make a difference? Look for information on one of these issues and write an essay or prepare

a speech about protection of the environment. Your essay or speech may be an argument, but it doesn't have to be: that is, you could explain your answer to any of these questions or argue a specific point. Either way, use examples and details from sources to support your ideas.

4. CONNECTIONS If you live in or have visited an urban area, you have probably seen people picking through Dumpsters or garbage cans, looking for items such as food, clothing, and bottles or cans that can be returned for a deposit. Consider your own experiences and observations as well as the information and ideas in Eighner's essay and in Barbara Lazear Ascher's "The Box Man" (p. 9). Write an essay proposing a solution to the social problems of extreme poverty and homelessness.

Barbara Kingsolver

Barbara Kingsolver is a well-known naturalist and best-selling author of more than a dozen novels, short-story and poetry collections, and nonfiction books, including *The Bean Trees* (1988), *The Poisonwood Bible* (1998), *Small Wonder* (2002), *Animal, Vegetable, Miracle* (2007), and *The Lacuna* (2009). She was born in 1955 in Annapolis, Maryland, grew up in rural Kentucky, and earned degrees in biology and ecology from DePauw University and the University of Arizona. Kingsolver worked briefly as a lab assistant before taking an office position at the University of Arizona and building a career as a writer. An activist with a strong sense of social justice, Kingsolver has written that "good art is political, whether it means to be or not, insofar as it provides the chance to understand points of view alien to our own." She lives in the Appalachian region of Virginia with her husband and two daughters.

Stalking the Vegetannual

Animal, Vegetable, Miracle documents a year in the life of Kingsolver and her family, when they moved to an ancestral farm and challenged themselves to eat only what they could produce themselves or obtain from local growers. In this excerpt from the book, Kingsolver advises how to recognize what vegetables are in season, a skill largely lost in a society accustomed to seeing strawberries and asparagus in the supermarket year-round.

If potatoes can surprise some part of their audience by growing leaves,   1
it may not have occurred to everyone that lettuce has a flower part. It does, they all do. Virtually all nonanimal foods we eat come from flowering plants. Exceptions are mushrooms, seaweeds, and pine nuts. If other exotic edibles exist that you call food, I salute you.

Flowering plants, known botanically as angiosperms, evolved from   2
ancestors similar to our modern-day conifers. The flower is a handy
reproductive organ that came into its own during the Cretaceous era,[1]
right around the time when dinosaurs were for whatever reason getting downsized. In the millions of years since then, flowering plants
have established themselves as the most conspicuously successful terrestrial life forms ever, having moved into every kind of habitat, in infinite variations. Flowering plants are key players in all the world's eco-
types: the deciduous forests, the rain forests, the grasslands. They are the
desert cacti and the tundra scrub. They're small and they're large, they
fill swamps and tolerate drought, they have settled into most every
niche in every kind of place. It only stands to reason that we would
eat them.

Flowering plants come in packages as different as an oak tree and a   3
violet, but they all have a basic life history in common. They sprout and
leaf out; they bloom and have sex by somehow rubbing one flower's
boy stuff against another's girl parts. Since they can't engage in hot pursuit, they lure a third party, such as bees, into the sexual act—or else
(depending on species) wait for the wind. From that union comes the
blessed event, babies made, in the form of seeds cradled inside some
form of fruit. Finally, sooner or later—because after *that*, what's the point
anymore?—they die. Among the plants known as annuals, this life history is accomplished all in a single growing season, commonly starting
with spring and ending with frost. The plant waits out the winter in the
form of a seed, safely protected from weather, biding its time until conditions are right for starting over again. The vegetables we eat may be
leaves, buds, fruits, or seeds, but each comes to us from some point along
this same continuum, the code all annual plants must live by. No variations are allowed. They can't set fruit, for example, before they bloom.
As obvious as this may seem, it's easy enough to forget in a supermarket
culture where the plant stages constantly present themselves in random
order.

To recover an intuitive sense of what will be in season throughout   4
the year, picture a season of foods unfolding as if from one single plant.
Take a minute to study this creation—an imaginary plant that bears
over the course of one growing season a cornucopia of all the different
vegetable products we can harvest. We'll call it a vegetannual. Picture its

---

[1] Roughly 145–65 million years ago. [Editors' note.]

life passing before your eyes like a time-lapse film: first, in the cool early spring, shoots poke up out of the ground. Small leaves appear, then bigger leaves. As the plant grows up into the sunshine and the days grow longer, flower buds will appear, followed by small green fruits. Under midsummer's warm sun, the fruits grow larger, riper, and more colorful. As days shorten into the autumn, these mature into hard-shelled fruits with appreciable seeds inside. Finally, as the days grow cool, the vegetannual may hoard the sugars its leaves have made, pulling them down into a storage unit of some kind: a tuber, bulb, or root.

So goes the year. First the leaves: spinach, kale, lettuce, and chard 5 (here, that's April and May). Then more mature heads of leaves and flower heads: cabbage, romaine, broccoli, and cauliflower (May–June). Then tender young fruit-set: snow peas, baby squash, cucumbers (June), followed by green beans, green peppers, and small tomatoes (July). Then more mature, colorfully ripened fruits: beefsteak tomatoes, eggplants, red and yellow peppers (late July–August). Then the large, hard-shelled fruits with developed seeds inside: cantaloupes, honeydews, watermelons, pumpkins, winter squash (August–September). Last come the root crops, and so ends the produce parade.

Plainly these don't all come from the same plant, but each comes 6 from a *plant*, that's the point—a plant predestined to begin its life in the spring and die in the fall. (A few, like onions and carrots, are attempting to be biennials, but we'll ignore that for now.) Each plant part we eat must come in its turn—leaves, buds, flowers, green fruits, ripe fruits, hard fruits—because that is the necessary order of things for an annual plant. For the life of them, they can't do it differently.

Some minor deviations and a bit of overlap are allowed, but in gen- 7 eral picturing an imaginary vegetannual plant is a pretty reliable guide to what will be in season, wherever you live. If you find yourself eating a watermelon in April, you can count back three months and imagine a place warm enough in January for this plant to have launched its destiny. Mexico maybe, or southern California. Chile is also a possibility. If you're inclined to think this way, consider what it took to transport a finicky fruit the size of a human toddler to your door, from that locale.

Our gardening forebears meant watermelon to be the juicy, bare- 8 foot taste of a hot summer's end, just as a pumpkin is the trademark fruit of late October. Most of us accept the latter, and limit our jack-o'lantern activities to the proper botanical season. Waiting for a watermelon is harder. It's tempting to reach for melons, red peppers, tomatoes, and other late-summer delights before the summer even arrives. But it's actually possible to wait, celebrating each season when it comes, not fretting about its being absent at all other times because something else good is at hand.

If many of us would view this style of eating as deprivation, that's 9 only because we've grown accustomed to the botanically outrageous condition of having everything, always. This may be the closest thing we have right now to a distinctive national cuisine. Well-heeled North American epicures are likely to gather around a table where whole continents collide discreetly on a white tablecloth: New Zealand lamb with Italian porcinis,[2] Peruvian asparagus, and a hearty French Bordeaux.[3] The date on the calendar is utterly irrelevant.

I've enjoyed my share of such meals, but I'm beginning at least to 10 notice when I'm consuming the United Nations of edible plants and animals all in one seating. (Or the WTO,[4] is more like it.) On a winter's day not long ago I was served a sumptuous meal like this, finished off with a dessert of raspberries. Because they only grow in temperate zones, not the tropics, these would have come from somewhere deep in the Southern Hemisphere. I was amazed that such small, eminently bruisable fruits could survive a zillion-mile trip looking so good (I myself look pretty wrecked after a mere red-eye from California), and I mumbled some reserved awe over that fact. I think my hostess was amused by my country-mouse naiveté. "This is New York," she assured me. "We can get anything we want, any day of the year."

So it is. And I don't wish to be ungracious, but we get it at a price. 11 Most of that is not measured in money, but in untallied debts that will be paid by our children in the currency of extinctions, economic unravelings, and global climate change. I do know it's impolite to raise such objections at the dinner table. Seven raspberries are not (I'll try to explain someday to my grandkids) the end of the world. I ate them and said "Thank you." ...

The business of importing foods across great distances is not, by its 12 nature, a boon to Third World farmers, but it's very good business for oil companies. Transporting a single calorie of a perishable fresh fruit from California to New York takes about eighty-seven calories worth of

---

[2] Mushrooms. [Editors' note.]
[3] Wine. [Editors' note.]
[4] World Trade Organization. [Editors' note.]

fuel. That's as efficient as driving from Philadelphia to Annapolis, and back, in order to walk three miles on a treadmill in a Maryland gym. . . .

In many social circles it's ordinary for hosts to accommodate vege-   13
tarian guests, even if they're carnivores themselves. Maybe the world would likewise become more hospitable to diners who are queasy about fuel-guzzling foods, if that preference had a name. Petrolophobes? Sea-sonaltarians? Local eaters, Homeys? Lately I've begun seeing the term *locavores*, and I like it: both scientifically and socially descriptive, with just the right hint of "Livin' *la vida loca*."[5]

Slow Food International has done a good job of putting a smile on   14
this eating style, rather than a pious frown, even while sticking to the quixotic agenda of fighting overcentralized agribusiness. The engaging strategy of the Slowies (their logo is a snail) is to celebrate what we have, standing up for the pleasures that seasonal eating can bring. They have their work cut out for them, as the American brain trust seems mostly blank on that subject. Consider the frustration of the man who wrote in this complaint to a food columnist: having studied the new food pyra-mid brought to us by the US Dietary Guidelines folks (impossible to deci-pher but bless them, they do keep trying), he had his marching orders for "2 cups of fruit, 2½ cups of vegetables a day." So he marched down to his grocery and bought (honest to Pete) eighty-three plums, pears, peaches, and apples. Outraged, he reported that virtually the entire lot was "rotten, mealy, tasteless, juiceless, or hard as a rock and refusing to ripen."

Given the date of the column, this had occurred in February or   15
March. The gentleman lived in Frostburg, Maryland, where they would still have been deeply involved in a thing called winter. I'm sure he didn't really think tasty tree-ripened plums, peaches, and apples were hanging outside ripe for the picking in the orchards around . . . um, *Frost*-burg. Probably he didn't think "orchard" at all—how many of us do, in the same sentence with "fruit"? Our dietary guidelines come to us without a roadmap.

Concentrating on local foods means thinking of fruit invariably as   16
the product of an orchard, and a winter squash as the fruit of an early-winter farm. It's a strategy that will keep grocery money in the neigh-borhood where it gets recycled into your own school system and local businesses. The green spaces surrounding your town stay green, and farmers who live nearby get to grow more food next year, for you. But

---

[5] Spanish: "the crazy life." [Editors' note.]

before any of that, it's a win-win strategy for anyone with taste buds. It begins with rethinking a position that is only superficially about deprivation. Citizens of frosty worlds unite, and think about marching past the off-season fruits: you have nothing to lose but mealy, juiceless, rock-hard and refusing to ripen.

Vocabulary

Some of the following words may be new to you. Before looking them up in a dictionary, try to guess their meanings from their context in Kingsolver's essay. Then use each new word in a sentence.

botanical (2, 8, 9)	tuber (4)	sumptuous (10)
conifers (2)	predestined (6)	temperate (10)
terrestrial (2)	biennials (6)	eminently (10)
ecotypes (2)	deviations (7)	untallied (11)
deciduous (2)	forebears (8)	boon (12)
tundra (2)	latter (8)	hospitable (13)
scrub (2)	fretting (8)	pious (14)
annuals (3, 6)	deprivation (9, 16)	quixotic (14)
continuum (3)	epicures (9)	invariably (16)
cornucopia (4)	discreetly (9)	

Key Ideas and Details

1. What, according to Kingsolver, is a *vegetannual*? What does it have to do with her purpose for writing?

2. Consider the possible meanings of the word *stalking* in Kingsolver's title. How does the word help preview the focus of her essay?

3. Kingsolver comments in paragraph 9 that "we've grown accustomed to the botanically outrageous condition of having everything, always." What does she mean? Why is this situation "outrageous"?

Craft and Structure

1. LANGUAGE Notice Kingsolver's use of personification to explain the life cycle of plants in paragraph 3. (If necessary, see p. 58 for a definition of personification.) What does this figure of speech add to (or detract from) her analysis?

2. Take a close look at the drawing that opens the essay. What does it represent? Where in her essay does Kingsolver discuss it, and what does it have to do with her subject?

3. Despite the fact that her purpose goes beyond mere explanation, does Kingsolver explain the process of plant growth clearly enough for you to understand how it works and why it matters? What are the main stages of the process?

4. OTHER METHODS The process analysis portion of "Stalking the Vegetannual" seems to come to an end at paragraph 9. Why do you suppose Kingsolver turns to example (Chapter 8), cause-and-effect analysis (Chapter 14), and argument and persuasion (Chapter 15) to complete her thoughts?

Integration of Knowledge and Ideas

1. Why does Kingsolver withhold her thesis statement until the very last sentence of her essay? How would you have reacted to her main idea if she had opened with it?

2. Kingsolver's chief assumption about her readers is evident in paragraph 9. What is it?

3. FOR DISCUSSION How does the author attempt to make her ideas accessible while also maintaining her sophistication? In your opinion, is this essay difficult to read, easy to read, or something in between? Why?

Writing Topics

1. Current dietary guidelines recommend eating at least five servings of fruits and vegetables a day. Assuming you wanted to follow this advice, how easy, or difficult, would it be for you to do so? What kinds of fruits and vegetables do you eat, and how often do you eat them? Now that you've read Kingsolver's essay, do you have any misgivings about your habits? Has she inspired you to change the way you look at food? Why, or why not? Explain your answers in a brief essay.

2. Our attitudes toward foods are often influenced by the family, community, or larger culture in which we grew up. Think of feelings that you have about a particular food that seem at least partly due to other people. In a short presentation or essay, describe the food and your feelings about it and explain the origins of your feelings as best you can.

3. RESEARCH How do you react to Kingsolver's essay? Do you agree with her that a person's food choices have broad-ranging environmental and economic consequences? Or do you think her solution is impractical and overly idealistic? Research the arguments for and against local foods and write an essay responding to Kingsolver's ideas. Be sure to include examples and expert opinions to support your view, citing your sources according to the guidelines on pages 63–82.

4. CONNECTIONS In "Dumpster Diving" (p. 253), Lars Eighner comments that he is accustomed to "gathering nuts and berries and such . . . according to the season and opportunity." But, unlike Kingsolver, he doesn't have much choice in what or when he eats. Or does he? Write an essay that considers what these two writers, who live under very different circumstances, share in their attitudes toward food and the environment.

WRITING WITH THE METHOD

PROCESS ANALYSIS

Select one of the following topics, or any other topic they suggest, for an essay developed by process analysis. Be sure to choose a topic you care about so that process analysis is a means of communicating an idea, not an end in itself.

Technology and the Environment

1. How an engine or other machine works
2. How the Internet works
3. How to set up a recycling program in a home or a school
4. How solar energy can be converted into electricity

Education and Work

5. How children learn to dress themselves, play with others, read, or write
6. Reading a newspaper
7. Finding a summer job
8. Succeeding in biology, history, computer science, or another course
9. Choosing a career

Entertainment and Hobbies

10. Performing a magic trick
11. Throwing a really *bad* party
12. Climbing a mountain
13. Playing a sport or a musical instrument
14. Making great chili or some other dish

Family and Friends

15. Offering constructive criticism to a friend
16. Driving your parents, brother, sister, friend, or teacher crazy
17. Minimizing sibling rivalry
18. Making new friends in a new place

WRITING ABOUT THE THEME

EATING WELL

1. All of the writers in this chapter offer techniques for overcoming difficulties with eating: Mark Fischetti shows how microwave ovens use dangerous energy waves to heat food (p. 238); L. Rust Hills equates an ice-cream cone with a live bomb (p. 241); Jane Brody emphasizes the challenges faced by dieters (p. 242); Firoozeh Dumas describes the frustrations of preparing intricate dishes with inadequate resources (p. 248); Lars Eighner reports experiencing "disgust and self-loathing" while scavenging (p. 253); and even Barbara Kingsolver faces social obstacles in her quest to avoid nonlocal foods (p. 258). Using these works as models, write a process analysis about an activity you find simultaneously difficult and rewarding, making sure to convey both feelings to your readers.

2. Firoozeh Dumas and Barbara Kingsolver host and attend dinner parties that feature exotic foods imported from around the globe, while Lars Eighner subsists on the food that other people throw away. How do you feel about this kind of discrepancy? Is eating well a basic human right, or is food just another commodity governed by the laws of supply and demand? Can the problem of world hunger be solved? Explain your answers in an essay. Be sure to back up your general statements with specific examples and other evidence.

3. Some writers in this chapter reveal mixed feelings about the business side of eating. Jane Brody expresses concern about the safety and effectiveness of commercial weight-loss plans. Firoozeh Dumas describes her mother's disdain for the low quality of the food sold in California supermarkets. And Barbara Kingsolver speaks of "fighting overcentralized agribusiness." How do you feel about the food and diet industries? Do you trust the companies that grow, process, and distribute the food you eat? What do you think accounts for your attitude? Drawing on the readings in this chapter and your own experience, write an essay that explains why you do, or don't, have faith in the food industry.

12

COMPARISON AND CONTRAST

▶

EXAMINING STEREOTYPES

An insomniac watching late-night television faces a choice between two vampire movies broadcasting at the same time. To make up her mind, she uses the dual method of comparison and contrast:

- **Comparison** shows the similarities between two or more subjects: the similar broadcast times and topics of the two movies force the insomniac to choose between them.

- **Contrast** shows the differences between subjects: the different actors, locations, and reputations of the two movies make it possible for the insomniac to choose one.

As in the example, comparison and contrast usually work together, because any subjects that warrant side-by-side examination usually resemble each other in some respects and differ in others. (Since comparison and contrast are so closely related, the terms *comparison* and *compare* will be used from now on to designate both.) You use the method instinctively whenever you need to choose among options—for instance, two candidates in a school election, three tiers of colleges, or several pairs of running shoes. You might also use comparison to make sense of competing proposals for preventing bullying, to explain how a shopping mall has changed in the past year, or to determine whether you should be more concerned about the sun's harmful rays or the chemicals in sunscreen. Writers, too, often draw on the method, especially when a comparison can explain something that may be unfamiliar to their readers.

Seeing Comparison and Contrast

You've probably seen *Freedom from Want*, Norman Rockwell's famous 1943 painting of an American family at the Thanksgiving table.

269

Commissioned for a poster promoting the sale of war bonds, Rockwell's painting illustrates one of the "Four Freedoms"—of speech, of worship, from want, from fear—whose protection President Franklin Delano Roosevelt cited as justification for entering World War II. You probably haven't seen Art Spiegelman's *Freedom from Want*, however. After the terrorist attacks on the United States of September 11, 2001, a wave of violence against Muslims spread across the country. Hundreds of innocent Arab Americans were assaulted, and several killed, because attackers believed their religion connected them with al Qaeda. Spiegelman, best known for *Maus*, a graphic novel about the Holocaust, responded to the misplaced hatred by reworking Rockwell's painting as a drawing of a Muslim family under attack. (He submitted it as cover art for the *New Yorker*, but the cover never ran.) Notice both the similarities and the differences in the two images. How does Spiegelman adapt an iconic American image to make a point about stereotypes? about freedoms? about wars? What argument does he seem to be making, and how do you react to his claim?

Reading Comparison and Contrast

Writers generally use comparison for one of two purposes:

- To *explain* the similarities and differences between subjects so as to make either or both of them clear
- To *evaluate* subjects so as to establish their advantages and disadvantages, strengths and weaknesses

The explanatory comparison does not take a position on the relative merits of the subjects; the evaluative comparison does, and it usually concludes with a preference or a suggested course of action. An explanatory comparison in a consumer magazine, for example, might show the similarities and differences between two popular music download services; an evaluative comparison on the same subject might argue that one service is better than the other.

Whether explanatory or evaluative, comparisons treat two or more subjects in the same general class or group: traffic accidents, religions, attitudes toward marriage, diseases, advertising strategies, diets, contact sports, friends. A writer may define the class to suit his or her interest—for instance, a television critic might focus on crime dramas, on cable news programs, or on situation comedies. The class likeness ensures that the subjects share enough features to make comparison worthwhile. With subjects from different classes, such as an insect and a tree, the similarities are so few and differences so numerous—and both are so obvious—that explaining them would be pointless.

In putting together a comparison, a writer selects subjects from the same class and then, using division or analysis, identifies the features shared by the subjects. These **points of comparison** are the characteristics of the class and thus of the subjects within the class. For instance, the points of comparison for music download services may be music selection, price per song, and device compatibility; for air pollutants they may be sources and dangers to plants, animals, and humans. These points help to arrange similarities and differences between subjects, and, more important, they ensure direct comparison rather than a random listing of unrelated characteristics.

In an effective comparison, a thesis or controlling idea governs the choice of class, points of comparison, and specific similarities and differences, while also making the comparison worthwhile for the reader.

With two or more subjects, several points of comparison, many similarities and differences, and a particular emphasis, comparison clearly requires a firm organizational hand. Writers have two options for arranging a comparison:

- *Subject by subject*, in which the points of comparison are grouped under each *subject* so that the subjects are covered one at a time.

- *Point by point*, in which the subjects are grouped under each point of comparison so that the *points* are covered one at a time.

The following brief outlines illustrate the different arrangements as they might be applied to music download services:

Subject by subject	*Point by point*
Tunelet	Music selection
Music selection	Tunelet
Price per song	Spindle
Device compatibilit	Price per song
Spindle	Tunelet
Music selection	Spindle
Price per song	Device compatibility
Device compatibility	Tunelet
	Spindle

Since the subject-by-subject arrangement presents each subject as a coherent unit, it is particularly useful for comparing impressions of subjects: the dissimilar characters of two good friends, for instance. However, covering the subjects one at a time can break an essay into discrete pieces and strain readers' memories, so this arrangement is usually confined to essays that are short or that compare several subjects briefly. For longer comparisons requiring precise treatment of the individual points — say, an evaluation of two proposals for a new subsidized meal program — the point-by-point arrangement is more useful. Its chief disadvantage is that the reader can get lost in the details and fail to see any subject as a whole. Because each arrangement has its strengths and weaknesses, writers sometimes combine the two in a single work, using the divided arrangement to introduce or summarize overall impressions of the subjects and using the alternating arrangement to deal specifically with the points of comparison.

Analyzing Comparison and Contrast in Paragraphs

Michael Dorris (1945–97) was a fiction and nonfiction writer who, as a member of the Modoc tribe, explored Native American issues and experiences. The following paragraph comes from "Noble Savages? We'll Drink to That," first published in the *New York Times*.

For centuries, flesh and blood Indians have been assigned the role of a popular-culture metaphor. Today, their evocation instantly connotes fuzzy images of Nature, the Past, Plight, or Summer Camp. War-bonneted apparitions pasted to football helmets or baseball caps act as opaque, impermeable curtains, solid walls of white noise that for many citizens block or distort all vision of the nearly two million Native Americans today. And why not? Such honoring relegates Indians to the long ago and thus makes them magically disappear from public consciousness and conscience. What do the 300 federally recognized tribes, and their various complicated treaties governing land rights and protections, their crippling teenage suicide rates, their manifold health problems have in common with jolly (or menacing) cartoon caricatures, wistful braves, or raven-tressed Mazola girls?

Subject-by-subject organization

1. The image in popular culture

Comparison clarified by transitions (underlined once) and repetition (underlined twice)

2. The reality of Native American life

Julia Álvarez (born 1950) is a novelist, poet, essayist, and teacher. Born in New York and raised in the Dominican Republic until the age of ten, Álvarez often writes about the complexities of immigration and bicultural identity. In this paragraph from her essay "A White Woman of Color," she examines class tensions within her immediate family.

It was Mami's family who were *really* white. They were white in terms of race, and white also in terms of class. From them came the fine features, the pale skin, the lank hair. Her brothers and uncles went to schools abroad and had important businesses in the country. . . . Not that Papi's family weren't smart and enterprising, all twenty-five brothers and sisters. (The size of the family in and of itself was considered very country by some members of Mami's family.) Many of Papi's brothers had gone to the university and become professionals. But their education was totally island—no fancy degrees from Andover and Cornell and Yale, no summer camps or school songs in another language. Papi's family still lived in the interior versus the capital, in old-fashioned houses without air conditioning, decorated in ways my mother's family would have considered, well, tasteless. . . . They were *criollos*—creoles—rather than cosmopolitans, expansive, proud, colorful. . . . Their features were less aquiline than Mother's family's, the skin darker, the hair coarse and curly. Their money still had the smell of the earth on it and was kept in a wad in their back pockets, whereas my mother's family had money in the Chase Manhattan Bank, most of it with George Washington's picture on it, not Juan Pablo Duarte's.

Point-by-point organization

1. Education

Comparison clarified by transitions (underlined once) and repetition (underlined twice)

2. Housing

3. Appearance

4. Money

Developing an Essay by Comparison and Contrast

▶ Getting Started

Whenever you observe similarities or differences between two or more members of the same general class—activities, people, ideas, things, places—you have a possible subject for comparison and contrast. Just be sure that the subjects are worth comparing and that you can do the job in the space and time allowed. For instance, if you have a week to complete a three-page paper, don't try to show all the similarities and differences between country music and rhythm and blues. The effort can only frustrate you and irritate your readers. Instead, limit the subjects to a manageable size—for instance, the lyrics of a representative song in each type of music—so that you can develop the comparisons completely and specifically.

To generate ideas for a comparison, explore each subject separately to pick out its characteristics, and then explore the subjects together to see what characteristics one suggests for the other. Look for points of comparison. Early on, you can use division or analysis (Chapter 9) to identify points of comparison by breaking the subjects' general class into its elements. A song lyric, for instance, could be divided into story line or plot, basic emotion, and special language such as dialect or slang. After you have explored your subjects fully, you can use classification (Chapter 10) to group your characteristics under the points of comparison. For instance, you might classify characteristics of two proposals for a new subsidized meal program into qualifications for eligibility, minimum and maximum amounts to be made available, and payment terms.

As you gain increasing control over your material, consider also the needs of your readers:

- Do they know your subjects well, or will you need to take special care to explain one or both of them?
- Will your readers be equally interested in similarities and differences, or will they find one more enlightening than the other?

▶ Forming a Thesis

While you are shaping your ideas, you should also begin formulating your controlling idea, your thesis. The first thing you should do is look over your points of comparison and determine whether they suggest an explanatory or evaluative approach.

The thesis of an evaluative comparison will generally emerge naturally because it coincides with your purpose of supporting a preference for one subject over another:

THESIS SENTENCE (EVALUATION)   Both download services offer a wide range of music, but Spindle is less expensive and more flexible than Tunelet.

In an explanatory comparison, however, your thesis will need to do more than merely reflect your general purpose in explaining. It should go beyond the obvious and begin to identify the points of comparison. For example:

> DRAFT THESIS SENTENCE (EXPLANATION)   Rugby and American football are the same in some respects and different in others.

> REVISED THESIS SENTENCE (EXPLANATION)   Though rugby requires less strength and more stamina than American football, the two games are very much alike in their rules and strategies.

These examples suggest other decisions you must make when formulating a thesis:

- Will you emphasize both subjects equally or stress one over the other?
- Will you emphasize differences, similarities, or both?

Keeping your readers in mind as you make these decisions will make it easier to use your thesis to shape the body of your essay. For instance, if you decide to write an evaluative comparison and your readers are likely to be biased against your preference or recommendation, you will need to support your case with plenty of specific reasons. If the subjects are equally familiar or important to your readers (as the music download services are in the previous example), you'll want to give them equal emphasis, but if one subject is unfamiliar (as rugby is in the United States), you will probably need to stress it over the other.

Knowing your audience will also help you decide whether to focus on similarities, differences, or both. Generally, you'll stress the differences between subjects your readers consider similar (such as music download services) and the similarities between subjects they are likely to consider different (such as rugby and American football).

▶ Organizing

Your readers' needs and expectations can also help you plan your essay's organization. An effective **introduction** to a comparison essay often provides some context for readers—the situation that prompts the comparison, for instance, or the need for the comparison. Placing your thesis sentence in the introduction also informs readers of your purpose and point, and it may help keep you focused while you write.

For the body of the essay, choose the arrangement that will present your material most clearly and effectively. Remember that the subject-by-subject arrangement suits brief essays comparing dominant impressions of the subjects, whereas the point-by-point arrangement suits longer essays requiring emphasis on the individual points of comparison. If you are torn between the two—wanting both to sum up each subject and to show the two side by side—then a combined arrangement may be your wisest choice.

A rough outline like the models on page 275 can help you plan the basic arrangement of your essay and also the order of the subjects and points of comparison. If your subjects are equally familiar to your readers and equally important to you, then it may not matter which subject you treat first, even in a subject-by-subject arrangement. But if one subject is less familiar or if you favor one, then that one should probably come second. You can also arrange the points themselves to reflect their importance and your readers' knowledge: from least to most significant or complex, from most to least familiar. Be sure to use the same order for both subjects.

Most readers know intuitively how comparison and contrast works, so they will expect you to balance your comparison feature for feature as well. In other words, all the features mentioned for the first subject should be mentioned as well for the second, and any features not mentioned for the first subject should not suddenly materialize for the second.

The **conclusion** to a comparison essay can help readers see the whole picture: the chief similarities and differences between two subjects compared in a divided arrangement, or the chief characteristics of subjects compared in an alternating arrangement. In addition, you may want to comment on the significance of your comparison, advise readers on how they can use the information you have provided, or recommend a specific course of action for them to follow. As with all other methods of development, the choice of conclusion should reflect the impression you want to leave with readers.

▶ Drafting

Drafting your essay gives you the chance to spell out your comparison so that it supports your thesis or, if you're still unsure of your thesis, to discover what you think by writing about your subject. You can use paragraphs to help manage the comparison as it unfolds:

- In a subject-by-subject arrangement, if you devote two paragraphs to the first subject, try to do the same for the second subject. For both subjects, try to cover the points of comparison in the same order and group the same ones in paragraphs.

- In a point-by-point arrangement, balance the paragraphs as you move back and forth between subjects. If you treat several points of comparison for the first subject in one paragraph, do the same for the second subject. If you apply a single point of comparison to both subjects in one paragraph, do the same for the next point of comparison.

This way of drafting will help you achieve balance in your comparison and see where you may need more information to flesh out your subjects and your points. If the finished draft seems too rigid in its pattern, you can always loosen things up when revising.

▶ Revising and Editing

When you are revising and editing your draft, use the following questions and the information in the focus box on pages 278–79 to be certain that your essay meets the principal requirements of the comparative method.

- *Are your subjects drawn from the same class?* The subjects must have notable differences and notable similarities to make comparison worthwhile—though, of course, you may stress one group over the other.

- *Does your essay have a clear purpose and say something significant about the subject?* Your purpose of explaining or evaluating *and* the point you are making should be evident in your thesis and throughout the essay. A vague, pointless comparison will quickly bore readers.

- *Do you apply all points of comparison to both subjects?* Even if you emphasize one subject, the two subjects must match feature for feature. An unmatched comparison may leave readers with unanswered questions or weaken their confidence in your authority.

- *Does the pattern of comparison suit readers' needs and the complexity of the material?* Although readers will appreciate a clear organization and roughly equal treatment of your subjects and points of comparison, they will also appreciate some variety in the way you move back and forth. You needn't devote a sentence to each point, first for one subject and then for the other, or alternate subjects sentence by sentence through several paragraphs. Instead, you might write a single sentence on one point or subject but four sentences on the other—if that's what your information requires.

FOCUS ON **Parallelism**

With several points of comparison and alternating subjects, a comparison will be easy for your readers to follow only if you emphasize likenesses and differences in your wording. Take advantage of the technique of parallelism discussed on page 55. Parallelism — the use of similar grammatical structures for elements of similar importance — will help you balance your comparisons and clarify the relation between elements.

All of the essays in this chapter use parallel structure for clarity and emphasis. Here are a few examples:

> [Neat people] wouldn't consider <u>clipping</u> a coupon, <u>saving</u> a leftover, <u>reusing</u> plastic nondairy whipped cream containers, or <u>rinsing</u> off tin foil and <u>draping</u> it over the unmoldy dish drainer.   — *Suzanne Britt*

> <u>I am not comfortably middle class; I am uncomfortably middle class.</u>
>   — *Leanita McClain*

> I have never had to choose <u>which streets I will walk down</u> and <u>which streets I will avoid.</u>   — *Cheryl Peck*

While parallelism can help readers follow a comparison, lack of parallelism can distract or confuse them. As you edit, look for groups of related ideas. To make the elements of a comparison parallel, repeat the forms of words, phrases, and sentences:

NONPARALLEL Both music services allow subscribers to download songs to their <u>computers</u>, <u>MP3 players</u>, or <u>a mobile device</u>.

PARALLEL Both music services allow subscribers to download songs to their computers, MP3 players, or <u>mobile devices</u>.

NONPARALLEL <u>Tunelet sells</u> songs individually, but <u>Spindle users can get</u> unlimited downloads for a monthly subscription fee.

PARALLEL Tunelet sells songs individually, but <u>Spindle allows</u> unlimited downloads for a monthly subscription fee.

For more on parallelism, see page 55.

Practice

Edit each of the following sentences or groups of sentences to repair instances of faulty parallelism.

1. Most people would rather get a tooth pulled than speaking in public.

2. The most popular country songs feature interesting characters and story lines that inspire people.
3. My sister wants to be a police officer, but my brother is interested in a career in nursing.
4. The city offers three kinds of public transportation: buses, taking a train, and the tram system.
5. Where will we go? What will we do? I wonder who will join us.

▶ For more practice editing for parallelism, visit Exercise Central at bedfordstmartins.com/exercisecentral.

A Note on Thematic Connections

Each writer represented in this chapter uses comparison and contrast to identify or challenge stereotypes that have been applied to a group of people. A drawing by Art Spiegelman refers to a painting by Norman Rockwell to compare assumptions about American freedoms (p. 268). A paragraph by Michael Dorris contrasts media images of Native Americans with reality (p. 272). Another paragraph, by Julia Álvarez, evaluates the differences between the "cosmopolitan"' and "creole" sides of a Dominican family (p. 273). Suzanne Britt defends slobs by examining the "moral" differences between sloppiness and neatness (next page), while Leanita McClain distinguishes her experience as a middle-class African American from the misperceptions of both blacks and whites (p. 284). And Cheryl Peck considers how hostility toward overweight people has affected her throughout her life (p. 289).

Suzanne Britt

Suzanne Britt has contributed essays and articles to the *New York Times*, *Newsweek*, and the *Boston Globe*, and she has published two collections of essays, *Skinny People Are Dull and Crunchy Like Carrots* (1982) and *Show and Tell* (1983). She has also authored two college English textbooks and published her poetry in literary magazines such as *Denver Quarterly* and *Southern Poetry Review*. Born in Winston-Salem, North Carolina, Britt teaches at Meredith College in North Carolina.

Neat People vs. Sloppy People

In "Neat People vs. Sloppy People," from *Show and Tell*, Britt explores the fundamental differences underlying these two kinds of people. She uses humor in her comparison to challenge the way we think about others.

I've finally figured out the difference between neat people and sloppy   1
people. The distinction is, as always, moral. Neat people are lazier and
meaner than sloppy people.

Sloppy people, you see, are not really sloppy. Their sloppiness is   2
merely the unfortunate consequence of their extreme moral rectitude.
Sloppy people carry in their mind's eye a heavenly vision, a precise plan,
that is so stupendous, so perfect, it can't be achieved in this world or
the next.

Sloppy people live in Never-Never Land. Someday is their métier.   3
Someday they are planning to alphabetize all their books and set up
home catalogs. Someday they will go through their wardrobes and mark
certain items for tentative mending and certain items for passing on to
relatives of similar shape and size. Someday sloppy people will make
family scrapbooks into which they will put newspaper clippings, postcards, locks of hair, and the dried corsage from their senior prom. Someday they will file everything on the surface of their desks, including the
cash receipts from coffee purchases at the snack shop. Someday they will
sit down and read all the back issues of the *New Yorker*.

For all these noble reasons and more, sloppy people never get neat.   4
They aim too high and wide. They save everything, planning someday
to file, order, and straighten out the world. But while these ambitious
plans take clearer and clearer shape in their heads, the books spill from
the shelves onto the floor, the clothes pile up in the hamper and closet,
the family mementos accumulate in every drawer, the surface of the desk
is buried under mounds of paper, and the unread magazines threaten to
reach the ceiling.

Sloppy people can't bear to part with anything. They give loving 5
attention to every detail. When sloppy people say they're going to tackle
the surface of a desk, they really mean it. Not a paper will go unturned;
not a rubber band will go unboxed. Four hours or two weeks into the
excavation, the desk looks exactly the same, primarily because the sloppy
person is meticulously creating new piles of papers with new headings
and scrupulously stopping to read all the old book catalogs before he
throws them away. A neat person would just bulldoze the desk.

Neat people are bums and clods at heart. They have cavalier atti- 6
tudes toward possessions, including family heirlooms. Everything is just
another dust-catcher to them. If anything collects dust, it's got to go
and that's that. Neat people will toy with the idea of throwing the children out of the house just to cut down on the clutter.

Neat people don't care about process. They like results. What they 7
want to do is get the whole thing over with so they can sit down and
watch the rasslin' on TV. Neat people operate on two unvarying principles: Never handle any item twice, and throw everything away.

The only thing messy in a neat person's house is the trash can. The 8
minute something comes to a neat person's hand, he will look at it, try
to decide if it has immediate use and, finding none, throw it in the trash.

Neat people are especially vicious with mail. They never go through 9
their mail unless they are standing directly over a trash can. If the trash
can is beside the mailbox, even better. All ads, catalogs, pleas for charitable contributions, church bulletins, and money-saving coupons go
straight into the trash can without being opened. All letters from home,
postcards from Europe, bills, and paychecks are opened, immediately
responded to, then dropped in the trash can. Neat people keep their
receipts only for tax purposes. That's it. No sentimental salvaging of
birthday cards or the last letter a dying relative ever wrote. Into the trash
it goes.

Neat people place neatness above everything, even economics. They 10
are incredibly wasteful. Neat people throw away several toys every time
they walk through the den. I knew a neat person once who threw away
a perfectly good dish drainer because it had mold on it. The drainer was
too much trouble to wash. And neat people sell their furniture when
they move. They will sell a La-Z-Boy recliner while you are reclining in it.

Neat people are no good to borrow from. Neat people buy every- 11
thing in expensive little single portions. They get their flour and sugar
in two-pound bags. They wouldn't consider clipping a coupon, saving a
leftover, reusing plastic nondairy whipped cream containers, or rinsing
off tin foil and draping it over the unmoldy dish drainer. You can never

borrow a neat person's newspaper to see what's playing at the movies. Neat people have the paper all wadded up and in the trash by 7:05 a.m.

Neat people cut a clean swath through the organic as well as the   12 inorganic world. People, animals, and things are all one to them. They are so insensitive. After they've finished with the pantry, the medicine cabinet, and the attic, they will throw out the red geranium (too many leaves), sell the dog (too many fleas), and send the children off to boarding school (too many scuff-marks on the hardwood floors).

Vocabulary

If any of the following words are new to you, try to guess their meanings from their context in Britt's essay. Check your guesses against a dictionary's definitions, and then use each word in a sentence of your own.

rectitude (2)	accumulate (4)	scrupulously (5)
métier (3)	excavation (5)	salvaging (9)
tentative (3)	meticulously (5)	

Key Ideas and Details

1. "Suzanne Britt believes that neat people are lazy, mean, petty, callous, wasteful, and insensitive." How do you respond to this statement?

2. What is meant by "as always" in the sentence "The distinction is, as always, moral" (paragraph 1)? Does the author seem to be suggesting that any and all distinctions between people are moral?

Craft and Structure

1. LANGUAGE How do you understand the use of the word *noble* in the first sentence of paragraph 4? Is it meant literally? Are there other words in the essay that appear to be written in a similar tone?

2. How does Britt use repetition to clarify her comparison?

3. Britt mentions no similarities between neat and sloppy people. Does that mean this is not a good comparison and contrast essay? Why might a writer deliberately focus on differences and give very little or no time to similarities?

4. OTHER METHODS Britt's essay does not lack for examples (Chapter 8). Study the examples in paragraph 11 and explain how they do and don't work the way examples should: to bring the generalizations about people down to earth.

Integration of Knowledge and Ideas

1. Is Britt writing primarily to neat people, to sloppy people, or to both? How do you think each group would react to the essay? What is *your* reaction?

2. Consider the following generalizations: "For all these noble reasons and more, sloppy people never get neat" (paragraph 4) and "The only thing messy in a neat person's house is the trash can" (8). How can you tell that these statements are generalizations? Look for other generalizations in the essay. What is the effect of using so many?

3. FOR DISCUSSION Is the author's main purpose to reverse stereotypes, to make fun of neat people, to assess the habits of neat and sloppy people, to help neat and sloppy people get along better, to defend sloppy people, to amuse and entertain, or to prove that neat people are morally inferior to sloppy people? What evidence from the essay leads you to your conclusion?

Writing Topics

1. What oppositions do you use to evaluate people? Smart versus dumb? Hip versus clueless? Fun versus dull? Choose your favorite opposition for evaluating people, and write an essay in which you compare and contrast those who pass your "test" with those who fail it. You may choose to write your essay tongue in cheek, as Britt does, or seriously.

2. Write a brief essay or create a brief presentation in which you compare and contrast two apparently dissimilar groups of people: for example, blue-collar workers and white-collar workers, runners and football players, readers and TV watchers, or any other variation you choose. Your approach may be either lighthearted or serious, but make sure you incorporate visuals and come to some conclusion about your subjects. Which group do you favor? Why?

3. Write a brief essay analyzing and contrasting the ways Britt characterizes sloppy people and neat people. Be sure to consider the connotations of the words, such as "moral rectitude" for sloppy people (paragraph 2) and "cavalier" for neat people (6). (If necessary, see *connotation* in the Glossary.)

4. Choose two characters in a novel, short story, or poem and analyze the similarities and differences between them. Which aspects of their personalities make them work well together, within the context in which they appear? Which characteristics work against each other, and therefore provide the necessary conflict to hold the reader's attention?

5. CONNECTIONS Write an essay about the humor gained from exaggeration, relying on Britt's essay, David Sedaris's "Me Talk Pretty One Day" (p. 160), and Brandon Griggs's "The Most Annoying Facebookers" (p. 217) for examples. Consider why exaggeration is often funny and what qualities humorous exaggeration often has. Use quotations and paraphrases from all three essays as your support.

Leanita McClain

An African American journalist, Leanita McClain earned a reputation for honest, if sometimes bitter, reporting on racism in America. She was born in 1952 on Chicago's South Side and grew up in a housing project there. She attended Chicago State University and the Medill School of Journalism at Northwestern University. Immediately after graduate school she began working as a reporter for the *Chicago Tribune*, and over the next decade she advanced to writing a twice-weekly column and serving as the first African American member of the paper's editorial board. Long suffering from severe depression, she committed suicide at the age of thirty-two.

The Middle-Class Black's Burden

McClain wrote this essay for the "My Turn" column in *Newsweek* magazine, and it was later reprinted in a collection of her essays, *A Foot in Each World* (1986). As her comparison makes disturbingly clear, McClain's position as an economically successful African American subjected her to mistaken judgments by both blacks and whites.

I am a member of the black middle class who has had it with being pat-   1
ted on the head by white hands and slapped in the face by black hands for my success.

Here's a discovery that too many people still find startling: when   2
given equal opportunities at white-collar pencil pushing, blacks want the same things from life that everyone else wants. These include the proverbial dream house, two cars, an above-average school, and a vacation for the kids at Disneyland. We may, in fact, want these things more than other Americans because most of us have been denied them so long.

Meanwhile, a considerable number of the folks we left behind in   3
the "old country," commonly called the ghetto, and the militants we left behind in their antiquated ideology can't berate middle-class blacks enough for "forgetting where we came from." We have forsaken the revolution, we are told, we have sold out. We are Oreos, they say, black on the outside, white within.

The truth is, we have not forgotten; we would not dare. We are   4
simply fighting on different fronts and are no less war weary, and possibly more heartbroken, for we know the black and white worlds can meld, that there can be a better world.

It is impossible for me to forget where I came from as long as I am   5
prey to the jive hustler who does not hesitate to exploit my childhood friendship. I am reminded, too, when I go back to the old neighborhood in fear—and have my purse snatched—and when I sit down to a busi-

ness lunch and have an old classmate wait on my table. I recall the girl I played dolls with who now rears five children on welfare, the boy from church who is in prison for murder, the pal found dead of a drug over-dose in the alley where we once played tag.

My life abounds in incongruities. Fresh from a vacation in Paris, I 6 may, a week later, be on the milk-run Trailways bus in Deep South back-country attending the funeral of an ancient uncle whose world stretched only fifty miles and who never learned to read. Sometimes when I wait at the bus stop with my attaché case, I meet my aunt getting off the bus with other cleaning ladies on their way to do my neighbors' floors.

But I am not ashamed. Black progress has surpassed our greatest 7 expectations; we never even saw much hope for it, and the achieve-ment has taken us by surprise.

In my heart, however, there is no safe distance from the wretched 8 past of my ancestors or the purposeless present of some of my contem-poraries; I fear such a fate can reclaim me. I am not comfortably middle class; I am uncomfortably middle class.

I have made it, but where? Racism still dogs my people. There are 9 still communities in which crosses are burned on the lawns of black families who have the money and grit to move in.

What a hollow victory we have won when my sister, dressed in her 10 designer everything, is driven to the rear door of the luxury high rise in which she lives because the cab driver, noting only her skin color, assumes she is the maid, or the nanny, or the cook, but certainly not the lady of any house at this address.

I have heard the immigrants' bootstrap tales, the simplistic reproach 11 of "why can't you people be like us." I have fulfilled the entry require-ments of the American middle class, yet I am left, at times, feeling unwel-come and stereotyped. I have overcome the problems of food, clothing and shelter, but I have not overcome my old nemesis, prejudice. Life is easier, being black is not.

I am burdened daily with showing whites that blacks are people. I 12 am, in the old vernacular, a credit to my race. I am my brothers' keeper, and my sisters', though many of them have abandoned me because they think that I have abandoned them.

I run a gauntlet between two worlds, and I am cursed and blessed 13 by both. I travel, observe, and take part in both; I can also be used by both. I am a rope in a tug of war. If I am a token in my downtown office, so am I at my cousin's church tea. I assuage white guilt. I disprove black inadequacy and prove to my parents' generation that their patience was indeed a virtue.

I have a foot in each world, but I cannot fool myself about either. I 14 can see the transparent deceptions of some whites and the bitter hopelessness of some blacks. I know how tenuous my grip on one way of life is, and how strangling the grip of the other way of life can be.

Many whites have lulled themselves into thinking that race rela- 15 tions are just grand because they were the first on their block to discuss crab grass with the new black family. Yet too few blacks and whites in this country send their children to school together, entertain each other, or call each other friend. Blacks and whites dining out together draw stares. Many of my coworkers see no black faces from the time the train pulls out Friday evening until they meet me at the coffee machine Monday morning. I remain a novelty.

Some of my "liberal" white acquaintances pat me on the head, hint- 16 ing that I am a freak, that my success is less a matter of talent than of luck and affirmative action. I may live among them, but it is difficult to live with them. How can they be sincere about respecting me, yet hold my fellows in contempt? And if I am silent when they attempt to sever me from my own, how can I live with myself?

Whites won't believe I remain culturally different; blacks won't 17 believe I remain culturally the same.

I need only look in a mirror to know my true allegiance, and I am 18 painfully aware that, even with my off-white trappings, I am prejudged by my color.

As for the envy of my own people, am I to give up my career, my 19 standard of living, to pacify them and set my conscience at ease? No. I have worked for these amenities and deserve them, though I can never enjoy them without feeling guilty.

These comforts do not make me less black, nor oblivious to the woe 20 in which many of my people are drowning. As long as we are denigrated as a group, no one of us has made it. Inasmuch as we all suffer for every one left behind, we all gain for every one who conquers the hurdle.

Vocabulary

If any of the following words are new to you, try to guess their meanings from their context in McClain's essay. Check your guesses against a dictionary's definitions, and then use each word in a sentence of your own.

proverbial (2)	nemesis (11)	amenities (19)
antiquated (3)	vernacular (12)	oblivious (20)
ideology (3)	gauntlet (13)	denigrated (20)
berate (3)	assuage (13)	
reproach (11)	tenuous (14)	

Key Ideas and Details

1. McClain states, "My life abounds in incongruities" (paragraph 6). What does the word *incongruities* mean? How does it apply to McClain's life?

2. What is the "middle-class black's burden" to which the title refers? What is McClain's main idea?

3. McClain writes that "there is no safe distance from the wretched past of my ancestors or the purposeless present of some of my contemporaries" (paragraph 8). What do you think she means by this statement?

Craft and Structure

1. LANGUAGE Notice McClain's use of parallelism in paragraph 8: "I am not comfortably middle class; I am uncomfortably middle class." Locate two or three other uses of parallelism. How does this technique serve McClain's comparison? (For more on parallelism, see p. 55, as well as *parallelism* in the Glossary.)

2. What exactly is McClain comparing here? What are her main points of comparison?

3. Paragraph 6 on "incongruities" represents a turning point in McClain's essay. What does she discuss before this paragraph? What does she discuss after?

4. McClain uses many expressions to make her comparison clear, such as "Meanwhile" (paragraph 3) and "different fronts" (4). Locate three more such expressions, and explain what relationship each one establishes.

5. OTHER METHODS McClain relies on many other methods to develop her comparison. Locate one instance each of description (Chapter 7), narration (Chapter 6), example (Chapter 8), and cause-and-effect analysis (Chapter 14). What does each contribute to the essay?

Integration of Knowledge and Ideas

1. What seems to be McClain's primary purpose in this piece? Does she simply want to express her frustration at whites and blacks, or is she trying to do something else?

2. Is McClain writing primarily to whites or to blacks or to both? What feelings do you think she might evoke in white readers? in black readers? What is *your* reaction to this essay?

3. FOR DISCUSSION McClain sets the tone for this essay in the very first sentence. How would you describe this tone? Is it appropriate, do you think? Why, or why not? Pick out some details from the essay to support your opinion and be prepared to defend it in class.

Writing Topics

1. Prejudice is so pervasive in our society that it is hard to avoid. Think of a time when somebody made an assumption about you because of your membership in a group (as an ethnic, religious, or sexual minority; as a club member; as a girl or boy; as a "jock," "nerd," and so on), and write a narrative in which you recount this experience in detail. How were you perceived, and by whom? What about this perception was accurate? What was unfair? How did the experience affect you? Write for a reader who is not a member of the group in question, being sure to include enough detail to bring the experience to life.

2. McClain's essay reports in part her experience of conflict resulting from her growth beyond the boundaries of her childhood and community. Think of a time when you outgrew a particular group or community. What conflicts and satisfactions did you experience? Write an essay comparing your experience with McClain's.

3. Are there any ways in which you feel, like McClain, that you have "a foot in each world" (paragraph 14)? These worlds might be related to race and affluence, as McClain's worlds are, or they might be aligned by gender, social class, religion, or some other characteristic. Write an essay describing your own experience in balancing these two worlds. Are there ways in which you appreciate having a dual membership, or is it only a burden? What have you learned from your experience?

4. CONNECTIONS Like McClain, Judy Brady, in "I Want a Wife" (p. 308), writes with strong emotion about the burdens of being oppressed by others. Both essays were written several decades ago. In an essay of your own, consider to what extent their perspectives are timely or dated. Could McClain and Brady make the same claims today?

Cheryl Peck

Cheryl Peck (born 1951) has always lived in Michigan — first with her parents and four younger siblings on a nonworking farm; now in Three Rivers with her "Beloved," Nancy, and her cat, Babycakes. She attended the University of Michigan and worked in a welfare office for twenty-five years. After friends encouraged her to write down the personal stories she was always amusing them with, Peck started submitting humorous and poignant articles to a Kalamazoo newsletter and giving readings at a community church. Her self-published essay collection *Fat Girls and Lawn Chairs* (2004) caught the attention of an editor at Warner Books, who brought the essays to a wider audience and cult-favorite status. Peck followed it a year later with *Revenge of the Paste Eaters: Memoirs of a Misfit* (2005) and took an early retirement so she could devote her time to writing. She is currently working on a novel and a third collection of essays.

Fatso

In most of her writing, Peck uses her ample size — "three hundred pounds (plus change)" — to fuel her self-deprecating brand of humor. This essay from *Revenge of the Paste Eaters*, however, takes a decidedly different approach to the weight issues that have plagued the author all her life.

My friend Annie and I were having lunch and we fell into a discussion of 1 people of size. She told me she had gone to the fair with a friend of hers who is a young man of substance, and while he was standing in the midway, thinking about his elephant ear,[1] someone walked past him, said, "You don't need to eat that," and kept on walking away. Gone before he could register what had been said, much less formulate a stunning retort.

And that person was probably right: he did not need to eat that ele- 2 phant ear. Given what they are made of, the question then becomes: Who *does* need to eat an elephant ear? And to what benefit? Are elephant ears inherently better for thin people than for fat ones? Do we suppose that that one particular elephant ear will somehow alter the course of this man's life in some way that all of the elephant ears before it, or all of the elephant ears to follow, might not? And last but not least, what qualifies any of us for the mission of telling other people what they should or should not eat?

I have probably spent most of my life listening to other people tell 3 me that as a middle-class white person, I have no idea what it is like to be discriminated against. I have never experienced the look that tells me

---

[1] Fried dough. [Editors' note.]

I am not welcome, I have never been treated rudely on a bus, I have never been reminded to keep my place, I have never been laughed at, ridiculed, threatened, snubbed, not waited on, or received well-meaning service I would just as soon have done without. I have never had to choose which streets I will walk down and which streets I will avoid. I have never been told that my needs cannot be met in this store. I have never experienced that lack of social status that can debilitate the soul.

My feelings were not hurt when I was twelve years old and the shoe   4
salesman measured my feet and said he had no women's shoes large enough for me, but perhaps I could wear the boxes.

I have never been called crude names, like "fatso" or "lard-bucket." . . .   5
My nickname on the school bus was never "Bismarck," as in the famous battleship. No one ever assumed I was totally inept in all sports except those that involved hitting things because—and everyone knows—the more weight you can put behind it, the farther you can kick or bat or just bully the ball.

I have never picked up a magazine with the photograph of a naked   6
woman of substance on the cover, to read, in the following issue, thirty letters to the editor addressing sizism, including the one that said, "She should be ashamed of herself. She should go on a diet immediately and demonstrate some self-control. She is going to develop diabetes, arthritis, hypertension, and stroke, she will die an ugly death at an early age and she will take down the entire American health system with her." And that would, of course, be the only letter I remember. I would not need some other calm voice to say, "You don't know that—and you don't know that the same fate would not befall a thin woman."

No one has ever assumed I am lazy, undisciplined, prone to self-   7
pity, and emotionally unstable purely based on my size. No one has ever told me all I need is a little self-discipline and I too could be thin, pretty—a knockout, probably, because I have a "pretty face"—probably very popular because I have a "good personality." My mother never told me boys would never pay any attention to me because I'm fat.

I have never assumed an admirer would never pay any attention to   8
me because I'm fat. I have never mishandled a sexual situation because I have been trained to think of myself as asexual. Unattractive. Repugnant.

Total strangers have never walked up to me in the street and started   9
to tell me about weight loss programs their second cousin in Tulsa tried with incredible results, nor would they ever do so with the manner and demeanor of someone doing me a nearly unparalleled favor. I have never walked across a parking lot to have a herd of young men break into song about loving women with big butts. When I walk down the street

or ride my bicycle, no one has ever hung out the car window to yell crude insults. When I walk into the houses of friends I have never been directed to the "safe" chairs as if I just woke up this morning this size and am incapable of gauging for myself what will or will not hold me.

I have never internalized any of this nonexistent presumption of who I am or what I feel. I would never discriminate against another woman of substance. I would never look at a heavy person and think, "self-pitying, undisciplined tub of lard." I would never admit that while I admire beautiful bodies, I rarely give the inhabitants the same attention and respect I would a soul mate because I do not expect they would ever become a soul mate. I would never tell you that I was probably thirty years old before I realized you really *can* be too small or too thin, or that the condition causes real emotional pain. 10

I have never skipped a high school reunion until I "lose a few pounds." I have never hesitated to reconnect with an old friend. I will appear anywhere in a bathing suit. If my pants split, I assume — and I assume everyone assumes — it was caused by poor materials. 11

I have always understood why attractive women are offended when men whistle at them. 12

I have never felt self-conscious standing next to my male friend who is five foot ten and weighs 145 pounds. 13

I am not angry about any of this. 14

Vocabulary

If any of the following words are new to you, try to guess their meanings from their context in Peck's essay. Check your guesses against a dictionary's definitions, and then use each word in a sentence of your own.

register (1)	crude (5)	demeanor (9)
retort (1)	prone (7)	gauging (9)
debilitate (3)	asexual (8)	presumption (10)

Key Ideas and Details

1. Throughout her essay Peck repeats that she has never experienced, done, or felt any of the things she describes. Is she telling the truth? How do you know?

2. How does Peck feel about the discrimination she faces as an overweight woman? Why does she feel this way?

3. Peck is cautious in the words she uses to refer to overweight people, preferring terms such as "woman of substance" (paragraphs 6 and 10) and "heavy

person" (10) over the judgmental terms that some people have used to describe her (and that she has caught herself thinking about others). Why, then, does she use the obviously insulting "Fatso" as the title of her essay?

Craft and Structure

1. LANGUAGE Peck uses the phrase "I have never" repeatedly (seventeen times, to be exact), as well as variations such as "I would never" and "I have not." What is the effect of this repetition?

2. What, precisely, is Peck comparing and contrasting in this essay? Identify a few of the points of comparison she uses to develop her main idea. Which of these points seem most important to her?

3. Where does Peck's comparison begin? How does she use a subtle shift in point of view to indicate that she does, indeed, know "what it is like to be discriminated against" (paragraph 3)? (If necessary, see *point of view* in the Glossary.)

4. OTHER METHODS Peck's comparison relies heavily on example (Chapter 8), focusing on a series of incidents from her own life. Choose two examples, and consider what each contributes to Peck's point.

Integration of Knowledge and Ideas

1. For whom is Peck writing? Fat people? Thin people? Herself? What clues in the essay bring you to your conclusion?

2. What lesson might readers take from Peck's essay?

3. FOR DISCUSSION What do you think of Peck's argument? For instance, how would you respond to her complaint that people treat overweight individuals unfairly? Does she overlook important considerations about health? Do you think she exaggerates any of her points? Prepare to agree or disagree with Peck, supporting your opinion with details from her essay as well as examples from your own experience.

Writing Topics

1. If you're like most people, you've probably been dissatisfied with your size at one point or another, whether you wanted to be taller or shorter, lose a few pounds, build some muscle, or simply avoid weight gain. Write a brief esssay in which you examine your attitude toward your body. What, if anything, would you change about it? Why? Where do you think that attitude came from? Was your self-image influenced in any way by your family, your friends, or the media? How?

2. Peck's essay is in some respects an imagined response to the person who insulted her friend's friend. Think of a time when a stranger made an inappropriate or insensitive comment directed at you or someone close to you (or of a time when you overheard such a remark intended for someone else). Write a speech that responds to the person in question, explaining why his or her comment was offensive.

3. RESEARCH American society is famously obsessed with people's size. Media outlets have focused recently on what has been described as an "obesity epidemic," and weight loss is a multibillion-dollar industry in this country. But in many cultures (Samoan and Polynesian, for example), large bodies are prized over small ones. Identify one such culture, and find two or three brief sources that explain that culture's attitudes toward body shape (a librarian can help you). Write an essay that compares that culture's standards of physical beauty with America's. Which set of ideals seem more reasonable to you? Express your preference in a clear thesis statement and support your evaluation with details. Be sure to document your sources, referring to pages 73–77 of Chapter 5 as necessary.

4. CONNECTIONS Peck suggests that discrimination against people of size is comparable, if not equivalent, to discrimination against people of color. In "The Middle-Class Black's Burden" (p. 284), Leanita McClain describes her own experiences with racial discrimination, and like Peck, she is angry. How do you think McClain would respond to Peck's characterization of race? Write an imaginary conversation between these two authors, inventing dialogue that mimics each writer's language and reflects the point of view she takes in her essay.

WRITING WITH THE METHOD

COMPARISON AND CONTRAST

Select one of the following topics, or any other topic they suggest, for an essay or presentation developed by comparison and contrast. Be sure to choose a topic you care about so that the comparison and contrast is a means of communicating an idea, not an end in itself.

Experience

1. Middle school and high school
2. Two experiences with discrimination
3. Your own version of an event you witnessed or participated in and someone else's view of the same event (perhaps a friend's or a reporter's)

People

4. Your relationships with two friends
5. An older relative before and after marriage or the birth of a child
6. Two or more candidates for public office
7. Two teachers

Places and Things

8. Your home as it is now and as it was years ago
9. Public and private transportation
10. Contact lenses and glasses
11. Two towns or cities

Art and Entertainment

12. The work of two artists or two works by the same artist
13. Movies or television today and when your parents were your age
14. An amateur football, baseball, or basketball game and a professional game in the same sport
15. The advertisements on two very different Web sites

Education and Ideas

16. Talent and skill
17. Learning and teaching
18. An English class and a science or mathematics class
19. A passive student and an active student

WRITING ABOUT THE THEME

EXAMINING STEREOTYPES

1. The authors in this chapter wrestle with questions of identity, addressing issues as diverse as the reality of life for members of a racial or ethnic minority (Michael Dorris, p. 272; Julia Álvarez, p. 273; Leanita McClain, p. 284), the impact of negative stereotypes (Art Spiegelman, p. 268; Dorris; McClain; Cheryl Peck, p. 289), and the relationship between outward appearance and social acceptance (Spiegelman; Suzanne Britt, p. 290; Peck). All the selections rely on comparison and contrast, but otherwise they go about their tasks very differently. Most notably, perhaps, their tones vary widely, from humor to vulnerability to anger. Choose the two works that seem most different in this respect, and analyze how the tone of each helps the author achieve his or her purpose. Give specific examples to support your ideas. Does your analysis lead you to conclude that one tone is likely to be more effective than another in comparing stereotypes with reality? (For more on tone, see pp. 43–44.)

2. Art Spiegelman, Michael Dorris, Leanita McClain, and Cheryl Peck refer to misperceptions of a minority group on the part of the dominant society. Think of a minority group to which you belong. It could be based on race, ethnicity, language, sexual orientation, religion, physical disability, or any other characteristic. How is your minority perceived in the dominant culture, and how does this perception resemble or differ from the reality as you know it? Write an essay comparing the perception of and the reality of your group.

3. All of the authors in this chapter suggest that stereotypes play a significant part in our perceptions of others and ourselves. Spiegelman reminds viewers that fear of others runs both ways, Dorris refers to the "white noise" of Indian images in the media, Álvarez to her parents' negative assessments of each other's extended families, Britt to assumptions that sloppiness is a weakness, McClain to a distorted image of African Americans, and Peck to perceptions about overweight individuals. To what extent, if at all, are these misconceptions the result of media hype or distortion, whether in advertising, news stories, television programming, movies, or elsewhere? What else might contribute to the misconceptions in each case? Write an essay explaining how such notions arise in the first place. You could use the misconceptions identified by the authors in this chapter for your examples, or you could supply examples of your own.

"I hope you realize that I'm the one who has to write about this stupid vacation next fall."

13

DEFINITION

▶
PURSUING HAPPINESS

Definition sets the boundaries of a thing, a concept, an emotion, or a value. In answering "What is it?" and also "What is it *not*?" definition specifies the main qualities of a subject and its essential nature. Since words are only symbols, pinning down their precise meanings is essential for us to understand ourselves and one another. Thus we use definition constantly, whether we are explaining a new word like *staycation* to someone who has never heard it, specifying what we're after when we say we want to do something *fun*, or clarify the diagnosis of a child as *hyperactive*.

We often use brief definitions to clarify the meanings of words—for instance, taking a few sentences to explain a technical term in an environmental study. But we may also need to define words at length, especially when they are abstract, complicated, or controversial. Drawing on other methods of development, such as example, analysis, or comparison and contrast, entire essays might be devoted to debated phrases (such as *family values),* to the current uses of a word (*monopoly* in business), or to the meanings of a term in a particular context (like *deviance* in sociology). Definition is, in other words, essential whenever we want to be certain that we are understood.

↰ Seeing Definition

The cartoon that opens this chapter is by Peter Steiner, a novelist, painter, and most of all, a popular cartoonist whose jokes and political drawings regularly appear in the *New Yorker*, the *Weekly Standard*, and the *Washington Times*. This cartoon, from the *New Yorker*, shows a family on vacation. Notice the way each person is dressed, the expressions on their faces, their postures. The couple's son, scowling in the back seat, is clearly not happy. Why? Because he seems to have a very different idea of what a vacation involves than his parents do. How does the teen define *vacation*? How do they? How can you tell? What, in your view, creates the humor in the situation?

Reading Definition

There are several kinds of definition, each with different uses. One is the **formal definition**, usually a statement of the general class of things to which the word belongs, followed by the distinction(s) between it and other members of the class. Here are some examples:

	General class	*Distinction(s)*
A submarine is	a seagoing vessel	that operates underwater.
A parable is	a brief, simple story	that illustrates a moral or religious principle.
Pressure is	the force	applied to a given surface.
Insanity is	a mental condition	in which a defendant does not know right from wrong.

A formal definition usually gives a standard dictionary meaning of the word (as in the first two examples) or a specialized meaning agreed to by the members of a profession or discipline (as in the last two examples, from physics and criminal law, respectively). Writers use formal definition to explain the basic meaning of a term so that readers can understand the rest of a discussion. Occasionally, a formal definition can serve as a springboard to a more elaborate, detailed exploration of a word. For instance, an essay might define *pride* simply as "a sense of self-respect" before probing the varied meanings of the word as people actually understand it and then settling on a fuller and more precise meaning of the author's own devising.

This more detailed definition of *pride* could fall into one of two other types of definition: stipulative and extended. A **stipulative definition** clarifies the particular way a writer is using a word: it stipulates, or specifies, a meaning to suit a larger purpose; the definition is part of a larger whole. For example, to show how pride can destroy personal relationships, a writer might first stipulate a meaning of *pride* that ties in with that purpose. Though a stipulative definition may sometimes take the form of a brief formal definition, most require several sentences or even paragraphs. In a physics textbook, for instance, the physicist's definition of *pressure* quoted above probably would not suffice to give readers a good sense of the term and eliminate all the other possible meanings they may have in mind.

Whereas a writer may use a formal or stipulative definition for some larger purpose, he or she would use an **extended definition** for the sake of defining—that is, for the purpose of exploring a thing, quality, or idea in its full complexity and drawing boundaries around it until its meaning is complete and precise. Extended definitions usually treat subjects so complex, vague, or laden with emotions or values that people misunderstand or disagree over their meanings. The subject may be an abstract concept like *patriotism*, a controversial phrase like *beginnings of life*, a colloquial or slang expression like *hype*, a thing like *nanobot*, a scientific idea like *continental drift*, even an everyday expression like *nagging*. Besides defining, the purpose may be to persuade readers to accept a definition (for instance, that life begins at conception—or at birth), to explain (what is continental drift?), or to amuse (nagging as exemplified by great nags).

As the variety of possible subjects and purposes may suggest, an extended definition may draw on whatever methods will best accomplish the goal of specifying what the subject includes and distinguishing it from similar things, qualities, or concepts. Several strategies are unique to definition:

- **Synonyms**, or words of similar meaning, can convey the range of the word's meanings. For example, a writer could equate *misery* with *wretchedness* and *distress*.

- **Negation**, or saying what a word does not mean, can limit the meaning, particularly when a writer wants to focus on only one sense of an abstract term, such as *pride*, that is open to diverse interpretations.

- The **etymology** of a word—its history—may illuminate its meaning, perhaps by showing the direction and extent of its change (*pride*, for instance, comes from a Latin word meaning "to be beneficial or useful") or by uncovering buried origins that remain implicit in the modern meaning (*patriotism* comes from the Greek word for "father"; *happy* comes from the Old Norse word for "good luck").

These strategies of definition may be used alone or together, and they may occupy whole paragraphs in an essay-length definition; but they rarely provide enough range to surround the subject completely. That's why most definition essays draw on at least some of the other methods discussed in this book. One or two methods may predominate: an essay on nagging, for instance, might be developed with brief narratives. Or several methods may be combined: a definition of *patriotism* might compare it with *nationalism*, analyze its effects (such as the actions people take on its behalf), and give examples of patriotic individuals. By drawing on the appropriate methods, a writer defines and clarifies a specific perspective on the subject so that the reader understands the meaning exactly.

Analyzing Definition in Paragraphs

Carlin Flora (born 1975) is a science journalist and the author of *Friendfluence: The Surprising Ways Friends Make Us Who We Are* (2013). The following paragraph is from "The Pursuit of Happiness," an article she wrote for the magazine *Psychology Today*.

What *is* happiness? The most useful definition—and it's one agreed upon by neuroscientists, psychiatrists, behavioral economists, positive psychologists, and Buddhist monks— is more like satisfied or content than "happy" in its strict bursting-with-glee sense. It has depth and deliberation to it. It encompasses living a meaningful life, utilizing your gifts and your time, living with thought and purpose. It's maximized when you also feel part of a community. And when you confront annoyances and crises with grace. It involves a willingness to learn and stretch and grow, which sometimes involves discomfort. It requires acting on life, not merely taking it in. It's not joy, a temporary exhilaration, or even pleasure, that sensual rush—though a steady supply of those feelings course through those who seize each day.

> Question introduces concept to be defined
>
> Synonyms
>
> Factors that contribute to happiness:
>   meaningful life
>   community
>   positive attitude
>   activity
>
> Concluding sentence states what happiness is not

Sarah Vowell (born 1969) is an essayist, a radio commentator, and the author of several books of popular history. This paragraph, adapted from Vowell's essay "Pop-A-Shot," explains what the arcade basketball game of the same name means to her.

I think Pop-A-Shot's a baby game. That's why I love it. Unlike the game of basketball itself, Pop-A-Shot has no standard socially redeeming value whatsoever. Pop-A-Shot is not about teamwork or getting along or working together. Pop-A-Shot is not about getting exercise or fresh air. . . . Pop-A-Shot has no point at all. And that, for me, is the point. My life is full of points—the deadlines and bills and recycling and phone calls. I have come to appreciate, to depend on, this one dumb . . . little passion. Because every time a basketball

> Topic sentence (underlined) previews definition
>
> Definition by negation:
>   no value
>   no teamwork
>   no exercise
>   no point
>
> Contrast with responsibilities

slides off my fingertips and drops perfectly, flawlessly, into that hole, well, swish, happiness found.

Developing an Essay by Definition

▶ Getting Started

You'll sometimes be asked to write definition essays, as when an earth science exam asks for a discussion of *photosynthesis* or a history assignment calls for an explanation of the term *totalitarianism*. To come up with a subject on your own, consider words that have complex meanings and are either unfamiliar to readers or open to varied interpretations. The subject should be something you know and care enough about to explore in great detail and surround completely. An idea for a subject may come from an overheard conversation (for instance, a reference to someone as "unpatriotic"), a personal experience (an accomplishment that filled you with pride), or something you've seen or read (another writer's definition of *jazz*).

Begin exploring your subject by examining and listing its conventional meanings (consulting an unabridged dictionary may help here, and the dictionary will also give you synonyms and etymology). Also examine the differences of opinion about the word's meanings—the different ways, wrong or right, that you have heard or seen it used. Run through the other methods to see what fresh approaches to the subject they open up:

- How can the subject be described?
- What are some examples?
- Can the subject be divided into qualities or characteristics?
- Can its functions help define it?
- Will comparing and contrasting it with something else help sharpen its meaning?
- Do its causes or effects help clarify its sense?

Some of the questions may turn up nothing, but others may open your eyes to meanings you had not seen.

▶ Forming a Thesis

When you have generated a good list of ideas about your subject, settle on the purpose of your definition. Do you mostly want to explain a word that is unfamiliar to readers? Do you want to express your own view so that readers see a familiar subject from a new angle? Do you want to argue in favor of a particular definition or perhaps persuade readers to look more critically at themselves or their surroundings? Try to work your purpose into a thesis sentence that summarizes your definition and—just as important—asserts something about the subject. For example:

> DRAFT THESIS STATEMENT   The prevailing concept of *patriotism* is dangerously wrong.

> REVISED THESIS STATEMENT   Though generally considered entirely positive in meaning, *patriotism* in fact reflects selfish, childish emotions that have no place in a global society.

(Note that the revised thesis statement not only summarizes the writer's definition and makes an assertion about the subject, but it also identifies the prevailing definition she intends to counter in her essay.)

With a thesis sentence formulated, reevaluate your ideas in light of it and pause to consider the needs of your readers:

- What do readers already know about your subject, and what do they need to be told so they will understand it as you do?

- Are your readers likely to be biased for or against your subject? If you were defining *patriotism*, for example, you might assume that your readers see the word as representing a constructive, even essential value that contributes to the strength of a country. If your purpose were to contest this view, as implied by the revised thesis statement, you would have to build your case carefully to win readers to your side.

▶ Organizing

The **introduction** to a definition essay should provide a base from which to expand and at the same time explain to readers why the forthcoming definition is useful, significant, or necessary. You may want to report the incident that prompted you to define, say why the subject itself is important, or specify the common understandings, or misunderstandings, about its meaning. Several devices can serve as effective beginnings: the etymology of the word; a quotation from another writer supporting or contradicting your definition; or an explanation of what the word does *not* mean (negation). (Try to avoid the overused opening that cites a dictionary: "According to the *American Heritage Dictionary*, _____ means. . . ." Your readers have probably seen this opening many times before.) If it is not implied in the rest of your introduction, you may want to state your thesis so that readers know precisely what your purpose and point are.

The body of the essay should then proceed, paragraph by paragraph, to refine the characteristics or qualities of the subject, using the arrangement and methods that will distinguish it from anything similar and provide your perspective. Here are some possibilities:

- You might draw increasingly tight boundaries around the subject, moving from broader, more familiar meanings to the one you have in mind.

- You might arrange your points in order of increasing drama.

- You might begin with your own experience of the subject and then show how you see it operating in your surroundings.

The **conclusion** to a definition essay is equally a matter of choice. You might summarize your definition, indicate its superiority to other definitions of the same subject, quote another writer whose view supports your own, or recommend that readers make some use of the information you have provided. The choice depends—as it does in any kind of essay—on your purpose and the impression you want to leave with readers.

▶ **Drafting**

While drafting your extended definition, keep your subject vividly in mind. Say too much rather than too little about it to ensure that you capture its essence; you can always cut when you revise. And be sure to provide plenty of details and examples to support your view. Such evidence is particularly important when, as in the earlier example of patriotism, you wish to change readers' perceptions of your subject.

In definition the words you use are especially important. Abstractions and generalities cannot draw precise boundaries around a subject, so your words must be as concrete and specific as you can make them. You'll have chances during revising and editing to work on your words, but try during drafting to pin down your meanings. Use words and phrases that appeal directly to the senses and experiences of readers. When appropriate, use figures of speech to make meaning inescapably clear; instead of "Patriotism is childish," for example, write "The blindly patriotic person is like a small child who sees his or her parents as gods, all-knowing, always right." The connotations of words—the associations called up in readers' minds by words like *home*, *ambitious*, and *generous*—can contribute to your definition as well. But be sure that connotative words trigger associations suited to your purpose. And when you are trying to explain something precisely, rely most heavily on words with generally neutral meanings. (See p. 58 for more on concrete and specific language and figures of speech. See pp. 57–59 for more on connotation.)

▶ Revising and Editing

When you are satisfied that your draft is complete, revise and edit it against the following questions and the information in the focus box on the next two pages.

- *Have you defined your subject completely and tightly?* Your definition should not leave gaps, nor should the boundaries be so broadly drawn that the subject overlaps something else. For instance, a definition of *hype* that focuses on exaggerated and deliberately misleading claims should include all such claims (some political speeches, say, as well as some advertisements), and it should exclude appeals that do not fit the basic definition (some public-service advertising, for instance).

- *Does your definition reflect the conventional meanings of the word?* Even if you are providing a fresh slant on your subject, you can't change its meaning entirely, or you will confuse your readers and perhaps undermine your own credibility. *Patriotism*, for example, could not be defined as "hatred of foreigners," for that definition strays into an entirely different realm. The conventional meaning of "love of country" would have to serve as the starting point, though your essay might interpret the meaning in an original way.

- *Does your essay have unity?* When drafting a definition, you may find yourself being pulled away from your subject by the descriptions, examples, comparisons, and other methods you use to specify meaning. Let yourself explore byways of your subject — doing so will help you discover what you think. But in revising you'll need to direct all paragraphs to your thesis, and within paragraphs you'll need to direct all sentences to the paragraph topic. One way to achieve unity is to focus each paragraph on some part of your definition and then to focus each sentence within the paragraph on that part. If some part of your definition requires more than a single paragraph, by all means expand it. But keep the group of paragraphs focused on a single idea. For more on unity in essays and paragraphs, see pages 38–40.

FOCUS ON **Restrictive and Nonrestrictive Elements**

A definition will be more understandable for readers if you insert modifying words, phrases, and clauses in your sentences to clarify your meaning and bring depth to your ideas. When you do so, be careful to punctuate restrictive and nonrestrictive sentence elements appropriately.

A modifier is *restrictive*, or essential, when it limits the word or phrase it modifies. If removing the modifier would change the fundamental meaning of the sentence, that element should not be set off with punctuation.

RESTRICTIVE I want a wife who will work and send me to school.
— *Judy Brady*

[The author of this sentence wants a particular kind of wife, not just any wife.]

RESTRICTIVE Happiness is a state of mind cultivated under a sophisticated understanding of a rapidly changing world.   — *Walter Mosley*

[The underlined phrase specifies the kind of state of mind Mosley means.]

A modifer is *nonrestrictive*, or nonessential, if it adds information to a sentence that would still make sense without it. Writers use commas, parentheses, or dashes to separate nonrestrictive elements from the primary meaning of a sentence. Here are some examples from the readings in this chapter:

NONRESTRICTIVE I want a wife who cooks the meals, a wife who is a *good* cook.   — *Judy Brady*

[The modifying phrase adds information about the kind of cook Brady wants but is not essential to her meaning.]

NONRESTRICTIVE Happiness is considered by most to be a subset of wealth, which is not necessarily true.   — *Walter Mosley*

[The second half of the sentence clarifies Mosley's assertion but does not change it.]

NONRESTRICTIVE The millionaires I know seem desperate to become multimillionaires, and spend more time with their lawyers and their bankers than with their friends (whose motivations they are no longer sure of).   — *Pico Iyer*

[The parenthetical remark adds a new idea; Iyer's sentence would still make sense without it.]

NONRESTRICTIVE So — as post-1960s cliché decreed — I left my comfortable job and life to live for a year in a temple on the backstreets of
Kyoto.
                                                                        — *Pico Iyer*

[The phrase set off by dashes is an aside that is not necessary to Iyer's
explanation.]

Notice that the same modifier might be restrictive or nonrestrictive, depending on the writer's intended meaning.

RESTRICTIVE The students who expressed optimism did well on the
exam.

NONRESTRICTIVE The students, who expressed optimism, did well on
the exam.

In the first sentence above, the phrase *who expressed optimism* identifies which students did well. The commas in the second sentence
indicate that the writer is referring to the entire group of students; the
phrase adds information about their attitudes. Both sentences are
correct, but their meanings are different.

For more on punctuating restrictive and nonrestrictive elements,
see page 54.

Practice

Fix the punctuation in the sentences below. Remove any commas
surrounding restrictive elements and add commas, parentheses, or
dashes to set off nonrestrictive elements.

1. Studies by psychologist, Dacher Keltner, have shown that
   maintaining a positive attitude can increase a person's chances for
   success.

2. But other scientists such as Barbara Ehrenreich question the
   findings of positive psychologists.

3. Ehrenreich a trained biologist who studies culture argues that a
   focus on positive thinking can have negative consequences.

4. She cites the example of customer service representatives who are
   often told that they need to stay upbeat if they want to keep their
   jobs.

5. Employees, forced to hide their true emotions, can become
   physically ill from the stress caused by lying.

▶ For more practice editing restrictive and nonrestrictive elements,
visit Exercise Central at bedfordstmartins.com/exercisecentral.

A Note on Thematic Connections

Happiness is the core topic of this chapter. The authors represented here all offer their own perspectives on the emotional and political meanings of an abstract concept that many of us take for granted. Peter Steiner, in a cartoon, shows how a vacation can make someone unhappy (p. 296). Carlin Flora, in a paragraph, presents the meaning of *happiness* as most psychologists understand it (p. 300). Sarah Vowell, in another paragraph, explains why playing a meaningless game fills her with joy (p. 300). In defining a wife, Judy Brady examines the traditional gender roles that made her miserable (next page), while Pico Iyer writes about the pleasures to be found in adapting to circumstance (p. 312). And Walter Mosley, a novelist turned activist, questions the government's commitment to the "pursuit of happiness" promised by the Declaration of Independence (p. 318).

Judy Brady

Judy Brady was born in 1937 in San Francisco. She attended the University of Iowa and graduated with a bachelor's degree in painting in 1962. Married in 1960, she was raising two daughters by the mid-1960s. She began working in the women's movement in 1969 and through it developed an ongoing concern with political and social issues, especially women's rights, cancer, and the environment. She believes that "as long as women continue to tolerate a society which places profits above the needs of people, we will continue to be exploited as workers and as wives." Besides the essay reprinted here, Brady has written articles for various magazines and edited *1 in 3: Women with Cancer Confront an Epidemic* (1991), motivated by her own struggle with the disease. She is also cofounder of the Toxic Links Coalition and serves on the board of Greenaction for Health and Environmental Justice.

I Want a Wife

Writing after a decade of marriage, and before divorcing her husband, Brady here pins down the meaning of the word *wife* from the perspective of one person profoundly unhappy with the role. This essay was first delivered as a speech at a San Francisco women's rally in 1970, then published in the premier issue of *Ms.* magazine in December 1971. It has since been reprinted widely. Is Brady's harsh portrayal of gender roles still relevant today?

I belong to that classification of people known as wives. I am A Wife. 1 And, not altogether incidentally, I am a mother.

Not too long ago a male friend of mine appeared on the scene fresh 2 from a recent divorce. He had one child, who is, of course, with his ex-wife. He is looking for another wife. As I thought about him while I was ironing one evening, it suddenly occurred to me that I, too, would like to have a wife. Why do I want a wife?

I would like to go back to school so that I can become economically 3 independent, support myself, and, if need be, support those dependent upon me. I want a wife who will work and send me to school. And while I am going to school I want a wife to take care of my children. I want a wife to keep track of the children's doctor and dentist appointments. And to keep track of mine, too. I want a wife to make sure my children eat properly and are kept clean. I want a wife who will wash the children's clothes and keep them mended. I want a wife who is a good nurturant attendant to my children, who arranges for their schooling, makes sure that they have an adequate social life with their peers, takes them to the park, the zoo, etc. I want a wife who takes care of the children when they are sick, a wife who arranges to be around when the children need special care, because, of course, I cannot miss classes at school. My wife must arrange to lose time at work and not lose the job. It may mean a small cut in my wife's income from time to time, but I guess I can tolerate that. Needless to say, my wife will arrange and pay for the care of the children while my wife is working.

I want a wife who will take care of *my* physical needs. I want a wife   4
who will keep my house clean. A wife who will pick up after my children, a wife who will pick up after me. I want a wife who will keep my clothes clean, ironed, mended, replaced when need be, and who will see to it that my personal things are kept in their proper place so that I can find what I need the minute I need it. I want a wife who cooks the meals, a wife who is a *good* cook. I want a wife who will plan the menus, do the necessary grocery shopping, prepare the meals, serve them pleasantly, and then do the cleaning up while I do my studying. I want a wife who will care for me when I am sick and sympathize with my pain and loss of time from school. I want a wife to go along when our family takes a vacation so that someone can continue to care for me and my children when I need a rest and change of scene.

I want a wife who will not bother me with rambling complaints   5
about a wife's duties. But I want a wife who will listen to me when I feel the need to explain a rather difficult point I have come across in my course of studies. And I want a wife who will type my papers for me when I have written them.

I want a wife who will take care of the details of my social life. When   6
my wife and I are invited out by friends, I want a wife who will take care of the babysitting arrangements. When I meet people at school that I like and want to entertain, I want a wife who will have the house clean, will prepare a special meal, serve it to me and my friends, and not inter-rupt when I talk about things that interest me and my friends. I want a wife who will have arranged that the children are fed and ready for bed before my guests arrive so that the children do not bother us. I want a wife who takes care of the needs of my guests so that they feel comfort-able, who makes sure that they have an ashtray, that they are passed the hors d'oeuvres, that they are offered a second helping of the food, that their wine glasses are replenished when necessary, that their coffee is served to them as they like it. And I want a wife who knows that some-times I need a night out by myself. . . .

If, by chance, I find another person more suitable as a wife than   7
the wife I already have, I want the liberty to replace my present wife with another one. Naturally, I will expect a fresh, new life; my wife

will take the children and be solely responsible for them so that I am left free.

When I am through with school and have a job, I want my wife to   8
quit working and remain at home so that my wife can more fully and completely take care of a wife's duties.

My God, who *wouldn't* want a wife?   9

Vocabulary

If any of the following words are unfamiliar, try to determine their meanings from the context of Brady's essay. Look up the words in a dictionary to check your guesses, and then use each one in a sentence or two of your own.

nurturant (3)   replenished (6)   hors d'oeuvres (6)

Key Ideas and Details

1. In one or two sentences, summarize Brady's definition of a wife. Consider not only the functions she mentions but also the relationship she portrays.

2. Brady provides many instances of a double standard of behavior and responsibility for the wife and the wife's spouse. What are the wife's chief responsibilities and expected behaviors? What are the spouse's?

Craft and Structure

1. LANGUAGE Why does Brady never substitute the personal pronoun "she" for "my wife"? Does the effect gained by repeating "my wife" justify the occasionally awkward sentences, such as the last one in paragraph 3?

2. Why does Brady repeat "I want a wife" in almost every sentence, often at the beginning of the sentence? What does this stylistic device convey about the person who wants a wife? How does it fit in with Brady's main idea and purpose?

3. Analyze the introduction to Brady's essay. What function does paragraph 1 serve? In what way does paragraph 2 confirm Brady's definition? How does the question at the end of the introduction relate to the question at the end of the essay?

4. OTHER METHODS Brady develops her definition primarily by classification (Chapter 10). What does she classify, and what categories does she form? What determines her arrangement of these categories? What does the classification contribute to the essay?

Integration of Knowledge and Ideas

1. Why do you think Brady wrote this essay? Was her purpose to explain a wife's duties, to complain about her own situation, to poke fun at men, to attack men, to attack society's attitudes toward women, or something else? Was she trying to provide a realistic and fair definition of *wife*? What passages in the essay support your answers?

2. What does Brady seem to assume about her readers' gender (male or female) and their attitudes toward women's roles in society, relations between the sexes, and work inside and outside the home? Does she seem to write from the perspective of a particular age group or social and economic background? In answering these questions, cite specific passages from the essay.

3. FOR DISCUSSION With "I Want a Wife," Brady clearly intended to provoke a reaction. What is *your* reaction to this essay: do you think it is realistic or exaggerated, fair or unfair to men, relevant or irrelevant to the present time? Why?

Writing Topics

1. Analyze a role that is defined by gender, such as that of a wife or husband, mother or father, sister or brother, daughter or son. First write down the responsibilities, activities, and relationships that define that role, and then elaborate your ideas into an essay defining this role as you see it. You could, if appropriate, follow Brady's model by showing how the role is influenced by the expectations of another person or people.

2. Combine definition and comparison (Chapter 12) in an essay or speech that contrasts a wife or a husband you know with Brady's definition of either role. Be sure that the point of your comparison is clear and that you use specific examples to illustrate the similarities or differences you see.

3. RESEARCH Brady's essay was written in the specific cultural context of the early 1970s. Undoubtedly, many cultural changes have taken place since then, particularly changes in gender roles. However, one could also argue that much remains the same. Write an essay in which you compare the stereotypical role of a wife now with the role Brady defines. In addition to your own observations and experiences, consider images of wives presented by the media—for instance, in television advertising or sitcoms—then and now.

4. CONNECTIONS Like Brady's "I Want a Wife," Sojourner Truth's "Ain't I a Woman?" (p. 443) is also notable for a strong, uncompromising tone. Write an analysis of the language Brady and Truth use to define women's role in society. How are their attitudes similar or different? Use specific examples from both works.

Pico Iyer

Travel writer Pico Iyer was born in 1957 in Oxford, England. The son of Indian college professors working abroad, he attended boarding schools in the United Kingdom and the United States, studied English literature at Oxford, and earned a master's degree in English and American language and literature from Harvard. Iyer worked as a staff writer for *Time* magazine for four years but felt constrained by office life; he quit so he could explore the world and has made his living as a freelance writer since 1986. His highly acclaimed books of travel essays include *Video Night in Kathmandu: And Other Reports from the Not-So-Far East* (1988), *The Global Soul: Jet Lag, Shopping Malls, and the Search for Home* (2000), and *Sun After Dark: Flights into the Foreign* (2004). Iyer is also the author of two novels, *Cuba and the Night* (1995) and *Abandon: A Romance* (2003), dozens of magazine pieces, and, most recently, *The Man within My Head* (2012), a critical meditation on the literature of British novelist Graham Greene. A self-described "perpetual foreigner" who cherishes his outsider perspective, Iyer lives in the suburbs of Kyoto, Japan.

The Joy of Less

In the fall of 2008, a global financial crisis plunged most of the world into an economic recession that left millions of people struggling. But as a practiced convert to frugal living, Iyer didn't mind. First posted as a blog entry for the *New York Times* in 2009, "The Joy of Less" offers his commentary on the benefits of doing without.

"The beat of my heart has grown deeper, more active, and yet more   1
peaceful, and it is as if I were all the time storing up inner riches. . . . My [life] is one long sequence of inner miracles." The young Dutchwoman Etty Hillesum wrote that in a Nazi transit camp in 1943, on her way to her death at Auschwitz two months later. Towards the end of his life, Ralph Waldo Emerson[1] wrote, "All I have seen teaches me to trust the creator for all I have not seen," though by then he had already lost his father when he was seven, his first wife when she was twenty and his first son, aged five. In Japan, the late eighteenth-century poet Issa is celebrated for his delighted, almost child-like celebrations of the natural world. Issa saw four children die in infancy, his wife die in childbirth, and his own body partially paralyzed.

---

[1] American writer Ralph Waldo Emerson (1803–82) was a leader of the transcendental movement, which rejected commercial culture and traditional religion in favor of self-reliance and intellectual growth. The line Iyer cites is from Emerson's 1875 essay "Immortality." [Editors' note.]

I'm not sure I knew the details of all these lives when I was twenty- 2
nine, but I did begin to guess that happiness lies less in our circumstances than in what we make of them, in every sense. "There is nothing either good or bad," I had heard in high school, from Hamlet, "but
thinking makes it so." I had been lucky enough at that point to stumble
into the life I might have dreamed of as a boy: a great job writing on
world affairs for *Time* magazine, an apartment (officially at least) on Park
Avenue, enough time and money to take vacations in Burma, Morocco,
El Salvador. But every time I went to one of those places, I noticed that
the people I met there, mired in difficulty and often warfare, seemed to
have more energy and even optimism than the friends I'd grown up with
in privileged, peaceful Santa Barbara, California, many of whom were on
their fourth marriages and seeing a therapist every day. Though I knew
that poverty certainly didn't buy happiness, I wasn't convinced that
money did either.

So—as post-1960s cliché decreed—I left my comfortable job and 3
life to live for a year in a temple on the backstreets of Kyoto. My high-
minded year lasted all of a week, by which time I'd noticed that the
depthless contemplation of the moon and composition of haiku I'd
imagined from afar was really more a matter of cleaning, sweeping and
then cleaning some more. But today, more than twenty-one years later,
I still live in the vicinity of Kyoto, in a two-room apartment that makes
my old monastic cell look almost luxurious by comparison. I have no
bicycle, no car, no television I can understand, no media—and the days
seem to stretch into eternities, and I can't think of a single thing I lack.

I'm no Buddhist monk, and I can't say I'm in love with renuncia- 4
tion in itself, or traveling an hour or more to print out an article I've
written, or missing out on the NBA Finals. But at some point, I decided
that, for me at least, happiness arose out of all I didn't want or need, not
all I did. And it seemed quite useful to take a clear, hard look at what
really led to peace of mind or absorption (the closest I've come to understanding happiness). Not having a car gives me volumes not to think or
worry about, and makes walks around the neighborhood a daily adventure. Lacking a cell phone and high-speed Internet, I have time to play
ping-pong every evening, to write long letters to old friends and to go
shopping for my sweetheart (or to track down old baubles for two kids
who are now out in the world).

When the phone does ring—once a week—I'm thrilled, as I never 5
was when the phone rang in my overcrowded office in Rockefeller
Center. And when I return to the United States every three months or
so and pick up a newspaper, I find I haven't missed much at all. While

I've been rereading P.G. Wodehouse,[2] or *Walden*,[3] the crazily accelerating roller-coaster of the 24/7 news cycle has propelled people up and down and down and up and then left them pretty much where they started. "I call that man rich," Henry James's Ralph Touchett observes in *Portrait of a Lady*,[4] "who can satisfy the requirements of his imagination." Living in the future tense never did that for me.

I certainly wouldn't recommend my life to most people—and my 6 heart goes out to those who have recently been condemned to a simplicity they never needed or wanted. But I'm not sure how much outward details or accomplishments ever really make us happy deep down. The millionaires I know seem desperate to become multimillionaires, and spend more time with their lawyers and their bankers than with their friends (whose motivations they are no longer sure of). And I remember how, in the corporate world, I always knew there was some higher position I could attain, which meant that, like Zeno's arrow,[5] I was guaranteed never to arrive and always to remain dissatisfied.

Being self-employed will always make for a precarious life; these 7 days, it is more uncertain than ever, especially since my tools of choice, written words, are coming to seem like accessories to images. Like almost everyone I know, I've lost much of my savings in the past few months. I even went through a dress-rehearsal for our enforced austerity when my family home in Santa Barbara burned to the ground some years ago, leaving me with nothing but the toothbrush I bought from an all-night supermarket that night. And yet my two-room apartment in nowhere Japan seems more abundant than the big house that burned down. I have time to read the new John le Carré,[6] while nibbling at sweet tangerines in the sun. When a Sigur Rós[7] album comes out, it fills my days

---

[2] Best known for creating the character of Jeeves the butler, English humorist Pelham George Wodehouse (1881–1975) wrote poems, song lyrics, short stories, novels, plays, and nonfiction works. [Editors' note.]

[3] Transcendental writer Henry David Thoreau's reflections (1854) on living alone for two years in a one-room cabin in the woods of Concord, Massachusetts. [Editors' note.]

[4] Henry James (1843–1916) was an American novelist and critic. *The Portrait of a Lady* (1881) is a novel about a New York woman who travels to Europe, inherits a fortune, and becomes trapped in an unhappy marriage. The character Touchett is the protagonist's invalid cousin. [Editors' note.]

[5] Zeno of Elea (approx. 495–430 BC) was a Greek philosopher famous for paradoxes, including his argument that if a moving object (in this case an arrow) is stationary at any point in time, and time is made up of a series of points, then a moving object must be stationary and will thus never reach its target. [Editors' note.]

[6] The pen name of English spy novelist David John Moore Cornwell (born 1931). [Editors' note.]

[7] An Icelandic rock band. [Editors' note.]

and nights, resplendent. And then it seems that happiness, like peace or passion, comes most freely when it isn't pursued.

If you're the kind of person who prefers freedom to security, who 8 feels more comfortable in a small room than a large one and who finds that happiness comes from matching your wants to your needs, then running to stand still isn't where your joy lies. In New York, a part of me was always somewhere else, thinking of what a simple life in Japan might be like. Now I'm there, I find that I almost never think of Rockefeller Center or Park Avenue at all.

Vocabulary

If you do not know the following words, try to determine their meanings from the context of Iyer's essay. Test your guesses in a dictionary, and then use each word in a sentence of your own.

mired (2)	Buddhist (4)	precarious (7)
decreed (3)	renunciation (4)	austerity (7)
haiku (3)	absorption (4)	resplendent (7)
monastic (3)	baubles (4)	

Key Ideas and Details

1. How does Iyer define *happiness*? Where in the essay is his definition expressed most clearly?

2. What is Iyer's thesis? Does he have a point he wants readers to take from his definition?

3. Why do you think Iyer comments that his "privileged" friends in California need therapy and the wealthy people he knows want even more money?

Craft and Structure

1. LANGUAGE In his last paragraph, Iyer shifts pronouns, from *I* to *you*. Why? What does this shift reveal about Iyer's reason for sharing his experience with readers?

2. Iyer begins with three examples rather than a statement of his main idea. What effect do these examples produce? How do they set up the main idea of the essay?

3. What is the effect of Iyer's expressions of uncertainty, such as "I'm not sure I knew" (paragraph 2) and "I wasn't convinced" (2)? Are these expressions sincere, do you think? What purpose, or purposes, do they serve?

4. OTHER METHODS Iyer draws on many methods to build his definition, among them narration (Chapter 6), example (Chapter 8), comparison and contrast

(Chapter 12), and cause-and-effect analysis (Chapter 14). What effects— positive and negative—does lack of luxuries have on Iyer?

Integration of Knowledge and Ideas

1. To whom does Iyer seem to be writing here? What assumptions does he make about his readers?

2. After explaining the benefits of simplicity, Iyer says, "I certainly wouldn't recommend my life to most people" (paragraph 6). Why not? What, then, could be his purpose in writing?

3. FOR DISCUSSION "The Joy of Less" abounds in literary references. Pick one or two such references and prepare to explain their meaning and significance to the rest of the class. Why does Iyer rely so heavily on other writers' ideas? To what extent do readers need to be familiar with their works to understand Iyer's meaning?

Writing Topics

1. How did you react to Iyer's essay? Do you agree that materialism makes people unhappy, or do you believe that acquiring wealth is a worthy goal? Why? Write an essay in which you describe your ambitions, pinpointing the beliefs and experiences that have influenced your expectations for your future. Do you believe that your desires will evolve? Do you think that they could ever change completely?

2. Before the invention of the phone and the Internet, people used to communicate almost exclusively by writing and mailing letters to each other, as Iyer still does. It seems as if hardly anyone writes letters anymore; our mailboxes are filled instead with flyers, junk mail, and bills. Write an essay in which you consider what has been gained or lost by modern forms of communication. Use examples from your own life to illustrate the benefits of communicating with others in different ways.

3. RESEARCH Iyer reports that he was "lucky enough" (paragraph 2) to be hired for his dream job shortly out of college, only to discover that he didn't like working in an office. What kind of work do you hope to do after you finish school? Using the Bureau of Labor Statistics' *Occupational Outlook Handbook* (*bls.gov/ooh*) as a starting point, research a career that interests you. What kinds of preparation (education, experience, and so on) are required to work in your chosen field? What are the chances of getting hired? What does the work entail? How much money could you make? How might taking on a particular job impact other aspects of your life, such as leisure, family, health, and overall satisfaction? Present your findings to the class.

4. CONNECTIONS Annie Dillard, in "Living Like Weasels" (p. 141), also writes about intellectual life, and like Iyer, she concludes that the key to happiness is to pursue one's passions. Write an essay analyzing both writers' attitudes toward thought and culture. What do their essays have in common? Where do their perspectives differ? How, if at all, do their ideas influence your own thinking about what it means to live well?

Walter Mosley

A former computer programmer turned writer, Walter Mosley (born 1952) is best known for his critically acclaimed Easy Rawlins detective novels, which explore the moral ambiguities of crime in the African American neighborhoods of Los Angeles. Mosley grew up in the Watts section of Los Angeles, attended Goddard College, and received a degree in political science from Johnson State College. He worked for Mobil Oil for several years before pursuing a master's degree in writing from the City College of the City University of New York. In addition to the Easy Rawlins series, Mosley has published a number of mystery and science-fiction novels notable for examining issues of race and class — among them *Blue Light* (1998), *Fearless Jones* (2001), *The Wave* (2006), and *The Last Days of Ptolomy Grey* (2010) — as well as several collections of short stories. An outspoken social critic and political activist, Mosley also writes provocative nonfiction, including regular essay contributions for the *New Yorker* and the *Nation* and two books that analyze capitalism and American culture: *Workin' on the Chain Gang: Shaking Off the Dead Hand of History* (2000) and *Twelve Steps Toward Political Revelation* (2011). He lives in New York.

Get Happy

In this essay Mosley proposes a political solution to what many would consider a personal problem. Most of us are unhappy, he claims, and our government needs to step in and help. "Get Happy" first appeared in the *Nation*, a magazine with a progressive political focus.

> *We hold these truths to be self evident, that all men are created equal, that they are endowed by their Creator with certain unalienable rights, that among these are Life, Liberty, and the pursuit of Happiness.*

Americans are an unhappy, unhealthy lot. From the moment we 1 declared our independence from the domination of British rule, we have included the people's right to pursue happiness as one of the primary privileges of our citizens and the responsibility of our government. Life and liberty are addressed to one degree or another by our executive, legislative and judicial branches, but our potential for happiness has lagged far behind.

As the quote above says (and does not say), freedom was once the 2 province of white men; now the lack of that freedom and the subsequent loss of the potential for happiness belongs to all of us. Our happiness is kept from us by prisonlike schools and meaningless jobs, un(der)-employment and untreated physical and psychological ailments, by political leaders who scare the votes out of us and corporate "persons" that buy up all the resources that have been created and defined by our labor.

Citizens are not treated like members of society but more like ³ employees who can be cut loose for any reason large or small, whether that reason be an individual action or some greater event like the downturn of the stock market. We are lied to by our leaders and the mass media to such a great extent that it's almost impossible to lay a finger on one thing that we can say, unequivocally, is true. We wage a "war on drugs" while our psychiatrists prescribe mood-altering medicines at an alarming rate. We eat and drink and smoke too much, and sleep too little. We worry about health and taxes and the stock market until one of the three finally drags us down. We fall for all sorts of get-rich-quick schemes, from the stock market to the lottery. We practice rampant consumerism, launch perpetual wars and seek out meaningless sex.

Through these studies we create aberrant citizens who glean their ⁴ empty and impossible hopes from television, the Internet and stadium sports. These issues, and others, form the seat of our discontent, a throne of nails under a crown of thorns.

Happiness is considered by most to be a subset of wealth, which is ⁵ not necessarily true. But even if it was true, most Americans are not wealthy, and most of those who are will lose that wealth before they die. Besides, money cannot buy happiness. It can buy bigger TVs and comelier sex partners; it can pay for liposuction and enough fossil fuel to speed away from smog-filled urban sprawls. Money can influence court verdicts, but it cannot buy justice. And without the bedrock of justice, how can any American citizen be truly happy?

Happiness is a state of mind cultivated under a sophisticated under- ⁶ standing of a rapidly changing world. In times gone by the world didn't change so fast. As recently as the early twentieth century it would take a generation or more for knowledge to double; now the sum total of our knowledge doubles each year, perhaps even less than that. As technology and technique change, so does our world and our reactions to it. The Internet, gene-splicing, transportation, overpopulation and other vast areas of ever-growing knowledge and experience force significant changes in our lifestyles every few years.

The pursuit of happiness implies room to move, but the definition ⁷ of that space has changed—from open fields to Internet providers, from talk with a friend or religious leader to psychotherapy and antidepression drugs.

If you are reading this essay and believe that you and the majority ⁸ of your fellows are happy, content, satisfied and generally pleased with the potentials presented to you and others, then you don't have to continue reading. I certainly do not wish to bring unhappiness to anyone who feels they fit into this world like a pampered foot into a sheepskin slipper.

Some of us are naturally happy; others have had the good fortune 9
to be born at the right moment, in the right place. But many of us suffer under a corporatized bureaucracy where homelessness, illiteracy, poverty, malnourishment (both physical and spiritual) and an unrelenting malaise are not only possible but likely.

One cure—for those who feel that their pursuit of happiness has 10
been sent on a long detour through the labor camps of American and international capitalism—is the institution of a government department that has as its only priority the happiness of all Americans.

At first blush this might seem like a frivolous suggestion. Each and 11
every American is responsible for her or his own happiness, whatever that is, you might say. Furthermore, even if a government department was designed to monitor, propagate and ensure the happiness of our citizens, that department should not have the power or even the desire to enforce its conclusions on anyone.

But the suggestion here is to
expand the possibilities for happiness, not to codify or impose these
possibilities. Our Declaration of Independence says that the pursuit of
happiness is an "unalienable right."
This language seems to make the
claim that it is a government responsibility to ensure that all Americans,
or as many as possible, are given a
clear path toward that pursuit.

12

This is not and cannot be some   13
rocky roadway through a barren landscape. Our world is more like the tropics, crowded by a lush forest of fast-growing knowledge. The path must be cleared every day. How can a normal person be happy with herself in this world, when the definition of the world is changing almost hourly?

What we need is a durable and yet flexible definition (created by 14
study and consensus) that will impact the other branches of government. If we can, through a central agency, begin to come to a general awareness of what we need to clear the path to the pursuit of happiness, I believe that the lives we are living stand a chance of being more satis-

fying. If we can have a dialogue based on our forefathers' declaration, I believe that we can tame the shadowy government and corporate incursions into our lives.

What do we need to be assured of our own path to a contented exis- 15 tence? Enough food to eat? Health? Help with childcare? A decent, fulfilling education? Should we feel that the land we stand on is ours? Or that our welfare is the most important job of a government that is made up by our shared citizenship?

These simple interrogations are complex in their nature. All paths 16 are not the same; many conflict. But we need a government that assures us the promise of the Declaration of Independence. We need to realize that the ever more convoluted world of knowledge can flummox even the greatest minds. We need to concentrate on our own happiness if we expect to make a difference in the careening technological and slovenly evolving social world of the twenty-first century.

Vocabulary

If you do not know the following words, try to determine their meanings from the context of Mosley's essay. Test your guesses in a dictionary, and then use each word in a sentence of your own.

domination (1)	cultivated (6)	consensus (14)
province (2)	corporatized (9)	incursions (14)
subsequent (2)	bureaucracy (9)	interrogations (16)
unequivocally (3)	malaise (9)	convoluted (16)
rampant (3)	frivolous (11)	flummox (16)
perpetual (3)	propagate (11)	careening (16)
aberrant (4)	codify (12)	slovenly (16)
comelier (5)	unalienable (12)	

Key Ideas and Details

1. What is the author's thesis? Where in the essay does he state his main idea?

2. What seems to be Mosley's understanding of what *happiness* is? What does he suggest a person needs to feel content?

3. Referring to the Declaration of Independence, Mosley writes, "freedom was once the province of white men; now the lack of that freedom and the subsequent loss of the potential for happiness belongs to all of us" (paragraph 2). What does he mean?

4. Who, according to Mosley, is to blame for our unhappiness? Why does he believe the government should do something to fix the problem?

Craft and Structure

1. LANGUAGE A novelist, Mosley uses figures of speech to make his definition vivid and immediate. Find two or three similes and metaphors and comment on their meaning and effectiveness. (If necessary, see pp. 00–00 and *figures of speech* in the Glossary for explanations of *simile* and *metaphor*.)

2. "Get Happy" begins with an epigraph, or quotation, from the Declaration of Independence. What function does this quoted passage serve?

3. Examine the structure of Mosley's essay. What is his focus in paragraphs 2–9? What does he emphasize in paragraphs 10–16? How are the two halves of his essay related?

4. OTHER METHODS Mosley uses definition to advance an argument (Chapter 15). Where in this essay does he address opposing viewpoints? How does he portray those who might disagree with him?

Integration of Knowledge and Ideas

1. What do you think Mosley's purpose is? Does he really believe that there should be a specific branch of government dedicated to ensuring citizens' potential for happiness? What details in the essay support your answer?

2. Who is Mosley's intended audience? How does he attempt to gain readers' support for his ideas?

3. Why do you think the *Nation* included the artwork on page 000 with the original publication of "Get Happy"? Does it add anything to (or take anything from) Mosley's ideas?

4. FOR DISCUSSION "Americans are an unhappy, unhealthy lot," says Mosley (paragraph 1). Why does he think so? What reasons does he give to support his opening claim?

Writing Topics

1. Write a response to Mosley's essay. What do you think of Mosley's proposal? Does his definition anger you? irritate you? reassure you? inspire you? make you feel something else? Does it lead you to rethink your own potential for happiness? Do you find his claims, reasons, and conclusions to be fair? Why, or why not? Support your response with details from Mosley's essay and examples from your own experience.

2. Mosley's essay in some ways questions the foundations of the American dream, which holds that a person from even the most humble circumstances can achieve prosperity and happiness through determination and hard work. How realistic, or not, do you think the American dream is today?

Write an essay answering this question. As evidence for your argument, you may want to discuss how, if at all, the American dream applies to you, given your social and economic background.

3. RESEARCH Mosley comments that "our psychiatrists prescribe mood-altering medicines at an alarming rate" (paragraph 3) and bemoans the rise of "psychotherapy and antidepression drugs" (7). Do library research on the psychological problem of depression. (A periodicals database can give you a start, and many books have been written on the subject.) Write a brief essay outlining the contemporary definition of depression and some of its treatments, including therapy and medication.

4. CONNECTIONS Both Walter Mosley and David Brooks, in "People Like Us" (p. 228), suggest that at least some of their readers are out of touch with the reality of daily life for most Americans. Although the two focus on different realities from nearly opposite points of view (Mosley is liberal; Brooks is conservative), they share similar concerns. Write an essay that compares and contrasts their positions. What do these writers have in common, and where do their perspectives differ? Is either writer more effective than the other at shaping his argument for a particular group of readers? Taken together, what do they tell you about the state of American society and culture?

WRITING WITH THE METHOD

DEFINITION

Select one of the following topics, or any other topic they suggest, for an essay developed by definition. Be sure to choose a topic you care about so that definition is a means of communicating an idea, not an end in itself.

Personal Qualities

1. Ignorance
2. Selflessness or selfishness
3. Loyalty or disloyalty
4. Responsibility
5. Hypocrisy

Experiences and Feelings

6. A nightmare
7. A good teacher, coach, parent, or friend
8. A good joke or a tasteless joke
9. Shame

Social Concerns

10. Poverty
11. Education
12. Domestic violence
13. Substance abuse
14. Prejudice

Art and Entertainment

15. Jazz or some other kind of music
16. A good novel, movie, or television program
17. Impressionism or some other art movement

Ideas

18. Freedom
19. Nostalgia
20. Feminism
21. Success or failure
22. A key concept in a class you're taking

WRITING ABOUT THE THEME

PURSUING HAPPINESS

1. The authors in this chapter approach the subject of happiness from very different perspectives, and each offers a unique definition as a result. Peter Steiner (p. 000) uses humor to express a teenager's unhappiness in a situation that most people find enjoyable. Carlin Flora (p. 300) offers a clinical explanation of a psychological state. Sarah Vowell (p. 300) considers the emotional benefits of play. Judy Brady (p. 308) examines her dissatisfaction from a feminist angle, while Pico Iyer (p. 312) draws on literature to consider the sources of contentment. And Walter Mosley (p. 318) takes a political look at the reasons behind unhappiness. How do these writers' perspectives influence their ideas? What do their definitions have in common, and where do they disagree? How do *you* define happiness? Answer in a brief essay, citing as examples the essays in this chapter and your own experiences and desires.

2. Many of the writers in this chapter identify education as a prerequisite to a happy life. Carlin Flora cites the importance of "a willingness to learn and stretch and grow, which sometimes involves discomfort." Judy Brady wants to go back to school, while Walter Mosley asserts that "prisonlike schools" prevent happiness and stresses the need for a "decent, fulfilling education." And Pico Iyer derives his joy from reading. The boy in Peter Steiner's cartoon, on the other hand, is frustrated by a traditional writing assignment. What, in your mind, constitutes a good education? Has school been a positive or a negative experience for you? How can you get the most out of your time as a student? Write an essay analyzing the role you think education will play in your potential for success and happiness as an adult.

3. Can money buy happiness? Pico Iyer and Walter Mosley both say no, although they acknowledge that lack of money can be a problem. Judy Brady, on the other hand, expresses a strong desire to "become economically independent." And Sarah Vowell feels a need to escape the pressure of paying bills. Drawing on these writers' ideas and your own observations, write an essay that examines the relationship between work, money, and happiness. Can work bring its own satisfaction, or is it simply a means to an end? How much income does a person need to live well? What other factors contribute to, or take away from, personal well-being?

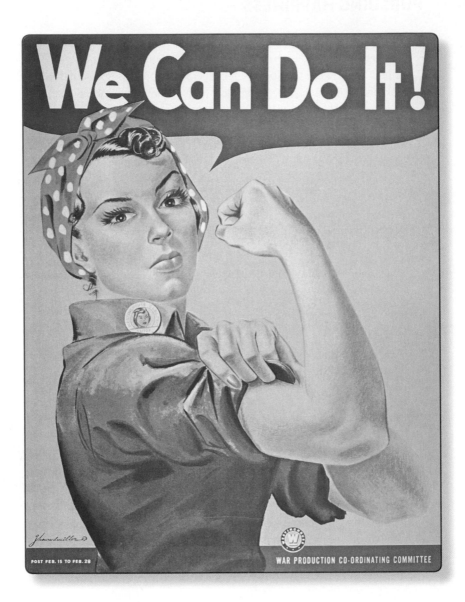

14

CAUSE-AND-EFFECT ANALYSIS

▶

INVESTIGATING THE WORKING WORLD

Why did free agency become so important in professional baseball, and how has it affected the sport? What caused the recent warming of the Pacific Ocean, and how did the warming affect the earth's weather? We answer questions like these with **cause-and-effect analysis**, the method of dividing occurrences into their elements to find relationships among them. Cause-and-effect analysis is a specific kind of analysis, the method discussed in Chapter 9.

Like everyone else, you probably consider causes and effects many times a day: Why is the traffic so heavy? What will happen if I take an elective in art rather than in business? In writing you'll also draw often on cause-and-effect analysis, perhaps explaining why the school's basketball team has been so successful this year, what made a bridge collapse, or how a new crosswalk has increased risks for pedestrians. You'll use the method for persuasion, too, as in arguing that families, not mass media, bear responsibility for children's violence (focusing on causes) or that illiteracy threatens American democracy (focusing on possible effects). Because cause-and-effect analysis attempts to answer *why* and *what if*—two of the most basic questions of human experience—you'll find the method often in your reading as well.

↰ Seeing Cause-and-Effect Analysis

Graphic artist J. Howard Miller (1918–2004) created the poster pictured here for Westinghouse Electric and Manufacturing in 1942, shortly after the United States entered World War II. The poster was displayed in the company's factories to encourage women to participate in the war effort by taking on the jobs left behind by the men fighting overseas. Traditionally discouraged from work outside the home or limited to service and clerical positions, millions of women accepted the challenge and proved that they could, indeed, do skilled industrial labor. After the war ended in 1945, however, most of them lost their jobs to the returning soldiers they had replaced and either settled for lower-paying fields or left the workforce altogether. Take a close look at Miller's image, keeping in mind Westinghouse's reasons for recruiting female workers and noticing how the woman (often referred to as "Rosie the Riveter") is portrayed. What— and whose—needs and desires does the poster address? In what ways does Rosie's appearance conform—or not—to ideals of femininity? What does the expression on her face suggest about how women might have felt about entering male-dominated fields during wartime? What results might they have expected? How do you imagine it affected women to be pushed back out of manufacturing after working for several years?

Reading Cause-and-Effect Analysis

Cause-and-effect analysis is found in just about every discipline and occupation, including history, social science, natural science, engineering, medicine, law, business, and sports. In any of these fields, as well as in writing done for school, the purpose in analyzing may be to explain or to persuade. In explaining why something happened or what its outcome was or will be, writers try to order experience and pin down connections. In arguing with cause-and-effect analysis, they try to demonstrate why one explanation of causes is more accurate than another or how a proposed action will produce desirable or undesirable consequences.

When writers analyze *causes*, they try to discover which of the events preceding a specified outcome actually made it happen: What caused Adolf Hitler's rise in Germany? Why have herbal medicines become so popular?

When writers analyze *effects*, they try to discover which of the events following a specified occurrence actually resulted from it: What do we do for (or to) drug addicts when we imprison them? What happens to our foreign policy when the president's advisers disagree over its conduct? These are existing effects of past or current situations, but effects are often predicted for the future: How would a cure for cancer affect the average life expectancy of men and women? How might the decision to quit a part-time job affect a student's college admissions prospects?

Causes and effects can also be analyzed together, as the questions opening this chapter illustrate.

The possibility of arguing about causes and effects points to the main challenge of this method. Related events sometimes overlap, sometimes follow one another immediately, and sometimes connect over gaps in time. They vary in their duration and complexity. They vary in their importance. Analyzing causes and effects thus requires not only identifying them but also judging their relationships accurately and weighing their significance fairly.

Causes and effects often do occur in a sequence, each contributing to the next in what is called a *causal chain*. For instance, an unlucky man named Jones ends up in prison, and the causal chain leading to his imprisonment can be outlined as follows: Jones's neighbor, Smith, dumped trash on Jones's lawn. In retaliation, Jones set a small brush fire in Smith's yard. A spark from the fire accidentally ignited Smith's house. Jones was prosecuted for the fire and sent to jail. In this chain, each event is the cause of an effect, which in turn is the cause of another effect, and so on to the unhappy conclusion.

Identifying a causal chain partly involves sorting out events in time:

- *Immediate* causes or effects occur nearest an event. For instance, the immediate cause of a town's high unemployment rate may be the closing of a large manufacturing plant where many townspeople work.

- *Remote* causes or effects occur further away in time. The remote cause of the town's unemployment rate may be a drastic decline in the company's sales or (more remote) a weak regional or national economy.

Analyzing causes also requires distinguishing their relative importance in the sequence:

- *Major* causes are directly and primarily responsible for the outcome. For instance, if a weak economy is responsible for low sales, it is a major cause of the manufacturing plant's closing.

- *Minor* causes (also called contributory causes) merely contribute to the outcome. The manufacturing plant may have closed for the additional reason that the owners could not afford to make repairs to its machines.

As these examples illustrate, time and significance can overlap in cause-and-effect analysis: a weak economy, for instance, is both a remote and a major cause; the lack of funds for repairs is both an immediate and a minor cause.

Since most cause-and-effect relationships are complex, several **falla-cies**, or logical errors, can weaken an analysis or its presentation. One is a confusion of coincidence and cause—that is, an assumption that because one event preceded another, it must have caused the other. This error is called **post hoc**, from the Latin *post hoc, ergo propter hoc*, meaning "after this, therefore because of this." Superstitions often illustrate post hoc: a basketball player believes that a charm once ended her shooting slump, so she now wears the charm whenever she plays. But post hoc also occurs in more serious matters. For instance, the office of a school administrator is vandalized, and he blames the incident on a recent speech by the student-government president criticizing the administration. But the administrator has no grounds for his accusation unless he can prove that the speech incited the vandals. In the absence of proof, the administrator commits the error of post hoc by asserting that the speech caused the vandalism simply because the speech preceded the vandalism.

Another potential problem in cause-and-effect writing is **oversim-plification**. An effective analysis must consider not just the causes and effects that seem obvious or important but all the possibilities: remote as well as immediate, minor as well as major. One form of oversimplification confuses a necessary cause with a sufficient cause:

- A *necessary* cause, as the term implies, is one that must happen for an effect to come about; an effect can have more than one necessary cause. For example, if emissions from a factory cause a high rate of illness in a neighborhood, the emissions are a necessary cause.

- A *sufficient* cause, in contrast, is one that brings about the effect by *itself*. The emissions are not a sufficient cause of the illness rate unless all other possible causes—such as water pollution or infection—can be eliminated.

Oversimplification can also occur if opinions or emotions are allowed to cloud the interpretation of evidence. Suppose that a writer is examining the reasons a gun-control bill she opposed was passed by the state legislature. Some of the evidence strongly suggests that a member of the legislature, a vocal supporter of the bill, was unduly influenced by lobbyists. But if the writer attributed the passage of the bill solely to this legislator, she would be exaggerating the significance of a single legislator and ignoring the opinions of the many others who also voted for the bill. To achieve a balanced analysis, she would have to put aside her personal feelings and consider all possible causes for the bill's passage.

For more about post hoc errors and oversimplification and for an overview of additional fallacies, see pages 371–73.

Analyzing Causes and Effects in Paragraphs

Barbara Ehrenreich (born 1941) is an investigative journalist with a PhD in biology. A contributing writer for a wide range of periodicals, she is probably best known for her books about contemporary class struggles in the United States, especially *Nickel and Dimed: On (Not) Getting By in America* (2001), the book in which the following paragraph appears.

The problem of rents is easy for a noneconomist, even a sparsely educated low-wage worker, to grasp. . . . When the rich and the poor compete for housing on the open market, the poor don't stand a chance. The rich can always outbid them, buy up their tenements or trailer parks, and replace them with condos, McMansions, golf courses, or whatever they like. Since the rich have become more numerous, thanks largely to rising stock prices and executive salaries, the poor have necessarily been forced into housing that is more expensive, more dilapidated, or more distant from their places of work. . . . Insofar as the poor have to work near the dwellings of the rich—as in the case of so many service and retail jobs— they are stuck with lengthy commutes or dauntingly expensive housing.

Cause (topic sentence underlined): competition for housing between rich and poor

Effects:

Rich buy inexpensive properties for themselves

Poor are forced to pay more, accept less, or move

Malcolm Gladwell was born in England in 1963 to an English father and a Jamaican mother and immigrated with his parents to Canada as a child. Now a staff writer at the *New Yorker*, he is known for his highly readable articles and books that synthesize complex research in the sciences and social sciences. This paragraph is from *Outliers* (2008), an exploration of why some people are more successful in their work than others.

[P]ersonal explanations of success don't work. People don't rise from nothing. We do owe something to parentage and patronage. The people who stand before kings may look

Effect (topic sentence under- lined): success

like they did it all by themselves. But in fact they are invariably the beneficiaries of hidden advantages and extraordinary opportunities and cultural legacies that allow them to learn and work hard and make sense of the world in ways others cannot. It makes a difference where and when we grew up. The culture we belong to and the legacies passed down by our forebears shape the patterns of our achievements in ways we cannot begin to imagine. It's not enough to ask what successful people are like, in other words. It is only by asking where they are *from* that we can unravel the logic behind who succeeds and who doesn't.

Causes:

Backgrounds

Opportunities

Influences

Developing an Essay by Cause-and-Effect Analysis

▶ Getting Started

Assignments in almost any class or line of work ask for cause-and-effect analysis: What caused the Vietnam War? What will be the effects of white-nose syndrome on the survival of North American bats? Why did costs exceed the budget last month? You can find your own subject for cause-and-effect analysis from your experiences, from observation of others, from your classwork, or from your reading outside school. Anytime you find yourself wondering what happened or why or what if, you may be onto an appropriate subject.

Remember that your treatment of causes or effects or both must be thorough; thus your subject must be manageable within the limits of time and space imposed on you. Broad subjects like those in the following examples must be narrowed to something whose complexities you can cover adequately.

BROAD SUBJECT   Causes of the decrease in American industrial productivity

NARROWER SUBJECT   Causes of decreasing productivity on one assembly line

BROAD SUBJECT   Effects of cigarette smoke

NARROWER SUBJECT   Effects of parents' secondhand smoke on small children

Whether your subject suggests a focus on causes or effects or both, list as many of them as you can from memory or from further reading. If the subject does not suggest a focus, then ask yourself questions to begin exploring it:

- Why did it happen?
- What contributed to it?
- What were or are its results?
- What might its consequences be?

One or more of these questions should lead you to a focus and, as you explore further, to a more complete list of ideas.

But you cannot stop with a simple list, for you must arrange the causes or effects in sequence and weigh their relative importance: Do the events break down into a causal chain? Besides the immediate causes and effects, are there also less obvious, more remote ones? Besides the major causes or effects, are there also minor ones? At this stage, you may find that diagraming relationships helps you see them more clearly. The following diagram illustrates the earlier example of the plant closing (see p. 329):

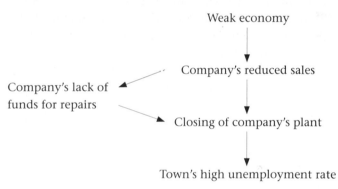

Though uncomplicated, the diagram does sort out the causes and effects and shows their relationships and sequence.

While you are developing a clear picture of your subject, you should also be anticipating the expectations and needs of your readers. As with the other methods of essay development, consider especially what your readers already know about your subject and what they need to be told:

- Do readers require background information?
- Are they likely to be familiar with some of the causes or effects you are analyzing, or should you explain every one completely?
- Which causes or effects might readers already accept?
- Which ones might they disagree with? If, for instance, the plant closing affected many of your readers—putting them or their relatives out of work—they might blame the company's owners rather than

economic forces beyond the owners' control. You would have to address these preconceptions and provide plenty of evidence for your own interpretation.

▶ Forming a Thesis

To help manage your ideas and information, try to develop a working thesis sentence that states your subject, your perspective on it, and your purpose. Here are two examples:

> EXPLANATORY THESIS SENTENCE   Unemployment has affected not only my family's finances but also our relationships.

> PERSUASIVE THESIS SENTENCE   Contrary to local opinion, the many people put out of work by the closing of Windsor Manufacturing were victims not of the owners' incompetence but of the nation's weak economy.

Notice that these thesis sentences reflect clear judgments about the relative significance of possible causes or effects. Such judgments can be difficult to reach and may not be apparent when you start writing. Often you will need to complete a draft of your analysis before you are confident about the relationship between cause and effect. And even if you start with an idea of how cause and effect are connected, you may change your mind after you've mapped out the relationship in a draft. That's fine: just remember to revise your thesis sentence accordingly.

▶ Organizing

The **introduction** to a cause-and-effect essay can pull readers in by describing the situation whose causes or effects you plan to analyze, such as the passage of a bill in the legislature or a town's high unemployment rate. The introduction may also provide background, such as a brief narrative of a family quarrel; or it may summarize the analysis of causes or effects that the essay disputes, such as townspeople blaming owners for a plant's closing. If your thesis is not already apparent in the introduction, stating it explicitly can tell readers exactly what your purpose is and which causes or effects or both you plan to highlight. But if you anticipate that readers will oppose your thesis, you may want to delay stating it until the end of the essay, after you have provided the evidence to support it.

The arrangement of the body of the essay depends primarily on your material and your emphasis. If events unfold in a causal chain with each effect becoming the cause of another effect, and if stressing these links coincides with your purpose, then a simple chronological sequence will probably be clearest. But if events overlap and vary in significance, their organization will require more planning. Probably the most effective way to arrange either causes or effects is in order of increasing importance. Such an arrangement helps readers see which causes or effects you consider minor and which major, while it also reserves your most significant (and probably most detailed) point for last. The groups of minor or major events may then fit into a chronological framework.

To avoid being preoccupied with organization while you are drafting your essay, prepare some sort of outline before you start writing. The outline need not be detailed so long as you have written the details elsewhere or can retrieve them easily from your mind. But it should show all the causes or effects you want to discuss and the order in which you will cover them.

In the **conclusion** of your essay, you may want to restate your thesis—or state it, if you deliberately withheld it for the end—so that readers are left with the point of your analysis. If your analysis is complex, readers may also benefit from a summary of the relationships you have identified. And depending on your purpose, you may want to specify why your analysis is significant, what use your readers can make of it, or what action you hope they will take.

▶ Drafting

While drafting your essay, strive primarily for clarity—sharp details, strong examples, concrete explanations. To make readers see not only *what* you see but also *why* you see it, you can draw on just about any method of writing discussed in this book. For instance, you might narrate the effect of a situation on one person, analyze a process, or compare and contrast two interpretations of cause. Particularly if your thesis is debatable (like the earlier example asserting the owners' blamelessness for the plant's closing), you will need accurate, representative facts to back up your interpretation, and you may also need quotations from experts such as witnesses and scholars. If you do not support your assertions specifically, your readers will have no reason to believe them. (For more on evidence in persuasive writing, see pp. 366–79. For more on finding and documenting sources, see Chapter 5.)

▶ Revising and Editing

While revising and editing your draft, consider the following questions and the focus box on the next two pages to be sure your analysis is sound and clear.

- *Have you explained causes or effects clearly and specifically?* Readers will need to see the pattern of causes or effects — their sequence and relative importance. And readers will need facts, examples, and other evidence to understand and accept your analysis.

- *Have you demonstrated that causes are not merely coincidences?* Avoid the error of post hoc, of assuming that one event caused another just because it preceded the other. To be convincing, a claim that one event caused another must be supported with ample evidence.

- *Have you considered all the possible causes or effects?* Your analysis should go beyond what is most immediate or obvious so that you do not oversimplify the cause-and-effect relationships. Your readers will expect you to present the relationships in all their complexity.

- *Have you represented the cause-and-effect relationships honestly?* Don't deliberately ignore or exaggerate causes or effects in a misguided effort to strengthen your essay. If a cause fails to support your thesis but still does not invalidate it, mention the cause and explain why you believe it to be unimportant. If a change you are proposing will have bad effects as well as good, mention the bad effects and explain how they are outweighed by the good. As long as your reasoning and evidence are sound, such admissions will not weaken your essay; on the contrary, readers will appreciate your fairness.

- *Have you used transitions to signal the sequence and relative importance of events?* Transitions between sentences can help you pinpoint causes or effects (*for this reason, as a result*), show the steps in a sequence (*first, second, third*), link events in time (*in the same month*), specify duration (*a year later*), and indicate the weights you assign events (*equally important, even more crucial*). (See also *transitions* in the Glossary.)

FOCUS ON **Conciseness**

While drafting a cause-and-effect analysis, you may need to grope a bit to discover just what you think about the sequence and relative importance of reasons and consequences. As a result, your sentences may grope a bit, too, reflecting your need to circle around your ideas in order to find them. The following draft passage reveals such difficulties:

WORDY AND UNCLEAR Employees often worry about negative comments from others. The employee may not only worry but feel the need to discuss the situation with coworkers. One thing that is an effect of harassment, especially verbal harassment, in the workplace is that productivity is lost. Plans also need to be made to figure out how to deal with future comments. Engaging in these activities is sure to take time and concentration from work.

Drafting this passage, the writer seems to have built up to the idea about lost productivity (third sentence) after providing support for it in the first two sentences. The fourth sentence then adds more support. And sentences 2–4 all show a writer working out ideas: sentence subjects and verbs do not focus on the main actors and actions of the sentences, words repeat unnecessarily, and word groups run longer than needed for clarity.

These problems disappear from the edited version below, which moves the main ideas up front, uses subjects and verbs to state what the sentences are about, and cuts unneeded words.

CONCISE AND CLEAR Verbal harassment in the workplace causes loss of productivity. Worrying about negative comments, discussing those comments with coworkers, planning how to deal with future comments — all these activities take time and concentration that a harassed employee could spend on work.

See pages 52–53 for more on editing for conciseness.

Practice

Revise the following sentences to eliminate wordiness. Try to emphasize the main ideas, put the meaning of each sentence into its subject and verb, and remove unnecessary words and phrases.

1. Another issue with verbal harassment is that the harassment can sometimes lead to physical abuse.
2. In many companies there have been incidents of employees shoving their coworkers, even of employees hitting other workers.
3. Some researchers say that the problem of harassment in the workplace is a result of the problem of bullying in schoolyards.
4. As a matter of fact, teenage bullies in schools are believed to simply grow up to be adult bullies in their jobs, according to those researchers.
5. It should go without saying that such behavior is clearly unacceptable regardless of the cause, so a way to prevent harassment must be found by employers.

▶ For additional practice editing for conciseness, visit Exercise Central at bedfordstmartins.com/exercisecentral.

A Note on Thematic Connections

Analyzing the workplace often prompts writers to ask what leads to success or failure or what may result from a business decision. The authors in this chapter all attempt to pinpoint a cause-and-effect relationship between business practices and their consequences for employees. In a recruitment poster (p. 326), J. Howard Miller encourages women to support war efforts by joining the industrial workforce. In a paragraph (p. 331), Barbara Ehrenreich considers how the real estate market makes housing difficult to find for low-wage workers. In another paragraph (p. 331), Malcolm Gladwell asserts that our chances for success are determined by hidden opportunities. In essays, journalist Dana Thomas (opposite) investigates the impacts our shopping choices have on workers around the globe. Ellen Goodman (p. 347) examines the results of overwork, while Charlie LeDuff (p. 352) contemplates what happens when there is not enough work to be had.

Dana Thomas

Fashion journalist Dana Thomas (born 1964) grew up in an upscale neighborhood of Philadelphia, attended the American University in Washington, DC, and taught journalism at the American University in Paris. She writes about style for *Newsweek* and has contributed articles to the *New York Times Magazine*, the *New Yorker*, *Harper's Bazaar*, *Vogue*, the *Wall Street Journal*, and several international newspapers. Noticing in the 1990s that high-end fashion brands such as Louis Vuitton, Gucci, and Prada had begun marketing low-end versions of their products, Thomas was inspired to research and write *Deluxe: How Luxury Lost Its Luster* (2007), an exposé of diminishing standards in the luxury industry that quickly became an international best-seller. She lives in Paris with her husband and daughter.

The Fake Trade

Thomas has been praised for offering an unexpected look at luxury merchandise and its impact on the people who make, sell, and buy it. In this article from *Harper's Bazaar Australia*, she explains why trading in counterfeit goods is not the victimless crime many shoppers assume it to be.

On a cool August evening, my family and I visited the preppy town of 1 Mill Valley, California, outside San Francisco. In the town square was an all-American sight: a couple of kids behind a card table selling homemade lemonade. My six-year-old wanted some, so I gave her a quarter and sent her over to the booth. After a few minutes, I joined the kids and noticed that one, a cute eight- or nine-year-old girl with a blonde blunt cut, had a little Murakami[1] pouch slung over her shoulder.

"Nice handbag," I said to her. 2

"It's Louis Vuitton," she responded proudly. 3

"No," I thought to myself as I gave it a good look-over. "It's a counterfeit Louis Vuitton. And it was probably made by a Chinese kid the same age as you in a slum halfway around the world." 4

Though the fashion business has muscled up its fight against counterfeiting, with many brands investing millions of dollars each year, the battle is ongoing. Since 1982, the global trade in counterfeit and pirated goods has grown from an estimated $5.5 billion to approximately $600 billion annually. Experts believe that counterfeiting costs American businesses $200 billion to $250 billion annually and is directly responsible for the loss of more than 750,000 jobs in the United States. 5

---

[1]Japanese artist Takashi Muramki designed a line of Louis Vuitton handbags. [Editors' note.]

What's counterfeited? Everything. A couple of years ago, a counter- 6
feit investigator discovered a workshop in the Thai countryside that produced fake versions of the classic Ferrari P4. Ferrari itself originally made
only three P4s back in 1967. The Food and Drug Administration has said
that counterfeit medicine could account for upwards of 10% of all drugs
worldwide. Unknowingly taking a fake version of your medicine could
have horrific effects on your health. European Union officials have seen
a dramatic rise in the seizure of counterfeit personal-care items such as
creams, toothpastes, and razor blades. The television series *Law & Order:
Criminal Intent* recently highlighted this problem in an episode in which
several children died after ingesting counterfeit mouthwash that had
been made with a poisonous chemical found in antifreeze. "There have
been counterfeit perfumes tested by laboratories that have found that a
major component was feline urine," says Heather McDonald, a partner at
the law firm Baker Hostetler in New York who specializes in anticounter-
feiting litigation. Counterfeit automotive brakes made with compressed
grass and wood have been found in US stores.

One of the primary reasons counterfeiting keeps flourishing is 7
that, as the little girl in Mill Valley proved, people keep happily buying
fakes. According to a study published last year by the British law firm
Davenport Lyons, almost two-thirds of UK consumers are "proud to tell
their family and friends that they bought fake luxury [fashion items]."
And according to a 2003 survey carried out by Market & Opinion Research
International in Great Britain, around a third of those questioned would
consider buying counterfeits. Why? Because we still think of counterfeiting as a "victimless crime." Buying a counterfeit Vuitton bag surely
doesn't affect the company, we reason. The parents of that Mill Valley
girl probably wouldn't have invested in a real Vuitton Murakami for her,
so it wasn't a loss of sales for the company.

But the reality is that we're all victims of counterfeiting, whether 8
from the loss of jobs or of tax revenue that could fund our schools and
our roads, or because by buying counterfeit goods, we are financing international crime syndicates that deal in money laundering, human trafficking, and child labor. Each time I read the horrid tales about counterfeiting from my book, *Deluxe: How Luxury Lost Its Luster*—like the raid
I went on in a clandestine factory in the industrial city of Guangzhou,
China, where we found children making fake Dunhill and Versace
handbags—audience members or radio listeners tell me they had no idea
it was such a dark and dangerous world and that by purchasing these
goods they were contributing personally to it. Then they invariably
swear that they will never knowingly buy another fake good.

Brands as well as law enforcement have cracked down on the coun- 9
terfeit business severely in the past few years, here in the US and abroad.
I saw a difference in Hong Kong, for example: a decade ago, you could
buy a fake Vuitton handbag or Burberry knapsack for a couple of bucks
from a vendor in the subway; today you can't even find them on the
street. There are still dealers, but now they lurk in doorways, whispering,
"Rolex? Chanel?" and you hurry down dark streets to armored hide-
aways to close the deal. To say it's scary is an understatement. "If you
can keep the stuff out of the public eye, you are halfway to winning the
battle," McDonald says. "The brands that are doing aggressive enforcement are hidden in back alleys and not on the street corners."

As long as there is a demand, however, there will be a supply. Tra- 10
ditionally, the supply chain worked like this: an order of ten thousand
handbags would be divided into ten groups of one thousand to be
made—often by children—in hidden workshops in Guangzhou. Once
completed, the items would be wrapped up and deposited in a neutral
place, like the courtyard of a local school, where they were picked up
by a local transporter, often simply a guy on a bike with a cart. The
transporter delivered the package to the wholesaler, who would take it
to another neutral place to be picked up by the international shipping
agent and put in a shipping container. The goods were often packed in
shipments of foodstuffs or legitimately manufactured clothing to escape
detection by receiving customs officials. Each time the goods changed
hands, the prices doubled. All transactions were done in cash.

But as fashion companies grew wise to the process and went after the 11
sources in China, leading to raids on workshops and busts at ports, the
counterfeit-crime rings came up with new routes to supply fake goods:
produce them, or at least finish them, in the destination country. Law
enforcement witnessed this firsthand during a big bust this past October. The New York Police Department raided a commercial building in
Queens, arrested thirteen, and seized around $4 million in counterfeit
apparel that carried the logos of major brands including Polo, Lacoste,
Rocawear, the North Face, and 7 for All Mankind. Officers also found a
stash of fake labels and buttons for Tommy Hilfiger, Nike, and Adidas
as well as embroidery machines. Investigators believe that the site was
a finishing facility. Workers took generic items that may have been
imported legally and sewed on fake logos and labels, turning the items
into counterfeit branded goods.

Another trick is to import counterfeit items that are hiding under a 12
legitimate face. "Some of the counterfeiters put a whole separate coat-
ing on the bag, and you peel it off like contact paper to see the logo fabric

underneath," McDonald tells me. "We seized a load of Lacoste men's dress shirts, and on the left breast pocket, where the alligator should be, there was a little generic label that read, 'Metro.' When you pulled out the threads and removed the Metro label, you found the alligator."

There's another method that is catching on rapidly: counterfeiters   13
who will take a legitimate logo, tinker with it slightly, apply for a trade-mark for the new design, then import those items under a false pretense of legality, showing the official application paperwork as their defense. For example, a company takes the Ralph Lauren polo-horse-and-rider logo and puts the polo mallet down instead of up in the air. The coun-terfeiter files a trademark application with the US Patent and Trade-mark Office and gets a document that states the application is pending. "It's a legitimate document fraudulently secured, and the application will probably be rejected in six months," the intellectual-property coun-sel for a luxury brand explains to me. "But between now and then, the customs agents will approve the importation of the items—believing, incorrectly, that the pending application proves the importer must have a legitimate right to the trademark."

By the time the brand realizes what's going on, the lawyer says, thou-   14
sands of items will have been imported and the counterfeiter will have "made millions" and fled. Luxury companies discovered one operation using this technique about two years ago, and now several more have popped up. "We must be doing a good job, since counterfeiters are look-ing for such complicated ways to get in," the lawyer says.

People often ask me, "How do you know it's fake?"   15

Well, if it's being sold at a fold-up table on a sidewalk corner or on   16
the back of a peddler on the beach, chances are it's fake. Or if it's at a flea market. Or a church fundraiser. Or in Wal-Mart or Sam's Club or other discount mass retailers. In June 2006, Fendi filed suit in a US district court against Wal-Mart Stores, Inc., asserting that the world's largest retailer was selling counterfeit Fendi handbags and wallets in its Sam's Club stores. For example, one bag was offered for $295; the legitimate Fendi handbag of the same design normally retailed for $925. In the suit, Fendi stated that Wal-Mart has never purchased Fendi products and never checked with Fendi to see if the items were real. The case was settled out of court last summer after Sam's Club agreed to pay Fendi an undisclosed sum.

If you want to guarantee that your luxury-brand purchases are   17
legitimate, don't shop in wholesale markets like those in Chinatown in Manhattan or Santee Alley in Los Angeles. "We'll go on raids on China-town wholesalers, and we'll find five or six suburban women standing

there—customers," New York security expert Andrew Oberfeldt has told me. "We'll say to these women, 'The dealers take you down dark corridors, through locked doors. The police say, "Open up!" The lights are turned out and everyone is told to be quiet. At what point did you realize that something was amiss here?'"

If you find an item for sale on the Internet for a price so low that 18 it seems too good to be true, it probably is too good to be true. Last fall, the UK-based Authentics Foundation, an international nonprofit organization devoted to raising public awareness about counterfeiting, launched *myauthentics.com*, a Web site that helps Internet shoppers determine if the products they are eyeing on the Web are real. It includes blogs and forums, news, myths, and tips on how to spot fakes; eBay now has links to the site. EBay also works with brands in its VeRO (Verified Rights Owner) program to find out if the items for offer on the site are genuine. If the brand deems a particular item to be counterfeit, the sale will be shut down. However, not all online sales sites have such verification processes in place. Besides, counterfeiters are known to post photos of genuine items to sell fakes. So as the old saying goes, buyer beware.

Of course, the best way to know if you are buying a genuine prod- 19 uct is to buy it from the brand, either in directly operated boutiques or in a company's shop in a department store. If you are curious about the authenticity of a used Vuitton item you purchased at a vintage shop or online, you can always contact one of the brand's boutiques.

Most important, we need to spread the word on the devastating 20 effects counterfeiting has on society today. I didn't tell the girl in Mill Valley that her bag was fake. It wasn't her fault her family had given it to her. But if I had met her parents, I would have said something. Awareness is key. Counterfeiting will never go away—it's been around since the dawn of time—but we can surely cut it down to size if we just stop buying the stuff. Without the demand, the supply will shrink. It's up to us.

Vocabulary

If any of the following words are new to you, try to determine their meanings from their context in Thomas's essay. Look up the words in a dictionary to check your guesses, and then use each word in a sentence of your own.

pirated (5)	flourishing (7)	pretense (13)
ingesting (6)	syndicates (8)	fraudulently (13)
feline (6)	clandestine (8)	counsel (13)
litigation (6)	invariably (8)	devastating (20)

Key Ideas and Details

1. Throughout her essay, Thomas repeats the words *counterfeit* and *legitimate*. How does she define these terms? Why is the distinction between the two important?

2. In paragraph 7, Thomas says that consumers believe counterfeiting is a "victimless crime." What does that mean? Does she believe it herself? Why does she bring it up?

3. "The Fake Trade" explores both causes and effects of counterfeiting. What, according to Thomas, are the main reasons for the practice? What are the most significant consequences?

Craft and Structure

1. LANGUAGE How would you characterize Thomas's tone? Is it appropriate, given her purpose and her audience?

2. How does Thomas use transitions to guide readers through her cause-and-effect analysis?

3. Analyze the organization of Thomas's essay by creating an outline of her major points. What is the effect of this structure?

4. OTHER METHODS Thomas provides many examples (Chapter 8) of counterfeit goods, and she uses process analysis (Chapter 11) to describe how they are manufactured, distributed, and sold. What does she accomplish by using these methods?

Integration of Knowledge and Ideas

1. What seems to be Thomas's primary purpose in this piece? Does she want to express her opinion about counterfeit goods? persuade consumers not to buy them? educate her readers? How can you tell?

2. To whom does Thomas seem to be writing here? Why do you think so?

3. Although Thomas stresses the importance of raising awareness of counterfeiting, she does not say anything to the girl with the fake designer handbag. Why not? Do you think she was right to keep quiet?

4. FOR DISCUSSION A journalist, Thomas supports her ideas with information from published studies and quotations from interviews with experts. Locate at least two examples of each. How effective do you find this evidence? Is it more, or less, persuasive than the examples she takes from her own experience? Why do you think so?

Writing Topics

1. Have you ever knowingly purchased something that pretended to be a luxury product but obviously wasn't, such as fake Versace sunglasses or an imitation Coach wallet? Did you have any reservations about making such purchases? Now that you've read "The Fake Trade," has your attitude changed in any way? Has Thomas persuaded you that counterfeiting has "devastating effects," or are you unmoved by her analysis? Why? Drawing on your own experience with fake goods and on what Thomas has to say, write an essay that argues for or against buying counterfeits. (If you share Thomas's concerns, be careful not just to repeat her points; look for additional examples of counterfeit products and add your own reasons for rejecting them.)

2. Thomas focuses on luxury goods, but in paragraph 6 she mentions that medicine is frequently counterfeited as well, compromising the health and threatening the lives of people who inadvertently buy ineffective or tainted drugs. Many supporters of health-care reform have raised the same point to argue that drug makers charge excessive prices for medications and that such costs should be controlled through government action. Write an essay that explores your thoughts on this issue. Should everyone have access to safe and effective medications, regardless of cost? Who should pay? Should some drugs be made available to all and other drugs provided only to those who can afford to pay for them? Do pharmaceutical companies have an obligation to make drugs affordable, or do they have a right to profit from the fruits of their research and development efforts? What, if anything, can be done to strike a fair balance between patients' and corporations' needs?

3. RESEARCH According to Thomas, the counterfeit industry not only leads to a loss of jobs in the United States, but also contributes to the problem of child labor in other countries, particularly China. What's wrong with child labor? Find a copy of Thomas's book *Deluxe: How Luxury Lost Its Luster* and track down one of the "horrid tales" she refers to in paragraph 8 of her essay. (If you can't locate a copy of the book in a library or bookstore, search the Web for information on child labor; see pp. 66–68 for tips on finding reliable sources online.) Based on what you discover, create a presentation that explains one aspect of the problem of child labor. For instance, in what kinds of work are children employed? Who hires them? How are they treated? Should children be permitted to work if their families need the income? Which countries are most affected? What is being done to protect child laborers, in the United States and abroad?

4. CONNECTIONS In "The Fake Trade," Thomas shows how efforts to get a bargain can impose high costs on workers in less affluent countries. Similarly, Barbara Kingsolver, in "Stalking the Vegetannual" (p. 258), asserts that importing off-season produce from distant parts of the world carries an environmental price tag. Write an essay that compares the two authors' beliefs about the benefits and drawbacks of a global economy. What assumptions, if any, do both writers share? Where do their perspectives diverge? How do their attitudes reinforce or conflict with your own views?

Ellen Goodman

Social commentator Ellen Goodman has had a distinguished career as a journalist and speaker. She was born in 1941, grew up in Boston, Massachusetts, and earned a degree from Radcliffe College (a part of Harvard University) in 1963. Goodman researched for *Newsweek* and reported for the *Detroit Free Press* and the *Boston Globe* before becoming a full-time syndicated columnist in 1974. Her observations on life and politics have been published in more than four hundred newspapers nationwide and collected in six volumes: *Close to Home* (1979), *At Large* (1981), *Keeping in Touch* (1985), *Making Sense* (1989), *Value Judgments* (1993), and *Paper Trail: Common Sense in Uncommon Times* (2004). One of the first American women to make a career as a columnist, Goodman won the Pulitzer Prize for distinguished commentary in 1980 and a lifetime achievement award from the National Society of Newspaper Columnists in 2008. She lives in Boston and spends summers with her family on the coast of Maine.

The Company Man

Goodman is known for her evenhanded thoughtfulness on contentious subjects ranging from the women's movement to bioethics. In this essay from *Close to Home*, she relates a story about one man's career to show how competitive office culture can damage lives.

1 He worked himself to death, finally and precisely, at 3:00 a.m. Sunday morning.

2 The obituary didn't say that, of course. It said that he died of a coronary thrombosis—I think that was it—but everyone among his friends and acquaintances knew it instantly. He was a perfect Type A, a workaholic, a classic, they said to each other and shook their heads—and thought for five or ten minutes about the way they lived.

3 This man who worked himself to death finally and precisely at 3:00 a.m. Sunday morning—on his day off—was fifty-one years old and a vice-president. He was, however, one of six vice-presidents, and one of three who might conceivably—if the president died or retired soon enough—have moved to the top spot. Phil knew that.

4 He worked six days a week, five of them until eight or nine at night, during a time when his own company had begun the four-day week for everyone but the executives. He worked like the Important People. He had no outside "extracurricular interests," unless, of course, you think about a monthly golf game that way. To Phil, it was work. He always ate egg salad sandwiches at his desk. He was, of course, overweight, by

twenty or twenty-five pounds. He thought it was okay, though, because he didn't smoke.

On Saturdays, Phil wore a sports jacket to the office instead of a 5 suit, because it was the weekend.

He had a lot of people working for him, maybe sixty, and most of 6 them liked him most of the time. Three of them will be seriously considered for his job. The obituary didn't mention that.

But it did list his "survivors" quite accurately. He is survived by his 7 wife, Helen, forty-eight years old, a good woman of no particular marketable skills, who worked in an office before marrying and mothering. She had, according to her daughter, given up trying to compete with his work years ago, when the children were small. A company friend said, "I know how much you will miss him." And she answered, "I already have."

"Missing him all those years," she must have given up part of her- 8 self which had cared too much for the man. She would be "well taken care of."

His "dearly beloved" eldest of the "dearly beloved" children is a 9 hard-working executive in a manufacturing firm down South. In the day and a half before the funeral, he went around the neighborhood researching his father, asking the neighbors what he was like. They were embarrassed.

His second child is a girl, who is twenty-four and newly married. 10 She lives near her mother and they are close, but whenever she was alone with her father, in a car driving somewhere, they had nothing to say to each other.

The youngest is twenty, a boy, a high-school graduate who has spent 11 the last couple of years, like a lot of his friends, doing enough odd jobs to stay in grass and food. He was the one who tried to grab at his father, and tried to mean enough to him to keep the man at home. He was his father's favorite. Over the last two years, Phil stayed up nights worrying about the boy.

The boy once said, "my father and I only board here." 12

At the funeral, the sixty-year-old company president told the forty- 13 eight-year-old widow that the fifty-one-year-old deceased had meant much to the company and would be missed and would be hard to replace. The widow didn't look him in the eye. She was afraid he would read her bitterness and, after all, she would need him to straighten out her finances—the stock options and all that.

Phil was overweight and nervous and worked too hard. If he wasn't 14 at the office, he was worried about it. Phil was a Type A, a heart-attack natural. You could have picked him out in a minute from a lineup.

So when he finally worked himself to death, at precisely 3:00 a.m.   15
Sunday morning, no one was really surprised.

By 5:00 p.m. the afternoon of the funeral, the company president   16
had begun, discreetly of course, with care and taste, to make inquiries
about his replacement. One of three men. He asked around: "Who's been
working the hardest?"

Vocabulary

If you do not know the following words, try to determine their meanings from
the context of Goodman's essay. Test your guesses in a dictionary, and then
use each word in a sentence of your own.

coronary (2)	conceivably (3)	discreetly (16)
thrombosis (2)	board (12)	

Key Ideas and Details

1. What killed Phil, according to his obituary? according to Goodman?

2. Why do you think Phil spent so much time at work? Did he love his job
   more than he loved his family, or does Goodman imply that there was
   some other reason (or reasons)?

3. "The Company Man" does not include a thesis statement. What is
   Goodman's point? Express the author's main idea in your own words.

4. Notice Goodman's frequent use of numbers: "five or ten minutes" (paragraph 2), "fifty-one years old" (3), "six vice-presidents" (3), and so on. What
   other numbers does she cite in this essay? What does the focus on such
   details contribute to her point?

Craft and Structure

1. LANGUAGE At several points in the essay Goodman quotes Phil's obituary as
   well as comments made by his family and coworkers. How do these quotations reinforce the main idea of her essay?

2. What cause does Goodman examine? What effects does she identify?

3. "He worked himself to death, finally and precisely, at 3:00 a.m. Sunday
   morning," Goodman says in paragraph 1, then again (with some variation)
   in paragraphs 3 and 15. Why does she stress these details? What other
   details does she repeat? What is the effect of her repetitions?

4. OTHER METHODS "The Company Man" is also a model of definition (Chapter 13). What does "Type A" (paragraphs 2 and 14) mean? What other details
   in the essay give you a clue to Phil's personality?

Integration of Knowledge and Ideas

1. Describing the reaction to Phil's death among his friends, Goodman says they "shook their heads—and thought for five or ten minutes about the way they lived" (paragraph 2). What does this comment reveal about her purpose for writing? about her intended audience?

2. Explain the irony of Goodman's conclusion. (If necessary, see the Glossary for an explanation of *irony*.)

3. FOR DISCUSSION Goodman gives no indication of what Phil's job was. Why not? What does leaving out this detail contribute to her meaning? What other details does she omit?

Writing Topics

1. Contemporary American society places great importance on work, encouraging people to find and devote themselves to jobs that entail responsibility and opportunity for advancement, to put in long hours if they are demanded, and to be available and productive at all times. In contrast, many other cultures emphasize leisure (in some European countries, for instance, businesses shut down for several hours every afternoon; in others, workers are entitled to eight weeks of paid vacation a year). Write an essay in which you consider the benefits and drawbacks of the American work ethic. What do we gain through hard work and determination? What do we lose?

2. Goodman writes that Phil's two sons took very different approaches to their independence as adults: The elder followed in his father's footsteps and became a "hard-working executive" (paragraph 9), while the younger chose to drift through "odd jobs" after finishing high school (12). How would you define *independence* for young adults? What freedoms does independence entail? What responsibilities? What problems can occur for the newly independent person?

3. RESEARCH Phil's oldest son "went around the neighborhood researching his father, asking the neighbors what he was like," Goodman writes in paragraph 9. How well do you know your parents? Even if you're close, you may not be fully aware of what they do with their time or how they get along with others. Pick a parent to research and interview several people—coworkers, for example, siblings, neighbors, or friends—to learn how others perceive him or her. In an essay, write a profile of your parent, focusing on how he or she interacts with the larger community.

4. CONNECTIONS While Goodman writes about a man who sacrificed his life and family to a demanding job, Pico Iyer, in "The Joy of Less" (p. 312), writes about leaving a prestigious job so he could pursue his own interests

and spend more time with his loved ones. In an essay, compare and contrast both writers' perspectives on work-life balance. What role does work play in a person's happiness? What role do personal relationships play? What changes in attitude do Goodman and Iyer hope readers will take from their essays? Is either more successful than the other at bringing readers around to a new point of view? How so?

Charlie LeDuff

Charlie LeDuff was born in 1967 in Virginia and grew up in the suburbs of Detroit, Michigan, where he is a registered member of the Sault Ste. Marie tribe of Chippewa. He earned a bachelor's degree in political science from the University of Michigan and a master's in journalism from the University of California at Berkeley. Before fully embarking on his writing career, LeDuff worked as a bartender, cannery worker, gang counselor, baker, carpenter, and middle-school teacher. He was a national correspondent for the *New York Times* from 1995 to 2007 and was awarded a Pulitzer Prize for his contributions to a series of articles about race in America. He branched out into television journalism and has written, produced, and hosted series for the Discovery Times Channel and the BBC. LeDuff is also the author of two books: *Work and Other Sins: Life in New York City and Thereabouts* (2004) and *US Guys: The True and Twisted Mind of the American Man* (2006). He is currently a multimedia reporter for the *Detroit News*.

End of the Line

For decades one of the largest employers in the United States, General Motors declared bankruptcy in June 2009, announcing that it would close many of its manufacturing plants and sending shockwaves throughout a country already stunned by global economic collapse. The company emerged from bankruptcy less than two months later, but many of its former employees and factory sites have not shared in its recovery. In September 2009, LeDuff wrote about the local effects of one GM plant closure for *Mother Jones* magazine. A photo essay by Danny Wilcox Frazier accompanied the essay, and we include some of the images here.

Driving through Janesville, Wisconsin, in a downpour, looking past the 1 wipers and through windows fogged up with cigarette smoke, Main Street appears to be melting away. The rain falls hard and makes a lonesome going-away sound like a river sucking downstream. And the old hotel, without a single light, tells you that the best days around here are gone. I always smoke when I go to funerals. I work in Detroit. And when I look out the windshield or into people's eyes here, I see a little Detroit in the making.

A sleepy place of 60,483 souls—if the welcome sign on the east side 2 of town is still to be believed—Janesville lies off Interstate 90 between the electric lights of Chicago and the sedate streets of Madison. It is one of those middle-western places that outsiders pay no mind. It is where the farm meets the factory, where the soil collides with the smokestack. Except the last GM truck rolled off the line December 23, 2008. Merry Christmas, Janesville. Happy New Year.

Janesville Assembly was one of General Motors' oldest plants, employing 4,000 people at its height, turning out classic Chevy and GMC vehicles. In December, the last GM truck rolled off the line. Photo: Danny Wilcox Frazier.

The Janesville Assembly Plant was everything here, they say. It was a birthright. It was a job for life and it was that way for four generations. This was one of General Motors' oldest factories—opened in 1919. This was one of its biggest—almost five million square feet. Nobody in town dared drive anything but a Chevy or a GMC. Back then GM was the largest industrial corporation in the world, the largest carmaker, the very symbol of American power. Ike's man at the Pentagon—a former GM exec himself—famously said, "What was good for our country was good for General Motors, and vice versa."[1] Kennedy, Johnson, Obama, they all campaigned here. People here can tell you of their grandparents who came from places like Norway and Poland and Alabama to build tractors and even ammunition during the Big War. Then came the Impalas and the Camaros. In the end they were cranking out big machines like the Suburban and the Tahoe, those high-strung, gas-guzzling hounds of the American Good Times.

Today, some $50 billion in bailouts later, GM is on life support and there is a sinking feeling that the country is going down with it. Those

---

[1] "Ike" was a popular nickname for Dwight D. Eisenhower, president of the United States from 1953 to 1961. LeDuff is referring to Eisenhower's secretary of defense, Charles Wilson, whose line was often misquoted as "What's good for GM is good for the country." [Editors' note.]

grandchildren are considering moving to Texas or Tennessee or Vegas. Who is to blame? Detroit? Wall Street? Management? Labor? NAFTA?[2] Does it matter? Come to Janesville and see what we've thrown away.

For years, the people here heard rumors that the plant was on its way   5
out. But no one ever believed it, really. Something always came along to save it. Gas prices went down or cheap Chinese money floated in. Janesville was too big to ignore. Too big to close.

And then they closed it.   6

Janesville was a company town, where generations of GM workers met at the VFW to cap off a hard day's work. Photo: Danny Wilcox Frazier.

The local UAW[3] union hall is quiet now. A photograph from a 1925   7
company picnic hangs there. The whole town is assembled near the factory, the women in petticoats, the children in patent leather, the men in woolen bowlers. The caption reads, "Were you there Charlie?"

Todd Brien's name still hangs in the wall cabinet—Recording Secre-   8
tary, it reads. But that is just a leftover like a coin in a cushion. Brien, forty-one, moved to Arlington, Texas, to take a temp job in a GM plant down there in April. He left his family up here. He is one of the lucky ones. Most of the other 2,700 still employed after rounds of downsizing

---

[2] The 1994 North American Free Trade Agreement removed restrictions and duties on goods and services exchanged between the United States, Canada, and Mexico. [Editors' note.]

[3] United Auto Workers. [Editors' note.]

had no factory to go to. But now, what with the bankruptcy of GM, he's temporarily laid off from Texas and back in Janesville to gather his family and head south.

"It was always in the back of my mind around here . . . They can 9 take it away," Brien says. "Well, they did. Now what? Can't sell my house. Main Street's boarding up. The kids around here are getting into drugs. You wonder when's the last train leaving this station? I just never believed it was going to happen." Today, freight trains leaving from Janesville's loading docks take auctioned bits and pieces of the plant to faraway places: welding robots, milling machines, chop saws, drill presses, pipe threaders, drafting tables, salt and pepper shakers.

Janesville is still a nice place. They still cut the grass along the river- 10 bank. The churches are still full on Sunday. The farmers still get up before dawn. But there are the little telltale signs, the details, the darkening clouds.

Janesville still looks like Heartland, USA—a giant fiberglass cow even marks the entrance into town. But restaurants are all but empty, and school enrollment is down. Photo: Danny Wilcox Frazier.

The strip club across the street from the plant is now an Alcoholics 11 Anonymous joint. There are too many people in the welfare line who never would have imagined themselves there. Dim prospects and empty buildings. A motel where the neon "Vacancy" sign never seems to say "No Vacancy."

The owner is Pragnesh Patel. He is thirty-six, looks a dozen years 12 older. He left a good job near Ahmedabad, India, as a supervisor in a television factory, he says. He came to try his luck in America. He got a job in a little factory in Janesville that makes electronic components for GM. He also bought the motel just up the hill from the assembly plant. Now with the plant closed, he's down to three shifts a week at the components factory and having to make $2,500 monthly payments on his motel on Highway 51. He charges forty-five bucks a night and today it's mostly the crackheads and the down-at-their-heels who come in for a crash landing. Welcome to America, except Patel has to raise his children amid this decay. "I'm trying, really trying to survive," he says. "I don't know anymore. I mean, I'm an American. I cast my lot here. But I have to tell you, on many days, I regret that I ever came."

There is a bar on the factory grounds that has become a funeral parlor. Yes, a bar on the factory grounds, not five-hundred feet from the time clock! Genius! It has been here since at least the Depression if the yellowed receipt from 1937 is to be believed. Five cases of beer for eight dollars and thirty cents. 13

And in some way, that bar on the factory grounds might explain what happened here. "We used to have a drive-through window," says one of the former UAW workers gathered at Zoxx 411 Club and drinking a long, cool glass of liquor at three in the afternoon. He is about fifty, about the age when a man begins to understand his own obsolescence. "Used to put two or three down and go back to work. Now those were the days, yes-siree." 14

You feel sorry for that autoworker until you hear he draws nearly three-quarters of his old salary for the first year of his layoff and half his salary for the second year of his layoff—plus benefits. 15

"It don't make sense to work," says the autoworker, buying one for the stranger. 16

If he finds a job, he says, they'll take his big check away. 17

"There ain't no job around here for $21 an hour," the autoworker says. "I might as well drink." 18

A taxpayer-funded wake. Good for him. Except you get the feeling that it's not good for a man to drink all day. Two years comes faster than a man thinks. 19

A little Detroit in the making, except Detroit has General Motors and Ford and Chrysler. Detroit is an industry town. Janesville had only General Motors. Janesville was a company town. You didn't have to go to college—but you might be able to send your kid there—because there was always GM. GM—Gimme Mine. GM—Grandma Moo, the golden cow. Now GM has Gone Missing. GM has Gone to Mexico. 20

"We took it for granted," says Nancy Nienhuis, seventy-six, a retired 21
factory nurse who farms on the outskirts of town. She did everything at
that plant a nurse could do: tended to amputations, heart attacks, shotgun wounds inflicted by a jilted lover, even performed an exorcism of
spiders from a crazy man's stomach. Whatever it took to keep those
lines moving.

"The rumor would start, they're talking about closing the plant. No 22
one would believe it. Then you saw the Toyota dealership open on the
east side of town and still they didn't believe it. The manager and the
worker sat next to each other in church, you see? They went to high
school together. Understand? The good worker got no recognition over
the bad worker. Nobody made waves about a guy drunk or out fishing
on the clock. In the end, the last few years, management rode them
pretty good. But by then it was a little too late."

Richard, a former welder at the plant, puts a pastry box in Nurse 23
Nancy's car. Richard begins to weep. He looks over his shoulder, wipes
his nose on his sleeve and says, "I don't want my wife to see this. I'm
sixty-two and I'm delivering doughnuts. What am I going to do?'"

Most laid-off GM assembly workers are paid severance for two years.
"There's going to be hell to pay when those unemployment checks stop
coming," says one resident. Photo: Danny Wilcox Frazier.

Desperation comes in subtler ways than a grown man crying. The 24
winner of the cakewalk at the local fair got not a cake—but a single,
solitary cupcake. Parents don't come to the PTA as much anymore. A lot

of kids will have left by the beginning of the school year, the superintendent says. Unemployment here is near 15%. The police blotter is a mix of Mayberry[4] and Big City: Truancy, Truancy, Shots Fired at 2 p.m., Dog Barking, Burglary at 5 p.m., Burglary at 6 p.m.

At 7 p.m. they fry fish at the VFW hall. Beers two bucks. Two-piece   25
plate of cod $6.95. Charlie Larson runs the place. You can see the factory from Charlie's parking lot, the Rock River running lazily beside it. Charlie tried the factory in 1966. His father got him in, but he was drafted into the jungles of Nam in 1967. "It's a discouraging thing," Charlie, sixty-one, says of the plant closing down, smoothing a plastic tablecloth. "It was the lifeblood of this town. It was the identity of this town. Now we have nothing, nothing but worry. Aw, there's going to be hell to pay when those unemployment checks stop coming."

Blame the factory worker if you must. Blame the union man who   26
asked too much and waited too long to give some back. Blame the guy for drinking at lunch or cutting out early. But factory work is a nine-to-five sort of dying. The monotony, the accidents. "You're a machine," says Marv Wopat. He put bumpers on trucks. A six-foot man stooping in a four-foot hole, lining up a four-foot bumper. Three bolts, three washers, three nuts. One every minute over an eight-hour shift. Wopat, sixty-two, has bad shoulders, bad knees, bad memories. "You got nightmares," he says. "You missed a vehicle or you couldn't get the bolt on. You just went home thinking nothing except the work tomorrow and your whole life spent down in that hole. And you thinking how you're going to get out. Well, now it's gone and alls we're thinking about is wanting to have it back."

And maybe they will have it back. The recession is loosening its   27
grip, some say. Some towns will rebound. Some plants will retrofit. Wind, solar, electric—that's the future, Washington says. But you get a pain-in-the-throat feeling that it is not the future. Not really. At least not as good a future as the past. There's no twenty-eight bucks an hour for life in that future. No two-car garage. No bennies.[5] No boat on Lake Michigan. Because in the new world they can build that windmill, or a solar panel, or an electric battery in India, where the minimum pay is less than $3 a day. Just ask Patel, the motel owner living at the edge of a dead factory in Janesville, Wisconsin. "You cannot compete with poverty unless you are poor."

---

[4] A fictional small town from the 1960s television series *The Andy Griffith Show.* [Editors' note.]

[5] Colloquial shorthand for *benefits.* [Editors' note.]

Vocabulary

If any of the following words are new to you, try to determine their meanings from their context in LeDuff's essay. Check your guesses in a dictionary, and then use each word in a sentence of your own.

birthright (3)	obsolescence (14)	cakewalk (24)
bailouts (4)	wake (19)	monotony (26)
petticoats (7)	amputations (21)	retrofit (27)
bowlers (7)	jilted (21)	
components (12)	exorcism (21)	

Key Ideas and Details

1. Why does LeDuff mention funerals in his opening paragraph? What do they have to do with his subject or his main idea?

2. Does LeDuff believe that Janesville will recover from the effects of the GM plant closure? Point to evidence from his essay to support your answer.

3. LeDuff's last sentence, "'You cannot compete with poverty unless you are poor,'" is quoted from a struggling motel owner. What does he mean? How does the line sum up LeDuff's underlying message?

Craft and Structure

1. LANGUAGE LeDuff's essay is full of sentence fragments, most notably in paragraphs 11, 19, 26, and 27. Choose one paragraph and edit it to eliminate the fragments, ensuring that every sentence is complete (for help with sentence fragments, see p. 49). Compare your edited version to LeDuff's original. Which is more effective, and why? How does LeDuff's deliberate use of fragments contribute to the overall effect of his essay?

2. In paragraphs 4 and 26, LeDuff lists several possible causes that might explain why General Motors went bankrupt, but he doesn't say anything more about them. Why does he devote his essay mainly to effects? What does he accomplish by dismissing causes as unimportant?

3. Examine the quotations from residents that LeDuff uses to explain the situation in Janesville. What do their own words convey that he could not? Why do you think he quotes them so extensively?

4. Take a close look at the photographs taken by Danny Wilcox Frazier. How would you characterize these images? What do they contribute to LeDuff's main idea?

5. OTHER METHODS In what ways does LeDuff use comparison and contrast (Chapter 12) as part of his cause-and-effect analysis? Why is this method important in developing his point?

Integration of Knowledge and Ideas

1. What seems to have inspired LeDuff to write this essay? How is "End of the Line" a reaction to a particular cultural moment?

2. What assumptions does LeDuff seem to make about his readers' familiarity with company towns and General Motors? What details help clarify the context of his analysis for those who don't already know it?

3. FOR DISCUSSION How do you react to LeDuff's essay? Do you agree that Janesville, Wisconsin, is dead, or is it simply on life support? Does it matter, as LeDuff asks, why the plant closed? Examine the writer's use of evidence and prepare to explain why you either agree or disagree with his conclusions.

Writing Topics

1. Think of a place to which you feel a special connection. The place may be rural or urban or suburban, and it need not be far away. Prepare an essay or presentation that describes the place for readers who are completely unfamiliar with it and who may be skeptical about your enthusiasm for it. Use concrete, specific details and, if possible, photographs and videos to show clearly why you value the place.

2. In the United States, people often define themselves—and others—by the work they do. Write about a job you have had. (If you have never held a job, imagine one you would like to have.) Was it something you did for money, because you wanted to, or because your parents forced you to? Did you enjoy the experience? What lessons did you learn from your employment? In what ways did your job influence your sense of who you are or who you want to become?

3. The United States—indeed, most of the world—officially entered a recession in 2008 (some economists say it has ended; others disagree). How, if at all, did the economic downturn affect you, your family, and your neighbors? Write an essay in which you analyze the effects of the recession on a person or a group of people you know. How did things change for these people, and what has been their response? To what extent are the individuals involved responsible (or not) for their situation? What can they do to improve it?

4. CONNECTIONS Both LeDuff and Ellen Goodman, in "The Company Man" (p. 347) explicitly link jobs with funerals, and both take a similarly dreary tone. Why? Is working—or not working—really so bad? Drawing on both essays for examples, write an essay that argues against these writers' negative portrayals of the working life. Consider, for instance, what Goodman's main character may have gained by working as hard as he did, or what the residents of Janesville, Wisconsin, might be grateful for. What do you look forward to experiencing as an adult with a full-time job and all the responsibilities that go along with it? How do those hopes counter those who would say that work is necessarily unpleasant?

WRITING WITH THE METHOD

CAUSE-AND-EFFECT ANALYSIS

Select one of the following questions, or any question they suggest, and answer it in an essay developed by analyzing causes or effects. The question you choose should concern a topic you care about so that your cause-and-effect analysis is a means of communicating an idea, not an end in itself.

People and Their Behavior

1. What makes a soldier, police officer, or firefighter a hero?
2. What does a sound body contribute to a sound mind?
3. Why is a particular celebrity or politician always getting into trouble?
4. Why do people root for the underdog?
5. What causes eating disorders such as anorexia or bulimia?

Work

6. Why should (or shouldn't) high-school students take part-time jobs?
7. What effects do you expect your education to have on your choice of career and your performance in it?
8. Why would a man or woman enter a field that has traditionally been filled by the opposite sex, such as nursing or engineering?

Art and Entertainment

9. Why did hip-hop music become so popular both here and abroad?
10. Does violence in video games lead to violence in real life?
11. What makes some professional sports teams succeed year after year while others consistently fail?
12. What impact has a particular television show or movie had on American culture?

Contemporary Issues

13. Why does the United States spend so much money on defense?
14. Is a college education worth the expense?
15. Why do marriages between teenagers fail more often than marriages between people in other age groups?
16. Why have political debates become so heated and angry?

WRITING ABOUT THE THEME

INVESTIGATING THE WORKING WORLD

1. The writers in this chapter seem to take a dim view of the working world. Barbara Ehrenreich (p. 331) portrays service workers as victims, and Malcolm Gladwell (p. 331) suggests that success in the workplace is determined by forces beyond our control. Dana Thomas (p. 339) describes the "horrid" reality of child labor in China and the dangers counterfeit workers face as they do their jobs. And Ellen Goodman (p. 347) and Charlie LeDuff (p. 352) both equate work with death. But as J. Howard Miller's poster (p. 326) suggests, for many people, working is a source of happiness, even joy. Some define themselves by the work they do; some take deep satisfaction in their efforts; others enjoy the benefits of employment even if they don't particularly like their jobs. What does work mean to you? Is it merely a means to a paycheck, or do you expect to get something more out of a job or career? Write an essay explaining how you perceive work, making sure to provide plenty of examples to support your claims. To get started, you might want to think about a job you particularly enjoyed or hated, or what kind of work you want to do when you finish school.

2. Several works in this chapter examine the unintended consequences of actions taken by businesses and consumers. Dana Thomas's exposé on counterfeiting (p. 339) is most notable in this respect, but even Barbara Ehrenreich's analysis of high rents (p. 331) suggests wealthier people's real-estate purchases can affect lower-income strangers, and Charlie LeDuff's look at the effects of a GM factory closing (p. 352) shows how business decisions can haunt a community. Think of a contemporary product or service that you believe holds the potential to do unexpected harm — or that could bring unanticipated benefits — and write an essay predicting its consequences. (Be sure to review the cause-and-effect guidelines on pp. 332–35 before beginning your analysis.)

3. Although the writers represented in this chapter all touch on questions of success and failure, their tones vary widely, from urgent to ironic to resigned. Choose the two authors who seem most different in tone, and analyze how their tones help clarify their points. Is one author's tone more effective than the other's? If so, why? (For more on tone, see pp. 43–44.)

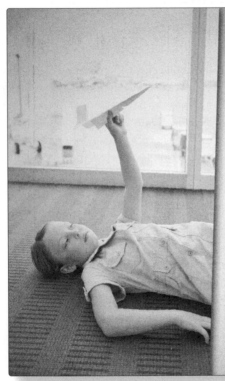

Katie is a
nine year old from Tulsa not a
terrorist.

Our current aviation security system sees everyone as a threat.
Tell Congress you want a Trusted Traveler Program to end the long
lines and one size fits all approach to securing our nation's airways.

Visit **BeTrustedNow.org**   Call **1-855-BE-TRUSTED**

15

ARGUMENT AND PERSUASION

DEBATING LAW AND ORDER

Since we argue all the time—with relatives, with friends, with a teacher or a shop clerk—a chapter devoted to argument and persuasion may at first seem unnecessary. But arguing with a teacher over the fairness of a grade is quite a different process from arguing with readers over a complex issue. In both cases we are trying to find common ground with our audience, perhaps to change its views or even to compel it to act as we wish. But the teacher is in front of us; we can shift our tactics in response to his or her gestures, expressions, and words. The reader, in contrast, is "out there"; we have to anticipate those gestures, expressions, and words in the way we structure the argument, the kinds of evidence we use to support it, even the way we think of the subject.

A great many assertions that are worth making are debatable at some level—whether over the facts on which the assertions are based or over the values they imply. Two witnesses to an accident cannot agree on what they saw; two economists cannot agree on what measures will reduce unemployment; two doctors cannot agree on what constitutes life or death. We see such disagreements play out in writing all the time, whether we're reading an accident report, a magazine article claiming the benefits of unemployment rates, or an editorial responding to a Supreme Court decision.

Seeing Argument and Persuasion

Shortly after terrorists hijacked three full airplanes and used them as bombs on September 11, 2001, new airport security procedures went into place across the country. Today all travelers must submit to random searches, metal detectors, physical pat-downs, and x-ray screenings before they may get on a plane or enter a boarding area. Some groups believe these screenings are a necessary precaution; others assert that they constitute an ineffective violation of civil liberties. The US Travel Association ran this advertisement, and several others like it, in 2011 to argue a third angle: that a "Trusted Traveler Program"—a system of background checks and advance security clearances—could eliminate hassles while ensuring public safety. Using a trick headline and an image of a bored girl in an airport, the ad appeals to readers' emotions—specifically, to their fear of terrorists, their concern for children's vulnerability, and their sense of frustration—to persuade them to demand change. But read the small print as well. The words extend the argument implied by the headline and photograph with additional claims and a call for action. How persuasive, overall, do you find the argument? Which evidence—visual or written—is more powerful?

Reading Argument and Persuasion

Technically, **argument** and **persuasion** are two different processes:

- *Argument* appeals mainly to an audience's sense of reason in order to negotiate a common understanding or to win agreement with a claim. It is the method of a columnist who defends a president's foreign policy on the grounds of economics and defense strategy.

- *Persuasion* appeals mainly to an audience's feelings and values in order to compel some action, or at least to win support for an action. It is the method of a mayoral candidate who urges voters to support her because she is sensitive to the poor.

But argument and persuasion so often mingle that we will use the one term *argument* to mean a deliberate appeal to an audience's reason and emotions in order to create compromise, win agreement, or compel action. Making an effective case for an opinion requires upholding certain responsibilities and attending to several established techniques of argumentation, most of them dating back to ancient Greece.

▶ The Elements of Argument

All arguments share certain elements.

- The core of any argument is an assertion, a debatable claim about the subject. Generally, this assertion is expressed as a thesis statement.

It may defend or attack a position, propose a solution to a problem, recommend a change in policy, or challenge a value or belief. Here are a few examples:

> The city should give first priority for summer jobs to students whose families need financial assistance.
>
> School prayer has been rightly declared unconstitutional and should not be reinstituted in any form.
>
> Smokers who wish to poison themselves should be allowed to do so, but not in any place where their smoke will poison others.

- The central assertion is broken down into reasons or subclaims, each one supported by evidence.

- Significant opposing arguments are raised and dispensed with, again with the support of evidence.

- The parts of the argument are organized into a clear, logical structure that pushes steadily toward the conclusion.

A writer may draw on classification, comparison, or any other rhetorical method to develop the entire argument or to introduce evidence or strengthen the conclusion. For instance, in a proposal arguing for raising a college's standards of admission, a dean might contrast the existing standards with the proposed standards, analyze a process for raising the standards over a period of years, and predict the effects of the new standards on future students' preparedness for college work.

▶ Appeals to Readers

Effective arguments appeal to readers: they ask others to listen to what someone has to say, judge the words fairly, and, as much as possible, agree with the writer. Most arguments combine three kinds of appeals to readers: ethical, emotional, and rational.

Ethical Appeal

The **ethical appeal** is often not explicit in an argument, yet it pervades the whole. It is the sense a writer conveys of his or her expertise and character, projected by the reasonableness of the argument, by the use of evidence, and by tone. A rational argument shows readers that the writer is thinking logically and fairly (see pp. 379–80). Strong evidence establishes credibility (see pp. 369–71 and 364–75). And a sincere, reasonable tone demonstrates balance and goodwill (see p. 379–80).

Emotional Appeal

The **emotional appeal** in an argument aims directly for the readers' hearts—for the beliefs, values, and feelings deeply embedded in all of us. We are just as often motivated by these ingrained ideas and emotions as by our intellects. Even scientists, who stress the rational interpretation of facts above all else, are sometimes influenced in their interpretations by emotions deriving from, say, competition with other scientists. And the willingness of a nation's citizens to go to war may result more from their patriotism and pride than from their reasoned considerations of risks and gains. An emotional appeal in an argument attempts to tap such feelings for any of several reasons:

- To heighten the responsiveness of readers
- To inspire readers to new beliefs
- To compel readers to act
- To assure readers that their values remain unchallenged

An emotional appeal may be explicit, as when an argument against capital punishment appeals to readers' religious values by citing the Bible's Sixth Commandment, "Thou shalt not kill." But an emotional appeal may also be less obvious because individual words may have connotations that elicit emotional responses from readers. For instance, one writer may characterize an environmental group as "a well-organized team representing diverse interests," while another may call the same group "a hodgepodge of nature lovers and profit-seeking businesspeople." The first appeals to readers' preference for order and balance, the second to readers' fear of extremism and disdain for greed. (See pp. 57–59 for more on connotation.)

The use of emotional appeals requires care:

- The appeal must be directed at the audience's actual beliefs and feelings.
- The appeal must be presented calmly enough so that readers have no reason to doubt the fairness in the rest of the argument.
- The appeal must be appropriate to the subject and to the argument. For instance, in arguing against a pay raise for city councilors, a legislator might be tempted to appeal to voters' resentment and distrust of wealthy people by pointing out that two of the councilors are rich enough to work for nothing. But such an appeal would divert attention from the issue of whether the pay raise is justified for all councilors on the basis of the work they do and the city's ability to pay the extra cost.

Carefully used, emotional appeals have great force, particularly when they contribute to an argument based largely on sound reasoning and evidence. The appropriate mix of emotion and reason in a given essay is entirely dependent on the subject, the writer's purpose, and the audience. Emotional appeals are out of place in most arguments in the natural and social sciences, where rational interpretations of factual evidence are all that will convince readers of the truth of an assertion. But emotional appeals may be essential to persuade an audience to support or take an action, for emotion is a stronger motivator than reason.

Rational Appeal

A **rational appeal** is one that, as the name implies, addresses the rational faculties of readers—their capacity to reason logically about a problem. It establishes the truth of a proposition or claim by moving through a series of related subclaims, each supported by evidence. In doing so, rational appeals follow processes of reasoning that are natural to all of us. These processes are induction and deduction.

Inductive reasoning moves from the particular to the general, from evidence to a generalization or conclusion about the evidence. It is a process we begin learning in infancy and use daily throughout our lives: a child burns herself the first two times she touches a stove, so she concludes that stoves burn; a moviegoer has liked four movies directed by Guillermo del Toro, so he forms the generalization that Guillermo del Toro makes good movies. Inductive reasoning is also very common in argument: a nurse administrator might offer data from hospital records to show that two hundred past patients in the psychiatric wards received drugs but no therapy and then conclude that the hospital relies exclusively on drugs to treat mental illness.

The movement from particular to general is called an *inductive leap* because we must make something of a jump to conclude that what is true of some instances (the patients whose records were examined) is also true of all other instances in the class (the rest of the patients). In an ideal world we could perhaps avoid the inductive leap by pinning down every conceivable instance, but in the real world such thoroughness is usually impractical and often impossible. Instead, we gather enough evidence to make our generalizations probable. The evidence for induction may be of several kinds:

- Facts: statistics or other hard data that are verifiable or, failing that, attested to by reliable sources (for instance, the types of drugs prescribed, derived from hospital records)

- The opinions of recognized experts on the subject, opinions that are themselves conclusions based on research and observation (for instance, the testimony of an experienced hospital doctor)
- Examples illustrating the evidence (for instance, the treatment history of one patient)

A sound inductive generalization can form the basis for the second reasoning process, **deductive reasoning**. Working from the general to the particular, we start with such a generalization and apply it to a new situation in order to draw a conclusion about that situation. Like induction, deduction is a process we use constantly to order our experience. The child who learns from two experiences that all stoves burn then sees a new stove and concludes that this stove also will burn. The child's thought process can be written in the form of a **syllogism**, a three-step outline of deductive reasoning:

> All stoves burn me.
> This is a stove.
> Therefore, this stove will burn me.

The first statement, the generalization derived from induction, is called the *major premise*. The second statement, a more specific assertion about some element of the major premise, is called the *minor premise*. And the third statement, an assertion of the logical connection between the premises, is called the *conclusion*. The following syllogism takes the earlier example about mental hospitals one step further:

> MAJOR PREMISE   The hospital relies exclusively on drugs to treat psychiatric patients.
>
> MINOR PREMISE   Drugs do not always cure mental illness.
>
> CONCLUSION   Therefore, the hospital does not always cure psychiatric patients.

Unlike an inductive conclusion, which requires a leap, the deductive conclusion follows necessarily from the premises: as long as the reasoning process is valid and the premises are accepted as true, then the conclusion must also be true.

In arguments, syllogisms are rarely spelled out neatly. Sometimes the order of the statements is reversed, as in this sentence paraphrasing a Supreme Court decision:

> The state may not imprison a man just because he is too poor to pay a fine; the only justification for imprisonment is a certain danger to society, and poverty does not constitute certain danger.

The buried syllogism can be stated thus:

MAJOR PREMISE   The state may imprison only those who are a certain danger to society.

MINOR PREMISE   A man who is too poor to pay a fine is not a certain danger to society.

CONCLUSION   Therefore, the state cannot imprison a man just because he is too poor to pay a fine.

Often, one of a syllogism's premises or even its conclusion is implied but not expressed. Each of the following sentences omits one part of the same syllogism:

All five students cheated, so they should be expelled. [Implied major premise: cheaters should be expelled.]

Cheaters should be punished by expulsion, so all five students should be expelled. [Implied minor premise: all five students cheated.]

Cheaters should be punished by expulsion, and all five students cheated. [Implied conclusion: all five students should be expelled.]

▶ Fallacies

Inappropriate emotional appeals and flaws in reasoning—called **fallacies**—can trap writers and speakers as they construct arguments. Watch out for the following errors.

- **Hasty generalization:** an inductive conclusion that leaps to include *all* instances when at best only *some* instances provide any evidence. Hasty generalizations form some of our worst stereotypes:

    Physically challenged people are mentally challenged, too.
    African Americans are good athletes.
    Italian Americans are volatile.

- **Oversimplification:** an inductive conclusion that ignores complexities in the evidence that, if heeded, would weaken the conclusion or suggest an entirely different one.

    The newspaper folded because it couldn't compete with the Internet.

    Although the Internet may have taken some business from the newspaper, other newspapers continue to thrive; thus the Internet could not be the only cause of the newspaper's failure.

- **Begging the question:** assuming a conclusion in the statement of a premise, and thus begging readers to accept the conclusion—the question—before it is proved.

> We can trust the president not to neglect the needy because he is a compassionate man.

This sentence asserts in a circular fashion that the president is not uncompassionate because he is compassionate. He may indeed be compassionate, but the question that needs addressing is what will he do for the needy.

- **Ignoring the question:** introducing an issue or consideration that shifts the argument away from the real issue. Offering an emotional appeal as a premise in a logical argument is a form of ignoring the question. The following sentence, for instance, appeals to pity, not to logic.

  > The superintendant was badly used by people he loved and trusted, so we should not blame him for the corruption in his administration.

- **Ad hominem** (Latin for "to the man"): a form of ignoring the question by attacking the opponents instead of the opponents' arguments.

  > O'Brien is married to a convict, so her proposals for prison reform should not be taken seriously.

- **Either-or:** requiring that readers choose between two interpretations or actions when in fact the choices are more numerous.

  > Either we imprison all drug users, or we will become their prisoners.

The factors contributing to drug addiction, and the choices for dealing with it, are obviously more complex than this statement suggests. Not all either-or arguments are invalid, for sometimes the alternatives encompass all the possibilities. But when they do not, the argument is false.

- **Non sequitur** (Latin for "it does not follow"): a conclusion derived illogically or erroneously from stated or implied premises.

  > The printer isn't working, so I couldn't complete the assignment.

The premise in this excuse does not support the claim. A broken machine might prevent someone from printing finished work, but it has nothing to do with the ability to do the work in the first place.

- **Post hoc** (from the Latin *post hoc, ergo propter hoc*, "after this, therefore because of this"): assuming that because one thing preceded another, it must have caused the other.

After the town banned smoking in closed public places, the incidence of vandalism went up.

Many things may have caused the rise in vandalism, including improved weather and a climbing unemployment rate. It does not follow that the ban on smoking, and that alone, caused the rise.

Analyzing Argument and Persuasion in Paragraphs

Jenny Price (born 1960) is an environmental historian and freelance writer. The following paragraph is from "Gun Violence at UC Irvine," a 2009 op-ed article she wrote for the *Los Angeles Times* in response to readers' shock that a woman was shot and killed in a neighborhood generally considered safe. The paragraph offers an inductive argument.

Twelve thousand people are shot to death in the United States every year—accounting for more than two out of every three killings. That's an average of 33 people daily. An additional 240 people get shot and injured every day, and more than 65 million Americans own a total of 283 million firearms. Where, exactly, do we expect the 12,000 homicides to happen? Do we really think that the places with gangs and high crime rates are the only places where people are going to use their guns? The widespread numbness to the especially high murder rates in our poor inner-city neighborhoods is egregious enough. But that's matched by the widespread denial that the epidemic of gun violence is playing out every day in every kind of neighborhood across America.

Evidence:
Number of gun-related homicides
Number of non-fatal shootings
Extent of gun ownership

The generalization (underlined): shootings can happen anywhere

John Stossel (born 1947) is a television host on Fox Business Network, an on-air analyst for Fox News, and a former co-anchor of the ABC news program *20/20*. In this paragraph adapted from "Guns Save Lives," a 2010 blog post for *townhall.com*, he uses deductive reasoning to argue in favor of increased gun ownership.

Now I know that I was totally wrong about guns. Now I know that more guns means—hold onto your seat—*less* crime. How can that be, when guns kill almost 30,000 Americans a year? Because while we hear about the murders and accidents, we don't often hear about the crimes *stopped* because

Major premise (implied): anything that prevents crime should be encouraged would-be victims showed a gun and scared criminals away. Those thwarted crimes and lives saved usually aren't reported to police (sometimes for fear the gun will be confiscated), and when they are reported, the media tend to ignore them. No bang, no news. This state of affairs produces a distorted public impression of guns. If you only hear about the crimes and accidents, and never about lives saved, you might think gun ownership is folly.

Minor premise: although the public doesn't realize it, gun ownership prevents crime

Conclusion: gun ownership should be encouraged

Developing an Argumentative and Persuasive Essay

▶ Getting Started

You will have many chances to write arguments, from defending or opposing a policy such as affirmative action in a social studies class to justifying a new procedure at work to persuading a company to refund your money for a bad product. To choose a subject for an argumentative essay, consider a behavior or policy that irks you, an opinion you want to defend, a change you would like to see implemented, or a way to solve a problem. The subject you pick should meet certain criteria:

- It should be something you have some knowledge of from your own experience or observations, from class discussions, or from reading, although you may need to do further research as well.

- It should be limited to a topic you can treat thoroughly in the space and time available to you—for instance, the quality of computer instruction at your school rather than in the whole nation.

- It should be something that you feel strongly about so that you can make a convincing case. (However, it's best to avoid subjects that you cannot view with some objectivity, seeing the opposite side as well as your own; otherwise, you may not be open to flaws in your argument, and you may not be able to represent the opposition fairly.)

Once you have selected a subject, do some preliminary research to make sure that you will have enough evidence to support your opinion. This step is especially important with heated issues like gun control or immigration, which we all tend to have opinions about whether we know the facts or not. Where to seek evidence depends on the nature of your argument.

- For an argument derived from your own experiences and observations, such as a recommendation that all students work part-time for the education if not for the money, gathering evidence will be primarily a matter of searching your own thoughts and also uncovering opposing views, perhaps by consulting others.

- Some arguments derived from personal experience can be strengthened by the judicious use of facts and opinions from other sources. An essay arguing in favor of vegetarianism, for instance, could mix the benefits you have felt with those demonstrated by scientific data.

- Nonpersonal and controversial subjects require the evidence of other sources. Though you might strongly favor or oppose a massive federal investment in solar-energy research, your opinions would count little if they were not supported with facts and the opinions of experts.

For advice on conducting research and using the evidence you find, see Chapter 5.

In addition to evidence, knowledge of readers' needs and expectations is absolutely crucial in planning an argument. In explanatory writing, detail and clarity alone may accomplish your purpose, but you cannot hope to move readers in a certain direction unless you have some idea of where they stand. You need a sense of their background in your subject, of course. But even more, you need a good idea of their values and beliefs, their attitudes toward your subject—in short, their willingness to be convinced. In an English class, your readers will probably be your teacher and your classmates, a small but diverse group. A good target when you are addressing a diverse audience is the reader who is neutral or mildly biased one way or the other toward your subject. This person you can hope to influence as long as your argument is reasonable, your evidence is thorough and convincing, your treatment of opposing views is fair, and your appeals to readers' emotions are appropriate to your purpose, your subject, and especially your readers' values and feelings.

▶ Forming a Thesis

With your subject and some evidence in hand, you should develop a tentative thesis. But don't feel you have to prove your thesis at this early stage; fixing it too firmly may make you unwilling to reshape it if further evidence, your audience, or the structure of your argument so demands.

Stating your thesis in a preliminary thesis sentence can help you form your idea. Make this sentence as clear and specific as possible. Don't resort to a vague generality or a nondebatable statement of fact. Instead, state the precise claim you want readers to accept or the precise action you want them to take or support. For instance:

VAGUE   Computer instruction is important.

NONDEBATABLE   Our school's investment in computer instruction is less than the average investment of the nation's public schools.

PRECISE   Money designated for new athletic facilities should be diverted to constructing computer facilities and hiring first-rate computer staff.

VAGUE   Cloning research is promising.

NONDEBATABLE   Scientists have been experimenting with cloning procedures for many years.

PRECISE   Those who oppose cloning research should consider its potentially valuable medical applications.

Since an argumentative thesis is essentially an opinion reached from evidence, you will probably need to do some additional reading to ensure that you have a broad range of facts and opinions supporting not only your view of a subject but also any opposing views. Though it may be tempting to ignore your opposition in the hope that readers know nothing of it, it is dishonest and probably futile to do so. Acknowledging and, whenever possible, refuting significant opposing views will enhance your credibility with readers. If you find that some counterarguments damage your own argument too greatly, then you will have to rethink your thesis.

▶ Organizing

Once you have formulated your thesis and evaluated your reasons and evidence against the needs and expectations of your audience, begin planning how you will arrange your argument.

The **introduction** to your essay should draw readers into your framework, making them see how the subject affects them and predisposing them to consider your argument. Sometimes a forthright approach works best, but an eye-opening anecdote or quotation can also be effective. Your thesis sentence may end your introduction. But if you think readers will not even entertain your thesis until they have seen some or all of your evidence, then withhold your thesis for later.

The main part of the essay consists of your reasons and your evidence for them. The evidence you generated or collected should suggest the reasons that will support the claim of your thesis—essentially the minor arguments that bolster the main argument. In an essay favoring federal investment in solar-energy research, for instance, the minor arguments might include the need for solar power, the feasibility of its widespread use, and its cost and safety compared with other energy sources. It is in developing these minor arguments that you are most likely to use induction and deduction consciously—generalizing from specifics or applying generalizations to new information. Thus the minor arguments provide the entry points for your evidence, and together they should encompass all the relevant evidence.

Unless the minor arguments form a chain, with each growing out of the one before, their order should be determined by their potential effects on readers. In general, it is most effective to arrange the reasons in order of increasing importance or strength so as to finish powerfully. But to engage readers in the argument from the start, begin with a reason that you think they will find compelling or that they already know and accept; that way, the weaker reasons will be sandwiched between a strong beginning and an even stronger ending.

The views opposing yours can be raised and refuted wherever it seems most appropriate to do so. If a counterargument pertains to just one of your minor arguments, then address it at that point. But if the counterarguments are more basic, pertaining to your whole thesis, you should address them either after the introduction or shortly before the conclusion. Bring up counterarguments early if the opposition is particularly strong and you fear that readers will be disinclined to listen unless you address their concerns first. Hold counterarguments for the end when they are generally weak or easily refuted once you've presented your case.

In the **conclusion** to your essay, you may summarize the main point of your argument and restate your thesis from your introduction, or state it for the first time if you have saved it for the end. An effective quotation, an appropriate emotional appeal, or a call for support or action can often provide a strong finish to an argument.

▶ Drafting

While you are drafting the essay, work to make your reasoning clear by showing how each bit of evidence relates to the reason or minor argument being discussed and how each minor argument relates to the main argument contained in the thesis. In working through the reasons and evidence, you may find it helpful to state each reason as the first sentence in a paragraph and then support it in the following sentences. If this scheme seems too rigid or creates overlong paragraphs, you can always make changes after you have written your draft.

Draw on a range of methods to clarify your points as you draft. For instance, define specialized terms or those you use in a special sense, compare and contrast one policy or piece of evidence with another, or carefully analyze the causes of a problem or the potential effects of your proposal.

▶ Revising and Editing

When your draft is complete, use the following questions and focus box to guide your revision and editing.

- *Is your thesis debatable, precise, and clear?* Readers must know what you are trying to convince them of, at least by the end of the essay if not up front.

- *Is your argument unified?* Does each minor claim support the thesis? Do all opinions, facts, and examples provide evidence for a minor claim? On behalf of your readers, question every sentence you have written to be sure it contributes to the point you are making and to the argument as a whole.

- *Is the structure of your argument clear and compelling?* Readers should be able to follow easily, seeing when and why you move from one idea to the next. To check the flow of your claims, try constructing an outline of your finished draft. Viewing your argument in its basic form can help you to identify any lapses in reasoning or gaps in evidence.

- *Is the evidence specific, representative, and adequate?* Facts, examples, and expert opinions should be well detailed, should fairly represent the available information, and should be sufficient to support your claim.

- *Have you slipped into any logical fallacies?* Detecting fallacies in your own work can be difficult, but your readers will find them if you don't. Double check the validity of your stated and implied syllogisms, and look for the following fallacies discussed earlier (pp. 371–72): hasty generalization, oversimplification, begging the question, ignoring the question, ad hominem, either-or, non sequitur, and post hoc. (All of these are also listed in the Glossary under *fallacies*.)

FOCUS ON **Tone**

Readers are most likely to be persuaded by an argument when they sense a writer who is reasonable, trustworthy, and sincere. A rational appeal, strong evidence, and acknowledgment of opposing views do much to convey these attributes, but so does tone, the attitude implied by choice of words and sentence structures.

Generally, you should try for a tone of moderation in your view of your subject and a tone of respectfulness and goodwill toward readers and opponents.

- State opinions and facts calmly:

    OVEREXCITED One clueless administrator was quoted in the newspaper as saying she thought many students who claim learning disabilities are "faking" their difficulties to obtain special treatment! Has she never heard of dyslexia, attention deficit disorder, and other well-established disabilities?

    CALM Particularly worrisome was one administrator's statement, quoted in the newspaper, that many students who claim learning disabilities may be "faking" their difficulties to obtain special treatment.

- Replace arrogance with deference:

    ARROGANT I happen to know that many parents would rather relax or just bury their heads in the sand than get involved in a serious, worthy campaign against the district's unjust learning-disabled policies.

    DEFERENTIAL Time pressures and lack of information about the issues may be what prevent parents from joining the campaign against the district's unjust learning-disabled policies.

- Replace sarcasm with plain speaking:

    SARCASTIC Of course, the administration knows even without meeting students what is best for every one of them.

    PLAIN SPEAKING The administration should agree to meet with each learning-disabled student to understand his or her needs.

- Choose words that convey reasonableness rather than negative emotions:

    HOSTILE The administration coerced some parents into dropping their lawsuits. [*Coerced* implies the use of threats or even violence.]

    REASONABLE The administration convinced some parents to drop their lawsuits. [*Convinced* implies the use of reason.]

See pages 43–44 for more on tone and pages 57–58 for more on connotation.

Practice

Rewrite each of the following sentences as necessary to adopt a tone appropriate for a formal argumentative essay.

1. Refusing to accommodate students with special needs is against federal law, whether the school district likes it or not.

2. Don't they know that the Individuals with Disabilities Education Act insists that students with learning disabilities have the right to a good education, even if it means giving them extra attention?

3. Administrators have some nerve pretending that the horrible learning-disabled policies aren't all about money.

4. The school board caved under pressure from a bunch of parents who were upset that funding the integration of special-needs students would take money away from their precious arts programs.

5. Well, too bad. Segregating students with learning disabilities from the rest of the student population is a form of discrimination that no decent human being should allow.

▶ For more practice revising for formal language, visit Exercise Central at bedfordstmartins.com/exercisecentral.

A Note on Thematic Connections

Argument and persuasion is the ideal method for presenting an opinion or a proposal on a controversial issue, making it a natural choice for the writers in this chapter, all of whom wanted to make a point about criminal or legal issues. In an advertisement, the US Travel Association (p. 364) urges readers to support proposed changes in airport security procedures. In paragraphs, Jenny Price (p. 373) warns that we should expect gun violence anywhere, while John Stossel (p. 373) argues that more people should carry guns. Anna Quindlen (next page) asserts that changing our attitude toward mental illness may help to prevent murders. Wilbert Rideau (p. 387) draws on his own experience as an inmate to make a case for prison reform. Marie Myung-Ok Lee (p. 392) tells a personal story to counter claims that American children born to illegal immigrants should not be granted automatic citizenship. And the final four essays all touch on rules regarding emerging technologies: Carolyn McCarthy (p. 398) and Radley Balko (p. 403) take opposing positions on banning texting while driving, while Nicholas Carr (p. 408) and Jim Harper (p. 415) square off on the problem of data mining on the Web.

Anna Quindlen

Winner of the Pulitzer Prize for commentary in 1992, Anna Quindlen writes sharp, candid columns on subjects ranging from family life to social issues to international politics. She was born in 1953 in Philadelphia, where she grew up, as she puts it, "an antsy kid with a fresh mouth." After graduating from Barnard College, Quindlen began writing for the *New York Post* and then joined the *New York Times*, where she worked her way up from a city hall reporter to a regular columnist. From 1999 to 2010 she wrote for *Newsweek* magazine. Her columns have been collected in *Living Out Loud* (1988), *Thinking Out Loud* (1993), and *Loud and Clear* (2004). Quindlen is also the author of the nonfiction books *How Reading Changed My Life* (1998), *A Short Guide to a Happy Life* (2000), and *Being Perfect* (2005); the novels *Object Lessons* (1991), *One True Thing* (1994), *Black and Blue* (1998), *Blessings* (2002), *Rise and Shine* (2006), and *Every Last One* (2010); and the memoirs *Good Dog. Stay.* (2007) and *Lots of Candles, Plenty of Cake* (2012).

The C Word in the Hallways

Quindlen wrote this selection in November 1999, a few months after students Eric Harris and Dylan Klebold killed twenty-two people, injured twenty-one others, and then committed suicide at Columbine High School in Colorado. Similar events since then have made her message as urgent as ever.

The saddest phrase I've read in a long time is this one: psychological   1
autopsy. That's what the doctors call it when a kid kills himself, and they go back over the plowed ground of his short life, and discover all the hidden markers that led to the rope, the blade, the gun.

There's a plague on all our houses, and since it doesn't announce   2
itself with lumps or spots or protest marches, it has gone unremarked in the quiet suburbs and busy cities where it has been laying waste. The number of suicides and homicides committed by teenagers, most often young men, has exploded in the last three decades, until it has become routine to have black-bordered photographs in yearbooks and murder suspects with acne problems. And everyone searches for reasons, and scapegoats, and solutions, most often punitive. Yet one solution contin-ues to elude us, and that is ending the ignorance about mental health, and moving it from the margins of care and into the mainstream where it belongs. As surely as any vaccine, this would save lives.

So many have already been lost. This month Kip Kinkel was sen-   3
tenced to life in prison in Oregon for the murders of his parents and a shooting rampage at his high school that killed two students. A psychia-

trist who specializes in the care of adolescents testified that Kinkel, now seventeen, had been hearing voices since he was twelve. Sam Manzie is also seventeen. He is serving a seventy-year sentence for luring an eleven-year-old boy named Eddie Werner into his New Jersey home and strangling him with the cord to an alarm clock because his Sega Genesis was out of reach. Manzie had his first psychological evaluation in the first grade.

Excuses, excuses. That's what so many think of the underlying   4 pathology in such hideous crimes. In the 1956 movie *The Bad Seed*, little Patty McCormack played what was then called a "homicidal maniac" and the film censors demanded a ludicrous mock curtain call in which the child actress was taken over the knee of her screen father and spanked. There are still some representatives of the "good spanking" school out there, although today the spanking may wind up being life in prison. And there's still plenty of that useless adult "what in the world does a sixteen-year-old have to be depressed about" mind-set to keep depressed sixteen-year-olds from getting help.

It's true that both the Kinkel and the Manzie boys had already been   5 introduced to the mental health system before their crimes. Concerned by her son's fascination with weapons, Faith Kinkel took him for nine sessions with a psychologist in the year before the shootings. Because of his rages and his continuing relationship with a pedophile, Sam's parents had tried to have him admitted to a residential facility just days before their son invited Eddie in.

But they were threading their way through a mental health system   6 that is marginalized by shame, ignorance, custom, the courts, even by business practice. Kip Kinkel's father made no secret of his disapproval of therapy. During its course he bought his son the Glock that Kip would later use on his killing spree, which speaks sad volumes about our peculiar standards of masculinity. Sam's father, on the other hand, spent days trying to figure out how much of the cost of a home for troubled kids his insurance would cover. In the meantime, a psychiatrist who examined his son for less time than it takes to eat a Happy Meal concluded that he was no danger to himself or others, and a judge lectured Sam from the bench: "You know the difference between right and wrong, don't you?"

The federal Center for Mental Health Services estimates that at least   7 six million children in this country have some serious emotional disturbance and, for some of them, right and wrong take second seat to the voices in their heads. Fifty years ago their parents might have surrendered them to life in an institution, or a doctor flying blind with an ice pick might have performed a lobotomy, leaving them to loll away their days. Now lots of them wind up in jail. Warm fuzzies aside, consider this from a utilitarian point of view: psychological intervention is cheaper than incarceration.

The most optimistic estimate is that two-thirds of these emotion-   8
ally disturbed children are not getting any treatment. Imagine how we would respond if two-thirds of America's babies were not being immu-nized. Many health insurance plans do not provide coverage for neces-sary treatment, or financially penalize those who need a psychiatrist instead of an oncologist. Teachers are not trained to recognize mental illness, and some dismiss it, "Bad Seed" fashion, as bad behavior. Parents are afraid, and ashamed, creating a home environment, and national atmosphere, too, that tells teenagers their demons are a disgrace.

And then there are the teenagers themselves, slouching toward   9
adulthood in a world that loves conformity. Add to the horror of creep-ing depression or delusions that of peer derision, the sound of the C word in the hallways: crazy, man, he's crazy, haven't you seen him, didn't you hear? Boys, especially, still suspect that talk therapy, or even heartfelt talk, is somehow sissified, weak. Sometimes even their own fathers think so, at least until they have to identify the body.

Another sad little phrase is "If only," and there are always plenty of   10
them littering the valleys of tragedy. If only there had been long-term intervention and medication, Kip Kinkel might be out of jail, off the tax-payers' tab, and perhaps leading a productive life. If only Sam Manzie had been treated aggressively earlier, new psychotropic drugs might have slowed or stilled his downward slide. And if only those things had hap-pened, Faith Kinkel, William Kinkel, Mikael Nickolauson, Ben Walker, and Eddie Werner might all be alive today. Mental health care is health care, too, and mental illness is an illness, not a character flaw. Insur-ance providers should act like it. Hospitals and schools should act like it. Above all, we parents should act like it. Then maybe the kids will believe it.

Vocabulary

If you are unsure of any of the following words used by Quindlen, try to deter-mine their meanings from their context in the essay. Check their meanings in a dictionary to test your guesses. Then use each word in a sentence of your own.

scapegoats (2)	lobotomy (7)	oncologist (8)
pathology (4)	loll (7)	derision (9)
ludicrous (4)	utilitarian (7)	psychotropic (10)
marginalized (6)	incarceration (7)	

Key Ideas and Details

1. What is Quindlen's main idea, and where do you find it in the essay?

2. What examples of teen violence does Quindlen give? What reason does she provide to explain these students' behavior?

3. In paragraph 6, Quindlen writes that William Kinkel's purchase of a gun for his son "speaks sad volumes about our peculiar standards of masculinity." What does she mean?

Craft and Structure

1. LANGUAGE How does Quindlen use parallel sentence structure in her conclusion to drive home her point?

2. Is Quindlen's appeal mostly emotional or mostly rational? Explain your answer with examples from the essay.

3. Where in the essay does Quindlen address opposing viewpoints? How fair is her depiction of people with conflicting opinions?

4. OTHER METHODS Quindlen supports her argument with other methods, such as example (Chapter 8), comparison and contrast (Chapter 12), and cause-and-effect analysis (Chapter 14). Locate one instance of each method. What does each contribute to the essay?

Integration of Knowledge and Ideas

1. Who do you think is the author's target audience? How does Quindlen engage these readers' support?

2. Although this essay was written only a few months after the tragedy at Columbine, Quindlen makes no mention of the shooters there, Eric Harris and Dylan Klebold. Why do you suppose she leaves them out of her discussion?

3. FOR DISCUSSION Quindlen makes two literary references in this essay: "a plague on all our houses" (paragraph 2) is an allusion to Shakespeare's play *Romeo and Juliet*, and "slouching toward adulthood" (9) is an allusion to William Butler Yeats's poem "The Second Coming." What is the effect of these references? (If necessary, look up *allusion* in the Glossary.)

Writing Topics

1. Write an essay or presentation that agrees or disagrees with one of Quindlen's points. Has the incidence of teenage suicide and homicide really "exploded" (paragraph 2) to the degree that Quindlen describes? How do you feel about the violence and its consequences? Are teenage killers victims of inadequate mental health care? Is better psychological treatment the answer to the

problem? Are there other solutions we should consider? You might answer any of these questions or argue a specific point. Either way, use examples and details to support your ideas.

2. At several points in her essay, Quindlen suggests that American ideas of masculinity are at least partly to blame for teenage boys' tendency toward violence. Write an essay that explores what our culture expects of boys and men, and how those expectations might translate into inappropriate behavior. How does American culture define manhood? Do we, in fact, pressure boys to keep silent about their emotions? To what extent is masculine aggression encouraged or rewarded? How does society respond to boys—and men—who don't conform to expectations? And to what extent are individuals responsible for their own behavior?

3. RESEARCH Although Quindlen demonstrates a large degree of compassion for troubled teenagers, some scholars and psychologists would caution that the cause-and-effect relationship she draws between mental illness and violence is oversimplified. Using the library or the Internet, research articles or studies concerning media stigmatization of the mentally ill. In an essay, discuss whether you think Quindlen's analysis of teen violence reflects negative stereotypes. If you find that it does, consider whether such stereotypes affect the persuasiveness of her argument. (For advice on finding and using research sources, see Chapter 5.)

4. CONNECTIONS Both Quindlen and Marie Myung-Ok Lee, in "I Was an Anchor Baby" (p. 392), write with strong emotion about a social issue—mental illness in Quindlen's case, illegal immigration in Lee's. In an essay, explore how the concept of personal shame, or social taboo, informs each writer's approach. How effective is each writer's strategy of tackling a controversial issue from an emotional perspective? What would these essays have lost (or gained) if they had been written from a more psychologically distant point of view?

Wilbert Rideau

Born in 1942 in Lawtell, Louisiana, Wilbert Rideau had a troubled youth. When he was just nineteen, an all-white jury convicted the African American teenager of murder for his role in the death of a bank teller during a robbery. After several appeals the conviction was overturned on the grounds of racial bias, and his sentence was switched to life imprisonment. In a 2005 retrial the verdict was reduced to manslaughter, and since Rideau had already served the maximum sentence for that crime, he was released. During his time on death row, the eighth-grade dropout educated himself through extensive reading; started his own publication, *Lifer*; wrote a syndicated weekly column for black newspapers in Louisiana and Mississippi; and became an award-winning editor of *Angolite*, the Louisiana State Penitentiary's newsletter. The coauthor of *The Wall Is Strong* (1991) and the editor of *Life Sentences* (1992), a collection of prison writing, Rideau is now a recognized authority on criminal justice. His autobiography, *In the Place of Justice: A Story of Punishment and Deliverance*, was published in 2010.

Why Prisons Don't Work

Not surprisingly, Rideau is an outspoken advocate for prison reform. Although crime prevention is important, he says, we're going at it the wrong way. He wrote this essay, commissioned by *Time* magazine, while he was still serving a sentence of life in prison.

I was among thirty-one murderers sent to the Louisiana State Penitentiary in 1962 to be executed or imprisoned for life. We weren't much different from those we found here, or those who had preceded us. We were unskilled, impulsive, and uneducated misfits, mostly black, who had done dumb, impulsive things—failures, rejects from the larger society. Now a generation has come of age and gone since I've been here, and everything is much the same as I found it. The faces of prisoners are different, but behind them are the same impulsive, uneducated, unskilled minds that made dumb, impulsive choices that got them into more trouble than they ever thought existed. The vast majority of us are consigned to suffer and die here so politicians can sell the illusion that permanently exiling people to prison will make society safe.

Getting tough has always been a "silver bullet," a quick fix for the crime and violence that society fears. Each year in Louisiana—where excess is a way of life—lawmakers have tried to outdo each other in legislating harsher mandatory penalties and in reducing avenues of release. The only thing to do with criminals, they say, is get tougher. They have. In the process, the purpose of prison began to change. The state boasts one of the highest lockup rates in the country, imposes the most severe penalties in the nation, and vies to execute more criminals per capita than anywhere else. This state is so tough that last year, when prison authorities here wanted to punish an inmate in solitary confinement for an infraction, the most they could inflict on him was to deprive him of his underwear. It was all he had left.

If getting tough resulted in public safety, Louisiana citizens would   3 be the safest in the nation. They're not. Louisiana has the highest murder rate among states. Prison, like the police and the courts, has a minimal impact on crime because it is a response after the fact, a mop-up operation. It doesn't work. The idea of punishing the few to deter the many is counterfeit because potential criminals either think they're not going to get caught or they're so emotionally desperate or psychologically distressed that they don't care about the consequences of their actions. The threatened punishment, regardless of its severity, is never a factor in the equation. But society, like the incorrigible criminal it abhors, is unable to learn from its mistakes.

Prison has a role in public safety, but it is not a cure-all. Its value is   4 limited, and its use should also be limited to what it does best: isolating young criminals long enough to give them a chance to grow up and get a grip on their impulses. It is a traumatic experience, certainly, but it should only be a temporary one, not a way of life. Prisoners kept too long tend to embrace the criminal culture, its distorted values and beliefs; they have little choice—prison is their life. There are some prisoners who cannot be returned to society—serial killers, serial rapists, professional hit men, and the like—but the monsters who need to die in prison are rare exceptions in the criminal landscape.

Crime is a young man's game. Most of the nation's random vio-   5 lence is committed by young urban terrorists. But because of long, mandatory sentences, most prisoners here are much older, having spent fifteen, twenty, thirty, or more years behind bars, long past necessity. Rather than pay for new prisons, society would be well served by releasing some of its older prisoners who pose no threat and using the money to catch young street thugs. Warden John Whitely agrees that many older prisoners here could be freed tomorrow with little or no danger to society. Release, however, is governed by law or by politicians, not by penal professionals. Even murderers, those most feared by society, pose little risk. Historically, for example, the domestic staff at Louisiana's Governor's mansion has been made up of murderers, hand-picked to work among the chief-of-state and his family. Penologists have long known that murder is almost always a once-in-a-lifetime act. The most dangerous criminal is the one who has not yet killed but has a history of escalating offenses. He's the one to watch.

Rehabilitation can work. Everyone changes in time. The trick is to influence the direction that change takes. The problem with prisons is that they don't do more to rehabilitate those confined in them. The convict who enters prison illiterate will probably leave the same way. Most convicts want to be better than they are, but education is not a priority. This prison houses 4,600 men and offers academic training to 240, vocational training to a like number. Perhaps it doesn't matter. About 90 percent of the men here may never leave this prison alive.   6

The only effective way to curb crime is for society to work to prevent the criminal act in the first place, to come between the perpetrator and crime. Our youngsters must be taught to respect the humanity of others and to handle disputes without violence. It is essential to educate and equip them with the skills to pursue their life ambitions in a meaningful way. As a community, we must address the adverse life circumstances that spawn criminality. These things are not quick, and they're not easy, but they're effective. Politicians think that's too hard a sell. They want to be on record for doing something now, something they can point to at reelection time. So the drumbeat goes on for more police, more prisons, more of the same failed policies.   7

Ever see a dog chase its tail?   8

Vocabulary

Some of the following words may be new to you. Try to guess their meanings from the context of Rideau's essay. Test your guesses in a dictionary, and then use each new word in a sentence of your own.

consigned (1)	infraction (2)	curb (7)
legislating (2)	incorrigible (3)	perpetrator (7)
vies (2)	abhors (3)	
per capita (2)	escalating (5)	

Key Ideas and Details

1. According to Rideau, what is the purpose of sending people to prison? Where in the text does he state the central assumption that grounds his argument?

2. Why don't prisons work? Locate the author's thesis statement or summarize his main idea in your own words.

3. How, according to Rideau, can we better protect society from violent criminals?

Craft and Structure

1. LANGUAGE Why does Rideau take such pains to describe himself and his fellow inmates as "unskilled, impulsive, and uneducated misfits" (paragraph 1)? How does he use repetition of key words to preview his solution to crime?

2. Explain how Rideau uses deductive and inductive reasoning to form his argument. How might his main idea be phrased as a syllogism (see pp. 370–71)?

3. What is the purpose of the question with which Rideau ends his essay?

4. OTHER METHODS In paragraphs 2 and 3, Rideau uses cause-and-effect analysis (Chapter 14) to examine the results of one instance of "getting tough" on crime. What were the consequences of Louisiana's strong stance on punishment? How does this cause-and-effect analysis further Rideau's argument for reform?

Integration of Knowledge and Ideas

1. In light of the fact that *Time* magazine asked Rideau to write this essay, what do you suppose his purpose is? Can an essay like this one, published in a magazine with a circulation in the millions, have an effect on legislation? What would the intermediary steps have to be?

2. How would you rate Rideau's ethical appeal? What strategies does he use to overcome readers' potential doubts about his objectivity?

3. FOR DISCUSSION How does Rideau handle opposing viewpoints? What is the effect of acknowledging some of the benefits of prisons in paragraphs 4 and 6?

Writing Topics

1. What is the purpose of prison in a civilized society? Do we jail people to punish them, to rehabilitate them, or to protect others from them? Are there other ways to respond to crime? Write an essay that explains and supports your thoughts on the uses of imprisonment in America. Do we, as Rideau argues, jail people in an effort to protect society from dangerous criminals, or do other motives come into play? Are such motives reasonable? Is imprisonment effective at accomplishing the purposes assigned to it? Is the institution abused or misused in any way? Whatever your position, be sure to support it with plenty of details and examples and to consider how others might disagree with you.

2. Laws reflect and reinforce basic social values: What behaviors are acceptable? What transgressions are punishable? How far should we go to enforce social norms? Although incarceration practices might seem reasonable in a contemporary cultural context, viewed from an outsider's perspective they can often be quite surprising. For much of American history, for instance, whole families—including dependent infants—were routinely placed in debtors' prisons for a father's failure to provide for them. And in the early twentieth century, unmarried women could be jailed for pregnancy. Think of a past or current law that strikes you as absurd or extreme and look for the underlying social value that it's meant to enforce. Then write an essay that explains the law to somebody from another culture, or another time, who might have trouble understanding it. You may be ironic or satiric, if you wish, or you may prefer a more straightforward informative approach.

3. RESEARCH Prison is a perennially popular subject in fiction. Find a novel, short story, or film that takes prison, or something related to prison (such as involuntary commitment to a mental hospital), as its subject. Create a presentation that compares and contrasts the novel's, story's, or film's attitudes toward prison with Rideau's views. Are the criticisms the same? Where do they differ?

4. CONNECTIONS Rideau and Anna Quindlen, in "The C Word in the Hallways" (p. 382), both impart a sense of urgency about crime prevention, but their approaches are as different as their last lines: Rideau's "Ever see a dog chase its tail?" (paragraph 8) versus Quindlen's "Then maybe the kids will believe it" (10). What do these lines and others like them reveal about these authors' attitudes toward their subjects and their readers? Are both approaches equally effective? Why, or why not?

Marie Myung-Ok Lee

Fiction writer Marie Myung-Ok Lee (born 1964) grew up the daughter of undocumented North Korean immigrants in Hibbing, Minnesota. Best known for her novels for teenagers — *Finding My Voice* (1992), *Saying Goodbye* (1994), *Necessary Roughness* (1996), and *Somebody's Daughter* (2005) — Lee has explained that she endured bullying and racial taunts in school and writes "coming-of-age stories of people who, for some reason, feel different than those around them." She has also written fiction for middle-school readers and regularly contributes short stories and essays to a wide range of adult publications, from *Slate* and the *New York Times* to the *Kenyon Review* and *TriQuarterly*. Lee is the winner of several literary prizes, including an O. Henry honorable mention for a story about Korean birth mothers of adopted children, adapted from a chapter in *Somebody's Daughter*. A former fiction judge for the National Book Awards and a founder of the Asian American Writer's Workshop, she currently teaches writing and ethnic studies at Brown University.

I Was an Anchor Baby

In the following essay published in the *Los Angeles Times* in 2010, Lee combines her family's story with a brief lesson in American history to counter recent arguments that children of illegal immigrants should not be given American citizenship at birth.

I was an "anchor baby." According to family lore, the day I was born at   1
Hibbing Memorial Hospital in Minnesota in the early 1960s was also
the day my parents received their deportation papers. They had come to
America from war-torn Korea on student visas that had run out. Laws
at the time prohibited most Asians from immigrating, so they were told
to leave, even with three American children.

The Fourteenth Amendment, with its guarantee that anyone born   2
here is an American, protected my siblings and me from being country-
less. Today, in the growing clamor over illegal immigration, there have
been calls to repeal this amendment, with the pejorative "anchor baby"
invoked as a call to arms. The words suggest that having a child in
America confers some kind of legal protection on illegal parents, that it
gives them a foothold here.

But in reality, merely having a baby on American soil doesn't change   3
the parents' status. As a so-called anchor baby, my existence did nothing to resolve my parents' situation; if anything, it only added to their
stress.

In Korea, my father was a talented physician who also happened to   4
speak fluent English. These skills led to his appointment as a medical

liaison officer with a MASH[1] unit during the Korean War. The assignment brought him to the attention of some American officers who, after the war ended, arranged for him and my mother to come to the US so my father could continue his education. He ended up training with Dr. C. Walton Lillehei, a pioneer of heart surgery; my father was one of the first anesthesiologists in the world capable of administering anesthesia during open-heart surgery.

Other wartime contacts led to his job as an anesthesiologist in   5 Hibbing, a northern Minnesota town that, because of its isolation and bitter winters, had trouble attracting doctors. My father was the sole anesthesiologist for miles, which meant that he spent long hours at the hospital, where he met with each patient the night before their surgeries and wouldn't leave until he'd answered all their questions. At home, a phone call during dinner—announcing springtime chain-saw accidents, appendectomies, emergency C-sections—often sent him rushing back to the hospital.

It wasn't until years later, when he made friends with another anes-   6 thesiologist who could cover for him—a German immigrant in Duluth, seventy miles away—that we could finally take a family vacation; until then, my father even had to be careful about drinking a beer at a cook-out in case the hospital should call with another emergency.

It was peculiar laws rather than criminal intent that made my par-   7 ents outlaws at the time of my birth. For most of American history, our country has had an open-door policy on immigration, restricting only people employed in certain kinds of occupations (such as prostitution) and those with communicable diseases. Then, in 1882, Congress passed the Chinese Exclusion Act out of fear that Chinese immigrants would take American jobs.

In 1924, the Immigration and Naturalization Act established quotas   8 that heavily favored "desirable" Western Europeans while banning immigration from Japan, Korea and other Asian countries. Had my father been from Germany—like his anesthesiologist friend in Duluth, also toiling away at a job American doctors eschewed—citizenship would have happened easily. The same if my father had been from Mexico, as the act placed no quota restrictions on immigration from countries in the Western Hemisphere.

Instead, my parents went through an awful period of uncertainty,   9 instability and stress, which included being swindled by a number of "immigration lawyers." In the end, self-interest won out. Not my parents'

---

[1] Mobile Army Surgical Hospital. [Editors' note.]

self-interest (although they did want to stay in the US) but the interest of a town that needed its anesthesiologist.

Another friend of mine, also Korean American—an academic who   10
has written groundbreaking books and nurtured a generation of schol-ars—mentioned to me that when her parents died, she opened a spe-cial box she'd always thought held secret, glittery treasures, only to find it stuffed with deportation warnings from the INS.[2] Many of my immi-grant and second-generation friends share this secret shame festering underneath the foil seals on our college and graduate degrees and our taxpaying lives. Studies show that immigrants, legal and not, are more law-abiding than the rest of the populace, and possibly more patriotic.

As a writer, I receive letters from readers who tell me how my work   11
has touched, even changed, their lives; as a child, I often heard my father's patients expressing similar sentiments of gratitude. Even the most anti-immigrant citizens have probably been touched by an illegal alien and/or an anchor baby in ways they probably cannot fully fathom.

Our Minnesota town, where people prided themselves on follow-   12
ing the law to the letter, did not rush to bring in the INS and run our illegal family out on a rail. People were instead so fearful of losing my father and his skills that the entire town signed a petition to protest the deportation order. This petition was brought to Congress by our local representative and eventually signed into a law to "provide relief" for my mother and father—but only them.

And although they were legal, they still weren't entitled to become   13
citizens. This satisfied the townspeople, who were happy we were anchor babies—that we anchored my father to this place where his skills were so needed. But my parents, even as "permanent alien residents" with three (later four) American-born children, were still left in legal limbo, inhabiting an America that allowed them to stay, work, pay taxes, but not vote.

As an alien, my father worked at a job that other Americans did not   14
want to do, and others like him have, too, harvesting crops, performing surgery, nurturing children, working in factories, making scientific dis-coveries, mopping floors.

In 1965, at the foot of the Statue of Liberty, President Lyndon   15
Johnson signed a new immigration act to correct "a cruel and enduring wrong in the conduct of the American nation." It meant my parents were no longer "aliens ineligible for citizenship." They passed their citi-zenship tests with flying colors and received passports with blue covers and gilt eagles that matched their children's. My father went on to work

---

[2] Immigration and Naturalization Service. [Editors' note.]

at Hibbing Memorial Hospital for three more decades. And finally, we were an American family.

Vocabulary

If you do not know any of the following words, try to determine their meanings from the context of Lee's essay. Test your guesses in a dictionary, and then use each word in a sentence of your own.

deportation (1)	liaison (4)	fathom (11)
visas (1)	communicable (7)	alien (13)
clamor (2)	quotas (8)	limbo (13)
invoked (2)	eschewed (8)	gilt (15)
confers (2)	festering (10)	

Key Ideas and Details

1. Where, if at all, does Lee state her thesis? What claim does she want readers to accept, and what does she want them to do or believe as a result of reading her essay?

2. What does an anesthesiologist do? Why, according to Lee, do most American doctors not want that job?

3. Why did Lee's parents immigrate to the United States? Why didn't they become citizens until after she was born?

Craft and Structure

1. LANGUAGE What does "anchor baby" mean? If the term is "pejorative," or insulting, as Lee claims in paragraph 2, why does she use it?

2. What subclaims does Lee make to support her defense of birthright citizenship? Do you find her reasons convincing? Why, or why not?

3. How does Lee present and handle opposing arguments? Does she seem fair? Why, or why not?

4. OTHER METHODS Lee combines narration (Chapter 6) and example (Chapter 8) to develop her argument. Where in the essay does she tell her family's story? Where does she explain the "peculiar laws" that affected their immigration status? How does she overlap personal history with American history to make her point?

Integration of Knowledge and Ideas

1. To whom does Lee seem to be writing? What assumptions does Lee make about her readers' values?

2. Why do you believe Lee wrote this essay? To share a painful personal experience? To express her indignation? To argue for or against something? (If so, what?) For some other purpose? What evidence from the text supports your answer?

3. FOR DISCUSSION Consider how Lee supports her argument. What kinds of evidence does she provide? How reliable is it, in your opinion?

Writing Topics

1. How do you react to Lee's essay? Do you agree with her assessment of immigration laws and their impact on families? Or do you find her evaluation of the issue one-sided, her examples and opinions too personal to form the basis of an argument? Write an essay that analyzes Lee's strategies and responds to her conclusions. Be sure to cite examples from her essay to support your analysis.

2. The United States is a country of immigrants, and each group has made an indelible mark on American identity. For example, consider just foods: salsa outsells ketchup, tacos are found everywhere, and cappuccino and sushi are now everyday food items for many Americans who have no Italian or Japanese heritage. Write an essay or presentation about the effects of immigration on your daily life: the food you consume, the music you listen to, the dress styles you prefer, and so forth. Include personal examples and historical information to bring your ideas to life, as Lee does.

3. In paragraph 14, Lee lists jobs taken by immigrants because "other Americans did not want to do" them. What is your response to her examples? Does she really mean to suggest that Americans do not want (or cannot do) work that involves "performing surgery, nurturing children, working in factories, [or] making scientific discoveries"? In an essay, consider the impact of foreign labor on the US job market. What are some sources of friction? What are some advantages? To what extent should the United States encourage immigration, and to what extent should the country restrict it? Why? Use examples from your own experience, observations, and reading.

4. RESEARCH Does the Fourteenth Amendment to the US Constitution really "guarantee that anyone born here is an American," as Lee claims in paragraph 2? Some people don't think it does. Locate the full text of the amendment as well as two or three competing interpretations of its meaning. In a short essay, paraphrase the first section of the amendment itself and summarize the controversy surrounding it. Based on the conflicting opinions and your own analyses, what do you interpret the Fourteenth Amendment to mean?

5. CONNECTIONS Both Lee and Anita Jain, in "A Nameless Respect" (p. 172), express strong feelings toward their fathers. In a brief essay, analyze how these writers convey their sense of pride and admiration so that their emotions are concrete, not vague. Focus on their examples, on their words, and especially on their figures of speech. (See pp. 58–59 for more on figures of speech.)

REGULATING TECHNOLOGY: DISTRACTED DRIVING

Carolyn McCarthy

A long-term Democratic representative in Congress, Carolyn McCarthy was born in Brooklyn, New York, in 1944, and has lived her whole life in her family's home on Long Island. She graduated from nursing school in 1964 and worked as a licensed practical nurse for more than three decades, specializing in chronically ill and intensive-care patients. After a 1993 incident in which a gunman shot twenty-five people on a commuter train, killing her husband and severely wounding her only child, McCarthy devoted herself to her son's recovery and started a campaign for tighter gun control in New York. When she discovered that her congressman intended to vote for repealing a ban on assault weapons that she had lobbied to enact, she decided to run for his position. In 1996 she was elected to the US House of Representatives, where the former Republican has gained a reputation as a champion and supporter of children and working families. Named by *Ladies Home Journal* as one of the "100 Most Important Women" in America, McCarthy has been reelected seven times.

Should Text Messaging While Driving Be Banned? Yes.

Although McCarthy is best known for her unyielding position on gun control, she is also outspoken on related issues of public safety. In this essay, first published in *US News Digital Weekly* in October 2009, she presents her argument in favor of a federal ban on texting while driving. The essay after this one, by Radley Balko (p. 403), responds directly to McCarthy in arguing against such bans.

Proponents of a law forbidding the use of hand-held devices behind the wheel say distracted motorists are far more likely to cause roadway accidents. Others argue that though texting while driving is dumb, laws against it are unenforceable. Is a ban the way to go?

As a member of Congress, I work to pass comprehensive, common-sense legislation that will benefit average Americans. With the same fervor I had when I was first sworn in to office in 1997, I seek common ground on issues that I believe will make our country stronger and safer each and every day. I had always known of the dangers of distracted driving, and it should come as no surprise to the American public that when drivers are preoccupied with tasks that take their eyes off the road and hands off the wheel, it most certainly creates unsafe and potentially fatal scenarios on the roadways.

On the heels of extended national coverage regarding the increased 3 incidence of distracted driving, I was shocked to learn that only a handful of states ban texting and driving. It was with this in mind that I was proud to introduce, along with my colleague, Rep. Nita Lowey of New York, HR[1] 3535, the Avoiding Life-Endangering and Reckless Texting by Drivers Act, a bill that would set in place guidelines that would lead to a nationwide ban on writing, sending, or reading text messages while operating a moving vehicle.

Today, we are all fully adept in multitasking. With the advent of 4 "smart" devices that provide access to e-mail, text messaging, the Internet, and more, individuals are becoming increasingly reliant upon mobile technology in their everyday lives. Frankly, it is rare to walk a few blocks without seeing someone using a hand-held device while performing another task. These devices have their benefits; I myself own one, and much like the countless mobile users across the country, I have seen it evolve into a nearly indispensable device that keeps me abreast of important developments in real time. Unfortunately, as these devices continue to evolve and become more affordable, their inappropriate and unsafe use continues to grow as well. I firmly believe that there is a time and place to be texting, but one situation where there is no excuse to be manipulating a hand-held device is while operating a moving vehicle.

Almost as rapidly as these devices have developed, so, too, have 5 hands-free and voice-activated technologies, each of which is designed to give individuals increased mobility and attentiveness while communicating. In line with this, the legislation that I introduced would exempt the use of voice-activated and vehicle-integrated devices. Explicitly, the bill directs the secretary of transportation to establish minimum texting-while-driving standards of protection that state legislatures must meet, while also allowing states to establish stricter standards as they see fit. And much like the laws that established the legal age to consume alcohol and blood-alcohol concentration limits for drivers, the bill would withhold a percentage of federal highway funding from those states that do not comply.

Not surprisingly, a recent CBS News / New York Times poll concluded 6 that 90% of adults believe texting while driving should be illegal. This overwhelming majority included men and women from across the nation and did not indicate any political bias. Promoting and setting

---

[1] House Resolution. [Editors' note.]

forth an agenda that improves roadway safety rises above political ideology. Whether one is a novice or experienced driver, actions that lead
to diverting one's eyes from the roadway and hands from the steering
wheel can, and often do, lead to roadway accidents.

It is hard to dispute the realities of distracted driving. In a study   7
published this summer, Virginia Tech University found that drivers are
twenty-three times as likely to get into an accident while texting. Another
study, published by *Car and Driver* magazine in June, concluded that
texting while driving can be more dangerous than drunk driving. Other
studies of distracted driving have yielded similar results.

While the problem of texting while driving has been recognized   8
across the country, questions and concerns arise over implementation
and enforcement. Recently, the Department of Transportation held a
two-day summit in Washington dedicated to vetting ideas, studies, and
policies relating to distracted driving. I appreciate and commend Secretary of Transportation Ray LaHood for his commitment to the cause and
believe that the summit and other forums of open discussion can yield
only positive results both by educating the public and by setting forth
sound policy initiatives. Similarly, I commend President Barack Obama,
who, in signing an executive order, effectively banned all federal employees from texting while driving on the job or behind the wheel of a federal vehicle. Both initiatives represent important steps toward cultivating
safety on our nation's roadways but fall short of applying these safety
precautions to each and every American driver.

While some states, including New York, have taken it upon them-   9
selves to ban the practice within their borders, others still lack effective
and prudent measures to curb this behavior. What makes a nationwide
ban so important is the fact that distracted driving is a practice that is
not isolated within particular states. Inconsistent laws across our country
serve only to confuse drivers and embolden those who text and drive.
Each day that passes without an effective nationwide ban represents a
day that drivers and passengers are put at risk.

Often, it is the legality of an issue that is the impetus to effect behav-   10
ioral change. For those in states that do not ban texting, there is little
incentive to encourage people to stop, aside from an accident itself. We
in Congress have an opportunity to create this law and keep our federal
regulations up to date with evolving technology's unintended dangers.

As a mother, nurse for over thirty years, and member of Congress,   11
I believe that the ALERT Drivers Act can and will deter roadway accidents
and fatalities for novice and experienced drivers alike. These preventable
risks simply cannot stand as they do today.

Vocabulary

If you do not know the following words, try to determine their meanings from the context of McCarthy's essay. Test your guesses in a dictionary, and then use each word in a sentence of your own.

proponents (1)	fervor (2)	advent (4)
legislation (2)	adept (4)	abreast (4)
legislatures (5)	summit (8)	cultivating (8)
novice (6)	vetting (8)	prudent (9)
implementation (8)	initiatives (8)	impetus (10)

Key Ideas and Details

1. In your own words, what is the thesis of McCarthy's argument? What main idea about texting while driving does she ask readers to accept?

2. Why is McCarthy so alarmed about distracted driving? What does she blame for the problem?

3. Explain the general idea of McCarthy's bill. What rules would the ALERT Drivers Act establish? How would they be enforced?

Craft and Structure

1. LANGUAGE How would you characterize McCarthy's tone in this essay? What does her language contribute to this tone? To what extent does the tone influence your receptiveness to her argument?

2. Locate examples of ethical, emotional, and rational appeals in McCarthy's argument. Which appeals do you consider most effective? least effective? Why?

3. Can you find any reference to opposing viewpoints in McCarthy's essay? How, if at all, does her treatment of alternative perspectives on the issue affect the persuasiveness of her argument?

4. OTHER METHODS Where in her essay does McCarthy use cause-and-effect analysis (Chapter 14) to develop her argument? Why is this method important to her purpose?

Integration of Knowledge and Ideas

1. In the next essay, which rebuts McCarthy's argument, Radley Balko implies that McCarthy's proposal for a texting ban is politically motivated: "A panic takes root in the media. Earnest editorialists scrawl urgent pleas for action. Politicians grandstand" (paragraph 2, p. 403). Does McCarthy's purpose in this essay seem political? Does she seem to be aiming for votes? Why, or why not?

2. Does McCarthy seem to expect her audience to agree or disagree with her position? In answering this question, consider the opening two paragraphs: what audience reaction does she seem to be seeking in her presentation of the issue and of herself?

3. FOR DISCUSSION What kinds of evidence does the author provide? Where does it come from, and is it reliable and convincing? Why, or why not? (See pp. 66–68 for information on evaluating sources.)

Writing Topics

1. Do you, or any of your friends, ever use a mobile phone while driving? Has anyone you know been involved in an accident that was blamed on driver distraction? Write an essay about driving habits among students at your school. Do you regard texting while driving as a critical problem? Do you believe that laws should ban the practice? Or do you believe that drivers can manage to multitask without risking their own and others' safety? In your essay, you might explain your answers to these questions or argue a specific point. Either way, use examples and details to support your ideas.

2. Choose a social or other kind of problem you care about—it could be overcrowding in public schools, violence in the media, child neglect, or anything else. Describe the problem as you understand it, particularly how it affects people. Then discuss your solution to the problem or some part of it. Be sure to acknowledge opposing views.

3. RESEARCH Congress did not pass McCarthy's bill. Use the library to investigate the status of distracted driving laws in your state, and report your findings in an essay. In your research, consider these questions: Is there a ban against texting while driving on the books? against phoning? If so, who may be pulled over for violating the rules and under what conditions? What punishments are meted out to offenders? How many drivers have been cited under the law? If there is no distracted driving law, has such legislation been proposed? What is its current status? In your essay, avoid taking sides on the issue. View your task as fact gathering for the purpose of providing yourself and others with objective background information.

4. CONNECTIONS Unlike McCarthy, Radley Balko, the author of the next essay ("Should Text Messaging While Driving Be Banned? No."), is strongly opposed to laws prohibiting distracted driving. Using the resources of the library as well as McCarthy's and Balko's essays, write an essay supporting or rejecting McCarthy's proposal. Make sure your own argument has a clear thesis and that it is supported to the extent possible by statistics, examples, and expert opinions. Remember to acknowledge arguments opposed to your own.

REGULATING TECHNOLOGY: DISTRACTED DRIVING

Radley Balko

Born in 1975 in Greenfield, Indiana, Radley Balko is an award-winning journalist who specializes in criminal justice. Currently an investigative reporter for the *Huffington Post*, he graduated from Indiana University in 1997 with a degree in journalism and political science. After studying gambling and the drug war as a policy analyst for a libertarian think tank, Balko for seven years wrote a biweekly political column for *FoxNews.com* and then took a job as senior editor for *Reason* magazine. His reports on police raids and wrongfully convicted death-row inmates have been cited in US and Mississippi Supreme Court decisions, and he has testified before Congress twice. Balko's articles appear in the *Los Angeles Times*, the *Washington Post*, *Slate*, and other newspapers and magazines. A strong advocate for civil liberties, Balko has been interviewed for several current affairs programs on both television and radio, including the Fox News Channel, MSNBC, and National Public Radio. He lives in Nashville, Tennessee.

Should Text Messaging While Driving Be Banned? No.

This essay was published in *US News Digital Weekly*, alongside Carolyn McCarthy's argument in favor of text-messaging bans (p. 398). In taking the view opposite McCarthy's, Balko lays out his own argument against her proposal — and others like it.

Forget flu season. Several times per year, America comes down with a national case of TOBAL-itis. 1

TOBAL is short for "There Oughtta Be a Law." Here's the progression of symptoms: Wrenching anecdotes about the effects of some alleged new trend make national news. A panic takes root in the media. Earnest editorialists scrawl urgent pleas for action. Politicians grandstand. Soon enough, we have our new law or regulation. It doesn't matter if the law is enforceable or may have unintended consequences. Nor does it matter if the law will have any actual effect on the problem it was passed to address. In fact, it doesn't even matter if the problem actually exists. The mere feeling that it exists is sufficient. 2

And so it goes with the panic over texting while driving. I'm not going to defend the act of clumsily thumbing out an e-mail while guiding a two-ton, gasoline-loaded missile down the highway at 70 miles per hour. That's foolish. Nor will I argue there's some right to drive while iPhone-ing tucked into a constitutional penumbra. I will argue that we 3 need to get over the idea that we can solve every bad habit with a new law. We can't, and this issue illustrates why.

Let's start with the alleged problem. Obviously, we have more people 4 texting behind the wheel today than we did in, say, 1985. And undeniably, those people pose a threat. But it's hard to find definitive empirical support for the idea that our highways are awash in BlackBerry-spilled blood. Since 1995, there's been an eightfold increase in cellphone subscribers in the United States, and we've increased the number of minutes spent on cellphones by a factor of 58. What's happened to traffic fatalities in that time? They've dropped—slightly, but they've dropped. Overall reported accidents since 1997 have dropped, too, from 6.7 million to 6 million.

Proponents of a ban on cellphones say those numbers should have 5 dropped more. "We've spent billions on air bags, antilock brakes, better steering, safer cars and roads, but the number of fatalities has remained constant," safety researcher David Strayer told the *New York Times* in July. "Our return on investment for those billions is zero. And that's because we're using devices in our cars."

Strayer would have a point if he were looking at the right statistics. 6 But we drive a lot more than we did in 1995. Deaths in proportion to passenger miles are a far better indicator of road safety than overall fatalities. In 1995, there were 1.72 deaths for every 100 million miles traveled. By 2007, the figure had dropped to 1.36, a 21% decline. That's hardly remaining constant.

But let's assume that even those numbers would be lower were it not 7 for texting drivers. It's still far from clear that banning texting will make us safer. There are countless other driver distractions that we'd never think of banning, from having kids in the back seat, to eating or drinking while driving, to fumbling with the radio. Certainly, it's foolish to type out text messages behind the wheel, but what about merely reading from your phone? Are you more impaired following MapQuest directions from your Palm Pre while driving than reading them from a sheet of paper? What if you're looking at a GPS navigation device that's only slightly larger than your cellphone? What if the GPS system is on your cellphone?

That brings us to the enforceability problem. Maryland just passed a 8 texting ban, but state officials are flummoxed over how to enforce it. The law bans texting while driving but allows for reading texts, for precisely the reasons just mentioned. But how can a police officer positioned at the side of a highway tell if the driver of the car that just flew by was actually pushing buttons on his cellphone and not merely reading the display screen? Unless a motorist is blatantly typing away at eye level, a car would need to be moving slowly enough for an officer to see inside, focus on the phone, and observe the driver manipulating the buttons. Which is to say the car would probably need to be stopped—at which point it ceases to be a safety hazard.

But let's say you're OK with a ban on reading cellphone messages,   9
too. How would you write that law? Would you prohibit so much as a glance in the general direction of a cellphone while driving? Should we mandate that cellphones be stored out of the driver's sight while the car isn't in park? What about other things that might distract him from the road, like navigation systems? Shiny objects? Pretty girls in the passenger seat? How would you prove a driver was looking at a cellphone and not something near it?

If you want to increase the penalties for reckless driving, go ahead.   10
If cellphone records show a driver was browsing baseball scores at the time he caused an accident, increase his fines and punishment. That at least makes some sense. But don't pass useless laws that will be arbitrarily enforced simply because "we have to do something." We've seen similar nonsense on display with the general use of cellphones while driving. Though several states have passed bans, all make exceptions for hands-free devices. But we know the level of impairment of drivers using hands-free devices is essentially the same as that of drivers holding a phone. These laws aren't about safety; they're about symbolism.

Here are two things these bans will do: They'll give police officers   11
another reason to pull people over, and they'll bring in revenue for the municipalities that aggressively enforce them. I think both are arguments against a ban. You may disagree, but the one thing these bans aren't likely to do is make the roads much safer. And if they won't accomplish that, there's no reason to enact them.

Vocabulary

If you do not know the meanings of the following words, try to determine them from the context of Balko's essay. Test your guesses in a dictionary, and then use each word in a sentence of your own.

wrenching (2)	factor (4)	arbitrarily (10)
alleged (2)	proponents (5)	symbolism (10)
scrawl (2)	proportion (6)	revenue (11)
penumbra (3)	flummoxed (8)	
empirical (4)	mandate (9)	

Key Ideas and Details

1. What is the thesis of Balko's argument? Where is this thesis stated most clearly? What is the relationship between Balko's thesis and McCarthy's thesis in the previous essay (beginning on p. 398)?

2. What does Balko mean by "TOBAL-itis" (paragraph 1)? Why does he believe that McCarthy's proposal is nothing but "symbolism" (10)?

3. Explain the "enforceability problem" (paragraph 8), as Balko presents it. Why would laws against texting while driving be difficult to enforce?

Craft and Structure

1. LANGUAGE Balko, more than McCarthy, relies on irony, saying one thing when he means another: for example, "it doesn't even matter if the problem actually exists" (paragraph 2). Locate other examples of irony. In your view, does irony strengthen or weaken Balko's argument? Why? (If necessary, consult *irony* in the Glossary.)

2. To what extent does Balko use rational appeals in refuting McCarthy? emotional appeals? Identify examples of each in your answer.

3. In paragraphs 4–9 Balko identifies and disputes a syllogism that he sees McCarthy and other proponents of texting bans relying on. Tease out the faulty syllogism and explain what Balko finds wrong with it.

4. OTHER METHODS Much of Balko's argument is developed by example (Chapter 8). What examples of driver distractions does he cite? Why does he stress them as he does?

Integration of Knowledge and Ideas

1. How does Balko present and handle opposing arguments? Does he seem fair? Why, or why not?

2. Whom does Balko seem to be addressing in this essay: Congresswoman McCarthy? those who support texting bans? those who oppose them? those who haven't made up their minds? some other group? What influence does he apparently hope to have on his readers' opinions? To what extent did he influence your opinions of laws against texting while driving and of McCarthy's argument supporting them?

3. FOR DISCUSSION Compare Balko's and McCarthy's accounts of the rise in accidents caused by distracted driving (paragraphs 4–6 in Balko; paragraphs 6–7, pp. 399–400, in McCarthy). Which is more detailed? How does each author's use of detail—and the details themselves—reflect the way in which he or she hopes to influence readers' opinions?

Writing Topics

1. "[W]e need to get over the idea that we can solve every bad habit with a new law. We can't, and this issue illustrates why," Balko writes in paragraph 3. Do you agree? Think of another law or regulation that has been proposed or enacted as a reaction to a perceived threat, such as bans on large sodas, limits on smoking in public spaces, or rules meant to prevent concussions among football players. Using Balko's argument against such laws as a starting point, explain in an essay why you think the law is or is not an effective solution to the problem. Is the problem as widespread as the media have reported? How real and serious is the threat? What other solutions suggest themselves? You may want to provide evidence from experts to support your opinion; see Chapter 5 for information on finding and using sources.

2. Some people believe that mobile devices can enhance connectivity and community among far-flung friends and relatives; others argue that electronic communication distances us from others, making us lonely and unhappy. What is your opinion of the social effects of technology? Do you think that today's communication habits have an overall positive or negative effect? Write an essay in which you explain how you think your mobile device affects you.

3. Although he opposes efforts to make texting while driving illegal, Balko acknowledges that the behavior is dangerous. Think of some other legal practice that could also be interpreted as risky or foolish, such as smoking, reducing weight through surgery, or tattooing. In an essay or presentation, argue for or against the practice on specific grounds: Is it indeed dangerous? Why, or why not? Why do those who engage in it do so? Does it affect society as a whole in any way? Is the behavior currently restricted? Should it be less or more restricted? How?

4. CONNECTIONS Both Balko and McCarthy invoke the dangers of texting while driving and examine the effectiveness of laws meant to stop the practice. But one aspect of the problem is merely hinted at in their essays: the *reasons* people use mobile devices while driving in the first place. What do you think those reasons are? How might addressing the causes of distracted driving help to prevent it? Drawing on these two authors' stated and unstated assumptions, your own experiences and observations, and any reading you have done on the subject, write an essay exploring this issue. Be sure to offer sufficient evidence to support your claims.

REGULATING TECHNOLOGY: INTERNET PRIVACY

Nicholas Carr

A former management consultant and executive editor for *Harvard Business Review*, and a current editorial adviser for *Encyclopaedia Britannica*, Nicholas Carr (born 1959) is best known for his often controversial articles and books examining the relationships between computers and culture. His work has been published in the *Guardian*, *Wired*, the *New York Times*, *Advertising Age*, and several other newspapers and business magazines. Carr's 2008 cover story for the *Atlantic* — "Is Google Making Us Stupid?" — generated such an overwhelming response that he extended his research to write *The Shallows: What the Internet Is Doing to Our Brains* (2011), a *New York Times* best-seller and a finalist for the Pulitzer Prize in general nonfiction. Carr has written two other books as well: *Does IT Matter? Information Technology and the Corrosion of Competitive Advantage* (2004) and *The Big Switch: Rewiring the World, from Edison to Google* (2008). He holds degrees in literature from Dartmouth College and Harvard University.

Tracking Is an Assault on Liberty

Carr has been particularly outspoken about the effects of the Internet on individuals and society. In this essay, first published in the *Wall Street Journal* in 2010, he presents an argument in favor of taking measures to protect privacy online. The essay after this one, by Jim Harper (page 415), dismisses Carr's concerns by insisting that businesses and individuals alike benefit from loss of privacy.

In a 1963 Supreme Court opinion, Chief Justice Earl Warren observed 1 that "the fantastic advances in the field of electronic communication constitute a great danger to the privacy of the individual." The advances have only accelerated since then, along with the dangers. Today, as companies strive to personalize the services and advertisements they provide over the Internet, the surreptitious collection of personal information is rampant. The very idea of privacy is under threat.

Most of us view personalization and privacy as desirable things, and 2 we understand that enjoying more of one means giving up some of the other. To have goods, services and promotions tailored to our personal circumstances and desires, we need to divulge information about ourselves to corporations, governments or other outsiders.

This tradeoff has always been part of our lives as consumers and citi- 3 zens. But now, thanks to the Net, we're losing our ability to understand and control those tradeoffs — to choose, consciously and with awareness of the consequences, what information about ourselves we disclose and what we don't. Incredibly detailed data about our lives are being harvested from online databases without our awareness, much less our approval.

Even though the Internet is a very social place, we tend to access it 4 in seclusion. We often assume that we're anonymous as we go about our business online. As a result, we treat the Net not just as a shopping mall and a library but as a personal diary and, sometimes, a confessional. Through the sites we visit and the searches we make, we disclose details not only about our jobs, hobbies, families, politics and health, but also about our secrets, fantasies, even our peccadilloes.

But our sense of anonymity is largely an illusion. Pretty much every- 5 thing we do online, down to individual keystrokes and clicks, is recorded, stored in cookies and corporate databases, and connected to our identities, either explicitly through our user names, credit-card numbers and the IP addresses assigned to our computers, or implicitly through our searching, surfing and purchasing histories.

A few years ago, the computer consultant Tom Owad published the 6 results of an experiment that provided a chilling lesson in just how easy it is to extract sensitive personal data from the Net. Mr. Owad wrote a simple piece of software that allowed him to download public wish lists that *Amazon.com* customers post to catalog products that they plan to purchase or would like to receive as gifts. These lists usually include the name of the list's owner and his or her city and state.

Using a couple of standard-issue PCs, Mr. Owad was able to down- 7 load over 250,000 wish lists over the course of a day. He then searched the data for controversial or politically sensitive books and authors, from Kurt Vonnegut's *Slaughterhouse-Five*[1] to the Koran. He then used *Yahoo! People Search* to identify addresses and phone numbers for many of the list owners.

Mr. Owad ended up with maps of the United States showing the 8 locations of people interested in particular books and ideas, including George Orwell's *1984*.[2] He could just as easily have published a map showing the residences of people interested in books about treating depression or adopting a child. "It used to be," Mr. Owad concluded, "you had to get a warrant to monitor a person or a group of people.

---

[1]A 1969 novel about alien abduction, time travel, and the bombing of Dresden, Germany, in World War II. [Editors' note.]

[2]A 1949 novel critical of communism and mind control. [Editors' note.]

Today, it is increasingly easy to monitor ideas. And then track them back to people."

What Mr. Owad did by hand can increasingly be performed auto- 9 matically, with data-mining software that draws from many sites and databases. One of the essential characteristics of the Net is the interconnection of diverse stores of information. The "openness" of databases is what gives the system much of its power and usefulness. But it also makes it easy to discover hidden relationships among far-flung bits of data.

In 2006, a team of scholars from the University of Minnesota 10 described how easy it is for data-mining software to create detailed personal profiles of individuals—even when they post information anonymously. The software is based on a simple principle: People tend to leave lots of little pieces of information about themselves and their opinions in many different places on the Web. By identifying correspondences among the data, sophisticated algorithms can identify individuals with extraordinary precision. And it's not a big leap from there to discovering the people's names. The researchers noted that most Americans can be identified by name and address using only their ZIP Code, birthday and gender—three pieces of information that people often divulge when they register at a website.

The more deeply the Net is woven into our work lives and leisure 11 activities, the more exposed we become. Over the last few years, as social-networking services have grown in popularity, people have come to entrust ever more intimate details about their lives to sites like *Facebook* and *Twitter*. The incorporation of GPS transmitters into cellphones and the rise of location-tracking services like *Foursquare* provide powerful tools for assembling moment-by-moment records of people's movements. As reading shifts from printed pages onto networked devices like the Kindle and the Nook, it becomes possible for companies to more closely monitor people's reading habits—even when they're not surfing the Web.

"You have zero privacy," Scott McNealy remarked back in 1999, 12 when he was chief executive of Sun Microsystems. "Get over it." Other Silicon Valley CEOs[3] have expressed similar sentiments in just the last few months. While Internet companies may be complacent about the erosion of personal privacy—they, after all, profit from the trend—the rest of us should be wary. There are real dangers.

---

[3] Chief executive officers. [Editors' note.]

First and most obvious is the possibility that our personal data will   13
fall into the wrong hands. Powerful data-mining tools are available not
only to legitimate corporations and researchers, but also to crooks, con
men and creeps. As more data about us is collected and shared online,
the threats from unsanctioned interceptions of the data grow. Criminal
syndicates can use purloined information about our identities to commit financial fraud, and stalkers can use locational data to track our
whereabouts.

The first line of defense is, of course, common sense. We need to take   14
personal responsibility for the information we share whenever we log
on. But no amount of caution will protect us from the dispersal of information collected without our knowledge. If we're not aware of what
data about us are available online, and how they're being used and
exchanged, it can be difficult to guard against abuses.

A second danger is the possibility that personal information may be   15
used to influence our behavior and even our thoughts in ways that are
invisible to us. Personalization's evil twin is manipulation. As mathe-
maticians and marketers refine data-mining algorithms, they gain more
precise ways to predict people's behavior as well as how they'll react
when they're presented with online ads and other digital stimuli. Just
this past week, *Google* CEO Eric Schmidt acknowledged that by tracking
a person's messages and movements, an algorithm can accurately predict
where that person will go next.

As marketing pitches and product offerings become more tightly tied   16
to our past patterns of behavior, they become more powerful as triggers of
future behavior. Already, advertisers are able to infer extremely personal
details about people by monitoring their Web-browsing habits. They can
then use that knowledge to create ad campaigns customized to particular
individuals. A man who visits a site about obesity, for instance, may soon
see a lot of promotional messages related to weight-loss treatments. A
woman who does research about anxiety may be bombarded with pharmaceutical ads. The line between personalization and manipulation is a
fuzzy one, but one thing is certain: We can never know if the line has
been crossed if we're unaware of what companies know about us.

Safeguarding privacy online isn't particularly hard. It requires that   17
software makers and site operators assume that people want to keep
their information private. Privacy settings should be on by default and
easy to modify. And when companies track our behavior or use personal
details to tailor messages, they should provide an easy way for us to see
what they're doing.

The greatest danger posed by the continuing erosion of personal   18
privacy is that it may lead us as a society to devalue the concept of
privacy, to see it as outdated and unimportant. We may begin to see privacy merely as a barrier to efficient shopping and socializing. That would
be a tragedy. As the computer security expert Bruce Schneier has observed,
privacy is not just a screen we hide behind when we do something
naughty or embarrassing; privacy is "intrinsic to the concept of liberty."
When we feel that we're always being watched, we begin to lose our sense
of self-reliance and free will and, along with it, our individuality. "We
become children," writes Mr. Schneier, "fettered under watchful eyes."

Privacy is not only essential to life and liberty; it's essential to the   19
pursuit of happiness, in the broadest and deepest sense. We human
beings are not just social creatures; we're also private creatures. What we
don't share is as important as what we do share. The way that we choose
to define the boundary between our public self and our private self will
vary greatly from person to person, which is exactly why it's so important to be ever vigilant in defending everyone's right to set that boundary as he or she sees fit.

Vocabulary

If you do not know the meanings of the following words, try to determine them
from the context of Carr's essay. Test your guesses in a dictionary, and then use
each word in a sentence of your own.

surreptitious (1)	algorithms (10)	purloined (13)
rampant (1)	incorporation (11)	dispersal (14)
divulge (2)	Silicon Valley (12)	stimuli (15)
disclose (3)	complacent (12)	pharmaceutical (16)
seclusion (4)	wary (12)	default (17)
peccadilloes (4)	unsanctioned (13)	intrinsic (18)
explicitly (5)	interceptions (13)	fettered (18)
implicitly (5)	syndicates (13)	vigilant (19)

Key Ideas and Details

1. What problem does Carr identify? What solution, if any, does he propose?

2. How, according to Carr, do "corporations, governments or other outsiders"
   (paragraph 2) obtain personal information about individual Internet users?
   Identify at least two ways.

3. "There are real dangers" to losing privacy online, Carr writes in paragraph 12. What are those dangers, as he sees them?

Craft and Structure

1. LANGUAGE How would you describe Carr's attitude toward his subject? What is the overall tone of his argument?

2. What does the author accomplish by opening with a discussion of the "tradeoffs" (paragraph 3) between privacy and personalization?

3. Does this essay appeal to emotion, or reason, or both? Give evidence for your answer.

4. OTHER METHODS Where and how does Carr use definition (Chapter 13) to clarify the meaning of *privacy*? By what means does the author bring his argument around to the subject of liberty?

Integration of Knowledge and Ideas

1. What seems to be Carr's purpose in writing this essay? Is he writing mainly to express a concern, offer a solution to a problem, influence government regulations, change individuals' attitudes, or do something else? What details from the text support your answer?

2. Why do you suppose Carr quotes or paraphrases Earl Warren (paragraph 1), Tom Owad (8), Scott McNealy (12), Eric Schmidt (15), and Bruce Schneier (18)? Who are these people? What does Carr achieve by using other writers' words and ideas to explain his points?

3. FOR DISCUSSION Why is Carr so concerned about "manipulation" (paragraphs 15–16)? What exactly does he think could happen if advertisers customize their messages to individual Web users' interests and behaviors? Do you think his concerns are valid, or do they seem overwrought? Why?

Writing Topics

1. "The more deeply the Net is woven into our work lives and leisure activities, the more exposed we become," Carr writes in paragraph 11. What does he mean? And do you agree? Draft a narrative account of an experience you have had using an online medium such as *Google, Facebook, Foursquare,* or another social-networking site in an attempt to discover whether you believe such tools encourage people to share "ever more intimate details about their lives" (11) and whether you think such exposure is a problem. Then expand your narrative to explain your assessment of the cause-and-effect relationship between the Internet and loss of privacy, being sure to define what you mean by *privacy*.

2. Write a paper in which you analyze and evaluate any one of Carr's ideas. For instance, do "[m]ost of us view personalization and privacy as desirable

things" (paragraph 2)? Are the dangers of online exposure as "real" (12) as he claims? Are we becoming resigned to lack of privacy as he says (18)? Do we really need privacy in the first place? Support your view with evidence from your experience, observation, or reading.

3. RESEARCH The novels Carr mentions—George Orwell's *1984* and Kurt Vonnegut's *Slaughterhouse-Five*—both present pessimistic visions of imagined societies in which governments control individual citizens' minds and behaviors. Choose one novel and read it, keeping Carr's argument in mind. Why do online searches for these novels represent particularly apt examples of the issues surrounding data tracking, given Carr's purpose and thesis? What might a government agency in particular infer about the motives and interests of a person who reads one of these works?

4. CONNECTIONS While Carr expresses deep concern about the implications of data mining online, Jim Harper, the author of the next essay ("Web Users Get as Much as They Give"), sees little reason to worry. On what major point do the authors agree and disagree? How do the tones of the two essays compare? Does either writer seem more convinced of being in the right? Which essay do you find more convincing, and why?

REGULATING TECHNOLOGY: INTERNET PRIVACY

Jim Harper

Jim Harper is director of information policy studies at the Cato Institute in Washington, DC; the editor of *Privacilla.org*, an online think tank focused on issues of privacy; and the Web master for *WashingtonWatch.com*, a site that monitors government spending. He began writing books, articles, and policy briefs about the challenges of adjusting laws to changing technologies shortly after he finished law school at the University of California at Hastings in 1994. Harper has published scholarly articles about privacy and security in the *Administrative Law Review*, the *Minnesota Law Review*, and the *Hastings Constitutional Law Quarterly*. His books include *Identity Crisis: How Identification Is Overused and Misunderstood* (2006) and *Terrorizing Ourselves: Why US Counterterrorism Policy Is Failing and How to Fix It* (2010), coedited with Benjamin H. Friedman and Christopher A. Preble. A founding member of the Department of Homeland Security's Data Privacy and Integrity Advisory Committee, he regularly provides testimony at congressional hearings and lectures on privacy issues.

Web Users Get as Much as They Give

A Web site producer himself, Harper strongly supports transparency online. As he sees it, privacy is not a right to be protected by laws but a preference to be controlled by individuals as they see fit. In this essay, published together with Nicholas Carr's argument (p. 408) in the *Wall Street Journal*, Harper argues that Internet tracking restrictons are both unnecessary and counterproductive.

If you surf the Web, congratulations! You are part of the information 1 economy. Data gleaned from your communications and transactions grease the gears of modern commerce. Not everyone is celebrating, of course. Many people are concerned and dismayed—even shocked— when they learn that "their" data are fuel for the World Wide Web.

Who is gathering the information? What are they doing with it? 2 How might this harm me? How do I stop it?

These are all good questions. But rather than indulging the natural 3 reaction to say "stop," people should get smart and learn how to control personal information. There are plenty of options and tools people can use to protect privacy—and a certain obligation to use them. Data about you are not "yours" if you don't do anything to control them. Meanwhile, learning about the information economy can make clear its many benefits.

It's natural to be concerned about online privacy. The Internet is 4 an interactive medium, not a static one like television. Every visit to a website sends information out before it pulls information in. And the information Web surfers send out can be revealing.

Most Web sites track users, particularly through the use of cookies, 5 little text files placed on Web surfers' computers. Sites use cookies to customize a visitor's experience. And advertising networks use cookies to gather information about users. A network that has ads on a lot of sites will recognize a browser (and by inference the person using it) when it goes to different Web sites, enabling the ad network to get a sense of that person's interests. Been on a site dealing with SUVs? You just might see an SUV ad as you continue to surf. Most Web sites and ad networks do not "sell" information about their users. In targeted online advertising, the business model is to sell space to advertisers—giving them access to people ("eyeballs") based on their demographics and interests. If an ad network sold personal and contact info, it would undercut its advertising business and its own profitability.

Some people don't like this tracking, for a variety of reasons. For 6 some, it feels like a violation to be treated as a mere object of commerce. Some worry that data about their interests will be used to discriminate wrongly against them, or to exclude them from information and opportunities they should enjoy. Excess customization of the Web experience may stratify society, some believe. If you are poor or from a minority group, for example, the news, entertainment and commentary you see on the Web might differ from others', preventing your participation in the "national" conversation and culture that traditional media may produce. And tied to real identities, Web surfing data could fall into the hands of government and be used wrongly. These are all legitimate concerns that people with different worldviews prioritize to differing degrees.

"Surreptitious" use of cookies is one of the weaker complaints. 7 Cookies have been integral to Web browsing since the beginning, and their privacy consequences have been a subject of public discussion for over a decade. Cookies are a surreptitious threat to privacy the way smoking is a surreptitious threat to health. If you don't know about it, you haven't been paying attention. But before going into your browser settings and canceling cookies, Web users should ask another question about information sharing in the online world. What am I getting in return?

The reason why a company like *Google* can spend millions and mil- 8 lions of dollars on free services like its search engine, Gmail, mapping tools, *Google* Groups and more is because of online advertising that trades in personal information. And it's not just *Google*. *Facebook*, *Yahoo!*, *MSN*, and thousands of blogs, news sites, and comment boards use advertising to support what they do. And personalized advertising is more valuable than advertising aimed at just anyone. Marketers will pay more to reach you if you are likely to use their products or services. (Perhaps online tracking makes everyone special!)

If Web users supply less information to the Web, the Web will supply less information to them. Free content won't go away if consumers decline to allow personalization, but there will be less of it. Bloggers and operators of small Web sites will have a little less reason to produce the stuff that makes our Internet an endlessly fascinating place to visit. As an operator of a small government-transparency Web site, *WashingtonWatch*, I add new features for my visitors when there is enough money to do it. More money spent on advertising means more tools for American citizens to use across the Web.

Ten years ago—during an earlier round of cookie concern—the Federal Trade Commission asked Congress for power to regulate the Internet for privacy's sake. If the FTC had gotten authority to impose regulations requiring "notice, choice, access, and security" from Web sites—all good practices, in varying measure—it is doubtful that *Google* would have had the same success it has had over the past decade. It might be a decent, struggling search engine today. But, unable to generate the kind of income it does, the quality of search it produces might be lower, and it may not have had the assets to produce and support all its fascinating and useful products. The rise of *Google* and all the access it provides was not fated from the beginning. It depended on a particular set of circumstances in which it had access to consumer information and the freedom to use it in ways that some find privacy-dubious.

Some legislators, privacy advocates and technologists want very badly to protect consumers, but much "consumer protection" actually invites consumers to abandon personal responsibility. The *caveat emptor*[1] rule requires people to stay on their toes, learn about the products they use, and hold businesses' feet to the fire. People rise or fall to meet expectations, and consumer advocates who assume incompetence on the part of the public may have a hand in producing it, making consumers worse off. If a central authority such as Congress or the FTC were to decide for consumers how to deal with cookies, it would generalize wrongly about many, if not most, individuals' interests, giving them the wrong mix of privacy and interactivity. If the FTC ruled that third-party cookies required consumers to opt in, for example, most would not, and the wealth of

9

10

11

---

[1] Latin for "buyer beware." [Editors' note.]

"free" content and services most people take for granted would quietly fade from view. And it would leave consumers unprotected from threats beyond their jurisdiction (as in Web tracking by sites outside the United States). Education is the hard way, and it is the only way, to get consumers' privacy interests balanced with their other interests.

But perhaps this is a government vs. corporate passion play, with 12 government as the privacy defender. The *Wall Street Journal* reported last week that engineers working on a new version of Microsoft's Internet Explorer browser thought they might set certain defaults to protect privacy better, but they were overruled when the business segments at Microsoft learned of the plan. Privacy "sabotage," the Electronic Frontier Foundation called it. And a *Wired* news story says Microsoft "crippled" online privacy protections. But if the engineers' plan had won the day, an equal, opposite reaction would have resulted when Microsoft "sabotaged" Web interactivity and the advertising business model, "crippling" consumer access to free content. The new version of Microsoft's browser maintained the status quo in cookie functionality, as does *Google*'s Chrome browser and *Firefox*, a product of the nonprofit Mozilla Foundation. The "business attacks privacy" story doesn't wash.

This is not to say that businesses don't want personal information— 13 they do, so they can provide maximal service to their customers. But they are struggling to figure out how to serve all dimensions of consumer interest, including the internally inconsistent consumer demand for privacy along with free content, custom Web experiences, convenience and so on.

Only one thing is certain here: Nobody knows how this is sup- 14 posed to come out. Cookies and other tracking technologies will create legitimate concerns that weigh against the benefits they provide. Browser defaults may converge on something more privacy-protective. (Apple's *Safari* browser rejects third-party cookies unless users tell it to do otherwise.) Browser plug-ins will augment consumers' power to control cookies and other tracking technologies. Consumers will get better accustomed to the information economy, and they will choose more articulately how they fit into it. What matters is that the conversation should continue.

Vocabulary

If you do not know the following words, try to determine their meanings from the context of Harper's essay. Test your guesses in a dictionary, and then use each word in a sentence of your own.

gleaned (1)	transparency (9)	status quo (12)
commerce (1)	assets (10)	converge (14)
static (4)	dubious (10)	augment (14)
demographics (5)	legislators (11)	articulately (14)
stratify (6)	jurisdiction (11)	
surreptitious (7)	sabotage (12)	

Key Ideas and Details

1. What connection does Harper make between personal data and the "information economy" (paragraph 1)? Express his main idea in a sentence or two of your own.

2. What are cookies, and how are they used? Why is Harper not bothered by them?

3. Where does Harper ultimately place the blame for the average American's loss of privacy online? What solution does he suggest?

Craft and Structure

1. LANGUAGE Harper uses figures of speech throughout his essay, such as "grease the gears of modern commerce" (paragraph 1), a metaphor, and "advertising that trades in personal information" (8), a personification. Locate a few more figures of speech and comment on their effectiveness. (See *figures of speech* in the Glossary.) What do they contribute to Harper's tone?

2. To understand Harper's strategy, make an outline of the main points in his argument. Which of these points directly counter points made by Nicholas Carr in the previous essay (beginning on p. 408)? Which of Carr's points does Harper not address directly? In what ways is his emphasis different from Carr's?

3. In paragraph 9 Harper discusses his role as "an operator of a small government-transparency Web site." What persuasive tactic is he employing here? Does it work, in your opinion?

4. OTHER METHODS Much of Harper's argument is developed by cause-and-effect analysis (Chapter 14). What does he claim would be the result of new regulations protecting privacy online?

Integration of Knowledge and Ideas

1. What seems to be the author's primary purpose in this essay: to discredit critics of Internet tracking? to reassure Web users that their personal information is safe? to advance an economic theory? Do you think Harper accomplishes his purpose? Why, or why not?

2. What assumptions does Harper seem to make about the readers of this essay? Are the assumptions correct in your case?

3. FOR DISCUSSION What examples of past efforts to protect consumer privacy does Harper present? What do these examples contribute to his point?

Writing Topics

1. Harper writes that "[s]ome people don't like . . . tracking, for a variety of reasons" (paragraph 6). He then lists several of these reasons and acknowledges that such concerns are legitimate, but doesn't go into them in any detail. Pick one of the issues he raises and explore it in an essay. Does it, for instance, "feel like a violation to be treated as a mere object of commerce" (6)? Could data mining lead to discrimination or stratification in society? What might happen if information falls into the wrong hands? You may wish to think broadly about this issue, but bring your essay down to earth by focusing on one specific concern—perhaps one that you've experienced or witnessed yourself.

2. Write an essay in which you compare and contrast two related types of communication or entertainment media: for example, print books and e-readers, television and *YouTube*, radio and streaming music services, laptops and tablets. Your approach may be either lighthearted or serious, but make sure you come to some conclusion about your subjects. Which technology do you favor? Why?

3. RESEARCH A "passion play" (paragraph 12) is a medieval Christian drama, usually performed around Easter, that celebrates the death and resurrection of Jesus. Use a reference work, such as a glossary of literary terms or an encyclopedia, to find out more about passion plays and the plot, characters, and themes they typically follow. What does Harper accomplish by making an allusion to this particular literary genre? Does it strengthen his argument, or weaken it? Why? (If necessary, look up *allusion* in the Glossary.)

4. CONNECTIONS Write a response to Harper's essay in which you establish your own position on the debate over Internet privacy. Do you agree with Harper that privacy is a reasonable price to pay for the content available online, or do you take Nicholas Carr's (p. 408) view that privacy is a fundamental right not to be given up lightly? Or does your opinion fall somewhere between the two extremes? As much as possible, use examples from your own experience (or from the experiences of those close to you) to support your argument.

WRITING WITH THE METHOD

ARGUMENT AND PERSUASION

Choose one of the following statements, or any other statement they suggest, and support or refute it in an argumentative essay. The statement you decide on should concern a topic you care about so that argument is a means of convincing readers to accept an idea, not an end in itself.

Popular Culture

1. Reality television has a negative influence on society.
2. Advertisements serve useful purposes.
3. Web sites encouraging anorexia or similar pathologies should be shut down.
4. Professional athletes should not be allowed to compete in the Olympics.

Health and Technology

5. Terminally ill people should have the right to choose when to die.
6. Private automobiles should be restricted in cities.
7. Laboratory experiments on dogs, cats, and primates are necessary.
8. Smoking should be banned in all public places, including outdoors.

Education

9. Students caught in any form of academic cheating should be expelled.
10. Student athletes should have to pay fees to participate in school sports.
11. Studying language arts is an impractical waste of time and resources.

Social and Political Issues

12. Corporate executives are overpaid.
13. Private institutions should have the right to make rules that would be unconstitutional outside those institutions.
14. Public libraries should provide free, unlimited access to the Internet.
15. When adopted children turn eighteen, they should have free access to information about their birth parents.

WRITING ABOUT THE THEME

DEBATING LAW AND ORDER

1. Several of the essays in this chapter discuss issues affecting children and young adults, yet the authors write from very different perspectives with widely varied purposes. The US Travel Association (p. 364), for instance, calls for changing airport screening practices that assume a child is a threat. Anna Quindlen (p. 382) takes an earnest tone in urging authority figures to do more to protect teenagers. Wilbert Rideau (p. 387) argues that people shouldn't have to spend their lives paying for the "dumb, impulsive choices" (paragraph 1) of their youth. Marie Myung-Ok Lee (p. 392) suggests that treating children of illegal immigrants as law breakers is unfair and harmful to families. And Carolyn McCarthy (p. 398) and Radley Balko (p. 403) debate whether laws should forbid drivers from using mobile devices behind the wheel. Think of an illegal or dangerous behavior typical of teenagers and write an essay that argues your position on how legal authorities should respond to it. For instance, you might write about tagging, underage drinking, or pirating music. How harshly should such behavior be punished, if at all? In your essay, be sure to consider the potential consequences of both the behavior and the response and to support your opinion with plenty of examples and details to explain your reasons.

2. Many of the writers in this chapter are concerned with guns and crime prevention. Jenny Price (p. 373) expresses concern that gun ownership leads to murder, while John Stossel (p. 373) argues that guns prevent crimes. Anna Quindlen cites examples of what happens when disturbed people have access to firearms. Wilbert Rideau, on the other hand, claims that putting shooters behind bars for life does not make society safer. What role do guns play in crime and public safety? Write about a recent time when you were aware of gun-control issues in your community — perhaps a noteworthy incident, a hunting accident, a controversy involving police methods, a report of rising or falling crime, even a personal experience. What did you read, hear, or experience, and what did you think about it? You could focus on a particular episode involving guns or on an issue of gun control in general. Do all American citizens have a constitutional right to bear arms, for instance, or do the needs of society outweigh individual rights? Should certain types of guns be banned or restricted? Why, or why not?

3. The four essays in the casebook all consider ways of adapting to new technologies. Carolyn McCarthy and Radley Balko debate the dangers brought by the common practice of texting while driving; Nicholas Carr (p. 408) and Jim Harper

(p. 415) examine privacy issues raised by increasingly sophisticated tracking tools online. Think of a newer technology that you dislike. (Examples might include RFID chips, GPS devices, friend locators, or streaming music services.) Why don't you care for it? In what ways is this technology harmful or just more trouble than it's worth? In an essay, explore the benefits and drawbacks of a modern convenience. When does technology help us? At what point does convenience become harmful or destructive to others? Write to persuade readers to change their behavior or from a narrower personal perspective. If you choose the latter course, however, be sure to make your experience meaningful to others with plenty of details and examples.

APPENDIX

HISTORIC SPEECHES

▶

You speak to people every day. In dinner conversations with family, gossip sessions with friends, classroom discussions with teachers and peers, you share your thoughts and experiences, instinctively adapting what you say and how you say it as others respond. But at work, in school, and in daily life you will sometimes be called on to speak to a group. You might be asked to give a **speech**, a spoken address that relies on words and gestures to inform, persuade, or entertain an audience of listeners, or a **presentation**, a speech combined with multimedia support such as visual slides or audio accompaniments. As a speaker you could, for instance, explain a theft prevention system to a group of new trainees, collaborate with your biology classmates to persuade residents at a community hearing that a proposed development will damage wildlife habitat, or give a toast at a wedding.

Speeches and presentations are more formal—and therefore more nervewracking—than casual chats, but the prospect of giving one needn't be a source of terror. Effective public speaking draws on communication skills you already possess, as well as the thinking and writing strategies addressed in this Appendix and throughout this book.

Reading and Listening to Speeches

Though each essay in this book illustrates one overall method of development, a speech is rarely developed by a single method alone. Even when speakers are purposefully narrating or arguing, say, they may also describe, compare, define, classify, or employ other methods. And often speechwriters use no dominant method at all but select whatever methods they need, in whatever sequence, to achieve their purpose.

As with any written text, you should read a transcript of a speech closely and attentively, as many times as needed to appreciate its style and grasp its deeper meanings. Using the critical reading strategies outlined in Chapter 1 and the checklist on page 8, examine the content for key ideas and details, analyze how the speaker applies craft and structure for a particular purpose and audience, and consider how the speech integrates knowledge and ideas from other sources as well as how it resonates with or challenges what you know about the subject.

Because speeches often have a persuasive purpose, take particular note of the speaker's rhetorical strategies and argumentative structure (see pp. 365–74). Does he or she, for instance, rely mainly on rational, emotional, or ethical appeals? Is the reasoning sound? What claim does the speaker want listeners to accept, and are the reasons compelling, the evidence adequate, the treatment of opposing views fair and balanced?

Of course, you won't always encounter speeches in written form. Many times, you'll be a listening member of a speaker's audience—maybe in person, through a live broadcast, or by way of a recording. At such times, you might not have the luxury of relistening to catch key ideas and details or to assess the speaker's strategies. When hearing a speech, then, you must focus on listening actively, following the speaking and listening guidelines listed on page 25. Be respectful and pay attention to what the speaker is saying, taking notes on key points if possible or appropriate. Speakers often conclude their presentations with a question-and-answer session, so if you have questions or objections, by all means raise them—politely and within reason.

Keys to Effective Speaking

Preparing a speech is similar to constructing an essay. Both kinds of writing involve the process of discovery, drafting, revising, and editing discussed in Chapters 2 through 4, and in both cases you may need to do some research to find evidence and details to support your points and main idea (see Chapter 5).

The major difference between writing an essay and writing a speech is that you'll deliver your speech live to a physical audience. In most cases you will be in the same room as your listeners, able to see the people you're addressing. You'll notice how the members of your audience are responding to your presentation (yawning or fidgeting, squinting in confusion, or nodding their heads in agreement), and you can and should adapt your speech accordingly—*as you are giving it*. Developing the flexibility and courage to revise your approach midspeech takes additional preparation, but with practice you can gain the confidence you need.

▶ Planning

As with writing an essay, writing a speech starts with a thorough consideration of what you hope to accomplish. You'll need to settle on a subject, of course, and you'll spend a fair amount of time exploring ideas, forming a thesis, and shaping your thoughts around your main point (see pp. 23–24). In preparing a speech, however, three elements of planning—audience, purpose, and time—are especially important.

- *Analyze your audience.* A successful presentation engages the audience by focusing on listeners' interests and needs, not the speaker's. Chances are you'll know many members of your audience personally—classmates and teachers in school, for instance, peers and supervisors at work, or neighbors and friends in a community setting—and so you'll be at least somewhat familiar with their values and attitudes. Whether or not you already know the people in your audience, however, you'll need to assess who your listeners are, what they know and don't know about your subject, where their interests lie, and what attitudes they may hold. Otherwise, you run the risk of boring or, worse, alienating your audience and failing to connect.

- *Determine your purpose.* Public speaking generally has one of three purposes: to inform, to persuade, or (on special occasions) to entertain. You'll need to decide early on what you want your listeners to understand, believe, or do after hearing you speak, so you can figure out how to bring them around to your perspective on the subject. You can't accomplish your goals if you don't know what they are.

- *Know your time limits.* Whether you are asked to deliver a five-minute speech or a half-hour presentation, be careful that the speech you prepare will stick to the time allotted. Especially if many people are slated to speak at a session, going over—or under—schedule will throw others off and strain listeners' patience.

▶ Structuring

To hold listeners' attention and to ensure that they can follow the speaker's points, an oral presentation requires a clear, simple organization. At its simplest, a speech consists of an introduction, a body, and a conclusion, with frequent repetition to keep listeners on track. As the public-speaking guru Dale Carnegie famously described the structure of an effective presentation, the goal is to "tell the audience what you're going to say, say it; then tell them what you've said."

Introduction

In your opening remarks, you first want to grab listeners' attention. Keeping the interests of your audience members in mind, you might try one of the techniques suggested under *introductions* in the Glossary. You could start with an anecdote, or brief narrative, that introduces your subject, for instance, with a pointed question, or with a surprising fact or statistic.

Once you have your audience's attention, you should clearly name the subject of your presentation and explain why it matters to your audience, preview your purpose by stating your thesis or main point, and provide a quick overview of the supporting points you will discuss. Be brief and try not to ramble.

Body

In the main part of a speech, the body, you provide as many reasons, bits of evidence, and examples as necessary to explain your main idea or prove your point.

You can use any of the methods addressed in Part Two to develop the body of a speech, but often you will find that combining methods is most effective because the methods provide different ways to introduce the details and other evidence needed to interest and convince an audience. Chapter 2 on developing an essay includes a set of questions that can aid your development of a subject (see p. 27). Say you are writing a speech on owls. Right off, several methods suggest themselves: a classification of kinds of owls, a description of each kind, a process analysis of an owl's life cycle or hunting behavior. But you want your presentation to go beyond the facts to engage listeners with your fascination with these birds of prey. Running through the list of questions, you find that "What is the story in the subject?" suggests a narrative of your first encounter with a barn owl, when your own awe and fear recalled the owl's reputation for wisdom and bad luck. Other questions lead you further along this path: "How can the subject be illustrated?" calls forth examples of myths and superstitions involving owls, and "Why did the subject happen?" leads you to consider why people see owls as symbols and omens. In the course of asking the questions, you have moved from a personal look at owls to a more imaginative and complex examination of their meaning and significance for other human beings.

With several elements and methods contributing to a presentation, a speech will be easy for listeners to follow only if you frequently clarify what point you are discussing and how it fits with your main idea. To help readers keep your presentation straight, aim for unity and coherence, relying especially on repetition and transitions.

- *Repetition or restatement* of key words and phrases helps an audience follow your points. Listeners have short attention spans; the more you can remind them of what you're saying and why, the better they can focus on your main idea. In her speech "I Want a Wife" (p. 306), for instance, Judy Brady relies on repetition and restatement to stress her point:

  I want a wife who will work and send me to school (paragraph 3). . . . I want a wife who will take care of *my* physical needs (4). . . . I want a wife who will not bother me with rambling complaints about a wife's duties (5). . . . I want a wife who will take care of the details of my social life (6). . . . When I am through with school and have a job, I want my wife to quit working and remain at home (8).

  Brady's repetition of "I want a wife" and the substitution of *who* for *wife* both emphasize the subject under discussion and clarify her thesis (that Brady is unhappy with her role as a wife). As you'll see, every speech in this Appendix uses a similar strategy, repeating key words and phrases to help listeners along.

- *Transitions* like those listed in the Glossary act as signposts to tell listeners where you, and they, are headed. Some transitions indicate that you are shifting between subjects, either finding resemblances between them (*also, likewise, similarly*) or finding differences (*but, however, in contrast, instead, unlike, whereas, yet*). Other transitions indicate that you are moving on to a new point (*in addition, also, furthermore, moreover*). In a speech especially, you can use full sentences as transitions to lead listeners along with you, reminding them of what you've just said and preparing them for your next point (*Now that we've looked at a few myths about owls, let's consider where those superstitions came from. . . . Superstitions like these provide some interesting clues into our relationship with nature.*)

See pages 38–42 for a fuller discussion of unity and coherence and additional examples of these techniques.

Conclusion

The conclusion to a speech should bring listeners back around to your main idea, usually by restating your thesis and summarizing the points you've provided to support it.

Any of the techniques suggested under *conclusions* in the Glossary can help you bring a presentation to a memorable close, but an especially effective strategy is to circle back to a detail from the introduction: If you opened with a story, for instance, bring it up again as you end; similarly, if you used a startling fact to introduce your speech, remind listeners of it in your conclusion. Be sure to mold your conclusion to your purpose for speaking. If your goal was to give the audience information, remind them what they've learned and suggest ways for them to put that knowledge to use. If your purpose was to persuade, end with a call to action, a direct challenge for listeners to do something or believe something.

▶ Integrating Multimedia

Most people process and remember verbal information better if the words are accompanied by visuals and sounds. By giving listeners something to look at while you speak, you can hold their attention and focus them on important points as you move along.

Many technologies enable presenters to enhance their speeches with visual and audio media, such as presentation slides, photographs, tables or charts, videos, and sound recordings. For such multimedia elements to be effective, however, they must be used for a specific purpose:

- To maintain audience interest
- To highlight or clarify key points
- To strengthen claims

For a presentation on owls, for instance, you might grab the audience's attention with an audio clip of a barred owl's screech, explain how owls hunt by screening a video, or prove a claim about the snowy owl's vital role in the ecosystem by showing an illustrated flowchart. When you do include any kind of multimedia in a presentation, be sure to tell the audience how it relates to your points. Projecting images or sounds merely for the sake of decoration will distract listeners, thereby defeating the purpose of using them.

Finally, keep visual elements as simple as possible. If you want to use PowerPoint slides to show an outline of your points as you speak, for instance, resist the temptation to cram full topic sentences with supporting details on each screen: aim, instead, for short bulleted lists with only a few key words on each line, and keep the number of slides limited (otherwise, your audience will read instead of listen). Be careful, also, that any text or image projected on a screen is large enough and legible enough that everyone in your audience—including the people at the back of the room—can see it clearly.

▶ Rehearsing

The most important element of a successful presentation is preparation. Once you've worked out the content and organization of a speech, and after you've selected any presentation aids, you'll need to practice.

Plan on rehearsing at least five or six times, if not more. Listeners are more receptive when a speaker looks at them, rather than at a written script, so you want to get to a point where you can speak from notes alone. The more you recite your speech, the more comfortable you'll become with the details within it, making it easier to shift gears during your presentation as necessary. At the same time, rehearsing a speech serves the same function as revising and editing an essay: it gives you the opportunity to adjust the details and hone your style.

It can help to rehearse with people you trust or in front a mirror. If you have access to a video or audio recording device, you might also try taping yourself to assess how you will look and sound to a live audience. As you practice, pay particular attention to your vocal and non-verbal delivery, aiming for clarity and ease.

- *Speak at a comfortable volume*, neither too loud nor too low. Try not to talk in a monotone: raise and lower your voice as appropriate, just as you do when speaking in a more casual setting.

- *Use a natural pace.* Some speakers rush their words when they're nervous; others slow down. Be aware if you tend to either extreme, and adjust your pace to the speed you would use in a normal conversation.

- *Avoid conversational fillers.* Verbal tics such as *like, um,* and *you know* distract listeners and reduce a speaker's credibility. Notice how often you utter such phrases and work to eliminate them.

- *Check your enunciation.* Speak articulately and clearly. Be sure that you know the correct pronunciations of the words you choose, and avoid mumbling.

- *Watch your body language.* Practice smiling and making eye contact with listeners. It's okay to move around and gesture as you speak (in fact, such motion will help to hold the audience's attention), but try not to fidget.

Everybody experiences some anxiety about speaking to a crowd—even actors and professional lecturers get nervous before they take the stage. When it's your turn to speak, stay calm. Breathe deeply, visualize success, and reassure yourself that you'll be fine. Remember: the more you rehearse, the more confident you will feel. Like any other skill, speaking gets easier with practice.

A Note on Thematic Connections

Besides combining the methods of development, the five speeches in this Appendix—all historic in their importance—reflect their speakers' ongoing concerns with the concept of liberty. Patrick Henry's speech to a gathering of patriots argues for American independence from British rule (next page). Elizabeth Cady Stanton (p. 437) and Sojourner Truth (p. 443) both address conventions of women's rights activists to demand equality. Abraham Lincoln's "Gettysburg Address" (p. 446) makes an impassioned call for the end of slavery and the young nation's survival. And "I Have a Dream," the enduring speech by Martin Luther King, Jr., expresses the frustrations and aspirations of African Americans during the civil rights movement of the 1960s (p. 449).

Patrick Henry

Patrick Henry was a lawyer and a representative in multiple forms of colonial government, but he is best known as a masterful orator with a sharp tongue and a deep resentment of injustice. He was born in 1736 to Scottish parents in rural Hanover County, Virginia, received only a minimal education, and served as a colonel in the state militia. After several failed attempts at business and farming, and despite his lack of legal knowledge, Henry was admitted to the Virginia Bar in 1760 and became involved in the political workings of revolutionary America. He was elected to the Virginia House of Burgesses (a legislative body under royal control) in 1765 and in 1776 became first governor of the commonwealth, where he served five nonconsecutive terms. Although a delegate to both Continental Congresses, Henry vigorously opposed ratification of the US Constitution until it included a Bill of Rights, fearing that federal powers would wield too much control over states and individuals. Once the new American government was established, he retired from politics and returned to private legal practice until his death in 1799.

Speech to the Second Virginia Convention

In Henry's time the American colonies had suffered a century of exploitation by the English government. Mostly from abroad, the English controlled much of the eastern seaboard's land and business, exacted taxes from the colonists without giving them representation in Parliament, and repressed the people in countless other ways. Henry, an early advocate of independence who had often lashed out at the tyrannies that he saw, was moved in 1775 to his most impassioned attack. Several new taxes had drawn angry protests, and the English sent military regiments to control the American crowds, resulting in multiple armed skirmishes. In response, Henry delivered this speech — a strongly worded call to war — to the Virginia House of Burgesses at St. John's Church in Richmond.

Mr. President:[1] No man thinks more highly than I do of the patriotism,   1
as well as abilities, of the very worthy gentlemen who have just addressed
the House. But different men often see the same subject in different
lights; and, therefore, I hope it will not be thought disrespectful to those
gentlemen if, entertaining as I do opinions of a character very opposite
to theirs, I shall speak forth my sentiments freely and without reserve.
This is no time for ceremony. The question before the House is one of
awful moment to this country. For my own part, I consider it as nothing less than a question of freedom or slavery; and in proportion to the
magnitude of the subject ought to be the freedom of the debate. It is

---

[1] Peyton Randolph, leader of the Second Virginia Convention. [Editors' note.]

only in this way that we can hope to arrive at truth, and fulfill the great responsibility which we hold to God and our country. Should I keep back my opinions at such a time, through fear of giving offense, I should consider myself as guilty of treason towards my country, and of an act of disloyalty toward the Majesty of Heaven, which I revere above all earthly kings.

Mr. President, it is natural to man to indulge in the illusions of hope.   2
We are apt to shut our eyes against a painful truth, and listen to the song of that siren till she transforms us into beasts. Is this the part of wise men, engaged in a great and arduous struggle for liberty? Are we disposed to be of the number of those who, having eyes, see not, and, having ears, hear not, the things which so nearly concern their temporal salvation? For my part, whatever anguish of spirit it may cost, I am willing to know the whole truth; to know the worst, and to provide for it.

I have but one lamp by which my feet are guided, and that is the   3
lamp of experience. I know of no way of judging of the future but by the past. And judging by the past, I wish to know what there has been in the conduct of the British ministry for the last ten years to justify those hopes with which gentlemen have been pleased to solace themselves and the House. Is it that insidious smile with which our petition has been lately received? Trust it not, sir; it will prove a snare to your feet. Suffer not yourselves to be betrayed with a kiss. Ask yourselves how this gracious reception of our petition comports with those warlike preparations which cover our waters and darken our land. Are fleets and armies necessary to a work of love and reconciliation? Have we shown ourselves so unwilling to be reconciled that force must be called in to win back our love? Let us not deceive ourselves, sir. These are the implements of war and subjugation; the last arguments to which kings resort. I ask gentlemen, sir, what means this martial array, if its purpose be not to force us to submission? Can gentlemen assign any other possible motive for it? Has Great Britain any enemy, in this quarter of the world, to call for all this accumulation of navies and armies? No, sir, she has none. They are meant for us: they can be meant for no other. They are sent over to bind and rivet upon us those chains which the British ministry have been so long forging. And what have we to oppose to them? Shall we try argument? Sir, we have been trying that for the last ten years. Have we anything new to offer upon the subject? Nothing. We have held the subject up in every light of which it is capable; but it has been all in vain. Shall we resort to entreaty and humble supplication? What terms shall we find which have not been already exhausted? Let us not, I beseech you, sir, deceive ourselves. Sir, we have done everything

that could be done to avert the storm which is now coming on. We have petitioned; we have remonstrated; we have supplicated; we have prostrated ourselves before the throne, and have implored its interposition to arrest the tyrannical hands of the ministry and Parliament. Our petitions have been slighted; our remonstrances have produced additional violence and insult; our supplications have been disregarded; and we have been spurned, with contempt, from the foot of the throne! In vain, after these things, may we indulge the fond hope of peace and reconciliation. There is no longer any room for hope. If we wish to be free—if we mean to preserve inviolate those inestimable privileges for which we have been so long contending—if we mean not basely to abandon the noble struggle in which we have been so long engaged, and which we have pledged ourselves never to abandon until the glorious object of our contest shall be obtained—we must fight! I repeat it, sir, we must fight! An appeal to arms and to the God of hosts is all that is left us!

They tell us, sir, that we are weak; unable to cope with so formidable 4
an adversary. But when shall we be stronger? Will it be the next week, or the next year? Will it be when we are totally disarmed, and when a British guard shall be stationed in every house? Shall we gather strength by irresolution and inaction? Shall we acquire the means of effectual resistance by lying supinely on our backs and hugging the delusive phantom of hope, until our enemies shall have bound us hand and foot? Sir, we are not weak if we make a proper use of those means which the God of nature hath placed in our power. The millions of people, armed in the holy cause of liberty, and in such a country as that which we possess, are invincible by any force which our enemy can send against us. Besides, sir, we shall not fight our battles alone. There is a just God who presides over the destinies of nations, and who will raise up friends to fight our battles for us. The battle, sir, is not to the strong alone; it is to the vigilant, the active, the brave. Besides, sir, we have no election. If we were base enough to desire it, it is now too late to retire from the contest. There is no retreat but in submission and slavery! Our chains are forged! Their clanking may be heard on the plains of Boston! The war is inevitable— and let it come! I repeat it, sir, let it come.

It is in vain, sir, to extenuate the matter. Gentlemen may cry, Peace, 5
Peace—but there is no peace. The war is actually begun! The next gale that sweeps from the north will bring to our ears the clash of resounding arms! Our brethren are already in the field! Why stand we here idle? What is it that gentlemen wish? What would they have? Is life so dear, or peace so sweet, as to be purchased at the price of chains and slavery?

Forbid it, Almighty God! I know not what course others may take; but as for me, give me liberty or give me death!

Vocabulary

If you do not know any of the following words, try to determine their meanings from the context of Henry's speech. Test your guesses in a dictionary, and then use at least ten of the words in sentences of your own.

reserve (1)	implements (3)	inviolate (3)
magnitude (1)	subjugation (3)	inestimable (3)
treason (1)	martial (3)	basely (3)
revere (1)	forging (3)	formidable (4)
arduous (2)	entreaty (3)	irresolution (4)
disposed (2)	supplication (3)	effectual (4)
temporal (2)	beseech (3)	supinely (4)
salvation (2)	remonstrated (3)	extenuate (5)
ministry (3)	prostrated (3)	brethren (5)
insidious (3)	interposition (3)	dear (5)
comports (3)	tyrannical (3)	

Key Ideas and Details

1. What is the "question . . . of awful moment" (paragraph 1) that Henry addresses? How does he answer it?

2. Outline the reasons Henry provides to support his call to arms.

3. Henry's concluding line—"give me liberty or give me death!" (paragraph 5)—is well known and often repeated. What does it mean? Why does he limit the options facing the colonists to two opposing choices?

Craft and Structure

1. LANGUAGE Henry uses several extended metaphors to bring depth to his ideas, especially "freedom or slavery" (paragraph 1) and "the lamp of experience" (3). Pick one of these metaphors, or another that catches your attention, and trace its development through the speech, explaining its meaning. (If necessary, see *figures of speech* in the Glossary for an explanation of *metaphor*.)

2. Point to some particular techniques that Henry uses to connect with a listening audience.

3. OTHER METHODS This speech uses cause-and-effect analysis (Chapter 14) to build an argument (Chapter 15). Where and how does Henry counter opposing views?

Integration of Knowledge and Ideas

1. Why did Henry deliver this speech to the Virginia House of Burgesses? What did he want his listeners to believe or do as a result of hearing him talk?

2. What is the effect of Henry's opening description of his motives for speaking? How does he present himself to his audience?

3. FOR DISCUSSION Analyze Henry's use of questions throughout his speech and be prepared to discuss them. What is the purpose of asking so many questions? Which questions does he answer, and how? Why does he end the speech with a series of unanswered questions?

Writing Topics

1. Just as Henry was outraged by the growing presence of the British military on American shores, you may be similarly moved by some current condition—perhaps climate change, increasing crime, a newly discovered health hazard, a dangerous traffic intersection that the authorities persist in ignoring. Imitate Henry's strategy and write a speech urging listeners to respond to the condition. Like Henry's your proposal should be fairly simple and argued with careful and detailed logic.

2. Examine Henry's use of argumentative appeals—ethical, emotional, and rational—and write a rhetorical analysis of his speech. Which elements are most effective, and why? (If necessary, see pp. 367–71 in Chapter 15, Argument and Persuasion, for an explanation of appeals.)

3. RESEARCH The "song of that siren" in paragraph 2 of Henry's speech is a reference to classical mythology and Homer's *The Odyssey*. Use a literary reference dictionary or database to learn what sirens are and what they do, then explain the meanings of Henry's allusion in a paragraph or two. (For a definition of *allusion*, see the Glossary.)

4. CONNECTIONS Like Patrick Henry, Walter Mosley, in "Get Happy" (p. 318) reveals unwavering dedication to the concepts of liberty and independence. How do Henry's arguments inform Mosley's definition of happiness? What values and assumptions do the two authors share? Where do their perspectives differ, and why? Explore your answers to these questions in a brief essay.

Elizabeth Cady Stanton

Elizabeth Cady Stanton (1815–1902) was born in Johnstown, New York, and lived most of her adult life in the Adirondack region of Seneca Falls. Her indulgent and progressive father, a lawyer, gave her a formal education of the sort normally reserved for boys, encouraging her to think for herself and opening her eyes to "the injustice and cruelty of the laws" affecting women. After completing her training at the Troy Female Seminary and being rejected admittance to Union College because of her gender, Stanton became a leader of the first women's rights movement in American history. She served as president of the National Woman Suffrage Association, edited the newspaper *Revolution*, wrote columns and articles for women's political magazines, and organized conventions — all while raising seven children. She is regarded as one of the most important figures of the nineteenth century for her insightful, impassioned arguments for women's independence and voting rights, some of which are recounted in her autobiography *Eighty Years and More* (1898), as well as the acclaimed three-volume *A History of Woman Suffrage* (1881–86), written with Matilda Joslyn Gage and Susan B. Anthony.

Seneca Falls Convention Keynote Address

Most historians mark the 1848 Seneca Falls Convention, which Stanton organized with Lucretia Mott, as the official launch of the women's rights movement of the nineteenth century. Married women at the time had no standing as American citizens: they could not own property, enter into contracts, or vote; by law they were controlled by their husbands. In this speech, the opening remarks for the convention, Stanton calls for reform by explaining that women had not consented to the rules that governed them.

We have met here today to discuss our rights and wrongs, civil and political, and not, as some have supposed, to go into the detail of social life alone. We do not propose to petition the legislature to make our husbands just, generous, and courteous, to seat every man at the head of a cradle, and to clothe every woman in male attire. 1

None of these points, however important they may be considered by leading men, will be touched in this convention. As to their costume, the gentlemen need feel no fear of our imitating that, for we think it in violation of every principle of taste, beauty, and dignity; notwithstanding all the contempt cast upon our loose, flowing garments, we still admire the graceful folds, and consider our costume far more artistic than theirs. Many of the nobler sex seem to agree with us in this opinion, for the bishops, priests, judges, barristers, and lord mayors of the first nation on the globe,[1] and the Pope of Rome, with his cardinals, too, all wear the 2

---

[1] England. [Editors' note.]

loose flowing robes, thus tacitly acknowledging that the male attire is neither dignified nor imposing.

No, we shall not molest you in your philosophical experiments with   **3** stocks, pants, high-heeled boots, and Russian belts.[2] Yours be the glory to discover, by personal experience, how long the kneepan can resist the terrible strapping down which you impose, in how short time the well-developed muscles of the throat can be reduced to mere threads by the constant pressure of the stock, how high the heel of a boot must be to make a short man tall, and how tight the Russian belt may be drawn and yet have wind enough left to sustain life.

But we are assembled to protest against a form of government exist-   **4** ing without the consent of the governed—to declare our right to be free as man is free, to be represented in the government which we are taxed to support, to have such disgraceful laws as give man the power to chastise and imprison his wife, to take the wages which she earns, the property which she inherits, and, in case of separation, the children of her love; laws which make her the mere dependent on his bounty. It is to protest against such unjust laws as these that we are assembled today, and to have them, if possible, forever erased from our statute books, deeming them a shame and a disgrace to a Christian republic in the nineteenth century. We have met to uplift woman's fallen divinity upon an even pedestal with man's. And, strange as it may seem to many, we now demand our right to vote according to the declaration of the government under which we live.

This right no one pretends to deny. We need not prove ourselves   **5** equal to Daniel Webster[3] to enjoy this privilege, for the ignorant Irishman in the ditch has all the civil rights he has. We need not prove our muscular power equal to this same Irishman to enjoy this privilege, for the most tiny, weak, ill-shaped stripling of twenty-one has all the civil rights of the Irishman. We have no objection to discuss the question of equality, for we feel that the weight of argument lies wholly with us, but we wish the question of equality kept distinct from the question of rights, for the proof of the one does not determine the truth of the other. All white men in this country have the same rights, however they may differ in mind, body, or estate.

---

[2] A stock was a wide, stiff necktie fashionable in the mid-nineteenth century. Some men also wore decorative narrow belts, similar in function to women's corsets, to make their shoulders seem broader by tightening their waists. [Editors' note.]

[3] The senator of Massachusetts from 1827–41, Daniel Webster was a famed diplomat and orator. [Editors' note.]

The right is ours. The question now is: how shall we get possession of 6 what rightfully belongs to us? We should not feel so sorely grieved if no man who had not attained the full stature of a Webster, Clay, Van Buren, or Gerrit Smith[4] could claim the right of the elective franchise. But to have drunkards, idiots, horse-racing, rum-selling rowdies, ignorant foreigners, and silly boys fully recognized, while we ourselves are thrust out from all the rights that belong to citizens, it is too grossly insulting to the dignity of woman to be longer quietly submitted to.

The right is ours. Have it, we must. Use it, we will. The pens, the 7 tongues, the fortunes, the indomitable wills of many women are already pledged to secure this right. The great truth that no just government can be formed without the consent of the governed we shall echo and re-echo in the ears of the unjust judge, until by continual coming we shall weary him.

There seems now to be a kind of moral stagnation in our midst. Phi- 8 lanthropists have done their utmost to rouse the nation to a sense of its sins. War, slavery, drunkenness, licentiousness, gluttony, have been dragged naked before the people, and all their abominations and deformities fully brought to light, yet with idiotic laugh we hug those monsters to our breasts and rush on to destruction. Our churches are multiplying on all sides, our missionary societies, Sunday schools, and prayer meetings and innumerable charitable and reform organizations are all in operation, but still the tide of vice is swelling, and threatens the destruction of everything, and the battlements of righteousness are weak against the raging elements of sin and death.

Verily, the world waits the coming of some new element, some puri- 9 fying power, some spirit of mercy and love. The voice of woman has been silenced in the state, the church, and the home, but man cannot fulfill his destiny alone, he cannot redeem his race unaided. There are deep and tender chords of sympathy and love in the hearts of the downfallen and oppressed that woman can touch more skillfully than man.

The world has never yet seen a truly great and virtuous nation, 10 because in the degradation of woman the very fountains of life are poisoned at their source. It is vain to look for silver and gold from mines of copper and lead.

It is the wise mother that has the wise son. So long as your women 11 are slaves you may throw your colleges and churches to the winds. You

---

[4] Henry Clay was an American statesman. Martin Van Buren was president of the United States from 1837–41. Gerrit Smith, Stanton's cousin and mentor, was a highly regarded reformer and philanthropist. [Editors' note.]

can't have scholars and saints so long as your mothers are ground to powder between the upper and nether millstone of tyranny and lust. How seldom, now, is a father's pride gratified, his fond hopes realized, in the budding genius of his son!

The wife is degraded, made the mere creature of caprice, and the foolish son is heaviness to his heart. Truly are the sins of the fathers visited upon the children to the third and fourth generation. God, in His wisdom, has so linked the whole human family together that any violence done at one end of the chain is felt throughout its length, and here, too, is the law of restoration, as in woman all have fallen, so in her elevation shall the race be recreated.   12

"Voices" were the visitors and advisers of Joan of Arc.[5] Do not "voices" come to us daily from the haunts of poverty, sorrow, degradation, and despair, already too long unheeded. Now is the time for the women of this country, if they would save our free institutions, to defend the right, to buckle on the armor that can best resist the keenest weapons of the enemy—contempt and ridicule. The same religious enthusiasm that nerved Joan of Arc to her work nerves us to ours. In every generation God calls some men and women for the utterance of truth, a heroic action, and our work today is the fulfilling of what has long since been foretold by the Prophet—Joel 2:28: "And it shall come to pass afterward, that I will pour out my spirit upon all flesh; and your sons and your daughters shall prophesy."   13

We do not expect our path will be strewn with the flowers of popular applause, but over the thorns of bigotry and prejudice will be our way, and on our banners will beat the dark storm clouds of opposition from those who have entrenched themselves behind the stormy bulwarks of custom and authority, and who have fortified their position by every means, holy and unholy. But we will steadfastly abide the result. Unmoved we will bear it aloft. Undauntedly we will unfurl it to the gale, for we know that the storm cannot rend from it a shred, that the electric flash will but more clearly show to us the glorious words inscribed upon it, "Equality of Rights."   14

Vocabulary

If you do not know the following words, try to determine their meanings from the context of Stanton's speech. Test your guesses in a dictionary, and then use each word in a sentence of your own.

---

[5] A folk hero and Catholic saint, Joan of Arc (1412–31) is famous for disguising herself as a boy and leading the French army in several battles against the English during the Hundred Years' War. [Editors' note.]

tacitly (2)	franchise (6)	keenest (13)
molest (3)	indomitable (7)	prophesy (13)
stocks (3)	licentiousness (8)	abide (14)
kneepan (3)	abominations (8)	undauntedly (14)
chastise (4)	battlements (8)	rend (14)
statute (4)	nether (11)	
stature (6)	caprice (12)	

Key Ideas and Details

1. What is the point of Stanton's speech? Where does she state her thesis directly?

2. What reasons does Stanton provide to support her argument?

3. "[W]e wish the question of equality kept distinct from the question of rights, for the proof of the one does not determine the truth of the other," says Stanton in paragraph 5. What does she mean? Why does the distinction matter?

Craft and Structure

1. LANGUAGE Locate instances of repetition and parallel structure in Stanton's speech. What do these devices contribute to her purpose?

2. Stanton introduces her speech with a discussion of men's clothes. Why? What does fashion have to do with her subject?

3. Stanton expresses outrage that "drunkards, idiots, horse-racing, rum-selling rowdies, ignorant foreigners, and silly boys" may vote but women may not (paragraph 6). Is she committing an ad hominem fallacy here? Where else does she resort to such attacks, and why do you think she uses this strategy? Does it strengthen or weaken her argument, in your opinion? (For a definition of *ad hominem*, see p. 372 and *fallacies* in the Glossary.)

4. OTHER METHODS Summarize the cause-and-effect analysis (Chapter 14) Stanton presents in paragraphs 8–12. What relationship between cause and effect does she assert? Do you find her analysis effective and convincing? Why, or why not?

Integration of Knowledge and Ideas

1. What seems to be Stanton's purpose in this speech: to complain about women's treatment in society? to welcome people to the convention? something else? Where in the speech does she most clearly reveal her reasons for speaking?

2. Is Stanton speaking to an audience whose views are similar to her own, or different? On what evidence do you base your response?

3. FOR DISCUSSION Stanton's speech is filled with metaphors, such as her intention to "uplift woman's fallen divinity upon an even pedestal with man's" (paragraph 4). Find two or three other metaphors and be prepared to explain how each one contributes to Stanton's meaning and helps convey her attitude toward women's rights. (If necessary, consult pp. 58–59 and *figures of speech* in the Glossary for an explanation of metaphors.)

Writing Topics

1. Using your answer to question 2 under "Key Ideas and Details" as a starting point, write an analysis of Stanton's speech as an argument, focusing on its ethical, emotional, and rational appeals. (See pp. 367–71 if you need help with these terms.) What makes the speech effective? What makes it ineffective?

2. American women obtained the right to vote in 1920, yet many women's rights issues continue to be a source of controversy and debate in this country: coeducation versus gender-specific classrooms, equal opportunities in sports, discrepancies between men's and women's earnings, parental roles within the family, medical research funding, gender stereotypes in the media, and so on. Investigate one such controversy that interests you, and in a speech present and defend your own position.

3. RESEARCH Stanton seems to accept, in paragraph 5, claims that men and women are naturally different—both mentally and physically. Do you agree? Spend some time in the library checking research into the differences between girls and boys. (An encyclopedia of psychology or sociology can get you started, as can a periodical index such as *Academic Search Premier* or the *Social Sciences Citations Index*.) Select a conclusion about difference that you find especially interesting or frustrating and write an essay that details your findings and relates them to your personal experience. Be sure the essay has a central, controlling idea about gender difference.

4. CONNECTIONS Patrick Henry's speech (p. 432), like Stanton's, outlines a list of grievances to support an argument. What do the two speakers' strategies have in common? Where do they differ? In an essay, analyze Stanton's use of the founding fathers' arguments for American independence to ground her claims for women's rights.

Sojourner Truth

Born Isabella in 1797 to slaves in Ulster County, New York, Sojourner Truth grew up speaking Dutch, bounced between several owners, and was sold to John Dumont of New Paltz Landing at the age of thirteen. She ran away in 1827, spent some time with a religious collective, and in 1843 became a traveling preacher. (She chose the name Sojourner Truth because she felt it was her duty "to travel up and down the land, showing the people their sins, and being a sign unto them.") As the antislavery and women's movements of the mid-nineteenth century gained steam, she embarked on a nationwide lecture tour, speaking unrehearsed and gaining fame as a powerful advocate for the dispossessed — a role she continued after the Civil War by counseling freed slaves and giving speeches on issues affecting women and African Americans. Although Truth was illiterate, she worked with Olive Gilbert to write her memoir *The Narrative of Sojourner Truth* (1850) and used the proceeds of the book's sales to purchase a home in Battle Creek, Michigan, where she died in 1883.

Ain't I a Woman?

Truth delivered her most famous speech at an 1851 women's rights convention in Akron, Ohio. After listening the first day to male ministers in the audience argue that women did not deserve rights because they lacked intelligence and religious standing, and frustrated that the white women hosting the meeting had said nothing to defend themselves, she stood up on the second day — uninvited — and gave her counterargument.

Well, children, where there is so much racket there must be something 1 out of kilter. I think that 'twixt the negroes of the South and the women at the North, all talking about rights, the white men will be in a fix pretty soon. But what's all this here talking about?

That man over there says that women need to be helped into car- 2 riages, and lifted over ditches, and to have the best place everywhere. Nobody ever helps me into carriages, or over mud-puddles, or gives me any best place! And ain't I a woman? Look at me! Look at my arm! I have ploughed and planted, and gathered into barns, and no man could head me! And ain't I a woman? I could work as much and eat as much as a man — when I could get it — and bear the lash as well! And ain't I a woman? I have borne thirteen children, and seen most all sold off to slavery, and when I cried out with my mother's grief, none but Jesus heard me! And ain't I a woman?

Then they talk about this thing in the head; what's this they call it? 3 [member of audience whispers, "intellect"] That's it, honey. What's that got to do with women's rights or negroes' rights? If my cup won't hold but a pint, and yours holds a quart, wouldn't you be mean not to let me have my little half measure full?

Then that little man in black there, he says women can't have as 4 much rights as men, 'cause Christ wasn't a woman! Where did your Christ come from? Where did your Christ come from? From God and a woman! Man had nothing to do with Him.

If the first woman God ever made was strong enough to turn the 5 world upside down all alone,[1] these women together ought to be able to turn it back, and get it right side up again! And now they is asking to do it, the men better let them.

Obliged to you for hearing me, and now old Sojourner ain't got 6 nothing more to say.

Vocabulary

If you do not know the meanings of the following words, try to determine them from the context of Truth's speech. Test your guesses in a dictionary, and then use each word in a sentence or two of your own.

kilter (1)	carriages (2)	obliged (6)
'twixt (1)	mean (3)	

Key Ideas and Details

1. What does Truth mean by "no man could head me" (paragraph 2)? What point is she making?

2. In your own words, what is Truth's thesis? Why does she withhold her main idea to the end of her speech?

Craft and Structure

1. LANGUAGE Truth speaks in nonstandard English, using words such as "'twixt" (paragraph 1) and "ain't" (2) and colloquial phrases such as "out of kilter" (1) and "in a fix" (1). What is the effect of her diction? Would her speech have been more or less powerful if she had used formal language? (If necessary, see *colloquial language* and *diction* in the Glossary.)

2. Locate instances of repetition in Truth's speech. Which ideas does she emphasize most strongly?

3. How does Truth organize her speech to build to an effective conclusion?

---

[1] Truth is referring to the biblical Eve, whose sin of eating an apple from the tree of knowledge resulted in expulsion from the Garden of Eden. [Editors' note.]

4. OTHER METHODS Paragraph 2 uses comparison and contrast (Chapter 12) to put forth a definition (Chapter 13). Based on what Truth says, how does her audience define *woman*? How does Truth define it?

Integration of Knowledge and Ideas

1. What prompts Truth to speak, and to whom does she direct her comments? How does she engage her audience's attention?

2. Why does Truth stress that she is a woman? Isn't that self-evident? Draw on details from her speech to support your answer.

3. FOR DISCUSSION What arguments against women's rights does Truth address? How does she counter them?

Writing Topics

1. Choose some aspect of your identity that others misunderstand or under-value, such as your gender, your race or ethnicity, your family structure, your membership in a team, your grade point average. Modeling Truth, write and deliver a short "Ain't I a _____?" speech of your own.

2. Write an essay in which you examine the state of racial discrimination in contemporary American politics or culture. You may wish to think broadly about this issue, but bring your essay down to earth by focusing on a specific form of discrimination—perhaps one that you've experienced or witnessed in your own life.

3. RESEARCH Truth's friend and colleague Frances Dana Gage published "Ain't I a Woman?" in 1863, twelve years after Sojourner Truth delivered her speech. Although Gage's version is the one most often taught, and the one Elizabeth Cady Stanton (p. 437) included in *A History of Woman Suffrage*, it is not an exact transcription. Search the Web for Marius Robinson's 1851 version of the speech, which was reported in Ohio's *Anti-Slavery Bugle* a few weeks after the convention. In an essay, compare the two versions. Which seems more authentic? What kinds of changes did Gage make to Truth's speech? In your mind, do those changes represent an improvement, or a violation of ethics? (Recall that Truth could neither read nor write.) Why do you think so?

4. CONNECTIONS In many ways, Truth's impromptu speech is a rebuke to mid-nineteenth century women's rights activists, who tended to focus on the needs of middle-class white women, acknowledging black women only in the context of antislavery reform. Read or reread Elizabeth Cady Stanton's "Seneca Falls Convention Keynote Address" (p. 437). On what issues did she focus? Why would Truth have felt left out of the discussion? In an essay, consider the ideals Stanton and Truth held in common, as well as where their perspectives diverged.

Abraham Lincoln

The sixteenth president of the United States, Abraham Lincoln was born in 1809 in Hodgenville, Kentucky, and moved frequently throughout his youth, following his impoverished family to the frontiers of Kentucky, Indiana, and Illinois. With only a year or so of formal schooling, he educated himself by reading voraciously. As a teenager he was put in charge of a mill store in the Illinois wilderness and quickly developed strong ties with the community, earning appointments as postmaster and county surveyor and, in 1834, election to the state legislature. While serving four consecutive terms, Lincoln took up an independent study of law and joined a private legal practice. Despite a disastrous term in Congress and a failed bid for the Senate, he developed a national reputation as a powerful speaker with strongly voiced opinions on the issues of the day, particularly slavery, which he considered a moral and legal abomination. In 1860 the Republican National Convention nominated Lincoln as a compromise candidate for the presidency; his election prompted seven slaveholding states to secede from the Union, ultimately leading to Civil War. He was elected for a second term in the midst of the fighting but, as the war came to an end and the work of reconstruction began, Lincoln was assassinated by John Wilkes Booth on April 14, 1865, just a month after his inauguration.

Gettysburg Address

In possibly the most famous (and shortest) speech ever delivered, Lincoln offered his remarks on the dedication of the Soldier's National Cemetery at Gettysburg, Pennsylvania, on November 19, 1863. Standing on a battlefield where more than 10,000 men had been killed and 30,000 wounded, Lincoln expressed gratitude for the Union troops' sacrifice with unparalleled eloquence. He prepared at least five drafts of the speech, refining the language even after he delivered the address.

1   Four score and seven years ago[1] our fathers brought forth on this continent, a new nation, conceived in liberty, and dedicated to the proposition that all men are created equal.

2   Now we are engaged in a great civil war, testing whether that nation, or any nation so conceived and so dedicated, can long endure. We are met on a great battle-field of that war. We have come to dedicate a portion of that field, as a final resting place for those who here gave their lives that the nation might live. It is altogether fitting and proper that we should do this.

3   But, in a larger sense, we can not dedicate—we can not consecrate—we can not hallow—this ground. The brave men, living and dead, who struggled here, have consecrated it, far above our poor power to add or

---

[1] "Score" means twenty. Four score and seven equals eighty-seven. [Editors' note.]

detract. The world will little note, nor long remember what we say here, but it can never forget what they did here. It is for us the living, rather, to be dedicated here to the great task remaining before us—that from these honored dead we take increased devotion to that cause for which they gave the last full measure of devotion—that we here highly resolve these dead shall not have died in vain—that this nation, under God, shall have a new birth of freedom—and that government of the people, by the people, for the people, shall not perish from the earth.

Vocabulary

If you do not know the following words, try to determine their meanings from the context of Lincoln's speech. Test your guesses in a dictionary, and then use each word in a sentence of your own.

conceived (1)	consecrate (3)	detract (3)
dedicated (1)	hallow (3)	perish (3)
proposition (1)		

Key Ideas and Details

1. Regarding the dedication of the cemetery, Lincoln says "we can not dedicate—we can not consecrate—we can not hallow—this ground" (paragraph 3). Why not?

2. What is Lincoln's main message? What does he want his listeners to believe or do after hearing him speak?

Craft and Structure

1. LANGUAGE Lincoln's speech is especially notable for its use of parallel structure. Locate at least three instances of parallelism and explain their effect. (See pp. 55, 278, and the Glossary for discussions of *parallelism*.)

2. The "Gettysburg Address" is a model of effective repetition in a speech. Which words does Lincoln repeat, and how often? How does the repetition drive home his main idea?

3. How does Lincoln organize his ideas?

4. OTHER METHODS Lincoln relies on cause-and-effect analysis (Chapter 14) to structure his speech. How does he explain the reasons for the Civil War? What does he hope will be its effect?

Integration of Knowledge and Ideas

1. What was Lincoln's reason for speaking? How does he shape his speech to fit the occasion?

2. Gettysburg is in Pennsylvania, a northern state that fought on the Union side. How does Lincoln appeal to his listeners' interests and beliefs?

3. FOR DISCUSSION Lincoln opens and closes his speech with a reference to the same historic moment. To what document is he alluding? How do the references enhance his meaning? (If necessary, look up *allusion* in the Glossary.)

Writing Topics

1. Reread the first paragraph of Lincoln's speech and examine each word closely, paying special attention to their connotations. Write a paragraph explaining how the opening sentence reflects, supports, and introduces Lincoln's main idea. (See the Glossary for an explanation of *connotation*.)

2. The "Gettysburg Address" is at heart a eulogy, words of praise and respect commonly delivered at funerals. Choose a person (living or dead) whom you admire: you might pick a historic figure, a family member, an athlete or a celebrity, or someone you know personally or from a distance. Write and deliver a three-minute speech that expresses your admiration for this person.

3. Lincoln speaks of the "honored dead" and the "devotion to that cause for which they gave their lives" (paragraph 2), but thousands of the men killed at Gettysburg fought for the South; their bodies were either buried in makeshift graves or removed from the site and interred elsewhere. How do you suppose their families might have responded to Lincoln's speech? In an essay, analyze the "Gettysburg Address" as a political argument.

4. RESEARCH The version of Lincoln's speech reprinted here is considered by most historians to be the authoritative, final copy. But Lincoln revised his address multiple times, and several versions exist. Locate at least one earlier draft and compare it to Lincoln's final draft. What kinds of changes did he make, and how did they improve (or weaken) his speech? Why do you think he paid such close attention to small details? Explain your conclusions.

5. CONNECTIONS Martin Luther King, Jr., opens "I Have a Dream" (opposite) with a subtle reference to the Gettysburg Address and a direct reference to the Emancipation Proclamation, the document with which Lincoln officially ended slavery in 1863. And like Lincoln, King refers to the Declaration of Independence. Read King's speech as a response to Lincoln. How had the situation for African Americans changed — for better and for worse — in the century since the end of the Civil War? How well, in King's estimation, had Lincoln and his followers completed "the great task remaining before" them?

Martin Luther King, Jr.

Born in 1929 in Atlanta, Georgia, the son of a Baptist minister, Martin Luther King, Jr., was a revered and powerful leader of the black civil rights movement during the 1950s and 1960s. He was ordained in his father's church before he was twenty and went on to earn degrees at Morehouse College (BA in 1948), Crozer Theological Seminary (BD in 1951), and Boston University (PhD in 1955). In 1955 and 1956, while he was pastor of a church in Montgomery, Alabama, King attracted national attention to the plight of Southern blacks by leading a boycott that succeeded in desegregating the city's buses. He was elected the first president of the Southern Christian Leadership Conference and continued to organize demonstrations for equal rights in other cities. By the early 1960s his efforts had helped raise the national consciousness so that the landmark Civil Rights Act of 1964 and Voting Rights Act of 1965 could be passed by Congress. In 1964 King was awarded the Nobel Peace Prize. When leading sit-ins, boycotts, and marches, King always insisted on nonviolent resistance "because our end is a community at peace with itself." But his nonviolence often met with violent opposition. Over the years he was jailed, beaten, stoned, and stabbed. His house in Montgomery was bombed. And on April 4, 1968, at a motel in Memphis, Tennessee, he was assassinated. He was not yet forty years old.

I Have a Dream

On August 28, 1963, one hundred years after Abraham Lincoln's Emancipation Proclamation had freed the slaves, 200,000 Americans marched on Washington, DC, to demand equal rights for blacks. It was the largest crowd ever to assemble in the capital for a cause, and the high point of the day was this speech delivered by King on the steps of the Lincoln Memorial (he revised it slightly for print publication). Always an eloquent and inspirational speaker, King succeeded in articulating the frustrations and aspirations of African Americans in a way that gave hope to the oppressed and opened the eyes of many oppressors.

Five score years ago, a great American, in whose symbolic shadow we   1
stand, signed the Emancipation Proclamation. This momentous decree came as a great beacon light of hope to millions of Negro slaves who had been seared in the flames of withering injustice. It came as a joyous daybreak to end the long night of captivity.

But one hundred years later, we must face the tragic fact that the   2
Negro is still not free. One hundred years later, the life of the Negro is still sadly crippled by the manacles of segregation and the chains of discrimination. One hundred years later, the Negro lives on a lonely island of poverty in the midst of a vast ocean of material prosperity. One hundred years later, the Negro is still languishing in the corners of American

society and finds himself an exile in his own land. So we have come here today to dramatize an appalling condition.

In a sense we have come to our nation's capital to cash a check. 3 When the architects of our republic wrote the magnificent words of the Constitution and the Declaration of Independence, they were signing a promissory note to which every American was to fall heir. This note was a promise that all men—yes, black men as well as white men— would be guaranteed the unalienable rights of life, liberty, and the pursuit of happiness.

It is obvious today that America has defaulted on this promissory 4 note insofar as her citizens of color are concerned. Instead of honoring this sacred obligation, America has given the Negro people a bad check, a check which has come back marked "insufficient funds." But we refuse to believe that there are insufficient funds in the great vaults of opportunity of this nation. So we have come to cash this check—a check that will give us upon demand the riches of freedom and the security of justice. We have also come to this hallowed spot to remind America of the fierce urgency of *now*. This is no time to engage in the luxury of cooling off or to take the tranquilizing drugs of gradualism. *Now* is the time to make real the promises of Democracy. *Now* is the time to rise from the dark and desolate valley of segregation to the sunlit path of racial justice. *Now* is the time to open the doors of opportunity to all of God's children. *Now* is the time to lift our nation from the quicksands of racial injustice to the solid rock of brotherhood.

It would be fatal for the nation to overlook the urgency of the 5 moment and to underestimate the determination of the Negro. This sweltering summer of the Negro's legitimate discontent will not pass until there is an invigorating autumn of freedom and equality; 1963 is not an end, but a beginning. Those who hope that the Negro needed to blow off steam and will now be content will have a rude awakening if the nation returns to business as usual. There will be neither rest nor tranquility in America until the Negro is granted his citizenship rights. The whirlwinds of revolt will continue to shake the foundations of our nation until the bright day of justice emerges.

But there is something that I must say to my people who stand on 6 the warm threshold which leads into the palace of justice. In the process of gaining our rightful place we must not be guilty of wrongful deeds. Let us not seek to satisfy our thirst for freedom by drinking from the cup of bitterness and hatred. We must forever conduct our struggle on the high plane of dignity and discipline. We must not allow our creative protest to degenerate into physical violence. Again and again we must rise to the majestic heights of meeting physical force with soul force. The marvelous new militancy which has engulfed the Negro community must not lead us to a distrust of all white people, for many of our white brothers, as evidenced by their presence here today, have come to realize that their destiny is tied up with our destiny and their freedom is inextricably bound to our freedom. We cannot walk alone.

And as we walk, we must make the pledge that we shall march ahead. 7 We cannot turn back. There are those who are asking the devotees of civil rights, "When will you be satisfied?" We can never be satisfied as long as the Negro is the victim of the unspeakable horrors of police brutality. We can never be satisfied as long as our bodies, heavy with the fatigue of travel, cannot gain lodging in the motels of the highways and the hotels of the cities. We cannot be satisfied as long as the Negro's basic mobility is from a smaller ghetto to a larger one. We can never be satisfied as long as a Negro in Mississippi cannot vote and a Negro in New York believes he has nothing for which to vote. No, no, we are not satisfied, and we will not be satisfied until justice rolls down like waters and righteousness like a mighty stream.

I am not unmindful that some of you have come here out of great 8 trials and tribulations. Some of you have come fresh from narrow jail cells. Some of you have come from areas where your quest for freedom left you battered by the storms of persecution and staggered by the winds of police brutality. You have been the veterans of creative suffering. Continue to work with the faith that unearned suffering is redemptive.

Go back to Mississippi, go back to Alabama, go back to South Caro- 9 lina, go back to Georgia, go back to Louisiana, go back to the slums and ghettos of our northern cities, knowing that somehow this situation can and will be changed. Let us not wallow in the valley of despair.

I say to you today, my friends, that in spite of the difficulties and 10 frustrations of the moment I still have a dream. It is a dream deeply rooted in the American dream.

I have a dream that one day this nation will rise up and live out the 11 true meaning of its creed: "We hold these truths to be self-evident, that all men are created equal."

I have a dream that one day on the red hills of Georgia the sons of 12 former slaves and the sons of former slaveowners will be able to sit down together at the table of brotherhood.

I have a dream that one day even the state of Mississippi, a desert 13 state sweltering with the heat of injustice and oppression, will be transformed into an oasis of freedom and justice.

I have a dream that my four little children will one day live in a 14 nation where they will not be judged by the color of their skin but by the content of their character.

I have a dream today.   15

I have a dream that one day the state of Alabama, whose governor's   16
lips are presently dripping with the words of interposition and nullifi-
cation, will be transformed into a situation where little black boys and
black girls will be able to join hands with little white boys and white girls
and walk together as sisters and brothers.

I have a dream today.   17

I have a dream that one day every valley shall be exalted, every hill   18
and mountain shall be made low, the rough places will be made plain,
and the crooked places will be made straight, and the glory of the Lord
shall be revealed, and all flesh shall see it together.[1]

This is our hope. This is the faith with which I return to the South.   19
With this faith we will be able to hew out of the mountain of despair a
stone of hope. With this faith we will be able to transform the jangling
discords of our nation into a beautiful symphony of brotherhood. With
this faith we will be able to work together, to pray together, to struggle
together, to go to jail together, to stand up for freedom together, knowing that we will be free one day.

This will be the day when all of God's children will be able to sing   20
with new meaning

> My country, 'tis of thee,
> Sweet land of liberty,
>   Of thee I sing:
> Land where my fathers died,
> Land of the pilgrims' pride,
> From every mountainside,
>   Let freedom ring.

So let freedom ring from the prodigious hilltops of New Hampshire.   21
Let freedom ring from the mighty mountains of New York. Let freedom
ring from the heightening Alleghenies of Pennsylvania. Let freedom ring
from the snowcapped Rockies of Colorado. Let freedom ring from the
curvaceous peaks of California.

But not only that. Let freedom ring from Stone Mountain of Georgia.   22
Let freedom ring from Lookout Mountain of Tennessee. Let freedom ring
from every hill and molehill of Mississippi. From every mountainside, let
freedom ring.

When we let freedom ring, when we let it ring from every village and   23
every hamlet, from every state and every city, we will be able to speed

---

[1] This paragraph quotes the Bible, Isaiah 40:4–5. [Editors' note.]

up that day when all of God's children, black men and white men, Jews and Gentiles, Protestants and Catholics, will be able to join hands and sing in the words of the old Negro spiritual, "Free at last! Free at last! Thank God almighty, we are free at last!"

Vocabulary

If you do not know the meanings of the following words, try to determine them from the context of King's speech. Test your guesses in a dictionary, and then use each word in a sentence of your own.

manacles (2)	gradualism (4)	interposition (16)
languishing (2)	degenerate (6)	nullification (16)
promissory note (3)	inextricably (6)	prodigious (21)
unalienable (3)	tribulations (8)	curvaceous (21)
defaulted (4)	redemptive (8)	hamlet (23)

Key Ideas and Details

1. In a sentence, state the main point of King's speech.

2. How does King depict the general condition of the nation's African Americans? What specific injustices does he cite?

3. What reasons does King give for refusing to resort to violence? What comfort does he offer those who have been jailed or beaten?

4. Summarize the substance of King's dream. What does he mean when he says, "It is a dream deeply rooted in the American dream" (paragraph 10)?

Craft and Structure

1. LANGUAGE King's speech abounds in metaphors, such as "manacles of segregation" and "chains of discrimination" (paragraph 2). Locate as many metaphors as you can (consulting the Glossary under *figures of speech* if necessary), and analyze what five or six of them contribute to King's meaning. Which metaphors are repeated or restated, and how does this repetition help link portions of the speech?

2. Analyze the organization of King's speech. What is the main subject of paragraphs 3–5? 6–9? 10–23? How does this structure suit King's purpose?

3. King depends heavily on two stylistic devices: repetition of sentence openings, as in "I have a dream" (paragraphs 11–18); and parallelism within sentences, as in "the manacles of segregation and the chains of discrimination" (2). Locate other instances of these two related devices. How do they contribute to the speech's effectiveness?

4. OTHER METHODS Paragraph 3 and the first half of paragraph 4 are developed by comparison and contrast. What are the main points of comparison, and what purpose does it serve? Do you think it is effective? Why, or why not?

Integration of Knowledge and Ideas

1. What do you think King wanted to achieve with this speech? How does each part of the speech relate to his purpose?

2. What group of people does King seem to be addressing primarily in this speech? Where does he seem to assume that they agree with his ideas? Where does he seem to assume that they have reservations or need reassurance?

3. What about King's purpose and audience leads him to rely primarily on emotional appeals? Where does he appeal specifically to his listeners' pride and dignity? to their religious beliefs? to their patriotism?

4. FOR DISCUSSION Where does King seem to suppose that doubters and opponents of the civil rights movement might also hear his speech? What messages about the goals and determination of the movement does he convey to these hearers?

Writing Topics

1. King's speech had a tremendous impact when it was first delivered in 1963, and it remains influential to this day. Pick out the elements of the speech that seem most remarkable and powerful to you: ideas, emotional appeals, figures of speech, repetition and parallelism, or whatever you choose. Write an essay in which you cite these elements and analyze their effectiveness.

2. Reread paragraph 6, where King outlines a strategy for achieving racial justice. In a speech of your own, briefly explain an unjust situation that affects you directly — in school, in your family, at work, in your community — and propose a strategy for correcting the injustice. Be specific about the steps in the strategy, and explain how each one relates to the final goal you want to achieve.

3. King says that his dream is "deeply rooted in the American dream" (paragraph 10). Write an essay in which you provide your own definition of the American dream. Draw on the elements of King's dream as you see fit. Make your definition specific with examples and details from your experiences, observations, and reading.

4. CONNECTIONS King delivered this speech in 1963. Leanita McClain wrote "The Middle-Class Black's Burden" (p. 284) in 1980, just seventeen years later, yet much had changed in American race relations. Write an essay comparing the attitudes of King and McClain toward the condition of African Americans, using the authors' own words as your evidence.

GLOSSARY

abstract and concrete words   An **abstract** word refers to an idea, quality, attitude, or state that we cannot perceive with our senses: *democracy, generosity, love, grief.* It conveys a general concept or an impression. A **concrete** word, in contrast, refers to an object, person, place, or state that we can perceive with our senses: *lawn mower, teacher, Chicago, moaning.* Concrete words make writing specific and vivid. See also pp. 58, 129, and *general and specific words.*

active reading   Direct interaction with a work to discover its meaning, the author's intentions, and your own responses. Active reading involves taking notes and annotating passages to reach a deeper understanding. See also pp. 6–7 and *critical thinking and reading.*

ad hominem argument   See *fallacies.*

allusion   A brief reference to a real or fictitious person, place, object, or event. An allusion can convey considerable meaning with few words, as when a writer describes a movie as "potentially this decade's *Star Wars*" to imply both that the movie is a space adventure and that it may be a blockbuster. But to be effective, the allusion must refer to something readers know well.

analysis (also called **division**)   The method of development in which a subject is separated into its elements or parts and then reassembled into a new whole. See Chapter 9 on division or analysis, p. 178.

anecdote   A brief narrative that recounts an episode from a person's experience. See, for instance, Peck, paragraph 1, p. 289. See also Chapter 6 on narration, p. 92.

annotation   The practice of reading actively by taking notes on a piece of writing. Notes typically include circles and underlines within a passage, markings such as brackets and checkmarks, and marginal comments and questions regarding the author's meaning and the reader's reactions. See also pp. 6–7 and *active reading.*

antecedent   The noun to which a pronoun refers: *Six days after Martin Luther King, Jr., picked up the Nobel Peace Prize in Norway, he was jailed in Alabama.* Antecedents should be clearly identified, and they should match their related pronouns. See p. 51.

argument   The form of writing that appeals to readers' reason and emotions in order to win agreement with a claim or to compel some action. This definition encompasses both argument in a narrower sense—the appeal to reason to win agreement—and **persuasion**—the appeal to emotion to compel action. See Chapter 15 on argument and persuasion, p. 364.

assertion   A debatable claim about a subject; the central idea of an argument.

audience   A writer's audience is the group of readers for whom a particular work is intended. To communicate effectively, the writer should estimate readers' knowledge of the subject, their interest in it, and their biases toward it and should then consider these needs and expectations in choosing what to say and how to say it. For further discussion of audience, see pp. 4, 8, 15–16, 23, and 24.

begging the question   See *fallacies.*

binary classification   See *classification.*

body   The part of an essay that develops the main idea. See pp. 98–99, 128.

brainstorming   Method to generate ideas by listing thoughts without judgment. See p. 27.

cause-and-effect analysis   The method of development in which occurrences are divided into their elements to find what made an event happen (its causes) and what the consequences were (its effects). See Chapter 14 on cause-and-effect analysis, p. 326.

chronological order   A pattern of organization in which events are arranged as they occurred over time, earliest to latest. Narratives usually follow a chronological order; see Chapter 6 on narration, p. 92.

classification   The method of development in which the members of a group are sorted into classes or subgroups according to shared characteristics. In a **binary** classification, two classes are examined in opposition to each other, typically when one group has a certain characteristic that the other group lacks. In a **complex** classification, each individual fits into one class because of at least one distinguishing feature shared with all members of that class but not with members of any other classes. See Chapter 10 on classification, p. 208.

cliché   An expression that has become tired from overuse and that therefore deadens rather than enlivens writing. Examples: *in over their heads, turn over a new leaf, march to a different drummer, as heavy as lead, as clear as a bell.* See p. 59.

climactic order   A pattern of organization in which elements—words, sentences, examples, ideas—are arranged in order of increasing importance or drama. See p. 42.

coherence   The quality of effective writing that comes from clear, logical connections among all the parts, so that the reader can follow the writer's thought process without difficulty. See pp. 41–42.

colloquial language   The language of conversation, including contractions (*don't, can't*) and informal words and expressions (*hot* for new or popular, *boss* for employer, *ad* for advertisement, *get away with it, flunk the exam*). Most dictionaries label such words and expressions *colloquial* or *informal.* Colloquial language is inappropriate when the writing situation demands precision and formality, as a formal term paper or a business report usually does. But in other situations it can be used selectively to relax a piece of writing and reduce the distance between writer and reader. (See, for instance, Tan, p. 116.) See also *diction.*

comma splice A sentence error in which two or more independent clauses run together with only a comma between them. See p. 50.

comparison and contrast The method of development in which the similarities and differences between subjects are examined. Comparison examines similarities and contrast examines differences, but the two are generally used together. See Chapter 12 on comparison and contrast, p. 269.

conclusions The endings of written works—the sentences that bring the writing to a close. A conclusion provides readers with a sense of completion, with a sense that the writer has finished. Sometimes the final point in the body of an essay may accomplish this purpose, especially if it is very important or dramatic (for instance, see Winik, p. 225). But usually a separate conclusion is needed to achieve completion. It may be a single sentence or several paragraphs, depending on the length and complexity of the piece of writing. And it may include one of the following, or a combination, depending on your subject and purpose:

- A summary of the main points of the essay (see Visser, p. 191; and Iyer, p. 315)
- A statement of the main idea of the essay, if it has not been stated before (see Dumas, p. 251), or a restatement of the main idea incorporating information from the body of the essay (see Dillard, p. 144; Mosley, p. 321; and McCarthy, p. 400)
- A comment on the significance or implications of the subject (see Jain, p. 173; Eighner, p. 255; McClain, p. 286; Lee, p. 389; and Carr, p. 412)
- A call for reflection, support, or action (see Griggs, p. 220; and Kingsolver, p. 263)
- A prediction for the future (see Thomas, p. 343; LeDuff, p. 358; Quindlen, p. 384; Balko, p. 405; and Harper, p. 418)
- An example, an anecdote, a question, or a quotation that reinforces the point of the essay (see Brooks, p. 233; Brady, p. 310; Britt, p. 282; Goodman, p. 349; and Rideau, p. 389)

Excluded from this list are several endings that should be avoided because they tend to weaken the overall effect of an essay: (1) an example, fact, or quotation that pertains to only part of the essay; (2) an apology for your ideas, for the quality of the writing, or for omissions; (3) an attempt to enhance the significance of the essay by overgeneralizing from its ideas and evidence; (4) a new idea that requires the support of an entirely different essay.

concrete words See *abstract and concrete words*.

connotation and denotation A word's **denotation** is its literal meaning: *famous* denotes the quality of being well known. A word's **connotations** are the associations or suggestions that go beyond its literal meaning: *notorious* denotes fame but also connotes sensational, even unfavorable, recognition. See p. 57.

contrast See *comparison and contrast*.

critical thinking and reading The practice of examining the meanings and implications of things, images, events, ideas, and written works; uncovering and testing assumptions; seeing the importance of context; and drawing and supporting independent conclusions. Critical reading applies critical thinking to look beneath the surface of a work, seeking to uncover both its substance and the writer's interpretation of the substance. See Chapter 1 on reading, especially pp. 5–8.

deductive reasoning The method of reasoning that moves from the general to the specific. See Chapter 15 on argument and persuasion, especially pp. 370–71. See also *syllogism*.

definition An explanation of the meaning of a word. A **formal**, or dictionary, definition identifies the class of things to which the word belongs then distinguishes it from other members of the class; a **stipulative** definition clarifies how a word or phrase is being used in a particular context; an **extended** definition may serve as the primary method of developing an essay. See Chapter 13 on definition, p. 296.

denotation See *connotation and denotation*.

description The form of writing that conveys the perceptions of the senses—sight, hearing, smell, taste, touch—to make a person, place, object, or state of mind vivid and concrete. See Chapter 7 on description, p. 122.

development The accumulation of details, examples, facts, opinions, and other evidence to support a writer's ideas. Development begins in sentences, with concrete and specific words to explain meaning. At the level of the paragraph, the sentences develop the paragraph's topic. Then, at the level of the whole essay, the paragraphs develop the governing thesis. See pp. 27–28 and 42–43.

dialogue A narrative technique that quotes the speech of participants in the story. See pp. 99–100.

diction The choice of words you make to achieve a purpose and make meaning clear. Effective diction conveys your meaning exactly, emphatically, and concisely, is appropriate to your intentions and audience, and follows the expectations of standard English. The vocabulary of standard English is large and varied, encompassing, for instance, both *comestibles* and *food* for edible things, both *paroxysm* and *fit* for a sudden seizure. In some writing situations, standard English may also include words and expressions typical of conversation (see *colloquial language*). But it excludes other levels of diction that only certain groups understand or find acceptable. Most dictionaries label expressions at these levels as follows:

- **Nonstandard:** words spoken among particular social groups, such as *ain't, them guys, hisself,* and *nowheres*.
- **Obsolete:** words that have passed out of use, such as *cleam* for smear.
- **Regional** or **dialect:** words spoken in a particular region but not in the country as a whole, such as *poke* for a sack or bag, *holler* for a hollow or small valley.

- **Slang:** words that are usually short-lived and that may not be understood by all readers, such as *bling* for jewelry, *bread* for money, and *honcho* for one in charge.

See also *connotation and denotation, standard English,* and *style.*

division or analysis   See *analysis.*

documentation   A system of identifying your sources so that readers know which ideas are borrowed and can locate the original material themselves. Papers written for English and other humanities classes typically follow the MLA (Modern Language Association) documentation system, which requires brief parenthetical citations within the body of the essay and a comprehensive list of works cited at the end. See Chapter 5 on working with sources, especially pp. 73–84.

dominant impression   The central idea or feeling conveyed by a description of a person, place, object, or state of mind. See Chapter 7 on description, especially p. 124.

drafting   The stage of the writing process in which ideas are tentatively written out in sentences and paragraphs. Drafts may be messy, incomplete, disorganized, and filled with misspellings and grammatical errors; such problems can be repaired during *revision* and *editing.* See pp. 33–36.

editing   The final stage of the writing process, in which sentences and words are polished and corrected for accuracy, clarity, and effectiveness. See Chapter 4 on editing, p. 48.

effect   See *cause-and-effect analysis.*

either-or   See *fallacies.*

emotional appeal   In argumentative and persuasive writing, the appeal to readers' values, beliefs, or feelings in order to win agreement or compel action. See pp. 368–69.

essay   A prose composition on a single nonfictional topic or idea. An essay usually reflects the personal experiences and opinions of the writer.

ethical appeal   In argumentative and persuasive writing, the sense of the writer's expertise and character projected by the reasonableness of the argument, the use and quality of evidence, and the tone. See p. 367.

etymology   The history of a word, from its origins and uses to changes in its meaning over time. See p. 299.

evidence   The details, examples, facts, statistics, or expert opinions that support any general statement or claim. See pp. 365 and 366–79 on the use of evidence in argumentative writing, pp. 63–70 on finding evidence in sources, and pp. 73–87 on documenting researched evidence.

example   An instance or representative of a general group or an abstract concept or quality. One or more examples may serve as the primary method of developing an essay. See Chapter 8 on example, p. 150.

exposition   The form of writing that explains or informs. Most of the essays in this book are primarily expository, and some essays whose primary purpose is self-expression or persuasion employ exposition to clarify ideas.

extended definition   See *definition*.

fallacies   Flaws in reasoning that weaken or invalidate an argument. Some of the most common fallacies follow (the page numbers refer to further discussion in the text).

- **Ad hominem** ("to the man") **argument**, attacking an opponent instead of the opponent's argument: *She is just a student, so we need not listen to her criticisms of foreign policy* (p. 372).

- **Begging the question**, assuming the truth of a conclusion that has not been proved: *Acid rain does not do serious damage, so it is not a serious problem* (p. 371).

- **Either-or**, presenting only two alternatives when the choices are more numerous: *If you want to do well in school, you have to cheat a little* (p. 372).

- **Hasty generalization**, leaping to a conclusion on the basis of inadequate or unrepresentative evidence: *Every one of the twelve students polled supports the change in the grading system, so the administration should implement it* (p. 371).

- **Ignoring the question**, shifting the argument away from the real issue: *A fine, churchgoing man like Charles Harold would make an excellent mayor* (p. 371).

- **Non sequitur** ("It does not follow"), deriving a wrong or illogical conclusion from stated premises: *Because students are actually in school, they should be the ones to determine our educational policies* (p. 372).

- **Oversimplification**, overlooking or ignoring inconsistencies or complexities in evidence: *If the United States banned immigration, our unemployment problems would be solved* (pp. 371, 378).

- **Post hoc** (from *post hoc, ergo propter hoc*, "after this, therefore because of this"), assuming that one thing caused another simply because it preceded the other: *Two employees left the company in the week after the new policies were announced, proving that the policies will eventually cause a reduction in staff* (pp. 371–72, 378).

figures of speech   Expressions that imply meanings beyond or different from their literal meanings in order to achieve vividness or force. Common figures of speech include *hyperbole, metaphor, paradox, simile*, and *personification*. See also pp. 58–59 for discussion and examples of specific figures.

flashback   In narration, an interruption of chronological sequence that shifts backward in time to recall or explore the significance of an earlier event. See p. 95.

formal definition   See *definition*.

formal style   See *style*.

freewriting   A technique for discovering ideas for writing: writing for a fixed amount of time without stopping to reread or edit. See pp. 26–27.

general and specific words   A **general** word refers to a group or class: *car, mood, book*. A **specific** word refers to a particular member of a group or class: *Toyota*, *irritation*, *dictionary*. Usually, the more specific a word is, the more interesting and informative it will be for readers. See also pp. 58, 60, and *abstract and concrete words*.

generalization   A statement about a group or a class derived from knowledge of some or all of its members: for instance, *Dolphins can be trained to count* or *Television news rarely penetrates beneath the headlines*. The more examples the generalization is based on, the more accurate it is likely to be. A generalization is the result of inductive reasoning; see pp. 152–57.

hasty generalization   See *fallacies*.

hyperbole   Deliberate overstatement or exaggeration: *The desk provided an acre of work surface*. See also p. 59. (The opposite of hyperbole is understatement, discussed under *irony*.)

ignoring the question   See *fallacies*.

image   A verbal representation of sensory experience—that is, of something seen, heard, felt, tasted, or smelled. Images may be literal: *Snow stuck to her eyelashes*; *The red car sped past us*. Or they may be figures of speech: *Her eyelashes were snowy feathers*; *The car rocketed past us like a red missile*. (See pp. 17–21.) Through images, a writer touches the readers' experiences, thus sharpening meaning and adding immediacy. See also *abstract and concrete words*.

independent clause   A word group that contains a subject and a verb and expresses a complete thought. A single independent clause can be punctuated as sentence; two independent clauses in a row need a clear separation: a period, a semicolon, or a comma along with and, *but, or, nor, for, so,* or *yet*. See p. 50.

inductive reasoning   The method of reasoning that moves from the particular to the general. See Chapter 15 on argument and persuasion, especially pp. 369–70.

inference   A conclusion about the meanings and implications of a work, applying the reader's own knowledge and ideas to textual evidence from the work itself. See also pp. 16 and 18 and *synthesis*.

infographics   Visual texts, such as tables, charts, and graphs, that make factual information easier to grasp. As with written texts, they should be read actively and critically. See pp. 18–21.

informal style   See *style*.

introductions   The openings of written works, the sentences that set the stage for what follows. An introduction to an essay identifies and restricts the subject while establishing the writer's attitude toward it. Accomplishing these purposes may require anything from a single sentence to several paragraphs, depending on the writer's purpose and how much readers need to know before they can begin to grasp the ideas in the essay. The introduction often includes a thesis sentence stating the main idea of the essay (see pp. 29–31). To set up the thesis sentence, or as a substitute for it, any of the following openings, or a combination, may be effective:

- Background on the subject that establishes a time or place or that provides essential information (see Douglass, p. 103; Gilb, p. 136; Sedaris, p. 160; Kingsolver, p. 258; and McClain, p. 284)

- An anecdote or other reference to the writer's experience that forecasts or illustrates the main idea or that explains what prompted the essay (see Tan, p. 116; Peck, p. 289; Brady, p. 308; and Rideau, p. 387)

- An explanation of the significance of the subject (see Mora, p. 199; Jain, p. 172; and Quindlen, p. 382)

- An outline of the situation or problem that the essay will address, perhaps using interesting facts or statistics (see Ballo, p. 85; de Zengotita, p. 194; Griggs, p. 218; LeDuff, p. 352; and King, p. 449)

- A statement or quotation of an opinion that the writer will modify or disagree with (see Johnson, p. 167; Brooks, p. 228; and Lee, p. 392)

- An example, quotation, or question that reinforces the main idea (see Dillard, p. 141; Iyer, p. 312; McCarthy, p. 398; Carr, p. 408)

A good introduction does not mislead readers by exaggerating the significance of the subject or the essay, and it does not bore readers by saying more than is necessary. In addition, a good introduction avoids three openings that are always clumsy: (1) beginning with *The purpose of this essay is* . . . or something similar; (2) referring to the title of the essay in the first sentence, as in *This is not as hard as it looks* or *This is a serious problem*; and (3) starting too broadly or vaguely, as in *Ever since humans walked upright* . . . or *In today's world* . . .

irony   In writing, irony is the use of words to suggest a meaning different from their literal meaning. An ironic statement might rely on reversal: saying the opposite of what the writer really means. But irony can also derive from understatement (saying less than is meant) or hyperbole (exaggeration). Irony can be witty, teasing, biting, or cruel. At its most humorless and heavily contemptuous, it becomes **sarcasm**: *Thanks a lot for telling Dad we stayed out all night; that was really bright of you.*

journal   A tool for discovering ideas for writing: an informal record of ideas, observations, questions, and thoughts kept in a notebook or electronic file for the writer's personal use. See pp. 25–26.

metaphor   A figure of speech that compares two unlike things by saying that one is the other: *Bright circles of ebony, her eyes smiled back at me.* See also p. 58.

modifier   A word, phrase, or clause that describes another word (or words) in a sentence. Modifiers can add emphasis and variety to sentences, but must be placed carefully to avoid confusing readers. See pp. 51 and 60.

narration   The form of writing that tells a story, relating a sequence of events. See Chapter 6 on narration, p.92.

negation   A technique for clarifying the definition of a word or phrase by explaining what it does *not* mean. See p. 299.

non sequitur   See *fallacies.*

nonstandard English   See *diction*.

objective writing   Writing that focuses on the subject itself and strives to be direct and impartial, without dwelling on the writer's perspective or feelings. Newspaper accounts, scientific reports, process analyses, and rational arguments are typical examples. See also p. 124 and *subjective writing*.

organization   The arrangement of ideas and supporting points in a piece of writing. See pp. 41–42, *chronological order*, *climactic order*, and *spatial organization*.

oversimplification   See *fallacies*.

paradox   A seemingly self-contradictory statement that, on reflection, makes sense: *Children are the poor person's wealth* (wealth can be monetary or spiritual). *Paradox* may also refer to a situation that is inexplicable or contradictory, such as the restriction of one group's rights to secure the rights of another group.

paragraph   A group of related sentences, set off by an initial indentation, that develops an idea. By breaking continuous text into units, paragraphing helps the writer manage ideas and helps the reader follow those ideas. Each paragraph makes a distinct contribution to the main idea governing the entire piece of writing. The idea of the paragraph itself is often stated in a topic sentence (see pp. 38–39), and it is supported with sentences containing specific details, examples, and reasons. Like the larger piece of writing to which it contributes, the paragraph should be unified, coherent, and well developed. For examples of successful paragraphs, see the paragraph analyses in the introduction to each method of development (Chapters 6–15). See also pp. 28–40 (unity), pp. 41–42 (coherence), and pp. 27–28 and 42–43 (development).

parallelism   The use of similar grammatical forms for ideas of equal importance. Parallelism occurs within sentences: *The doctor recommends swimming, bicycling, or walking.* It also occurs among sentences: *Strumming her guitar, she made listeners feel her anger. Singing lines, she made listeners believe her pain.* See also pp. 15, 40, 55, and 278–279.

paraphrase   A restatement—in your own words—of another writer's ideas. A paraphrase is about the same length as the original passage, but it does not repeat words, phrases, or sentence patterns. See also p. 69.

personification   A figure of speech that gives human qualities to things or abstractions: *The bright day smirked at my bad mood.* See also p. 58.

persuasion   See *argument*.

plagiarism   The failure to identify and acknowledge the sources of words, information, or ideas that are not your own. Whether intentional or accidental, plagiarism is a serious offense and should always be avoided. See pp. 72–73.

point of view   The position of the writer in relation to the subject. In description, point of view depends on the writer's physical and psychological relation to the subject (see pp. 125–26). In narration, point of view depends on the writer's place in the story and on his or her relation to it in time (see pp. 95–97). More broadly, point of view can also mean the writer's particular mental stance or attitude. For instance, an employee and an employer might have different points of view toward the employee's absenteeism or the employer's sick-leave policies.

points of comparison   The set of attributes used to distinguish and organize the elements of two or more subjects being compared to each other. See Chapter 12 on comparison and contrast, especially pp. 271–72.

post hoc   See *fallacies.*

premise   The generalization or assumption on which an argument is based. See *syllogism.*

presentation   A speech enhanced with multimedia support, such as audio and visual aids, to maintain audience interest, to highlight or clarify points, or to strengthen claims. See "Keys to Effective Speaking" in the Appendix, especially pp. 425–31, and *speech.*

principle of analysis   The interpretive framework or set of guidelines used to divide a subject into components. The choice of a principle depends on the writer's interest and will determine the focus and outcome of an analysis. One writer analyzing a contemporary television show set in the 1960s, for instance, might focus on historical context and implications, while another might emphasize production values, and yet another might focus on literary qualities such as plot and character. See Chapter 9 on division or analysis, especially pp. 180–81.

principle of classification   The distinctive characteristics used to sort things into categories or general classes. A writer's focus determines the principle, which in turn shapes and limits the contours of a classification. An essay about apartment dwellers, for example, might group them by noise (too loud, too quiet, just right), by income (poor, working class, middle class, wealthy), or by relationship status (bachelors, couples, widows); it should not, however, mix them into unrelated categories (too loud, middle class, widows). See Chapter 10 on classification, especially pp. 211–12.

process analysis   The method of development in which a sequence of actions with a specified result is divided into its component steps. Process analysis may be directive, telling how to do or make something; or explanatory, providing the necessary information for readers to understand how something happens. See Chapter 11 on process analysis, p. 238.

pronoun   A word that refers to a noun or other pronoun: *Six days after Martin Luther King, Jr., picked up the Nobel Peace Prize in Norway, he was jailed in Alabama.* The most common personal pronouns are *I, you, he, she, it, we,* and *they.* See also p. 40, and 51–60, 125, 129.

proposition   A debatable claim about a subject; the central idea of an argument. See also *thesis.*

purpose   The reason for writing, the goal the writer wants to achieve. The purpose may be primarily to explain the subject so that readers understand it or see it in a new light; to convince readers to accept or reject an opinion

or to take a certain action; to entertain readers with a humorous or exciting story; or to express the thoughts and emotions triggered by a revealing
or instructive experience. The writer's purpose overlaps the main idea—
the particular point being made about the subject. In effective writing,
the two together direct and control every choice the writer makes. See
also pp. 23–24 and 37–38, *thesis*, and *unity*.

quotation   The exact words of another writer or speaker, copied word for
word and clearly identified. Short quotations are enclosed in quotation
marks; longer quotations are set off from the text by indenting. See
pp. 69–71.

rational appeal   In argumentative and persuasive writing, the appeal to
readers' rational faculties—to their ability to reason logically—in order
to win agreement or compel action. See pp. 369–70.

repetition and restatement   The careful use of the same words or close
parallels to clarify meaning and tie sentences together. See also p. 40.

revision   The stage of the writing process devoted to "re-seeing" a draft,
divided into fundamental changes in content and structure (revision) and
more superficial changes in grammar, word choice, and the like (editing).
See Chapter 3 on revising, p. 36, and Chapter 4 on editing, p. 48.

rhetoric   The art of using words effectively to communicate with an audience, or the study of that art. To the ancient Greeks, rhetoric was the art
of the *rhetor*—orator, or public speaker—and included the art of persuasion. Later the word shifted to mean elegant language, and a version of
that meaning persists in today's occasional use of *rhetoric* to mean preten-
tious or hollow language, as in *Their argument was mere rhetoric.*

run-on sentence   A sentence error in which two or more independent
clauses run together without punctuation between them. See p. 50.

sarcasm   See *irony.*

satire   The combination of wit and criticism to mock or condemn human
foolishness or evil. The intent of satire is to arouse readers to contempt
or action, and thus it differs from comedy, which seeks simply to amuse.
Much satire relies on irony—saying one thing but meaning another (see
irony).

sentence   See *independent clause.*

sentence fragment   A word group that is punctuated like a sentence but is
not a complete sentence because it lacks a subject, lacks a verb, or is just
part of a thought. See pp. 15 and 49.

simile   A figure of speech that equates two unlike things using *like* or *as*:
The crowd was restless, like bees in a hive. See also p. 58.

slang   See *diction.*

source   Any outside or researched material that helps to develop a writer's
ideas. A source may be the subject of an essay, such as when you are writing about a reading in this book, or it may provide evidence to support a

particular point. However a source is used, it must always be documented. See Chapter 5 on working with sources, p. 63.

spatial organization   A pattern of organization that views an object, scene, or person by paralleling the way we normally scan things—for instance, top to bottom or near to far. See also p. 41.

specific words   See *general and specific words*.

speech   A verbal address delivered to a live audience. Most speeches are prepared in advance and shaped to accomplish a specific goal, such as informing, persuading, or entertaining listeners. See "Keys to Effective Speaking" in the Appendix (pp. 425–31).

standard English   The formal written language of educated native speakers, expected in all writing for school, business and the professions, and publication. Standard English encompasses correct use of grammar and punctuation and appropriate diction. See Chapter 4 on editing (pp. 48–62) and *diction*.

stipulative definition   See *definition*.

style   The *way* something is said, as opposed to *what* is said. Style results primarily from a writer's characteristic word choices and sentence structures. A person's writing style, like his or her voice or manner of speaking, is distinctive. Style can also be viewed more broadly as ranging from formal to informal. A very formal style adheres strictly to the conventions of standard English (see *diction*); tends toward long sentences with sophisticated structures; and relies on learned words, such as *malodorous* and *psychopathic*. A very informal style, in contrast, is more conversational (see *colloquial language*); tends toward short, uncomplicated sentences; and relies on words typical of casual speech, such as *smelly* or *crazy*. Among the writers represented in this book, Douglass (p. 103) writes quite formally, Sedaris (p. 160) quite informally. The formality of style may often be modified to suit a particular audience or occasion: a formal term paper, for instance, demands a more formal style than an essay narrating a personal experience. See also *tone* and Chapter 3 on revising, especially pp. 43–44.

subject   What a piece of writing is about. The subject of an essay is its general topic, such as nature (Didion, p. 131; Gilb, p. 136; Dillard, p. 141), language (Sedaris, p. 160; Johnson, p. 167; Jain, p. 172), or food (Dumas, p. 248; Eighner, p. 253; Kingsolver, p. 258). Because writers narrow a subject until they have a specific point to make about it, multiple essays on the same subject will typically be very different from one another. See also pp. 23–24, *purpose*, and *thesis*.

subjective writing   Writing that focuses on the writer's own perspectives, feelings, and opinions. Memoirs, personal reflections, and emotional arguments, for example, tend to be subjective. See also p. 124 and *objective writing*.

summary   A condensed version—in your own words—of the main idea of a longer work. A summary is much shorter than the original and leaves out most of the supporting details. See also p. 68.

syllogism   The basic form of deductive reasoning, in which a conclusion derives necessarily from proven or accepted premises. For example: *The roof always leaks when it rains* (the major premise). *It is raining* (the minor premise). *Therefore, the roof will leak* (the conclusion). See Chapter 15 on argument and persuasion, especially pp. 370–71.

symbol   A person, place, or thing that represents an abstract quality or concept. A red heart symbolizes love; the Golden Gate Bridge symbolizes San Francisco's dramatic beauty; a cross symbolizes Christianity.

synonym   A word that carries a meaning similar, but not exact, to another word. For example: *angry* and *furious*, *happy* and *ecstastic*, *skinny* and *thin*.

synthesis   The practice of combining elements into a new whole. In writing, synthesis usually involves connecting related ideas from multiple sources to form an original idea of your own. See pp. 68–72.

thesis   The main idea of a piece of writing to which all other ideas and details relate. The main idea is often stated in a **thesis sentence** (or sentences), which asserts something about the subject and conveys the writer's purpose. The thesis sentence is often included near the beginning of an essay. Even when the writer does not state the main idea and purpose, however, they govern all the ideas and details in the essay. See also pp. 28–31, 37–38, and *unity*.

tone   The attitude toward the subject, and sometimes toward the audience and the writer's own self, expressed in choice of words and sentence structures as well as in what is said. Tone in writing is similar to tone of voice in speaking, from warm to serious, amused to angry, joyful to sorrowful, sympathetic to contemptuous. For examples of strong tone in writing, see Griggs (p. 218), McClain (p. 284), Peck (p. 289), and Brady (p. 308). See also pp. 43–44 and 379–80.

topic sentence   A statement of the main idea of a paragraph, to which all other sentences in the paragraph relate. See pp. 38–39.

transitions   Links between sentences and paragraphs that relate ideas and thus contribute to clarity and smoothness. Transitions may be sentences beginning paragraphs or brief paragraphs that shift the focus or introduce new ideas. They may also be words and phrases that signal and specify relationships. Some of these words and phrases—but by no means all—are listed here:

- **Addition or repetition**: again, also, finally, furthermore, in addition, moreover, next, that is
- **Cause or effect**: as a result, consequently, equally important, hence, then, therefore, thus
- **Comparison**: also, in the same way, likewise, similarly
- **Contrast**: but, even so, however, in contrast, on the contrary, still, yet
- **Illustration**: for example, for instance, specifically, that is
- **Intensification**: indeed, in fact, of course, truly

- **Space**: above, below, beyond, farther away, here, nearby, opposite, there, to the right

- **Summary or conclusion**: all in all, in brief, in conclusion, in short, in summary, therefore, thus

- **Time**: afterward, at last, earlier, later, meanwhile, simultaneously, soon, then

understatement   See *irony*.

unity   The quality of effective writing that occurs when all the parts relate to the main idea and contribute to the writer's purpose. See also pp. 28–40.

visual   A non-verbal text or image created to convey a message or present information, either by itself or as a supplement to written text. Visuals include photographs, paintings, and drawings, as well as tables, charts, and graphs. See pp. 18–21, 43, and *infographics*.

writing process   The series of activities involved in creating a finished piece of writing. Rather than produce a polished essay in one sitting, most writers work back and forth in a series of overlapping stages: analyzing the writing situation, discovering ideas, forming a thesis, organizing, drafting, revising, and editing. See pp. 22–23.

ACKNOWLEDGMENTS

of Random House, Inc. Any third party use of this material, outside of this publication, is prohibited. Interested parties must apply directly to Random House, Inc. for permission.

Thomas de Zengotita. *"American Idol* Worship," originally titled "Why We Worship *American Idol,"* from *The Los Angeles Times,* February 17, 2006. Copyright © 2006 Thomas de Zengotita. Reprinted by permission of the author.

Art Credits

p. 18, "Homeless Man." Photo by Colin Gregory Palmer Grey.

p. 20, "Summary of Homeless Persons by Subpopulations Reported." By US Department of Housing and Urban Development.

p. 20, "Homeless Population and Subpopulations, 2011." By Peter Witte, in "State of Homelessness in America," National Alliance to End Homelessness, January 2012.

p. 92, "The Return." From *Persepolis 2: The Story of a Return* by Marjane Satrapi, translated by Anjali Singh. Translation copyright © 2004 by Anjali Singh. Used by permission of Pantheon Books, a division of Random House, Inc. Any third party use of this material, outside of this publication, is prohibited.

p. 117, "Amy Tan at Age Twelve." Photo courtesy of Amy Tan. Reprinted by permission of the author and the Sandra Dijkstra Literary Agency.

p. 122, *Aspens, Northern Mexico.* Photo by Ansel Adams. Copyright © Ansel Adams Publishing Rights Trust/CORBIS.

p. 150, *Important Notice.* Photo by, and copyrighted by, Julie Mbaisa, courtesy of Bethany Keeley, unnecessaryquotes.com.

p. 150, *No Dogs.* Photo by, and copyrighted by, Rachel Hadiashar, courtesy of Bethany Keeley, unnecessaryquotes.com.

p. 150, *Do Not Put Nothing Here.* Photo by, and copyrighted by, Amy Spencer, courtesy of Bethany Keeley, unnecessaryquotes.com.

p. 150, *Dear Customers.* Photo by, and copyrighted by, Eric Reinarman, courtesy of Bethany Keeley, unnecessaryquotes.com.

p. 150, *Cheaper Than Cheaper.* Photo by, and copyrighted by, Tito Perez, courtesy of Bethany Keeley, unnecessaryquotes.com.

p. 178, "Balance Your Media." Photo by Steven Leckart/Wired.com/Conde Nast.

p. 208, "National Population by Race." Photo courtesy of the United States Census Bureau.

p. 232, *Nascar/Fox v. NPR*/New York Times. Cartoon by Steve Brodner, 2003.

p. 238, "How the Microwave Oven Works." By © George Retseck Illustration.

p. 258, *Vegetables.* From *Animal, Vegetable, Miracle* by Barbara Kingsolver with Steven L. Hopp and Camille Kingsolver. Copyright © 2007 by Barbara Kingsolver, Steven L. Hopp, and Camille Kingsolver. Reprinted by permission of HarperCollins Publishers.

p. 258, *Freedom from Want.* Art by Norman Rockwell. Printed by permission of the Norman Rockwell Family Agency. Copyright © 1943 The Norman Rockwell Family Entities. Norman Rockwell Museum Collection.

p. 258, *Freedom from Want.* Cartoon by Art Spiegelman, currently collected in BLOWN COVERS: *New Yorker Covers You Were Never Meant to See* by Françoise Mouly. Copyright © 2011 by Art Spiegelman, used by permission of The Wylie Agency LLC.

p. 296, *"I Hope You Realize . . ."* Cartoon by Peter Steiner/ The New Yorker Collection/ www.cartoonbank.com.

p. 320, "Illustration for 'Get Happy'." Photo by Karen Caldicott. Reprinted with permission from the October 5, 2009 issue *of The Nation*, "Illustration for 'Get Happy'" by Karen Caldicott. For subscription information, call 1-800-333-8536. Portion's of each week's *Nation* magazine can be accessed at http://www.thenation.com.

p. 327, *We Can Do It!* World War Two poster, c. 1942, Bridgeman Art Library International.

p. 353, *GM Plant.* Photo by Danny Wilcox Frazier/Redux Pictures.

p. 354, *Car Outside VFW.* Photo by Danny Wilcox Frazier/Redux Pictures.

p. 355, *GM Reading Room.* Photo by Danny Wilcox Frazier/Redux Pictures.

p. 327, *GM Prayer.* Danny Wilcox Frazier/Redux Pictures.

p. 364, *Katie Is a Terrorist.* Photo by U.S. Travel Association (www.ustravel.com).

INDEX OF AUTHORS
AND TITLES

GUIDE TO THE ELEMENTS OF WRITING

The Common Reader offers advice on writing from the general, such as organizing and revising, to the particular, such as tightening sentences and choosing words. Consult the page numbers here for answers to questions you may have about the elements of writing. To find the meaning of a particular term or concept, consult the Glossary on pages 000–000.